Handbook of
Educational
Supervision

HANDBOOK of EDUCATIONAL SUPERVISION

A Guide for the Practitioner

second edition

Sir James Robert Marks

*Professor, Behavioral Sciences Division, and
Supervising Director, Instructional Center*
West Los Angeles College

Emery Stoops

*Professor Emeritus, Educational
Administration and Supervision*
University of Southern California

Joyce King-Stoops

Associate Professor of Education
University of California

Allyn and Bacon, Inc.
Boston ▪ London ▪ Sydney

Library of Congress Cataloging in Publication Data

Marks, James R
    Handbook of educational supervision.
    Bibliography: p.
    Includes index.
    1. School supervision. I. Stoops, Emery,
joint author. II. King-Stoops, Joyce, joint
author. III. Title.
LB2805.M283 1978   371.2   77-18000
ISBN 0-205-06020-X

Second printing . . . July, 1979

Contents

Foreword   xi

Preface   xiii

I   PLANNING FOR THE SUPERVISORY PROGRAM   1

Chapter

1   Background for School Supervision   3

Need for the Improvement of Instruction 3,   Definitions and Principles 4,   Democratic Supervision in American Education 6,   A History of Educational Personnel Administration for the Supervisor 14,   Do 19, Don't 19,   Trends 19, Supervisory Problems (In Basket) 21,   Questions and Suggested Activities 22,   Selected Bibliography 24

2   Special Problems: The Role of the Intermediate Unit in Supervision   26

Intermediate Unit Variations, Functions, and Organizational Status 26, Supervisory Services Performed by the Intermediate Unit Staff 31,   Do 36,   Don't 36,   Trends 37,   Supervisory Problems (In Basket) 38, Questions and Suggested Activities 38,   Selected Bibliography 40

3   Special Problems: The Role of the State and Federal Government in School Supervision   42

The Role of the Federal Government in Supervision 42,   The American School System 43,   History of Governmental Aid and Support for Supervision 45,   General Federal Activities Affecting Supervision 46, Historical Development of the State Departments of Education 50,   The Position of Chief State School Officer 50, Functions of the State Departments of Education 53,   Special Problems at the State Level 63,   Do 69,   Don't 70,   Trends 70,   Supervisory Problems (In Basket) 71, Questions and Suggested Activities 72,   Selected Bibliography 74

4   Organizing the Supervisory Program   76

Basic Principles of Organization for the Supervisor 76,   Authority and Organization: How to Organize and Implement a Supervisory Program 80,   A Shared Responsibility 83,   A New Type of Supervisor and a

Chapter

New Type of Supervision 94,   How to Plan Your Work as a Supervisor 94,   How to Provide for Managerial Coordination: The Roles of the Principal and the Superintendent 97,   Conflicting Organizational Demands 103,   Do 106,   Don't 106,   Trends 107,   Supervisory Problems (In Basket) 108,   Questions and Suggested Activities 110, Selected Bibliography 112

5   How to Be a Successful Supervisor through Leadership and Human Dynamics   116

How Leaders Succeed 118,   How to Criticize: Leadership, Criticism, and Human Nature 121,   How to Be a Successful Change Agent 123, How to Work with the Group and with the Individual 126,   How to Communicate Effectively 131,   How to Be a Success as a Leader in a Social Setting 136,   Some Psychological Implications of Your Supervisory Behavior 143,   Do 150,   Don't 151,   Trends 151,   Supervisory Problems (In Basket) 152,   Questions and Suggested Activities 154,   Selected Bibliography 156

II   IMPLEMENTING THE SUPERVISORY PROGRAM   161

Chapter

6   How to Promote Staff Development and Handle Some Special Problems   163

How to Develop Programs for Instructional Development and Staff Development 163,   Principles of the Program for In-Service Education 169,   Individual Endeavors for In-Service Education 173,   How to Help the Beginning Teacher 174,   How to Help the Superior Teacher 187,   How to Help the Senior Teacher 188,   How to Work with the Dissenting Teacher 188,   How to Work with the "Undemocratic" Staff Member 189,   Behavioral Guidelines for Working in Groups 190,   Do 202,   Don't 203,   Trends 204,   Supervisory Problems (In Basket) 204,   Questions and Suggested Activities 206,   Selected Bibliography 207

7   How to Improve Supervisory Visits   211

Principles and Purposes of Supervisory Visits 211,   How to Plan for Classroom Visitation 213,   Mechanics of Observation 214,   Techniques in Visitation 218,   How to Use the Technique of Interschool Visitation 234,   Individual Visits 234,   Group Visitation 235,   Do 238,   Don't 238,   Trends 238,   Supervisory Problems (In Basket)

Chapter

239, Questions and Suggested Activities 240, Selected Bibliography 241

8   How to Improve Supervisory Follow-Up Conferences   243

Principles and Purposes of Supervisory Conferences 243,   How to Conduct a Successful Conference 244,   Recording the Conference Results 248,   How to Interview 248,   Do 254,   Don't 255,   Trends 256, Supervisory Problems (In Basket) 257,   Questions and Suggested Activities 258,   Selected Bibliography 259

9   How to Provide Successful Faculty Meetings   261

Principles and Practices 262,   How to Improve Workshops and Institutes 267,   How to Conduct the Meeting 270,   Do 279,   Don't 282, Trends 282,   Supervisory Problems (In Basket) 283,   Questions and Suggested Activities 285,   Selected Bibliography 287

10   How to Measure Teacher Effectiveness and Improve Methods and Techniques of Instruction   289

Basic Principles 290,   How to Get Started in Measuring Teacher Effectiveness: Organizational Plans 291,   Teacher Evaluation and Appraisal: How the Principal Should Initiate the Evaluation Program 292, How to Select Criteria 295,   How to Evaluate Instructional Efficiency 299,   How to Organize for Instruction 307,   How to Help the Teacher Plan for Instruction 314,   Gaming 326,   Do 326,   Don't 327,   Trends 328,   Supervisory Problems (In Basket) 330,   Questions and Suggested Activities 331,   Selected Bibliography 333

11   How to Select, Organize, and Facilitate the Use of Instructional Media and Library Facilities   337

Principles and Practices 338,   Curriculum Improvement through the Use of Instructional Materials and Systems 342,   How to Evaluate and Improve the Instructional Media Center 342,   How to Improve the Use of Instructional Materials 349,   How to Select and Evaluate Instructional Materials 355,   How to Improve Library Services 382,   Do 391,   Don't 393,   Trends 394,   Supervisory Problems (In Basket) 395,   Questions and Suggested Activities 397,   Selected Bibliography 399

12   How to Help the Staff Understand and Guide Children   403

Need for Improving the Staff's Understanding of Children 404,   How to Help the Staff Understand Children through the In-Service Education Program 407,   Interplay of Sociological Factors 409,   How to Help

Chapter

the Teacher Plan for More Effective Parent Conferences 412, How to Help the Staff Understand Children through Health Records, Observation, Anecdotal Records, and Related Techniques 417, How to Help the Staff Understand Students through Intervisitation 424, How to Help the Staff Understand Students through the Interstaff Conference 425, How to Help Teachers Understand Students through Cumulative Records 434, Case Studies 437, How to Supervise the Assignment of a Student to a Classroom 444, Do 446, Don't 447, Trends 447, Supervisory Problems (In Basket) 449, Questions and Suggested Activities 450, Selected Bibliography 453

13   How to Help the Staff Study and Improve the Curriculum   457

Basic Principles and History of Curriculum Development 458, The Supervising Principal's Role in Curriculum Change 474, How to Use the Systems Analysis Cycle in Curriculum Development 477, How to Determine Resources 485, The Supervision of Cocurricular Activities 488, Do 490, Don't 492, Trends 492, Supervisory Problems (In Basket) 494, Questions and Suggested Activities 495, Selected Bibliography 497

14   How to Improve the Work of Classified Personnel   500

Principles of Classified Service Improvement 501, How to Select, Assign, and Orient Classified Personnel 502, How to Improve the Quality of Office Management 506, How to Improve the Morale of Classified Personnel 507, How to Evaluate Classified Personnel Performance 509, How to Do It: Techniques that Work 510, How to Plan for More Efficient Classified Personnel Performance 515, How to Get the Most Out of In-Service Education Programs for Classified Employees 516, Do 527, Don't 528, Trends 528, Supervisory Problems (In Basket) 530, Questions and Suggested Activities 531, Selected Bibliography 533

III   SUPPORT, SUPERVISORY PERSONNEL,
       PROFESSIONAL RESPONSIBILITIES, AND THE
       FUTURE OF EDUCATIONAL SUPERVISION   537

Chapter

15   How to Supervise the Program for Obtaining Community
     Support   539

Definitions and Functions 539, Basic Principles 540, How the Staff Can Participate 544, How to Build a Community Relations Program

Chapter

549,   How to Evaluate the Community Relations Program 553,   Do
559,   Don't 560,   Trends 561,   Supervisory Problems (In Basket)
562,   Questions and Suggested Activities 564,   Selected Bibliography 565

16   How to Select Personnel for Supervisory Positions   568

Selection and Recruitment 568,   How to Appraise Candidates for Supervisory Positions 572,   How to Set Priorities for Candidate Qualities 578,   How to Match Candidate with Position 578,   How to Decide Whether to Reject or Accept the Candidate 579,   How to Make Probationary Assignments 580,   How to Evaluate the Selection Process 581,   Do 582,   Don't 582,   Trends 583,   Supervisory Problems (In Basket) 584,   Selected Bibliography 586

17   How to Make Effective Decisions and Evaluate a Supervisory Program   587

Principles for the Evaluation of Supervision 587,   Psychological Aspects of Decision Making for the Supervisor 589,   Stages in Decision Making 590,   How to Develop and Appraise Written Evaluations of Performance 600,   How to Describe and Appraise the Status of the Supervisory Program 600,   Teachers and Principals View Supervision in Action 602,   Evidence of an Effective Supervisory Program 604,   Some Questions the Supervising Principal Can Ask 605,   Do 606,   Don't Forget 607,   Trends 607,   Supervisory Problems (In Basket) 608,   Questions and Suggested Activities 609,   Selected Bibliography 611

18   Professional Responsibilities of the Supervisor   614

Requirements for Professional Status 615,   Qualities of a Profession 616,   The Educator's Responsibilities 617,   Ethics for the Supervisor in Handling Personnel Matters 619,   Professional Organizations 621,   Moving Toward Professional Status 623,   Do 624,   Don't 624,   Trends 625,   Supervisory Problems (In Basket) 626,   Questions and Suggested Activities 627,   Selected Bibliography 629

19   Further Trends and Issues: The Supervisor Looks to the Future   632

Factors Producing Changes 632,   New Directions in Educational Supervision 635,   The Supervisor Faces the Issues of Today and Tomorrow 636,   Trends 640,   Supervisory Problems (In Basket) 645,   Selected Bibliography 647

APPENDICES

A   Useful Sources for the Supervisor   648

Publications and Films Related to Human Relations for the Supervisor 648,   Films 650,   Major Published Sources for Educational Research 651,   Educational Bibliographies 651,   Educational Dictionaries 651, Educational Encyclopedias 652,   Educational Yearbooks and Government Publications 652,   Periodical Sources 652,   Other Sources 654

B   Flanders System of Interaction Analysis and Accompanying Forms for Recording and Charting Results   655

C   Program Evaluation Checklist for Staff and Instructional Development Programs   658

D   Applied Educational Psychology for the Supervisor: Growing, Learning, and Testing   661

Principles of Growth and Development for the Supervisor 661,   How to Help the Teacher Test, Assign Marks, and Understand Statistical Measures 675,   A Look at the Future 685

AUTHOR INDEX   687

SUBJECT INDEX   691

Foreword

In the revised edition of this handbook, and especially through its practical suggestions—the "how-to's"—Sir James Robert Marks, Emery Stoops, and Joyce King-Stoops have insured higher quality education in depth for our children. The fundamental aim of the book is to improve instruction through the approach of assisting, supplementing, and encouraging the teacher—to inspire, not to impose; to strengthen, not to criticize harshly or destructively. The practical suggestions for action on the part of the educational supervisor are the result of more than thirty years of work and research.

Completely updated and reorganized, the handbook deals with all elements of the learning situation; it dignifies the teacher as a cooperating member of the supervisory team.

I have personal knowledge of the competencies of the authors. Dr. Joyce King-Stoops, whose latest book is *The Child Wants to Learn: Elementary Teaching Methods,* has served as teacher, principal, and professor-in-charge of the Honors Intern Program, Teacher Education Department, University of Southern California.

Dr. Emery Stoops has been teacher, counselor, supervisor, principal, and superintendent, and has filled administrative and supervisory assignments in the Office of the Los Angeles County Superintendent of Schools. He has served as Professor of Education Administration and Supervision at the University of Southern California. During the past several years, he has served as administrative consultant to the Riverside County Schools and was named as a member of the survey team for the California State Department of Education.

As past international president of Phi Delta Kappa, professional education association and honor society for men and women, Dr. Stoops traveled and studied supervisory programs in all parts of the country. His numerous articles and textbooks reflect his unusual skill and deep understanding of the broad field of school supervision. His latest publication, *Handbook of Educational Administration,* with M. L. Rafferty and R. Johnson, has become a leader in its field.

Dr. Sir James R. Marks, who did the lion's share of the writing, has been outstanding in general supervision, staff and instructional development, personnel and educational psychology, curriculum development, and administration. He currently is Professor of Psychology and Education and Supervising Director of the Instructional Center at West Los Angeles College. In the capacity of superintendent, he organized and administered a teacher education program for the Armed Forces. As Coordinator at the California State Polytechnic College's Kellogg Campus, in addition to serving as Professor of Psychology and Education, he organized and supervised a teacher education and credentialing program. He has taught extensively through the graduate level. He has written and lectured widely in the areas of supervision, including instructional and staff development; curriculum; educational and personnel psychology; administration; and in instructional technology and teaching techniques. He has received numerous awards and honors related to his work in directing graduate level supervisory seminars and workshops in California, at Idaho State University, at the University of Hawaii, at the University of British Columbia, and in Puerto Rico. Extensive experiences and contributions in educational therapy and in psychological services have enhanced his insight into educational supervision. His pioneering research in "Assignment Specifications" yielded perspective in the area of educational personnel psychology and in the selection, assignment, and supervision of certificated employees.

Dr. Marks recently was knighted by royal decree in recognition of his untiring and significant contributions to education and improved instruction for all people on an international basis. He is the recipient of numerous awards and honors, both from within and outside of his profession. His television program on supervision was selected by the American Broadcasting Company for replay as its *Scope* "Program of the Year." Dr. Marks is listed in the Cambridge University *Men of Distinction* as well as in the *International Who's Who of Authors and Writers*.

The high quality material that comprises this handbook by Marks, Stoops, and King-Stoops will enable supervisors to help teachers do a better job more efficiently and with more facility. It emphasizes practical "how-to" suggestions for supervisory action. It suggests patterns of usable techniques that should prove invaluable to both the beginning and the experienced supervisor.

Maynard Bemis
Executive Secretary Emeritus
Phi Delta Kappa

Preface

Today's supervisor faces a task—a challenge—that demands that he or she be both creative in the approach and competent in the knowledge of the skills and techniques employed by successful colleagues in their practice of the art and science of supervision. The authors have drawn the basic principles of supervision from the results of scientific research; and from the caldron of experience in current practices and trends the "how-to" sections of the work, which comprise the major portions of our recipes for the successful supervisor, have been elicited.

As was true of the first edition, the purpose of this book is to provide specific, practical assistance to on-the-job supervisors in the successful realization of their main job: the improvement of instruction. John Dewey told us that theory must not be divorced from practice. Theory and research are present: they are included as the backdrop on which the "Do-Don't" sections are projected.

Staff development, decision making, selecting supervisory personnel, gaming, instructional development, coordinated instructional systems, individualized instruction, and developments in instructional media and technology, issues the supervisor must face, and a look to the future of educational supervision are among the many new sections that have been added to the text. Bibliographies have been completely updated. Nonprint media listings that note multimedia kits, films, cassettes, and the like have been added. The new check sheet for evaluating instructional and staff development programs should prove especially helpful to the supervisor.

In each task-area, we have included patterns for supervision: definite procedures, techniques, and devices that have been proved in the fires of experience. Just as the seamstress must alter and adapt a pattern she purchases at the department store to fit her needs, similarly the supervisor must adapt the patterns in supervision to the situation at hand: to himself, to the individuals he supervises, and to those with whom he works. The important point is that the patterns are here for the supervisor to sample. The pitfalls are noted; the musts are listed.

Graduate students of supervision will find in this book ideas that will help solve many of the problems they will confront on the supervisory firing line. They will be aided by the practical *simulated "in-basket" supervisory problems,* by the clear statements of expert opinion and research finds that flavor each section of the book, and by the *questions and suggested activities,* which include questions for analysis and discussion and suggested class activities. New and continuing *trends* are specifically identified.

In order to implement the important aspects of school supervision, the authors have identified certain unifying threads, such as human relations, effective communication, and team work. This fabric has been interwoven with a sound theory of supervision in an effort to produce a well-balanced book readily adaptable to varied needs—a book that can be used with confidence by all who are engaged in school supervision.

To produce a well-balanced book readily adaptable to varied needs—and in an attempt to make more concrete the principles discussed—numerous charts, tables, and figures have been included that qualify the techniques and procedures developed in the book. It is hoped that such a book will benefit the students of the schools and the democratic communities in which they live

It would be impossible to list all of the individuals who contributed to this work. The authors do, however, wish to express their appreciation to several outstanding contributors.

Recognition goes to the supervising principals and other specialists in the field of educational supervision who participated; to cartoonist Judy Wyner; to Shirley Marks, Rose Rotter, Jean Bates, Norman Chapman, Doris Webb, Herbert Zeitlin, Robert Gates, and David A. V. Moody; and to Sol Rotter, Seymour I. Marks, and Robert Williams. A special thanks to Diana, Glenn, Bruce, Gary, and Deborah Marks who were so patiently attentive while their father was in authorship.

James Robert Marks
Emery Stoops
Joyce King-Stoops

Handbook of
Educational
Supervision

PART

I

Planning for the Supervisory Program

1

Background for School Supervision

Mr., Mrs., Ms. Supervisor, beware! The technological and sociological forces that are abroad in the land demand of you a continuous, powerful program of instructional improvement.

Before you can implement such a program, employing the tools and techniques presented in later chapters of this book, you must understand and appreciate the general nature of supervision. The following points are discussed in this chapter:

Need for the improvement of instruction
Definitions and principles
Emergence of democratic supervision
History of educational personnel administration
Do—Don't
"In-Basket" supervisory problems
Questions and suggested activities

Need For the Improvement of Instruction

Primitive societies generally are not concerned with mass education; complex societies demand organized, formal school experiences. In a primitive society, only the privileged few are selected to receive instruction; in a complex democracy, it is hoped that all will be given an opportunity to progress in relation to their abilities. Equal opportunity, rather than identical experiences, is stressed.

In a democracy we have the freedom *to become;* we need not be content with the *status quo.* If the youth of today are to receive the best possible education, teachers and supervisors must keep pace with the tremendous advances made in institutions and in technology. Each society tends to measure the products of an educational system in terms of observable changes in behavior. Allport[1] noted that it is the maintaining, actualizing, and enhancing of the capacities of the individual organism that are the basic motives of life in the individual. We cannot deny that education at all levels is based on behavioral anticipations.

Definitions and Principles

The value of supervision lies in the development and improvement of the teaching-learning situation and is reflected in the development of the student. Before listing the basic principles of supervision that will serve as a guide to the superstructure of this work, let us consider a few basic definitions.

Staff Development and Instructional Development

Staff development focuses on the professional and classified staff and attempts to provide the means for the total staff to meet better the needs of students. These needs include personal, social, intellectual, and career requirements that students (and others) see as essential to their life styles and goals. Staff development, then is a comprehensive, school-wide program that provides for improvement in organization and communication structures, in instructional programs and processes, and in human interrelationships and personal attitudes.

    Instructional development concentrates on curriculum and instruction. Its goal is to create a more effective, systematic way of providing efficient and meaningful instruction based on clearly specified objectives. Both programs (staff and instructional development) are the same as the general goal of educational supervision—the improvement of instruction. The changes in organization and in human relationships must be measured by their influences on the instructional setting.

Curriculum

The school's curriculum is composed of all experiences that the individual receives under the school's guidance. Our dynamic society requires that these experiences be organized and presented efficiently. If teachers are to keep pace with these changes and perform to the best of their abilities, the supervision of instruction must be democratic in nature. Provisions for helping the professional staff improve the curriculum must be made by the supervising principal.

---

[1] Gordon W. Allport, *Becoming: Basic Considerations for a Psychology of Personality* (New Haven: Yale University Press, 1955), pp. 16–17.

The Supervising Principal
and the Specialist-Consultant

The terms *principal, supervising principal,* and *specialist-consultant* appear throughout the text. As used in this work, the terms *supervising principal* and *principal* are synonymous. Both refer to the executive leader at the individual school level.

The specialist-consultant serves in a staff capacity. He usually is assigned at the school system offices and gives service at many schools within the system.

The term *supervisor* refers to any individual rendering supervisory services, including the supervising principal, the assistant principal, the department head, the assistant dean, the dean, the specialist-consultant, and the assistant consultant or master teacher-consultant.

Principles of Supervision

Some basic principles of supervision that may serve as guideposts for further discussion follow:

1. Supervision, an integral part of an educational program, is a cooperative, team-type service.
2. All teachers need, and are entitled to, supervisory help. This service is the chief responsibility of the supervising principal.
3. Supervision should be adapted to meet the individual needs of school personnel.
4. Classified as well as certified personnel need, and should benefit from, supervision.
5. Supervision should help clarify educational objectives and goals and should illuminate the implications of these objectives and goals.
6. Supervision should help improve the attitudes and relationships of all members of the school staff and should help develop good rapport with the community.
7. Supervision should assist in the organization and proper administration of cocurricular activities for students.
8. The responsibility for improving the program for school supervision rests with the teacher for his/her classroom. In a like manner, this responsibility rests with the principal for the school, and with the superintendent for the school system.
9. There should be adequate provision for supervision in the annual budget.
10. Both long- and short-term planning for supervision is essential. All affected, including certificated and classified personnel, professional associations, the school community, and the students should participate or be represented, in varying ways and degrees, in planning sessions and in the program for supervision.
11. The supervisory program, being serviced by administration and by staff personnel, should, at all levels below that of the community college, utilize

consultant help from the intermediate unit superintendent's (county) office, the state department of education, colleges and universities, and other local, state, and national agencies.

12. Supervision should help interpret and put into practice the latest findings of educational research.

13. The effectiveness of the program for supervision should be evaluated by both the participants and outside consultants.

Democratic Supervision in American Education

European Backgrounds

EDUCATION IN EARLY GREECE.   In the time of Homer there was no systematic education in Greece. It is suspected[2] that there might have been some private tutoring. With the cultural development of the Dorian Greeks, learning to write became a necessity, and it is suspected that schools for teaching writing were established prior to 500 B.C. The Greeks provided some public support for the education of poor children, but only boys were permitted to attend school. From 400 B.C. to 350 B.C. reading and writing were taught in most schools.

SPARTAN EDUCATION AND ITS SUPERVISION.   S. E. Frost reported:

Near the eighth century B.C. a Dorian tribe of Greeks pushed into Laconia and conquered the original inhabitants of the area. They settled in a fertile plain, 5 by 18 miles, and isolated by high mountains. Here they established small villages which were little more than military barracks.[3]

Education was a chief concern of the Spartan state. The purpose of education was to enhance, develop, maintain, and protect the Spartan state. The authority for education was placed in the hands of the chief rulers of the city who were called *Ephors*. Frost[4] noted that a *Paidonomous* was chosen for a period of one year from among the chief magistrates. It was the duty of the *Paidonomous* to supervise the training of the students. He was in absolute control and was assisted by whip bearers called *Bidioi*. There were no teachers or tutors. The student was given no freedom. Each citizen was responsible for the teaching of the young.

EDUCATION IN LATER GREECE.   In later Athenian-led Greece the ideal of education was the development of the golden mean; professionalism and specialization were discouraged.

[2] S. E. Frost, *Essentials of History of Education* (New York: Barron's Educational Series Inc., 1947), p. 22.

[3] Ibid.

[4] Ibid., p. 23.

The famous teachers—Socrates, Plato, and Aristotle—were astounding all with their brilliant new ideas and concepts. Apollonius Dyscholus, who lived during the second century B.C., developed the science of grammar. During the same century, Eratosthenes did his great work in the science of geography.

EDUCATION IN ROME.   When the Romans took over much of the Greek empire, they assimilated in themselves much of the Greek heritage of art, science, and education. We suspect that the Greeks originally had obtained much of their scientific, artistic, and educational ideals from the early travelers of the Aegean Sea and that these early Aegean travelers had been highly influenced by the early Phoenicians and Hebrews. All this rich heritage they gave to the Romans.

When the liberal brothers Gracchus came into political power approximately 140 B.C., schools of Latin grammar arose. Many books to be used in these schools appeared and research into the Latin language was increased. Since much Latin literature was created, Latin grammar took form and substance. Suddenly there was a need for the improvement of instruction and curriculum in this subject! During the fourth and fifth centuries, elementary and Latin grammar schools were to be seen everywhere throughout the empire.

EDUCATION AND ITS SUPERVISION IN THE MIDDLE AGES.   The elementary "Reading and Writing Schools" of the Middle Ages that grew out of the Reformation were attended by both boys and girls. Instruction was in the vernacular language. Teachers were selected by the elders of the city and were paid out of the public treasury.

During the sixteenth century in England, many patrons contributed money to grammar schools, and English catechisms and primers were given to the schools. The Song Schools were eliminated, and government supervision of both schools and teachers was begun. Many patrons provided additional funds to the English public schools in order to provide a free education for poor boys. These schools were "public" because they prepared students from many burgs and hamlets of England to become state officials.

Supervision rendered by the government appointee was, naturally, concerned that instruction be in line with the best interests of the state, and the supervising clergyman was interested in the religious and moral content of instruction. Little attention was paid to the quality of instruction, nor was a great deal of effort expended in attempting to improve educational conditions in general.

New World Precedents

The increasingly liberal ideas concerning religion and education for children in the Colonies of North America originated not only from within the newer religious sects, such as the Quakers and Anglicans, but also from within others of the more established or traditional sects. There was an increasing emphasis on gentle control rather than on harsh discipline in the Colonies. Many argued, even in those early days, that children varied in their individual aptitudes and interests. The spirit of Penn and Benezet was invading the community of fear established by Cotton Mather, Increase Mather, and Jonathan Edwards.

R. F. Butts and L. A. Cremin[5] noted that when the colonists came to the New World in 1600, a study of literature and languages, especially Latin, Hebrew, and Greek, was well imbedded in the educational system, primarily in secondary and higher education. The Protestant revolution produced scholars who found that they had to do holy battle with the learned Catholic philosophers and theologians. Those who controlled education found that they must provide time for supervision.

In 1647, the Massachusetts General Court passed one of the most important laws in the educational history of our country. This law required towns containing fifty or more families to establish schools. A teacher of such a school was to give instruction in reading and writing, and his pay was to come from taxes, contributions from the parents, or fees levied on the parents. A Latin grammar school was to be established if there were 100 or more families in the town. The important principle here is that government had the right to require the establishment of schools and to control these schools.

During the Colonial period, the elementary schools were designed mainly for the children of the lower classes, who were taught reading and writing. The Latin grammar schools and colleges were designed strictly for the upper classes. There was instruction in religion in both types of schools. In the latter part of the eighteenth century, the private "English schools" and then the academies were established.

The school curriculum was well set during the early Colonial period. Children who planned to enter grammar schools were expected to have obtained the basic fundamentals of reading and writing by the age of eight. Apprentices were expected to learn from their masters, and the poorer children could attend publicly or privately endowed schools or religious schools.

Children of the upper classes might attend a private dame school. A woman would have many children come to her house and would instruct them, a few times a week, in reading and writing.

The Evolution of Supervision
in the United States

In 1654, the General Court of the Massachusetts Bay Colonies passed a law that required the elders of a town, as well as the overseers of Harvard University, to insure that no teachers were hired who were "unsound in faith or scandalous in their lives." Teachers were required to sign an oath of allegiance to the states

---

[5] R. Freeman Butts and Lawrence A. Cremin, *A History of Education in American Culture* (New York: Henry Holt and Company, 1953), p. 75.

when the War of Independence began, long before the advent of loyalty oaths during the so-called Cold War.

In 1709, Committees of Laymen were appointed in Boston. These committees were to inspect and approve teachers, courses of study, and classroom instructional techniques.

The supervisory authority of the principal was acquired slowly.[6] In many instances, the town committee was reluctant to surrender its authority. Furthermore, the principal was looked on as a super-teacher rather than as a person with sufficient skill and knowledge to act as a supervisor of instruction.

The superintendent, when he finally gained power, was unwilling to delegate authority to the principal, and there was no clear statement of who had the responsibility and authority for supervision in the new school organization. This confusion often led to resentment and to malpractice among those who struggled for control.

The improvement of instruction was not emphasized; rather, as seen in Table 1–1, the discipline of the students was observed, the school plant was scrutinized, and the performance of the teacher received superficial attention and appraisal.

The nation's growth during the nineteenth century demanded that the supervisory responsibilities be given to professional school administrators. The position of principal teacher (or principal) emerged during this period when the board members discovered that they could no longer administer or "supervise" the rapidly growing school systems. Although the principalship was the first administrative position to emerge, it was the last to secure responsibility and authority for instructional improvement. The principal's duties at first were clerical, then disciplinary, then administrative, and—finally—supervisory. Even at this late date, "supervision" is taken by many to mean an emphasis on inspection and control.

The early 1900's, especially from the turn of the second decade of the century to approximately 1935, was marked by intensive interest in measurement, classroom management, and operation. There was little professional literature of note that championed the cause of the improvement of instruction through supervision. One of the most influential works was H. W. Nutt's *The Supervision of Instruction* (Boston: Houghton Mifflin Co., 1920).

"Efficiency!"—the keynote of the time—resulted in the application of tremendous pressure to "find something to improve" in each classroom visited. Mental testing movements gained momentum; visitation became a mechanical process; elaborate rating systems were devised. The evidence shows that the classroom visitations and criticisms rarely served as a basis for improvement or guidance. Nonetheless, supervision of instruction was viewed as a worthy function, and expenditure of school funds for supervisory purposes was authorized; effort was sincere; techniques were developed that were to lead, eventually, toward the development of a program for the improvement of instruction.

[6] Butts and Cremin, *A History of Education in American Culture*, pp. 115–137.

In the Middle and Late 1900's, supervision emerged as a democratic function, with supervisory assignments becoming broader in scope and purpose. The *human factor* finally was considered.

There was an increasing awareness of the need for positive, adequate programs of community relations in an attempt to reach the several publics involved with the school. It finally was recognized that the best program of "public relations" is open, two-way communication, especially concerning evidence of the best possible instructional program.

Table 1-1 shows the historical periods in the evolution of supervision. The goals of supervision were, at first, administrative in character. Later, there

TABLE 1-1.   Historical Periods in the Development of American School Supervision.[a]

CONCEPTS OF SUPERVISION IN AMERICAN EDUCATION	PERIOD OF INFLUENCE	PARTIES DOING THE SUPERVISION	NATURE OF THE SUPERVISORY PROGRAM
1. Inspection of school and classroom	Colonial period through the Civil War	Laymen: clergy, school wardens, trustees, selectmen, citizens' committees.	Inspection for the sake of control. Emphasis upon observing rules and maintaining existing standards.
2. Inspection of school and classroom	Nineteenth century	State, intermediate unit (county) local superintendents.	Inspection for the sake of control. Emphasis upon regulations, with leadership for improvement.
3. Supervision of classroom instruction	1910–1935	Responsibility divided between principals and special supervisors or "helping teachers."	Improvement of instruction through direct classroom observation and demonstration with attention focused upon the teacher's weaknesses.
4. Cooperative educational leadership	1935–1963	Responsibility of principals and special supervisors, shared with coordinators, curriculum directors, consultants, and others.	Program centered in cooperative study enterprises, such as curriculum development, and in-service education courses, aiming toward improvement of instruction.

TABLE 1-1. Continued

CONCEPTS OF SUPERVISION IN AMERICAN EDUCATION	PERIOD OF INFLUENCE	PARTIES DOING THE SUPERVISION	NATURE OF THE SUPERVISORY PROGRAM
5. Supervision as cooperative effort, stimulated by democratic leadership and influenced by the availability of federal grants and interest of the community	1964 to Present	Responsibility of teachers and principals, and, in certain cases specialist-consultants, special supervisors, coordinators, curriculum directors, consultants, research personnel and public relations specialists.	Program still centered in cooperative study enterprises with the addition of community participation. Awareness of utilization of federal monies to best advantage. Systems approaches to staff development and instructional development emerging. Management by performance objectives supports the participation/involvement approach to problem solving and conflict resolution.[a]

[a] Harold Spears, *Improving the Supervision of Instruction* (Englewood Cliffs, New Jersey: Prentice-Hall, Inc., 1953) p. 38.

appeared a shift toward establishing goals that were more supervisory in nature and were concerned with the democratic improvement of instruction.[7]

The meaning of democracy as applied to educational supervision was well stated by the National Education Association Commission on the Reorganization of Secondary Education:

. . . Democracy sanctions neither the exploitation of the individual by society, nor the disregard of the interests of society by the individual . . .
. . . This ideal demands that human activities be placed upon a high level of efficiency; that to this efficiency be added an appreciation of the significance of these activities. . . .[8]

[7] Jack C. Goodwin, "Principles and Practices of Teacher Evaluation Programs in the Schools of the United States" (Doctoral dissertation, University of Southern California, 1956).

[8] R. Freeman Butts and Lawrence A. Cremin, *A History of Education in American Culture*, p. 131.

If we accept the idea that the educator's goal is to develop each student's highest potentialities, then we, as teachers and supervisors, must learn to produce such qualities within ourselves. These qualities must include independent thinking, initiative, self-reliance, democratic cooperation with others, and intellectual honesty. Boardman, Douglass, and Bent[9] noted that if supervision's goal is the ideal of democracy, then supervision must be democratic. The older supervisory techniques, which inhibited initiative, must be replaced by techniques that encourage experimentation and creativity. If teachers are to develop the ability to adapt materials and procedures to the objectives of education, then the supervising principal must use every means at his disposal in order to develop the *initiative, self-reliance, originality,* and *independence of thought* of the professional staff.

Traditional supervision centered on the teacher and the classroom situation and was based on the misconception that teachers, being undertrained, needed constant direction and training. Modern supervision is seen as a cooperative service that is primarily concerned with identifying and solving professional problems. Rather than focusing attention on the teacher and the classroom situation, attention is focused on the total learning-teaching situation. The trend is away from supervision as superinspection and superrating, and toward the newer concepts of supervision as providing cooperative services, consultation, and inservice education.

Traditional and Modern Supervision Compared

Burton and Brueckner[10] summarized six major points in comparing traditional and modern practices in school supervision.

Traditional school supervision, then, consisted largely of inspection of the teacher, was poorly planned, and was authoritarian. Modern supervision,

Traditional Supervision	*Modern Supervision*
1. Inspection	1. Pragmatic study and analysis
2. Teacher-focused	2. Goal, material, techniques, method, teacher, student, and environment—(total teaching-learning situation)—focused
3. Visitation and conference	3. Many diverse functions
4. Poorly planned or a meager formal plan	4. Definitely organized and planned, with specific objectives
5. Imposed and authoritarian	5. Derived and cooperative
6. Usually by one person	6. By many persons

[9] Charles W. Boardman, Harl R. Douglass, and Rudyard K. Bent, *Democratic Supervision in Secondary Schools* (Boston: Houghton Mifflin Company, 1953).

[10] William H. Burton and Leo J. Brueckner, *Supervision, A Social Process* (New York: Appleton-Century-Crofts, Educational Division, Meredith Corp., 1955.) Reprinted by permission of the publisher.

in sharp contrast, is based on research and analysis of the total teaching-learning environment and its many functions by many individuals. Modern supervision is objective, systematic, democratic, creative, growth-centered and producing, and accentuates the spirit of inquiry by emphasizing experimentations and continuous evaluation. Democratic principles should control supervision and evaluation in the school.

At the same time that the concept and practices of supervision were developing, leadership research was progressing from an emphasis on traits to situations to an emphasis on social role theory. No matter what the theoretical emphasis, the success of supervision seems to depend more on the element of good human relations than on any other single factor. Keep in mind that supervision is primarily the responsibility of the principal. Although teachers do have a part in the supervisory process, the extent of teacher participation in supervision, especially below the level of the community college, is still in question. Most school systems have some type of evaluation, with the larger systems having the more formal type. Smaller school systems tend to avoid the more formalized programs of evaluation.

Supervision's Administrative Heritage

H. J. Otto[11] wrote that in the operation of schools it is difficult, if not impossible, to draw fine lines between the administrative, supervisory, and leadership functions. Many activities in which supervising principals participate do fall in one or another of these three categories, but many activities overlap the borders between these three functions.

When considering either a supervisory or an administrative program, we start with a *needs assessment,* followed by a statement of an educational *philosophy.* We *identify* the *audience, environment,* and real-world *constraints,* and then state the broad, long-range *goals* and *management tasks.* We develop *strategy(ies)* by defining objectives, preparing criterion measures, specifying resources needed, and constructing a prototype program. Then we *evaluate,* analyze the evaluation data, and *revise* the specific supervisory or administrative program.

Perhaps the best way to distinguish between supervision and administration is to look at the *purpose* of the activity. If the purpose is to improve instruction, then the activity may be put in the supervisory column. If, on the other hand, the purpose of the activity is primarily concerned with areas other than improving instruction, then the activity could be termed administrative.

For example, Shirley Rotter, principal of Pemberton High, visited Diana Bruce's classroom on Tuesday for the purpose of helping Diana to initiate a unit in geography. Realizing that one goal of supervision is to help professionals grow and become independent, she brought many materials to Diana before the class session. She scheduled a follow-up conference after her visit so that she could

---

[11] Henry J. Otto, *Elementary School Organization and Administration* (New York: Appleton-Century-Crofts, Inc., 1954), p. 296.

discuss other resources, with an eye toward helping Diana become proficient in locating her own materials giving her specific ideas that would help her to make her instruction more effective and efficient.

The following day, Mrs. Rotter visited the same teacher, but for a different purpose. It was May, and the class schedules for the following term were being prepared. She wished to determine the possibility of Mrs. Bruce's teaching a course on elementary Spanish to sixth-grade students.

The class assignment rating function was administrative in character; the Tuesday unit initiation visit and follow-up conference were supervisory in nature.

For our purposes, then, let us consider any activity that is *primarily concerned with improving classroom instruction* as a supervision activity.

A History of Education Personnel Administration for the Supervisor

Public personnel supervision in the United States began "when the government became large enough to require a considerable number of employees."[12]

Nearly a century after public personnel administration was inaugurated in the United States, industry, spurred by the ever increasing stimulus of competition, initiated personnel administration as a definite function of management. By 1920, personnel administration was becoming a formidable complex. Powerful labor organizations forced industry to develop strong and adequate personnel departments emphasizing the human dynamics aspect of personnel management. According to J. M. Pfiffner, the "differences between private and public personnel practices are drawing closer together."[13]

Comparing the personnel function in industry with that in the public school, A. H. Simons wrote that "personnel administration in industry is years ahead of public school personnel administration."[14]

Early selection of teachers was by local lay boards of education. "The superintendent as a professional executive did not exist. The only specification for a teacher was that he would be considered competent 'if he could discipline.' "[15]

In New England, teachers were appointed at regular town meetings. Since the schools were so closely related to the church, the minister's approbation was essential. Selection was based on finding someone who was qualified and willing to teach, and who would accept the meager salary that had been voted for the purpose. Many teachers received payment "in kind," that is, in goods or services.[16]

[12] Marshall Edward Dimock and Gladys Ogden Dimock, *Public Administration* (New York: Rinehart Company, 1953), p. 146.

[13] John M. Pfiffner, *Public Administration* (New York: The Ronald Press Company, 1947).

[14] Aubrey Hays Simons, "An Evaluation of Recruitment Methods in Medium-Sized School Districts in California" (Doctoral dissertation, University of Southern California, 1956), p. 18.

[15] Ibid., p. 19.

[16] William A. Yeager, *Administration and the Teacher* (New York: Harper and Brothers, 1954), pp. 132–134.

TABLE 1-2. Developmental Trends That Have Influenced Educational Personnel Supervision.

THE PAST		THE PRESENT
Education for few	⟶	Education for all
Private, parochial, and pauper schools	⟶	Common schools for all, regardless of economic status or "social class"
Instruction in religion	⟶	Practical instruction for life in society
Education preserving class and social distinctions	⟶	Education aimed at equalization or harmonizing different social and economic groups; education as a social ladder

The instructors were usually male school masters, since few women were employed. Since the demand exceeded the supply, a man had an excellent chance of being hired if he could "keep school." While his statement concerning his own ability normally was accepted, a letter of recommendation from a minister usually was sufficient to meet the qualifications for the office.

W. A. Yeager commented: "We cannot deny that favoritism, both political and social, had its place in the selection of teachers whose [other] qualifications were often quite lacking."[17] This condition led to E. H. Reisner's contention that teaching was the "last measure of professional and business incompetence. It was not even a well-defined trade with standards of preparation and fitness."[18]

Upgrading from these lowly origins has been a long and tedious process. Table 1-2 reflects developmental trends in education that have influenced the practice of educational personnel supervision. Improvement in quality became noticeable only after the selection process became a professional function. Three factors have influenced this movement: (1) the development of educational leaders; (2) the beginnings of the normal schools; and (3) the beginnings of local and later state controls over trainees both as to preparation and certification requirements.[19]

What Is The Role of Supervision Today?

The broad modern interpretation of the role of supervision is action and experimentation aimed at improving instruction and the instructional program. Using this definition, supervision should be the concern of superintendents, principals, specialists, directors, consultants, deans, coordinators, chairmen, and teachers.

[17] Ibid., p. 67.
[18] Edward H. Reisner, *The Evaluation of the Common School* (New York: The Macmillan Company, 1930), p. 393.
[19] Yeager, p. 66.

The following ways of improving the instructional program are used more frequently today:

1. Sharing ideas, procedures, and materials in order to evaluate and develop the curriculum
2. Developing materials and procedures to implement the curriculum
3. Planning for instructional improvement through in-service education, institutes, research, workshops, and projects
4. Organizing a staff of professional specialist-consultants
5. Directing teachers toward goals through democratic processes by supplying specific directions based on a sound background in individual and group dynamics
6. Allowing—indeed encouraging—teachers to participate in planning and organization
7. Evaluating curriculum, materials, and procedures in the light of basic objectives and the findings of scientific research

Whose Job Is It?

The superintendent, staff members, specialists, principal, consultants, and department heads and teachers are all concerned with improving the instructional program in the schools. However, this area is more the total responsibility of the principal and his staff.

The principal's job is to fulfill the objectives for the school's supervisory program. The ultimate responsibility for the program rests with the principal for his school, and with the superintendent for the school system.

Surely the hallmark for supervision today would include the factors of objectivity, systematic planning and procedures, a democratic approach, a creative atmosphere, pragmatic orientation, and a lot of experimentation and evaluation. It should include a spirit of cooperative inquiry, empathy, service, creativity, openmindedness, appraisal, and skill in group processes. It is at once an expert, technical service concerned with studying and improving all conditions inherent in the teaching-learning process, and a supportive function, a service function, a human relations function.

BASIC CHANGES IN THE FUNCTIONS OF SCHOOL SUPERVISION IN THE LOCAL SCHOOL SYSTEM.   The following list illustrates some of the more basic changes in school supervision that have occurred at the local level:

1. Supervision includes more than it did in the past. This expansion is the result of continual critical thinking in connection with the nature of education and its relation to the individual and to society.
2. Supervision methods are becoming more objective and experimental. This change stems from the scientific movement in education.

3. Supervision is increasingly participatory and cooperative. Policies and plans are formulated through group discussion, with participation by all concerned. This alteration in approach and technique is the result of increasing insight into the nature of democracy and of democratic methods.
4. Supervisory activities and opportunities are distributed among an ever-increasing number of persons as all come to contribute and to accept the challenge to exercise leadership.
5. Supervision is increasingly derived from the given situation, rather than imposed from above.

Everything in a school system is (or should be) designed for the ultimate purpose of stimulating learning and growth. Supervision deals with items that primarily directly condition learning and growth.

LOCAL SUPERVISION: A PROBLEM IN LEADERSHIP AND COOPERATION. Barr et al.[20] formulated the following outline of leadership functions for the school supervisor at the local level:

1. Evaluating the educational products in the light of accepted objectives of education.
   a) The cooperative determination and critical analysis of aims
   b) The selection and application of the means of appraisal
   c) The analysis of the data to discover strength and weakness in the product.
2. Studying the teaching-learning situation to determine the antecedents of satisfactory and unsatisfactory student growth and achievement.
   a) Studying the course of study and the curriculum-in-operation
   b) Studying the materials of instruction, the equipment, and the socio-physical environment of learning and growth
   c) Studying the factors related to instruction (the teacher's personality, academic and professional training, techniques)
   d) Studying the factors present in the learner (capacity, interest, work habits, intellectual development, and others).
3. Improving the teaching-learning situation.
   a) Improving the course of study and the curriculum-in-operation
   b) Improving the materials of instruction, the equipment, and the socio-physical environment of learning and growth
   c) Improving the factors related directly to instruction
   d) Improving factors present in the learner which affect his growth and achievement.
4. Evaluating the objectives, methods, and outcomes of supervision.
   a) Discovering and applying the techniques of evaluation
   b) Evaluating the results of given supervisory programs, including factors which limit the success of these programs
   c) Evaluating and improving the performance of the personnel of supervision.

[20] Barr, et al., *Supervision*, pp. 9–11.

The National Education Association[21] delineated the following functions of the school supervisor:

PER CENT	FUNCTIONS
100	Attending meetings of professional associations
97	Discussing educational philosophy, objectives, and techniques
96	Holding group conferences to discuss common problems
96	Making classroom visitations

Serving as a resource person also should be added to this list. In performing these functions, the supervisor should call on specialists from the intermediate and state units. Local system supervisors in a geographical area should cooperate in area meetings and in sharing materials.

THE IMPORTANCE OF SELF-SUPERVISION.   The transition from imposed supervision, coupled with the desirable modern emphasis on cooperative group endeavor, sometimes obscure an important implication of modern philosophy and thinking in supervision—the possibilities for self-direction, self-guidance, and self-supervision. The mature individual not only will serve as a leader in group enterprise and make contributions to group discussions and decisions; he/she also often will engage in a program for self-improvement.

Specialists engage in such a program when they work independently on a frontier problem. A member of the rank and file does this when studying his/her own needs, or trying new methods in the classroom, or pursuing a problem of his own through the available literature. Self-initiated attention to any problem usually grows out of group activities.[22]

The Principal as the Chief Supervisor in the Local School

The building principal must accept responsibility for all that transpires in the local school. This means that the principal is the chief supervisory officer. General, special, intermediate unit, and state supervisors always must work through, and in harmony with, the principal. Before visiting teachers individually or in groups, the staff supervisor (the specialist-consultant) should check with the principal's office. The functions of the supervisors at the state and intermediate unit levels are discussed in chapters 2 and 3.

[21] Association for Supervision and Curriculum Development of the National Education Association, "Leadership through Supervision," *1946 Yearbook of the Association* (Washington, D.C.: The Association, 1946), pp. 37–38.

[22] Barr et al., *Supervision,* p. 13.

Do

1. Combine efforts of teachers and supervisory personnel.
2. Offer and accept new ideas.
3. Work toward the optimum utilization of all instructional materials.
4. Respect staff opinions and suggestions.
5. Recognize that support and loyalty form a two-way street.
6. Have a sincere concern for staff members as professional individuals.
7. Praise and encourage good attitudes and procedures for specific accomplishments.
8. Use effective measures of evaluation.
9. Support the staff in relations with the community.
10. Accept the teacher as an equal, charged with specific responsibilities.
11. Enlist the cooperative efforts of the entire staff in studying the school's educational problems.
12. Provide opportunities from which teachers can develop potential leadership.
13. Accept deviations from the established order of doing things.
14. Conduct a continuous search for better and more effective ways of performing your duties.
15. Enlist the services of the specialist-consultants at the local, intermediate, and state levels.
16. Believe always that no best way has yet been found.

Don't

1. Assume the role of a *superior*-visor.
2. Assume that the curriculum and the methods of implementing and teaching it are fixed.
3. Consider experimentation by teachers to be insubordination.
4. Make a standard, scheduled supervisory visit without making an appointment ahead of time.
5. Be afraid to make an informal, *brief* visit.
6. Look upon yourself as a threat rather than as a helper.
7. Be afraid to call on neighboring principals, specialist-consultants, and teachers for additional help.
8. Fail to devote at least 50 percent of your time to the vital business of supervision.

TRENDS: THE FUTURE OF SUPERVISION

Toward ⟶   Acceptance of the Supervisor

as a Facilitator, Aid, Consultant,

and Professional Advisor

As noted in the past the supervising principal was considered to be a super-inspector. It is hoped that in the future the supervisor will be accepted as facilitator, an aid, consultant, and professional advisor to the classroom teacher and to classified personnel. Signs indicate that this change has begun. The road is uncertain, however, and slow. Perhaps this journey will be speeded with the cooperative development of assignment specifications and with granting tenures to supervisors.

Toward ⟶ Increased Research and Experimentation in Supervision

We are not content to hope that we are using the best methods and materials available in our program of supervision. We are turning more to the results of research and experimentation for direction.

In the past, the type of supervision often was up to the individual supervising principal, as were the suggestions concerning how an individual teacher might improve his/her instructional performance. At times these "suggestions" bore the weight of command, and many a "supervisor" would proudly point to some common action being taken by the teachers under despotic control. Unfortunately, these common actions often lacked two important factors, for (1) they would be based, partially or totally, on off-the-cuff "intuition," and/or (2) they would be applied to all teaching-learning situations and all teachers, with all classes.

We now recognize that teachers are individuals, that children are individuals, and that no two groups possess the same dynamics. We also are beginning to recognize the invaluable service of research and experimentation, although disappointingly little research has been accomplished in the area of supervision.

The professional supervising principal must provide the spirit and the force for such experimentation. We must forcefully assume our professional responsibilities. As the techniques and methods of scientific investigation are developed and made known to more people engaged in supervision, we shall see an increase in the amount of research in this area.

Toward ⟶ Increased Activity of the United States Office of Education in Elementary School Supervision

Since 1867, the role of the United States Office of Education has been expanding. In light of today's needs, it is safe to predict increased federal research in instructional techniques and technology. A system of education that can do the job required for modern institutions requires national coordination. This does not necessitate a system managed from Washington.

Supervisory Problems

In Basket

Throughout the text, the reader will encounter "In-Basket (simulated) Supervisory Problems." These problems may be considered as representative of situations and problems a supervisor in the field may encounter as he/she goes about everyday tasks. In establishing the ground rules for handling the problems, the seminar group may wish to indicate that the individuals assigned to provide a solution for the problem may assume any data they wish, when no information to the contrary is provided. Group leaders may wish to encourage the seminar members to bring in their own in-basket (simulated) supervisory problems. If so, the general scope of the problem and a few basic references should be presented to the participants before the problem is presented to permit adequate preparation for the seminar. The seminar leader (the student presenting the problem) should introduce the topic, set the environmental background, and summarize at the end of the session.

The seminar leader should provide a systematic progression in the discussion of the problem, somewhat as follows:

    A.   Statement of the immediate problem
    B.   Underlying problem(s)
    C.   Facts as stated in the problem
    D.   Solution(s)—options (short-, intermediate-, and long-range)

Problem

The school district by which you are employed has a small but vocal teacher's union local. Most teachers in the district belong to the District Teacher's Association and to the parent state and national associations. There has been some talk of establishing a professional relations committee, but no action has been taken.

Your superintendent believes that all probationary teachers should be rated once per month. As principal of Edward Elcott High, you have complied.

You have received a note in your in-basket that reads:

"Dear Snooper: Your supervisory techniques are deplorable: You must be living in the past! We want you to know that we can take just so much! If you continue to visit the probationary teachers once per month and, therefore, fail to permit them to relax and teach, without worrying about putting on a show for you, we shall be forced to take this problem further."

What would you do?

(NOTE: *You may assume anything, but you may not change the facts, nor may you indicate that in the past you would have done something to avoid the problem. The question is, what will you do, given the facts as listed in the problem?*)

Questions and Suggested Activities Concerning Principles of Supervision

Questions

1. What have been your experiences and reactions to supervision? Can you account for your reactions? Were valid principles employed in the supervisory program?
2. How can the supervisor best gain the confidence and cooperation of teaching personnel? What principles are involved?
3. What are the advantages of democratic, cooperative supervision? The disadvantages?
4. How can desired changes best be effected by the supervisor?
5. The role of the supervisor is viewed differently by supervisors, teachers, administrators, and the school board. How can the supervisor best resolve these differences of opinion?
6. What are some principles that a supervisor can use to gain rapport and cohesiveness within a group?
7. Can a school be known for its supervisory program, or is it restricted by the policies of the school system?
8. How much should a school be swayed by community pressures to which it is subjected?

Suggested Activities

1. List the ways by which a supervisor can observe basic principles in aiding teachers.
2. List the basic principles of supervision violated by a group of teachers who have become tyrannical and unpleasant in their classes.
3. List some "do's" and "don't's" for the beginning supervisor. Refer to the list of basic principles.
4. List the qualifications of the ideal supervisor in training, experience, and personal qualities. What principles are involved?
5. List the differences in supervision that might be found between a small, rural district and a large, city school system.
6. List the changes currently taking place in education and their possible effects on supervision.
7. List the qualities of an ideal supervisor.
8. List recent articles on supervision. Write a short critique of each. Note where the authors are working.
9. Write a short article suitable for publication in a professional journal. It should be related to one of the topics covered in this chapter.
10. Trace the evolution of supervision in the old world. Compare supervision in the old world, prior to the French Revolution, with supervision today in England and France.

11. Trace the evolution of supervision in the United States. Be sure to include Colonial precedents compared with supervision today.
12. Trace the history of the acquisition of supervisory authority by the superintendent; by the principal.
13. Prepare two skits to be presented in class. In one skit, show the traditional supervision in action; in the other, show how the supervisor of tomorrow will perform.
14. Indicate the major organizations concerned primarily with educational supervision, and trace the development of these organizations.
15. Indicate briefly how developing social movements have influenced supervision. Prepare charts, graphs, and/or diagrams that will assist in interpretation. Be sure to include demography, sociology, and theories of educational sociology, government, communication, transporation, and agrarian movement.
16. Indicate how developing philosophies of education have influenced supervision.
17. Indicate what you believe to be the proper role of the federal government in (1) education in general; (2) either community college, secondary, or elementary education; and (3) the supervision of either community college, secondary, or elementary education.

Selected Bibliography

Books

Allport, Gordon W. *Becoming: Basic Considerations for a Psychology of Personality.* New Haven: Yale University Press, 1955.

Barr, A. S., William H. Burton, and Leo J. Brueckner. *Supervision, Principles and Practices in the Improvement of Instruction.* New York: D. Appleton-Century Company, 1938.

Bartky, John A. *Supervision as Human Relations.* Boston: D. C. Heath and Company, 1953.

Boardman, Charles W., Harl R. Douglass, and Rudyard K. Bent. *Democratic Supervision in Secondary Schools.* Boston: Houghton Mifflin Company, 1953.

Burton, William H., and Leo J. Brueckner. *Supervision, A Social Process.* New York: Appleton-Century-Crofts, 1955.

Butts, R. Freeman, and Lawrence A. Cremin. *A History of Education in American Culture.* New York: Henry Holt and Company, 1953.

Fieldler, Fred E., and Martin M. Chemers. *Leadership and Effective Management.* Glenview, Illinois: Scott, Foresman and Co., 1974.

Frost, S. E. *Essentials of History of Education.* New York: Barron's Educational Series Inc., 1947.

Gwynn, J. Minor. *Theory and Practice of Supervision.* New York: Dodd, Mead, & Company, 1961

Lucio, William H., and John D. McNeil. *Supervision.* New York: McGraw-Hill Book Company, 1969.

Morphet, Edgar L., Roe L. Johns, and Theodore L. Reller. *Educational Administration.* Englewood Cliffs, New Jersey: Prentice-Hall, Inc., 1959.

Otto, Henry J. *Elementary School Organization and Administration.* New York: Appleton-Century-Crofts, 1954.

Plunkett, W. Richards. *Supervision: the Direction of People at Work.* Dubuque, Iowa: Wm. C. Brown Co., 1975.

Ryan, Doris W., et al. *The Individualized System: Administration and Leadership.* (H. S. I. Studies) Toronto: The Ontario Institute for Studies in Education, 1974.

Smith, Vernon H. *Alternative Schools: The Development of Options in Education.* Lincoln, Neb.: Professional Educators Publications, Inc., 1974.

Spears, Harold. *Improving the Supervision of Instruction.* Englewood Cliffs, New Jersey: Prentice-Hall, Inc., 1953.

Stoops, Emery, Max Rafferty, and Russell E. Johnson. *Handbook of Educational Administration.* Boston: Allyn and Bacon, Inc., 1975.

Wiles, Kimball, and John T. Lovell. *Supervision for Better Schools.* 4th ed. Englewood Cliffs, New Jersey: Prentice-Hall, Inc., 1975.

Audio Cassettes

Broadwell, Martin. *The New Supervisor Cassette Program.* Addison-Wesley, 1973. Designed to acquaint supervisors new to the job with their new responsibilities. Audio cassettes plus text and gaming.

The New Manager of the Training Function. Development Digest, 1975. Available from Thompson-Mitchell, Atlanta, Georgia.
The New Supervisor. Thompson-Mitchell, Atlanta, Georgia, 1970. A set of five sound filmstrips that treats matters of immediate concern to the beginning supervisor.

Film

The Everyday Supervisory Skills Series. Thompson-Mitchell, Atlanta, Georgia, 1974. A set of six sound filmstrips concerning the principles of good supervision.

Periodicals

Bradfield, Luther E. "Basic Principles Underlying Techniques of Supervision." *American School Board Journal* CXXVIII (June 1954) : 21–23.
Farley, Genevieve J., and John J. Santosuosso. "Techniques of Supervision." *Educational Administration and Supervision* XLIII (April 1957) : 249–252.
Simpson, Roy E. "The Place of the State Superintendent in Public Education." *California Schools* XXI (September 1950) : 307–312.

Other Sources

Alexander, William Marvin. "State Leadership in Improving Instruction." Unpublished Doctoral dissertation, Teachers College, Columbia University, 1940.
American Association of School Administrators. "Leadership at the State Level," Chapter XIII in *The American School Superintendent.* Thirtieth Yearbook of the Association. Washington, D.C.: The Association, 1952.
Association for Supervision and Curriculum Development of the National Education Association. "Leadership through Supervision," *1946 Yearbook of the Association.* Washington, D.C.: The Association, 1946.
Goodwin, Jack C. "Principles and Practices of Teacher Evaluation Programs in the Schools of the United States." Doctoral dissertation, University of Southern California, 1956.
Marks, James R. "An Analysis of Assignment Specifications for Certificated School Personnel in the United States." Doctoral dissertation, University of Southern California, 1962.
National Education Association. *Rural Supervision at Work.* Edited by Marchia Everett. 1949 Yearbook. Washington, D.C.: National Education Association, 1949.
Trillingham, C. C. *The County Superintendent and County Service Foundation.* Second Report of Assembly Interim Committee on Public Education. Sacramento: Assembly of the State of California, 1949.
U.S. Department of Health, Education, and Welfare. *Curriculum Responsibilities of the States.* Washington, D.C.: Government Printing Office, 1968.
———. *Curriculum Responsibility of State Departments of Education.* Washington, D.C.: Government Printing Office, 1958.

2

Special Problems:
The Role of the Intermediate
Unit in Supervision

The intermediate unit now plays a vital role in school supervision. The supervisor must be aware of the following major points, which are discussed in this chapter:

Intermediate unit variations, functions, and organizational status
Supervisory services performed by the intermediate unit staff
Do—Don't
Trends
"In-Basket" supervisory problems
Questions and suggested activities

Intermediate Unit Variations, Functions, and Organizational Status

Variations

Public education in this country has become more and more a local operation, a state responsibility, and a national concern.[1] The intermediate unit lies between the state department of education and the local systems. There are several types of intermediate units, and probably no two are exactly alike. The United States has county units, parishes, townships, supervisory unions, and other political entities acting as intermediate units. These various administrative units can be classified into four general divisions: (1) state; (2) county unit, where the county unit is the local school district; (3) supervisory union or township; and (4) county intermediate unit.

[1] Emery Stoops, M. L. Rafferty, and Russell E. Johnson, *Handbook of Educational Administration* (Boston: Allyn and Bacon, Inc., 1975), p. 3.

The National Education Association has defined the intermediate unit:

[The intermediate unit is an] area comprising the territory of two or more basic administrative units and having a board, or officers, or both, responsible for performing stipulated services for the basic administrative units or for supervising their fiscal, administrative, or educational functions.[2]

This definition can be shortened to say that an intermediate administrative school unit is any agency operating as a "middleman" between the local school district and the state department of education. The intermediate unit is the state agent that enforces minimum standards. It is the agent between the local school system and the state department through which information and leadership are disseminated in operating and improving local problems. No single definition can include all types.

THE STATE CENTRAL SYSTEM.   The state central system exists only in Delaware, Alaska, and Hawaii. Delaware might truly be called the state department of education central system. Here the state directly administers most public schools as one district. Excluded from this system are the cities of Wilmington and Dover, and fifteen special districts.[3]

All school districts in Alaska are independent and report directly to the state department of education; however, the local school board is governed by state standards of operational procedure.

In Hawaii, education is controlled by the Hawaiian Department of Public Instruction in Honolulu, which has suboffices in various sections of the state.[4]

THE COUNTY UNIT SYSTEM.   Twelve states are organized on the county unit system; schools in these states operate under the control of an elected county board of education. The good systems follow the general boundaries of the county civil unit.[5]

In some of these states, the larger cities are excluded from the county unit and operate as independent districts. The county unit is a recent invention in the field of local public school administration. Most county-unit systems were established during the last half of the nineteenth century.[6] States organized on this system are Alabama, Florida, Georgia, Kentucky, Louisiana, Maryland, New Mexico, North Carolina, Tennessee, Utah, Virginia, and West Virginia.

[2] William P. McClure, *The Intermediate School District in the United States* (Urbana: University of Illinois Press, 1956), p. 1.

[3] Arthur B. Moehlman, *School Administration* (Boston: Houghton Mifflin Company, 1951), p. 123.

[4] Stoops *et al.*, *Handbook*, p. 66.

[5] In only two states, Florida and West Virginia, the school systems and county unit boundaries are coterminous. In these states there are no independent school districts.

[6] Shirley Cooper and Charles O. Fitzwater, *County School Administration* (New York: Harper and Brothers, 1954), p. 173.

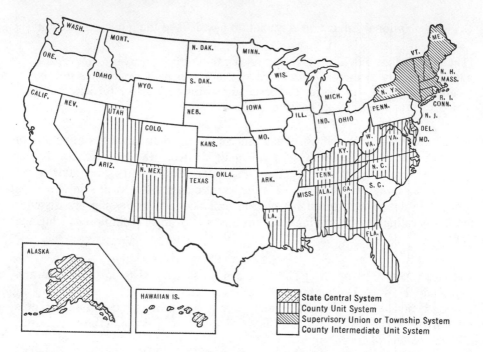

FIGURE 2-1.   Forms of Intermediate Unit Organization in the United States.

SUPERVISORY UNION OR TOWNSHIP.   Township administrative units have been present since the beginning of public education in America.[7] Sometimes referred to as supervisory unions, these units are formed when two or more towns become a single school unit for administrative purposes. These units are not necessarily coterminous with civil county boundaries. Generally, the supervisory union is found in the northeastern section of the nation. Michigan is an exception to the rule. It provides for township districts on a permissive basis.[8] In addition to Michigan, other states allow high-school districts to be formed; in some instances, these districts include an entire county.

The states considered to be true supervisory unions are Connecticut, Maine, Massachusetts, New Hampshire, New York, Rhode Island, and Vermont. New York has 175 such systems. The unions are responsible to their state departments of education and are governed by state codes. As populations have increased, some large cities have formed their own independent supervisory unions.

COUNTY INTERMEDIATE UNIT.   As the map in Figure 2-1 shows, more states (28) use the county intermediate plan than any other type of unit. A sample organization chart for this type of intermediate unit appears in Figure 2-2. All of these states are in the West, Southwest, and Midwest. They are Arizona, Arkan-

---

[7] Ibid.
[8] Moehlman, *School Administration,* p. 124.

FIGURE 2–2 Organization Chart for Office of Los Angeles County Superintendent of Schools.

sas, California, Colorado, Idaho, Illinois, Indiana, Iowa, Kansas, Michigan, Minnesota, Mississippi, Missouri, Montana, Nebraska, Nevada, New Jersey, North Dakota, Ohio, Oklahoma, Oregon, Pennsylvania, South Carolina, South Dakota, Texas, Washington, Wisconsin, and Wyoming.

General Functions of the Intermediate Unit

An intermediate unit provides educational service in an area composed of two or more local school systems. The intermediate unit operates between the state and the local school system and provides service for both the state and the system. The state code establishes regulations and standards governing these services. The intermediate unit provides professional services to the local system and serves as a supervisory standards agency for the state. Some researchers believe that this type of organization gives the local community the highest degree of autonomy while providing an effective means of upholding state standards.

Limited Functions

The office of the intermediate unit superintendent has been limited in function; however, the office has been of vital importance in the improvement of local education and has been of significant value to the rural school more than to urban areas. In many rural areas, the intermediate unit superintendent is the educational leader of the community. He advises and helps coordinate many civic, cultural, and educational activities, including the juvenile court, health and welfare programs, and fund-raising drives.[9]

Organizational Status

Most of the school administrative units in this country are located in unincorporated territories. Generally, these school systems do not include any civil metropolitan incorporated units of noteworthy size, such as a city or township, within the system boundaries. Many of these schools are one- or two-room buildings. Most enlightened citizens of the space age accept the concept that a modern learning environment cannot be developed in a one-room schoolhouse.

All American states except Alaska are divided into civil intermediate units for purposes of public administration. The smallest unit is Arlington County, Virginia, and the largest is San Bernardino County, California. Despite this wide range in size, almost half of the intermediate units in the nation are between 500 and 1,000 square miles in area.[10]

[9] Stoops et al., Handbook, p. 71.

[10] Fred Engelhardt, Public School Organization and Administration (Boston: Ginn and Company, 1931), p. 12.

Differences in the population density of the nation's intermediate units are even more striking than are differences in the area of these units. One might compare, for example, the population of Hinsdale County, Colorado, with that of Los Angeles County, California.[11]

Since the nation's beginnings, the intermediate unit has been a local unit of government. At the county seat are many agencies and officials such as the sheriff, the courts, and the county recorder. These agencies and officials are actually state agencies and state officials; the state has authorized them to help carry out state functions. It was decided, in the past, that the state was too removed from the problems of the local areas and that the intermediate unit could best operate as the agent of the state in a given geographic area.

In some northeastern states the only functions of the intermediate unit are in judicial, highway, and welfare matters. However, in some areas of the South, the intermediate unit is an active and highly important subdivision of the state. Between these extremes the intermediate units of the rest of the nation function at different levels of authority and importance.[12]

Supervisory Services Performed by the Intermediate Unit Staff

Public Relations

The *special services division* of an intermediate unit generally is concerned with public relations. The task of this division is to communicate effectively with the citizens of the community. In so doing, this division uses all of the mass communications media available in the community—radio, television, public meetings, and the assistance of civic service organizations.

Effective Communication

In striving to provide internal communication, it is advantageous to publish newsletters, pamphlets, and reports to be distributed to the staff of the schools within the area in the intermediate unit.

In conducting a truly effective two-way communications system with the public, the special services division should help the electorate express its needs and desires to the schools. The services of the division should be utilized to coordinate the efforts of lay groups to work with the schools.

---

[11] It should be noted that New York City, which is divided into five boroughs, occupies parts of five different counties.

[12] Engelhardt, *Public School Organization,* p. 14.

Teacher Personnel Placement

This division also might maintain a teacher personnel placement service and provide for credential registration and evaluation of training. In one large county in Southern California, the Personnel Placement Office is involved in a majority of the selected interviews conducted by the several school districts in the county. An adequate file of assignment specifications is essential to the successful operation of such departments, as is an adequate, up-to-date, and readily accessible filing system. The use of the information retrieval capacities of a computer system, such as the IBM–360 series, is becoming more and more a need of the personnel placement office.

In a small intermediate unit the superintendent probably would be responsible for the special services division.

Curricular Services

The curricular services division is the largest and the one associated most closely with the classroom. In large- or medium-sized intermediate units, the work of this division is divided into several general areas. Educational specialists direct the operations of each department. Some services offered by this division include instructional media, child study programs, research and guidance, attendance and counseling, and student transportation. The intermediate unit should maintain an instructional materials laboratory.

Special Assistance

Some intermediate units can offer the assistance of specialists in such areas as school nursing, audiometry and psychological testing, and dental hygiene. Sometimes intermediate units can offer assistance providing programs for exceptional children. Special interest intermediate units, such as *special education service units* and *computer service units* recently have emerged.

Supervision: the Final Goal

It seems that the final outcome of all the efforts of the intermediate unit staff is supervision in one form or another. To the school system, this supervision takes the form of service. Three factors are necessary in order to carry out an effective program:

1. The superintendent
2. The staff
3. Supporting services of the intermediate unit

Trained specialists of the intermediate unit can do much to coordinate and improve instructional operations of local school systems. Cooper and Fitzwater[13] stated that the intermediate unit superintendent's most important task is to select a capable staff; and that wealth can never overcome a weakness in the professional staff.

Since one aspect of good supervision is leadership, the intermediate unit superintendent and his staff must: (1) be educational leaders; (2) be resource persons who are informed on up-to-the minute developments in their fields and can make quick, sound decisions; (3) maintain an uninterrupted two-way communication system between their office and the people they serve; (4) command the respect and confidence of the people with whom they work; (5) be able to motivate the people with whom they work to achieve their fullest potential; (6) possess the skill and know-how to effectively carry on their professional specialties; (7) have personalities to fit into social and cultural life of the community in which they serve; and (8) have the courage to stand for their professional convictions and principles.[14] The intermediate unit superintendent, then, is not a 'regular' local school system superintendent of schools.

To develop a successful intermediate unit staff and to provide effective service, the superintendent must instill a feeling of cooperation and teamwork. Teamwork becomes an unseen force as the staff members join together to accomplish the task of the intermediate unit.

It is sound to use accepted standards of appointment in securing these specialists. An application should show evidence of qualification and, if possible, appointments should be made from eligibility lists. Staff members should be selected on the basis of fitness rather than personal influence.

THE SPECIALIST-CONSULTANT AT THE INTERMEDIATE LEVEL WEARS MANY HATS   Supervision has many different meanings and reflections, depending on individual backgrounds. To some it means another unnecessary frill in the budget; to others it means an effective way of increasing the effectiveness of instruction. The Department of Rural Education of the National Education Association stated:

> Supervision is not the sole responsibility of . . . one person. It is a function that is carried on by many people in many ways at many different times in many different places. There should be one or more persons whose primary responsibility is to make it possible for supervision to take place.[15]

One person, the supervisor, is essential to make this guidance and leadership become a reality. In many areas, this person is known as a helping teacher, a coordinator, or a consultant. Spears stated:

[13] Shirley Cooper and Charles O. Fitzwater, *County School Administration* (New York: Harper and Brothers, 1954), p. 173.

[14] Ibid., p. 272.

[15] National Education Association, *Rural Supervisor at Work*, edited by Marchia Everett, 1949 Yearbook (Washington, D.C.: National Education Association, 1949), p 12.

Good supervision stimulates . . . personnel to the highest endeavor. It coordinates . . . efforts and facilitates . . . work. . . . It evaluates the whole undertaking.[16]

Often the specialist from the intermediate unit can help teachers and the school by providing the school board with timely and adequate information that they may need to make wise decisions. Such data may include statements concerning the achievements of the staff and children of the school and accounts of staff meetings, in-service education, committee work, and items of general interest.

CASE 1.   Another role in which the supervisor may find himself is that of community helper. The Department of Rural Education of the National Education Association reported that an intermediate unit specialist-consultant helped a small isolated New Mexico community rehabilitate itself. This task was accomplished partly by bringing the community together, assisting in the problem of self-evaluation, helping to plan a solution, securing an expert to provide needed training, and coordinating the outside resources available.[17]

CASE 2.   This National Education Association department also reported that a specialist-consultant from a rural area in New Jersey helped a county to establish a visual aids library, despite tremendous obstacles.

The work necessitated coordinating the resources of parents, teachers, school boards, other governmental agencies, and the citizens. This project required the services of all involved. As a result of the intermediate unit specialist-consultant's skill in coordination, the entire community was able to work together to provide a means of improving classroom education.[18]

PROBLEMS.   The most logical step to take in providing good supervision, particularly in rural areas, is furnishing an adequate number of specialists. Since funds and personnel are limited, both should be used wisely. The provision for specialist-consultants at the intermediate unit level of supervision developed in the 1930's and 1940's. With increased competition for the tax dollar, the appropriation of significantly large additional funds for this field does not seem likely in the future. It will be necessary to use the existing supervisory services to the best possible advantage.

SERVICE.   Supervision is not law enforcing but rather a program of leadership. By sharing a teacher's problem and offering technical advice, a supervisor may give service as effectively as in classroom visits.

The supervisor at the intermediate unit level should be more than a classroom visitor. He/she should be a teacher's consultant. He/she should provide in-service education, help prepare courses of study, secure instructional aids,

[16] Harold Spears, *Improving the Supervision of Instruction* (Englewood Cliffs, New Jersey: Prentice-Hall, Inc., 1953), p. 236

[17] Ibid., pp. 62–63.

[18] Ibid., pp. 64–65.

preview new educational films, and help teachers keep abreast of research findings.

An intermediate unit consultant's task may be to bring teachers together to observe a fellow teacher who has developed an outstanding teaching technique. All of these activities are aimed at securing growth, competence, and independence to improve instruction. One of the greatest services that a specialist-consultant can provide is operating a curriculum laboratory center where teachers conveniently can gather to work and where they can discover new materials.

Many states have encouraged intermediate units to assume the supervisory service function needed to help make possible equality of education for the children of both rural and urban school systems. In all instances the emphasis is on service, not on control. C. C. Trillingham reported:

> We try to lean over backwards to work, under the philosophy that the center of gravity of education is within the local district. It is not in the county office. We do not try to run the districts—we try to serve the districts.[19]

FURTHER PROBLEMS.   E. McGovern[20] reported that teachers generally fear the intermediate unit specialist-consultant and do not understand his/her function. Teachers rated classroom activities of the intermediate unit supervisors very low, although the intermediate unit personnel expressed confidence in their program.

McGovern went on to note that teachers wanted concrete methods and techniques of instruction; that group discussion techniques were needed; that local school system superintendents gave low ratings to intermediate unit centered activities whereas the intermediate unit superintendents preferred activities that were centered in the intermediate unit offices. Educators in general desired more democratic leadership from the intermediate unit supervisors, and they stressed the importance of cooperation between the specialists at the intermediate unit office and the teacher-training institutions.

Summary of Services

The following outline summarizes the supervisory services rendered by the intermediate unit:

A.   Services in the area of school supervision:
1. Curricular services
2. Communications
3. Operation of schools
4. Consultant services

[19] C. C. Trillingham, *The County Superintendent and County Service Foundation*. Second Report of Assembly Interim Committee on Public Education (Sacramento: Assembly of the State of California, 1949), p. 113.

[20] Elcy McGovern, "A Critical Evaluation of California General County School Supervisors" (Doctoral dissertation, University of Southern California, 1948).

5. Instructional technology (audio-visual) services and leadership
6. Library services
7. Guidance services
8. Special services
   a) Public relations
   b) Teacher personnel placement
   c) Others

B. Other services:
1. Business management
2. Auditing and accounting
3. School district reorganization
4. Purchasing

As a Supervisor at the Intermediate Level

Do

1. Be an educational leader.
2. Be a resource person who is informed on up-to-the-minute developments in his/her field(s) and can make quick, sound decisions.
3. Maintain an uninterrupted two-way communication system between the office and those served.
4. Actively work to command the respect and confidence of the people with whom you work.
5. Learn to stimulate the people with whom you work to work up to their full potentials.
6. Have the courage to stand for your professional convictions and principles.
7. Develop a successful intermediate unit staff and provide effective service, work to instill a feeling of cooperation and teamwork. This teamwork becomes an unseen force as the staff members join together to accomplish the task of the intermediate unit.
8. Continuously evaluate the level and effectiveness of the services of the intermediate unit office. Criteria may be developed cooperatively with the local schools served. State department of education personnel can help develop criteria and can provide the means to be used in the assessment process.
9. Work *with* the local districts and school systems to help them better serve their students. One major responsibility of the intermediate unit is to help the local school system help itself.

Don't

1. Attempt, at the intermediate unit level, to help strengthen education by exerting punitive regulations.
2. Approach the local school system and its personnel as an omnipotent oracle of the truth in education.

3. Forget that wealth can never overcome a weakness in the professional staff. No service can exceed the quantity, quality, and capacity of the staff.
4. Perform functions that readily could be performed on the local school system level.
5. Select staff members on a basis of personal influence. Use accepted standards of selection in securing these specialists. An applicant should show evidence of qualifications and, if possible, appointment should be made from eligibility lists. Staff members should be approved on a basis of fitness rather than personal influence.

TRENDS: AN EVOLVING OFFICE

Toward ⟶ Increased Activities by Intermediate

Unit Offices in Instruction and Staff Development

The changes that will affect the intermediate unit will be the result of new needs and problems. As school systems become larger, the services that they will be able to provide for themselves probably will alter the configuration of the intermediate unit. Intermediate units could become higher echelon organizations coordinating and supplying complex research services. Perhaps these services will be in the areas of educational television and programmed learning, or in the research into special problems, such as methods of teaching brain-damaged children.

Toward ⟶ A Vehicle for Providing Some State

Office Services

Intermediate units are acknowledged as arms of the state government. The educational complex of the future will demand that the kinds of communications required by activities mentioned above be readily available. People will not want to communicate with and obtain needed services from an office located at a considerable distance. Their demand for more immediate access to resources will cause the further development of intermediate unit services and a shifting of the housing of several research and instructional and staff development supervisory services that now are provided at state offices. Under some circumstances, it would be sensible for the intermediate unit office to share facilities with the state unit.

Supervisory Problems

In Basket

Problem 1

As specialist-consultant in the office of the intermediate unit superintendent of schools, you have been asked to help evaluate and deveolp instructional technology (audio-visual) and library collections services. The superintendent indicated that he and the assistant superintendent favor the development of a professional library collection as a part of the instructional media complex, which will include the regular library collection and the now separate instructional technology collection.

> *How will you proceed?*
> *What priorities will you establish?*
> *What standards will you recommend?*

Problem 2

In accordance with a recently enacted state law, the Lourose School District's governing board has ordered that students in grades three through six be taught about the contributions to the development of community, city, state, and country made by men and women of various ethnic, racial, and cultural origins and backgrounds. The district does not employ subject matter supervisors but depends on the intermediate unit staff for its supervisory assistance. The superintendent of the Lourose District telephoned while you, the Assistant Superintendent for Instructional Services, were at a meeting of the County Board of Supervisors. Upon your return to the office, you discovered a memo in your in-basket informing you of this message. The intermediate unit office does not presently employ a multicultural heritage, affirmative action, or other specialist in the required area.

> *What would you do? Assume that you must provide the assistance needed, and that adequate funds are available to carry out your plans.*
> *How would you proceed, especially as concerns curriculum, staff, instructional materials, and in-service educational activities?*
> *How would you evaluate the success of your activities?*

Questions and Suggested Activities Concerning the Role of the Intermediate Unit

Questions

1. What are the major activities of your local intermediate unit in the area of educational supervision?

2. How would you change the form of services given by your local intermediate unit?
3. What legal basis is there for the operation of the intermediate unit? What court decisions have been influential in this area?
4. How would you, as a junior high school supervisor, obtain the assistance of the consultants on the intermediate unit staff? What type of assistance would you expect from such specialists?
5. Do you believe that the intermediate unit can perform certain functions with more efficiency and/or economy than can the local school system? List such functions and indicate your reasons for including them in your list.
6. What services should the intermediate unit perform that it is now not providing? Indicate your reasons.
7. What training specifications would you recommend for the intermediate unit superintendent? The specialists?
8. What are the functions of the intermediate unit as related to elementary education? to secondary education? to community colleges?
9. What should a supervisor know about the opinions of the state attorney general?
10. Should the state give financial aid to parochial and other private schools for staff and instructional development?
11. Is the intermediate unit the most satisfactory for school supervision, organization, and administration, or is some other geographical area more favorable? Indicate your reasons.

Suggested Activities

1. Indicate your reasons for believing the intermediate unit board of trustees and superintendent should be elected or appointed.
2. List all services that the local school system should perform and compare these to the services of the intermediate unit and/or the state.
3. Develop a chart showing the ratio or number of recommended intermediate unit specialists to the number of elementary, junior high school, and senior high school teachers in the county or intermediate unit areas.
4. Analyze the relationship of the salaries of the administrators and specialist-consultants in the local school systems to those of the intermediate unit superintendent and his specialists.
5. Outline the organization of the intermediate unit nearest your houme. Diagram line and staff functions.
6. Criticize the intermediate unit educational organization for your state, and propose improvements.
7. Distinguish between the county as an intermediate unit and the "county unit system" in education.

Selected Bibliography

Books

Byron, George, and D. A. Howell. *The Government and Management of Schools.* Atlantic Highlands, New Jersey: Humanities Press, Inc., 1974.

Cooper, Shirley, and Charles O. Fitzwater. *County School Administration.* New York: Harper and Brothers, 1954.

Cubberley, Ellwood P. *Public Education in the United States.* Boston: Houghton Mifflin Company, 1934.

Engelhardt, Fred. *Public School Organization and Administration.* Boston: Ginn and Company, 1931.

Fiedler, Fred E., and Martin M. Chemers. *Leadership and Effective Management.* Glenview, Illinois: Scott, Foresman and Co., 1974.

Jacobson, Paul B. *The American Secondary School.* Englewood Cliffs, New Jersey: Prentice-Hall, Inc., 1952.

McClure, William P. *The Intermediate School District in the United States.* Urbana: University of Illinois Press, 1956.

Moehlman, Arthur B. *School Administration.* Boston: Houghton Mifflin Company, 1951.

Morphet, Edgar L., Roe L. Johns, and Theodore L. Reller. *Educational Administration.* Englewood Cliffs, New Jersey: Prentice-Hall, Inc., 1959.

Mort, Paul R., and Donald H. Ross. *Principles of School Administration.* 2d ed. New York: McGraw-Hill Book Company, 1957.

Spears, Harold. *Improving the Supervision of Instruction.* Englewood Cliffs, New Jersey: Prentice-Hall, Inc., 1953.

Stoops, Emery, Max Rafferty, and Russell E. Johnson. *Handbook of Educational Administration.* Boston: Allyn and Bacon, Inc., 1975.

Stoops, Emery, and M. L. Rafferty, Jr. *Practices and Trends in School Administration.* Boston: Ginn and Company, 1961.

————, and Russell E. Johnson. *Elementary School Administration.* New York: McGraw-Hill Book Company, 1967.

Trillingham, C. C. *The County Superintendent and County Service Foundation.* Second Report of Assembly Interim Committee on Public Education. Sacramento: Assembly of the State of California, 1949.

Other Sources

Butterworth, Julian E. *The New Intermediate School District for New York State.* Albany: State Department of Education, *Bulletin 4,* No. 1336, 1947.

Clowes, Richard N. "An Appraisal of the Functions of the Elected Lay County Board of Education in California." Doctoral dissertation, University of Southern California, 1960 (unpublished).

Fine, Thomas W. "An Analysis of Systematic Planning and Development in the Organizational Patterns of the Intermediate Units in California." Doctoral dissertation, University of Southern California, 1968 (unpublished).

Gresham, Olin R. "The Impact of Selected School Legislation on the Organization and Operation of the County Office of Education in California." Doctoral dissertation, University of Southern California, 1970 (unpublished).

Hoffmann, Glenn W. "An Investigation of Cooperative Educational Activities Among County Offices of Education in California." Palo Alto: Doctoral dissertation, Stanford University, 1966 (unpublished).

Isenberg, Robert M. *The Community School and the Intermediate Unit.* Washington, D.C.: Department of Rural Education, Yearbook, NEA, 1954.

Marks, James S. "An Analysis of Assignment Specifications for Certified School Personnel in the United States." Doctoral dissertation, University of Southern California, 1962.

McGovern, Elcy. "A Critical Evaluation of California General Elementary County School Supervisors." Doctoral dissertation, University of Southern California, 1948.

National Education Association, *Rural Supervision at Work,* ed. Marchia Everett. 1949 Yearbook. Washington, D.C.: National Education Association, 1949.

Rosander, Gerald A. and the Committee of Ten. *The Future Role and Function, Size, Structure and Organization of the Intermediate Unit in California.* N. P.: California Association of County Superintendents of Schools, 1966.

3

Special Problems:
The Role of the State
and Federal Government
in School Supervision

Each state has established basic standards of organization, supervision administration, certification of teachers, curricula, and school plant layouts either as suggested guides or as requirements. However, over the past several years the approach of the state in school supervision and administration has moved increasingly from an emphasis on inspection toward an emphasis on leadership. During this quarter century, great strides have been made toward equalizing the quality and quantity of education available to our children.

   A backward view of the accomplishments already effected in this monumental task of elevating and equalizing our school program tempts one to believe that the goal has been reached. However, as in all systems subject to sociological forces, our school system is characterized by dynamism and restiveness; movement is inevitable. The continuing development and improvement of our educational program are the only alternatives to social decadence. Merely to keep pace with technological and economic progress in this space age, the state must exert even greater energy in educational leadership.

   The topics discussed in this chapter are:

   The role of the federal government in supervision
   The American school system
   History of govermental aid and support for supervision
   General federal activities affecting supervision
   Historical development of the state departments of education
   The position of chief state school officer
   Functions of the state departments of education
   Special problems at the state level
   Do—Don't
   "In-Basket" supervisory problems
   Trends
   Questions and suggested activities

The Role of the Federal Government in Supervision

Education, a function of the state and the responsibility of the local school system, is a national concern of great proportion. Yet as E. Benedetti emphasized, "It is incredible that a problem of such magnitude received no specific mention in the Federal Constitution."[1]

Any intention relating to supervision of instruction that the Federal Government entertained under the implied powers of the Constitution disappeared when the Tenth Amendment was adopted. This amendment confirmed that the powers not delegated by the Constitution of the United States, nor prohibited by it to the states, are reserved to the states, respectively, or to the people.

The Federal Government is endowed only with enumerative powers; since education is not specifically designated as a federal function, the Tenth Amendment has been interpreted as granting to the individual states plenary control over the administration of public education.[2]

The general welfare clause of the Federal Constitution, Article I, Section A, did render some federal participation in education possible; it stipulated, "Congress shall have power to . . . provide for the common defense and general welfare. . . ." In 1962, the Supreme Court of the United States enjoined the schools of the State of New York from requiring pupils to participate in a morning prayer. This prayer had been prepared under the supervision of, with the approval of, the New York State Board of Regents. The Federal Government, then, does have some role in education in general, and in school supervision in particular.

The American School System

American Education: A Most Complex Industry

AMERICAN EDUCATION BECOMES BIG BUSINESS. E. Stoops and M. L. Rafferty stressed that more and more people go to school each year. From a meager beginning in the colonies, with Dame Schools or Bible study for a negligible percentage of the population, school enrollments rose to about the 42 million mark in 1957–58, and were more than 59 million in 1973–74.[3]

1 Eugene Beneditti, "Legal Aspects of School Administration" (Duplicated material copyrighted by the author. Los Angeles: 1956), p. 2.
2 Ibid.
3 U.S. Department of Health, Education, and Welfare, Digest of Education Statistics (Washington: The Department, 1975), p. 6.

Relationships between Federal, State,
and Local Governments

THE AMERICAN SCHOOLS ARE A PRODUCT OF, ARE RESPONSIBLE TO, AND ARE OWNED BY THE PEOPLE. Stoops and Rafferty noted that the underlying principle of the American system of public education is its lack of system:

> It is at once the despair of the logical French, the scientific German, and the traditional English. In other lands the schools belong to the government and are administered by government bureaus and appointees. They are financed through national taxes and directed by a Secretary of Education. This enables the school systems in these countries to operate independently of local whims and upheavals and . . . insures a maximum of uniformity in school procedures. Indeed, some can state with confidence the subject, unit, and text chapter being studied in every classroom of the nation. Such uniformity . . . involves the granting of huge powers to the national government in the field of education, and a corresponding lessening of local control.[4]

Where other nations have proudly set up educational superstructures of gigantic proportions, the United States proudly points to a system of education in which the separate states of the union are completely independent; there is no national school system in the United States.

RELATIONS AND FUNCTIONS. One distinctive feature of the American public schools is the relationship between the federal, state, and local levels of control. In Colonial times, poor transportation made it difficult to supervise instruction in the schools located at opposite sides of the township. Thus, small separate districts and school systems developed.

State governments are responsible for the educational systems, with certain powers delegated to local school districts. All states have established machinery to administer and supervise the school systems, and most states have state boards of education and a chief state school officer.

IMPLICATIONS FOR THE SUPERVISION OF INSTRUCTION. The implications of the relationships between the federal, state, and local governments in the educational enterprise are many. The supervising principal must acquaint the professional staff with the obligations concerning mandatory, permitted, and prohibited instruction and classroom organization derived from laws, rules, regulations, and judicial decisions at the federal, state, and local levels.

For example, in the famous Oregon case the United States Supreme Court indicated that even though the states could require school attendance, they could not require attendance in a public school. In the Everson case, the court further declared that public funds could be used to provide free transportation for paro-

---

[4] Emery Stoops and M. L. Rafferty, Jr., *Practices and Trends in School Administration* (Boston: Ginn and Company, 1961), p. 15

chial school students under certain conditions. In the McCollum case, it stated that released and dismissed time for religious education programs could not be conducted on public school property.

The Supreme Court had claimed jurisdiction in these cases by virtue of the First and Fourteenth Amendments to the Constitution. The First Amendment states that "Congress shall make no law respecting an establishment of religion or prohibiting the free exercise thereof . . . or the right of people peaceably to assemble. . . ." The Fourteenth Amendment stipulates "nor shall any state deprive any person of life, liberty, or property without due process of law; nor deny to any person within its jurisdiction the equal protection of the laws."[5] The supervising principal must be aware of federal court decisions that have implications for the instructional program of the school, for the teacher, and for the student. Certainly he/she must keep abreast of laws that would authorize federal funding of programs aimed at improving instruction.

History of Governmental Aid and Support for Supervision

A grammar school teacher's salary in Colonial New England probably ranged from twenty to sixty pounds a year—roughly equivalent to $50 to $100. Meals and lodging also were provided. The higher paid teachers were in the middle socioeconomic class; the more poorly paid teachers were in the lower class status and were comparable to tradesmen. "Salaries were often irregular in payment and often were paid in produce or livestock rather than in cash."[6]

In the Colonial period, teachers did not think of themselves as part of a professional group. There were no professional organizations and no standards concerning preparation. By 1860, America's state school system had taken form. Twenty years before then, it was the rule for New England children to have formal education.

R. F. Butts and L. A. Cremin noted that one of the most bitter stuggles in securing public common schools was the struggle for public support. Different states and sections of the country progressed at different rates. Some of the many kinds of public support for the schools included income from public lands, the Federal Government, fines and license fees, and public lotteries.

The Land Ordinance of 1785, passed by the Continental Congress, provided that the sixteenth section of every township must be dedicated for the maintenance of public schools within the said township. In the Northwest Ordinance of 1787, Congress included Article III that stated "religion, morality, and

---

[5] See Eugene Benedetti, "Federal Government Has a Bigger Stake in Schools," *Nation's Schools* LV (March 1955), 61; and Newton Edwards, *The Courts and the Public Schools* (Chicago: University of Chicago Press, 1955).

[6] R. Freeman Butts and Lawrence A. Cremin, *A History of Education in American Culture* (New York: Henry Holt and Company, 1953), p. 134.

knowledge being necessary to good government and the happiness of mankind, schools and the means of education shall forever be encouraged."

In 1827, the Massachusetts legislature made compulsory the support of schools entirely by taxation. In 1834, a common school fund was established. In New England, the principle of public support had been accepted by the time of the Civil War.

Public Law 864, the National Defense Education Act of 1958, provided for loans to students and institutions of higher education; financial assistance for strengthening instruction in science, mathematics, and modern languages; national defense scholarships; funds for research and experimentation; more effective use of television, radio, and motion pictures for educational purposes; authorization for a national science foundation to establish a science information service and a science information council; and authorization of funds to improve the statistical services of state agencies.

General Federal Activities Affecting Supervision

The U.S. Office of Education

HISTORY OF THE OFFICE. The common school revival, as expounded in the 1840's by its champion Horace Mann in Massachusetts, caused the people of the several states to think in terms of education and the improvement of the educational enterprise.

Henry Barnard led the movement for a national education agency. C. A. DeYoung[7] noted that in 1866 President James A. Garfield presented a history-making proposal to Congress. This proposal was adopted by the National Association of State and City School Superintendents, which is now the American Association of School Administrators. It advocated the establishment of a federal bureau of education.

A public law authorizing the Department of Education was approved on the 2nd of March 1867. Originally adopted during the presidency of Andrew Johnson, it reads:

> Be it enacted *by the Senate and the House of Representatives of the United States of America, in Congress Assembled,* that there shall be established in the city of Washington, a department of education, for the purpose of collecting such statistics and facts as shall show the condition and progress of education in the several states and territories, and of diffusing such information respecting the organization and management of schools and school systems and methods of teaching as

[7] Chris A. DeYoung, *Introduction to American Public Education* 2d ed. (New York· McGraw-Hill Book Company, Inc., 1950), p. 23.

shall aid the people of the United States in the establishment and maintenance of efficient school systems, and otherwise PROMOTE THE CAUSE OF EDUCATION throughout the country.

> 39th Congress, 2nd Session
> Approved by President Andrew Johnson
> 2 March 1867

In 1869, due to the opposition of several of the states, the department was made an office of education in the Department of Interior. This title was changed in 1870 to the Bureau of Education, but was restored in 1929 as the Office of Education. On July 1, 1939, the Office of Education was transferred from the Department of the Interior to the Internal Security Agency, and in the 1950's was placed under the Department of Health, Education, and Welfare.

ACTIVITIES OF THE U.S. OFFICE OF EDUCATION IN THE FIELD OF SUPERVISION. The major duties enumerated in the basic law include the collection of statistics and facts promoting the cause of education in general, and the diffusion of information concerning the schools. Collecting, sifting, and organizing statistics and facts in a country as far-flung and as full of school districts and systems as is the United States is a colossal task![8] The office diffuses information through its many conferences, exhibits, publications, letters, broadcasts, telecasts, and surplus property information center, and through the exchange of books, radio and television scripts, transcriptions, tape recordings, and motion picture material. The monthly periodical *American Education* and mimeographed circulars are printed by the Superintendent of Documents, Government Printing Office, Washington, D.C. 20025.

THE U.S. OFFICE AS A CLEARING HOUSE. From 1867 through 1906, a lot of biographical historical research was published by the office. Since Alaskan Indians came under the jurisdiction of the office at this time, the office provided for the education of Indian children. Since 1917, the establishment of vocational education, under the Smith-Hughes Act, has added many responsibilities to the Office of Education.

Stoops and Rafferty emphasized:

> It is in the field of services, however, that the office probably will play its most important role. A city . . . superintendent of schools today owes much of his success as an . . . [educator] to the research findings released at periodic intervals by the United States Office of Education. Statistics on almost every conceivable subject . . . related to education are painstakingly collected, correlated, and charted by the office personnel and made available, without cost, to educators. . . .[9]

---

[8] Ibid., p. 25.
[9] Stoops and Rafferty, *Practices and Trends,* pp. 22–23.

Services such as these help remove much of the guesswork from the field of school supervision and have made possible scientific planning on the part of the school supervisor. Individuals and organizations who have used the United States Office of Education's services are: (1) service clubs; (2) patriotic societies; (3) farmers' organizations and associations; (4) business and professional associations; (5) state school systems; (6) local school systems; (7) private schools; (8) colleges and universities; (9) public libraries; (10) foreign students and educators; (11) radio and television broadcasting stations and systems; (12) national, state, and local parent's associations; (13) educational associations; (14) labor groups; and (15) social- and service-civic organizations.

FURTHER ACTIVITIES OF THE U.S. OFFICE OF EDUCATION, AND IMPLICATIONS FOR SUPERVISION.   A. J. Burke and C. Alexander described the U.S. Office of Education publications as gold mines for both the practical school person and the research worker: "Sooner or later research in every phase of education is sure to be discussed and supplied with references in these publications."[10] In addition to the many bulletins, circulars, and pamphlets, the U.S. Office of Education also issues the *Biennial Survey of Education,* including statistical and textual résumés of educational conditions in the United States, the *Education Directory,* the *Vocational Division Bulletins, Higher Education,* and *School Life.* The office also has issued many biographies that apply to the field of supervision, as well as Guidance Leaflets, Higher Education Circulars, Home Economics Circulars, Industrial Circulars, International Education, Kindergarten Circulars, and posters and charts. *Research Studies in Education,* published from 1926 to 1940, was a valuable series.

The supervising principal should write to the Librarian, U.S. Office of Education, Department of Health, Education, and Welfare, Washington, D.C., 20025, and to the Superintendent of Documents, Government Printing Office, Washington, D.C. 20025, for lists of publications referring to particular topics. The request should include complete information on the data needed.

The Role of U.S. Commissioner
of Education in Supervision

Many illustrious individuals have served as commissioner of the Office of Education. The first commissioner was Henry Barnard, who took office in 1838. The first secretary of the Department of Health, Education, and Welfare was Oveta Culp Hobby.

Some educators have suggested that the Commissioner of Education should become a national superintendent of schools. The U.S. Office of Education would be established as a nonpartisan, independent agency, governed by a national board of education. This board would be composed of individuals as-

[10] Arvid J. Burke and Carter Alexander, *How to Locate Educational Information and Data* (New York: Bureau of Publications, Teachers College, Columbia University, 1958), p. 247.

signed for overlapping terms by the president, with the consent of the Senate. The commissioner would serve as the executive officer and the secretary of the board.

The office would coordinate educational functions for the Federal Government, but all federal participation and publications in education would be transmitted through the individual state's departments of education.

Other individuals have suggested the need for a national curriculum and for national control to the extent that the states now control education. The specifics of administration, curriculum, instruction, and student personnel services would remain with the individual school systems, within certain prescribed limits. The functions now served by the state legislatures would continue within prescribed limits established by Congress and the national board of education. Still others in the areas of school supervision and administration have suggested that all federal support for education should be distributed directly to the state departments of education on the basis of need, combined with a basic aid formula.

Surprisingly, an overwhelming percentage of federal monies is spent on education through agencies other than the Office of Education. Such agencies govern the military academies and the Department of Defense; the Department of Justice and prison education; the school for postal inspectors in the Post Office Department; the Library of Congress; the Copyright Office; the Government Printing Office; the Pan-American Union; the Office of Indian Affairs; the Smithsonian Institute; the National Academy of Sciences; the Commission of Fine Arts; the American Printing House for the Blind in Louisville, Kentucky; and the Columbia Institute for the Deaf in Washington, D.C.

The Tennessee Valley Authority maintains public schools and educational facilities for children as well as for adults and special schools have been established overseas, where there is a large concentration of federal employees.

Other U.S. Government Agencies Involved in Supervision

The Department of Agriculture has been active in the areas of home economics, biology, and agriculture. The 4H Clubs have been sponsored by the department and have furnished many new ideas through bulletins, films, books, pamphlets, and circulars.

The Department of Commerce includes the Bureau of the Census. Its reports regarding student age, sex, and geographical distribution are very valuable. The Coast and Geodetic Survey, Bureau of Standards, and Environmental Sciences Division (Weather Bureau) also are in the Department of Commerce. It is obvious that this department and its agencies provide a wealth of material with which the elementary school principal should be familiar.

The Department of Labor provides a useful service to vocational counselors and teachers through long-range employment outlook in industry. One of its chief publications is the *Dictionary of Occupational Titles*.

Conclusions

The present system of American public education, decentralized as it is, does not and should not preclude an improved federal program of cooperation, leadership, and support. The Advisory Committee on Education stated:

> Education is, in a large sense, an individual matter, but individuals compose neighborhoods and communities, communities compose states, and in the United States the states compose the nation. As are the neighborhoods so will be the states and nation.
>
> Since the formation of the Union, Americans have been citizens both of the state and of the nation. Most Americans now feel that their federal government is their agent as much as is their state government.[11]

Historical Development of the State Departments of Education

J. M. Gwynn[12] reported that after 1870 the rapid expansion of the state normal school stimulated the development of the position of general supervisor in the public elementary schools. The most important task facing the normal school during the 1800's was improving the professional education curriculum for teachers. One way in which the state normal schools planned to perform this function effectively was to have the general supervisor supervise the elementary grade teacher training program at the normal schools.

The state departments of education also influenced the direction taken by supervision, for early in the 1900's the state departments provided inspectional and supervisory services. These services were rendered primarily at the secondary school level.[13] After 1917, an increasing number of special subject supervisors was added to the professional staff.

The Position of Chief State School Officer

A Limiting Factor

The state constitutions provide for the educational program in some manner in all fifty states. Some constitutions specify that education has first call on the funds of

---

[11] Advisory Committee on Education, *Report of the Committee* (Washington, D.C.: Superintendent of Documents, Government Office, 1938), p. 35.

[12] J. Minor Gwynn, *Theory and Practice of Supervision* (New York: Dodd, Mead & Company, 1961), pp. 7–9.

[13] Ibid., p. 8.

the states, and some indicate the teacher's minimum salary. The constitution can be changed only by vote of the people. The constitution; statutes, including the education code or school code of the state, the various other administrative codes of the state, the administrative code containing the rules of the state board of education; local board rules and regulations; and court decisions—all act to determine the structure of education.

Growth of the Position

The Tenth Amendment to the United States Constitution reserved the power for jurisdiction over education to the several states. By the early 1800's, most functions of education were being served by local school systems. Shortly thereafter began a struggle wherein the states attempted to regain much of their lost power. New York was the first to develop a centralized school system with statutes restricting local districts.

R. F. Butts and L. A. Cremin emphasized the importance of a centralized state system for education in New York:

> Moreover, New York was also the first state to create the office of superintendent of common schools. His duties, according to the Law of 1812, involved preparation of plans for improving the common school system, reporting and superintendence of school monies, and the providing of information concerning the schools to the legislature.[14]

A few states followed New York and created similar offices in the next two decades; but not until 1850, when every northern state and some of the southern states created similar offices, did the position become firmly established. In reality, many of these early state superintendents of public instruction were really *ex officio* superintendents,[15] wherein an individual who was already an official of the state had certain limited school responsibilities added to his other duties. Other chief state school officers of the time were secretaries of the state boards of education. As the office grew in importance and stature, visitation and advisement functions in local school systems were added to the duties of the chief state school officers. One state's organization for education is represented graphically in Figure 3-1.

The Position Today

Excepting Hawaii, Delaware, and Alaska, where the whole state is virtually one school system, and New York, where the chief state school officer is very powerful, the position of chief state school officer has been weakened by the elective

---

[14] R. Freeman Butts and Lawrence A. Cremin, *A History of Education in American Culture* (New York: Henry Holt and Company, Inc., 1953), pp. 225–256.

[15] Ibid.

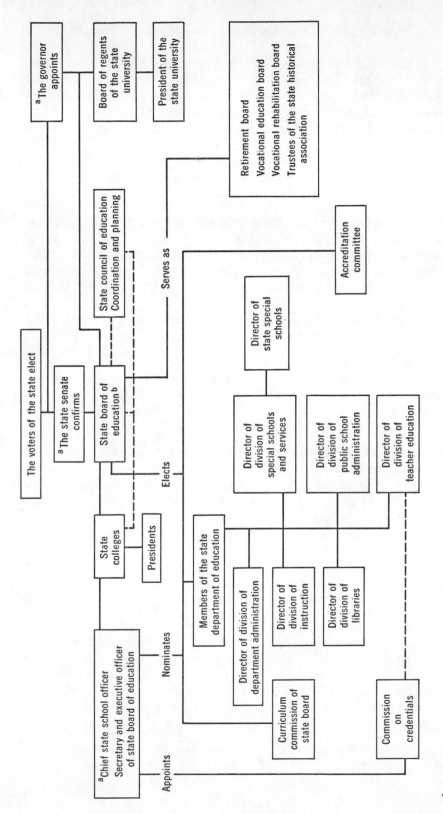

The voters of the state elect

[a]The governor appoints

Board of regents of the state university

President of the state university

[a]The state senate confirms

State board of education[b]

State council of education — Coordination and planning

Retirement board
Vocational education board
Vocational rehabilitation board
Trustees of the state historical association

Serves as

Accreditation committee

Elects

Director of state special schools

State colleges

Presidents

Members of the state department of education

Director of division of special schools and services

Director of division of public school administration

Director of division of teacher education

[a]Chief state school officer — Secretary and executive officer of state board of education

Nominates

Director of division of department administration

Director of division of instruction

Director of division of libraries

Curriculum commission of state board

Commission on credentials

Appoints

[a]Elected

[b]Performs policy-making functions. The members are appointed by the governor.

[c]From Edward H. La Franchi, "School Organization and Administration" (Department of Administration and Supervision, School of Education, University of Southern California, Los Angeles, 1954), p. 14.

nature of the office. The position offers little security because the chief state school officer must seek election. Therefore, it is difficult to obtain a well-qualified person for the position.

Functions of the State Departments of Education

Approval and Accreditation

HISTORICAL DEVELOPMENT.   Accreditation, narrowly defined to include schools whose graduates were acceptable to a university without prior examination, can be traced to 1873, when the Indiana state board of education assumed this responsibility. Although accreditation applies mainly to the secondary school level, it has deep implications for the supervisor.

In 1837, state universities rather than state boards of education accredited schools. Around the turn of the century, it was more practical to have the state board take over this responsibility. The system spread rapidly. Its effect was a trend toward standardizing education within a given state, thus giving equal opportunities for college preparation.

APPROVAL PROGRAMS.   Many approval programs of state departments of education stemmed from responsibilities delegated to them by the legislature in conjunction with allocation of state funds to aid education. For instance, in 1878, the Minnesota State Legislature established a board whose responsibility was to visit and inspect each school receiving $400 or more in state aid.

The objective in Minnesota was to provide better preparation for college. As state boards of education were charged with the dispersal of funds and accumulated responsibilities for regulating local schools, programs of approval or accreditation became necessary. Approval programs became the principal tool through which the state boards could exercise a regulatory function over management and operation on the local school level.

Approval programs differed widely. This disparity was a natural consequence of the variation in regulatory responsibilities as delegated by the state legislatures. In all cases, the state could exercise a regulatory function over management and operation at the local school level.

During the early part of the twentieth century, a widespread method of exercising approval of schools was by inspection. The *school inspector,* in a unique position to observe a given number of schools at the "grass-roots" level, and to compare one with the other, saw the need for establishing standards. In all areas of programming, administration, and facilities the school inspector pioneered in developing standards by which local schools could be rated, graded or classified. A few states and the provinces of Canada still have standards or criteria that refer to the inspection of schools or to the school inspector. Accreditation and approval at the community college level has been a shared responsibility of the state and the several regional accrediting organizations that one encounters in higher education.

INCREASING FINANCIAL SUPPORT.   Over the years, state legislatures have gradually increased their financial support of education. Deeper financial involvement has been paralleled by growing concern about the prudent expenditure of funds. This heightened concern sparked the growth of statewide standards during the first half of this century. In many states, legislative statutes have effected control of funds in areas separate from school approval programs; other states include control of funds within the approval program. This practice has serious overtones for the supervising principal. In the latter case, the purpose appears to insure economy and efficiency in the operation of local schools. Formal standards for approval of schools were further encouraged by state requirements regarding the audit of school funds, insurance on school buildings, location and construction of school buildings, and provisions for economy and safety in the use and custody of school funds.

COMPULSORY ATTENDANCE LAWS.   Laws that made attendance compulsory focused attention on what was available to the children who were compelled to attend schools. Charged with carrying out compulsory attendance laws, the state boards of education necessarily became concerned with academic programs and with minimum standards that would fulfill the intent of the compulsory attendance laws.

DEVELOPMENT AND IMPROVEMENT OF EDUCATIONAL PROGRAMS.   As the stress on the inspection of schools changed to an emphasis on the development and improvement of educational programs in which state and local school officials were partners, local school authorities were more willing to conform to state minimum standards when they, the local officials, had a part in developing these standards. Supervisors played a leading role in this development.

A UNIFIED APPROACH.   The concept that one school or one level of the school program should not be improved at the expense of another has resulted in a trend to evaluate and improve the total school program throughout the school system. In early accrediting programs, it was apparent that steps enabling high schools to achieve accredited status often were taken at the expense of the elementary schools. This fact often encouraged the state education agency to develop approval or accreditation programs that included both elementary and secondary schools.

When accreditation standards were first developed, they tended to emphasize physical facilities and the other facets of the school program that could be measured objectively, such as the number of students per teacher, the number of books in the library, the number of units offered in various subjects, and the number of classrooms. Modern accreditation processes include provisions for more subjective judgments emphasizing the quality of the school, its administration, its program, and its facilities.

APPROVAL, ASSESSMENT, AND ACCREDITATION.   The meaning and use of the terms "approval," "assessment," and "accreditation" vary considerably in different states. What is understood to be an accreditation program in one state may, in a neighboring state, be an approval program. Within a given state, the state education agency may approve some schools and accredit others. Certain states with approval type programs refer to their schools as commissioned, classified, registered, recognized, chartered, or standardized.

Approval of a school may or may not be based on a judgment of the quality of the school on the part of the state department of education; almost invariably *assessment* programs and the *accreditation* of a school require such judgment. The term "approval" may be used when the state education agency is administering a state statute that allows financial support if certain criteria are met, such as being open a specified number of days and employing only certified teachers. The department simply ascertains that the school has complied with the law and will approve the school for receipt of aid. In such a situation the department makes no attempt to inquire into or judge the quality of a school's program and facilities.

A state department of education might approve only certain phases of a school's program, such as the course of study, textbooks, or buildings. The department might administer one or several such approval programs without, however, exercising a judgment on the quality of the total school and its instruction, administration, or facilities.

PROGRAMS FOR APPROVAL IN THE FIFTY STATES.   The practices of state departments of education with respect to their approval or accreditation programs fall into three categories: (1) those requiring *no state approval or accreditation* of public schools; (2) those making approval or accreditation *voluntary* and extending it only on application by local public schools; and (3) those *requiring* approval or accreditation.[16] As the academic ladder is ascended from nursery school to higher education, the trend throughout the country is to follow either plan (2) or (increasingly) plan (3). Even though 80 per cent of public nursery schools are without approval, only 6 per cent of high schools fall into this category. Unapproved elementary schools are found in 34 per cent of the states.

Table 3-1 also indicates that if approval or accreditation is considered at all there is a tendency to make it required rather than voluntary.

AUTHORITY TO APPROVE SCHOOLS AND SCHOOL PROGRAMS.   State legislatures commit legal authority to accredit or approve schools to one of three agents: the

---

[16] See W. B. Rich, *Approval and Accreditation of Public Schools* (OE-20013) (Washington, D.C.: Government Printing Office, 1960); and H. H. Cummings and H. K. Mackintosh, *Curriculum Responsibilities of State Departments of Education* (Washington, D.C.: Government Printing Office, 1958).

TABLE 3-1.   State Requirements Concerning Approval (In per cents)

	NURSERY[a]	KINDERGARTEN	ELEMENTARY	HIGH SCHOOL
No approval necessary	80	54	34	6
Approval voluntary; extended on application	8	14	28	42
Approval required	10	32	38	52
Total	98	100	100	100

[a] New Jersey has no public nursery schools.

state board of education, the chief state school officer, the state department of education or to a combination of these three. This authority is exercised exclusively by the state board of education in twenty-six states, by the chief state school officer in seven states, and by the state department of education in three states. Sharing authority by the state board of education and the chief state school officer occurs in eight states.

Combined authority is exercised by the state board of education and the state department of education in two states. Tripartite authority is delegated in four states to the state board, the state department, and the chief state school officer.

The wording of state statutes with regard to authority to approve schools varies; most statutes direct that the schools will be approved, accredited, commissioned, recognized, chartered, classified, graded, standardized, or rated. California and Hawaii stand alone—they have no terms or categories that describe the type or level of approval.

PURPOSES OR OBJECTIVES OF APPROVAL PROGRAMS.   Clues to the purposes of approval programs can be had from reading state manuals or handbooks and legislative statutes themselves. Most are written to be helpful and stimulating and do not make rigid, inflexible standards that must be met to the ultimate detail. In fact, mandatory standards occasionally are so closely interrelated with recommendations that exactness is sacrificed in attempting to achieve a salutary style. The primary purpose of these publications is to assist local school officials with their administrative problems and to improve educational programs as a whole.

With regard to more specific purposes, eighteen states include as one purpose the authorization of a school or school district to collect tuition from other districts for nonresident students.

Enforcing legal requirements or state board rules or regulations seems almost too obvious to mention, but only forty-three states outline this as a distinct responsibility. Coordinating the instructional programs throughout the state is set forth as a purpose of forty-one states. Forty-eight states encourage self-evaluation by local schools, although only rarely is this practice required. State financial aid is related directly to the approval program in thirty-three states.

SIGNIFICANCE OR EFFECT OF APPROVAL OR ACCREDITATION.   As has been emphasized, the actual significance of approval varies among the states, but all fifty do agree that an approved school is one in which minimum acceptable standards are met or exceeded. A few states do not base their approval on fulfilling a comprehensive set of standards or criteria. Throughout the country, schools are encouraged, but not necessarily required, to meet minimum state standards. Though an indication of the *extent* of the standards may be found in published form, it is difficult, if not impossible, to determine the *degree* to which minimum acceptable standards are either enforced or met. This primarily is determined by state supervisory policies and activities. The same applies to endorsement of the quality of a school's program. The *degree* to which endorsement is carried remains, in most cases, rather obscure. Exceptions are states that categorize or classify schools, endorsing quality on two or more levels. At the college level, denial of accreditation or approval could mean that a student would not be able to transfer his credits to another institution, or that his degree would not be recognized.

PUBLISHED STANDARDS.   The following outline gives an idea of the scope and areas on which attention most frequently seems to be focused in these published standards:

		Number of States
1.	Organization	
	a) Grade organization	29
	b) Length of school year	39
	c) Length of school day	35
	d) Length of class periods	35
	e) Size of classes	27
	f) Student-teacher ratio	28
	g) Enrollment in school or ADA	18
2.	Administration	
	a) School board policies, meetings, and minutes	15
	b) Self-evaluation	13
	c) Financial records and reports	18
	d) Internal accounting or auditing of activity funds	21
	e) Student transportation	17
	f) Records and reports required	34
	g) Philosophy and/or objectives of school or system	14
	h) School-community relations	9
	i) Supervision	26
3.	Personnel	
	a) Minimum number of teachers	34
	b) Certification, qualifications, or preparation of teachers	43
	c) Certification, qualifications, or preparation of administrators	39
	d) Salaries of teachers	13
	e) Salaries of administrators	8

		Number of States
f)	Personnel policies of school board	10
g)	In-service training programs	16
h)	Employment practices	10
4.	Pupils	
a)	Admission and attendance	29
b)	Health	20
c)	Promotion	11
d)	Examinations, grading and/or reporting to parents	12
e)	Extracurricular activities	12
f)	Student record	39
g)	Student load	35
5.	Program of studies	
a)	Graduation requirements	39
b)	Curriculum and/or instruction	39
c)	Instructional materials, including textbooks	30
d)	Guidance and counseling	32
e)	Activity program	19
f)	Libraries	41
g)	Teacher load	34
6.	Plant and equipment	
a)	Site and location of school plant	29
b)	Size or adequacy of school plant	28
c)	Construction of school plant	25
d)	Sanitation and hygienic conditions	33
e)	Equipment	30
f)	Lighting, heating and/or ventilating	30
g)	Administrative space	20
h)	Classroom space	29
i)	Maintenance and/or custodial services	30
j)	Laboratory space	27
7.	Other items	
a)	Community use of school plant	7
b)	Space for special instruction such as music, art, and physical education	27
c)	Safety regulations	30
d)	Requirements for special schools and programs such as summer schools, night schools, veteran's programs	26
e)	Approval of vocational programs	27

Suggestions or recommendations have not been interpreted as requirements, although in practice they often are fulfilled as if they were actual requirements. The absence of a written recommendation should not be construed to mean that a state does not have requirements covering the area.

TEACHER PREPARATION STANDARDS.   The most frequently encountered item pertains to the certification, qualifications, or preparation of teachers. All but one of the forty-four states that publish standards have requirements ranging from a simple statement that teachers must be certificated to a detailed listing of the training required for teaching specific subjects. Requirements to be met by administrators are published by thirty-eight states. Specifications run the gamut from a statement requiring that the supervisor hold an administrative certificate, to descriptions of the amount of graduate work and experience a candidate must have completed or acquired. The situation is similar for superintendents of school districts.

STANDARDS FOR INSTRUCTIONAL SUPPLIES AND TEXTS.   Forty-one states have standards for libraries; of these, about one-third are brief and general, stating that adequate library facilities will be provided and listing a few basic requirements. Another third go into moderate detail, listing requirements that cover up to a full printed page. The remaining third are extensively detailed, outlining specific requisites with regard to space, equipment, books, periodicals, cataloguing, records, expenditures, staff, and aids to be used by the librarian in selecting library material.

EVALUATING STANDARDS OF THE STATE DEPARTMENTS OF EDUCATION.   Review of standards or criteria for the approval of public schools occurs periodically in accordance with established policies in thirty-seven states. A few of these policies specify the interval between reviews. For example, five states review their standards annually. In Florida, revisions are made approximately every three years, and in Wyoming about every five years. All states rely on the advice of local professional advisers to some extent before standards are revised. Seventeen states specifically mention accrediting committees, standards committees, or advisory commissions.

WORKSHOPS AND NEWSLETTERS.   It is widespread practice for state departments of education to initiate consultation with local school supervisors and administrators aimed at preventing or correcting violations of the standards or criteria for the approval or accreditation of the schools. Forty states sponsor periodic workshops or conferences to foster understanding of, to engender support for, and to improve more accurate compliance with state standards. Such services overlap the areas of service stressed in Figure 3-2.

These workshops usually are given as part of the state's supervisory or regulatory program. Activities such as these are supplemented by letters itemizing deficiencies and pointing out any violations that might exist. Some departments of education publish periodic newsletters or memoranda that discuss problems in all spheres of education that relate to approval programs. Local schools frequently are encouraged to request special consultative visits from the state's supervisory personnel for help in preventing or correcting a transgression of the established standard. In at least one state a progress report citing steps taken to correct a standards violation is required from a school whose status is questionable.

FIGURE 3-2.   The Many Strong Arms of the State Department of Education Serve the Supervisor.

FAILURE TO MEET MINIMUM STANDARDS.   Of twenty-five states in which approval has been discontinued or accreditation status lowered, nine withheld funds from schools for failure to meet the minimum standards. Funds were withheld from a kindergarten in one state, from elementary schools in four states, and from high schools in seven states. In any one state, the total number of schools from which funds were withheld ranged from one to forty.

During a recent school year, twelve states rejected or postponed applications for approval of schools. The number of schools applying in any one state ranged between one and 175.

These data lend support to the impression that the states move slowly in making changes in status in their schools. It also is apparent that even though the state boards of education of thirty-four states are empowered by the legislature to withhold funds where minimum standards are not met, it is rather unusual for them to do so.

STATE SUPERVISORY VISITS AND INSPECTION.   Inspection and/or a visit to the school as part of the approval procedure is required by thirty-nine states. In twenty-six states, the valuation is made by state professional personnel only. Eleven other states include local and state professional personnel in the evaluation. In rare instances, community representatives participate with the state and local educators in the approval procedure. In all cases, state professional personnel participate in the required evaluation procedures.

The Texas Education Agency has adopted self-evaluation as part of its procedures for evaluating accredited school systems:

> *Self-evaluation.* Each local school system, through its own initiative, determines whether or not it wants to be accredited by the State Department of Education. When it decides to become accredited, it automatically accepts responsibility of meeting at least the minimum standards prescribed for accreditation. The initial

responsibility, therefore, for meeting the standards for accreditation rests with the local school officials. Consequently, self-evaluation is the first step in the evaluative process. Each accredited school system shall establish and maintain in its own way a system of self-evaluation.[17]

There are various methods of notification of approval by the state authority. Official state bulletins listing approved or accredited schools are published by forty states. Notification by letter to the school occurs in forty states. About half the states send annual notices of approval; one state sends notices biannually. All states send out notifications regarding approval in some form or other.

Figure 3-3 indicates the organization of the major divisions of a state department of education. In general, then, the state departments of education perform the following tasks in the areas of approval and accreditation.

1. Standards are established
2. These standards are evaluated and revised
3. State personnel participate in visiting and evaluating schools
4. Standard evaluations are corrected and a program for prevention and remediation of evaluations is approved
5. Forms and reports are issued and processed

Curriculum and Supervision Responsibilities of the State Department of Education

As state departments of education have moved from an inspection role to a leadership role, the curriculum guide has become much more than a course of study with a listing of subject matter that students are expected to learn. The increasing tendency to incorporate the term "guide" in the title indicates a growing acceptance of the idea that the instructional bulletin is suggestive and not prescribed.

Significant achievements in the field of curriculum development have been brought about by state departments of education as well as by local school systems.

STATE CURRICULUM WORKSHOP. The curriculum workshop is now the most important method of developing curricula. Representatives of many groups come together to participate in workshops to produce a wide variety of material for the classroom teacher. Although the output of ideas in a workshop is important, the changes that take place in the members who participate may be even more important in influencing the successful implementation of the curriculum in the classroom.

[17] Texas Education Agency, *Principles and Standards for Accrediting Elementary and Secondary Schools,* Bulletin No. 560 (Austin: Texas Education Agency, July 1951).

FIGURE 3-3.   Organization of the Major Divisions of One State Department of Education.

THE INSTRUCTIONAL PROGRAM AND THE STATE DEPARTMENT OF EDUCATION. State departments of education are almost uniformly responsible for maintaining an elementary school program that provides instruction in reading, literature, spelling, handwriting, oral and written expression, arithmetic, American history, geography, science, health, physical education, art, and music.[18] Such subjects

[18] Lee C. Deighton, *The Encyclopedia of Education* (New York: Crowell-Collier Education Group, 1971), Vol. 8, pp. 466–470.

usually are mandated by law but frequently are required by rulings of the state board or the state department of education and, with few exceptions, have been a part of the elementary school curriculum for many years. In general, the state laws are less specific for the programs in grades 9 to 12, and similar degrees of freedom are permitted in the selection of textbooks in the high schools. Community colleges enjoy even more autonomy.

TEXTBOOK SELECTION.   The states handle the selection of textbooks in many different ways. Over the years, the trend has been away from adopting a single textbook in each subject and toward multiple adoptions on both state and local levels. Twenty-four states permit local school authorities to adopt textbooks without control from any state or intermediate authority. Seven states place control in the hands of state textbook commissions or committees. Other states give control to the state board of education.

Eleven states present a list of textbooks to local authorities, who may choose one textbook for each subject. This list is compiled by the state board of education or the textbook commission. Thirteen states permit multiple adoptions from such a list, and five permit multiple adoptions only for certain subjects.

ORGANIZATION FOR CURRICULUM DEVELOPMENT.   Leadership in curriculum development programs usually comes from the state department of education. Involved are directors of curriculum; directors of elementary, secondary community college and vocational education; and supervisors in special subject fields.

Special Problems at the State Level

The state departments of education use several methods to involve as many individuals and groups as possible in curriculum development.[19] These methods include workshops, work conferences, meetings, and committee work. In some states, these projects begin on a statewide level and then progress to similar conferences and workshops on a local level. Other states begin projects on the local level and later work up to a large statewide meeting. Either route is effective, depending on the nature of the curriculum problems.

Some state committees work in fields broader than any single subject at any one time. For example, early elementary education, adult education, and such topics as exceptional children, evaluation, and development of materials of instruction were covered at the time of a survey in one large Midwestern state. Other commonly occurring statewide committees were related to conservation, guidance, safety, instructional technology (audio-visual) programs, library service, supervision, and accreditation.

[19] The authors are grateful to the U.S. Department of Health, Education, and Welfare, *Curriculum Responsibilities of the States* (Washington, D.C.: Government Printing Office, 1968), for much of the data in this section.

The responsibilities of these committees can be divided into three groups:

1. Those that advise the state department on supervisory problems
2. Those that survey supervisory needs
3. Those that help to provide supervisory publications and curriculum materials

Individual teachers, administrators, and supervisors who have served on these committees have found them stimulating. The experiences in cooperative thinking and planning appear valuable. The pattern of development in committee work tends to follow a sequence:

1. Orientation
2. Study and research
3. Development of point of view
4. Listing basic assumptions
5. Determination of objectives
6. Development of a plan for the project
7. Production of a tentative manuscript

The most common difficulties experienced by the state committees are usually related to three factors. (1) *Funds are short.* Committee work is costly. Providing travel funds for committee members, hiring substitute teachers while committee members are away, and printing reports or syllabi are the major expenses. (2) *There is a shortage of personnel or time.* Busy teachers, supervisors, and administrators find it difficult to take part in long and exhaustive committee work projects. Research, a basic need of the committee, takes both time to assemble and training to interpret. People with such time and training are not available in sufficient numbers. (3) *There is difficulty in reaching a common working philosophy.* Harmonizing diverging points of view and reconciling different beliefs must occur before the committee can function productively.

Workshops and Work Conferences at the State Level

The workshop and work conference are widely used techniques for dealing with problems at the state level that range from the elementary school to the community college level. A *workshop* may be defined as a work situation in which the participants, with expert consultant help, attempt to solve their problems by many activities. A workshop usually lasts for a week or more. A *work conference,* on the other hand, may be similar to a workshop in techniques used, but its scope is limited to a specific problem and reduced to a day or two. It is similar, then, to the institute, which will be discussed in a later chapter.

Expenses for workshops and work conferences usually come from state funds (seventeen states), from local school systems (in more than half of the states), and from the participants themselves (twenty-two states). Consultants to the workshop or conference are paid from state funds in thirty-six states, by organizations in twenty-eight states, or by other methods in the remaining states.

Statewide Conferences

The statewide conference, usually a more formally organized meeting, is a third method used in supervision at the state level. Speeches usually occur at the beginning of the conference and serve the purpose of orientation. Panel discussions frequently are used in general meetings. Smaller groups analyze and discuss problems, and there is a closing general session or summary.

Some states have evaluating committees work while the conference is in progress and/or fulfilling follow-up functions to increase the effectiveness of statewide conferences. These evaluating committees have illuminated the factors important to the success of conferences:

1. The specific purpose of the conference should be determined by representatives of the groups that attend.
2. Consultants should be selected for their experience and skill in working with groups.
3. Orientation programs should be provided for the conferees; a variety of meetings should be planned; everyone should be encouraged to participate actively.
4. Preplanning should be provided for the comfort of the conferees and for activities to develop fellowship.

Sectional Conferences

A fourth method for dealing with problems at the state level is the sectional conference. The pattern of organization is similar to that of the statewide conference except that participants are more likely to be drawn from special groups such as superintendents, principals, specialist-consultants, and teachers in special subject fields. Some sectional meetings include all teachers, supervisors, and administrators from an area in one meeting.

These smaller sectional conferences are numerous in the larger and more populous states. California reported 477 sectional conferences during a recent five-year period. Fifteen states held fifty or more each during the same interval, and sixteen states held none.

The sectional conference has been successful in reaching many teachers and administrators. Purposes served include drawing ideas from as many educators as possible, discussing and refining ideas, and carrying them back to the classroom. Problems encountered are the common ones of time, funds, and personnel.

Specialist-Consultants Provide Assistance at the State Level

Specialist-consultants are drawn from various sources that commonly include (1) educational institutions and (2) state departments of education either from within the state or from another state. Specialist-consultants also are called from industry, from the United States Office of Education, and from other federal sources as well as from the several national and state associations.

Specialist-consultants provide many services at the state level; they:

1. Make presentations dealing with specific content, with trends, with the interpretation of research, with objectives, and with methods of teaching
2. Discuss reasonable standards of achievement
3. Lead discussion groups
4. Advise on textbooks, present instructional technology materials, give demonstration lessons, demonstrate teaching techniques, and, in the case of the consultant from industry, demonstrate vocational skills
5. Help produce curriculum guides
6. Edit material
7. Evaluate the activities involved in a conference

Curricular Materials: Production, Distribution, and Application

State departments of education all believe that producing curricular materials is an important function, if not a major responsibility, of supervision at the state level. Such materials usually are considered as guides for the schools to use on a voluntary basis. These curricular materials are produced to define the requirements of law and the desires of the state department of education and to suggest content and methods that are considered as most appropriate and useful. As the established standards are met, most state departments permit considerable local variation in organizing and teaching courses; indeed, the trend is toward more local autonomy in this area.

The Supervisor at Work at the State Department of Education

There are three typical patterns of state-local cooperation:

1. Conferences or worshops with local teachers, followed by editorial work by a small committee
2. Workshops of local teachers to consider tentative drafts of instructional materials and to follow up with a revision of the manuscripts
3. A preliminary period of cooperative work between state and local people using workshops and conferences before the final manuscripts

The supervisor at the state level acts as leader, organizer, reporter, consultant, evaluator, and director. The material is then distributed to teachers, who apply the course of study for a year in the classroom. On the basis of criticisms received from the teachers, revisions are made by an editorial committee. Except in a very general way, most state department supervisors have not developed an effective follow-up procedure to determine the impact of new courses of study on the instructional program.

Most state departments of education employ one or more supervisors to maintain an instructional materials library. The supervisor must:

1. Organize a distribution system for films, tapes, and other materials of instructional technology so that all schools receive these materials (without charge) at regular intervals.
2. Organize instructional centers (or libraries) of these materials.
3. Help teachers make wider and better selection and use of instructional media and materials in the classroom.
4. Cooperate in the production of films, filmstrips, tape recordings, programmed materials, and radio and television programs to meet needs peculiar to the state.

Research and Experimentation

Research and experimentation in supervision fall into two general categories at the state level: (1) research and fact-finding studies, and (2) state-testing programs. Schools are chosen to participate in the study with the subject to be studied in mind. Criteria on which schools are selected involve geographic locations, size of the community, and the social and economic backgrounds of the students. When more than one school is used, the point of view is expressed that a variety of situations is desirable. Interest in the project, plus facilities and personnel to carry on the work, seem to be essential.

E. L. Morphet and C. O. Ryan[20] described various programs of state leadership in improving instruction:

1. Attempts were made to coordinate the functions of the state departments only recently.
2. Staff positions in each state were usually filled by persons holding supervisory or administrative positions within the state.
3. Principals indicated less satisfaction with the program of supervision provided by the state than did supervisors and superintendents.
4. Cooperative, directive, and indirect programs were identified. In the cooperative program, local participation and planning were secured and no direct attempts to secure statewide participation were made.

[20] See Edgar L. Morphet and Charles O. Ryan, *Designing Education for the Future,* No. 3: "Planning and Effecting Needed Changes in Education" (New York: Citation Press, 1967), and William Marvin Alexander, "State Leadership in Improving Instruction" (Doctoral dissertation, Teachers College, Columbia University, 1940).

5. The cooperative program, more than the directive, stressed the importance of stimulating local initiative.
6. The indirect programs made little provision for study, experimentation, and appraisal, whereas the directive program provided for a study of instructional problems by local groups.
7. The clearinghouse   pect of state leadership was an essential phase of the cooperative program.

The following recommendations can be derived from the findings above:

1. Local workers should have ultimate responsibility for procedure in programs to improve instruction.
2. Each program should provide means for facilitating local study.
3. The improvement of instruction should be regarded as a common problem of local and state educators. State supervisors should coordinate the work of groups.
4. The type of service needed by the locality, and for modifying state activity accordingly, should be determined. The cooperative program should be employed; the direct program becomes authoritarian, and the indirect program is ineffective.

From a practical point of view, the major responsibility of state departments of education is to assure the opportunity for all children to acquire a basic education. The fundamental program must be continually revised, augmented, and improved in order to keep abreast of changing times. The most successful approach to this goal has been to enlist the help of people with first-hand experience and to bring them together in large numbers in workshops and conferences, with the state's responsibility being exercised in the role of leader and coordinator. Modern transportation, the high level of teacher education, and the growing number of people with supervisory training have been important factors in making such meetings productive and highly successful.

All efforts to improve education in general, by the nature of the problems, must be experimental. Courses of study or curriculum guides should be revised at least every five years. These periodic revisions, together with the experimental method, make for a state of dynamic flux, ever striving toward improvement in our educational system.

One of the most important by-products that accrues in a democratic society is the progress made through the best use of our human resources. Teamwork between the educational specialist and the classroom teacher, between state departments and private educational organizations, and between state and local administrators results in more effective education.

Persistent Problems in the State Program
for Supervision

Two persistent problems burden and tend to decelerate the rate of progress in supervision at the state level. One is communication. Part of the problem exists between specialist-consultants and people who apply the suggested principles. Part of the difficulty is in effectively disseminating results of current research to teachers and to principals. Furthermore, there is a need for continuous evaluation of public opinion and its effects on the success or failure of a program. There is a great need not merely to keep the public informed, but to interest the general public in the welfare of the schools and to gain support for programs: *to communicate*. All means available are being used: the press, radio, television, recordings, private publications, and organizations.

Another persistent problem is the compelling need for repeated fact-finding studies and research geared to answer the following questions:

1. What is the nature of the school problems in this state?
2. What has research made available to help us solve these problems?
3. How can sufficiently trained and experienced people be made available to handle these studies?

In summary, effective communication, intensive and extensive research, and a continuously applied program of evaluation are essential to progress. The state department of education has a vital role in the area of educational legislation. It must perform the research needed to outline legislation and must recommend such legislation to the elected representatives of the people.

Professional organizations concerned with school supervision should bring needed legislation to the attention of state departments of education. Through cooperation between all agencies seeking better education it is possible to secure needed legislation. In this way, the state can exert leadership toward better instruction for children.

As a Supervisor at the State Level

Do

1. Work to outline and obtain support for passing needed legislation.
2. Maintain an adequate curriculum materials and instructional media laboratory and information retrieval system.
3. Provide needed specialist-consultant services to the offices of the several intermediate unit superintendents and, if authorized, to the local school systems. Channel such services through the intermediate unit.
4. Provide for a liaison with university education departments.

5. Serve as a clearinghouse for instructional research and special programs throughout the state.
6. Provide essential liaison with the U.S. Office of Health, Education, and Welfare and with other federal agencies.
7. Beware of performance contracting, management by objectives, and the like. Education is an art as well as a science; some children and groups cannot meet some goals or objectives.
8. Study accountability programs and laws and assessment designs carefully.

Don't

1. Fail to provide for full-time staff personnel assignments to handle federally funded programs.
2. Fail to help local school systems and community colleges become aware of keeping up to date concerning and applying for the several federal and state grants that may be available.
3. Bypass the intermediate unit by giving direct service to the local system, except in special authorized circumstances and with wholehearted support from the intermediate unit staff.
4. Be slow in responding to questions and requests from local school system and intermediate unit personnel.

TRENDS IN THE ROLE OF THE STATE AND FEDERAL GOVERNMENT IN SCHOOL SUPERVISION

| Toward | ⟶ Greater Support for Instructional and

Staff Development

State and national support for supervision will increase; specific funds will be allocated for staff and instructional development. These funds will provide for improved state programs as well as for a significant expansion of the supervisory programs of local school systems and intermediate level offices.

| Toward | ⟶ Significantly Increased Influence of

Educators on State and National Legislation

Educators and educators' organizations are responsible for sponsoring legislation that affects supervision and education in general. In the future, they will make a greater effort and be more influential.

Toward ⟶   Implementing Statewide
Assessment Programs

The states have shown a tendency to implement *statewide assessment programs.* This trend probably is an offshoot of the *accountability movement. Phi Delta Kappan,* the journal of the professional honor society Phi Delta Kappa, regularly publishes summaries of research concerning assessment and accountability programs. *Audio Visual Instruction* (Dec. 1975) also includes several articles on this topic.

Supervisory Problems

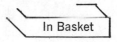

In Basket

Problem 1

The Deputy Superintendent of Public Instruction has written you indicating her interest in establishing an adequate "really complete and functioning curriculum materials center" in the State Department of Education and asks that you accept the assignment. How would you go about your task, assuming that the State Board of Education has authorized release time for you and two assistants and has provided the necessary funding for the project?

What steps would you take?
What materials and services would you recommend be available in such a curriculum center at the state level?
How would you determine the adequacy of your suggestions?
How would you provide for evaluation and feedback concerning these factors?

Problem 2

The Educational Finance Committee of the State Legislature has asked you to appear as a resource person at its current budget hearings. You have one week to prepare for your appearance. You know that there is much sentiment on the committee to "economize," especially in what one assemblyman termed "the flowery frills of schooling nowadays." Further, you have heard that several committee members are dissatisfied with "those ethnic—so-called—studies programs," as a senior assemblyman put it. As curriculum specialist for the State Department of Education:

How would you prepare for your appearance before the legislative committee?
What areas would you anticipate as being most vulnerable to the economy thrust?
What points would you plan to emphasize during your appearance?

Questions and Suggested Activities Concerning
the Role of the State and Federal Government

Questions

1. How can your state constitution be amended?
2. Differentiate between the type of material included in your state constitution, your state education or school code, and the rules and regulations of your state board of education.
3. What part do the courts play in establishing educational practices for the entire state?
4. What qualifications do you believe the members of the state board of education should possess?
5. What qualifications do you believe the chief state school officer and/or the U.S. Commissioner of Education should possess?
6. Do you believe that your state should refuse to give supervisory assistance to a private or parochial school? Why?
7. Requirements for a high-school diploma are issued in written form by thirty-nine states. Should such requirements be listed for elementary school graduation as well? For a community college degree? Indicate your reasons.

Suggested Activities

1. Outline the functions of the state in educational supervision.
2. Distinguish between the terms chief state school officer, state department of education, state board of education, and state legislature.
3. List general principles for the state's role in educational supervision.
4. Trace the historical development of the state departments of education.
5. Indicate the responsibilities of the chief state school officer. From the list of responsibilities, decide how the chief state school officer should be selected.
6. List the functions of the state department of education for your state. Prepare a chart indicating relationships between the various offices of the state department of education.
7. List the curriculum and supervision responsibilities of the state department of education for your state. Consider textbook selection; organization for curriculum development; organization for supervision; subject area consultive services and techniques used; workshops and work conferences, statewide, sectional, and local conferences; consultant services; grants of funds for special programs; curriculum materials, instructional technology (audiovisual aids) and programmed learning, research, and experimentation.
8. Analyze the role that your state department of education has played in submitting proposed legislation to the state legislature. Cite examples of laws passed that the state department recommended.
9. Prepare a bibliography of material that has appeared in the periodical litera-

ture during the last year concerning the role of the state and/or federal government in supervision.

10. Differentiate between the terms approval and accreditation; give specific examples of each term.

11. Study the form of the accreditation and approval program(s) employed by your state department of education. Show how they could be improved.

Selected Bibliography

Books

Baron, George, and D. A. Howell. *The Government and Management of Schools.* Atlantic Highlands. New Jersey: Humanities Press, Inc., 1974.

Beach, F. F. *The Functions of State Departments of Education.* Washington, D.C.: Government Printing Office, 1950.

Butts, R. Freeman, and Lawrence A. Cremin. *A History of Education in American Culture.* New York: Henry Holt and Company, Inc., 1953.

Campbell, Roald F., ed. *Strengthening State Departments of Education.* Danville, Illinois: Interstate Printers, 1967.

Council of Chief School Officers. *Responsibilities of State Departments of Education for Approval and Accreditation of Public Schools.* Washington, D.C.: Council of Chief State School Officers, 1960.

Cummings, L. L., and Donald P. Schwab. *Performance in Organizations: Determinants and Appraisal.* Glenview, Illinois: Scott, Foresman and Co., 1973.

DeYoung, Chris A. *Introduction to American Public Education.* New York: McGraw-Hill Book Company, Inc., 1950.

Frey, Sherman H., and Keith R. Getschman. *School Administration: Selected Readings.* New York: Thomas Y. Crowell Company, 1969.

Grieder, Calvin, and W. E. Rosenstengle. *Public School Administration.* New York: The Ronald Press Company, 1954.

Gwynn, J. Minor. *Theory and Practice of Supervision.* New York: Dodd, Mead, & Company, 1961.

Harris, Ben M. *Supervisory Behavior in Education.* Englewood Cliffs, New Jersey: Prentice-Hall, Inc., 1975.

Moehlman, Arthur B. *School Administration.* rev. ed. Boston: Houghton Mifflin Company, 1951.

Morphet, Edgar L., and Charles O. Ryan. *Designing Education for the Future.* Bulletin, No. 3. New York: Citation Press, 1967.

Morrisett, Lloyd N., Sr. *Power Play for Control of Education.* Denver: Education Committee of the States, 1967.

Reeder, Ward G. *The Fundamentals of Public School Administration.* New York: The Macmillan Company, 1951.

Stoops, Emery, Max Rafferty, and Russell E. Johnson. *Handbook of Educational Administration.* Boston: Allyn and Bacon, Inc., 1975.

Stoops, Emery. *Report of the Study Title III, ESEA.* Sacramento: California State Department of Education, 1970.

Periodicals

Atkinson, Byron H. "What Is a Modern State Board of Education?" *American School Board Journal* CXXVII (November 1953):25–26.

Fuller, Edgar. "Public Schools and Separation of Church and State." *School Executive* LXVIII (February 1949):11–18.

Goold, G. H. State Aid: *A Matter of Putting First Things First.* New York State Education 57 (January 1970):48.

Simpson, Roy E. "The Place of the State Superintendent in Public Education." *California Schools* XXI (September 1950):307–312.

"Trends: Accountability, Competencies, and Instruction," *Audio Visual Instruction* XX (December 1975), Special Issue.

Other Sources

Alexander, William Marvin. "State Leadership in Improving Instruction." Doctoral dissertation, Teachers College, Columbia University, 1940.

American Association of School Administrators. "Leadership at the State Level." Chapter XIII in *The American School Superintendent.* Thirtieth Yearbook of the Association. Washington, D.C.: The Association, 1952.

Council of State Governments. *The Forty-Eight State School Systems.* Chicago: The Council, 1949.

Cummings, H. H., and H. K. Mackintosh. *Curriculum Responsibilities of State Departments of Education.* Washington, D.C.: Government Printing Office, 1958.

Rich, W. B. *Approval and Accreditation of Public Schools.* Washington, D.C.: Government Printing Office, 1960.

Texas Education Agency, *Principles and Standards for Accrediting Elementary and Secondary Schools,* Bulletin No. 560. Austin: Texas Education Agency, July 1957.

U.S. Department of Health, Education, and Welfare. *Curriculum Responsibility of State Departments of Education.* Washington, D.C.: Government Printing Office, 1958.

4

Organizing the Supervisory Program

The organizational plan for supervision must clearly define the responsibilities, functions, and relationships of the professional staff. The following topics are treated in this chapter:

Basic principles of organization for the supervisor
Authority and organization: how to organize and implement a supervisory program
A shared responsibility
A new type of supervisor and a new type of supervision
How to plan your work as a supervisor
How to provide for managerial coordination: the roles of the principal and the superintendent
Conflicting organizational demands
Do—Don't
Trends
"In-Basket" supervisory problems
Questions and suggested activities

Basic Principles of Organization for the Supervisor

In modern organization for school supervision, the direction is toward improving the total teaching-learning process, which subsumes the total setting, rather than toward the more limited aim of improving teachers in service. Modern supervision directs attention toward the fundamentals of education and the improvement of learning. The focus of supervision is on the teaching-learning situation, with the groups and individuals working to improve the total complex. The teacher in this type of supervision becomes a cooperating member of a group dedicated to the improvement of instruction. Before this dedication can be translated into action leading to positive results, the prime requisite of *planning* must receive consideration.

The Need for Coordination

The all-pervasive element in the process of both administration and supervision and that is evident in the total management process is coordination. Without coordination, effective planning cannot occur.

A POLICY SYSTEM APPROACH TO SUPERVISORY ORGANIZATION. Generally accepted policies, especially when those policies are in written form and have been adopted by the governing board, allow the supervisory system to function properly. They facilitate planning, encourage the delegation of authority and responsibility, and permit personnel to develop a clearer, more definite conception of their responsibilities and authority.

Policies, of course, can be general in nature, touching only on the broad outlines of the supervisory organization. They may be more detailed, taking the form of standard operating procedures, which can provide exact methods for accomplishing nearly every task. As policies are developed, the supervisor must insure that they can be amended so that the system does not stagnate. There must be room for individual initiative; administrative flexibility must not be denied.

A POLICY HANDBOOK. The development of a policy handbook that deals with the system for supervision should be initiated. Such a handbook exerts a stabilizing effect on the organization, serves as a guide to performance, and provides a standard against which to measure accomplishment. It provides a goal and direction for the supervisory system.

PLANNING, COORDINATION, STIMULATION, AND GROWTH. In supervision, there should be planning, coordination, stimulation, and growth of teachers. The student should be encouraged to exercise his talents toward a richer and more intelligent participation in the society and the world in which he lives. Only when supervision is organized, both as a creative art and as a science, will instruction and instructional procedures be improved.

Educational supervision must be organized to:

1. Help the professional staff see more clearly the goals of education; help those working in supervision at each level of education (elementary, secondary, and higher) see the special role of each level in achieving these goals.
2. Help teachers see the problems and needs of children and youth.
3. Provide effective democratic leadership in promoting the professional improvement of the school and its activities in fostering harmonious and cooperative staff relations, in stimulating professional in-service education of teachers, and in enhancing school-community relations.

4. Build strong group morale and unify teachers into an effective team working to achieve the same general goals.
5. Determine the work for which each teacher is best suited, assign him/her to such work, and encourage him/her to develop his/her capabilities.
6. Help the professional staff develop greater competence in teaching.
7. Assist teachers new to the school system.
8. Evaluate the results of each teacher's efforts in terms of student growth toward predetermined goals.
9. Aid teachers in the diagnosis and remediation of learning difficulties.
10. Interpret the instructional program to the community.
11. Protect the professional staff from unreasonable demands and from unwarranted, negative criticism.

The organizational format for the supervisory program must be clear as to what is to be achieved. The means used must be chosen because they are appropriate for achieving the desired results. The program must have purpose and organization, related activities, and consistent objectives. Without these three, the system breaks down.

A program of supervision must be a program of educational improvement. Although many kinds of supervision are possible, supervisory activities may be organized according to four general classifications: (1) creative, (2) constructive, (3) preventative, and (4) corrective.[1]

The Systems Approach to Supervisory Organization: Guidelines for Implementation

The following list of basic principles may be used as a guide by the professional staff in organizing for school supervision:

1. All major functions to be performed must be grouped with administrative or management positions to direct them. Such functions should be combined in closely related groups of similar functions to insure their coordination.
2. The number of persons directly responsible to a school system administrative officer should not exceed what can be given reasonably adequate supervision. No position should be responsible to more than one higher position.
3. Titles should indicate the level of control assigned to the several administrative positions. Titles for school level positions should not be the same as for school system level positions. Similarly, titles for the classified management positions should not be the same as those for certified positions. Such consistency can help school system personnel and the general public understand the staff organization.
4. School system level administrative and supervisory positions should be staffed on a full-time basis, as should special service and special teaching positions, although not quite to the same degree.

[1] See William H. Burton and Leo J. Brueckner, *Supervision,* 3d ed. (New York: Appleton-Century-Crofts, 1955), chapter V.

5. School system level administrative personnel should be employed on a twelve calendar month basis. Principals should be employed on a twelve school months basis. Other supervisory, special service, and special teaching positions typically should be staffed on the basis of eleven school months annually. Clerical positions generally should be assigned on the same annual service basis as the management position to which they are attached.

6. All administrative and supervisory positions should receive help from an appropriate number of clerical employees. In no instance should well-paid, highly trained personnel have to do a lot of their own clerical work.

7. An efficient organization must be planned to meet the needs of the school system, and personnel must be employed to fit the organization, rather than providing a plan around the personnel that a school system may happen to have in its employ at any given time.

8. An organizational pattern should be sufficiently flexible to allow the addition of staff members in existing types of positions and to permit the creation of new types of positions as required to care for school system growth, without altering the basic design of the organization. Patterns of organization should be designed to permit full compliance with this standard.

9. Good school system organization requires a plan for the coordination of administrative and supervisory functions, as well as of special service and teaching functions. This normally is accomplished, in part, by a schedule of regular meetings between staff members.

10. Administrative-supervisory staff, special service personnel, and clerical assistants should have a place to work under conditions of comfort and efficiency. This means adequate office space with modern facilities and good conditions for effective and harmonious relationships. Lack of adequately planned and interrelated office spaces, adequate workrooms, and adequate lounge and restroom facilities for the school system level staff definitely reduces the efficiency of the staff. Similarly, inadequate provisions for maintenance and warehousing make these services less efficient.[2]

11. Authority should be delegated commensurate with the assignment of responsibility. High level supervisory and administrative positions should be free to provide a high level type of leadership rather than to be occupied with details appropriate for delegation to lower level positions. Enough authority and responsibility should be delegated to prevent the bottlenecks that occur when too much detail must cross the desk of top administrators.

12. Efficient functioning of school system organization largely depends on effective channels of communication. Such channels should be clear-cut, two-way, short, and direct.

Coordination: a Universal Requirement

O. Tead[3] reported that a growing organization arises from a deliberate association of persons desiring to accomplish something together; to realize certain de-

[2] Irving R. Melbo et al., "Report of the Survey, Taft City School District" (Los Angeles: July 1960).

[3] Ordway Tead, *The Art of Administration* (New York: McGraw-Hill Book Company, Inc., 1951).

fined objectives that, as individuals, the persons either could not do for themselves or could not do so well. The customary outcome of intensive human relations is the development of a satisfying camaraderie. Keeping this sentiment flourishing is a challenge to supervisory skill.

Authority and Organization: How to Organize and Implement a Supervisory Program

General Principles of Organization

The supervisory principal should be familiar with four basic general principles of organization:

1. The learning situation for students can be improved by the proper administrative organization of personnel engaged in supervisory services.
2. Organization for supervision should be based on a generally accepted philosophy of education for the school system.
3. The governing board, as a policy-making body, has full authority over the supervisory program and should delegate responsibility and authority for administration of the program to the superintendent.
4. The school's organization for supervision should be appraised continuously and revised in the light of the appraisal.

Principles of External Organization

The generally accepted principles of *external* organization are essentially as follows:

1. Authority is centralized in the legally appointed person at the head.
   a) The superintendent of schools is, in the last analysis, responsible for the general instructional policy of the school system.
   b) The superintendent in a large school system should delegate the supervisory responsibility to a single assistant.
   c) The assistant superintendent in charge of instruction should serve in behalf of the superintendent in dealing with the supervising principal.
   d) The principal should be the administrative executive-in-charge of instruction within the school unit. He should be directly responsible to the superintendent.
   e) Supervisory staff members, including general supervisors, special subject supervisors, psychologists, research specialists, and others, should serve both teachers and the principal in an advisory relationship, and they

should be responsible to the superintendent or the assistant superintendent.

2. The teacher should be responsible directly to the principal for the instructional program within the classroom.

3. The lines and channels through which delegated authority and responsibility flow should be defined sharply and unambiguously.

   a) The delegation of responsibility should follow clearly defined policies and should be set forth in writing.

   b) By means of periodic reports, members of the supervisory staff should keep the superintendent informed about activities and achievements related to delegated responsibilities; the superintendent also should keep the staff informed concerning board policies related to supervision.

   c) Provisions must be made so that each individual or area in the organization may be reached expeditiously from any higher administrative level.

   d) Provision must be made for appeal from any individual or level to higher administrative levels.

   e) No individual should receive complete directions covering precisely the same item from more than one person. (Assignments, notices, and directions to teachers should originate with the principal.)

   f) The performance of duties assigned to any level must be checked by the next higher levels throughout the system.

4. Staff officers are instructional experts and consultants; they are thus differentiated from the line officers. Further, they have no executive power.

   a) A principal is both an administrative and a supervisory officer.

   b) The principal, in his supervisory capacity, can be most effective through direct assistance: visiting and conferring with individual teachers; helping with individual students; making immediate suggestions; helping with lesson plans, devices, and units.

   c) The general or special supervisors or "specialist-consultants" from the central office can be most effective through indirect and more remote assistance: making or taking leadership in preparing courses of study, providing materials, interpreting standards, and helping principals and groups of teachers.

   d) The bulk of everyday classroom visitation may be taken over by the principal; the central office supervisor's visits usually occur on request.[4]

These principles are practically self-explanatory and will be familiar to advanced students and workers in the field.

Principles of Internal Organization

The principles of *internal* organization are:

1. Facility for cooperation and coordination must be provided.
   a) A common theory of education, a common technology, and common goals must be established.

[4] Burton and Bruecker, *Supervision*, p. 103.

b) The work of the line officers and the staff officers must be coordinated by common planning under a deputy superintendent or some form of supervisory council.

c) Many interlocking committees, conference groups, and small subcommittees should exist below the level of general coordination.

d) Cases of conflict or disagreement between any officers or groups must be settled by the next higher administrative officer, and ultimately by the superintendent.

2. There must be flexibility of operation.

a) Adjustment of strictly logical lines and duties must be made when local circumstances demand it (type of community, size of system, traditions, previous policies, training, experience and personalities).

b) Line officers, in some instances, perform duties that ordinarily are assigned to staff officers. The reverse is true only on special occasions.

c) A clear distinction should be made between authoritative (line) and advisory (staff) relationships.

d) *A linear responsibility chart,* which would go beyond the usual, simple display of lines of authority and communication, should be developed. With special symbols, this chart can indicate job title–responsibility couplings such as: (1) advisory–consultive, (2) technical, (3) informational, (4) managerial, (5) operational, (6) supervisory, and (7) specialty.

VERTICAL AND HORIZONTAL ORGANIZATION.   In vertical organization, supervisors are advisers on instructional conditions in a given subject or curriculum area throughout all grades. In horizontal organization, supervisors work only in given school divisions such as primary, upper elementary, secondary, or higher education.

Vertical supervision is strong in securing unity, coordination, integration, and articulation of materials and methods within each field. It is weak in that it tends to keep subjects or areas separate and provides less correlation between subjects or areas. It sometimes fails to secure integration of subjects or areas required by the objectives of the school.

Horizontal supervision is strong in securing unity and integration between subjects or areas within the delimitations of divisional levels. Its weaknesses lie in its possible failure to articulate between levels and in a possible lack of provision for expert specialist-consultant services in the individual subject matter fields.

Choice between the systems depends on the training and attitudes of the given staff and on local traditions. Staff specialist-consultants in conventional line-and-staff serve all principals and teachers.

A schematic representation of dualistic line organization for school supervision is included as Figure 4-1. In this type of organizational plan, both superintendent and business manager report directly to the governing board. The superintendent, then, who should be the champion of the instructional program, does not have the power of the purse (or the ear of the governing board concerning that power), whereas the individual who *does* have that power (or ear) may

FIGURE 4-1. Dualistic Line Organization for Supervision—Not Recommended.

lack an instructional orientation. Such a dualistic plan can lead to problems in communications and in goals determination.

A Shared Responsibility

The program for school supervision is one in which the entire professional staff must assume certain duties and responsibilities.

The best type of school system organizational plan supports the instructional program. Instruction is the only reason a school system has for existing. All other functions are supportive and facilitating. They are not independent, nor are they justified in their own right. An organizational pattern that fulfills these requisites for a small school system is represented in Figure 4-2. It recognizes the integral nature of all phases of the educational program. In this *unit plan,* the several supportive functions are coordinated under a central administration in order to exert the efforts of many individuals toward a common goal: more effective instruction. Figures 4-3 and 4-4 present organization charts for medium and large systems.

Figure 4-5 illustrates various relationships within the school system.

Legal Bases for Supervisory Organization

A public school teacher, supervising principal, specialist-consultant, or superintendent is subject to the authority of state codes and of the governing board. The

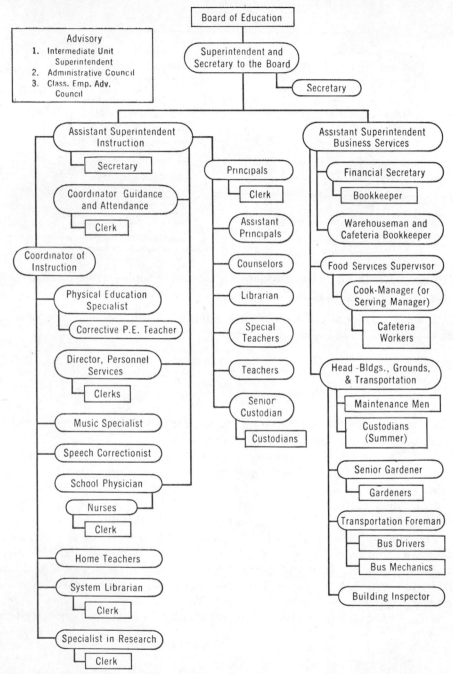

FIGURE 4-2.   Recommended Organization and Relationships: A Small School System.

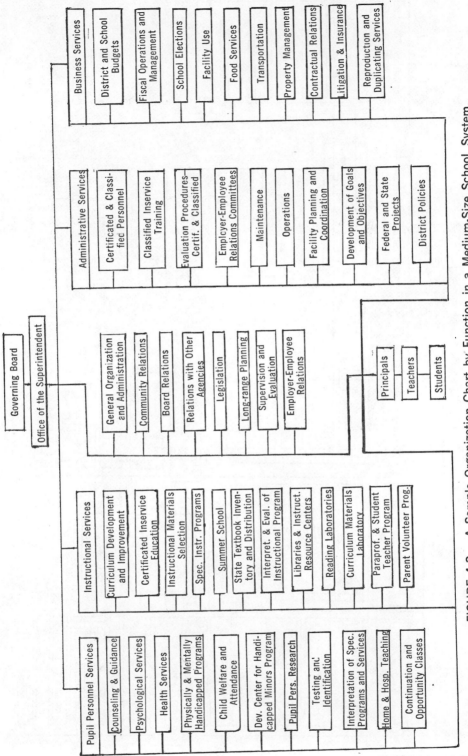

FIGURE 4-3. A Sample Organization Chart by Function in a Medium-Size School System.

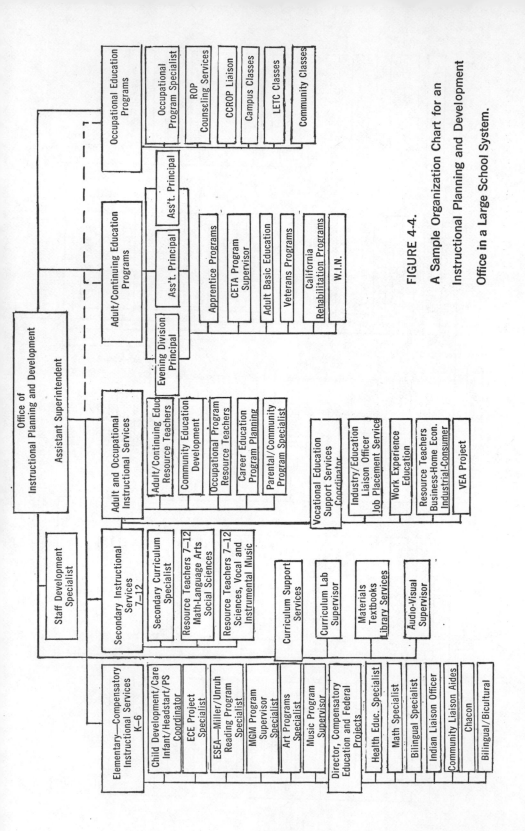

FIGURE 4-4.

A Sample Organization Chart for an
Instructional Planning and Development
Office in a Large School System.

The School Board

Superintendent

Assistant Superintendent

Principal | within the school | Director or Coordinator

Teachers

Assistant Director or Assistant Coordinator } Staff

In-Service Education

Consultants and Specialists

– – – – – – – – – – = Lines of communication, rather than authority

FIGURE 4-5.   The Staff Works Together in School Supervision.

legal responsibilities of certified employees have been defined in general by the judiciary:

1. Public school teachers must be under the actual control and supervision of responsible school authorities,[5] and they must perform their labors and duties under the control and direction of the school board in conformity to such lawful rules and regulations as the board may adopt or as may be imposed by statute.[6]

2. The duties of school teachers are not defined or created by statute but arise directly from the contract of hiring entered into them with the school board,[7] and their power and duties are prescribed and limited thereby.[8]

3. It is the duty of a teacher to conduct himself so as to command the respect and good will of the community, even though one result of the choice of a

[5] New Mexico, Zellers v. Huff, 236 P. 2nd 949, 55 N. M. 501.

[6] New York, Parrish v. Moss, 106 N.Y.S. 2nd 5773, affirmed 107 N.Y.S. 2nd 580, 279 App. Div. 608.

[7] Pennsylvania, Malone v. Hayden, 197 A. 344, 329 Pa. 213.

[8] Iowa, Whitney v. Rural Independent School District No. 4 of Lafayette Township. 4 N.W. 2nd 394, 140, A.L.R. 1376.

teacher's vocation may be to deprive him of the same freedom of action enjoyed by persons of other vocations.[9]

4. A supervising principal or a superintendent of a public school is subject at all times to the supervision and control of the school board or governing body of the school in all activities connected with the business of the school. The school specialist-consultant also is under the supervision and control of the governing board.[10]

5. A principal has the right to make and enforce proper and reasonable rules and regulations for teachers to follow,[11] but he cannot, in violation of statute, act as principal of any school other than the one for which he has been legally employed.[12]

6. The teacher is responsible, not to the public nor to the patrons of the school, but to the proper school officers, the trustees or board of education, the intermediate superintendent, and the state superintendent of public instruction.[13]

7. A superintendent has general supervision over the schools of the system.[14] The same decision also stated that the school system superintendent performs functions different from those of a teacher.

8. The duty of a teacher in the public schools is to exercise proper supervision over students in his charge,[15] and to exercise reasonable care to prevent injury to them.[16] The school supervising principal must help the teacher comply with the meaning and intent of this decision.

9. The teacher's duty is to exercise care in the tasks assigned to students.[17] The relationship of a teacher to a student with respect to the law applicable to the duties of a teacher in the care and custody of the student is one of *in loco parentis*.[18] This relationship may be reflected in the assignment specifications developed for the position of school teacher. The teacher must exercise such care of his students as a parent of ordinary prudence would exercise under comparable circumstances.[19]

10. Where required by statute, it is the duty of teachers to observe the conduct of students to and from school, on the playground, and during any intermission.[20] The organization for school supervision must provide for assistance in this area.

[9] Donald Piety, "Legal Aspects of Recruitment, Selection, and Assignment of Certified Personnel in Public Schools as Shown by Court Devisions, 1956" (Doctoral dissertation, University of Southern California, 1956), p. 146.

[10] Massachusetts, Russell y. Gannon, 183 N.E. 736, 281 Mass. 398.

[11] Pennsylvania, Appeal of Cable, 61 Pa. Dist. and County 298.

[12] California, Cloverdale Union High School District v. Peters, 264 P. 273, 88 Cal App. 731.

[13] Heath v. Johnson, 15 S.E. 980, 36 W. Va. 782.

[14] Montana-State ex rel. Howard v. Ireland, 138 P. 2nd 569.

[15] New York, Miller v. Board of Education, Union School District No. 1, Town of Albion, 50 N.E. 2nd 529.

[16] New York, La Dalley v. Stamford, 272 App. Div. 183.

[17] New York, Gobel v. Board of Education of the City of Albany, 48 N.Y.S. 2nd 299, 267 App. Div. 621, affirmed 60 N.E. 2nd 133.

[18] Gaincott v. Davis, 275 N.W. 299.

[19] Ohman v. Board of Education of the City of New York, 90 N.E. 2nd 474. Reargument denied: 93 N.E. 2nd 927.

[20] Nevada, Nevada Industrial Commission v. Leonard, 68 P. 2nd 576.

11. Teachers may *not* be required to perform janitorial services, police service (traffic duty), or school bus driving service.[21]
12. The term principal, or supervising principal, is commonly applied to the head of the school,[22] and it has been held to apply equally to elementary and high schools.[23]
13. A school principal, supervising principal, or specialist-consultant is the servant and agent of the school board.[24]
14. Although a superintendent is an executive officer and a public officer,[25] he also is an employee.[26]

Organizing the Work of the Supervisors of the School System

Knowing the teaching personnel is as necessary to the determination of policies as is knowing the community. Democratic organization also demands that the teachers help establish policies for the system as a whole, as well as for their individual schools. It is, therefore, important that there be direct contact between the *supervisory team* (the specialist-consultant, principal, resource personnel, master teachers, and others) and the teaching staff.

THE ASSISTANT SUPERINTENDENT IN CHARGE OF INSTRUCTION. Only a few school systems employ assistant superintendents. These officials are not always strictly instructional supervisors. The italicized words in the sample policy included as Figure 4-6 clearly show this; this section is typical of most statements defining the duties of the assistant superintendent.

One item stands out clearly in the situation regarding the assistant superintendent: since the assistant is to act under the immediate direction of the superintendent, the superintendent may delegate to the assistant most administrative duties and thus be free to give more personal attention to instruction.[27]

FUNCTIONS OF THE ASSISTANT SUPERINTENDENT. In order to be of greatest assistance to the superintendent of schools and to be most effective in improving instruction, the assistant superintendent should be assigned rather broad authority and responsibility in the area of instructional services. I. Melbo et al.[28] recommended the following functions:

[21] Parrish v. Moss. Reasonable hours for teachers are covered in 85 N.E. 2nd 792.

[22] A. S. Barr, William H. Burton, and Leo J. Brueckner, *Supervision* (New York: D. Appleton-Century Company, Inc., 1947), p. 11.

[23] Ibid., p. 12.

[24] Pennsylvania, Howell v. Kingston Township School District, 161 A. 559.

[25] Kansas-State ex rel. Hill v. Sinclair, 175 P. 41.

[26] Ibid.

[27] Hubert Wilbur Nutt, *Current Problems in the Supervision of Instruction* (New York: Johnson Publishing Company, 1928), pp. 172–173.

[28] Melbo et al., "Report of the Survey," p. 50.

FIGURE 4-6.   Sample Policy.

(School System), ARTICLE IV
Assistant Superintendent

SECTION 1.   *Duties.* The duties of such assistant shall be those ordinarily incident to such position. He shall work and cooperate with the superintendent in all matters pertaining to school work and shall be under the direction of the superintendent in all such matters, and in the absence or disability of the superintendent, shall perform his duties.

SECTION 2.   He shall, *in all matters pertaining to the financial and business interests of the schools, be under the general supervision of the superintendent alone, and shall make all reports directly to the superintendent.*

---

1.   Assist the superintendent in the program for community relations and in the development of educational policies and programs for the entire school system.
2.   Assist the superintendent in the recruitment, selection, employment, induction, and assignment of certified personnel (both regular and substitute) and in the maintenance of necessary school system personnel records for these employees.
3.   Direct curriculum development, evaluation, textbooks and supplementary book adoptions, instructional procedures, and instructional material selection.
4.   Direct the in-service education program.
5.   Direct and coordinate the school system's program of health services and the program of education for physically handicapped children and for the home bound.
6.   Supervise and coordinate the work of all personnel assigned to attached positions.

The reader can compare the duties of the assistant superintendent and the superintendent as instructional leaders with the help of the thirty-fifth yearbook of the American Association of School Administrators.[29]

T. Freese[30] reported that the position of assistant superintendent in charge of instruction originally was established to aid the superintendent. Little attention was given to the position until approximately 1945. Within a decade, the position was widely used in cities of over 25,000 census population and was growing rapidly. The chief reasons for justifying the existence of the position have been the coordination and improvement of instruction and the relief given to the superintendent.

Freese recommended that the position of assistant superintendent be created for instructional services in all school systems of over 20,000 population

[29] American Association of School Administrators, *The Superintendent as an Instructional Leader,* Departmental Thirty-Fifth Yearbook (Washington, D.C.: The Association, 1957).

[30] Theron Freese, "A Study of the Position of Assistant Superintendent in Charge of Instruction: Its History, Status, and Functions" (Doctoral dissertation, University of Southern California, 1955).

and that curriculum development, supervision of instruction, and in-service education receive major emphasis.[31]

DIRECTOR OF RESEARCH.   The director of research gives services such as:

1. Helping the assistant superintendent in charge of instruction in the two broad areas of research and curriculum development.
2. Directing and coordinating various research projects including the retrieval, assembly, analysis, and discussion of information, and the development of graphic and tabular representations of research results.
3. Directing and coordinating experiments in improving instructional methods and materials.
4. Directing and coordinating the development of an instructional materials center.
5. Directing and coordinating the use and evaluation of the instructional technology materials and of teaching laboratory programs.
6. Supervising attached personnel as required.

THE ASSISTANT PRINCIPAL.   G. M. Weller[32] stated that 50 per cent of a vice-principal's time was spent in the general area of student direction and control. He suggested a more meaningful classification of duties, broken down into six primary areas: (1) student control, (2) student activity direction, (3) instructional supervision, (4) plant management, (5) community relations, and (6) miscellaneous administrative duties.

The assistant principal's responsibilities in teacher evaluation were stressed by the authors in a symposium on evaluation and merit rating. The use of assignment specifications was implied and the area of human dynamics was given prime focus:

For a successful evaluation program, the administrator *must* accept the responsibility for acquainting the teacher with what is expected of [him/her] . . ., and what appraisal techniques are being used.
. . . .
In conclusion, evaluation cannot achieve its objective unless it is cooperatively approached by both teacher and administrator alike . . . supervision is a human relations study. . . . It seems . . . [the] main tasks, therefore, are determining

[31] The research of Freese may be compared with the findings of the research by Harold J. Smith, "Practices and Procedures in Recommending and Screening Candidates for the Position of Superintendent for Public School Districts in California" (Doctoral dissertation, University of Southern California, 1960), while administrative policies and practices, and their relation to teaching efficiency, are covered in a report of the research by Wilburn Smith, "Administrative Policies and Practices and Their Relation to Teaching Efficiency" (Doctoral dissertation, University of Southern California, 1954). General principles and practices in elementary supervision have been reported by Jack C. Goodwin, "Principles and Practices of Teacher Evaluation Programs in the Elementary Schools of the United States" (Doctoral dissertation, University of Southern California, 1960).

[32] Gerald M. Weller, "The Role of the Boys' Vice-Principal," *Educational Administration and Supervision* XXIV (December 1938): 705–708.

ways of [stimulating] . . . teachers, attempting to fit method to teacher personality, and encouraging self-evaluation.[33]

ROLE OF THE SPECIALIST-CONSULTANT. In a larger school system, the major responsibilities of the specialist-consultant are services arranged on a school system basis rather than those designed for a single school. Several schools may participate in the programs, and the specialist-consultant aids in the following ways:

1. Organizing and conducting workshops, institutes, and demonstrations.
2. Directing research in instruction.
3. Providing facilities for curriculum development.
4. Planning testing and evaluation programs.
5. Arranging for outside consultants and resource persons.
6. Informing school personnel about instructional trends and developments.
. . . .
8. Making recommendations as to instructional policy.
9. Assisting with planning school buildings and facilities.
. . . .
11. Working with colleges to plan courses for teachers and to co-ordinate practice teaching.[34]

The relationship of the specialist-consultant to the classroom teacher appears to be changing. The idea of supervision is assuming broader dimensions. With this change in theory and practice comes a new emphasis:

1. The human relationship aspect of professional guidance and leadership as well as leadership in interpreting content and method.
2. The use of the team approach with the principal, teacher, and specialist-consultant working cooperatively in small group conferences, workshops, and in-service education classes for the improvement of classroom instruction.
3. Maintaining a resource team for the coordination of central office services with the school's staff to maintain and improve quality education.

THE SPECIALIST-CONSULTANT AND THE SUPERVISORY ORGANIZATION. The specialist-consultant usually is attached to the office of the assistant superintendent, but when entering a school, he automatically assumes the role of a staff member assisting the school's principal. There are three categories of specialist-consultants: (1) specialists in specific subjects, (2) general consultants, and (3) curriculum directors or coordinators. Some school systems use experienced master teacher-consultants. The work of the curriculum specialists is discussed in Chapter 12.

[33] Emery Stoops and James R. Marks, "What About Teacher Evaluation?" *The School Executive* LXXVII (September 1957): 97.

[34] Clarence Fielstra, "Student Reviews of Selected Literature in the Field of Instructional Supervision," Mimeographed Monograph. (University of California at Los Angeles, 1961), p. 37.

If a school system wishes to emphasize the improvement of teaching in a specific subject, it can appoint a specialist-consultant for that subject. It is practically impossible to make specialist-consultants understand that other subjects are at least as significant as theirs to the curriculum.

The general consultant is specialized more by grade level than by subject. Thus we find primary or lower grade consultants, middle grade consultants, and upper grade consultants.

THE ROLE OF THE MASTER TEACHER-CONSULTANT.   The master teacher, helping teacher, or teacher-consultant, under the principal's direction, helps the individual classroom teacher improve the instructional program. This function is, perhaps, most effectively accomplished by providing for direct and practical help in the classroom.

The master teacher-consultant, by assisting the teacher with lesson plans and evaluation, becomes more aware of the teacher's immediate needs. The consultant quickly can learn the classroom needs and can help develop the teacher's strengths. By assisting in the teaching-learning program, the consultant becomes more a partner than an observer.

The teacher-consultant helps the teacher select and use teaching materials and equipment. For example, by setting up a multimedia listening center in a classroom, both the children and the teacher can be introduced to a new concept. Sharing the new idea often results in the continuance of the teaching technique.

By demonstrating specific techniques and procedures, the teacher encounters new methods of instruction. Valuable teacher time is saved, and the children's learning experience shows growth.

Beginning teachers often will ask a question more readily when they feel they are working with someone who will not participate in their evaluation.

The master teacher-consultant aids the supervisory program by working with groups of teachers in orientation and grade-level meetings and workshops. The teachers often request more meetings on specific subjects. The master teacher-consultant shares in planning, presenting, and evaluating these meetings.

ORGANIZATION FOR SCHOOL SUPERVISION THROUGH THE PARTICIPATION OF THE ENTIRE PROFESSIONAL STAFF.   The supervisory organization should be formulated cooperatively as an expression of the combined thinking of the superintendent, principals, supervisors, teachers, and lay members of the community. The organization should provide a planned, effective system of communication including adequate records, information retrieval, and policy systems, through which all members can be kept informed. Assignment specifications should be a vital part of the organization for supervision. These specifications permit balancing work load of the professional staff both with respect to time allotted and in the number of relationships or span of control designated to each supervisor and administrator. The administrator of the future will have fewer individuals directly responsible to him. Supervisory organization in the future thus will be permanent and consistent but will be sufficiently flexible to permit revision to meet changing needs. Information retrieval systems, coupled with advanced business data processing techniques, will be commonplace in the school system.

A New Type of Supervisor and a New Type of Supervision

The creative supervisor will continuously foster creative activity and self-leadership within his staff, helping the teachers become less dependent on outside direction and more reliant on their own resources. The supervisor should feel free to advise, criticize, and make suggestions, but by directing his/her help toward growth in personal and professional stature he/she will promote and enrich the understanding and the program of his/her school.

In discussing the use of staff members in a supervisory program, W. S. Elsbree and H. J. McNally stated:

> The process of discovering and utilizing the talents of staff members is the function of the principal and poses a more challenging problem than giving direct counsel to teachers on how to improve their instructional methods.[35]

How to Plan Your Work as a Supervisor

Basic Aspects of Supervisory Planning

The great French industrialist and pioneer student of organization and management, Henri Fayol, reported that "if foresight is not the whole of management, at least it is an essential part of it. To foresee, in this context, means both to assess the future and make provision for it; that is, forecasting is itself action already."[36] Planning involves, then:

1. The process of fact interpretation.
2. Determining a line of action to be taken in light of all data available and of objectives sought.
3. Detailing the steps to be taken in keeping with the action determined.
4. Making provisions to carry through the plan to a successful conclusion.
5. Establishing and maintaining a system of evaluation to see how close performance comes to plans.

[35] Willard S. Elsbree and Harold J. McNally, *Elementary School Administration and Supervision* (New York: American Book Company, 1959), p. 59.

[36] Henri Fayol, *General and Industrial Management* (New York: Pittman Publishing Corporation, 1949), p. 43.

Planning, then, requires a lot of supervisory foresight and a high degree of constructive analysis. Certainly, ability and willingness to plan are essentials of supervisory leadership. If a supervisor is not willing to plan ahead to facilitate and improve instruction, he/she does not deserve the confidence of the educators with whom he/she works.

One way for the supervisor to plan ahead is to handle routine administrative matters by bulletin or note, saving the staff meetings and conference sessions before and after school for discussion of instructional matters. If the supervisor is a teaching principal, he/she may wish to arrange for a substitute teacher on a regular basis to permit time for classroom visitations, conferences, meetings, and other supervisory activities. A substitute teacher should handle the principal's class at least two days per week.

The teaching principal may be able to employ older students on a part-time basis, using school district funds and/or the funds provided by special federal programs for payroll demands of individuals so employed. These students can handle many of the routine responsibilities in office, supply room, and cafeteria and could relieve the office clerk from telephone answering duties.

The principal should plan his/her time by scheduling supervisory visits and conferences on a weekly schedule chart such as is found in Figure 4-7.

A school is organized that it may be administered; it is administered that instruction may take place. The supervisor's major responsibility is to lead teachers to the steady, continuous, and progressive improvement of the curriculum,

FIGURE 4-7. Program Schedule for Planning Supervisory Visits and Conferences.

	School Month				
Week of School Month	Day				
	M	T	W	T	F
First					
	(A.M. P.M.)	(A.M. P.M.)	(A.M. P.M.)	(A.M. P.M.)	(A.M. P.M.)
Second					
	(A.M. P.M.)	(A.M. P.M.)	(A.M. P.M.)	(A.M. P.M.)	(A.M. P.M.)
Third					
	(A.M. P.M.)	(A.M. P.M.)	(A.M. P.M.)	(A.M. P.M.)	(A.M. P.M.)
Fourth					
	(A.M. P.M.)	(A.M. P.M.)	(A.M. P.M.)	(A.M. P.M.)	(A.M. P.M.)

KEY: V = Visit[a]   A = Other Appointment
      C = Conference   PR = Probationary Rating
      R = Request   T = Teaching Assignment for Principal

[a] School principals usually find it difficult to schedule more than one supervisory visit per day. The principal should attempt to visit for an entire lesson.

instructional media, and teaching techniques that enable children best to profit from it. Leadership must be democratic, constructive and creative, and professionally informed.

How to Organize

A principal must ask him/herself many questions before deciding to organize a supervisory program. He/she must decide what should and can be done to improve education. He/she must question the extent that these efforts and those of colleagues can contribute to the improvment of supervision.

T. H. Briggs and J. Justman[37] have outlined certain steps to use in organizing a program of supervision, recognizing that each situation and each program must be approached in a unique manner:

1. Estimate or survey the situation.
2. Plan the way.
3. Prepare the way. (Organize, identify, and budget for necessary staff, supplies, equipment, and facilities.)
4. Share the responsibility.
5. Get under way.
6. Guide the development.
7. Relate the program to the community.
8. Measure and evaluate progress. Plan for further action. Report!
9. Provide for educational continuity.

In order to estimate the situation, it is necessary to know about the school and its program, the students, the teaching personnel, and the community. A supervisor must know the interest, needs, attitudes, problems, accomplishments, and characteristics of various groups. Plans must fit situations and must be suited to the school. To insure a sound program, program planning should be a cooperative enterprise.

Abilities Prerequisite to Effective Planning

Many supervisors make the mistake of too much personal operation and too little constructive planning. Since planning requires prediction—looking ahead in terms of present and anticipated facts—it is evident that planning requires analysis—an ability to project activities that are yet to take place.

The prerequisites to effective planning include:

1. The ability to see the entire situation—the *gestalt*.
2. The ability to analyze a problem—to break it down into its simplest elements.

[37] Thomas H. Briggs and Joseph Justman, *Improving Instruction through Supervision* (New York: The Macmillan Company, 1952).

3. Resourcefulness, a constructive imagination, and versatility, combined with the willingness to convert old methods into new, if warranted.
4. An impersonal analytical approach that is not dominated by either the idols of the cave or the idols of the marketplace.
5. The willingness and ability to evaluate the effectiveness of a given plan or procedure.
6. Fortitude, personality, and capacity that permits one to avoid becoming so entangled in the daily details of the educational enterprise that no time is left for planning.

How to Provide for Managerial Coordination: the Roles of the Principal and the Superintendent

The Principal as Instructional Leader

If we accept the premise that the prime purpose of the school is to establish a creative environment wherein the learning process can most effectively be achieved, then we must conclude that the principal's chief role lies in being able to effect such an environment through dynamic leadership.

Principals place high priority on their role in the improvement of instruction. Although the increasing demands on the principal's time tend to erode this role as an instructional leader, research[38] has indicated this area is the one to which principals would most like to devote themselves.

B. C. Browning and H. J. Otto[39] reported that the superintendents view the principal as the key person in the improvement of instruction. Lack of time, involvement in many other duties, and a feeling of personal inadequacy have hampered the achievement of this goal. Nevertheless, most principals strive to develop their professional capacities as dynamic, creative, and effective instructional leaders.

If we accept the concept of leadership in the improvement of the instructional program for the supervising principal, then the definition of responsibility becomes more meaningful and less overpowering. The principal then becomes a coordinator of knowledge and abilities who strives to develop and improve the total instructional program.

The instructional program's general structure is a major concern of the principal, requiring that he/she assume certain vital responsibilities. Primarily, the principal must have a broad understanding of the basic purpose of education in our democratic society.

---

[38] National Education Association, "The Principal and Supervision," *The National Elementary Principal*, Thirty-Seventh Yearbook (Washington, D.C.: National Education Research Division, 1958).

[39] Bruce C. Browning and Henry J. Otto, *Organization for Instructional Supervision in Elementary Schools*, A Monogram (Austin: University of Texas, 1957).

THE PRINCIPAL AND THE TEACHERS.   If a principal is to practice a democratic form of leadership, certain attitudes must precede practice. The principal should:

1. See him/herself as a member of the group; a colleague and co-worker working with other staff members. They are in the process of learning. He/she should approach any problem-solving situation as a co-learner, working with the group to achieve a satisfactory solution.
2. Be sensitive to the feelings and needs of others. Those most frequently chosen for leadership in supervision have insight into the needs of co-workers. The principal who wants to become sensitive to the feelings of others must first develop listening skills.
3. Listen to fellow staff members and be available to hear the complaints and the praises of the people with whom he/she works. He/she also should become an inquisitive observer. People reveal their feelings through their physical behavior and casual conversation in informal and formal situations. The principal should make a continuous observation of conditions and attitudes in the classroom, the staffroom, and at faculty meetings.
4. Recognize that he/she is not the only person attempting to improve instruction, although he/she does have the primary responsibility for such improvement. No leader can be successful if he/she thinks that improvement will come only when *he/she* initiates programs, practices, and techniques.
5. Exhibit respect for and faith in other staff members. He/she should recognize their professional integrity and their desire to improve themselves and the profession.
6. Recognize and understand that teachers are individuals, as are children. Educators have talked long about meeting the individual needs of children, but little attention has been paid to the importance of meeting the individual needs of teachers.

THE PRINCIPAL CREATES A CLIMATE CONDUCIVE TO PRODUCTIVITY.   The principal must help create a psychologically healthful organizational climate[40] that is free from fear, threats, and coercion. He/she can do this, first of all, by accepting that diverse opinions are an asset rather than detriment. If people are to feel free to express their opinions, they also must feel that these opinions will be heard and that they will not be penalized, however diverse these opinions may be from the norm of the group. Effective solutions to simple and complex problems come out of the true dialectic of free discussion.

When the principal does give problems to the faculty for discussion of possible solutions, he/she must never overrule these decisions by the sheer weight of status authority. This action will result in cessation of communication. Further, it will cause members of the group to revert to the position of attempting to please the status leader. The principal continuously must foster creative action and experimentation by members of the staff.

[40] See Andrew W. Halpin, *Theory and Research in Administration* (New York: The Macmillan Company, 1966), chapter 4, for a discussion of research and theory concerned with the organizational climate of schools.

Ten commandments for the humane administrator were listed by D. E. Lawson:[41]

1. Do not rebuke or correct any teacher in the presence of students or any other persons.
2. Praise teachers, and in the fields of their special preparation walk humbly.
3. Deal not lightly with any person's problem, but treat it as if it were your own.
4. Forget not the days of your youth. Keep a sense of humor.
5. Honor your custodians and your teachers, that your days may be long in the job that the governing board has given you.
6. Let no child be judged by his behavior alone, but seek the causes of such behavior that they may be corrected.
7. Strive to see each child through the eyes of his parents, and treat that child with love as if it were your own.
8. When you have a teacher who is old in the service so that he no longer teaches well, deal with him tenderly and understandingly. (Teachers do grow older—and they don't just fade away.)
9. Be sensitive to the needs of your whole community and faith in its people, for in that faith you will find your strength.
10. Have vision as well as devotion, that you might use all your talents for the benefit of all humanity.

Unfortunately, the first of these commandments often is broken. When a teacher is rebuked or corrected by the principal in the presence of students or adults, the principal is guilty of a gross breach of professional ethics.

By appreciating the teachers' strengths and recognizing their needs, the principal builds rapport. Many teachers consistently do an outstanding job, and they need recognition for such work. The principal builds on this strength.

It is assumed that the teacher is the most important single factor in the educative process. The kind of behavior that he/she exhibits in the classroom determines the kind of learning that will take place. The teacher should try to improve his/her professional competencies. It is further assumed that only the teacher can alter him/herself. In other words, the principal can help best by setting up situations whereby the teacher can be stimulated, see the need for innovation and, as a result, experiment with new ideas and techniques, internalizing them as his/her own, and not as techniques superimposed by the principal.

The principal must exhibit an implicit belief in the professional staff, at the same time stressing that there is no field of human endeavor in which there cannot be improvement.

CHANGE: A SLOW PROCESS. Any modification of practice, any improvement in techniques, will be a slow process. If change takes place, it must come from the

41 Douglas E. Lawson, an Address at Southern Illinois University, Carbondale, Illinois, 1955.

teacher's desire for change. When contemplating new techniques, the teacher judges them in the light of experience. What has worked? What will work best for students? The teacher must have faith in new techniques before he honestly can accept them.

The principal must not assume that teachers will modify their behavior simply as a result of a logical presentation.

Teacher Individuality

There is no one style of teaching, no one pattern of classroom organization, no special technique of teaching that should be universally adopted by all. One of the principal's major functions is to help teachers reach agreement on problems of instruction, and then to give these teachers an opportunity to work together. The principal must keep in mind that teachers are busy, and that any improvement of instruction will result from a supervisory program that is an integral part of the regular school program.

THE PRINCIPAL COORDINATES WITH OTHERS IN THE IMPROVEMENT OF INSTRUC-TION.   The people who contribute to the instructional program are the most important resource for continued improvement. Consequently, the principal must possess skill in human relations in order to secure the maximum contributions from each individual.

The principal must know these persons well. What things does each do well? What special talents and abilities do individuals possess? Do they have skill in organizing, writing, speaking, dramatics, or in working with others? What are the personality qualities of each one?

Kyte[42] maintained that all supervisory officers, other than the superintendent of schools, the assistant superintendent in charge of instruction, and the principal, are technical advisers to the superintendent, the assistant superintendent in charge of instruction, the principal, and the teacher.

The specialist-consultant is responsible for aiding teachers within the specialty and performs under the principal's direction. The principal always maintains the responsibility and authority for school supervision.

TRENDS IN THE EVOLVING ROLE OF THE PRINCIPAL AS AN INSTRUCTIONAL LEADER.   Although there is a trend toward accepting the principal as a supervisor of instruction as well as the administrative leader in the school, this role in supervision is in jeopardy. As school systems grow, the principal's role as the supervisor of instruction erodes. Further clerical assistance is needed to handle many routine duties, formerly performed by principals. This practice gives the principal more time for the supervision of instruction. The "specialist-consultant" or "coordinator" or "director," working out of the school system's central office

---

[42] George C. Kyte, *The Principal at Work,* rev. ed. (Boston: Ginn and Company, 1952).

is being called on as a resource person to assist the principal; he/she should not replace the principal in the area of supervision.

Perhaps the principal of the future will be recognized as a *chief-of-staff* officer—an instructional leader—a plan termed *the academic equivalent*. Under this plan, most of the purely administrative and pseudoadministrative functions presently performed by many principals would be put in the hands of assistants and classified employees. As educational leader, the supervising principal must spend at least fifty per cent of his/her time actively supervising instruction. To be a leader, he/she must be willing to evaluate and be evaluated. This evaluation activity is essential to his/her success as an instructional principal.

PREPARATION FOR THE PRINCIPAL.   The principal of the future will be highly trained in forming small study groups and curriculum committees; in orienting substitute teachers and teachers new to the school; in keeping the staff informed concerning new materials, methods, techniques, and ideas; in curriculum construction; in instructional techniques; and in methods of coordinating the efforts of resource people and specialists. The principal also will be expected to be generally conversant in broad cultural areas, including the natural sciences, the fine arts, the social sciences, foreign languages, and the humanities. No one individual can be expert in several areas, but the principal should be broadly educated as well as being a specialist in *how* to educate.

EXPERIENCE AND EDUCATION FOR THE SUPERVISING PRINCIPAL.   More principals will go on toward an advanced two-year degree in education or for the Doctoral degree. More preparing universities offer advanced programs leading to the advanced degree of Master of Education in school supervision. This degree requires one to two years of preparation in addition to that required for the basic Master of Science or Master of Arts degree.

The potential principal's background should include not less than five years of successful classroom experience at the level he/she expects to supervise. In addition to the increase in the amount of education is an increase in the amount of teaching experience required by the local school systems for the position of supervising principal.

DELEGATION OF DUTIES BY THE SUPERVISING PRINCIPAL.   The past twenty years have seen a change in the duties generally recommended for the principalship. The main functions retained by principals should be policy-making and supervision. Routine administrative and supervisory functions, such as those listed below, should be delegated to the assistant principal as soon as he/she can administer them:

1.   Assistance in planning with individual teachers and in observing classroom teaching
2.   Orienting and guiding new teachers

3. Working with small groups of teachers and with grade level or department group on instructional problems
4. Helping teachers provide for individual differences
5. Conducting faculty meetings
6. Helping select equipment and supplies
7. Initiating and coordinating research programs

Principals tend to delegate supervisory tasks such as these to the assistant principal:

1. Directing and coordinating the school program for guidance and psychological services
2. Developing and maintaining student personnel records
3. Directing student welfare work and attendance accounting
4. Directing the program of student co-curricular activities
5. Directing and coordinating the program for school health and safety
6. Coordinating student transportation at the school level
7. Coordinating the school's food services program

The Superintendent as Instructional Leader

Leadership is the superintendent's major in-service responsibility. Individual teachers should be encouraged to identify problems, to seek help, and to try out solutions. The superintendent should create an atmosphere in which he/she helps others see problems, get started, make decisions, put plans into action, evaluate, and improve both group and individual performance. Experimentation is good.

THE SUPERINTENDENT ORGANIZES TO IMPROVE INSTRUCTION. The superintendent must develop a framework for a cooperative approach to effective supervision. Time and materials must be provided, staff relationships taken into account, and a flexible organization provided that will develop staff potential through shared responsibility. The superintendent should try to improve the instructional program so that:

1. Each individual teacher is given broad authority for adapting content, method, and organization of learning experiences to student needs.
2. Each school is given wide authority and responsibility for improving instruction.
3. The school system can establish general policies as *guideposts* to each school in exercising the autonomy granted to it.

The superintendent should encourage the formulation and adoption of written policies as guides to action when any problem concerning the instructional program recurs or involves more than one individual, so that:

1. Delegating responsibility and authority is facilitated
2. Favoritism is avoided
3. Responsibilities are fixed
4. The authority of the governing board is utilized constructively

Staff Relations and Quality of Instruction

The school system is no better than the classroom teachers it employs, and the teachers are no better than the quality of staff relations maintained by the school system. The superintendent must be aware of forces that motivate human behavior, factors affecting group work, procedures for working together for individual growth, working conditions and staff relations, economic and community status of staff members, and ways in which the professional staff can work together for good school-community relations.

Conflicting Organizational Demands

Job Demands[43]

Because he/she is evaluated in so many areas, the supervisor often faces conflicts in demands for time, conflicts of interests among those with whom he/she must work, and conflicts between personal needs and the job requirements. He/she sees discrepancies between how the boss treats him/her and how he/she is supposed to treat workers. He/she complains that administration or management fails to make its policies clear about supervisor-subordinate relations:

> Personal dependence upon the judgments and decisions of his superiors so characteristic of the subordinate-superior relation in modern industry makes the . . . situation basically insecure. . . . In some cases this preoccupation with what the boss thinks becomes so acute that it accounts for everything [said or done] . . .[44]

Time Demands

How much time executives say they spend in supervision correlates negatively with the amount of authority they say they have. However, reported supervisory

[43] The authors are grateful to Bernard M. Bass for his reflections on supervisory behavior in industry [Bernard M. Bass, *Organizational Psychology* (Boston: Allyn and Bacon, Inc., 1965)] and for much of the material in this section.

[44] F. J. Roethlesberger, "The Foreman: Master and Victim of Double Talk," *Harvard Business Review* XXIII (1945): 285–295.

time does not correlate with how much responsibility they feel they have nor with how often and to what extent they delegate authority. Higher level executives seem to be able to spend more time in innovation, in attending to personnel relations, and in coordination, according to a survey of 96 management personnel. The first-line foreman, however, usually must devote more of his attention to quantity of production if he is to be evaluated highly, particularly by his superiors.

Some supervisors bury themselves or are buried in paperwork and have little time left for such important functions as stimulating subordinates.

An unpublished study of the contact patterns of 80 members of management indicated that the executive heading a productive department was never at either extreme in how he distributed his time. He avoided being tied up all day in meetings but spent more time in meetings than a supervisor of an unproductive department. Compared to ineffective supervisors the effective supervisor did not spend more time with one subordinate than another or with his superiors rather than his subordinates.

Conflicting Loyalties

Superiors want the supervisor to demonstrate more initiative in organization; subordinates evaluate a supervisor more highly when he/she exhibits more consideration. The effective supervisor must be able to resolve the incompatibility of superiors' and subordinates' interests. The supervisor must initiate an organizational structure that requires more energy expenditure by subordinates and offers more reward potential for superiors if successful. At the same time, he/she must be seen as considerate by subordinates.

The supervisor who solves the dilemma of being caught in the middle is praised by both superiors and subordinates. Of those supervisors who were judged immediately promotable by their bosses, 75 per cent were seen as "pulling for the company and the men" by their subordinates. On the other hand, among those supervisors judged questionable or unsatisfactory by their superiors, only 40 per cent were seen by their subordinates as pulling both for the company and the workers.

Conflicting Channels of Communication

Thirty-two executives indicated to what extent they consulted with their boss, peers, subordinates, outsiders, rulebooks, or only themselves when faced with various kinds of problems such as whether to participate, how to plan something, or how to assign rewards. No matter what the problem, some executives attended strongly to the rule books; others did not. Consistent differences also existed in how often these executives consulted with their boss, peers, subordinates, and themselves, but not with persons outside their organization. On the other hand, the nature of the problem led to no consistent response differences.

In a laboratory simulation of the pressures confronting the person-in-the-middle, this differential attention was a function of the general orientation of subjects. When the boss threatened and subordinates were dissatisfied, *self-oriented* and *interaction-oriented* supervisors increased their communications to the boss. *Task-oriented* supervisors increased their communications to their subordinates.

The supervisor is a member of a formal organization based on the patterns of formal relations between job occupants above and below him. He also is in an informal organization based on relations between persons regardless of the jobs they occupy. The informal organization is likely to diverge from the formal, particularly when formal upward channels of communication are "noisy" or blocked. The person-in-the-middle is a central relay station, and the development of conflicting informal patterns may depend to a considerable degree on his/her performance. He/she must learn to accommodate and to use the informal organization, if a strong one is present. What he/she receives from superiors, subordinates, peers, and others will depend on how much attention he/she pays to each source of communication.

Who Evaluates?

"If you try to please everybody, you may not please anybody"; there appears to be no correlation between the evaluations supervisors receive from their subordinates and from their superiors.

Above and beyond these considerations is the lack of agreement between what the supervisor thinks he/she does and what subordinates say he/she does. Table 4-1 shows this glaring discrepancy by comparing supervisors' descriptions of their own behavior with the experience reported by workers in the same utility company. For example, while 52 per cent of the supervisors said that they give privileges very often, only 14 per cent of the workers said they received such privileges.

IMPORTANCE OF IMMEDIACY. Another complicating factor is the probability that the evaluations to which a supervisor gears his/her actions direct how he/she spends time; and how he/she concentrates efforts depends on relatively immediate evaluations. Yet ten years after a supervisor is discharged, associates may reflect that he/she was the best executive they ever had on that job.

The administration, teacher, and staff must work together with the governing board and the community to correct conditions that block the improvement of staff relations. One place to start is the long after-school faculty meeting, especially if it is devoted to reading announcements.

TABLE 4-1. Comparison of Supervisors' Description of Their Behavior With Employees' Description of Their Experience[a]

	ASKED OF SUPERVISORS: "HOW DO YOU GIVE RECOGNITION FOR GOOD WORK DONE BY EMLOYEES IN YOUR WORK GROUP?"	ASKED OF EMPLOYEES: "HOW DOES YOUR SUPERVISOR GIVE RECOGNITION FOR GOOD WORK DONE BY EMLOYEES IN YOUR WORK GROUP?"
	PERCENTAGE OF SUPERVISORS WHO SAID "VERY OFTEN":	PERCENTAGE OF EMPLOYEES WHO SAID "VERY OFTEN":
Gives privileges	52	14
Gives more responsibility	48	10
Gives a pat on the back	82	13
Gives sincere and thorough praise	80	14
Trains for better jobs	65	9
Gives more interesting work	51	5

[a] After Likert, 1961, p. 91.

Do

1. As superintendent, see that the principal is delegated sufficient authority, has the necessary time for supervision, and is given adequate stimulation, direction, support, and help.
2. As superintendent, work cooperatively with school principals in effecting educational improvement—stimulating, encouraging, and guiding rather than ordering and criticizing.
3. As supervisor, maintain a relationship with fellow educators (superintendent, principals, and teachers) based on mutual respect, trust, and recognition of responsibilities.
4. Clarify beliefs and goals, and reflect continuously on how they can be applied.
5. Develop the will to grow.
6. Analyze assignments and determine which can be done best.
7. Write articles for publication in professional journals. The superintendent and principal also should read the professional literature.
8. Learn from public administration and from industry.
9. Discuss problems with others and participate actively in small discussion groups.

Don't

1. As supervising principal, tell anyone, nor imply by deed or tone of voice, that you do not support the superintendent's instructional policies. Policies

that you believe are in error can be revised, but until such time as they are altered they deserve your support.

2. Omit your own supervisory practices from reflection.
3. Fail to enroll for courses in higher institutions of learning on a regular basis.
4. As supervisor, avoid rating yourself occasionally. You may wish to invite teachers to evaluate your performance.

TRENDS: ORGANIZATION FOR EDUCATIONAL SUPERVISION IN THE FUTURE

Toward ────→   The Provision of Adequate

Funds for Staff and Instructional Development

The governing board of the future will budget sufficient funds to provide for adequate personnel, equipment, and supplies in order to attain its educational aims and objectives through the organization for school supervision. Adequate funds will be provided for not only by the local school system, but also by the state and by the federal government. A portion of the budget will be used for institutes, workshops, child study groups, consultants, and specialists in order to promote the in-service education of all employee personnel.

Toward ────→   Organization for

School Supervision through the

Participation of the Entire

Professional Staff

An increased number of the supervisory organizations of the future will be formulated cooperatively as an expression of the combined thinking of the superintendent, principals, specialist-consultants, teachers, and lay members of the community. The organization will provide a planned system of communication through which all members may be kept informed.

Toward ────→   Adequate Policy Systems

for the Organization of Supervisory

Services

Adequate policy systems and developing assignment specifications will be a vital part of the organization for supervision in more and more school systems. The work load of the professional staff will be balanced both with respect to time allotted and in the number of relationships or span of control designated to each administrator. As a part of this continuing trend, the supervisors and administrators of the future will have fewer individuals directly responsible to them.

The organization thus will be permanent and consistent, but will be sufficiently flexible to permit revision to meet changing needs.

Supervisory Problems

Problem 1

Assume that you are the supervising principal of a large junior high school in a district that includes three other junior high schools and two high schools. The district superintendent has asked you to organize and coordinate the supervisory efforts of the district in solving the following problem:

Twelve members of the district's liberal arts faculties participated in a summer workshop that developed an "English and Literature Guide" to accompany the newly adopted textbooks to be used for the coming school year. The district paid the summer workshop registration fees for the participants.

These guides were developed for each grade, seven through twelve, on three levels of difficulty. A copy of the appropriate guide was presented to each English and literature teacher at the start of the fall term.

The superintendent asked supervising principals to inform the teachers involved that these guides would be collected at the end of the school term along with their corrections, recommendations, suggestions, and evaluation of each unit of work included therein.

As the supervisory concerned, how would you follow through on the superintendent's request and organize the supervisory forces of the district to obtain full participation and cooperation on a professional basis when:

1. Many members of each faculty did not approve the adopted text
2. Some schools were not represented at the summer workshop
3. There was a great deal of resistance on the part of the faculty—"what was good enough was good enough!"

Problem 2

The Arrowhead Valley Unified School District lies in a peaceful recreational center in the foothills of the Sierra Nevada. The average daily attendance for the district is 2,800. Superintendent Lawrence Alan Douglas, who majored in psychology and education at Rochelle State Teachers, prides himself on the "relaxed, friendly, informal administrative atmosphere" of the district.

The Board of Education of the school district, on motion of Mr. Ross, its president, asked Superintendent Douglas to summarize the District's organization for instructional and staff development.

At the administrative council's weekly meeting, the superintendent asked those present to select from the topics listed below:

1. The advantages of centralized vs. decentralized supervisory programs in the district.
2. The advantages of horizontal vs. vertical supervision as pertains to the district.
3. Agencies and levels of education other than the local district that provide supervisory service to the district.
4. The organization of the staff of the assistant superintendent for instruction for the district, and recommendation for reorganization.
5. The schedule and program for the supervision of probationary teachers in the district.
6. Provisions for research and experimentation in the district.

Each individual was asked to prepare a short survey of that topic and to propose a program of improvement for that aspect of the organization for supervision.

The superintendent also requested that each supervising principal be prepared to present his/her recommendations, along with the values and pitfalls, concerning the extent to which teachers should participate in planning for supervision.

As supervising principal:

1. *Which topic would you select?*
2. *How would you proceed in organizing to prepare your response? What would you do?*
3. *What would be contained in your response?*
4. *How would you respond to the superintendent's query concerning teacher participation in planning for the organization of supervisory services?*

Problem 3

Three teachers in the elementary school where you are supervising principal asked to visit with you this morning. You discovered that they believe that several of their students need to improve skills in writing sentences and paragraphs, which are essential to English composition.

How would you organize an instructional development program to satisfy their needs? *Exactly* what would you do?

Questions and Suggested Activities Concerning How to Organize for School Supervision

Questions

1. Can a "helper" relationship exist between the supervisory staff and the teacher if periodic written evaluations of the teacher's performance are required?
2. Who is responsible for the character and quality of the instructional program?
3. How can a school system organize for supervision with clear lines of authority and still be democratic?
4. What factors are responsible for the newer democratic approach to supervision?
5. What is the relationship of *line* officers to *staff* officers? Is it essentially democratic? Efficient?
6. What weaknesses are most apparent in the line and staff system of organization? Are the same weaknesses present in *linear responsibility charting*?[45]
7. What is the proper relationship between administration and supervision?
8. What is the supervising principal's role in the supervisory program? The superintendent's? The specialist-consultant's? The teacher's? The student's?

Suggested Activities

1. Chart the line of authority in supervisory practice from the board of education to the teacher in: (a) an authoritarian type of organization, and (b) a democratic type of organization. Discuss the strengths and weaknesses of each type of organization.
2. List the apparent trends that are emerging in the organization of supervisory services.
3. Discuss the relationship of the supervisor to other staff and line officers and present a plan of coordination between these positions.
4. Compose a good job description for a supervisory position in your school system. Include duties, qualifications, and title of the position.
5. From personal experience, give examples of organization that are operating effectively, whether authoritarian or democratic.
6. Describe the use of a standing committee to strengthen your supervisory program. Be sure to include the tasks and composition of the committee.
7. List the ways in which the superintendent provides supervisory help for the school. How may the teacher or lay person aid in this program?
8. Report on how the organizational structure can be changed while feelings of insecurity are kept to a minimum.
9. Determine where laymen and classified personnel should be placed in the organization chart for purposes of supervision.

[45] See David I. Cleland and William R. King, *Systems Analysis and Project Management* (New York: McGraw-Hill Book Company, 1968) Ch. 9.

10. List the main topics that should be included in a policy manual on supervision.
11. Discuss the various duties that will be delegated to the assistant superintendent in charge of instruction by the superintendent of schools.
12. List five reasons for preferring modern supervisory services to the more traditional, authoritarian type.

Selected Bibliography

Books

Baron, George, and D. A. Howell. *The Government Management of Schools*. Atlantic Highlands, New Jersey: Humanities Press, Inc., 1974.

Barr, A. S., William H. Burton, and Leo Brueckner. *Supervision*. New York: D. Appleton-Century Company, Inc., 1947.

Bass, Bernard M. *Organizational Psychology*. Boston: Allyn and Bacon, Inc., 1965.

Briggs, Thomas H., and Joseph Justman. *Improving Instruction through Supervision*. New York: The Macmillan Company, 1952.

Browning, Bruce C., and Henry J. Otto. *Organization for Instructional Supervision in Elementary Schools*. A Monogram. Austin: University of Texas, 1957.

Burton, William H., and Leo J. Brueckner. *Supervision*. *A Social Process*, 3rd edition. New York: Appleton-Century-Crofts, Inc., 1955.

Cleland, David I., and William R. King. *Systems Analysis and Project Management*. New York: McGraw-Hill Book Company, 1968.

Crosby, Muriel. *Supervision as Co-operative Action*. New York: Appleton-Century-Crofts, Inc., 1957.

Elsbree, Willard S., and Harold J. McNally. *Elementary School Administration and Supervision*. New York: American Book Company, 1959.

Fayol, Henri. *General and Industrial Management*. New York: Pitman Publishing Corporation, 1949.

Frey, Sherman H., and Keith R. Getschman. *School Administration: Selected Readings*. New York: Thomas Y. Crowell Company, 1969.

Halpin, Andrew W. *Theory and Research in Administration*. New York: The Macmillan Company, 1966.

Iannaccone, Laurence, and Frank W. Lutz. *Politics, Power and Policy: The Governing of Local School Districts*. Columbus, Ohio: Charles E. Merrill Publishing Co., 1970.

Kirst, Michael W. *Politics of Education at the Local, State and Federal Levels*. Berkeley: McCutchan Publishing Co., 1970.

————. *State, School, and Politics*. Lexington, Massachusetts: D. C. Heath and Co., 1972.

Kyte, George C. *The Principal at Work*. rev. ed. Boston: Ginn and Company, 1952.

Lutz, Frank W., and Laurence Iannaccone. *Understanding Educational Organizations: A Field Study Approach*. Columbus, Ohio: Charles E. Merrill Publishing Co., 1969.

McCarty, Donald J., and Charles E. Ramsey. *The School Managers*. Westport, Connecticut: Greenwood Publishing Corporation, 1971.

McCloskey, Gordon. *Education and Public Understanding*. New York: Harper & Row Publishers, 1967.

Mintzberg, Henry. *The Nature of Managerial Work*. New York: Harper & Row, 1973.

Nutt, Hubert Wilbur. *Current Problems in the Supervision of Instruction*. New York: Johnson Publishing Company, 1928.

Owens, Robert G. *Organizational Behavior in Schools*. Englewood Cliffs, New Jersey: Prentice-Hall, Inc., 1970.

Reeder, Ward G. *The Fundamentals of Public School Administration.* New York: The Macmillan Company, 1951.
Stoops, Emery, Max Rafferty, and Russell E. Johnson. *Handbook of Educational Administration.* Boston: Allyn and Bacon, Inc., 1975.
Tead, Ordway. *The Art of Administration.* New York: McGraw-Hill Book Company, Inc., 1951.

Audio Cassettes

Broadwell, Martin. *The New Supervisor Cassette Program.* Addison-Wesley, 1973. Designed to acquaint supervisors new to the job with their responsibilities. Audio cassettes plus text and gaming.
The New Manager of the Training Function. Development Digest, 1975. Available from Thompson-Mitchell, Atlanta, Georgia.

Periodicals

Adelsbach, Cleo G. "Small Districts Offer a Better Way of Life." *California Teachers Association Journal* LVII (March 1961): 8.
Carpenter, C. C. "Large Districts Offer Professional Growth." *California Teachers Association Journal* LVII (March 1961): 9.
Roethlesberger, F. J. "The Foreman: Master and Victim of Double Talk." *Harvard Business Review* XXIII (1945): 285–295.
Stoops, Emery, and James R. Marks. "What About Teacher Evaluation?" *The School Executive* LXXVII (September 1957): 97.
Warmke, Roman F. "A Concept of Supervision." *National Business Education Quarterly* XXIX (May 1961): 3.
Weller, Gerald M. "The Role of the Boys' Vice-Principal." *Educational Administration and Supervision* XXIV (December 1938): 705–708.

Films

Assessing Management Potential. Bureau of National Affairs Films (5615 Fishers Lane, Rockville, Maryland 20852), 1976.
Points up problems relating to managerial succession, promotion policy and practice, managerial selection techniques, career counseling and the like.
Making Human Resources Productive. Bureau of National Affairs Films, 1976.
Job enrichment, climate, trust, motivation, feedback, and performance.
Management by Objectives. Thompson-Mitchell, Atlanta, Georgia.
Clearly defines the steps for an MBO system. Limited application to educational supervision. A sound filmstrip.
Management by Participation. Bureau of National Affairs Films, 1976.
Treats issues such as organizational climate, leadership style, participation vs. "permissiveness," group involvement in problem solving, and altering managerial and employee attitudes toward new management practices.

Management of Time Series. Thompson-Mitchell, Atlanta, Georgia, 1974.
Setting priorities, analysis of time usage, delegating, setting time limits. A sound filmstrip.
Management of Work Series. Thompson-Mitchell, Atlanta, Georgia, 1975.
A sound filmstrip.
Managing Time. Bureau of National Affairs Films, 1968.
Peter Drucker, educator and management consultant, illustrates how executive time is wasted, much of it being taken up by decisions that others can make. The effective executive stays out of the "time trap" by concentrating only on problems that require his decision and by not allowing his time to be wasted in routine tasks. (25 minutes)
Organization Development Series. Thompson-Mitchell, Atlanta, Georgia, 1972.
A sound filmstrip series.
Pay for Performance. Bureau of National Affairs Films, 1976.
Pay practices, performance appraisal, goal setting, motivation, and morale.
Team Building. Bureau of National Affairs Films, 1976.
Conflict and cooperation, group communication, interpersonal relations.
What Every Manager Needs to Know About Long-Range Planning. Bureau of National Affairs Films, 1974.
Discusses strategic planning techniques. (20 minutes)

Other Sources

American Association of School Administrators. *The American School Superintendency*. Departmental Thirtieth Yearbook. Washington, D.C.: The Association, 1952.
――――. *Staff Relations in School Administration*. Departmental Thirty-Third Yearbook. Washington, D.C.: The Association, 1955.
――――. *The Superintendent as an Instructional Leader*. Departmental Thirty-Fifth Yearbook. Washington, D.C.: The Association, 1957.
California. Cloverdale Union High School District v. Peters, 264 P. 273, 88 Cal. App. 731.
Fielstra, Clarence. "Student Reviews of Selected Literature in the Field of Instructional Supervision." Mimeographed Monograph. Los Angeles: University of California at Los Angeles, 1961.
Freese, Theron. "A Study of the Position of Assistant Superintendent in Charge of Instruction: Its History, Status, and Functions." Doctoral dissertation, University of Southern California, 1955.
Gaincott v. Davis, 275 N.W. 299.
Heath v. Johnson, 15 S.E. 980, 36 W. Va. 782.
Iowa, Whitney v. Rural Independent School District No. 4 of Lafayette Township, 4 N.W. 2nd 394, 140 A.L.R. 1376.
Kansas-State ex rel. Hill v. Sinclair, 175 P. 41.
Lawson, Douglas E. An Address at Southern Illinois University, Carbondale, Illinois, 1955.
Massachusetts, Russell v. Gannon, 183 N.E. 736, 281 Mass. 398.
Melbo, Irving R. et al. "Report of the Survey, Taft City School District." Duplicated material copyrighted by the author. Los Angeles: July 1960.

Montana-State ex rel. Howard v. Ireland, 138 P. 2nd 569.

National Education Asociation. "The Principal and Supervision," *The National Elementary Principal*. Thirty-Seventh Yearbook. Washington, D.C.: National Education Research Division, 1958.

Nevada, Nevada Industrial Commission v. Leonard, 68 P. 2nd 576.

New Mexico, Zellers v. Huff, 236 P. 2nd 949, 55 N.M. 501.

New York, Gobel v. Board of Education of the City of Albany, 48 N.Y.S. 2nd 299, 267 App. Div. 621, affirmed 60 N.E. 2nd 133.

New York, La Dalley v. Stamford, 272 App. Div. 183.

New York, Miller v. Board of Education, Union School District No. 1, Town of Albion, 50 N.E. 2nd 529.

New York, Parrish v. Moss, 106 N.Y.S. 2nd 5773, affirmed 107 N.Y.S. 2nd 580, 279 App. Div. 608.

Oakes, Keith Ronald. "Statutory Responsibilities of District Superintendents in the United States." Doctoral dissertation, University of Southern California, 1954.

Ohman v. Board of Education of the City of New York, 90 N.E. 2nd 474. Reargument denied: 93 N.E. 2nd 927.

Parrish v. Moss, 85 N.E. 2nd 792.

Pennsylvania, Appeal of Cable, 61 Pa. Dist. and County 298.

Pennsylvania, Howell v. Kingston Township School District, 161 A. 559.

Pennsylvania, Malone v. Hayden, 197 A. 344, 329 Pa. 213.

Piety, Donald. "Legal Aspects of Recruitment, Selection, and Assignment of Certificated Personnel in Public Schools as Shown by Court Decisions, 1956." Doctoral dissertation, University of Southern California, 1956.

Smith, Harold J. "Practices and Procedures in Recommending and Screening Candidates for the Position of Superintendent for Public School Districts in California." Doctoral dissertation, University of Southern California, 1960.

Smith, Wilburn. "Administrative Policies and Practices and Their Relation to Teaching Efficiency." Doctoral dissertation, University of Southern California, 1954.

5

How to Be a Successful
Supervisor Through
Leadership
and Human Dynamics

Have you ever been criticized by *your* supervisor in front of people with whom you work?

Have *you* ever received a supervisory bulletin you did not understand?

Have *you* ever suggested a change and met with a brick wall of opposition?

Have *you* ever worked in a situation where morale seemed to be low and dropping fast—where *loyalty* seemed to be nonexistent?

One result of common intention is common effort. If common intention is to operate, certain commonly accepted and acceptable goals are required. These goals are, in turn, the result of needs, desires, and satisfactions that are shaped by the professional or occupational staff. Ordway Tead, in his book *The Art of Administration*,[1] commented that the degree of individual commitment to common effort varies according to the degree of satisfaction experienced on the job.

The main responsibility for supervision in an industrial enterprise may rest with the department manager; in a governmental service agency, it may rest with a division supervisor; in a hospital, it may rest with a chief of staff for medical personnel and with a supervising nurse; in a school, it rests with the principal. Whatever his title, the supervisor, along with specialists working as consultants in staff positions, must realize that *loyalty is a two-way street*.

If the school or company or service agency or hospital administration expects loyalty and support from the staff employees, it must produce evidence of being loyal to the staff. Genuine solicitude must be shown for the staff's interests, aims, and satisfactions. Opportunity must be provided for individual creativity and development. There must be sufficient freedom for personal initiative.

We are obliged, then, to understand human nature. Only with this knowledge will people's activities fall into a meaningful pattern. The supervising principal should be among the first to use the results of specialists' findings in such

[1] Ordway Tead, *The Art of Administration* (New York: McGraw-Hill Book Company, Inc., 1951).

FIGURE 5-1.   Primary Purposes of Supervisory Leadership.

allied fields as psychology and sociology in the areas of leadership and human dynamics, since his/her goal is to make things happen through the efforts of people. As seen in Figure 5-1, this ultimate goal of making things happen through the efforts of people is operational whether the goal of the organization be in the area of service, profitable production (as in private industry), or teaching and learning.

If the supervisor is to be an effective leader, he/she must understand his/her own place and function in the organization and the requisites for strong, resourceful leadership.

This chapter includes a discussion of the following topics:

How leaders succeed
How to criticize: leadership, criticism, and human nature
How to be a successful change agent
How to work with the group and with the individual
How to communicate effectively
How to be a success as a leader in a social setting

Some psychological implications of your supervisory behavior
Keys to leadership for the supervisor
Do—Don't
Trends
"In-Basket" supervisory problems
Questions and suggested activities

How Leaders Succeed

Leadership is necessary for a local school system to carry on a successful educational program. This leadership is a corequisite of effective supervision.

Educational leadership has been defined as "that action or behavior among individuals and groups which causes both the individual and the group to move toward educational goals that are increasingly acceptable to them."[2]

With this concept of educational leadership, it is the responsibility of the local school system to perform various leadership tasks:

1. The superintendent and the supervising principal must inform the community as to the needs and purposes of the school.
2. The community needs help in defining its educational goals. This help should come from the supervising principal.
3. The role of educational leadership is to facilitate instruction so that teaching and learning become more effective and efficient.
4. Leadership, if it is truly democratic, helps to create growth and to stimulate the development of new leadership.

The supervisor is a part of a team. As such, he/she should be interested in the characteristics possessed by successful enterprises. The basic characteristics of an organization that are essential to its efficient functioning are:

1. Strong, resourceful leadership
2. Clearly defined responsibilities
3. A staff that has been carefully selected, educated, trained, and assigned
4. Methods that have been standardized to reduce redundancy
5. An accurate, adequate, and reliable record-keeping system
6. An efficient information retrieval system coupled with two-way open channels of effective communication
7. An atmosphere of high morale and its concomitant, cooperation.

As a strong, resourceful leader, the supervisor must possess the ability to recognize and anticipate problems. He/she must have the capacity to develop

---

[2] Association for Supervision and Curriculum Development, *Leadership for Improving Instruction* (Washington, D.C.: National Education Association, 1960).

sound solutions to these problems and the ability and willingness to take decisive action to put the solution into effect. The supervisor must possess confidence in his/her own ability, tact, and self-control if he/she is to win the confidence of fellow educators. He/she must have the ability to develop the staff into a hard-hitting, well-coordinated unit. The patrons of the schools demand this degree of efficiency in their educational enterprise. Leadership is essential in the largest organization and in the smallest department in the school, if the goals are to be met successfully.

Most of the most effective people who have climbed the executive ladder to success have possessed personal characteristics such as the following:

1. Technical competence for the job to be done
2. Social competence—being able to work well and competitively with others
3. A knowledge of to whom to go to get things done
4. Both the ability and willingness to delegate responsibilities and commensurate authority
5. A strong sense of and skill in organization, so that tasks can be completed and goals realized
6. Skill in designating objectives and the ability to plan to achieve these objectives
7. A sound, working knowledge of leadership dynamics.[3]
8. A strong drive for achievement and job competence and a desire for recognition
9. The distinct ability to make many sound, rapid-fire decisions among several alternative courses, and to translate these decisions into action
10. Strong motivation and strong orientation to what is real, practical, and useful, and an aggressive, active desire to participate in the struggle for status and prestige—to be a part of the authority system, and even to dominate it
11. A strong respect for, but not dependence on, one's own considered judgment; and decisive and self-directional orientation within the frameworks of school system policy and organization[4]

How to Be a Successful Leader

Being a leader requires one to be true to one's own ideals but, at the same time, to be sufficiently flexible so as to be able to perform the many specialized duties and functions for a group or organization in a continuously changing environment. Leadership is the performance, in various and variable situations, of the functions of a leader, while at the same time meeting the expectations, aspirations, needs, and demands of the group. The successful leader is:

[3] See William R. Spriegel, Edward Schulz, and William B. Spriegel, *Elements of Supervision* (New York: John Wiley & Sons, Inc., 1966), especially pp. 19–22.

[4] See especially Russell H. Ewing, *The Leadership Functions of Executives and Managers: An Evaluation of Current Leadership Theory and Practice* (Beverly Hills, California: National Institute of Leadership, 1962), pp. 10–11.

1. Sensitive to the feelings of others while being at once considerate, helpful, responsive, and friendly
2. Loyal to one's ideas and ideals and respectful of the beliefs, rights, and dignity of others
3. Strong in his/her feelings of self-confidence and the ability to identify easily with co-workers, including those who supervise him/her and those whom he/she supervises
4. Consistent, generous, humble, modest, fair and honest in dealing with others
5. Enthusiastic in informing others about the policies and regulations of the school system
6. Interested in the improvement of the group while at the same time possessing the ability to get the job done quickly and in the most economical, efficient, and correct manner
7. Aware of the need to avoid envy, jealousy, and indulging in personalities while at the same time being willing to take the blame for one's own mistakes
8. Certain to give co-workers the benefit of the doubt and the advantage whenever possible
9. Firm but not stubborn in judgments and decisions
10. Apparently sincere, straightforward, approachable, easy to talk to, alert to getting the best out of people without aggressive shouting, open to suggestion, encouraging, enthusiastic, stimulating, inspiring, relaxed, and, finally, an interested dynamic leader who has maintained his sense of humor[5]

Delegation

Many supervisors are unwilling or reluctant to deputize or delegate. Others will willingly delegate *responsibilities,* but fail to give the necessary *authority* to get results. Still others will delegate authority and responsibility and then attempt to abdicate their own ultimate responsibility for what happens. No supervisor can say, "the responsibility is yours," and then forget it. The amount of follow-up is a function of the amount and type of work and of the individual to whom the responsibility has been delegated. Bruce, who joined the faculty two days ago, will require more follow-up than will Gary, who has been with the school for twenty years.

Recall, the supervisor is primarily responsible for making things happen through the efforts of people. Only when he/she perceives this facet of the position will he/she be successful in improving instruction. Supervising calls for:

1. Building morale and cooperation
2. Using sound techniques of supervision
3. Basing decisions on a sound knowledge of human nature
4. Developing the ability and willingness to delegate

The supervisor must possess the ability and willingness to delegate in order to be successful in improving instruction. Recall the story of the school superintendent of a relatively wealthy school system in Orange County, Cali-

5 Ibid.

TABLE 5-1.   *Supervisory Delegation*

DO DELEGATE	DO NOT DELEGATE
1. Accident prevention SHARE	1. The responsibility for delegating
2. Maintaining quality, quantity of production; cost control SHARE	2. Maintaining appropriate relationships with other departments; ultimate responsibility for quality and quantity control
3. Proper use and control of materials; training beginning employees SHARE	3. Personnel procurement and *planning* for the in-service education and train- of new personnel
4. Maintenance of proper *records* on which reports are based	4. Reports to *your* supervisor(s)
5. Inspection and care of materials, equipment, tools	5. Settlement of basic disagreements between subordinates
6. Encouraging cooperation and teamwork SHARE	6. Discharges; final responsibility for promotion
7. Recording employees' working time	7. Consideration of absences, tardinesses, discipline (control)
8. Health, sanitation factors: inspection and planning	8. Final responsibility for maintaining a safe environment[a]

[a] William R. Spriegel, Edward Schulz, and William B. Spriegel, *Elements of Supervision* (New York: John Wiley and Sons, Inc., 1966).

fornia. Superintendent Raboy followed the old axiom, "If you want it done right, do it yourself." Superintendent Raboy did almost everything himself, then he had a heart attack himself, and the only thing he could not do himself was to read his own eulogy. Table 5-1 lists some responsibilities that can be delegated, some that cannot, and some that should be shared.

One reliable measure of a supervisor's leadership ability is how he/she delegates. A successful leader has the courage to delegate to others and the organizational ability to institute controls (checks) to see that delegated responsibilities are accomplished according to plan. Supervisors who are weak in the skill of delegation usually are weak in organization. They do not realize that proper organization provides natural channels for delegating and fixing responsibilities.

The supervising principal must keep in mind that although he/she may deputize someone to perform a continuing task, the supervisor is, in the last analysis, responsible for seeing that the task is accomplished—for getting it done.

How to Criticize: Leadership, Criticism, and Human Nature

Leadership is necessary for an enterprise to carry on its function successfully. This leadership is a corequisite of successful supervision. We have defined supervisory leadership as the action or behavior among individuals and groups that causes both the individual and the group to move toward goals that are increasingly acceptable to them. Moreover, democratic leaders help to create growth and to stimulate new leadership; they do not *stifle,* inhibit, and slash or control others through destructive criticism. In their book, *The Human Side,* J. Beckley and R. Baldwin[6] emphasized that it is easy to criticize, but it is not easy to criticize skillfully. Offering corrective criticism without arousing resentment is a fine art in human relations. Few supervisors master this art.

The problem is that all psychologically normal human beings have an intense desire to protect the ego, or self. In all of us there is a certain amount of vanity. Beckley and Baldwin reported:

> The trouble is that most of us . . . —whether we admit it or not—are born with a fat streak of vanity. We like to criticize—it takes the other fellow down a peg and makes us feel superior, but when the shoe is on the other foot, that's a different story.[7]

Destructive Criticism

An unfortunate error made by many supervising principals is using severe criticism. Such criticism is of a destructive nature and usually does not get results.

Criticism is most effective when it is done in a relaxed manner. Experienced supervisors have found this to be one of the most important keys to leadership. *It is not necessary to criticize severely in order to obtain results.* Severe criticism does more harm than good.

Planning for Constructive Criticism

When it is necessary to criticize, one should do so with careful prior planning. Beckley and Baldwin[8] reported that the supervisor who is about to criticize, must realize that he/she is about to tackle one of the most ticklish tasks in the field of personnel management. Many supervisors bungle it badly. The supervising principal must remember this: the purpose of criticism is neither to show anger, nor to punish, nor to create unhappiness. The purpose is to help the individual to understand what can be improved and to make him/her anxious to do better.

PROTECTING THE TEACHER'S EGO.   Criticism, to be effective, although it be constructive, should be softened with praise. *This praise must,* of course, *be deserved.*

---

[6] J. Beckley and R. Baldwin, *The Human Side—A Fine Art,* Bulletin No. 229 (New London, Conn.: National Foreman's Institute, 1960).

[7] Ibid., p. 2; see also Harry Mier and Joan Mier, *If the Shoe Fits* (Beverly Hills, California: Merit Publishers, 1967).

[8] Ibid., p. 5.

. . . What a marvelous lesson! And you obviously have such a fine relationship with the students! Glenn really understood the meaning of . . . ! Perhaps your lesson would be even more effective if you would try. . . . I know it would be easier and take you less time to prepare for the lesson demonstration if you would . . . great work! Let me know if I can help in any way or get you some of those . . .

Before anyone is criticized, time must be taken to appreciate positive aspects of the individual's performance. Criticism is much easier to take when there is a good deal of praise mixed into the recipe.

OPPORTUNITY FOR SELF-CRITIQUE.   Before offering suggestions for solving a professional problem, the teacher should be given a chance to criticize him/herself. The subject probably should be brought up in an incidental manner. Remember— a good technique is to bring up the subject and see what the employee thinks about it. If the individual is aware of the need for improvement, he/she may prefer to admit shortcomings, at least to oneself, rather than have the supervisor point them out.

When offering constructive criticism, the supervising principal must use due caution. He/she must not seem to act superior nor appear insincere. All human beings make mistakes. Administrative performance is somewhat short of perfect. Supervisors can set an example by recognizing their own mistakes—and tactical errors—and correcting them as promptly as possible.

When discussing a particular point with a teacher, the supervisor could recall having made a similar error himself. One cannot turn a poor worker into a good one by whipping him with words. Criticism must aim at the dual goals of good will and improved performance; it is used to assist the professional staff, not to punish it.

How to Be a Successful Change Agent

As human beings, we have a strong instinct for self-preservation and for security. Most human beings are conservative, security-seeking creatures and resist change almost instinctively. Beckley and Baldwin[9] stated that regardless of the rut we are in, it is a familiar rut, and we are adjusted to it. There are no unknown or unexpected angles.

Don't Try to Change the World in a School Year

A child can change the shape of an inflatable, plastic globe by opening a valve and squeezing, but the supervising principal must not attempt to change the world in a

---

[9] J. Beckley and R. Baldwin, *The Human Side—Step by Step*, Bulletin No. 302 (New London, Conn.: National Foreman's Institute, 1960).

work week nor in a school year. If the reader is, or is going to be, a beginning supervisor or a supervisor new to the scene, he/she must realize that the mere fact that he/she has arrived is enough to cause feelings of insecurity and anxiety on the part of the staff. The proposal to alter things that are familiar will (not may, *will*) immediately arouse fear of the unknown. Many good ideas, which should have worked, have failed miserably because they were put into effect too quickly.

A Case in Point

Let us consider a case from the field of industrial supervision. The principles are the same; only the setting has changed. Lewis Rose was appointed to the position of supervisor three days ago. Today, at his first formal meeting with his staff, disaster struck. He had suggested a few changes, such as introducing a team quota system for increasing production through incentives, which was to be preceded by a time-motion study and followed by a statistical, cost control analysis. He announced that he planned to delegate many of his responsibilities to the production team leaders. These modifications would necessitate half the employees changing production assignments, specific duties, and/or shifts.

The employees were not receptive. As Lew's system went into operation, it became apparent that some of his ideas had value. But the employees were not cooperating. A grievance committee was formed. Many resignations were submitted.

Proceed Slowly, and with Caution

The same plan or at least portions of it, introduced more gradually, with time to adjust the thinking of the professional individuals involved, might have been a success.

When the supervisor is thinking of changing any of the standard operating procedures of the school, such changes should be made gradually, step by step. The staff must be prepared, carefully and expertly, for that which is to follow. They should have time to develop *enthusiasm* for the change.

Steps in Obtaining Support for a Change

When the supervisor intends to try something new, he/she must not announce it abruptly, without warning. After first establishing rapport, the supervisor should:

1. Discuss the problem several times, with several individuals, and get a commitment from indigenous group leaders
2. Attempt to stimulate the staff to realize that *some* sort of change may be desirable. Aim for a consensus, rather than for majority approval

FIGURE 5-2. "I Understand Your Point, Mr. Horn, and Perhaps We Should Evaluate that Portion of the Plan Again After We've Had a Chance to See How It Works, But I Really Don't Think You Have Anything To Worry About."

3. Attempt to draw the suggestions from the staff. A suggestion from the staff will be easier to put across than would a proclamation from above
4. Avoid presenting the new idea as an accomplished fact. The idea should be presented as a suggestion—as something for the staff to consider and to discuss, whenever possible
5. Take the time, even if he/she plans to proceed in spite of objections raised by the staff. People must become accustomed to the idea and have an opportunity to overcome some of their impulsive resistance to change. This concept is illustrated graphically in Figure 5-2.

How to Use the Staff's Brainpower

Making changes gradually instead of abruptly helps lessen opposition and often results in a better solution to the problem. Even the most appealing plan probably has some limitations in design or concept that have not occurred to the originator of the idea. We know that group effort has a good chance of being superior to individual endeavor. The brainpower of the professional staff should be tapped to accrue the greatest benefit to the students of the school.

Even when we are convinced that our ideas will work as we have planned, we must not rush headlong into such changes. These changes must be made slowly. Any plan has a better chance for success (and survival) if the professional staff has had a chance to adjust its thinking and to cooperate in its production.

This is not to imply that the supervisor should avoid taking a stand. He/she is responsible for all that transpires within the scope of his/her assignment and must be forthright. Rather, the *manner* in which ideas are put into action is important. If a group of employees proposes an idea that the supervisor is convinced will not work, or that is against the policy of the organization (i.e., the governing board) or state law or regulation, he/she must say so. He/she must have the capacity to "stick to his guns" while still maintaining an open mind. If the idea has merit, policy can be changed. In supervision, we strive toward strong, democratic leadership, not toward anarchy or tyranny. The principal should use caution in rejecting an idea. He/she must *never* imply that the superintendent does not like the idea, but that he/she, as supervisor, approves of it. The principal must support the superintendent if he/she expects to receive support in kind. The teachers soon lose faith in a principal who implies that he/she does not support the superintendent or the governing board.

How to Work with the Group and with the Individual

Tead, in *The Art of Administration,*[10] reported that a common factor runs through the activities of all organizations: the close association of individuals, under direction, to accomplish certain stipulated tasks—to realize certain goals. But the relationships involved in these organized activities do not necessarily produce harmonious, productive results.

The problem is that people do not work together naturally and eagerly. There is friction, misunderstanding, indifferences, and conflict between individuals and between groups. "Illogical" employee reactions sometimes can be understood if the possible cause of the illogical reaction, be it environmental or as stated by the individual, is analyzed with an eye to the personal preferences, sentiments, desires, and group pressures. These forces may account for the behavior that may not seem logical in terms of the possible cause as related by the individual. Both the social past and social present must be considered, as may be seen in Figure 5-3.

In addition to the required personal adjustments, divergent or conflicting group relations may arise. High morale is not universal; eager and informed cooperation is atypical. Loyalty and partnership receive a lot of lip service, but seldom are in operation. When indifference and conflict between individuals and between groups do exist, there is cooperation of sorts, as may be seen in Figure 5-4, or no productive outcomes would result. Unfortunately, this cooperation often could be described as passive acquiescence, or as antagonistic submission.

[10] Tead, *The Art of Administration,* pp. ix, 223.

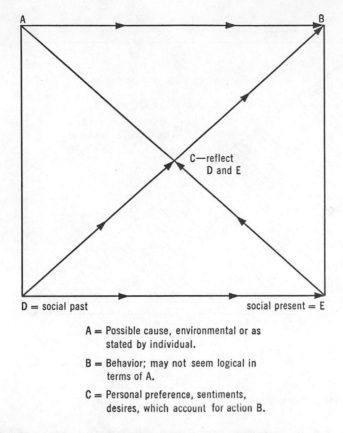

A = Possible cause, environmental or as
     stated by individual.

B = Behavior; may not seem logical in
     terms of A.

C = Personal preference, sentiments,
     desires, which account for action B.

FIGURE 5-3.   Understanding "Illogical" Employee Reactions.

Supervision at its best exhibits a finite fragment of human creativity and at its worse can be a serious social liability. Or, as Tead[11] noted, it can be boring, impersonal, and domineering. As such, it could be stifling and could operate in opposition to the best interests of society. Supervision is, then, both an art and a science. It operates (1) through organizations, (2) through human beings, (3) through groups, and (4) within the democratic political-social-economic society. For information concerning leadership techniques in problem solving, decision making, and program evaluation, see chapters 6 and 18.

Human Dynamics: A Social Product

A lot depends on how we appeal to others. Human dynamics is largely a social product. This means it is malleable to a degree, variable in its responses, and often predictable.

[11] Ibid., chapter XIII.

Increasing Conflict

CONFLICT
(between group members
as to goal or means of
attaining it)

GROUP
EFFECTIVENESS

Decreasing Effectiveness

FIGURE 5-4.   Conflict vs. Effectiveness.

How to Understand Individual Differences

Each person is seeking to become established as a self, and thus continuously is shaped by the standards, values, expectations, and restrictions that are confronted in home, school, community, nation, and professional societies.

EGO DEFENSE.   We all have a two-way interest in maintaining our psychological integrities. The desire for a sense of personal worth is tremendously strong. People want to be identified and acknowledged as individuals with meritorious qualities.

Constructing an Image of the Self

When an individual's interests, associations, and creative participations extend into social channels with distinctive, productive social results, the quality of the ego is manifestly enhanced. Sincere, friendly attitudes tend to beget friendship and cooperation. The more inclusive the fronts on which the person registers and finds worthwhile expressions, the better adjusted, more productive, and more mature he/she may be.

If a staff member discovers that job relations are stultifying and finds little satisfying expression in the course of employment, he will invest as little energy as possible in the job or will invest it in a destructive manner. A dangerous situation would be one in which a supervisor was thrwarted and stifled at home. He might attempt to compensate for home frustrations by being unduly harsh, aggressive, and domineering with the staff.

The supervisor must be alert to the following criteria in detecting individual differences:

1. No supervisor should rely entirely on personal ability to judge personnel by interviewing or talking with them
2. Actual, on-the-job performance is probably the best method for measuring individual differences, but only for the specific task at hand
3. The same teacher changes from year to year and from day to day in performance and interests, both in degree and kind
4. If we grant equal ability (and skill), different kinds of work are best performed by individuals who are particularly interested in them
5. Changes in the environment (both physical and social) and in the complex of factors that govern individual reactions, as indicated in Figure 5-5, can exert a decided influence on individual reactions and, therefore, on human relations
6. The supervisor must recognize the emotional, mental, and physical differences between individuals as to nature, extent, and influence, and must appreciate the influence that the attitudinal complex and morale of the group have on individual staff members

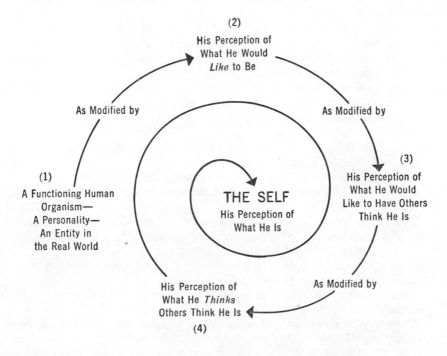

FIGURE 5-5.   Four Factors Governing Individual Reactions.

7. In general, a group tends to change more slowly than does the individual; the group possesses more stability than the individual staff members
8. Power reclines in the fads and fancies that appear to be harmonious with the group's sentiments, with irrational emotions tending to influence the group's actions along lines manifested by its sentiments, with individuals responding to slogans that may tend to unite the sentiments of the staff members and to direct group effort toward objectives associated with the slogans and sentiment
9. Individuals tend to respond positively when they have the whole story, which tends to displace the individual's irrational reactions to rumor.

How to Be Alert to Potential Trouble: Symptoms of Problems to Come

J. Minor Gwynn[12] listed several symptoms that may indicate when a teacher has a developing personal problem. These typical warning signs include:

1. When a teacher cannot sit down and talk quietly and at length, but has to stand up, and perhaps walks about while talking with the principal or another colleague.
2. When a teacher who has normally been rather talkative becomes suddenly and unexplainably more silent than talkative; and the reverse of this, when a teacher who is normally prone to be rather silent changes radically into a very talkative person.
3. When a teacher's classes have a much larger number of "personality conflicts" than usual between teacher and students.
4. When a teacher who has been consistently pleasant and mild in attitude becomes "snappy" and fault-finding with his students.
5. When a teacher who has a record of promptness gets into the habit of not being able to complete tasks or responsibilities on time.
6. When a teacher suddenly develops a tic or nervous mannerism which he did not have before.
7 When little things or irrelevant matters irritate a teacher easily and assume an importance that is not warranted.
8. When a teacher begins to tell the same story, the same episode over and over again to the same person with the same details, not realizing that he is doing it.
9. When a teacher who is normally rather calm and of moderate voice changes and starts each day on a higher key, with his voice getting louder, until the children are keyed up and talking excitedly too.
10. When a teacher begins to lose or gain weight steadily and noticeably when not on a diet under a physician's care.
11. When a teacher consistently cannot wait for someone to finish before he interrupts.
12. When a teacher begins to blame someone or some thing else for his own failure to perform a task well or to carry out a responsibility.

[12] Reprinted by permission of Dodd, Mead & Company, Inc., from *Theory and Practice of Supervision* by J. Minor Gwynn. Copyright © 1961 by Dodd, Mead & Company, Inc.

13. When a teacher who is well known for his liking and love for children changes his attitude to one of constant criticism of students.
14. When a teacher who is a temperate person begins to drink more or less steadily.
15. When a teacher who likes social life and contacts begins to withdraw more and more into privacy and solitude.
16. When a teacher who formerly seemed to love and enjoy his work dreads going to school in the morning, no longer finds joy or satisfaction in his work, and thinks only of dismissal on Friday.

You, Too, Have Needs, My Dear Supervisor

It is important for all supervisors to remember that they have a personal life. How much one involves, shares, and communicates school concerns with one's spouse should be a function of the couple's relationship and is a personal matter.

The supervisor needs to maintain a balance in life by having variety, relaxation, and adventure. By so doing he/she is more effective and productive. How hard one works, as evidenced in apparent effort, and the amount of time one stays on the job (how late in the day one leaves) are not factors that determine a supervisor's success. Supervisors' needs have been summarized as including a feeling of accomplishment, security, friendship, and service, as shown in Table 5-2.

How to Communicate Effectively

Have you ever thought to yourself:

1. "All of my good ideas stick in my throat whenever I get up at a meeting. I sit down feeling like a fool." OR

TABLE 5-2. *Needs of Supervisors*

PERSONAL OFF-THE-JOB NEEDS	ON-THE-JOB NEEDS	
	EGOISTIC	SOCIAL
Good standard of living	Accomplishment	Friendship
Family	Feeling important	Identification
Social life	Feeling for whole	Team work
Recreation	Skill	Helping others
Sexual fulfillment	Program	Being helped
Financial security	Completion	Fair treatment
Community recognition	Autonomy	Praise
Reputation	Knowledge	Acceptance
	Security	Attention
	Job advancement	*Knowledge of where one stands*

2. "On my way home from the faculty meeting I think of all the things I should have said." OR

3. "I often think how much more effective I could be as a supervisor if I could just communicate!"

Recall Aristotle's maxim, "It is not enough to know what to say; it is necessary also to know how to say it." Leadership is practically impossible for a person who lacks the ability to express ideas.

Effective Communication for the Supervisor

Putting even the few hints listed below into practice right now can help you become a more effective communicator of ideas and, therefore, a more successful school supervisor:

1. Speak wisely and well—the following anonymous lines offer a bit of good advice:
   "If wisdom's ways you wisely seek,
   Five things you will observe with care;
   Of whom you speak, to whom you speak;
   And how and when and where."

2. Develop a liking for people—whether you speak to one person or a thousand, they can tell in a split second whether or not you are eager to share good ideas with them or if your words come only from your lips, not from your heart.

3. Keep informed—this task is not easy and often means sacrificing leisure time. But you will be a much more effective supervisory leader if you keep abreast of what is going on in education in general and in supervision in particular; in the social and professional organizations to which you belong; and on the local, national, and international scenes.

4. Go and keep going—if you belong to an organization or group, be informed and play an active role in its meetings and programs. Above all else, make your voice heard. Remember that *unexpressed ideas are of no more value than the kernels in a nut before it is cracked.*

5. Think before you speak—take a few seconds to organize your thoughts, rather than blurting out a gush of words that do not know where they are going. Clear thinking must precede clear speaking. *A moment's thinking is worth an hour in words.*

6. Keep the other fellow in mind—
   - Try to understand the other person's point of view
   - Avoid sarcasm, barbed remarks, and personal insults, for the use of these weapons is an indication of weakness, not of strength
   - Display a calm manner and clear, sound thinking in the midst of heated discussion.
   Let these qualities be manifest:
   - In your tone of voice
   - In your facial expression and your posture
   - In the volume and rate at which you speak.

7. Concentrate on your message, not on yourself—focus attention on what you have to say and you automatically will forget yourself. Fear of being misunderstood, taken with a grain of salt, or even laughed at, will be put in the background once you realize you are an instrument for serving children by bringing helpful ideas to others.

8. Collect material for your discussions—look for facts and "slices of life" that can be used in your talks. Tear out items in newspapers and magazines and underscore passages in books; collect materials that teachers may wish to see, rather than hear about, that pertain to your topic. Jot down your ideas on index cards or keep a small notebook with you.

9. Be brief and precise—
   - Do not bite off more than you can chew or more than your listeners can digest
   - Omit long and unnecessary explanations
   - Select your point and get to it
   - Use short sentences. Be economical in your use of words, never using three or four where one would do.

10. Make nervousness work for you—most people are a bit frightened when speaking before a group. The beginning supervisor especially may be fearful when addressing a first faculty meeting or parent association get together. But a little fear can be an asset. It can sharpen your talks and make them sparkle. Before you begin, consciously relax your muscles and quietly look around at your audience for ten or fifteen seconds.

11. Be enthusiastic. Recall that the word "enthusiasm" comes from two Greek words, *en* and *theos*, meaning "in God." So let the divine spark show through when you want to communicate constructive ideas; but do not confuse enthusiasm with bombast, wild gestures, or emotional display. You can be enthusiastic in a whisper or without moving so much as a finger.

12. Let gestures help you—they can be an outward expression of inner convictions and add dimension to your words. A wave of the arm, a raising of the eyebrow, shrugging the shoulders, nodding the head, are types of gestures.

13. Communicate with your eyes. "Eye communication" means more than "eye contact." It implies looking directly at your listeners and actually talking with your eyes. Sweep the audience gently with a warm, friendly gaze, allowing your glance to rest here and there for a brief second or two. It is far easier to know whether you are making your point if you look at your listeners, rather than at the floor or ceiling.,

14. Keep trying—the type of leadership we stress offers little in the way of ease, honor, or personal gain. In fact, it usually involves hardship, misunderstanding, personal risk, and sometimes personal loss.

15. Be a good listener. Learn from the thoughts and ideas of others. Recall from Epictetus: "Nature has given to man one tongue, but two ears, that we may hear from others twice as much as we speak."

16. Know when to stop—as this verse puts it:
    "I love a finished speaker;
    Oh yes indeed I do.
    I don't mean one who's polished,
    I just mean one who's through."

FIGURE 5-6.   The Successful Listener's Requirements.

Specialists in the language arts, in psychology, in supervision, and in communication theory have listed the principles of effective communication. R. C. Borden's[13] four major principles, which are prerequisite to making communication effective toward improving human relations, are illustrated in Figures 5-6 and 5-7.

Those who are receiving the communication, be they listeners or readers, appreciate:

1. Specific examples included in the communication:
    a) Examples involving either familiar individuals or the recipients of the communication
    b) Examples making more concrete the ideas that the communicator is attempting to present
    c) Colorful analogies
    d) Important statistical material, well dramatized or illustrated
    e) Examples presented through the use of the materials of instructional technology.
2. Terminology that is free from superlatives, trite expressions, groping expressions, repetitious expressions, and the words "et cetera" or "and so forth."

Listeners dislike statements such as, "Of course, it's only my opinion, . . ." Naturally it is your opinion, that is why you are expressing it. Naturally "it seems to you," or you would not be saying it. They also dislike punch-pulling phrases such as "more or less," or, "to a greater or lesser degree."

[13] Richard C. Borden, *Public Speaking as Listeners Like It!* (New York: Harper and Row, Publishers, 1935).

THE
COMMUNICATOR *MUST...*

1. GET DOWN TO CASES, KEYING
   THE BODY OF THE MATERIAL TO
   THE DEMAND OF THE RECEIVER
   FOR CONCRETE EXAMPLES

2. AT THE CONCLUSION...

| ASK FOR **ACTION** | ANSWER THE QUESTION... **"SO WHAT?"** | INCLUDE A **POINT** |

FIGURE 5-7.   The Successful Communicator's Requirements.

Recipients of communication appreciate phraseology that is grammatically sure-footed and easily understood. Sentences should not exceed twenty words in the usual communication. Periods should be inserted when a sentence begins to crumble under its own weight, or when a dependent clause starts to miss on one grammatical cylinder. Listeners appreciate phraseology that is:

- Conversational
- Specific
- Picturesque
- Clear
- To the point

Written Personnel Policies Are Vital to Effective Communication

Without clear information employees are likely to be confused, do not know what is expected of them, and are apt to believe that favoritism or pull is the major factor in assignment, in obtaining instructional materials, and even in selecting and rating. Such beliefs are devastating to good human relations and morale. It is here that heated disputes are most likely to develop within the school organization and between school and community.

The school system is charged with the task of setting forth such personnel policies in writing so that they may be *adhered to carefully* to enhance effective communication and serve as a means of eliminating favoritism, poor morale, and much ill will. Governing boards must not bow to the pressures of militant, aggressive groups within the community to avoid establishing a written personnel policy system nor should governing boards yield to pressures to violate their own policies.

The supervising principal should take the lead in developing a teacher's handbook containing major policies. Such handbooks help human relations and should be available to all teachers in the school system. Such a handbook should include sections concerning:

1. School system organization and point of view
2. Assignment specifications
3. Auxiliary services
4. Specialized instructional services
5. Student management
6. Management of forms, supplies, and equipment
7. Certificated personnel policies
8. Special services
9. Professional responsibilities and ethics

In order to acquire free expression and maximum cooperation, the staff must work together in an atmosphere of freedom. A system of instructional policies should be cooperatively formulated, and assignment specifications should be officially adopted by the governing boards. Morale will be elevated in many ways, including the use of teacher committees, cooperatively planned policies, effective two-way communication, timely information, and due consideration to personal problems.

B. O. Smith, W. O. Stanley, and J. H. Shores reported that good communication must be regarded not from a standpoint of the dissemination of information, but rather as a means of developing perspective. If that perspective is distorted, the information will be interpreted incorrectly. If instruction is to be improved, the channels of communication must work more effectively than they do today.

How to Be a Success as a Leader in a Social Setting

If a supervisor is to be effective in improving instruction, he/she must show initiative in drawing out the creative abilities of the staff. He/she realizes that groups have both status leaders and emergent leaders in a democracy. The status leader occupies this position because of his/her professional assignment, such as superintendent of schools or supervising principal, whereas emergent or shared leadership provides an opportunity for each member of the group to occupy the

Types of Leaders

FIGURE 5-8.   Types of Leaders.

leadership position temporarily because each one can make a contribution. It is essential that the status leader, especially:

1. Attempt to improve human relations within the professional staff
2. Encourage free discussion
3. Assist in developing cooperative techniques for getting the job(s) done and the goal(s) met
4. Assist in developing future leaders
5. Coordinate functions of the staff
6. Provide advice as needed.

How to Recognize Types of Leadership and Identify Pleasing and Displeasing Leadership Behavior

Specialists in the field traditionally have identified four major types of leaders. *laissez faire* leaders, democratic leaders, and two types of autocratic leaders— hard-boiled autocrats and benevolent autocrats. The democratic leaders, who could be represented graphically as occupying the central position in the leadership continuum as may be seen in Figure 5-8, provide the best possible type of leadership. Ewing[14] differentiated between the charismatic, symbolic, head man, expert, theorist, agitator, authoritarian, and groupocratic types of leadership behavior, as outlined in Table 5-3.

Regarding the type of leadership behavior indicated as Group VIII in Table 5-3 (the absence of leadership), the reader should recall that the people will support the tyrant rather than live in a state of anarchy.

Perhaps of more vital concern to the supervisor were the findings of research concerning pleasing and displeasing leader behavior.

[14] Russell H. Ewing, *The Leadership Functions of Executives and Managers* (Beverly Hills, California: National Institute of Leadership, 1969), p. 6.

TABLE 5-3. *Types of Leadership Behavior*[a]

GROUP	CHARACTER	COMMENTS AND BEHAVIORAL CHARACTERISTICS	EXAMPLES
I	Charismatic	Introduced by the German sociologist Max Weber, denotes leadership based on supposedly divine or supernatural powers	Jesus, Mohammed, Joan of Arc, the Pope, Father Divine
II	Symbolic	A leader with prestige but little power, symbolizing a nation or an institution which has symbolic value	The remaining European Kings and Queens
III	Head man	An institutional leader who fills a traditional position and whose authority is derived from custom and tradition	The chancellor of a university is often the head man type of leader
IV	Expert	Based solely on achieved eminence in a certain field	Darwin, Einstein, Beethoven
V	Administrative leader or Theorist	This kind of leader is found in all societies and functions chiefly in business, politics, and government	Bismarck, Lincoln, F. D. Roosevelt
VI	Agitator or Reformer	Rests on persuasive and propagandastic ability rather than on executive or administrative skill, although these two factors may be present	Thomas Paine, William Jennings Bryan, Hitler, Norman Thomas
VII	Authoritarian	Individuals who have conscious or unconscious drives toward dogmatism, absolutism, and an inflexible exercise of power	Hitler, Stalin
VIII	Groupocratic	An offbeat system of leadership which some students of the subject label "anarchy." Has been called upside-down leadership or management in which the subordinate may dictate to his supervisor. Although these theories are shrouded in the cloak of democracy, many specialists[a] indicate that this character of leadership could result in anarchy or chaos if practiced in any wide scale in government, business, industry, education, or military organizations.	Sensitivity trainers, group dynamics theorists, unstructured training theorists

[a] Russell H. Ewing, *The Leadership Functions of Executives and Managers* (Beverly Hills, California: National Institute of Leadership, 1969), p. 7.

Pleasing Leadership Behavior

Clifford Campbell[15] reported the types of pleasing supervising principal behavior, as viewed by his staff and by parents' association presidents, in order, as indicated below:

1. Shows an interest in work and offers assistance
2. Possesses pleasing personality traits, such as courtesy, firmness, high integrity
3. Praises personnel and passes on compliments
4. Supports actions and decisions of personnel
5. Is a good organizer
6. Assumes authority and stands by convictions
7. Allows self-direction in work and shows confidence in ability
8. Makes wishes clearly known
9. Allows participation in decision making
10. Is firm with school standards and student discipline, and considerate of employees' work load

Displeasing Leadership Behavior

The types of supervising principal leadership behavior that Campbell[16] classified as displeasing included, in rank order:

1. Possesses poor personality traits, such as rudeness, unfairness, low integrity, and moral offensiveness
2. Is a "fence-sitter" and seems afraid to assume authority rightfully his
3. Is a poor disciplinarian
4. Is not a good organizer
5. Does not allow participation in decision making
6. Is not considerate of the work load of personnel
7. Does not support personnel in decisions or actions
8. Does not make wishes clearly known
9. Does not show an interest in, or offer assistance with work
10. Does not allow self-direction in work or show confidence in ability
11. Allows too much parental influence
12. Is hypercritical, too demanding about details
13. Shows inadequate job knowledge and does not praise personnel

15 Clifford W. Campbell, "The Elementary School Principal as Viewed by His Staff and Parent-Teacher Association Presidents," Doctoral dissertation (University of Southern California, 1964), pp. 223–227.
16 Ibid.

The Importance of a Sense of Humor
in Leadership Behavior

A sense of humor can help keep good leaders from taking themselves too seriously.[17] It can make their efforts in dealing with others less tense and more amiable: it helps people to retain a sense of proportion between activity and effort. As an aspect of leadership behavior, a sense of humor is invaluable, for it often can lessen tensions as no other remedy can. Abraham Lincoln was a master at this technique of leadership.

The following films are recommended:

1. "Democracy"—Encyclopedia Britannica Films (ten minutes)
2. "Despotism"—Encyclopedia Britannica Films (ten minutes)
3. "Role-Playing in Human Relations"—Department of Adult Education, National Education Association, Washington, D.C. (twenty-five minutes)
4. "We Plan Together"—Teachers College, Columbia University (twenty minutes)

How the Power of the Supervisor Is Secured

Personal power over others may be acquired in three ways: (1) by *inheritance,* (2) by *seizure,* and (3) by demonstrated expertise or other influence leading to *appointment or election.* The effectiveness of the supervisor apparently depends more on how well he/she deals with people than on how he/she obtained the position. Supervisors can demonstrate their power by being ruthless, domineering, and autocratic in command, or they can gain cooperation by their expertise and by their friendly, helpful, persuasive leadership. The effects of democratic and authoritarian atmospheres are compared in Table 5-4.

Leadership that is ruthless, domineering, and autocratic may be reflected in indifference and in passive, reluctant obedience.

Security, confidence in one's own competence, job satisfaction, and absence of frustrations in the home are essential conditions in the lives of those who are to wield their personal power over others in wholesome productive ways.

The supervisor exercises power with integrity when he/she is solicitous of the welfare of the staff. The response of the staff to *sincere* and competent effort is confidence in judgment, admiration and respect for technical resourcefulness, and pride in the profession. In a democratic atmosphere, then, the leader operates within established policies, attempts to improve human relations within the staff, encourages free discussion, assists in the development of future leaders, coordinates functions and activities, provides advice, and assists in the development of cooperative techniques for problem-solving.

[17] Emery Stoops, M. L. Rafferty, and Russell E. Johnson, *Handbook of Educational Administration* (Boston: Allyn and Bacon, Inc., 1975), p. 38.

TABLE 5-4.   Comparison Between Effects of Democratic and Authoritarian Atmosphere

EFFECTS OF DEMOCRATIC ATMOSPHERE	EFFECTS OF AUTHORITARIAN ATMOSPHERE
1. More "we-feeling"; more frequent use of "we" and "our."	1. More "I-feeling"; more frequent use of "my" and "I."
2. Group-minded suggestions; relatively few demands for individual focus of attention.	2. Suggestions more designed to focus attention from leader on self.
3. Positive identification with whole group, including leaders and non-leaders.	3. No group identification; leader identification rather than group identification.
4. Positive group identification and unity.	4. Relatively less group unity, members may temporarily unite to defy leader, but this does not necessarily indicate existence of genuine group identification.
5. Activity and productivity begins before leader arrives and continues during his/her absence.	5. Activity and productivity decreases with absence of leader and increases during his/her presence.
6. Greater job satisfaction and morale with few or no rumors.	6. Less job satisfaction and morale, with relatively more anxiety about the present and future, leading to formation and spreading of rumors.
7. Relatively little aggression toward leader and other group members; generally more friendly behavior when frustrated, aggression is directed toward real source of aggression.	7. Considerable aggression toward other members. Tendency to displace aggression to scapegoats, outsiders, "beginners"; when frustration is very great, apathy and inwardly directed aggression are evident.
8. Fewer "gripe sessions."	8. More "gripe sessions."
9. Relatively less obvious dependence on leader, who is admired.	9. Overdependence on and submission to leader, who is less liked; in extreme situations there may be regression toward childlike dependence.
10. Relatively broader perspective of problems and their possible solutions.	10. Piecemeal perception of problems.
11. More variability and flexibility of behavior.	11. More stereotyped, inflexible behavior.

Supervisory Leadership in the Good Old Days

We have come a long way. The following list of rules for teachers was posted by a New York City principal in 1872:

1. Teachers each day will fill lamps, clean chimneys, and trim wicks.
2. Each teacher will bring a bucket of water and a scuttle of coal for the day's session.
3. Make your pens carefully; you may whittle nibs to the individual tastes of the children.
4. Men teachers may take one evening each week for courting purposes, or two evenings a week if they go to church regularly.
5. After ten hours in school, the teachers should spend the remaining time reading the Bible or other good books.
6. Women teachers who marry or engage in *other unseemly conduct* will be dismissed.
7. Every teacher should lay aside from each pay a good sum of his earnings for his benefit during his declining years so that he will not become a burden on society.
8. Any teacher who smokes, uses liquor in any form, frequents pool or public halls, or gets shaved in a barber shop, will give good reason to suspect his worth, intentions, integrity, and honesty.
9. The teacher who performs his labors faithfully and without fault for five years will be given an increase of twenty-five cents per week in his pay providing the board of education approves.

Of course trimming wicks or carrying coal has not been a part of the education profession for some time, but many teachers remember vividly the role that was expected of them:

1. The educator was a purveyor of learning, or more directly, a person who distributed knowledge. Of course, this knowledge must not have been in opposition to the accepted community mores. He was not to be controversial nor an "all round" human being. He was not permitted to expound new social theories.
2. He had to be active in community affairs, that is, in youth groups, church activities, community welfare drives, and the like. He was expected to be a "do-gooder." He must not, under any condition, have been a competitor for top community honors; he could not run for office. He was expected to operate actively at the "second level" in the social life of the community.
3. The teacher's personal life was under constant community scrutiny. If he was male, he was expected to be married to a girl who did not work. A female teacher was expected to be single, dress very conservatively, and wear little or no make-up. One superintendent insisted that any teacher who wanted to leave town for the weekend get special permission from him.

Some Psychological Implications of Your Supervisory Behavior

Democratic Leadership Implies General Rather than Close Supervision

By not supervising too closely, the democratic leader generates and maintains feelings of freedom among subordinates. Translated into behavior, these feelings affect how the democratic leader feels toward subordinates.

CLOSE SUPERVISION AND MISTRUST.   In a laboratory experiment, two "subordinates" were monitored by a subject who served as the laboratory "supervisor." High output was required on a dull task. One subordinate was monitored closely, the other was checked infrequently. Both subordinates performed equally well, but the attitude of the supervisor towards the two subordinates was quite different because of how he had to supervise them. The supervisor reported that the subordinate he monitored closely was less trustworthy, less dependable, and complied with the supervisor's requests only because he was being watched. On the other hand, the supervisor felt that the subordinate who was checked very little complied because "he was a nice guy" or he "wanted to."

Mistrust tends to be reciprocal; it feeds on itself. If a supervisor feels compelled to supervise a subordinate closely, he/she increases his/her belief in the need for close supervision of that same subordinate. If conditions are democratic and the subordinate works equally well, then the supervisor increases his/her belief in the trustworthiness of the subordinate and presumably is able to become even more permissive in dealing with that subordinate.

CLOSE SUPERVISION AND PRODUCTIVITY.   According to a similar laboratory experiment, tension is lower in workers and productivity higher under general rather than close supervision.

A benefit of general supervision is the extent to which *mixed* or *partial reinforcement* effects can keep workers at their tasks in the absence of the supervisor. Experiments suggest that the learner who is checked as correct or incorrect after each trial in the learning process will extinguish or forget more quickly what he/she has learned if the correction suddenly ceases than will the learner who has been corrected intermittently. Some schedule of partial or "mixed" reinforcement is most powerful and efficacious. This conclusion logically follows the observation that the permissive, general, supervisor can be absent from a work group with less deleterious effects on the productivity of the group than the close supervisor. When the close supervisor leaves, one is likely to see an increase in time wasting, wandering off the job, and "horseplay" among the workers.

Democratic Leadership Promotes Productivity

In addition to fostering acceptance, agreement, change, satisfaction, and trust, democratic supervision often seems to contribute to the quality and quantity of output by subordinates. Work groups in an insurance company were more productive among first-line supervisors who encouraged workers to participate in decisions, were more democratic in dealing with them, and supervised less closely. The ease and freedom that employees feel in communicating with superiors correlates highly with productivity. Employees permitted to set goals, whether in office or factory operations, are significantly more productive, and feel (1) more influential and (2) more likely to be supported by their supervisors.

Democracy, Not License!

Critics confuse democratic leadership with lax, uncontrolled, unrestrained supervision. In this case, the supervisor avoids attempting to influence subordinates and shirks supervisory duties:

> . . . [and] has no confidence in his ability to supervise and consequently buries himself in paper work or stays away from employees. He may also be the one who believes that to be a "good fellow" means license. He leaves too much responsibility with the employees; set no clear goals toward which they may work; is incapable of making decisions or helping the group arrive at decision; and tends to let things drift . . .[18]

Such laissez faire leadership should not be confused with the activities of the democratic supervisor who:

> . . . whenever possible, . . . shares with his group the decision-making about work planning, assignment, and scheduling. Where a decision must be made by him, he helps the group to understand clearly the basis for his decision. He is careful to develop as much participation, opinion-giving . . . and a feeling of responsibility for the success of the work on the part of everyone. He is concerned that each employee clearly understand his work and have opportunities for success in it . . . He encourages worthwhile suggestions and the development of new procedures . . ."[19]

Democratic Participation Does Not
Necessarily Lower Decision Quality

Critics also argue that if a supervisor permits subordinates to participate in the decision-making process, the group product will be inferior. The supervisor, with

[18] L. P. Bradford and R. Lippitt, "Building a Democratic Work Group," *Personnel* XXII (1945): 142–148.
[19] Ibid.

special knowledge and training, is in the best position to evaluate the situation and can make the best decision. The compromises resulting from group discussions are regarded by critics as likely to reduce the quality of solutions. But the evidence runs counter to the criticism. Experiments generally show that group decisions are superior to decisions reached by the average member of that group, although it also is true that the group decision may not be as good as that of the best member in the group. But how often is the supervisor the best? If excellence could be guaranteed, then decision quality might be better when decisions were made by the supervisor alone. When 66 air force officers wrote decisions before discussion and then met as an *ad hoc* staff to write the decisions, the decisions written by the staff were superior to the average quality of decisions written by individuals without discussion. At the same time, the quality was the same after discussion whether the decision was written by the staff or by the commander who had listened to the staff discussion. Group discussions contributed to better decision-making, whether or not the final decision was written by the group or by the person leading the group. See chapter 18 for a more complete discussion of the decision-making process.

Some Negative Consequences of Permissiveness

Even though the usual concerns that democratic leadership will promote licentiousness, lowered standards, anarchy, and less control are unfounded, there are some potential negative consequences. The person who shares in the decision-making process not only derives greater self-satisfaction from the job, he/she also develops greater frustration with it, according to nationwide American mental health survey:

> [Having] a personal stake in the outcomes of decisions taken . . . can be a satisfying, even an exhilarating experience, but it can also lead to sleepless nights.
> This mixed blessing which power sometimes represents is illustrated by the experiment in a large clerical organization . . . in which about 200 clerks were given greater responsibility to make decisions about some of the things that affected their work groups. In general, morale increased in these divisions as a result of the change in control. Clerks felt more satisfied with the company, with supervision, with their work in general. They were, in large measure, favorable toward the increased control which they were able to exercise. However, despite the general increase in satisfaction, the clerks felt less of a sense of accomplishment at the end of the work day. They were also less satisfied with their present level in the organization. . . . In acquiring an increased feeling of responsibility for the work through the added control which they were able to exercise, the clerks no doubt developed standards of achievement which are harder to satisfy.[20]

[20] A. S. Tannenbaum, "Control in Organizations: Individual Adjustment and Organizational Performance," *Seminar on Basic Research in Management Controls* (Palo Alto: Stanford University, 1963), p. 184.

When Permissiveness Is Contraindicated

Permissive, and to some extent, persuasive supervision appear, in general, most effective in promoting satisfaction and productivity among employees. Nonetheless, numerous circumstances require more authoritative action by the supervisor, more direct application of his/her power to reward or punish, and more decisions without consulting subordinates.

WHEN INTERACTION IS RESTRICTED.   When contact between superior and subordinate is restricted because of the size of the group, infrequent meetings between superior and subordinate, or poor communications, the supervisor must be ready to direct and to structure the situation—to give orders and see that they are obeyed. In small, intimate groups, where interaction between supervisor and all members is quick and easy, the supervisor can remain permissive. In the small, intimate, communicative group, more attempted leadership acts can occur in a given amount of time than in the large, distant group. Each leadership attempt must "count more" in the large group since relatively fewer attempts are possible. As groups become larger than 30, the demands from subordinates for strong, central leadership become stronger. Subordinates place more reliance on whoever is appointed leader, regardless of who he/she is personally. There is more tolerance of leadercentered direction in larger groups.

Figure 5-9 shows how the productivity of scientists in a medical research laboratory is greatest when they have daily contact with their group chief, but only

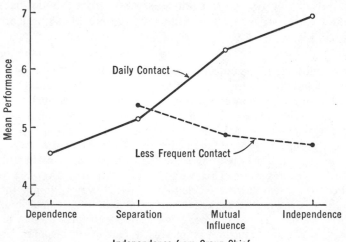

FIGURE 5-9.   The Relationship of Scientific Performance to Independence from Group Chief and Contact with Chief.[21]

[21] Bernard M. Bass, *Organizational Psychology* (Boston: Allyn and Bacon, Inc., 1965), p. 184.

if they are treated democratically and allowed to share in decision-making or given the freedom to make most of their own decisions. This approach works best when meetings are frequent. But when contact between supervisor and subordinates is only a few times a week or less, productivity falls off with this same permissiveness by the supervisor. Permissiveness is thus contraindicated when interaction is low between leader and led.

THE NATURE OF THE TASK.   The nature of the task may mitigate against permissive approaches, particularly if it restricts interaction. A person at the center of a network of communications from four peripheral locations will promote the fastest, clearest, most accurate communication system if he/she accepts the responsibility for making the decisions for the network. Although those in the periphery may be unsatisfied with this arrangement, the system works most effectively if the central person is authoritative. On the other hand, if all locations are interconnected, more equalitarian decision-making becomes possible.

Whether the task is simple or complex may make a difference. If the task is easy and uncomplicated for the worker, close supervision is likely to be detrimental, since the worker already knows what to do and how to do it. On the other hand, if the task is complex or the worker has little understanding of how to tackle it, permissiveness may be contraindicated. The worker may prefer a lot of guidance and attention from the supervisor until he/she has mastered the job, particularly if it does not involve much creativity from the worker but only attention to routine details which must be learned.

Higher Authority

Both in a progressive petrochemical refinery and in a national food processing firm the extent to which a supervisor felt he should be considerate correlated positively with how highly he was rated by his superiors.[22] Yet in other companies no such correlation has been found, and one can easily imagine settings in which considerate, permissive superiors would be severely downgraded by *their* supervisors. A conflict is likely if top management insists on sacrificing all else in the interests of maximizing productivity, accountability, and managing by (performance) objectives and has the power to coerce workers to that end.

EXPECTATIONS OF SUBORDINATES.   If custom restricts what the worker is permitted to decide, the supervisor will define and structure the work. Thus, whether Norwegian factory employees participated in decisions depended on whether they deemed that the activity was legitimate for them. Similarly, Israeli sailors who expected that their commander would be authoritarian were as satisfied with him as they were with a permissive commander.

Studies in other more traditional cultures such as Japan and Great Britain

[22] Ibid., p. 185.

generally support the utility of permissive techniques, but more analyses repeating American experiments need to be done abroad.[23] Military field studies indicate that more important to the effectiveness of the team is whether the leader conforms to the role expected by subordinates, not whether he/she is permissive or coercive.[24]

PERSONALITY AND ABILITY OF SUBORDINATES.   Supervisors will have difficulty promoting participation in decisions among their subordinates if the subordinates do not know what they could contribute. Subordinates may dislike making decisions. They may dislike (1) living without immediate decisions from supervisors and (2) remaining in ambiguous, unstructured circumstances. Such intolerance for ambiguity is one characteristic associated with authoritarian attitudes. A survey of Philadelphia residents disclosed that highly authoritarian personalities wanted powerful, prestigeful leaders who would direct them strongly. On the other hand, equalitarian persons preferred leaders who could help them solve their problems. They wanted warmth and consideration in their leaders.

PERSONALITY AND EXPECTATIONS OF WOULD-BE PERMISSIVE LEADERS.   An authoritarian manager who cannot tolerate uncertainty, who has strong power needs, and who cannot accept equalitarian attitudes toward other people may be more effective if he/she does not try to disguise these true feelings by a superficial display of permissive practices. A manager who maintains a consistent authoritative position allows subordinates to develop a consistent, reasonably tolerable way of getting along with him/her. They know what to expect and, although they may react to coercion in the ways described earlier, they will react possibly even more strongly to the executive who forcefully declares, "We'll be democratic around here, or else. . . ."

What we are saying is that it pays to be democratically permissive, but that some supervisors may be unable to bring themselves to think and behave as is required for a true sharing of leadership between supervisor and subordinate. In such cases, they may be better off maintaining practices with which they, at least, will be more comfortable. Otherwise, their own conflicts in what they prefer to do and what they actually do may generate more difficulties with subordinates. For example, the professor who lectures to classes for the full 50 minutes and refuses to allow time for discussion because he cannot tolerate or deal with questioning or skeptical students may be more effective in refusing to have open discussions with students than he would be if he allowed time for interaction which was likely to arouse hostility, anxiety, and conflict in himself and, in turn, the students. This professor might effectively solve this dilemma by informal discussions with individual students outside of class.

EMERGENCIES.   Subordinates want to be told what to do in a hurry when danger threatens. Time does not always permit a democratic discussion of alternatives.

---

[23] Ibid., p. 186.
[24] Ibid.

Rapid, decisive leadership may be demanded. From one-half to two-thirds of 181 airmen who were asked their opinions concerning missile teams, rescue teams, scientific teams or other small crews facing emergencies strongly agreed that they should respond to the orders of the commander with less question than they usually do. In an emergency, the commander was expected to "check more closely to see that everyone is carrying out his responsibility." One-half to three-fourths felt that "the commander should not be 'just one of the boys.' "

Analyses of the survival experiences of 200 crews who had to fight hunger, cold, fatigue, and the enemy suggests that the effective leader in such stressful circumstances differs from the ineffective leader in the extent to which he exercises power, maintains communications in the group, rapidly restructures the situation, and maintains the group's goal orientation so that panic will be avoided. Panic occurs when members suddenly seek individual goals—the everyone-for-himself syndrome.

Summary

Although the best decisions occur when the leader seeks and accepts information, ideas, and opinions of members for evaluation, still he/she must express his/her own opinions, assume responsibility for making decisions, and, when required, make decisions without consulting the group.

Supervisors vary from each other in many ways. Most significant in effects on their organization are the extent to which they initiate structure, show consideration for their subordinates, and balance their objectives and loyalties. They differ in how they use their abilities to persuade subordinates, yet often this is an effective style of leadership. They can use their power to coerce subordinates with promises and threats, but this practice has open and hidden costs. With power and ability they can treat subordinates democratically: setting the constraints liberally within which their subordinates can pursue objectives, sharing in decisions with subordinates, and discussing with them matters that affect all concerned. However, such permissiveness is less effective when groups are large, when time is limited, and in other circumstances limiting interaction possibilities between the supervisor and subordinates. Yet, in the aggregate, where it is feasible, democratic leadership (*not* anarchy) pays off, particularly in the small, face-to-face working situation.[25]

Keys to Leadership for the Supervisor

To be effective in our democratic society, a supervisor must show initiative in drawing out the abilities of the staff. We know that individuals are more produc-

[25] Science Research Associates have published a paperback that has significance for the psychology of supervisory behavior. (Elwood N. Chapman, *Supervisor's Survival Kit* [Chicago: Science Research Associates, 1976].)

tive and perform most effectively when they operate within a familiar framework, use familiar techniques and methods, and proceed toward a readily obtainable goal.

The production of the staff is enhanced both qualitatively and quantitatively when the individals involved have had an opportunity to help establish goals.

The leader must be concerned, then, not only with the profitable and efficient attainment of desired objectives, but also with the *methods employed* and with the *individuals participating*.

Thus is loyalty won. Thus is the educational or institutional or industrial product advanced, enhanced, and elevated.

The potential for leadership is inherent, and all persons have some potential. But we are chiefly concerned with leadership characteristics that are learned. These we can improve. Here are some factors that can improve leadership performance.

Do

1. Work beyond requirements—and do not call on subordinates for tasks that you are unwilling to undertake yourself.
2. Report to work on time, regularly, and without obvious effort or complaint.
3. Keep your mind focused on work to be done instead of watching the clock. You should excuse a subordinate for a dental appointment sooner than you would take the privilege for yourself.
4. Supervise by policy, and remember that you are subject to the policy that you helped to create.
5. Appreciate difficulties involved in puzzling assignments and offer praise when a colleague solves the problem.
6. Express concern through action, not mere verbalization, for the welfare of the staff, as a means of maintaining high morale.
7. Maintain faith in the staff (if you doubt them, they will doubt you).
8. Involve others in policy decisions. Wait out the slowness of group problem solving, for if you pressure too hard, the slower members of the group will lose interest.
9. Improve programs by starting with worker dissatisfactions and help find an answer, as opposed to belittling their dissatisfactions or giving them ready-made solutions.
10. Keep all members of the staff fully informed and look on some internal disagreement as the doorway to further growth.
11. Solve a problem rather than sell a solution.
12. Stress what is right rather than who is right.
13. Allow time for consensus rather than ramming through a majority vote.
14. Accept responsibility for the outcomes of the group's decisions.
15. Agree with Walter Lippmann that "the final test of a leader is that he leaves behind him in other men the conviction and the will to carry on."
16. Delegate authority, responsibility, and function. *The leader is effective only as he works through people.*

The leader must avoid certain behaviors if he/she is to maintain the "leader goose" position at the head of the flock.

Don't

1. Show favoritism, but do recognize individual differences in the group and capitalize on them. Where is the fine line between recognizing ability and showing favoritism? The leader must find and follow it.
2. Tend toward intimacy. When students call a teacher by his first name, or nickname, respect and leadership qualities tend to evaporate. The oriental philosopher, Laotzu, said, "A leader is best when people hardly know he exists."
3. Take criticisms personally. Keep calm and weigh all criticisms objectively.
4. Expect social concourse; accept loneliness. The crowd has company, but the leader stands by himself.
5. Be tempted by power. The strong, effective leader must beware of the temptation to exert power. Paraphrasing Lord Acton, "power tends to corrupt; absolute power corrupts absolutely." Plato saw this danger when he said in *The Republic,* "people always have some champion whom they set over them and nurse into greatness . . . this and no other is the root from which the tyrant springs; when first he appears he is a protector . . . In the early days of his power, he is full of smiles, and he salutes everyone whom he meets." Beware the temptations to exert power.
6. Fail to avoid the temptation to feel tall by cutting down enemies, much less fellow workers, and much, much less a subordinate staff member. This kind of person can hold power only through status positions, or the methods of coercion, and not through the loyalty and respect of devoted staff.

Leadership, then, is not moral; neither is it immoral. It is amoral. Leaders can be good or bad. It is the direction and results of leadership that count. Genghis Khan, Alexander, Napoleon, Tojo, and Hitler were leaders, but to destruction. Moses, Socrates, Jesus, Mohammed, Gandhi, Horace Mann, and Florence Nightingale were leaders, but to a better life.

TRENDS: PREPARING FOR EDUCATIONAL SUPERVISION—A FURTHER LOOK

Toward ⟶   Training School

Executives in the Use of

Techniques Derived from a Study

of Human Relationships

An increasingly large number of elementary supervising principals will attend laboratories, such as that of the National Training Laboratories for Human Relations. Comprehensive courses in human dynamics and group processes designed especially for the supervisor will be offered in the preparing institutions. As the supervising principal becomes more aware of the technique of scientific management as applied to groups, the efficiency with which educational supervision is accomplished will be enhanced.

Toward ⟶   an Increase in the Skill

of the Supervising

Principal in Effective Communication

To achieve free expression and to acquire maximum cooperation, the staff must work together in an atmosphere of freedom. A system of personnel policies will be cooperatively formulated, and assignment specifications will be officially adopted by the governing boards. Morale will be elevated in many ways, including the use of teacher committees, cooperatively planned policies, effective two-way communication, and due consideration to personal problems.

Good communication must be regarded not from a standpoint of the dissemination of information, but rather as a means of developing perspective. If that perspective is distorted, the information will be interpreted incorrectly. If instruction is to be improved, the channels of communication must work more effectively than they do today.

Toward ⟶   the Professional Team

Approach to Educational Supervision

The alert superintendent of the future will see the trend toward team action that is beginning to develop today and will seek opportunities to develop teachers as leaders. He/she will include all of the professional staff in planning, executing, and evaluating educational experiences. Team action for better human relationships and higher morale will be a major goal.

Supervisory Problems   In Basket

Problem 1

A large elementary school has four first-grade teachers. Each has her own problems:

Mrs. Horn is quiet, keeps to herself, and rarely shares ideas with other teachers. Her classroom door is always closed. She is, nevertheless, very efficient and handles her students well. She always complies with the principal's requests and her reports are always in on time.

Mrs. Brown is a widow. Her personality has changed noticeably of late. At school she tends to mother Mrs. Douglas, a young first-grade teacher. Her reports are accurate and on time. She thinks mainly of her class and her students. However, she is willing to share ideas and materials.

Mrs. Green is the oldest of the four first-grade teachers. According to others, she offers too much advice and much of it has little meaning. She would be willing to share materials, but has trouble finding them in the chaotic conditions that usually exist in her room. Her reports usually are late and at times incorrect.

Mrs. Douglas is a young teacher who wants to do a good job. She turned to Mrs. Brown for help. This caused hard feelings between Mrs. Brown and Mrs. Green, who had been coworkers for many years.

At last the problem boiled over. On the afternoon of March 6, seven teachers were gathered in the faculty room having soft drinks during recess. Mrs. Brown and Mrs. Douglas were seated together talking about the approaching First Grade Spring Music Festival. Mrs. Green entered the teacher's room and went directly to the vending machine and got a soft drink. She added a comment to the conversation. Mrs. Douglas turned to Mrs. Brown and made a remark. Mrs. Green did not hear the remark, and she assumed it was about her. Becoming enraged at the two, she threw her coke bottle on the floor, breaking it. Mrs. Douglas' foot was cut, and the relationships of the teachers were shattered.

How would you, as the supervising principal, work to re-establish a positive relationship between the four first-grade teachers?

Problem 2

Miss Ross has been teaching for ten years in several different schools. This year she is teaching in a school whose faculty is made up of 50 per cent "freshmen" teachers. She has a very dominating personality, loves to talk and complain, and is unhappy when she does not get things done her way. Whenever any new ideas are brought up for discussion, Miss Ross immediately gives her views on why the idea is without merit. This causes an uneasy feeling among the teachers. The younger teachers are afraid to speak up. Because of Miss Ross' behavior, communications between teachers and between faculty and administration are strained.

As the supervising principal, what would you do to help ease this situation?

Problem 3

A faculty group comes up with an idea that, if put into action, would be contrary to governing board policy.

How would you handle the situation? Indicate how this difficulty could have been avoided.

Problem 4

A parent complains to you that because her son was kept after school, he missed his bus. He had to walk home in the rain, and now is quite sick. The parent demands a meeting with you and the teacher, at which the teacher will be asked to defend his actions.

Note how you, as supervising principal, would proceed.

Questions and Suggested Activities Concerning How to Provide Instructional Leadership

Questions

1. What are the areas of instructional concern for the supervisor? In which areas is leadership most needed?
2. Whose responsibility is it to see that instructional leadership is provided in a school?
3. What recent changes and developments in the world have made leadership in curriculum construction and implementation more important?
4. What is the function of the local school superintendent in instructional leadership? Of the board of education? Of the specialist-consultant? The supervising principal? The teacher?
5. How do lay groups function in instructional leadership? How are leaders for lay groups procured?
6. How are community-school relations improved when mutual leadership is exercised between school and community?
7. How do you cope with pressure or interest groups whose intentions would not be for the general good?

Suggested Activities

1. List representatives from professional and lay groups whom you feel should comprise an instructional leadership council and discuss the roles of the professional and lay leaders of this council.

2. List some advantages for having cooperative leadership shared by the principal or supervisor and the certificated staff.

3. Discuss problems that may arise between the principal and teachers in relation to curriculum construction, revision, implementation, and evaluation.

4. Discuss the reactions of teachers when instructional leadership is initiated entirely by administration.

5. Outline methods of obtaining faculty participation in instructional improvement.

6. Devise a model for evaluating the effectiveness of instructional leadership.

7. List the areas of the curriculum that you feel need revision as a result of technological, economic, social, and political trends.

8. Present a skit in which you and two others attempt to solve a problem as a group. Use the role-playing technique.

9. Make a list of recent references that will help the supervising principal in the area of human dynamics.

10. Indicate your opinion on why some specialists express themselves negatively concerning the "Group Dynamics Movement" whereas they support the use of techniques based on a knowledge of human dynamics in group processes.

11. Outline the topics that you believe should be included in a handbook of school system policies that is to be designed especially for teachers. How would this content differ from the topics contained in a handbook designed especially for the elementary school principal?

12. List the advantages and pitfalls of a "management by objectives" or "performance contracting" approach to educational supervision.

Selected Bibliography

Books

Bartky, John A. *Supervision as Human Relations*. Boston: D. C. Heath and Company, 1953.

Baxter, Bernice, and Rosalind Cassidy. *Group Experience—The Democratic Way*. New York: Harper and Brothers, 1943.

Benne, Kenneth, and Bozidar Muntyan. *Human Relations in Curriculum Change*. New York: The Dryden Press, 1951.

Berne, Eric. *The Structure and Dynamics of Organizations and Groups*. Philadelphia: J. B. Lippincott Company, 1963.

Boardman, Charles W., Harl R. Douglass, and Rudyard K. Bent. *Democratic Supervision in Secondary Schools*. Boston: Houghton Mifflin Company, 1953.

Bonner, Hubert. *Group Dynamics: Principles and Practices*. New York: The Ronald Press Company, 1959.

Borden, Richard D. *Public Speaking as Listeners Like It!* New York: Harper and Brothers, 1935.

Bradfield, Luther E. *Supervision for Modern Elementary Schools*. Columbus, Ohio: Charles E. Merrill Books, Inc., 1964.

Campbell, Clyde M. *Practical Applications of Democratic Administration*. New York: Harper and Row, Publishers, Inc., 1952.

Cartwright, Dorwin, and Alvin Zander. *Group Dynamics: Research and Theory*. White Plains, New York: Row, Peterson and Company, 1953.

Chase, Stuart. *Roads to Agreement*. New York: Harper and Brothers, 1951.

Clement, J. A., and J. H. Clement. *Cooperative Supervision in Grades Seven to Twelve*. New York: The Century Company, 1930.

Collins, Barry E., and Harold Guetzkow. *A Social Psychology of Group Processes for Decision Making*. New York: John Wiley & Sons, Inc., 1964.

Corbally, J. E., T. J. Jenson, and F. W. Staub. *Educational Administration: The Secondary School*. Boston: Allyn and Bacon, Inc., 1961.

Ewing, Russell H. *The Leadership Functions of Executives and Managers: An Evaluation of Current Leadership Theory and Practice*. Beverly Hills, California: National Institute of Leadership, 1962.

Fiedler, Fred E., and Martin M. Chemers. *Leadership and Effective Management*. Glenview, Illinois: Scott, Foresman and Co., 1974.

Frey, Sherman H., and Keith R. Getschman. *School Administration: Selected Readings*. New York: Thomas Y. Crowell Company, 1969.

Gordon, Thomas. *Group Centered Leadership*. Boston: Houghton Mifflin Company, 1955.

Gorton, Richard A. *Conflict, Controversy and Crisis in School Administration Supervision: Issues, Cases and Concepts for the 70's*. Dubuque, Iowa: Wm. C. Brown, 1972.

Gwynn, J. Minor. *Theory and Practice of Supervision*. New York: Dodd, Mead & Company, 1961.

McCloskey, Gordon. *Education and Public Understanding*. New York: Harper & Row, 1967.

McGregor, Douglas. *Human Side of Enterprise.* New York: McGraw-Hill Co., 1960.
————. *The Professional Manager.* New York: McGraw-Hill Co., 1967.
Maslow, Abraham H. *Eupsychian Management.* Homewood, Illinois: Richard D. Irwin Inc., 1965.
Mier, Harry, and Joan Mier. *If the Shoe Fits.* Beverly Hills, California: Merit Publishers, 1967.
Riesman, David. *The Lonely Crowd.* New Haven: Yale University Press, 1950.
Ryan, Doris W. et al. *The Individualized System: Administration and Leadership.* (H. S. I. Studies) Toronto: The Ontario Institute for Studies in Education, 1974.
Saunders, Robert L., et al. *A Theory of Educational Leadership.* Columbus: Merrill Books, Inc., 1966.
Sigband, Norman B. *Communication for Management and Business.* 2nd ed. Glenview, Illinois: Scott, Foresman and Company, 1976.
Smith, B. Othanel, William O. Stanley, and J. Harlan Shores. *Fundamentals of Curriculum Development.* New York: The World Book Company, 1960.
Spriegel, William R., Edward Shulz, and William B. Spriegel. *Elements of Supervision.* New York: John Wiley & Sons, Inc., 1966.
Stinnett, Timothy M. *Turmoil in Teaching.* New York: The Macmillan Co., 1968.
Stoops, Emery, and Russell E. Johnson. *Elementary School Administration.* New York: McGraw-Hill Book Company, 1967.
Tead, Ordway. *The Art of Administration.* New York: McGraw-Hill Book Company, 1951.
Toffler, Alvin. *Future Shock.* New York: Random House, Inc., 1970. (Paperback, Bantam, 1971).
Townsend, Robert. *Up the Organization.* New York: Alfred A. Knopf, Inc., 1970.
Zaleznik, A. *The Human Dilemmas of Leadership.* New York: Harper & Row, 1966.

Periodicals

Philippi, Harlan A., and Jack R. Childress. "The School Administrator and Organizational Groupings." *The Clearing House* XLII (September 1967):54–56.
Sargent, Edward H., Jr. "Ground Rules for Group Process." *Adult Leadership* XV (October 1966): 122, 145.
Singer, Laura J. "The Development and Use of Teaching Materials for the Training of Discussion Leaders." *The Family Coordinator* XVIII (October 1969): 318–321.

Films

Avoiding Communication Breakdown. BNA Films. (A Division of the Bureau of National Affairs, Inc., 5615 Fishers Lane, Rockville, Maryland 20852), 1975. This film discusses some causes of communication breakdown and how they can be predicted and corrected. A dramatization of how a key account is lost points out that communication breakdown costs money, affects employee morale, and results in lost sales. Dr. David Berlo points out some warning signals and how they can be used to avoid breakdown.

Changing Attitudes Through Communication. BNA Films, 1975. Some insights into human behavior in the face of change are given to show why people behave as they do—when and how and why they accept or reject attempts at persuasion. Rejection, distortion, and avoidance must be anticipated and corrected through effective communication.

Communicating Management's Point of View. BNA Films, 1975. Changing people's beliefs and attitudes and behavior. Demonstrates the principal ingredients of effective persuasion: empathy and credibility.

Communication Feedback. BNA Films, 1975. Dramatizations show nonuse and misuse of feedback: a typical staff-confused secretary, a resentful employee. Effective communication means getting results by affecting behavior; it is impossible when feedback is ignored, distorted, avoided or not perceived.

Confronting Conflict. BNA Films, 1976. Team building, group dynamics, group communication processes, conflict, cooperation, male-female relationships in the work setting, the woman executive, leadership style. (28 minutes)

Coping with Change. Bureau of National Affairs Films, 1969. Prof. Gordon Lippitt, George Washington University, describes how to prepare for and bring about planned change, and discusses several factors that cause people to resist change. (25 minutes)

Delegating Work. McGraw-Hill Films, 1959. Shows how a supervisor's failure to delegate work properly can have serious effects on the efficiency of his workers. (9 minutes)

Enforcing Rules and Procedures. McGraw-Hill Films, 1959. A case study. (9 minutes)

Effective Leadership. Educational Media Center, University of California, Berkeley, 1968. Dr. Robert Tannenbaum, behavioral scientist, lectures on the characteristics of effective leadership. Relationships that threaten or embarrass us, or that create hostility or anxiety due to misunderstanding have to be met by effective responses. An effective leader must have "social sensitivity," which comes through trying to understand how another person views his/her problems. An effective leader must also possess "action flexibility," the ability to behave appropriately in response to one's perceptions, and to communicate that response to another. The only tool an individual can use in a leadership role is oneself. Dr. Tannenbaum concludes that considerable personal learning and development is the principle way to truly effective leadership. (32 minutes)

The Goya Effect. Roundtable Films, 1975. Encourages supervisors to be aware of the needs of their subordinates.

Human Considerations in Management. University of California Extension Media Center, Berkeley, California, 1969. A lively and spontaneous lecture stressing the simple but often neglected fact that managers are human beings. Prof. Abraham Kaplan, University of Michigan, pinpoints the problems of morale, productivity, and turnover that cannot be negotiated, contracted, or manipulated. He suggests that managers, as well as their employees, hide behind conventional patterns of behavior that alienate others and actually interfere with the goals of management. When people break through depersonalized responses and express their true feelings, even if these feelings are frustration or irritation, the result can be a welcome relief and may clear the air for future cooperation. (29 minutes)

Human Nature and Organizational Realities. BNA Films, 1977. Employee apathy and lack of effort may be reactions by normal people to an unhealthy environment created by management. This film describes how interpersonal relations may be improved. (28 minutes)

Individuality and Teamwork. Bureau of National Affairs Films, 1969. Prof. Gordon Lippitt describes needs of individual and group in a teamwork situation, and discusses eight considerations in determining how well groups work together. (25 minutes)

Introduction to Change. Thompson-Mitchell, Atlanta, Georgia, 1974. A set of three sound filmstrips.

Making Human Resources Productive. BNA Films, 1976. Job enrichment, climate, trust, motivation, feedback, and performance.

Management by Participation. BNA Films, 1976. Treats issues such as organizational climate, leadership style, participation vs. "permissiveness," group involvement in problem solving, and altering managerial and employee attitudes toward new management practices.

Pay for Performance. BNA Films, 1976. Pay practices, performance appraisal, goal setting, motivation, and morale.

Personality Conflict. McGraw-Hill Films, 1960. An older but excellent film designed to stimulate discussion on adjustments that supervisors must make when two conflicting personalities have to work together. (7 minutes)

Productivity and the Self-Fulfilling Prophecy: the Pygmalion Effect. CRM, 1975. Shows how supervisors affect employee morale and performance.

Team Building. Bureau of National Affairs Films, 1975. Conflict and cooperation, group communication, interpersonal relations.

Audio Cassettes

Guide to Better People Management. Seminars in Sound (Nation's Business, 1615 H Street, N.W. Washington, D.C. 20006), 1975. Dramatizes a variety of "people problems" and how they are solved. Topics include spotting potential leaders, settling interoffice conflicts, and the best ways for handling the delicate details of dismissal.

Make the Most of Your Time. Seminars in Sound, 1975. Helps capture wasted hours. Suggested techniques aim at turning wasted hours into productive effort so the supervisor truly can control his time, with a less harried approach as the welcome result.

Mastering the Art of Delegating. Seminars in Sound, 1975. This taped seminar offers successful methods in the art of delegating responsibility. Includes case studies.

Your Role as a Decision Maker. Seminars in Sound, 1975. Sheds new light on the important decision-making function as it affects the supervisor. Both personal and psychological effects are reported. Techniques used by experienced supervisors in evaluating data and minimizing risks are discussed.

Other Sources

Association for Supervision and Curriculum Development. *Group Planning in Education.* Washington, D.C.: The Association, 1945.

————. *Group Processes and Supervision.* Washington, D.C.: The Association, 1948.

————. *Leadership for Improving Instruction.* Washington, D.C.: National Education Association, 1960.

Beckley, J., and R. Baldwin. *The Human Side—A Fine Art.* Bulletin No. 229. New London, Conn.: National Foremen's Institute, 1960.

————. *The Human Side—Step by Step.* Bulletin No. 302. New London, Conn.: National Foremen's Institute, 1960.

Benne, Kenneth D. et al. *Role-Playing and Discussion Method.* Washington, D.C.: National Education Association, 1950.

Calvert, Leonard, and Myron S. Olson. *Secondary Education: A Resource Syllabus.* Los Angeles: University of Southern California, 1965.

Campbell, Clifford W. *The Elementary School Principal as Viewed by His Staff and Parent-Teacher Association Presidents.* An Unpublished Dissertation. Los Angeles: University of Southern California, 1964.

Grambs, Jean D. *Group Processes in Intergroup Education.* New York: National Conference of Christians and Jews [n.d.].

Marks, James R. "An Analysis of Assignment Specifications for Certificated School Personnel in the United States." Doctoral dissertation. University of Southern California, 1962.

Taba, Hilda, and Deborah Elkins. *With Focus on Human Relations.* Washington, D.C.: American Council on Education, 1950.

Implementing the Supervisory Program

6

How to Promote
Staff Development
and Handle
Some Special Problems

The rapidly changing scene in the instructional program is a challenge to instructional leadership in our school systems. It must be met with increased skills and understandings through professional growth.

The competency with which the principal, through skill in leadership, inspires teachers to participate in group and individual programs for professional growth will be reflected in the operational efficiency success of the instructional program.

This chapter includes a discussion of the following topics:

How to develop programs for instructional development and staff development
Principles of the program for in-service education
Individual endeavors for in-service education
How to help the beginning teacher
How to improve orientation meetings for the beginning teacher
How to help the superior teacher
How to help the senior teacher
How to work with the dissenting teacher
How to work with the "undemocratic" staff member
How to use group problem-solving techniques in supervision
Behavioral guidelines for working in groups
Do—Don't
Trends
"In-Basket" supervisory problems
Questions and suggested activities

How to Develop Programs for Instructional
Development and Staff Development

Staff development focuses on the staff. It attempts to provide the means for the total staff to meet the students' needs—the academic, personal, social, intellectual, and career objectives that are perceived as essential to the goals of students and society.

Instructional development concentrates more narrowly on the objectives concerned with curriculum and instruction. Its objectives include developing a more effective, systematic way of providing efficient meaningful, effective instruction based on clearly specified objectives.

Although these two programs may take different approaches, they are both strongly linked to improving instruction. Staff development is the comprehensive program that provides for improvement in organizational structures, instructional processes, and personal attitudes toward helping the total staff— teachers, administrators, clerical, custodial, and others—better meet students' needs. Staff improvement usually includes such strategies as preservice selection and orientation, and many in-service education programs.

Instructional development is the systematic use of objective and empirical methods to design, develop, and implement curricular and instructional programs and experiences in order to reach specified instructional objectives. It answers three questions:

1. What should the learner know or feel or be able to do and how well? (Instructional objective)
2. How can the student reach the instructional objective? (Strategies + media + programs + experiences)
3. How will we know when the student has achieved the objective(s)? (Evaluation)[1]

Staff development and instructional development begin with a need to solve curricular and instructional problems.

How to Stimulate Faculty to be Involved in Instructional Development

No matter how forward looking a supervising principal may be, he/she cannot suddenly institute and activate an instructional development system. A careful study must be made to determine the best strategies for change. If the institution is new and has adequate financial resources available for development, an assault on the media problem might be most beneficial. That is, an approach could be designed into the educational and architectual plans, with administrators and faculty being hired specifically to work in this area.

In established institutions, where established faculties and staffs tend to be more set in their ways, other strategies must be used. The broken-front approach is most likely to succeed. It requires that the supervisor seek out individuals who appear receptive to change, encourage them to innovate, provide them

[1] Based on materials developed in part at the De Anza Workshop on Staff and Instructional Development, Squaw Valley, California, 1975.

with release time from normal assignments, and protect them from the jealousies and objections of their fellows.

A systems approach to problem solving can be applied to developing specific solutions to staff and instructional development problems. A systems approach is outlined below.

PHASE I.   *Build a Relationship with the Client(s)*
Establish communication links, develop empathy, and develop dialogue. Communicate!

PHASE II.   *Needs Assessment*
A needs assessment determines the difference between the knowledge, skills, and attitudes required and those that presently exist

A.   *Needs Assessment Objectives*
After completing the needs assessment, the supervisor should know how to meet the need—by changing the environment, by increasing motivation, and/or by education.

B.   *Needs Assessment Procedure*
1.   Identify the educational needs or problems. What gap exists between present knowledge, skills, and attitudes and those required at a base-line mastery level? These discrepancies are grouped and synthesized, and the needs further clarified.
2.   Identify the audience and environment and real-world constraints.
3.   State goals (broad, long-range).
4.   Specify management tasks needed for this phase, such as budget, housing, resources, staffing, clerical support, equipment, and media.
5.   Note procedures for collecting additional information about the staff's present knowledge, skills, and attitudes. Consider such techniques as hiring an outside consultant, interviews, open-ended, and questionnaires.
6.   Identify and record the specific *staff development needs.* Use behavioral or performance terms. Label each need listed as being met by changing the work environment (e), increasing motivation (m), an instructional program (i), or combinations of any or all three.
7.   Determine which needs can be met through means other than education.
8.   Record or code the needs to be handled in other ways.

PHASE III.   *Strategies and Media Development—The Action Phase*
Once objectives have been determined, the supervisor analyzes each objective to determine the primary type of learning specified, what instructional strategy is necessary, and what media is to be used.

A.   *Objectives for Strategies and Media Development*
After completing this phase, the supervisor will have identified three methods for accomplishing the objectives specified in the needs assessment phase. The supervisor will:

1. List the resources needed for objectives that can be accomplished through *individualized or self-directed study*.
2. Determine alternative methods for accomplishing objectives that require *interaction*.
3. Identify and select strategies and media that are readily available for instructional and staff development.

B. *Procedure for Strategies and Media Development*

ELEMENT 1: *Strategies for individualized, self-directed study.*

    a. List objectives that could be accomplished by providing resources such as books, programmed instruction, attending conferences, coordinated instructional systems, and other individualized (self-instruction) forms of media. Define objectives by listing terminal behavior(s) first.

    b. Prepare criterion (evaluation) measures and the level of mastery required.

    c. State strategies necessary to reach the objective(s).

    d. List the resources that need to be provided for each objective. (The reader may wish to see chapter 11 on Instructional Technology.)

    e. If the problem is to be solved at least partially through a *coordinated instructional system,* refer to the appropriate sections on "Coordinated Instructional Systems" and on "Individualized Instruction" in chapter 10 "How to Measure Effectiveness, Improve Methods and Techniques of Instruction." Be sure to include: an introduction; descriptive objectives; study resources and related directions that *really* direct; practice items and related directions; a discussion of the practice items (feedback); a self-test and discussion; and a study unit post test.

    f. Specify (again) and acquire resources needed.

    g. Gain acceptance for the tentative program.

ELEMENT 2: *Strategies involving interaction, problem solving, games, simulations, etc.*

    a. List the objectives that require *interaction* —those that would *not* be handled through individualized, self-directed study.

    b. Suggest alternatives for accomplishing each objective. Consider instructional games, staff self-awareness seminars, group retreats, simulations, lectures, and gaming. (Scan chapter 11.) Star the strategy(ies) considered optimal.

ELEMENT 3:   *Identify and select required resources that are readily available.*

Note coordination/management functions, strategies and media that must be developed. List the additional resources necessary to accomplish the strategies, such as budget personnel, facilities, and equipment.

PHASE IV.   Evaluation

Gronlund[2] noted that evaluation is the systematic process for determining the extent or degree to which the target population achieves its stated instructional objectives. Evaluation implies both qualitative and quantitative measures of learner behavior as well as value judgments relating to the desirability of the specified behavior.

In instructional or staff development, there are two major purposes for evaluation:

1. To determine if the learner (staff member or student) did achieve the criterion measure stated in the instructional objective, and

2. To determine the *validity* of the instructional strategy and its components; that is, to ascertain the extent to which the strategy accomplished what it was designed to accomplish: to improve learning and/or teaching and/or performance.

The key principle in designing an appropriate evaluation program is that the evaluation measures must test the same performance or behaviors that were specified as objectives. Thus, if one wants a learner to *demonstrate* a skill or to *construct* a model, evaluation measures must reflect and be congruent with these anticipated outcomes (competencies).

A. As the first step in the *validation* of instructional modules, state evaluation techniques (tests—informal and formal, oral, written, performance, speed, power; interviews, rating scales, and questionnaires; observation techniques and anecdotal records).

B. Read each instructional objective, and for each one ask:

1. To what *questions* do I want the learner to be able to respond, and how well?

2. What *problems* do I want the learner to be able to solve, and how well?

3. What *actions* or *tasks* do I want the learner to be able to perform, and how well?

C. Construct or select available evaluation instruments that effectively appraise the specified learning outcomes.

[2] Norman E. Gronlund, *Measurement and Evaluation in Teaching,* (New York: Macmillan, 1965), p. 6.

    D. Assess the extent to which the program accurately does what it is supposed to do (validity) through a *pilot* or *prototype program.*

        1. Construct the prototype program. In this step, the program's essential elements are initially analyzed to ensure that all key components are present and fit into the program.

        2. Conduct the prototype program. Field test for validity.

        3. Obtain self-evaluation and practice exercise responses from the learners.

        4. Have learners identify difficult, ambiguous, confusing, or inadequate instructions or activities and whether rapid and effective feedback (knowledge of results) were provided.

        5. Ask learners to comment on the use, interest, and value of the program.

        6. Get comments during field tryouts from objective observers!

    E. Organize, analyze, and summarize.

    The result of the tryout is identifying possible changes to make in the original program in order to make the program (or program element) do what it was supposed to do—that is, to help most learners effectively accomplish a set of specified program objectives.

PHASE V. *Program Revision*

    A. Review the prototype evaluation summary. How well did learners perform? What problems surfaced during the tryout? Base revisions on legitimate inferences from pilot study field test data. Plan for an outside observer to assess the tryout data and to offer revision recommendations. Program revisions must be made from criterion data taken from program objectives. Therefore, evaluate end results in terms of whether performance on the criteria measures has been achieved.

    B. If stated objectives are not achieved, re-examine the instructional (or staff development) program and modify it—add or delete strategies and activities, check sequence, assess whether feedback and motivation are maintained, etc.

    C. Redesign/modify the program to elevate learner performance.

    D. Implement the redesigned program for staff or instructional development. Provide for continuous trial re-evaluation and redesign. In other words, stabilize the change and generate self-renewal.

    Successful staff and instructional development will occur only as a result of concentrated, organized team effort to solve specific problems—to reach clearly specified objectives. The focus must be on the potential learner and/or the individual(s) who will use the program, rather than on the system or process itself. In this process, the supervisor should serve as a catalyst, a process helper, a resource person, a solutions giver, an enabler, and a facilitator. (The supervisor should refer to Appendix C for a Staff Development Processing Check Sheet.)

Principles of the Program for In-Service Education

In-service education includes all activities of school personnel that contribute to their continued professional growth and competence. The following may be considered as a set of basic principles:

1. The in-service education program emerges from recognized needs of the school and community.
2. All school personnel need in-service education.
3. Proper supervision is an effective means of accelerating the in-service professional growth of personnel.
4. Improving the quality of instruction is the immediate and long-range objective of in-service education.
5. In-service education leads to a continuous process of re-examination and revision of the educational program. Additionally, it encourages participants to attain self-realization through competence, accomplishment, and security.
6. In-service education has become an increasing concern of state agencies, colleges and universities, school boards, school administrators, and teachers.
7. Supervisors should create an atmosphere that will stimulate a desire on the part of teachers for in-service growth.
8. The in-service program should keep personnel abreast of research and advances in education.
9. An in-service education program is most effective when cooperatively initiated and planned.

The in-service program is one in which both supervisors and teachers grow in improving the learning situation of children. According to H. Spears,[3] certain principles of the in-service program have become apparent:

1. The professional education of the teacher does not cease as he leaves college.
2. Professional development cannot be adequately served by teaching experience alone.
3. Although it is reasonable to expect a teacher to guide his own future development, it is the obligation of the school system to stimulate advancement by providing opportunities for in-service growth. These opportunities, properly planned and coordinated, constitute the in-service education program of the school system.

[3] Harold Spears, *Curriculum Planning through In-Service Programs* (Englewood Cliffs, New Jersey: Prentice-Hall, Inc., 1957), p. 315.

4. The provision of staff leadership for this program is a legitimate school expenditure.
5. The test of the in-service program lies in its consequences in instruction and student development.

As this text has stated, the basic functions of supervision are instructional and staff development. Conversely, improving instruction and the instructional program constitute goals of supervision, with the principal helping the teacher perform more effectively and efficiently. The means used to realize these goals constitute a program of in-service education.

Many clues can help ascertain what type of in-service education is needed. One clue might come from the supervising principal's evaluation of the staff; another clue might come from faculty experiences (and competencies) in curriculum development; and still another might come from ever-changing community needs and problems.

How to Plan for Supervision

Planning is the most essential factor for effective leadership in a supervisory program. Planning for supervision must provide for: (1) adequate budgeting of the supervising principal's day so that he/she can spend the most time on supervision, (2) determining the methods and techniques that will insure the effective use of available time, and (3) constructing adequate schedules and definite plans so that available time can be used efficiently.

Care and skill in continuous, comprehensive, flexible, and cooperative planning are the keys to effective instructional improvement. Without planning, a constructive and comprehensive program cannot be developed.

Even though all plans must be considered as tentative, both long- and short-term planning are required. Short-term plans emphasize but one or two major goals. Planning must be creative, for each school system, school, classroom, teacher, and class offers unique circumstances, capabilities, and personalities. Applying the techniques of supervision, then, is not merely a mechanical procedure.

Most Beneficial Techniques

According to the *Twelfth Yearbook* of the Department of Supervisors and Directors of Instruction,[4] supervision is planning for all-around improvement of school factors that seem to affect seriously the teacher-learning process, especially the school building and its equipment, the materials of instruction, the organization and management of the school, the curriculum, the methods of teaching, and the

[4] Department of Supervisors and Directors of Instruction, *Newer Instructional Practices of Promise*, Twelfth Yearbook (Washington, D.C.: National Education Association, 1940), pp. 328–349.

personality of the teacher. The Department reported that most beneficial techniques for supervision include:

1. *Faculty meetings.* These faculty meetings include curriculum meetings, institutes, workshops, study groups and clubs, excursions, travel, seminars, committee work, curriculum revision, experimentation, and research.

   A faculty meeting offers many opportunities in a program of in-service education because usually it is the major means of communication within a school. Despite its many advantages, evidence indicates that these meetings usually are not popular with the teachers. If properly planned and executed, staff meetings can create an atmosphere of working relationships and improve the quality of education within the school.

2. *Supervisory visits.* Visits generally should be followed by conferences. The supervisor should study the total learning situation, giving attention to all factors that affect student growth.

3. *Professional bulletins.* Unfortunately, most professional bulletins are prepared by people engaged in supervision. If they were teacher-prepared, they might have more meaning. These bulletins constitute effective communication media and may include announcements, summaries of research, analyses of presentations at professional association meetings, acknowledgments, and developments in the various subject matter fields.

4. *Professional libraries.* A convenient source of information is the school professional library. Teacher contributions could become a part of this repository of information. The professional library provides not only a source of information, but also is an incentive for personal satisfaction. Books on the professional point of view, plays, newer supplementary readers, and many professional periodicals should be available to all teachers.

5. *Materials center or curriculum laboratories.* Curriculum laboratories supply instructional guides, sample materials of instructional technology, and textbooks.

Additional methods used in supervision include:

1. *Teacher assignment.* For optimum success, the assignment of a particular teacher to a certain class, grade level, and subject should be determined on the basis of staff needs, training, experience, personality, and the desire of the teacher. Anything the principal does to make the teacher more secure will improve the teacher's results with the students.

2. *Demonstration teaching.* Demonstration teaching is a valuable technique. Prepared plans, printed in advance, emphasizing important points or the value of certain teaching techniques, are helpful. A conference following the demonstration may clarify many points. An analysis of the observation is necessary.

3. *Curriculum development.* Curriculum planning offers an excellent opportunity for staff participation. It is up to the principal to create the interest and desire for this important and continuous work.

4. *Development of instructional guides.* This enterprise explores and lists suggestions aimed at helping the teacher in instructional planning. Unfortu-

nately, in many schools teachers are given little opportunity for assisting in determining the objectives of instruction, the subject matter content, or in selecting instructional materials including textbooks. Since the democratic movement, more teachers are encouraged to participate in cooperative curriculum development.

5. *Excursions.* Trips to the community and local industries are excellent methods of education, especially in the teacher-student relationship.
6. *Workshops and institutes.* Workshops provide for group cooperation, for pooling ideas, for discussing mutual or specific problems, and for personal and professional growth in the various subject matter areas. (Specific suggestions concerning workshops and institutes appear later in this chapter.)
7. *Intervisitation of classes.* Studies reveal that intervisitation is quite popular and effective. These visits usually are planned on the teacher's request. This technique is more effective when a careful analysis follows each observation.
8. *Professional reading.* Professional reading is widely encouraged by specialists. Teachers should be urged to read on various topics, by many authors, and not restrict themselves to a particular author.
9. *School-community survey.* A comprehensive study of the community will help the teacher and the supervising principal understand more clearly the type of program that will meet the needs and interests of the students.

There is no single method. The first problem is to determine needs. Then the problem is to determine how the teachers can be helped. There are many techniques, and those selected should contribute in a marked degree to a particular aim or objective.

Barr, Barton, and Brueckner referred to all methods of supervision as "subsidiary techniques in improvement programs."[5] This appears to be an appropriate phrase, since any method used to promote teacher growth is subsidiary to the basic objective—student growth and development. Under separate classifications, they have listed some devices for personnel growth and improvement in the educational program, as follows:

I. *Group Devices*
   A. *Doing Techniques*
      1. Workshops
      2. Committees
   B. *Verbal Techniques*
      1. Staff Meetings
      2. Group Counseling
      3. Course Work
      4. Documentary Aids
      5. Directed Reading
   C. *Observational Techniques*
      1. Directed Observation
      2. Field Trips

[5] A. S. Barr, W. S. Burton, and L. J. Brueckner, *Supervision* (New York: Appleton-Century-Crofts, 1938), chapters I and IV.

      3. Travel Seminars
      4. Audio-Visual Aids
II. *Individual Devices*
  A. *Active Techniques*
      1. Participation in the total teaching act
      2. Individual problem-solving
  B. *Verbal Techniques*
      1. Individual conferences
      2. Adjustment counseling
  C. *Observational Techniques*
      1. Directed observation
      2. Intervisitation[6]

Other effective techniques include experimental studies, study of tests and measurements, research, and use of the professional library and learning or instructional center.

The Specialists Agree

Specialists are in general agreement that staff relations based on democratic leadership provide the key to successful attainment of supervisory objectives. There is some general agreement on many techniques and methods used in instructional improvement, but many leading specialists do not agree on the degree of effectiveness of certain techniques.

Planning appears to be the most essential factor for effective leadership in a supervisory program. It is agreed that planning must have these three factors present:

1. It cannot be standardized.
2. It must be comprehensive.
3. It must be flexible.

Specialists tend to agree that an effective program needs the full cooperation of staff, teachers, and resource persons, and that selection of method depends on many variables and is a function of need.

Individual Endeavors for In-Service Education

One objective of supervision is to achieve self-directed growth. C. T. McNerney[7] said that teacher improvement can be achieved only through teacher effort.

---

[6] Ibid., p. 465.

[7] Chester T. McNerney, *Educational Supervision* (New York: McGraw-Hill Book Company, Inc., 1951), p. 297.

The individual teacher initiates growth in professional competency in many ways. The principal can help by securing annotated bibliographies to facilitate professional and general reading. Some teachers, under pressure of time from different sources, would rather investigate at their convenience areas in which a need is felt. Periodicals, particularly, help the supervisor and the teacher keep abreast of immediate thinking in curriculum improvement, pointing out changing ideas and giving food for thought.

The supervising principal can suggest further graduate courses. Here he/she can stimulate the teacher by noting that the product of additional learning would benefit the entire school. Recent research and theory, brought out in the university class, could be reported to the faculty.

Conference Attendance and Experimental Research Programs

Principals should encourage teachers to attend conferences on trends in education, curriculum development, subject matter, or any programs that may help the teacher to grow in service. Some teachers work in experimental programs, discovering new ideas or exploring the possibilities of untried projects.

Professional Writing

Professional writing is another way for individuals to share valuable experiences or new ideas with other teachers. Since each person contributes to the growth of the profession and to his/her personal development in a unique manner, writing creates an outlet for talents that may stimulate other educators to respond. The supervising principal must encourage and assist the writer in any manner possible.

How to Help the Beginning Teacher

The teachers most in need of help, and the ones who should profit most by the help given, are the beginning teachers. A principal often fails to appreciate the difficulties that a beginning teacher encounters. For many reasons, the beginning teacher may experience difficulties before the principal realizes that a problem exists. A beginning teacher, with little experience in the profession, soon finds that adjustment to the school society, administration, and supervision is not easy. The orientation of the beginning teacher must be thorough and constructive. At the start, a new teacher should not be given extra responsibilities, such as work on committees.

Greeting the Beginning Teacher

A hearty welcome to the beginning teacher by the principal and encouraging words by the "old timers" on the staff may alleviate the difficulties of integrating into the faculty. Teachers' suggestions often are more effective and acceptable to the beginning teacher than is the principal's help, for the teacher may feel too uncomfortable to be frank with the principal. When the beginning teacher feels more at home in the new environment, he/she should be encouraged to visit, voluntarily, an experienced colleague's room for observation purposes.

Specialists agree that no matter how well trained the new teachers are, they still need supervision and in-service education. E. H. Reeder explained:

> The problem of harmonizing theory and practice in a highly complicated and creative activity like teaching is a confusing and difficult one, not likely to be solved by individuals working alone.[8]

Growth in teaching ability is not assured merely by obtaining experience. There must be evaluation and in-service education. Barr and Burton, writing in their classic work on supervision, stated:

> There is no teacher at present, nor is there likely to be for a long time any teacher who is so expert and so well trained that . . . [he/she] cannot profit by some of the improvement devices.[9]

Supervision has a responsibility toward helping the beginning teacher, who is entitled to all the assistance necessary to do a good job. This help should be given as the teacher's needs arise, and in a way that will benefit him most. The supervising principal must remember to acquaint the beginning teacher with the breadth of supervisory services available.

Parent-Teacher-School Relationships

The beginning teacher should understand the basic factors of the parent-teacher relationship. Teachers frequently feel that parents exercise undue and unnecessary control over school activities, whereas parents often view teachers as different from other human beings. Teachers without children of their own may not understand the perspective with which most parents view their own children; parents, however, measure the value of their child's school program against what they remember of the one they followed as children.

[8] Edwin H. Reeder, *Supervision in the Elementary School* (Boston: Houghton Mifflin Company, 1953), p. 270.

[9] A. S. Barr et al., *Supervision, Democratic Leadership in the Improvement of Learning* (New York: D. Appleton-Century Company, 1947), p. 415.

Successful parent-teacher relations are based on empathy, understanding, and acceptance. Differences should be welded into an approach based on the student's welfare. Seldom is any conflict caused by one side being interested in the student and the other being indifferent. Problems usually arise from disagreement concerning what is the best approach to aiding the student, rather than over the extent of interest the teacher or parent has in the student's welfare.

The principal should encourage the beginning teacher to observe the following points in conducting parent-teacher conferences:

1. Be a good listener.
2. Remember empathy. Say, "I certainly can understand why you would be upset."
3. Be sincere. Do not use vocabulary with which the parent is unfamiliar.
4. Be honest, yet be diplomatic.
5. Do not discuss other teachers, departments, or students.
6. Let the solution to a problem be "our" solution.

A teacher should not encourage a parent to ask questions regarding specific teaching techniques. The parent should be welcomed as an observer. Neither a teacher nor a supervising principal should try to teach a parent in a fifteen-minute conference what it took five or more years of higher education plus experience to learn. Suggest that the parent may visit the classroom. Such observations probably should be delimited to a maximum of twenty minutes.

A more complete discussion of parent-teacher conferences is included in chapter 12.

How Students View the Beginning Teacher and Student Relations

The beginning teacher may profit from the following students' comments, gathered by E. Stoops and A. R. Evans,[10] in an effort to gain and maintain student respect:

1. The teacher should keep the class in a studious attitude.
2. The teacher should be someone who has his heart in the work. He/she should not be someone who is doing it just to have some income.
3. Beginning teachers should joke—not all the time, but once or twice in the lesson. They should look happy and smile!
4. Teachers should be neat and clean.
5. Someone who keeps order, so as to have the attention of the whole class when he/she wants it, and who is consistent, will be respected.

[10] Emery Stoops and Albert R. Evans, "Helping the Beginning Teacher," *The Nation's Schools* LVII (April 1956): 74.

6. The teacher should make the subject interesting.
7. The students want a teacher to say frankly, "I don't know, but I'll find out."

How to Help Beginning Teachers with Classroom Control Problems

The beginning teacher usually encounters his/her first trouble with classroom control or "discipline." The principal's job is not to do the disciplining, but rather to analyze the difficulty and to tell the teacher why the methods and techniques used have failed. The principal should point out better methods and bolster the teacher's courage by showing confidence in his/her ability ultimately to pull through.

Helpful forms, such as the one included as Figure 6-1, should be available to the beginning teacher.

The supervising principal, in a conference with the beginning teacher, should stress the following points:

1. Know each individual student through the cumulative card and health card. Have the student sit where he/she can see and hear. Determine the general socioeconomic background by taking a drive around the community. Study the general characteristics of the community and of the age group.
2. Maintain a neat room environment. Provide furniture of the right height, proper ventilation and lighting, and attempt to arrange the room so students can move around without disturbing one another. Bulletin boards should be on the eye level of students, properly grouped, with natural colors for the background. A smooth organization of routines should be planned and agreed on by teachers and students. See Figure 6-2 for a sample homework assignment plan. In the elementary school, it is helpful to have a pencil monitor sharpen pencils in the morning. Then allow no sharpening during the day unless it is an emergency. Supplies and equipment should be arranged conveniently. Even the simplest organization of routine activities pays off.
3. Plan for the group, but consider the individual. Keep the lesson length within the attention span of the group and provide maximum opportunity for student participation. The lesson should be interesting, varied, challenging, and presented with confidence.
4. Be prepared by having all necessary materials on hand. Anticipate routine needs, including passing and collecting materials. Anticipate clean up.
5. When teaching a lesson, stimulate, provide variety, use different methods of presentation, be sure each student knows what to do, allow time for asking and answering questions, and provide for slow learners and gifted children. Do not ask questions that could result in a chorus answer. Instead of "Did we do that?" say "Did we do that, Bill?"
6. When the need arises, students evaluate behavior and build standards through teacher guidance. It is the teacher's responsibility to see that each student adheres to the group's standards. One standard could be chosen for emphasis at the beginning of a lesson. The class could evaluate how well they did with

Name of School and Address

Date _____

Dear _____

     I wish to inform you that up to this time _____'s accomplishment in _____ has not been up to the average standard expected at this grade level.

     I shall be happy to discuss his/her work with you and to plan for its improvement.

_____   A personal conference is desirable, but is not essential at this time.

_____   An appointment has been made for our conference at _____on

                       _____

                       If this appointment is not convenient, please so indicate below, noting a more preferable time.

     Thank you for your kind attention to this matter. Please sign below and return this correspondence to school.

                       Cordially,

                       _____

                       Teacher

                       _____

                       Principal

Please sign and return

_____

Parent's Signature

FIGURE 6-1.   Form to Inform Parents of Student's Unsatisfactory Work.

reference to the standard at the end of the lesson. A sample procedure for building room standards is included as Figure 6-3.

7.   Obtain attention through a signal that says, "May I have your attention, please?" *Obtain undivided attention.* Establish the fact that the signal is given *once.* *Never* teach to inattention. Compliment those who are ready—who

Monday: History/geography/science
Tuesday and *Thursday:* Reading and spelling
Monday and *Wednesday:*   Language and mathematics

FIGURE 6-2.   Sample Elementary School Homework Assignment Schedule.

really are helping the group. Remember to speak definitely, firmly, with confidence and authority, yet softly. Give one direction at a time, clearly, using
a minimum of words. Give students an opportunity to ask legitimate questions. *Expect the best!*

A principal of a high school that incorporates grades 7 and 8 prepared the
following classroom control techniques:

1. Get a good start. Be in your room early and make preparations to start
    class activities as soon as the bell rings. Do not permit any student to
    monopolize your time at the beginning of a class. Establish a routine for roll
    taking and getting into the activities of the day. If you know what you are
    going to do, and the students know what you are going to do and what is
    expected of them, the battle is half won.
2. Teach on your feet as much as possible. Not only are you in a position to
    see and hear what goes on, but students can see and hear you better. A
    student who can only half hear what you say and who is unable to see you
    is not likely to be very attentive.
3. Change your pace. It is overly optimistic to expect a group of students to
    give complete attention to a given line of work for an hour. Plan changes
    in pace and different methods of attacking the problem at hand. A change
    is almost as good as a rest. Alternate quiet study periods with periods of
    class activity.
4. Be fair. Students are particularly sensitive to any injustice, real or imagined.
    Do not have obvious pets. Give each student a chance to gain some recog-
    nition. Marks are the paycheck that students receive from you for their
    work. Be sure the grades are fair. When a question concerning the fairness
    or accuracy of a grade arises, nothing can be lost by discussing the matter
    with the student. If there is any doubt in your mind after the discussion, no
    harm can come in giving the student the benefit of the doubt.
5. Do not harangue an entire class. It usually is fruitless. If an entire class
    seems to be in error, the trouble may be at least partly your own doing.
    If a disciplinary matter arises in which several students are involved, you
    probably will be more successful in handling them one at a time. Pick the
    most flagrant offender first, and ignore the others until you have finished
    with him/her. This procedure may take a little longer, but in the long run
    it will be worth it.
6. Reprimand in private. Do not call down a student for a minor infraction
    in front of the class. Accord him/her the courtesy of a private dressing
    down.

SAMPLE PROCEDURE

Step 1: Discuss the idea that the more people there are living together in one place, the more problems. What are some of the problems?

	Number of Rooms in Home	People (Living There)
Leo	5	3
Billy	5	2
Rose	3	4
Our room	1	31

Step 2: Through discussion and questions, have students state their contributions regarding room standards.
Write them on chalkboard.
Transfer to chart at a later date.

Step 3: "So many people living in one room leads to problems, therefore room standards are **important.**"
(Compare chart of standards from last term. Check off those no longer applicable.)

Step 4: Teacher reminds class of standard to walk quietly before dismissing.

OUR STANDARDS

(Sample Standards Chart)

1. Work harder
2. Be quieter walking in halls
3. Keep pencils where they belong
4. Take turns talking
5. Listen to the speaker
6. Be polite
7. Do not be a waster of time or supplies

FIGURE 6-3.   Building Room Standards.

7. Learn the names of your students as quickly as possible, and let them see that you have a sincere interest in their work and that you respect them as individuals even as you demand respect from them. A seating chart is indispensable.

8. Comraderie vs. familiarity. Be consistent. There is a fine distinction between comradeship with your students that breeds familiarity and that which commands respect. There is no known formula that will help you to attain the latter, but by all means avoid the former.

9. Do not threaten any action that you might not be able to carry out. It is better not to threaten at all. Act! Act with consistency. A particular type of behavior always brings the same result. Save the talk. Students understand *fair, consistent,* and *certain* action better.

10. Work for *esprit de corps.* When the class participates as a group, try to have each student feel his responsibility for the conduct of the group.

How to Use the Group Conference to
Help Beginning Teachers

SUGGESTED TOPICS FOR DISCUSSION IN THE GROUP CONFERENCE.   The following
topics are recommended for discussion in the weekly conference:

1. Becoming acquainted with the background of the children.
2. Becoming acquainted with the school and classroom routines.
3. Learning to plan (see Figure 6-4), including long-range plans for a semester and planning for shorter periods. Semester plans, weekly plans, and daily plans should be discussed.
4. *Suggestions for self-evaluation,* such as those included in Table 6-1.
5. Becoming acquainted with teaching aids, including the materials of instructional technology (such as computer-assisted learning, instructional modules including tape recordings, graphic materials, single-concept 8mm film loops, and slides), teaching machines, and programmed instruction.
6. Helping teachers to understand children.

Periods or Times	Subjects	Monday	Tuesday	Wednesday	Thursday	Friday
I						
II						
VI						
VII						
VIII						

Name _____   Dates _____

Grade _____   Received _____

(List Objectives, Pages, Assignments, Special Materials)

FIGURE 6-4.   Sample Weekly Plan Block Form.

7. Learning about the use of time in the daily program, including legal requirements.
8. Learning about reports to parents.
9. Learning about attendance accounting.
10. Learning to conduct a parent-teacher conference.
11. Learning about the ethics of the profession.
12. Discussing matters of personal effectiveness.
13. Learning about the school health program.
14. Learning about the safety program.
15. Planning to help the child who is below grade level in accomplishments, and how to plan corrective, remedial, and developmental activities.
16. Developing class organization and environment.

TABLE 6-1. *Points in Self-evaluation for the Beginning Teacher*

ITEM	COMMENTS
1. Were the preparation and organization of subject matter adequate?	
2. Were goals (objectives) clearly stated in operational terms?	
3. Was the presentation satisfactory?	
4. Were the social controls of the class satisfactory?	
5. Were the students interested? If so, how was the interest secured and maintained?	
6. Was there a maximum of participation on the part of the students?	
7. Were there valuable contributions from the class? If so, were they capitalized on? How?	
8. Were new situations utilized to the best advantage?	
9. Was student growth apparent? If so, along what lines was this growth? Was it in: Development of skills and abilities? Gain in knowledge of subject matter? Development of wholesome attitudes? Development of independent thinking?	
10. Was there student growth in terms of the teacher's objectives? To what extent?	
11. Was there self-improvement on the part of the teacher? What further needs are evident?	

How to Help the Beginning Teacher Work
with the Disturbed Child in the Classroom

The beginning teacher needs specific assistance in meeting the needs of the disturbed child and in protecting the other students from aggressive acts or other actions of an emotionally disturbed individual. At all times the rights of the group must be preserved. One child must not be permitted to keep thirty or thirty-five other children from learning effectively and efficiently. A supervising principal suggested the following three methods:

1. Releasing tension
2. Giving recognition
3. Building interest

A possible pattern for working with the emotionally disturbed child in the classroom follows:

1. Have individual talks with the student before problems arise
2. Speak directly to the child
3. Isolate him/her from the group if necessary; always give the child an opportunity to come back when ready
4. Bring him/her close to the teacher
5. Differentiate between disapproval of activity and disapproval of the child
6. Do not become so upset that you punish the whole group
7. Avoid too much talking and watch the pitch of your voice, raising it only when needed
8. Prevent problems by proper timing and rapid movement from one activity to another
9. Have private conferences with offenders
10. Use praise whenever deserved
11. Speak with firmness to insure attention but do not shock; obtain the student's undivided attention so far as possible
12. Remember: causes of poor self-control should be analyzed.

Suggestions for classroom control that the supervising principal may wish to communicate to the beginning teacher are included later in the chapter.

How to Help the Beginning Teacher Prepare
for the Beginning of the School Term

The time of decision in an educator's professional life occurs during the first two months of teaching. Serious problems should be solved by the end of this time.

The beginning teacher requires specific assistance in preparing for the initial days of this vital period—the beginning of the school term. One large city school system offered suggestions covering the following topics:

1. Before school begins:
   a) Find the answers to vital questions.
   b) Make a lesson plan for the entire day.
   c) Have instructional materials ready.
2. The first day:
   a) With the children
   b) With the parents
   c) Room organization
   d) Work habits
   e) Control
3. The first week:
   a) Find the answers to vital questions.
   b) Make a general plan for the first two weeks.

How to Improve Orientation Meetings for Beginning Teachers

There are several categories of beginning teachers who come into a school system every year: the teacher fresh from teacher training who has never taught before, the experienced teacher from another state or system, and the teacher within the school system who is changing grade levels or schools. All of these teachers will require some help from the supervising principal to acquaint them with local policies and procedures as well as help in planning for instruction.

Orientation programs are designed to welcome beginning teachers to the school and community, to help them develop professional confidence, and to help them solve both personal and professional problems. The terms "orientation" and "induction" are used synonymously.

One aim of an orientation program is to give the teacher specific information regarding the teaching assignment. Teachers should be shown around the school plant and should be given full information to acquaint them with the services available to them. Help in ordering appropriate equipment, materials, and supplies also is needed. A study completed by the American Association of School Administrators[11] warned against distributing an excessive quantity of professional publications.

K. Wiles[12] cited as good practice the scheduling or orientation or induction programs for a period of one week before school begins. The new teachers meet with their principals, discuss the educational goals of the system, and make plans. Summer workshops also help the teacher prepare for a successful start. Salary should be paid for the week's course. Conducting in-service education classes on the employee's own time following the end of a work day is at best a questionable practice.

[11] American Association of School Administrators, *Off to a Good Start* (Washington, D.C.: The Association, 1956).

[12] Wiles, *Supervision for Better Schools*, p. 225.

Most specialists who have worked with beginning teachers agree that these teachers need help in relating theories learned in teacher-training institutions to their own situations. They must learn content, methods, and procedures, and classroom routines and control. Inexperienced teachers are not always certain as to what constitutes acceptable standards of work and behavior in the various learning situations.

While he observed that in a broad sense all supervision is in-service education, J. A. Bartky[13] narrowed his definition of the latter to be teacher education that is accomplished in small groups under the direction of the supervisor, possibly with specialist-consultant help. It is coordinated with the overall supervision program.

Initial orientation meetings, which should include small group meetings of the various grade levels, are vital to success. Here teachers will learn what is expected of them and will become acquainted with the people in the field who can give them assistance and an interpretation of the instructional program.

Different programs, materials, and goals are found at each grade level. The overall philosophy of the school system, however, will remain the same. Induction meetings are held for various subject areas, thus acquainting the faculty with a background of knowledge for preparation for the first day of school.

Wiles reported:

> An explanation to new teachers of the way the program has developed enables them to understand the things that have already been attempted, the types of difficulties that have been encountered, and the compromises that have been made.[14]

Instilling confidence and courage within new teachers at the orientation meetings paves the way for greater receptivity later on. The principal helps new teachers not only to appreciate their own capabilities, but also to realize their valued contribution to the community. The principal strengthens the new teachers' long-range objectives, gives them an insight into the standards and ethics of the profession, and makes them feel proud to be members of the team.

In one school system, the preschool orientation meetings are the first of the services provided for beginning teachers. Their purpose is to orient new teachers to the school system and to assist them in initial planning for their teaching assignments. Several members of the professional staff help plan and prepare for these meetings, which are scheduled for three days during the week prior to the opening of school.

The teachers are welcomed by the superintendent, who briefly describes professional responsibilities and opportunities for advancement. The superintendent then introduces the specialist-consultants. During the remainder of the induc-

[13] John A. Bartky, *Supervision as Human Relations* (Boston: D.C. Heath and Company, 1953), p. 28.

[14] Wiles, *Supervision for Better Schools*, p. 221.

tion period, an opportunity is provided for the teachers to meet by grade level with their principal and with specialist-consultants.

The content of the group meetings is designed to give practical, specific help in the areas most needed by the new teacher. The following is a list of the activities frequently included in these meetings:

1. Suggestions for the first day of school
2. Suggestions for the first two weeks of school
3. Instructions for ordering supplementary books
4. Instructions for ordering audio-visual material
5. Suggestions for organizing classroom materials
6. An overview of the content in the various subject fields
7. Tours to see arranged classroom environments in the school adjoining the system office
8. Distribution of supervisory bulletins and curriculum publications (caution!)
9. Seeing video-tape recordings and filmstrips of teaching techniques in various subject fields
10. Suggestions for initiating units of work.

In another school system, orientation classes are scheduled approximately two weeks after the beginning of every school term for the inexperienced teachers in the school system. The classes are organized by master teachers under the direction of the specialist-consultant of the appropriate grade level. The classes are intended to provide information about materials, techniques, methods, and content in the subject fields. Classroom routines, control techniques, and individual problems are also within the scope of the classes. Meeting after school, each class consists of eight two-hour sessions, and the participants receive two points of credit applicable to advancement on the salary schedule.

Various group activities are used in the meetings: lectures relating theory and practice, discussions, workshops, role-playing, and demonstrations. The assignments for outside preparation extend the ideas gained in class for use in the classroom. Suggested techniques are tried, and materials are made and used to supplement the lessons.

During orientation, new teachers should be encouraged to request the services of the specialist-consultant, whose first duty is to the inexperienced teacher. The type of help provided depends on the individual and the situation. The specialist-consultant help through:

1. Consultation
2. Observation and conference
3. Demonstration
4. Coteaching with the teacher
5. Workshops
6. Grade-level meetings
7. Providing materials

The following recommendations for improving the program of supervision for inexperienced employees require the cooperation of the entire professional staff:

1. Positive attitudes should be developed toward supervisory assistance. Seeking such assistance indicates strength rather than weakness.
2. The principal should plan for an initial conference between the specialist-consultant and the beginning teacher during the first two weeks of the term. The first conference helps build rapport and provides the basis for future planning and cooperative action.
3. The goals of induction meetings should be delimited to meeting the immediate needs of beginning teachers. Attention to teaching procedures in each of the subject fields is more meaningful after the teacher has met his/her class and discovered needs for more specific techniques.
4. Well-constructed, brief questionnaires could be used to evaluate orientation meetings.
5. Specialist help should be provided in art and music, as well as in physical education and the academic subjects.
6. Demonstrations should be planned in connection with the orientation classes, and principals should be encouraged to release their beginning teachers to observe these demonstrations.
7. Teacher participation in the orientation classes should be encouraged. Cooperative group techniques should be developed specifically to meet the needs and interests of the teachers.
8. Provision should be made for developing the leadership potentials of all members of the professional staff. Beginning teachers who show promise of becoming outstanding educators should be encouraged to continue to work with the supervisor after the semester of orientation. They should be included in leadership classes after completing their first year of teaching.

In conclusion, many people in a school system are responsible for organizing supervisory services to teachers. The entire professional staff is concerned with helping teachers work more effectively in the classroom. Each individual plays a different role, but all are striving for the fundamental goal of a better system of education through enlightened supervision.

How to Help the Superior Teacher

While giving due attention to the beginning teachers and/or to the weak teachers, the supervising principal may tend to forget to encourage and help the superior teachers. Perhaps as a consequence of their apparent competency in teaching or supervising other school activities, the principal may consider that their abilities need no further growth. Such an idea, or unconscious negligence, may result in complacency, which could result in the creation of a static condition that would be injurious to a member of any profession.

Teaching is an on-going business and not a job to be learned once and for always.[15] Whenever new research discoveries are made and ideas are developed, a short refresher course should be given to the superior teachers along with the rest of the staff.

The experienced teacher should be used as a supervising master teacher. He/she should assist the less experienced or the beginning teacher through demonstration teaching, through supervisory conferences, and—perhaps more importantly—through friendship and through examples at informal get-togethers.

How to Help the Senior Teacher

Teachers do grow older—and they don't just fade away. Some of our best teachers are older teachers. The supervisor may feel that some of them are seeking the easiest way to complete their final years in service, or even that they may wish to prevent change through dictation on the basis of their seniority.

The supervising principal must realize that it is important to recognize and utilize the worth of each teacher, including the older teacher. It is the supervisor's responsibility to insure that the older teacher does not lose a sense of leadership and importance.

The supervising principal can help teachers who are older in service by:

1. Recalling that older teachers have information about the school that is not possessed by the beginning staff member, and such information should be put to use in solving professional problems
2. Securing the advice of the older teacher, demonstrating that the teacher is respected, but not asking for suggestions in such a manner that the supervisor or staff is placed in the position of being forced to follow the advice
3. Encouraging beginning teachers to seek the advice of the more experienced teachers on the staff
4. Considering the teacher older in service as one who can provide a feeling of continuity and tradition to the institution and to its staff
5. Giving due consideration to any problems of a physical nature in programming and scheduling.

How to Work with the Dissenting Teacher

In any school situation there will be staff members who are not in total agreement with the supervising principal; indeed, recent thinking has focused on the necessity

---

[15] Harold Spears, *The Teacher and Curriculum Planning* (Englewood Cliffs, New Jersey: Prentice-Hall, Inc., 1951), p. 83.

of divergent and conflicting (but logically derived and not ritualistic) opinions for professional growth. Such disagreement may be quite obviously on the suface or, more seriously, it may be of a repressed, sullen nature. A supervising principal in Montana reported that he had used the following techniques successfully in working with the "dissenting" teacher:

1. He was concerned with teacher growth rather than with winning his own way
2. He was not concerned that he would "lose" an argument, since the emphasis was upon development of teachers
3. At times he would suspend judgment on the point in question
4. He made it a practice never to lose his dignity in an attempt to "battle it out" with a dissenting staff member
5. He refused to permit a situation to develop to the point where winning an argument or—more specifically—winning the other person over to his point of view—became the primary goal
6. He recognized that disagreement must not be considered as a personal affront, and worked as closely with those who disagreed with his point of view as those who were most enthusiastically "with him"
7. He recognized that the teacher might be correct in his point of view, and that dissension could be healthy, since without it little fruitful discussion would take place, and problems would be handled conveniently rather than solved after adequate investigation and consideration.[16]

How to Work with the "Undemocratic" Staff Member

If the supervising principal believes that a teacher is not operating in a "democratic" manner in the classroom, or that the teacher may wish to force his/her own ideas on the faculty through undemocratic procedures, he/she should look at:

1. The in-service education program, determining whether he/she has brought to the staff teachers or specialist-consultants who stress democracy in their presentations
2. Faculty-planning sessions and discussions to determine whether democratic values have received sufficient attention
3. The procedures he/she has established for the staff meetings
4. The professional library, determining whether it contains professional journals and texts that contain subject matter related to democratic faculty and classroom procedures
5. Administrative and supervisory procedures that might violate democratic principles, and therefore provide ammunition to those who have become bitter and resentful

[16] See Wiles, *Supervision for Better Schools*, pp. 118–120; and Ross L. Neagley and N. Dean Evans, *Handbook for Effective Supervision of Instruction* (Englewood Cliffs, New Jersey: Prentice-Hall, Inc., 1951), pp. 154–159.

6. His/her relationship with the faculty association, insuring that he/she is not in reality attempting to manipulate the faculty through control of the association
7. His/her own supervisory practices—and whether he/she insists that the staff operate in a democratic manner, "or else!"

Behavioral Guidelines for Working in Groups

Much of the individual's behavior can be understood only in the context of the small group in which he/she works. Commitment to goals, acceptance of leadership, satisfaction with work, and effectiveness of performance all tend to depend on the relations of the individual with his/her immediate face-to-face coworkers.[17]

Any group, whether it be participating in a supervisory conference or in another group activity, reaches maturity when members learn to accept and trust each other; when they can communicate openly and share in decisions about the group; when they can identify their individual goals with the group's objectives; and when the governance of their behavior is based on mutual support and restraint.

Groups can be too large or too small depending on the task. The task determines whether it will be efficacious to assemble employees into groups according to their similarities or differences in ability and attitude.

Decisions are reached in groups in many ways, but it is profitable to strive for genuine consensus rather than settle for majority vote or decision by a single person. A group also will be more effective to the extent that (1) expectations of the members' roles are clear, (2) the members are cooperative rather than competitive, (3) the members are tolerant of each other, and (4) the members provide mutual feedback as a self-corrective mechanism for learning. Consider the following case taken from Bass:

> The mechanization of English coal mines destroyed the traditional face-to-face teams of two to four miners. As a supposed move toward greater efficiency, the new "longwall" method broke the operation in a series of steps—cutting, ripping, and filling—to be completed during three shifts by about 40 men. But the expected increases in productivity failed to materialize. Instead there were increases in absenteeism, turnover, sickness, and the incidence of psychosomatic disorders. Remedial action was taken. Small, stable, responsible teams were reestablished with some opportunity to set their own pace. Following this social modification there was as much as a 30 percent increase in output.[18]

[17] The authors are grateful to Bernard M. Bass, *Organizational Psychology* (Boston: Allyn and Bacon, Inc., 1965), especially chapter VI, for much of the data in this section.

[18] B. M. Bass, "Feelings of Pleasantness and Work Group Efficiency," *Personal Psychology* VII (1954): 81–91.

This case illustrates how the primary work group often determines what its members will do. Management may set quotas, but the primary work group of peers may decide whether its members will meet those or some other standards established by the group, with or without management's blessing. The extent to which the group can set and maintain standards for its members depends on its cohesiveness, which strongly influences how hard they will work and how they feel about their jobs.

Group Character and Member Performance

The character, composition, and history of a work group will strongly affect the performance and attitudes of its members.

IMPORTANCE OF GROUP EFFORT.   "A camel is a horse designed by a committee." So quip critics of group effort. But work in groups both by management and workers is as commonplace in industry as it is in education. Why? A primary reason is that modern technology usually makes it difficult for one man to assemble, organize, and digest the facts necessary to make an appropriate decision or complete an operation. An individual very often finds him/herself, as in the case of steel fabrication, forced to depend on peers, and they find they must depend on him/her in order to complete their mutual tasks successfully. In such situations, no individual has the knowledge or capability to deal with the problem alone. Thus, it is not a question of whether groups are better than individuals in problem solving and in quality of performance than individuals working alone. Rather, there are numerous working situations in which it is impossible or most inefficient for an individual to attempt to handle the problems involved alone. Supervision, at all levels, is a group effort.

Group Development

As individuals learn, so groups learn. The eventual performance of a group depends on the individual learning of its members and on how well the members learn to work with each other, how well they capitalize on the talents of their fellow group members, and how well they coordinate their efforts. A group's performance will be impaired if members are too hasty and superficial in their agreement, substituting their initial unanimity for a rational analysis of the problem they face. Performance also will be impaired if decisions are compromises to resolve conflicts to "save face," rather than if the decisions are based on a careful deliberation of the problem and a thorough exploration and evaluation of all other alternatives. Taking a quick vote before any really serious discussion has been completed often "short-circuits" formulating a high-quality solution to a problem by a group that has the resources to come to such a solution. Groups can and must learn how to use the resources their members bring to the group. Four stages have been described in the learning process for committees, discussion groups, and many kinds of work groups.

STAGES IN GROUP DEVELOPMENT.   A four-stage learning process describes the development and maintenance of typical management committees or conference groups responsible for innovation, planning, operating decisions, sharing information, or evaluating. First, members must learn to accept each other and to develop mutual confidence and trust. Only then can they proceed to communicate openly and freely and to act and react with their full resources to set and achieve desired goals at a high rate of productivity. The members move from concern about trusting each other to concern about how to communicate effectively. From there they proceed to concern about what goals to set and finally to concern about how controls shall be maintained.

FIRST STAGE: DEVELOPING MUTUAL ACCEPTANCE AND MEMBERSHIP.   Members initially are hampered by their mistrust of each other (which they quickly deny). They respect the motives of others, but they fear their own inadequacies as well as those of other members. Protection is sought in cliques and mutual admiration pairings. They resist initiating new ways of operating through legalism and quibbling. Remaining defensive, they restrict the range of permitted behavior through conformity and ritual.

When members learn to accept each other and themselves, they more easily can express their feelings and conflicting attitudes. They become more *goal* and *task oriented* and less *ego oriented*. Norms are established about how they will proceed, but individual differences are tolerated. Legitimate influence is accepted, and members develop a liking for each other.

SECOND STAGE: MOTIVATION AND DECISION MAKING.   During this phase, what first were ambiguous expressions are clarified in meaning. Strategy, gimmicks, and tricks are replaced by problem-solving behavior. Caution, pretense, and protective phraseology give way to open communications and reactions. Sufficient time is spent in reaching decisions.

THIRD STAGE: MOTIVATION AND PRODUCTIVITY.   The group has reached maturity in resolving problems of its members' motivation when creativity is observed in sustained work, when members are involved in the work, when extrinsic or irrelevant rewards are not needed to maintain a high level of productivity, and when members are cooperative rather than competitive.

FOURTH STAGE: CONTROL AND ORGANIZATION.   A group has succeeded in organizing effectively when work is allocated according to abilities and by agreements among those involved. Members are interdependent, but the organization remains flexible and ready to change in the face of new challenges. Informality and spontaneity are stressed with little expression of concern about the form of the organization.

The Effective Group

Thus, in the effective work group, the individual members are highly interdependent, coordinated, and cooperative in their efforts. They are capable and highly motivated as individuals, goal or task oriented, and information flows freely among them.

We shall now look at conditions conducive to creating and maintaining an effective work group. Two basic questions confront us: How large should a group be? and Who should be grouped with whom? *If reaching the goal depends on smooth, cooperative, conflict-free, coordinated efforts* among the members, then a homogeneous membership where people are alike, should be more productive.

In a related experiment, groups were formed on the basis of the Guilford-Zimmerman Temperament Survey scores of individual members. Groups with members who were similar in personality profiles had less difficulty in regulating their internal relations but more difficulty in creative problem-solving than groups of heterogeneous membership. Where members differed in personality, they more often rejected an easy choice of two superficial alternatives to a problem offered to them. On their own, these members developed a third, more creative, integrated solution.

OPTIMUM MIX.   As there is an optimum size for groups depending on the task, so there also is an optimum mix of people for a given group task. If people are too different, they have so much trouble interacting that they cannot use their varied resources to solve a complex problem. If people are too similar, they reach agreement too easily and too often on the same wrong answers. They are more likely to fail to consider various alternatives and to explore the problem as widely. For simple, routine assignments, the optimum mix is composed of fairly similar types of people. For complex tasks with creative demands, the optimum becomes a more diversified assemblage. For assignments requiring easy, cooperative interaction, the optimum again is of similar people. But when such cooperation is less important, the members can differ more.

How to Compose Groups to Promote Interaction

In addition to considering the number and homogeneity of employees to assign to a group, we can foster interaction and the ease with which individuals can work together by grouping together members who are already familiar with each other, who already are attracted to each other, who esteem each other, who are geographically and socially close to each other, and who can communicate fluently, accurately, and rapidly with each other.

FAMILIARITY BREEDS INTERACTION.   If we are intimate, familiar, or experienced with other persons, we feel more comfortable about initiating and maintaining interaction with them. Our familiarity makes it possible to predict, with less risk of error, their likely reactions to us. We feel more secure about interacting with them. In turn, continued interaction breeds familiarity, so we are more likely to interact with those we have interacted with before. At a gathering we usually approach friends before strangers.

Since they interact more readily, friends can work together more quickly than strangers. Thus an experiment disclosed that pairs of close friends could solve codes, puzzles, and arithmetic problems more quickly than could pairs of strangers.

Consensus: False, Forced, and True

Full participation of all concerned, resulting in complete agreement on a decision, is the ideal toward which an effective group strives.

False consensus may be mistaken for true agreement. For example, silence does not mean consent. When relatively few members speak out on issues, it is just as reasonable to assume that they are against a proposition as it is to assume that they are for it. Each member must express his/her view (if he/she has any) if the group is to achieve true consensus, or he/she must indicate that he/she does not care how a matter is decided. At the same time, it is the responsibility of the group or its chairperson to see that everyone has an opportunity to speak before a decision is made.

Consensus cannot be forced. If members are silent, it is unwise for a chairperson or leader to point a finger at each member in turn to ask them how they stand on a matter. It is equally unsound for the group to agree, "Let's go around the table to see what each person thinks we ought to do." A member may be forced to render an opinion when he/she does not really have one, or he/she may have to offer an evaluation before having an opportunity to hear what some more knowledgeable coworkers have to say. An individual's best potential contributions may be inspired after her turn to speak has passed, and she may now hesitate to interrupt "going around the table" since she feels she has been given a chance—although it was not fully used.

True consensus comes only when members feel free to express their opinions and are willing to keep working together to develop a decision that satisfies the desires of the whole group. True consensus occurs when members may use fully whatever resources they can bring to bear on the group's problems. Mechanical procedures such as voting or taking turns to force contributions are avoided, but everyone who has something to contribute has a chance to do so and a chance to see his/her contribution considered and if possible worked into the final decision.

Groups that strive for true consensus must be ready to settle for less than complete agreement on all matters. Yet a group is more likely to operate effectively if it knows how its members stand in disagreement than if it obscures the situation with majority decisions or forced or false consensus. Then, if agreement is impossible, the members at least feel that the matter has been fully examined; and they may be more willing to commit themselves to an alternative solution.

The supervisor can help the group achieve decision-making consensus in many ways. He/she can block members who seem to be monopolizing the group's activities or trying to dominate the group. By using suitable questions, the supervisor can challenge a member who continually argues and opposes without logical consistency. He/she may bring into the discussion members who seem to be uninterested by asking them for their advice and opinion. The supervisor may do nothing more than show willingness to share his/her power to provide the arena in which the group, including him/herself, can explore together the basis for obtaining group agreements. He/she may provide the kinds of information to the group not formerly available to it that will serve to set the boundaries of the group's responsibilities and authority.

Further Impediments to Effective Utilization of Group Resources

In addition to the inadequate decision-making processes and interaction difficulties mentioned earlier, such as those caused by enlarging a group, other causes of group ineffectiveness have been demonstrated. Removing these impediments should result in improving a group's performance.

UNCLEAR ROLE EXPECTATIONS.   Trouble arises when members are unclear about what others expect of them. Moreover, they become defensive if they cannot forecast what other members are likely to do.

COMPETITIVENESS.   If members see each other as competing for the supervisor's favor, or as competing for promotion, recognition, or pay raises, self-interest will conflict with the need to cooperate with other members to work toward group goals. When such self-oriented needs become dominant, consensus becomes difficult. Competitors see each other as less similar in personality than those who can achieve mutual rewards through cooperation. Therefore, competition among members increases perceived differences in a group and consequently reduces the potential to interact and the likely effectiveness of the members as a group. In comparison to groups in which members must cooperate with each other to achieve personal rewards, members who must compete for rewards are less coordinated and vary more in what they contribute. They are less productive in quantity and quality, less friendly, and less favorable to the group, its products, and its functioning.

INTOLERANCE.   When one group member takes an unpopular position, different and opposed to that maintained by all others, the dominant majority first tries to convert the deviant; then, if he/she will not convert, they psychologically eject him/her from the group. They act as if he/she did not exist, paying little or no attention thereafter. The rejection is even more severe if the group—except for the deviant—is highly cohesive. Yet the deviant may be the one member in the group with the right idea, the pioneering attitude, the most original outlook on the problem. Where members are highly task-oriented, deviant opinion is more likely to be tolerated.

ABSENCE OF SPECIALIZED RESOURCES OR ACTIVITIES.   Ordinarily, effective groups may suffer lowered productivity and dissatisfaction owing to the failure of the administration to provide resources to the group. For instance, inadequate secretarial service was a strong factor in retarding the effectiveness of 72 observed conferences. Groups need supplies, time, and support personnel.

Absence of Positive Feedback

Groups are less likely to solve problems effectively, and members are likely to be more dissatisfied with their work, if feedback is not provided. Knowledge of results is as important in group work as it is in individual endeavors. The performance of individuals working as a group improves most when they receive constructive information concerning their individual efforts as well as about the group's success as a whole, particularly if the tasks are complex and the goals difficult to achieve. Yet merely emphasizing what is wrong with an individual member's performance serves only to increase his/her defensiveness in the group, particularly if remarks are personal.

So What?

So, the key to effective supervision and satisfied employees lies in forming and maintaining active, efficient, and effective work groups. If one enters an educational organization in which the groups are already committed to inadequate processes or to goals that conflict with the aims of the organization as a whole, one may be able to bring about desired changes in the individual employee only after one's group has first examined and accepted the possibilities of changing procedures and directions.

Understanding group life is essential in promoting effective supervision, for modern supervision is seen as a cooperative team effort aimed at improving instruction, and it must take place in groups.

How to Use Group Problem-Solving Techniques in Supervision

Whether at the conference workshop, institute, staff conference, or in the area of general research, the supervising principal should insure that a system analysis

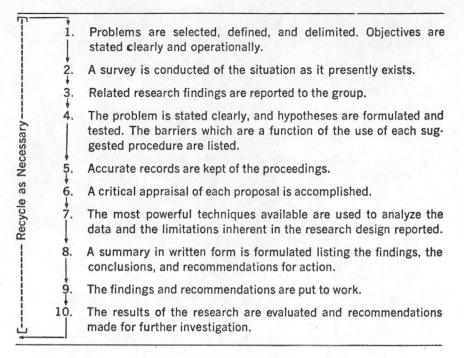

1. Problems are selected, defined, and delimited. Objectives are stated clearly and operationally.

2. A survey is conducted of the situation as it presently exists.

3. Related research findings are reported to the group.

4. The problem is stated clearly, and hypotheses are formulated and tested. The barriers which are a function of the use of each suggested procedure are listed.

5. Accurate records are kept of the proceedings.

6. A critical appraisal of each proposal is accomplished.

7. The most powerful techniques available are used to analyze the data and the limitations inherent in the research design reported.

8. A summary in written form is formulated listing the findings, the conclusions, and recommendations for action.

9. The findings and recommendations are put to work.

10. The results of the research are evaluated and recommendations made for further investigation.

FIGURE 6-5.   Steps in Helping Groups Solve Supervisory Problems.

approach to problem-solving is employed. The steps to be followed in helping groups in supervisory problem-solving are indicated in Figure 6-5.

Case Study

Stone W. Jackson, principal of school No. 1 of the Sierra Way Union School District, was cautious in how he led the faculty in attacking a problem that had arisen at the previous staff meeting through group discussion. Being well versed in the area of group processes, Jackson initiated the following procedures:

1. The problem was defined
2. The implications, possibilities, and hazards implicit in each of the suggested possible solutions were considered by the group
3. Knowledge and experience from outside specialists, as well as from literature, interviews, and other sources, were utilized
4. The information bearing on the problem was brought together, and tentative and final conclusions were developed
5. A report of the proceedings was carefully prepared.

Jackson guided the members of his faculty through the following techniques:

Preparation

1. Were members notified about meeting time, place, and topic? _____

2. Were the physical arrangements right for good discussion? _____

3. Did I prepare an outline for the discussion? _____

4. Did I provide sufficient background and factual material? _____

5. Were the visual or other aids in place and ready for use? _____

6. Was a friendly, personal atmosphere developed before the discussion started? _____

Leading the Discussion

7. Did my introduction state the topic? _____
   Define the areas of discussion? _____
   Relate them to the interest of the group? _____

8. Was it too long? _____

9. Did it insure that the group had enough information on which to base the discussion? _____

10. Did the group come right into the discussion after the introduction? _____

11. How did I "toss the ball" to the group? _____

12. Did I keep the discussion moving by frequent transitional summaries?_____Checking repetitions?_____Calling attention to digressions and irrelevancies?_____Pointing up differences of opinion?_____Clarifying the discussion?_____Allowing sufficient time for each major area of the topic? _____

13. Were the questions and other methods I used to guide the discussion:
    Aimed at bringing out reasons, opinions, causes? _____
    Designed to bring out all shades of opinion? _____
    Presented objectively (not slanted or argumentative)? _____
    Worded briefly and clearly? _____
    Thought-provoking (not rhetorical or "yes-no" in form)? _____
    Fairly and tactfully distributed among all members? _____

14. Did I encourage participation by:
    Keeping any one member from "hogging the show"? _____
    Drawing out the reticent members? _____
    Expressing appreciation of individual contributions? _____
    Re-directing questions to other members? _____
    Maintaining good humor and fair play? _____

FIGURE 6-6.   Checklist for Group Leaders.

15. Did I bring the discussion to a clear and definite conclusion? _____

16. Did my final summary fairly review all points of view expressed? _____
State the agreements reached? _____
And the points of disagreement? _____
Call attention to sources of information? _____
Announce the next meeting? _____

Results

17. Were there any indications of satisfaction from members of the group? _____
Any indications of dissatisfaction from members of the group? _____

18. Were there any unusual problems? _____
Did I handle them properly? _____

19. How many members did not participate at all? _____

20. Was the topic suitable for discussion? _____

21. Were any important aspects of the question omitted? _____

22. Was there a clearer understanding of the subject after the discussion? _____

23. What conclusions did the group reach?
_____

24. What could I have done better?
_____

1. He helped individual members of the group establish their places within the group.
2. He saw to it that information concerning each member was exchanged, that strong leadership was available, and that cohesiveness was developed between group members.
3. Finally, he was able to stimulate the group due to the real problem they were attacking. The result was an increase in responsibility in each individual.

Finally, Jackson evaluated his own performance as a group leader by using a technique similar to that which appears in Figure 6-6. He kept his study groups to a reasonable size. D. Cartwright and A. Zander[19] reported a study that seemed to indicate that the optimum size of a group for the study of a problem is approximately five, with the upper limit approximately twelve. Jackson was aware of the major functions that must be accomplished if any group is to meet with success. These functions are illustrated in Figure 6-7.

[19] Dorwin Cartwright and Alvin Zander, *Group Dynamics: Research and Theory* (New York: Harper and Row, Publishers, 1953).

FIGURE 6-7.   Four Major Functions.

Guidelines for Evaluating Group Action

Every group needs guidelines if its deliberations are to be successful. Good human relations in group processes are as dependent on rules as is a baseball game. The leader or chairperson must referee the conference with specific rules in mind. The rules of fair play and full participation must be understood and accepted by the group lest the process end in conflict and futility. The following guidelines furnish more than adequate bases for formulating criteria that can be used in evaluating group endeavors in problem-solving:

1. Was the meeting attended by all representatives concerned?
2. Did the participants stick to the point in question?
3. Were preliminary plans formulated, and was a tentative outline of procedure followed?
4. Did the individuals work as a group?
5. Was democratic cooperation with truly strong leadership present?
6. Were suggestions of previous groups followed or noted?
7. Did the individuals arrive on time for the meeting?
8. Did any one individual spend more time working at attacking the problem than did the other participants?
9. Did any one individual not perform to the best of his ability?
10. Were individual tasks accomplished?
11. Was the problem attacked with an open mind?
12. Were possible solutions checked?
13. Was each member made to feel that he was needed and wanted as a member of the group?
14. Were the rules, mechanisms, procedures, and policies determined by the group or were they imposed from above the group?[20]
15. Was there a stimulating environment, rich in experiences and materials, designed to facilitate maximum interaction?
16. Were conditions arranged that afforded opportunities for individuals to make special contributions through their particular interest and talents, and were these contributions utilized in group deliberations?

[20] Charles A. Stone, "The Teachers' Institute in American Education" (Doctoral dissertation, Stanford University, 1950).

17. Did the members have an opportunity to evaluate the outcomes of their planning, and was their evaluation continuous?
18. Was the contribution of each member recognized and evaluated?
19. Were the contributions of the members relevant to the problem solution?
20. Were the conflicts in points of view resolved into common understanding?
21. Were the worth and dignity of each member of the group fully recognized?
22. Did all share the responsibility of leadership and duties?
23. Did all the members of the group participate, and was the fullest participation from all concerned secured?
24. Were cooperative attacks made on the problem and did the group reach a decision as a result of group planning, discussion, action, and evaluation?
25. Were good human relations and satisfactory personal interactions developed within the group so that a cooperative, permissive atmosphere was characterized in its functioning?
26. Did the group aim at achieving unity in general purpose, and diversity in ways of achieving that purpose?
27. Did the group have sufficient interest and/or adequate knowledge to pursue and expedite their attainment?
28. Was the problem worthy of individual and group consideration?

Many supervising principals have found an end-of-the-conference "suggestion slip" invaluable. An example of such a slip is included as Figure 6-8. See chapter 18 for a more complete discussion of decision-making and problem-solving techniques.

What did you think of this meeting? Please be frank. Your comments can contribute a great deal to the success of our meetings.

1. How did you feel about this meeting?

	(Check)		
		Without value	( )
		Poor	( )
		Mediocre	( )
		Good	( )
		Excellent	( )

2. What were the weaknesses?

_____

3. What were the strong points?

_____

4. What improvements would you suggest?

_____

FIGURE 6-8.   End-of-the-Conference Suggestion Slip.

The following list of techniques may prove useful in planning for in-service education:

Do

1. Hold conferences before the opening of school in the fall. These meetings will orient new staff members and act as a reorientation for returning members of the faculty.
2. Open the way for faculty meetings concerned with educational problems that have been planned by teacher-principal committees to enhance in-service growth.
3. Encourage visitation within the system or with neighboring school systems.
4. Stress the better understanding of educational problems and improved articulation between grades that should result from subject matter area meetings that include teachers from all levels of education.
5. Assign staff members to conduct a survey of various educational problems of the school and to report their findings to the faculty.
6. Help the school staff interpret effectively the school program to the public through articles, talks, student presentations, open-house activities, and demonstration teaching.
7. Encourage attendance at graduate school and professional conventions in order that school personnel may continue their professional growth and keep abreast of educational progress.
8. Conduct teacher-principal rating conferences, by using a form designed by teachers that indicates strengths and areas in each teacher's training that need improvement.
9. Make available professional literature that pertains to the interests and needs of teachers, supervisors, and administrators.
10. Make all personnel aware of school handbooks, monographs, manuals, and guides on policies and procedures.
11. Make provision in the budget that could encourage in-service education of teachers. Remuneration should be provided for summer school, educational travel, consultant services, professional meetings, sabbatical leave, workshops, and institutes.
12. As you begin to work on staff and instructional development:
    a. Work initially with a small, select staff.
    b. Try to select a staff of eager, interested, innovative persons.
    c. Select a problem that is generally recognized as a *real problem*, so that the idea of change will be more readily accepted.
    d. Select a project that can be handled easily.
    e. Do not burden the staff with unnecessary clerical work, trivial chores, nonessential reports, and tasks that less expert persons can do. Furnish your expert staff with total administrative and clerical support.
    f. Encourage the staff to select areas of responsibility whenever possible.
    g. Encourage a variety of open channels of communication. Encourage suggestions and permit free, constructive criticism. Get all of the "feedback" possible. Staff development can be accomplished best by face-to-face or cross-table communication with "enablers" and "advisors," rather than in a more formal approach.

h. Pick a problem that is easily structured. Let the staff members choose the area they feel needs work.
i. Provide the staff with a library of handy reference material relating to all aspects of the problem.
j. Hold planning sessions as necessary, but *keep them short.*
k. Reward the staff involved. Build into the project a system of incentives, such as extra compensation.
l. Recognize work well done as often as possible, preferably publicly.
m. Fix responsibility. Everyone should be clear about his/her goals and share of the responsibility.
n. Set definite time limits. It is too easy to delay and procrastinate when time is open-ended.
o. Short-term goals and short-term time limits, sequentially assigned, are preferable to complex goals and longer time limits.
p. Do not rush the project. Start early and have a lead time that will allow for the involvement and development of all personnel involved.
q. Be flexible. When errors occur, correct them. The best plans are not perfect, so change plans when necessary. Dead-ends will occur. When they do, do not hesitate to scrap one idea in favor of another.
r. Encourage production. Whether it is plans, idea lists, outlines, drafts of software (instructional materials), criterion tests, or other materials that are developed, try to get something written as soon as possible. It is easier and more productive to correct, change, and proof imperfect drafts than it is to wait until the production is likely to be perfect. Many people hesitate to produce, and as a result they delay to the point of nonproduction and only worry about the enormity of the problem.
s. Provide for helpful supervision. Supervisors should be resource persons rather than merely overseers.

Don't

1. Rebuke or correct any teacher in the presence of students or other staff members.
2. Tread heavily in the field of teacher's specialty.
3. Deal lightly with any person's problems, but treat them as if they were your own.
4. Forget the days of your youth—keep a sense of humor.
5. Deal harshly with a teacher who is old in the service—deal with him/her kindly and with understanding.
6. Set a time limit when working with a new teacher. Give all the help needed now over a period of time; even if he/she requires a major portion of the supervisor's time for three days, three weeks, or three months. Recall that, after all, the teacher was hired on the basis of capabilities and potentialities, qualifications and promise. Do not let her fail.[21]
7. "*Nit-pick.*" *Keep the major problem in focus,* and many of the minor irritations will cure themselves.

21 See J. Minor Gwynn, *Theory and Practice of Supervision* (New York: Dodd, Mead, 1965), pp. 215–218.

TRENDS CONCERNING THE APPLICATION
OF SUPERVISORY TECHNIQUES

Toward ⟶ Released Time for In-service Education

There is a definite trend toward providing for the release of employees from their regular assignments during the work day so that they can attend staff development and other supervisory programs. Learning is not optimal when employees attend such programs after the conclusion of their regular work day, when they are fatigued and rushed. The principles of learning apply to supervisory programs as well as to classroom learning environments!

Toward ⟶ School System Grants
to Individual Teachers and Other Employees
for Tuition

More school systems have a policy whereby the cost of classes in which teachers and other employees enroll in order to improve professional skills and abilities will be borne by the school system. This practice is desirable and should be sought by the supervisor.

The supervisor of the future will work diligently for adequate financial support for staff development and the improvement of instruction through all legitimate avenues.

Toward ⟶ Improved Orientation Programs

The teacher who is new to a school system will be introduced into the system through an improved orientation program that takes into account the general and specific needs of beginning teachers as outlined in this chapter. The program will include an introduction to specific system policies, to the community, to the school plant, to the students, to materials of instruction, to curriculum and instructional guides, to techniques of instruction, and to an outline of subject matter content.

Supervisory Problems

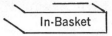

Problem 1

Mr. Angel is a dynamic young man in his first year of teaching. He is a Phi Delta Kappan and graduated from his state university with honors. He is a person with a "strong ego." He tends to dominate most discussions, and although he produces many good ideas he quickly has become obnoxious to the staff. He has not yet learned to listen. He apparently is having problems in orienting himself to his role as a member of a professional staff.

How should the supervising principal handle Mr. Angel in order to utilize his strength and to minimize his weakness?

Problem 2

Mr. Raboy has returned to the teaching profession after an absence of twenty years. He was a very successful teacher in his early professional career and was active in both his state and local professional organizations. During his absence, he has had little contact with his profession and has done little professional reading, nor has he returned to the university for study. His activities during his absence have been in different areas. He is certain that the innovations that he finds in the school, such as team teaching and the individualization of instruction and the use of the materials of instructional technology including computer-supported instruction and programmed instructional aids, are but "fads" and transitory and a "waste of the taxpayers' money." He is critical of his fellow teachers and often is arrogant. He uses the methods he was trained to use well in his classroom. Both students and teachers are cowed by his temper.

How can the supervising principal help Mr. Raboy to grow and at the same time protect his psychological integrity?

Questions and Suggested Activities Concerning How to Supervise the In-Service Education Program

Questions

1. What is the principal's role in organizing an in-service program?
2. What means can be found for identifying the great variety of needs and interests of teachers for setting up in-service programs?
3. What is the relationship between the principal and the curriculum coordinator in the in-service program? The consultants and the teachers?
4. What kind of in-service program should principals encourage beginning teachers to take? Highly experienced teachers?
5. What resources are available, either within or outside the school and/or school system to aid in the in-service program?
6. As a supervisor, what results of the in-service training program would you use to justify the appropriation of more funds?
7. What should be done at the local school system level and what should be the relationship of this program to the district or county program?

Suggested Activities

1. Select, describe, and make recommendations for the solution of a specific instructional problem in your school that lends itself to an on-going, in-service program.
2. Interview twenty-five or more teachers and report on the following: what they like and dislike most about in-service education; how in-service education practices, procedures, and interaction can be improved.
3. List the steps necessary for reorganizing in-service training programs to meet teacher and administrator needs.
4. Discuss in-service programs and their implications for (a) the new teacher, (b) the transfer teacher, (c) the ineffective teacher, and (d) the "old-fashioned" teacher.
5. List several methods and develop criteria that could be used effectively to evaluate an in-service training program.

Selected Bibliography

Books

Adams, Harold P., and Frank Dickey. *Basic Principles of Supervision*. New York: American Book Company, 1953.

Barr, A. S., William H. Burton, and Leo J. Brueckner. *Supervision, Democratic Leadership in the Improvement of Learning*. New York: D. Appleton-Century Company, Inc., 1947.

Bartky, John A. *Supervision as Human Relations*. Boston: D. C. Heath and Company, 1953.

Briggs, Thomas H., and Joseph Justman. *Improving Instruction through Supervision*. New York: The Macmillan Company, 1952.

Burton, William H., and Leo J. Brueckner. *Supervision, A Social Process*. New York: Appleton-Century Crofts, Educational Division, Meredith Corp., 1955.

Campbell, Clyde M. *Practical Application of Democratic Administration*. New York: Harper and Brothers, 1952.

Cartwright, Dorwin, and Alvin Zander. *Group Dynamics: Research and Theory*. New York: Harper and Row, Publishers, 1953.

Dale, Edgar. *Audio-Visual Methods in Teaching*. New York: Dryden Press, 1954.

Elsbree, Willard S., and Harold J. McNally. *Elementary School Administration and Supervision*. New York: American Book Company, 1959.

Evans, Dean. *Supervision for Better Schools*. Englewood Cliffs, New Jersey: Prentice-Hall, Inc., 1951.

Frey, Sherman H., and Keith R. Getschman. *School Administration: Selected Readings*. New York: Thomas Y. Crowell Company, 1969.

Gwynn, J. Minor. *Theory and Practice of Supervision*. New York: Dodd, Mead, 1965.

Kelley, Earl C. *The Workshop Way of Learning*. New York: Harper and Brothers, 1951.

McNerney, Chester T. *Educational Supervision*. New York: McGraw-Hill Book Company, Inc., 1951.

Miles, M. B. *Learning to Work in Groups*. New York: Columbia University, Teacher's College Press, 1969.

Neagley, Ross L., and N. Dean Evans. *Handbook for Effective Supervision of Instruction*. Englewood Cliffs, New Jersey: Prentice-Hall, Inc., 1968.

Reeder, Edwin H. *Supervision in the Elementary School*. Boston: Houghton Mifflin Company, 1953.

Saint, A. M. *Supervision of Employees—Study and Teaching*. Chicago: Nelson-Hall Co., 1974.

Spears, Harold. *The Teacher and Curriculum Planning*. Englewood Cliffs, New Jersey: Prentice-Hall, Inc., 1951.

————. *Improving the Supervision of Instruction*. Englewood Cliffs, New Jersey: Prentice-Hall, Inc., 1953.

————. *Curriculum Planning through In-Service Programs*. Englewood Cliffs, New Jersey: Prentice-Hall, Inc., 1957.

Stoops, Emery, and John Dunworth. *Classroom Disciplines*. Montclair, New Jersey: The Economics Press, 1958.

Thomas, George I. *Administrator's Guide to the Year-Round School.* Englewood Cliffs, New Jersey: Prentice-Hall, Inc., 1973.

Thompson, Robert B. *A Systems Approach to Instruction.* Hamden, Connecticut: Shoe String Press, Inc., 1971.

Unruh, Adolph, and Harold E. Turner. *Supervision for Change and Innovation.* Boston: Houghton Mifflin, 1970.

Wiles, Kimball. *Supervision for Better Schools.* Englewood Cliffs, New Jersey: Prentice-Hall, Inc., 1951.

Wilhelms, Fred T. *Supervision in a New Key.* Washington, D.C.: Association for Supervision and Curriculum Development, 1973.

Yauch, Wilber A. *Improving Human Relations in School Administration.* New York: Harper and Brothers, 1949.

Periodicals

Abrahamson, S. "Toward Better In-Service Education." *Educational Leadership* XI (November 1953): 82–85.

Anderson, George F. "Evaluating Teacher Education." *American Association Health, Physical Education, and Recreation Journal* XXIV (February 1953): 11.

Baker, T. P. "What Is an Effective In-Service Education Program?" *National Association of Secondary School Principals* XXXV (March 1951): 46–48.

Cory, N. Durward. "Incentives Used in Motivating Professional Growth of Teachers." *North Central Association Quarterly* XXVII (April 1953): 385–409.

Harnly, P. W. "In-Service Education of Teachers." *North Central Association Quarterly* XXIII (January 1949): 273–275.

Hightower, H. W. "In-Service Education." *Educational Administration and Supervision* XXXVIII (April 1952): 243–246.

Mackenzie, G. N. "In-Service Teacher Education: A Challenge to College and Schools. *Educational Outlook* XXIV (March 1950): 144–150.

Mallison, Jacqueline V. "The Current Status of Science Education in the Elementary Schools." *School Science and Mathematics* LXI (April 1961): 252–270.

Moffit, J. C. "Administration of In-Service Education." *Educational Administration and Supervision* XXXVII (October 1951): 355–361.

Murphy, Rose M. "Troy Plans for In-Service Training." *The American School Board Journal* CXXII (June 1951): 26.

Stoops, Emery, and Albert R. Evans. "Helping the Beginning Teacher." *The Nation's Schools* LVII (April 1956): 74.

Weber, C. A. "Reactions of Teachers to In-Service Education in Their Schools." *School Review* LI (1943): 234–240.

Wood, Hugh B. "In-Service Education of Teachers." *Journal of Teacher Education* II (December 1951): 243–247.

Audio Cassettes

Conference Planning and Leadership. Thompson-Mitchell, Atlanta, Georgia, 1973. Some do's and don't's. Includes an interview with Gloria Fauth.

Glasser, William. *Glasser on Discipline*. North Hollywood, California: New Views Unlimited (5557 Cahuenga Blvd., Los Angeles, California 91601), 1975. A series
of six audio cassettes by Dr. William Glasser on control and discipline.

Films

Anger at Work. International Film Bureau, 1956. Explains one mental mechanism of
man's personality—his displacement of his own anger onto other men—and how
this impairs his efficiency in everyday living. Five incidents show some techniques
that people have developed for handling anger, resentment, and frustration. (21
minutes)

Controlling Absenteeism. BNA Films (a division of the Bureau of National Affairs,
Inc., 5615 Fishers Lane, Rockville, Maryland 20852), 1975. Saul Gellerman
zeros in on the causes of absenteeism and offers practical measures to curb it.

Designing Effective Instruction. General Programmed Teaching (a division of Commerce Clearing House, San Rafael, California), 1970. Sound filmstrips, workbooks, and leader's guide.

Managing In a Crisis. BNA Films, 1975. In addition to crisis management, this is an
excellent film to teach group problem solving, team work, conference leadership,
group dynamics, decision making and conflict management.

Personal Problem. McGraw-Hill, 1959. Stimulates effective discussion about the nature
and extent of the help a supervisor must be prepared to give an employee with
a personal problem that affects teaching efficiency. (6 minutes)

Problem Solving in Groups. Educational Media Center, University of California, Berkeley, 1961. Illustrated lecture by Dr. Richard Wallen on management committees and how they function, with particular emphasis on solving problems.
Explains the problem-solving process, how committees usually deal with problems, and how their methods can be improved. (25 minutes)

Working With Troubled Employees. BNA Films, 1975. Harry Levinson illustrates two
common types of troubled behavior—the depressed employee and the overly aggressive employee—and gives tips on how to distinguish emotional troubles from
behavior associated with disciplinary action or low morale. He also outlines the
supervisor's role in dealing with troubled employees.

Other Sources

American Association of School Administrators. *Off to a Good Start*. Washington,
D.C.: The Association, 1956.

Council of Directors and Supervisors. "Supervision, Los Angeles City Schools." Duplicated material. Los Angeles: Operating Division, Division of Elementary
Education, 1953.

Denver Public Schools. *Denver Serves Its Children*. Denver: Board of Education, 1948.

Department of Supervisors and Directors of Instruction, *Newer Instructional Practices
of Promise*. Twelfth Yearbook (Washington, D.C.: National Education Association, 1940), 328–349.

Dunworth, John, Lavona Dunworth, and Emery Stoops. *Discipline—Bi-Weekly Newsletter,* Fairfield, New Jersey: The Economics Press, Inc., 1975 ed.

Instructional Objectives Exchange (IOX). (Address: P.O. Box 24095, Los Angeles, California 90024.) Provides objectives-based test sets in the areas of Reading, Language Arts, Social Studies, and Mathematics. IOX also has gathered "Measurable Objectives Collections." Collections range from "Language Arts—The Decoding Skills of Reading (K–12)," and "Mathematics—Numbers and Their Operations," to "Spanish (7–12)," "Self Concept (K–12)," "U.S. History (10–12)," and "Sex Education (K–12)." These books can be useful aids in drawing up criteria-referenced tests and materials, in writing instructional plans, and also for evaluation procedures. A "product listing" with prices will be sent on request.

Mitchell, James Russell. "The Workshop as an In-Service Education Procedure." Doctoral dissertation, Indiana University, 1954.

Stone, Charles A. "The Teachers' Institute in American Education." Doctoral dissertation, Stanford University, 1950.

Teacher Education Workshop. "Report of the Teacher Workshop." Duplicated material. Nashville: The George Peabody College for Teachers, 1945.

7

How to Improve
Supervisory Visits

The supervising principal must give considerable thought to classroom visitation for supervisory purposes. This chapter analyzes this important function of the supervisor and proposes a model for the supervisory visit that will help the supervising principal conduct the visit in a manner in keeping with the encompassing goal of any modern supervisory program—improving instruction. The natural companion of the supervisory visit—the follow-up conference—is studied in chapter 8.

This chapter includes a discussion of the following topics:

Principles and purposes of supervisory visits
How to plan for classroom visitation
Mechanics of observation
Techniques in visitation
How to use the technique of interschool visitation
Do—Don't
Trends
"In-Basket" supervisory problem
Questions and suggested activities

Principles and Purposes of Supervisory Visits

Even though the emphasis placed on the supervisory visit is not as great as that exhibited from the 1930's through the 1960's, it still is considered a part of the program of supervision. Classroom visitation successfully fulfills many needs when performed by someone who is aware of the responsibilities.

In terms of general values, consider first the theory that teaching is not a stagnated, routine function, but rather that it is both a science and creative skill, ever growing, ever capable of improvement. As the creative teacher seeks to improve skills, it becomes obvious that one cannot examine, in a truly objective fashion, one's own performance as well as can another individual who has been trained for this function on a professional level. The need for having a competent instructional leader constructively evaluate—but not inspect—the performance of the teacher is recognized as essential to the acceptance of the supervisory visit and its corollary, the follow-up conference.

Basic Principles and Purposes

Teachers want supervision that is well planned, constructive, and democratically applied. If these expectations are to be realized, the following criteria should be met:

1. Supervisory visits should focus on all elements of the teaching-learning situation, not merely on the teacher.
2. The chief purpose of supervisory visits should be the improvement of learning; they should be inspirational and instructive rather than inspectional and repressive.
3. Supervisory visits should afford each teacher a definite and concrete basis for improvement.
4. The principal, not the staff specialist-consultant, should be responsible for rating teachers. The principal is responsible for what transpires in the classroom. He/she is responsible for the improvement of instruction in all areas, at all levels.
5. The principal's first concern should be for the safety, welfare, and development of the students; and then for the safety, welfare, and development of the staff.
6. The principal should help the teachers use various measures of self-evaluation.
7. Teachers should feel free to discuss their problems and to make suggestions. The principal must respect the opinions and points of view of the professional staff.

A Democratic Approach to Classroom Observation

When the head master contemplated visiting a classroom in colonial days, the visit was an inspectional tour, and the conference following the visit was fraught with negative, destructive connotations. Since that time, there have been numerous modifications with regard to the supervisory visit and follow-up conference.

Today, the acknowledged purpose of these visits and conferences is the improvement of the instructional program. Despite this shift from focus on the teacher toward an emphasis on the total teaching-learning situation, a problem still exists. Many teachers fear a visit by the principal, often with good reason. They dislike having to defend methods and techniques that they have found successful.

They object to being told what to do. They fear being rated by someone who too frequently drifts into and out of the classroom on an unannounced, unplanned visit.

Many shortcomings in the program for classroom visitation have been emphasized by M. S. Norton,[1] who stressed such items as perfunctory visits, failure to establish rapport, poor conference techniques, lack of worthwhile assistance with classroom problems, and insufficient planning. Any one of these reasons could cause deep dissatisfaction with the program. The problem facing the supervisor is not a question of the need for supervisory visits and conferences, but rather one of how to improve the practice in order to increase its effectiveness. Perhaps the increasing concern of various professional associations to improve instruction using the techniques described in this chapter bodes well for the future of the supervisory evaluation of instruction.

How to Plan for Classroom Visitation

The improvement of instruction is the primary duty of a supervising principal. If he/she is to perform this function effectively he/she must become proficient in the use of modern techniques for supervisory visits and conferences.[2] Careful planning by the supervisor should precede a classroom visit. From the following list, the supervisor might select activities that are applicable to a specific visit:

1. The supervisor will know the purpose of the visit and will insure that the teacher clearly understands the purpose.
2. The supervisor will know as much as possible about the teaching-learning situation prior to the visit.
3. The supervisor will discuss with the teacher the area of the instructional program with which the teacher has requested help prior to the visit.
4. The supervisor will review all available pertinent materials, including records of previous visits and follow-up conferences that might pertain to the proposed visit.
5. The supervisor will refer to any pertinent professional material.
6. Before the supervisory visit, the supervisor will plan with the teacher for a follow-up conference.
7. The supervisor will complete a monthly schedule of supervisory visits and conferences, such as included in chapter 4 and which is reported here as Figure 7-1, so that he/she will know when and for how long he/she will be in the classroom. Another form that may be helpful in programming classroom visits and follow-up conferences is included as Figure 7-2.

[1] Monte S. Norton, "Are Classroom Visits Worthwhile?" *The Clearing House* XXV (September 1960): 41.

[2] See Edwin H. Reeder, *Supervision in the Elementary School* (Boston: Houghton Mifflin Company, 1953), pp. 197–199; and Reba M. Burnham and Martha L. King, *Supervision in Action* (Washington, D.C.: Association for Supervision and Curriculum Development, National Education Association, 1961), p. 56.

FIGURE 7-1.   Sample Planning Schedule for Supervisory Visits and Conferences.

SUPERVISORY VISITS* AND CONFERENCES
SCHEDULE
_____School Month

Week of School Month	Day				
	M	T	W	T	F
First	___ (A.M. P.M.)	___ (A.M. P.M.)	___ (A.M. P.M.)	___ (A.M. P.M.)	___ (A.M. P.M.)
Second	___ (A.M. P.M.)	___ (A.M. P.M.)	___ (A.M. P.M.)	___ (A.M. P.M.)	___ (A.M. P.M.)
Third	___ (A.M. P.M.)	___ (A.M. P.M.)	___ (A.M. P.M.)	___ (A.M. P.M.)	___ (A.M. P.M.)
Fourth	___ (A.M. P.M.)	___ (A.M. P.M.)	___ (A.M. P.M.)	___ (A.M. P.M.)	___ (A.M. P.M.)

KEY: V = Visit   A = Other Appointment
KEY: C = Conference   PR = Probationary Rating
KEY: R = Request   T = Teaching Assignment for Principal

* Elementary school principals usually find it difficult to schedule more than one supervisory visit per day. The principal should attempt to visit for an entire lesson. An average visit may be thirty minutes in length.

Mechanics of Observation

Duration and Frequency

The duration of the supervisory visit will be determined both by the type of teaching-learning situation being observed and by the type of visit—whether it is the standard or survey variety and whether it is scheduled. Establishing the purpose for the visit in advance enables the principal to gauge the length of the visit accordingly. If the teaching-learning situation happens to be a lesson in political science, the principal may want to be in the classroom for a full hour. A music lesson in an elementary school probably would consume less than half that time.

If the teacher took the initiative by inviting the principal to visit, or if the principal had informed the teacher of an intention to visit, the principal will be expected to remain until the lesson is completed. In the preplanning session with the teacher, the duration of the principal's visit should be discussed. Certainly the principal will be in a better position to discuss the lesson intelligently in the follow-up conference if the total lesson has been observed.

FIGURE 7-2.   Supervisory Visit and Follow-Up Conference Programming Form.

---

1. Preparation for the visit:
   a) Obtain information, check previous notes_____
   _____
   b) Preconference and results_____
   _____
   c) Contact_____

2. The classroom visit:
   a) Time allotment_____
      (Check teacher's daily program)
   b) Method_____
   c) Planned objective_____
   d) Other_____

3. Analysis of the observed performance:
   _____
   _____
   _____

4. The follow-up conference:
   a) Preceding activities
   b) When_____
   c) Where_____
   d) What discussed_____
   e) Written report_____
   f) Plans/materials to bring_____
   _____
   g) Teacher's reactions_____
   h) Closing_____

The frequency of supervisory visits will depend on (1) the purpose of the visit and (2) who initiates the visit. If the supervising principal is observing a teacher who has requested help with a specific area of the instructional program, the principal may want to contemplate a return visit within a short time following the initial observation in order to gather more data or to demonstrate a teaching technique. The principal's function will be to provide as much help as is needed when it is needed.

If the principal initiates the supervisory visit, it is possible that he/she will plan to visit the teacher a minimum of once per month; whereas if the teacher initiates the visit, visits could occur either more or less frequently, depending on the function of the visitation. The frequency of supervisory visits should be a function of an effective program. H. Spears[3] clearly stated the need for a regular

[3] Harold Spears, *Improving the Supervision of Instruction* (Englewood Cliffs, New Jersey: Prentice-Hall, Inc., 1953), p. 62.

program of visitation, commenting that perhaps fear of supervision occurs because visits are infrequent and improperly handled.

Types of Visits

Both scheduled ana unscheduled visits need to be made by the supervising principal to beginning teachers. The supervising principal should concentrate on establishing rapport with th꞉ teacher to be visited. For this reason alone, it might be best to *schedule* at least the initial visits, so that the teachers involved may prepare carefully. They will appreciate the principal's thoughtfulness. Standard scheduled visits are in order for both experienced and beginning teachers.

The beginning teacher realizes that he/she will be rated by the principal. The principal's dropping in unexpectedly will only add to the teacher's feelings of insecurity. Once rapport has been established, the teacher will accept the supervising principal's visit as a matter of course.

If the principal wishes to learn more about a particular phase of the instructional program through observation, then he/she will want to plan especially carefully for the visit. M. S. Norton wrote:

> . . . [the supervisor] must arrange for visitations at times when he/she can best analyze the learning situation and obtain the best cross-section of a particular unit of study.[4]

This principle alsꞈ should be applied to visits to experienced teachers.

Not all scheduled visits are proposed by the principal. Rather, as E. H. Reeder suggested, "some of the principal's visits will be the result of invitations from the new teachers, if the 1ight supervisory relationships have been established."[5]

Once 1apport has been ꞈstablished, the principꞈ꞉ ꞈhould feel free to make ꞈn unscheduled visit. If he/she ha꞉ demonstrated a sincere interest in what happeꞈs within thꞈ ꞉lassroom, the ꞈeacher will welcome hꞈs/her presence and look forward to a conꞈꞈrence later ꞉n the day. The unscheduled visit can serve to reinforce any conclusions the ꞉rincipal may have formꞈlated concerning the instructional program. Conversely, it may result in a change of opinion. Whatever the result, if the supervisor has responded negatively to what he/she has observed in the classroom, he/she should reserve final judgment until he/she has discussed the lesson with the teacher.

Helping the Experienced Teacher through Visitation

Standard *unscheduled* visits to competent, experienced teachers with tenure have been termed a questionable practice by specialists in this area. The principal

[4] Norton, "Are Classroom Visits Worthwhile?", p. 41.
[5] Reeder, *Supervision in the Elementary School,* p. 197.

should plan for standard *scheduled* visits and for scheduled and unscheduled *survey type* visits to the classrooms of experienced teachers. The supervising principal must remember that he/she must account for all that transpires within the school. If a situation involving an experienced teacher arises that the supervising principal cannot ignore, quite properly he/she might have to handle it in a different manner and through established channels. The supervising principal always must remember the safety, welfare, and development of students and staff. Improvement in the instructional program is a means of reaching the goals concomitant to these functions of the principalship.

Scheduled and Unscheduled Survey Visits to the Experienced Teacher

At times a teacher will request that the principal make a complete survey of his/her instructional techniques. It is then that the principal will want to schedule and provide for a scheduled survey visit to the classroom. The *scheduled* survey type visit should be made to the experienced teacher *only* on the invitation of the teacher.[6] These visits will be planned:

1. When the teacher is conducting one phase of study of a problem that was established by group decision and is seeking judgment concerning the effectiveness of certain aspects of the program of action research
2. When an experienced teacher asks for help with a specific area of the instructional program.

It is general practice for supervising principals to complete what is termed an unscheduled survey visit to all classrooms approximately four times each school year. The purpose of the unscheduled survey visit is to give the principal a general overview of the general status of the school and of its instructional program. It is not the purpose of the unscheduled survey visit to focus attention on individual teachers and/or problems. Unscheduled survey visits are too short in duration for the principal to formulate judgments based on individual situations.

Unscheduled survey visits should be planned by the principal. They are made without the invitation of the teachers, whereas the scheduled survey visit is made on invitation *only*. Good human relations require that the supervising principal usually prepare the faculty to expect a visit within a designated period, and to offer an explanation of the purpose for the visit. In summation, the supervising principal plans both scheduled and unscheduled survey type visits to the experienced teacher. The scheduled survey visit involves an *exhaustive* analysis of teaching techniques in instructional programs, and occurs only on invitation. The *unscheduled* survey visit does not involve a critique of progress of the individual teacher, but it is designed to present an overall picture of the general status of the entire school with regard to one or more variables.

[6] Ibid., p. 199.

TABLE 7-1. *Interrelationships Between the Various Major Types of Supervisory Visits*

	To Experienced Teachers	To Beginning Teachers	May Be "On Call"	Usually Only upon Request	Observation Time Determined by Length of Lesson	Shortest Observation Time	Longest Observatior. Time	Critique o, Individual Performance
Unscheduled Survey Visits	X	X				X		
Scheduled Survey Visits	X	X	X	X			X	X
Standard Unscheduled Visits		X			X			X
Standard Scheduled Visits	X	X	X		X			X

In the case of the beginning teacher, the principal probably will wish periodically to apply both types of survey visits. He/she also will employ the standard supervisory visit both of the scheduled and unscheduled variety. Standard visits, especially those that are unscheduled, are designed to aid teachers who have not as yet reached as high a degree of instructional proficiency as have the experienced, permanent professional educators. ᴗee Table 7-1 for a representation of these relations.

Techniques in Visitation

Responsibilities of the Visitor

Discussing how the supervising principal conducts him/herself in the classroom is important only insofar as the teacher and the class are affected by what he/she does.

In conducting the visit, the supervising principal should:

1. Have arranged the time of the visit with the teacher during the previsit conference
2. Enter the classroom quietly and avoid drawing unnecessary attention to him/herself (in a secondary school the interval between classes would be a good time)
3. Smile, to let the teacher and the class know that he/she is glad to be there
4. Try to become a temporary part of the class.

FIGURE 7-3.   Too Many Visits May Spoil the Supervisory Broth.

Some points to consider concerning the management of the observation phase include:

1. The supervisor should gauge mobility by the activity taking place in the class. If the class is engaged in the stimulation and planning phase of a creative writing lesson, the supervising principal will wish to observe at close hand.
2. The supervising principal will make observation practice known to teacher in the previsit planning conference.
3. *Notes should not be made in the classroom* but should be recorded directly after the visit, in private. If the scheduled survey type of visit is being made and notes are taken by agreement in the previsit conference, the teacher should be shown the notes in the follow-up conference.
4. The supervising principal must keep an accurate and detailed record of the strengths and weaknesses of the lesson for follow-up conferences.
5. Emphasis should be placed on the teaching-learning situation and not on the teacher and should gather data for the follow-up conference evaluation.

What to Look for During the Visit

The supervising principal should prepare in advance for the observation by completing a listing of points to be observed. The following outline was prepared by one supervising principal and may prove helpful:

1. Do the students participate in the selection and/or formulation of classroom standards of conduct? Is self-control encouraged?
2. Do students recognize the reasons for their being corrected? Are the observable or predictable consequences of an action stressed? Is disciplinary action considered a form of constructive criticism?

3. What is the teacher trying to accomplish? Is there a definite objective? Does the teacher seem to be guided by it?
4. Is the teacher's attitude friendly and accepting? Does the teacher ridicule or threaten? Is he/she overly familiar?
5. Is the teacher's voice well modulated and of sufficient volume?
6. Does the teacher have leadership qualities? Is he/she confident, positive, and consistent?
7. Does the teacher know the subject matter? Is the teacher well prepared? Does he/she have adequate lesson plans? Does he/she plan for varied activities? Does he/she have materials and instructional technology aids readily available? Is the teacher well organized? Does he/she post an agenda for the period? Does he/she have a seating plan? Does he/she have an efficient way to handle routines? Does he/she have a definite place to write assignments? Are assignments clear, reasonable, pertinent, and varied? Do they meet individual and group needs?
8. What teaching method or combination of methods and techniques are observed? Is the method used skillfully? What is the reaction of the class? Is there much participation? Caution: participation (or the lack of it) does not necessarily make a lesson. How much disturbance is there? How much enthusiasm?
9. Does the lesson come to a useful conclusion? Does the teacher provide for enrichment activities for fast workers? Does he/she show how the lesson relates to the present and/or future psychosociological world of the student?

Interaction Matrices and the Use of Video-Tape Recordings in Instructional Supervision

INTERACTION MATRICES: THE FLANDERS SYSTEM.   During visitation, the supervisor can help the teacher increase effectiveness by using different interaction matrices, such as that developed by Flanders and by Medley, by Withall, and by Perkins.[7] Interaction analysis schemes attempt to quantify and categorize the spoken-verbal communications during a lesson, and to record and chart the results of the analysis. The categories generally differentiate between teacher-originated and student-originated vocal communications. The categories and three forms used in recording and charging the results of the application of this technique are included as Appendix B.

The supervisor must beware the temptation to apply the interaction matrix technique without considering its limitations. There is a tendency to fail to

[7] Ned Flanders, "Intent, Action, and Feedback: A Preparation for Teaching," *Journal of Teacher Education* XIV (September 1963), no. 3; Donald M. Medley, "Experience with the OSCAR Technique," and John Withall, "Mental Health: Teacher Education Report," both in *Journal of Teacher Education* XIV (September 1963), no. 3; and Hugh Perkins, "A Procedure for Assessing the Classroom Behavior of Students and Teachers," *American Educational Research Journal* (November 1964).

differentiate between an analysis or how much "teacher-talk" is occurring in a classroom and the prescription of how much *should* be in evidence: "Perhaps the . . . percentage of teacher questioning and confirming should be increased— at least in some learning situations," as noted by Lucio and McNeil.[8] Further- more, the supervisor must keep in mind that this technique does not analyze all teacher effectiveness, but only an aspect of student-teacher verbal behavior.

USE OF VIDEO-TAPE RECORDINGS AND MICRO-TEACHING TECHNIQUES IN SUPER- VISION. A video-tape recording can work wonders in the area of supervision. The technique of recording a lesson on a video-tape recorder can, if handled properly, permit the teacher to visit his/her own classroom at leisure. The video- tape recorder not only provides direct aid to the student, as in micro-teaching, but also permits instructors to appraise the quality and effectiveness of their presenta- tions to their classes, and to analyze their lessons at a higher level than the traditional visit and "hearsay" follow-up conference.

The video-tape recorder should be set up in the classroom several days before the visit (or its intended use as prescribed above) to permit the teacher to become acquainted with the equipment and its operation and to minimize the "on-stage" syndrome. The superior should emphasize that the tape will be avail- able for the teacher's use ONLY, that the supervising principal will view the results ONLY if requested to do so by the teacher, and that the tape becomes the property of the teacher and is in his/her custody immediately on recording. The authors recommend that the supervisor encourage the purchase of color video-recording equipment. The small price differential is more than compensated for by the added dimension and impact of the color programming.

Checklist for Recording Data about Observed Instruction

The supervising principal may wish to involve the staff in the preparation of a checklist instrument for recording data obtained during observation. One such visitation record is included as Figure 7-4.

Shorter Continuous Records of Observed Instruction

The three observation report forms that have been helpful are illustrated in Figures 7-5, 7-6, 7-7.

If, by district policy, the supervising principal must complete a teacher evaluation sheet that will be considered as pertinent in determining whether the teacher is to be rehired, forms such as the three that are included as Figues 7-8, 7-9, and 7-10 might be used.

[8] William H. Lucio and John D. McNeil, *Supervision* (New York: McGraw-Hill Book Company, 1969), p. 314.

FIGURE 7-4. Sample Visitation Record

VISITATION RECORD

Name of staff member
making visit: _____ Date _____

Name of teacher visited: _____

School where teacher employed: _____

Grade and/or subjects being taught: _____

Previsitation interview: _____

Postvisitation conference: _____

Observation Criteria	Superior	Good	Average	Needs Impr.
General appearance and poise				
Room appearance and physical condition				
Teaching materials and procedures				
Student-teacher relationship				
Interest and activity of students				
Classroom management				
Attitude toward teaching				
Command of language: effective communication				
Chalkboard ability				

Comments and suggestions resulting from visit:

FIGURE 7-5. Sample Observation Report Form

OBSERVATION REPORT

School _____

Teacher_____Grade_____Date_____

Subject observed_____Time_____

1. STUDENTS:
   a) Attitude_____
   b) Attention_____
   c) Discipline_____

   d) Effort_____
   e) Seating_____
   f) Number in room_____

2. TEACHER:
   a) Preparation_____
   b) Following plan_____
   c) Response of students_____
   d) Skill_____

   e) Speech_____
   f) Voice quality_____
   g) Appearance_____

3. LESSON:
   a) Topic_____
   b) Technique_____

   c) Student participa-
      tion_____
   d) Use of Instruc-
      tion aids_____

4. ROOM:
   a) Bulletin boards/
      displays_____
   b) Writing aids posted_____
   c) Environment_____

   d) Ventilation_____
   e) Lighting_____
   f) General appear-
      ance_____

5. OVERALL EVALUATION:
   a) Strong points_____
   c) Additional suggestions_____

   b) Weak points_____

Follow-up conference held:

No_____Yes_____ Date_____Observer's signature

_____

FIGURE 7-6.   Sample Observation Report

JOINT SCHOOL DISTRICT NO. 407
St. Marcus, Idaho
OBSERVATION REPORT

School _____ Instructor _____

Date _____ No. of Students _____ Subject or Grade _____

Lesson Title _____ Observer _____

NOTES: _____

1. Room appearance

2. Personal appearance

3. Emotional climate of room

4. General classroom management

5. Presentation of material

6. Lesson preparation

7. Assignments

8. Student-teacher relations

9. Punctuality

10. Supervisory work

11. Administration-teacher relations

12. Lesson Plan Book

13. Grade Book

14. Comments

Signed: _____
            Teacher   Date   Principal

FIGURE 7-7.   Sample Report of Principal's Classroom Visit

REPORT OF PRINCIPAL'S CLASSROOM VISIT

Teacher _____ Class _____ Hour _____ Date _____

I. *Physical Characteristics of Classroom:*

   1. Ventilation _____

   2. Lighting_____

   3. Temperature _____

   4. Seating arrangements _____

   5. Decorations _____

   6. Displays _____

   7. Orderliness _____

II. *Teaching:*

   1. Are classroom activities in line with stated objectives:

_____

_____

   2. Student reactions:

_____

_____

   3. Work in progress:

_____

_____

   4. Evaluation:

_____

_____

_____

                                        _____

                                                Principal

FIGURE 7-8.   Teacher Evaluation Sheet for Instructional Improvement

---

Name and Place of School System

Teacher's name _____ Grade _____

School _____ Date _____

Subject being taught during observation
   or evaluation _____

Conditions: 1. Excellent   3. Weak, needs improvement
              2. Satisfactory   4. Unsatisfactory, needs improvement

FACTORS OF EVALUATION

       1 2 3 4   *A. Objectives*

1.   . . . .   Objectives clearly defined (long-term and immediate)?
2.   . . . .   Instruction guided by objectives?

B. Planning

3.   . . . .   Evidence of careful and definite planning?
4.   . . . .   Evidence of following plan?

C. General Room Atmosphere

5.   . . . .   Does the room atmosphere encourage intellectual activity?
6.   . . . .   Does the arrangement of furniture give unity in the room?
7.   . . . .   Are there present pictures, flowers or other conditions
                      which tend to make the classroom pleasant?

D. General Room Appearance

8.   . . . .   Clean?
9.   . . . .   Well ventilated?
10.   . . . .   Students' desks and room clean and tidy?
11.   . . . .   No evidence of willful destruction of desks or other school
                      property?

E. Personal Characteristics

12.   . . . .   Dressed appropriately and well groomed?
13.   . . . .   Speaks clearly and uses good English?
14.   . . . .   Is physically able to perform duties?
                    Is not handicapped by too frequent absence or illness?
15.   . . . .   Maintains sound emotional adjustment; has good self-control?
16.   . . . .   Has a sense of humor?
17.   . . . .   Is a resourceful person?
18.   . . . .   Can accept deserved criticism and praise with poise?

FIGURE 7-8.   (Continued)

1 2 3 4
19. . . . . Shows understanding and concern for individual students?
20. . . . . Punctual to work and with reports and assignments?
21. . . . . Attempts to correct personal habits and mannerisms that de-
            tract from effective teaching?
22. . . . . Displays knowledge of subject being taught?

F. *Classroom Control: Teaching*

Methods and Tools

23. . . . . Handles behavior problems individually as far as possible?
24. . . . . Is consistently fair and firm in dealing with classroom be-
            havior problems?
25. . . . . Is respected by students and secures voluntary cooperation?
26. . . . . Adapts to the teaching-learning situation?
            (Underline method used: Lecture, Recitation, Drill, Story-Tell-
            ing, Project or Laboratory, Audio-Visual, Dramatic or Role
            Playing, Group Discussion, Manual.)
27. . . . . Skillful and timely use of teaching aids?
28. . . . . Avoids scolding, nagging, shouting, or loud talking?
29. . . . . Belives in, maintains, or helps maintain good order in the
            classroom, halls, and all parts of the building?

G. *Instructional and Guidance Skills*

30. . . . . Provides for individual differences?
31. . . . . Provides for effective class and group work?
32. . . . . Encourages good work and study habits?
33. . . . . Insists on thorough and neat work; done on time?
34. . . . . Evidence of students mastering skills being taught?
35. . . . . Students are being taught self-direction and democratic prin-
            ciples?
36. . . . . Provides opportunities for working effectively in groups or as
            individuals?
37. . . . . Inspires eager responses from students; many participating?
38. . . . . Exercises care, supervision, and provides special instruction
            in health, safety, moral, and spiritual values?
39. . . . . Respects students' suggestions and opinions?
40. . . . . No favoritism; no pets?
41. . . . . Praise and criticism based on fact; no hasty conclusions?
42. . . . . Students devoid of tensions and free to speak, express opin-
            ions?

H. *Assignments*

43. . . . . Assignments definite and clear, reasonable in length and
            difficulty?
44. . . . . Establishes a link between the new lesson and the past lesson?

FIGURE 7-8.   (Continued)

45. . . . . Explains and motivates for assignments, rather than mere page and chapter assignments?

I. Professional and Staff Characteristics

46. . . . . Conducts relations with students and teachers on a high plane?
47. . . . . Aids in developing and maintaining faculty and student morale?
48. . . . . Actively supports local, state, and national professional organizations in accordance with district policies and directions of superiors?
49. . . . . Does not talk unethically about other teachers, administrators, parents, or students?

J. Classroom Mechanics

50. . . . . Follows school policies in marking roll books?
51. . . . . Proper and timely assignment and correction of written assignments (including work books)?
52. . . . . Proper and timely follow-up of written work?
53. . . . . Accuracy in accomplishing routine details and assignments?

Remarks: (Feel free to make remarks on any factor above. When so doing, list letter and number.)

Use of Goal-Based, Cooperatively Developed Rating Instruments

The several evaluation forms available, then, differ in detail, but essentially focus on performance in the eight areas listed below. These forms should focus on individual or team goals. They should be developed cooperatively following the establishment of jointly agreed on district and school criteria.

1. Classroom management and disciplinary control
2. Knowledge of subject matter
3. Teaching techniques and instructional skills
4. Dependability and record keeping
5. Personal characteristics such as appearance, punctuality, tact, voice, cooperation, sense of humor, initiative, enthusiasm, poise, and good grooming
6. Personal fitness for the job
7. Human relationships with students, parents, other staff members, and the community
8. Professional conduct, ethics, and evidence of professional growth.

FIGURE 7-9.   Sample Teacher Evaluation Form

EVALUATION FOR PROFESSIONAL GROWTH

This form will be used as a guide for teacher eveluation. It should prove helpful both for self-evaluation and for evaluation by the principal or superintendent or both. Summaries are to be mutually agreed upon and will be recorded as an indication of progress. These summaries should indicate teacher strengths and points of improvement. The intent is not negative but to give a positive approach to mutual growth. All interviews will be held in strict confidence.

This form is to be used as often as necessary but at least one interview is required each year for all teaching staff members. One copy completed is retained by the principal and one copy is retained by the superintendent.

The five areas listed below form the basis for the improvement and evaluation of professional services

TEACHER EVALUATION FORM

	Superior	Good	Satis-factory	Needs Improvement
I. Personal Characteristics Statement: A superior teacher has a wholesome personality, a sound character, and enjoys good physical, mental, and emotional health. a. Personal appearance				
b. Emotional stability (self-control)				
c. High ethical and moral standards				
d. Punctuality				
e. Dependability				
f. Poise				
g. Tact				

FIGURE 7-9.   (Continued)

	Superior	Good	Satis-factory	Needs Im-provement
h. Voice				
i. Health				
j. Fulfills obligations				
II. Instruction Skills Statement: A superior teacher controls all classroom activities to assure that work of individuals and groups is orderly and effective; that each student contributes according to his ability; and that each one gains a sense of worth through achievement. a. Classroom control (discipline)				
b. Knowledge of subject matter				
c. Preparation				
d. Leadership				
e. Ability to stimulate student				
III. Teacher—Staff Relationships Statement: A superior teacher is a good team worker who is conscious that his attitudes affect all others on the school staff. He is loyal to the school's program and its policies. a. Cooperation with staff administration				
b. Adheres to school regulations				
c. Loyalty				
d. Serves willingly				

FIGURE 7-9.   (Continued)

	Superior	Good	Satis-factory	Needs Im-provement
IV. Self-Improvement Statement: A superior teacher takes responsibility for, and participates in, various types of student and faculty activities; takes responsibility for formal and informal guidance beyond regular classroom contacts; appears always as an important and valuable member of the professional "team" operating the school. a. Cultural interests				
b. Evidences of professional growth				
c. Participation in professional and/or subject area organizations				
V. Social and Community Participation Statement: A superior teacher will utilize community resources and take part in community activities. a. Professional relationship with students				
b. Participation in activities, community affairs				
c. Relationships with parents				

General comments:

Teacher's Signature _____ Signature of Evaluator _____

Date of Evaluation _____

FIGURE 7-10. Teacher Observation Record Sheet

Name of School System

Name of Teacher _____ Status _____ File or Employee Number _____

School _____ Principal _____

Subject/Grade Taught _____ Date _____ Time _____

Directions: Please indicate by a check in the appropriate parentheses the description which fits best.

	Unsatis-factory	Weak	Satis-factory	Strong	Out-standing	No Oppor-tunity to Observe
Personal Qualities:						
1. Appearance, manner, and bearing	( )	( )	( )	( )	( )	( )
2. Mental alertness	( )	( )	( )	( )	( )	( )
3. Effectiveness of voice and speech	( )	( )	( )	( )	( )	( )
4. Oral and written expression	( )	( )	( )	( )	( )	( )
5. Emotional poise	( )	( )	( )	( )	( )	( )
6. Health and physical condition	( )	( )	( )	( )	( )	( )
Professional Competence:						
1. Knowledge of subject matter	( )	( )	( )	( )	( )	( )
2. Knowledge and use of basic skills (reading, spelling, language usage, arithmetic)	( )	( )	( )	( )	( )	( )
3. Development of classroom control (discipline) and morale	( )	( )	( )	( )	( )	( )
4. Leadership qualities	( )	( )	( )	( )	( )	( )
5. Success in planning for instruction	( )	( )	( )	( )	( )	( )
6. Effectiveness of teaching procedures	( )	( )	( )	( )	( )	( )
7. Management of classroom environment and routine	( )	( )	( )	( )	( )	( )

8. Assumption of share or responsibility
   for school activities ( ) ( ) ( ) ( ) ( )

9. Ability to work with others (members of school
   staff, parents, community leaders) ( ) ( ) ( ) ( ) ( )

10. Reaction to constructive criticism
    of a professional nature ( ) ( ) ( ) ( ) ( )

Comments: Be Objective:

1. Attitude _____
2. Relations with people/ability to adjust _____
3. Professionalism: ethics and acts _____
4. Poise/appearance _____
5. Organization _____
6. Sense of humor/manner with children _____
7. Discipline (control) _____
8. Understanding of principles of educational psychology and guidance _____
9. Honesty and consistency _____
10. Cocurricular activities _____
11. Community relations _____
12. Further comments _____

*Conferences held on _____
                        (dates)

Recommend continued employment _____

Recommend dismissal _____
Recommend transfer _____

Special recommendations _____
to teacher: _____
                (optional)

Overall Rating: Unsatisfactory ( )   Weak   ( )
                 Satisfactory   ( )   Strong ( )
                 Outstanding   ( )

Date _____ Signed _____
                                    (Principal)

* The remainder of the form usually would be completed only after numerous administrative (not supervisory) visits and follow-up conferences, aimed primarily at rating and at determining the teacher's qualifications for reemployment purposes, had been held.

Limitations

The practitioner in supervision should keep in mind the many limitations of such checklists and rating scales. No foolproof method of evaluation has yet been (nor shall be) developed. Too many variables and judgment decisions are involved.

There is a lack of hard research data concerning what really constitutes good teaching performance. Two observers of the same classroom lesson will not agree on its effectiveness in every detail. One may look for quiet, controlled participation of students, whereas another may look for dynamic, challenging discussion with many students trying to present their ideas—often at the same time. Would either technique indicate best teaching in all classrooms at all times for all teachers and students? Certainly not!

No form has yet been developed that is acceptable to all supervisors. Rating scales inherently include errors and, if used without awareness of their many limitations, can rate a teacher unfairly. Unreliable evaluation is worse than no evaluation.

How to Use the Technique of Interschool Visitation

An improved program of supervisory visits includes individual and group visitation opportunities for teachers and principals. If carefully planned and managed, it is one of the best ways to present the use of desirable methods and techniques. Principals and teachers alike can benefit by this type of experience.

Teachers who are new to a school system and who need an opportunity to learn about a particular phase of the program should find demonstration lessons helpful. This also is an excellent way to familiarize all staff members with a new way of working. They can adapt it to their own needs, or reject it, once they have seen it in action.

The supervising principal can help in providing demonstration lessons for group observation purposes and can direct an individual to a master teacher for observation of a particular lesson.

Individual Visits

When a need arises, if there is no one in the principal's school to whom he/she can send the teacher to observe, he/she can turn to the principal of a neighboring school for assistance. A principal may be able to suggest two or three teachers who would be willing and able to present the kind of lesson desired.

The principal should make final arrangements for a teacher's visit to another school. These arrangements should include contacting the principal of the other school and receiving approval of the proposed visit. The other principal, in turn, can discuss the visit with the host teacher. Usually the demonstration teacher's regular schedule would be observed in planning a time for the visit.

If possible, the supervising principal should accompany the observing teacher on the visit. The observing teacher should take notes to help remember successful techniques, and a conference should follow the observation. Asking the demonstration teacher to participate in the discussion is a desirable practice.

When the teacher must visit without the principal, it is still desirable to have the visiting teacher and his/her principal discuss the lesson when the teacher returns to his/her school. The teacher should decide on a course of action that will result from the observation experience.

Group Visitation

One noteworthy aspect of the group visitation program is the amount of learning that results for all who participate. Teachers, principals, and specialist-consultants benefit.

Group visitations involve more extensive planning by the principal than is involved in scheduling individual visitations. Planning includes (1) determining the type of lesson to be presented, (2) selecting the demonstration teacher, (3) scheduling the visit, (4) preparing the class for the visit, (5) selecting the observation techniques to be used, and (6) scheduling the preplanning and evaluation conferences for the observers.

In making a decision on the type of lesson to be presented, the most common determining factor is a general need for improving a particular area of the instructional program. An awareness of this need can occur as a result of conferences such as the grade-level meeting or through supervisory visits.

The following suggestions may be given to the group prior to the visit:

1. Be aware of class differences, especially where there is homogeneous grouping and type class.
2. Become acquainted with the demonstration teacher before the visit.
3. Create as little disturbance as possible in entering and leaving the classroom. The observers should be present at the beginning of the class period and remain in the room until the period is over.
4. Observe the reactions of the pupils.
5. Observe the use of the materials of instructional technology and the techniques of programmed learning.
6. Note all steps in the lesson and the amount of time spent on each step. Observe how the teacher stimulates the students.
7. Remember to appear happy, relaxed, and free from strain or uneasiness before, during, and after the visit.

Preparing for the Visit

When arrangements have been made for a group to observe a demonstration lesson, the observation period always should be preceded by a preplanning conference with the observers. In this conference period the purpose of the demonstration is established, pertinent background information is provided about the children to be observed, and group activities that have led up to the lesson to be presented are listed.

SOME HELPFUL DEVICES.   A valuable preplanning technique involves using a carefully prepared observation sheet on which the observers may make notes as the lesson is developed. Questions on the observation sheet will add to the observer's awareness of techniques employed by the demonstration teacher and will help make the teaching-learning situation more meaningful.

The principal should be familiar with the various types of fact-gathering techniques that can be used during observations. He/she also should be aware of their limitations. He/she must be skillful in choosing techniques to apply in a given situation.

SETTING THE DATE AND TIME.   Once the school and the teacher have been selected, a date for the visitation is arrived at cooperatively by the principals and the teachers involved. Usually the host principal suggests one or two dates that will not conflict with the master calendar. Then the visiting principal and the teachers select one of the dates suggested. An effort is made to plan the visit for when teachers will not have to be away from their classroom for a prolonged period.

The visit may be planned for the first instructional period of either the morning or afternoon session so that the planning conference can be held during the half hour before school begins, thus not cutting into the instructional time. Or it may be held the last period of the morning or of the afternoon, allowing for the evaluation conference after the children have been excused.

PREPARING THE HOST CLASS.   To prepare the class for the visit, the principal must work closely with the teacher and the class in developing readiness for the teaching-learning situation to be demonstrated. This preparation may involve several supervisory visits to the classroom, followed by conferences.

If the purpose of such visits is to help the visiting teachers use new techniques and to help the class learn how to handle new ways of working, the teacher and the class should have enough time to adjust to the changes.

A class should not practice or rehearse the lesson that will be presented during the demonstration. It must in no way be an artificial situation. However, the host principal may want to review the teacher's final plans with him/her and help in every way possible to prepare for the lesson.

It is suggested that the host principal select observation techniques that will guide the observers toward the intended goal—namely, discovering ways to utilize in their own classrooms the techniques that are to be demonstrated.

Plan to Schedule a Pre-Visit Conference

In scheduling the group visitation, adequate time should be provided for discussing the lesson with the master teacher. A visitation without these conferences has little value.

An important part of preparing for a group visitation is making sure that all individuals included or affected by the visit are properly notified. Usually a supervisory memorandum is prepared that includes all essential information. The memorandum should contain a brief description of the type of lesson to be presented, information about the grade level for which it is planned, and the place and time of visitation. The principal should make sure that teachers receive the information and should expedite plans for their attendance.

The Visitors Arrive

Common courtesies should be observed by the visiting principal, the host principal, and the teachers during a group interschool supervisory visit. A courteous principal can make the visit a welcome event; and a courteous host principal and teaching staff, in turn, make their school a pleasant place to visit.

The dictates of good supervisory practices demand that the visiting principal announce the arrival at the host school both as a matter of courtesy and to keep his whereabouts known in case of an emergency. He should introduce himself to the school clerk, who should be expecting him. The host principal should be present to greet the group and to accompany the guests throughout the visit.

In either conference situation, the principals will need to remember that the purposes of the conference are to discuss good ways of working with children and to encourage teachers to experiment with different techniques, to keep abreast in subject matter, and to adapt what is observed to their particular situations.

Plan for a Post-Visit Conference

As the visit draws to a close, the principals may wish to hold a short conference to review the day's work. Any discussion of individual situations remains on a highly professional level and must not become a supervisory rating session. If good planning preceded the visit, and good practices were followed during the visit, much has been accomplished.

Do

1. Evaluate the job (performance)—not the person.
2. Base evaluations on *firsthand* observations.
3. Use a positive approach; consider what will help improve the teacher's effectiveness.
4. Combine the measurement of personality traits, student progress, and teacher performance in your program of teacher evaluation.
5. Keep the evaluation program flexible enough to meet changing conditions.
6. Consider evaluation as an important means toward achieving goals—not an end in itself.
7. Be thoroughly familiar with the teacher's abilities and background, as well as those of the students in the class to be observed.
8. Record observations immediately and arrange a conference with the teacher to analyze findings cooperatively.
9. Smile; maintain a cheerful and sincere attitude.
10. Plan your work—work your plan—and evaluate.
11. Discuss what appear to be the strong and weak aspects of the teacher's performance, and make definite plans for correction and improvement.
12. Remember to schedule a previsitation conference. (This practice constitutes a very important aspect of the supervisory visitation-conference complex.)
13. Encourage an experimental environment in which teachers and supervisors feel free to explore, to experiment, and to test methods, processes, and materials used in teaching.

Don't

1. View the visit as an inspection tour.
2. Direct criticism at the individual.
3. Make a visit without first establishing good rapport.
4. Criticize a teacher's work in front of others.
5. Discuss a teacher's problems with other teachers.

TRENDS CONCERNING SUPERVISORY VISITS

Toward ⟶ Broader Participation in the

Evaluation Process

Several trends are becoming apparent in teacher evaluation. Rating devices are becoming less rigid and more constructive. Cooperatively developed goals, criteria, techniques, and rating instruments are becoming more common. There will be more coevaluation by teachers and supervisors. The principle of multiple evaluation will be used more extensively, with professional associations joining in the evaluation process.

Due to the integral nature of the topics, further trends concerning supervisory visits and follow-up conferences are included in the following chapter.

Supervisory Problems

In-Basket

Problem 1

The problem develops in a fourth-grade classroom in an elementary school of about 600 students. The teacher involved (Miss Iseri) had one year of experience before her assignment to this school. She seems to do an excellent job. The students like her and work hard for her. She plans her work well and is an enthusiastic teacher. She is not unattractive, but is slightly "dowdy" in her appearance.

It is the policy of the principal (her immediate supervisor) to visit the classrooms of all teachers at least twice during the school year. The first visit is always a standard scheduled visit; the second visit usually is of the unscheduled standard variety.

When the supervising principal entered Miss Iseri's classroom for the first time he noticed that she was, apparently, quite disturbed by his presence. She rapidly became more flustered until she finally embarrassed herself and the principal before he could leave the room. She was extremely upset when the principal tried to hold a conference with her. He learned later that she was upset whenever *any* adult entered her room, and was especially distraught if that adult was another educator.

How can the supervising principal develop the kind of rapport with the teacher that will allow him to visit her classroom in his capacity as a supervisor?

Problem 2

A principal at a neighboring school has asked for advice. He described a severe situation regarding a teacher who has become antagonistic and resentful toward supervisors and supervision.

Describe the procedures that you would suggest for handling the situation.

Questions and Suggested Activities Concerning
How to Improve Supervisory Visits
and Follow-Up Conferences

Questions

1. What are some important objections to visiting the classroom only on the teacher's invitation?
2. What techniques might be effectively employed for recording classroom activities? Could video recordings be helpful? How?
3. How can the supervisor insure that his/her presence is not threatening to the teacher or distracting to the students?

Suggested Activities

1. List the most promising techniques for improving supervisory visits and conferences.
2. Contrast supervisory visits in a small district with those in a large city school system.
3. Outline a plan for supervisory visits and follow-up conferences in a nineteen-teacher school.
4. Suggest techniques that a supervisor can use to get invitations from teachers for supervisory visits and conferences.
5. Indicate when, and under what conditions, supervisory visits should be conducted.
6. Describe and compare the advantages and disadvantages of the announced and the unannounced supervisory visit.
7. Distinguish between the standard scheduled visit, the standard unscheduled visit, the scheduled survey visit, and the unscheduled survey visit. Indicate the circumstances under which you, as the supervising principal, would employ each type.
8. Indicate when and under what conditions consultants from outside the local school system should be called on to make classroom visits.

Selected Bibliography

Books

Adams, H. P. et al. *Basic Principles of Supervision.* New York: American Book Company, 1953.

Anderson, Richard C. et al. *Current Research on Instruction.* Englewood Cliffs, New Jersey: Prentice-Hall, Inc., 1969.

Ayer, Fred C. *Fundamentals of Instructional Supervision.* New York: Harper & Row, Publishers, 1954.

Bartky, John A. *Supervision as Human Relations.* Boston: D. C. Heath and Company, 1953.

Criscualo, Nicholas P. *Supervising the Reading Program.* Midland, Michigan: Pendell Publishing Co., 1973.

Douglas, H. R. et al. *Democratic Supervision in Secondary Schools.* Cambridge: The Riverside Press, 1961.

Drucker, Peter F. *Managing for Results.* New York: Harper & Row Co., 1964.

Faunce, Roland C. *Secondary School Administration.* New York: Harper and Brothers, 1955.

Griffith, Francis J. *A Handbook for the Observation of Teaching and Learning.* Midland, Michigan: Pendell Publishing Co., 1973.

Harris, Ben M. *Supervisory Behavior in Education.* 2nd ed. Englewood Cliffs, New Jersey: Prentice-Hall, Inc., 1975.

Hicks, Hanne J. *Educational Supervision in Principle and Practice.* New York: The Ronald Press Company, 1960.

Lucio, William H. et al. *Supervision: A Synthesis of Thought and Action.* New York: McGraw-Hill Book Company, 1962.

Morgan, James E. *Supervision of Employees.* Englewood Cliffs, New Jersey: Prentice-Hall, Inc., 1973.

Neagley, Ross L., and N. Dean Evans. *Handbook for Effective Supervision of Instruction.* Englewood Cliffs, New Jersey: Prentice-Hall, Inc., 1968.

Nolte, Mervin Chester. *Duties and Liabilities of School Administrators.* Los Angeles: Parker & Son Publications, Inc., 1973.

Reeder, Edwin H. *Supervision in the Elementary School.* Boston: Houghton Mifflin Company, 1953.

Spears, Harold. *Improving the Supervision of Instruction.* Englewood Cliffs, New Jersey: Prentice-Hall, Inc., 1953.

Stoops, Emery, and James R. Marks. *Elementary School Supervision.* Boston: Allyn and Bacon, Inc., 1965.

Stoops, Emery, and Russell E. Johnson. *Elementary School Administration.* New York: McGraw-Hill Book Company, 1967.

Torrance, E. Paul. *Guiding Creative Talent.* Englewood Cliffs, New Jersey: Prentice-Hall, Inc., 1962. Especially chapter X.

Periodicals

Flanders, Ned. "Intent, Action, Feedback: A Preparation for Teaching," *Journal of Teacher Education* XIV (September 1963), No. 3.

Gross, R. S. "Teachers Want Supervision." *School Executive* LXXII (August 1953)
  52–53.
Harman, A. C. "Classroom Visitation as a Phase of Supervision." *American Schoo
  Board Journal* CXVIII (June 1949) : 39–40.
Medley, Donald M. "Experience with the OSCAR Technique," and John Withall
  "Mental Health: Teacher Education Report," both in *Journal of Teacher Edu-
  cation* XIV (September 1963), No. 3.
Norton, Monte S. "Are Classroom Visits Worthwhile?" *The Clearing House* XXV
  (September 1960) : 41.
Perkins, Hugh. "A Procedure for Assessing the Classroom Behavior of Students and
  Teachers," *American Educational Research Journal* (November 1964).

Other Sources

Association for Supervision and Curriculum Development. *Leadership for Improving
  Instruction.* 1960 Yearbook. Washington, D.C.: National Education Association,
  1960.
Burnham, Reba M., and Martha L. King. *Supervision in Action.* Washington, D.C.:
  Association for Supervision and Curriculum Development. National Education
  Association, 1961.
Southwest Cooperative Program in Educational Administration. *The Role of the Ad-
  ministrator in the Analysis and Improvement of Instruction.* Austin: University
  of Texas Press, 1954.
Steel, Sanger. *Improving Instruction.* New York: Metropolitan School Study Council,
  1954.

8

How to Improve Supervisory Follow-Up Conferences

Most specialists in supervision suggest that the principal have some kind of follow-up conference shortly after classroom visitation. This chapter presents specific suggestions on how the supervising principal can improve the supervisory conference. The following topics will be discussed:

> Principles and purposes of supervisory conferences
> How to conduct a successful conference
> How to interview
> Do—Don't
> Trends
> "In-Basket" supervisory problem
> Questions and suggested activities

Principles and Purposes of Supervisory Conferences

Objectives of Follow-Up Conferences

Five criteria to be followed by the supervising principal in the formal follow-up conference:

1. First, the principal should establish rapport with the teacher at the beginning of the conference.
2. The principal should include a general commendation of the lesson as a whole, and specific approval of a specific aspect of the lesson.
3. The principal should commend the teacher on his/her skill.
4. The principal should help further the teacher's confidence in him/herself and his/her work.
5. The principal should include constructive suggestions whereby the teacher's good work can be further improved.

243

The goal of a follow-up conference between a supervisor and a teacher is cooperative planning, not the imposition of a plan on the teacher. A conference is an attempt to reach a union of minds and purposes.[1]

The individual conference probably is the most important supervisory technique for use in the specific improvement of instruction. If correctly employed, it gives each teacher the special help needed to become proficient in self-analysis, self-appraisal, and self-improvement. As a form of personal interview, the individual conference provides an excellent opportunity for the two participants to define the subject to be discussed, to agree on the educational point of view, to recognize the need for improvement, and to solve the problem cooperatively.

The supervisory conference is a difficult activity because of the personal element involved. Misgivings are faced by both the principal and the teacher, regardless of the amount of experience each has had. The principal wonders if the teacher will understand the professional purposes and if his/her assistance will be thorough and clear.

New and experienced teachers alike panic at the thought of an individual conference. They will wonder what is wrong with their work. Was the lesson really all right? If not, will they be given a chance to improve?

The Nature of the Conference

No set plan for holding conferences can be outlined. However, there are some factors that will determine the need for scheduling a conference. The need exists:

1. When the principal has visited a classroom.
2. When a teacher has requested an individual conference.
3. When participants in a group project need to meet. Such a conference can be scheduled several weeks in advance or on a regular basis.
4. When a beginning teacher is employed.
5. When the principal wishes to discuss a problem with an individual staff member or with a group.

How to Conduct a Successful Conference

Preparing for the Conference

Preparing for the supervisory conference is just as important as preparing for a supervisory visit. Great knowledge, skill, and understanding are required to carry

---

[1] See George C. Kyte, *The Principal at Work,* rev. ed. (Boston: Ginn and Company, 1952). Chapters XIV and XV are especially helpful.

on a successful conference. It will be to the advantage of the principal to have every available resource within reach.

Some of the following suggested activities may apply more to one specific type of conference than to another. The principal should select those that will help in a particular situation.

1.   Recall the purpose of the conference.
2.   Review all records pertinent to this conference.
3.   Develop tentative hypotheses by anticipating probable conclusions and recommendations.
4.   Note possible courses of action.
5.   Review and assemble additional professional materials that will help the teacher.
6.   Assemble instructional materials that the teacher may use and evaluate.
7.   Check with the custodian to learn if the room is ready.
8.   Remind all participants of the conference time and place.
9.   Plan to provide simple refreshments.

Teacher committees might assist with some of the preparations, particularly refreshments, if this is a group conference. For an individual conference, a teacher will appreciate the principal's thoughtfulness if some refreshment is planned. Refreshments create a more relaxed, informal atmosphere that is conducive to the sharing of ideas.

Scheduling a Time and a Place for the Conference

More importance seems to be attached to the time for which the principal sets the conference than to where it will be held. Both decisions can be arrived at cooperatively by the principal and by the teachers involved.

OPTIMUM CONFERENCE TIME. When the conference concerns a visit to a classroom, it is wise to arrange for the conference to be held as soon as possible following the visit. The discussion will have more meaning if the details of the teaching-learning situation are not allowed to fade because too much time has elapsed. However, it is important to schedule the conference at an hour when enough time can be allotted in order to allow for a discussion that is satisfying to all participants. Many times a conference before school or after school will be best for this reason. In the event that a teacher has a free work period, a conference could be scheduled at that particular time.

Conferences that are most likely to be held after school include the group conference (with the exception of the group visitation conference, which will be discussed later) and the individual conference that is not related to a recent visitation. The individual conference easily might be held before school, if time permits.

CONFERENCE LOCATION. As to where the conference is held, the size of the group that will meet with the principal is a determining factor. Obviously, an individual conference can be held in a place that would not be suitable for a group conference.

Individual conferences following visitations frequently are held in the classroom. It often is easier to visualize the total situation when discussing the lesson in the same environmental setting.

Although the teacher should have a choice as to the meeting place, usually *he/she will feel more secure within his/her own classroom* than in the principal's office. Other individual conferences most likely will be held in the office unless the principal asks to come to the classroom. The principal may wish to talk about the use of new materials and will feel that where they will be used is the best place to hold the conference.

Group conferences often are held in the faculty conference room or workroom. However, if the group plans to work with the various materials of instructional technology, such as a motion picture projector, the choice might be either the audio-visual room or the auditorium. Some classrooms used by older children serve the purpose very well.

The important points with which the principal needs to be concerned are: (1) insuring privacy, (2) being careful to protect the ego of all, and (3) making certain that every teacher involved is informed of the time and place for the conference. The information could be posted or could be included in a weekly bulletin.

The Principal's Actions and Reactions During a Conference

The principal is responsible for the success of the conference. As the instructional leader of the school, the principal should typify certain personal qualities and professional abilities if he/she is to establish rapport with staff members and if he/she is to maintain a superior instructional program within the school. Professional conduct begets professional conduct.

The following are suggestions for working with teachers in a conference situation. If conscientiously followed, they should result in a fruitful conference period. The principal should:

1. Be friendly.
2. Listen carefully.
3. Invite participation from all present.
4. Share the responsibility of analyzing techniques and prescribing a subsequent course of action.
5. Offer suggestions.
6. Keep adequate records of plans and suggestions.
7. Make certain that some course of action has been decided on.

8.   Summarize findings, conclusions, and decisions.
9.   Provide for adequate evaluation.

Following a classroom visit from the principal, the teacher will expect an evaluation of the lesson observed during the supervisory visit because he/she desires to improve his/her skills as a teacher. An awareness that professional associates care about his/her service and wish to help may determine the difference between a mediocre teacher and a skilled educator.

The importance of including the teacher in the process of analyzing and prescribing must be emphasized. If the teacher and the supervising principal are to perform as a professional team, it is important that they share a common professional orientation. Additionally, the teacher and the supervising principal must jointly accept effective methods and techniques of objective analysis. Only then can the factors observed during the course of the supervisory visit be treated adequately; only then can the teacher and the supervisor be capable of professional consultation that may determine a program leading to improvement of instruction.

Deciding on a program of action does not imply necessarily that a final decision has been reached. It might mean that the conference group plans to engage in further exploration along the lines already agreed on before finding a solution. An individual staff member might decide to try out a suggestion that is mutually acceptable. In this instance, the principal must make the teacher's problems his/her own. He/she should plan a follow-up visit on the day the teacher tries the suggestion.

The principal who displays a sincere interest in improving the program of supervisory conferences within the school will be rewarded by the increased cooperation and enthusiasm of the staff members. Educators naturally respond to recognition of their worth as contributing members of the profession.

It is hoped that in the process of helping to evaluate a teaching-learning situation supervising principals will grow in their ability to apply objective criteria of self-evaluation. As supervising principals visit the classroom and have the opportunity to compare the learning situation that exists in one class with what exists in others, and their skills in handling various problems with the skills of others, they can make a better use of criteria of self-evaluation.

The following are some points to consider while holding a follow-up conference:

1.   Remember to be understanding. Try not to upset the teacher. Use the Golden Rule. The principal should ask him/herself, "How would I feel if I were the teacher?" Empathy should be emphasized. Show interest in the teacher as an individual.
2.   Be sincere and friendly. Approach the teacher as a peer and as a qualified member of the profession.
3.   Use all of the time necessary; do not appear to be rushed.
4.   Start the conference with a positive approach. *Something* must be all right!
5.   If criticisms are necessary, criticize methods and techniques rather than the

teacher. The individual's psychological integrity must be protected and pre-served. Proper rapport places the teacher at ease.

6. Help the teacher by leading the way. "How do you feel about teaching now?" "What has been the easiest?" "Where and when do you find it least easy?"

7. Accept and start with the teacher's problems as he/she sees them. Analyze difficulties together.

8. Discuss possible solutions, such as:
   a) Constructing lesson plans together.
   b) Discussing ways to stimulate students.
   c) Suggesting various types of assignments and their appropriateness.
   d) Discussing how to help students to participate.
   e) Reviewing steps in a lesson.
   f) Suggesting ways to check and evaluate.

9. Consider the possibility of this being an "off" day. Try a new approach.

10. Do not be afraid to suggest. The teacher would rather have an idea ex-pressed than to wonder what you are thinking.

11. Do not bluff. If you do not know something, say so! The teacher may learn later that you really did not know.

12. Summarize together the ideas brought out during the conference.

13. Close the conference on a friendly note with praise or commendation. *Be encouraging.* Leave the teacher with something to grow on, something to go on, and something to glow on.

Recording the Conference Results

It is important that an adequate record of the supervisory conference be main-tained for further reference to serve as a vehicle for planning future supervisory visits and follow-up conferences. Two convenient conference report forms that the supervising principal may find useful are included as Figures 8-1 and 8-2.

How to Interview

The Supervisor and the Orientation Interview

In some large school systems, the employment and assignment phases of the personnel process may be completed without the participation of the supervising principal. Such an unenlightened personnel practice places the principal in the position of having to discover the new employee's interests, experiences, educa-tional and other personal data through an exploratory interview. It is important

FIGURE 8-1. Sample Conference Report Form

CONFERENCE REPORT FORM

Date _____

Name of Teacher _____

Grade _____

Subject _____

Time: From _____ to _____

Good points of the lesson: _____

_____

Physical and learning environment: _____

_____

Detailed, specific suggestions for improvement: _____

_____

Questions: _____

_____

Statements: _____

_____

---

that the supervising principal remember that this first interview with the beginning teacher establishes a pattern for future relations.

At the time of the initial interview, the new employee should be told about the important phases of his/her work, what his/her specific assignment will be the location of various offices and facilities in the school, and anything else that a new employee should know (see chapter 6 for a more complete description of the orientation process). If the supervising principal is pressed for time and cannot give the new teacher the attention he/she deserves, the principal should say that they will talk later but that for the present time he/she will have to place the teacher in the hands of the assistant principal, a department head, or another teacher. In this event, the supervising principal should make a point of visiting the new employee as soon as possible. At that time, the principal must indicate a sincere interest in the new employee and a desire to help. There is no substitute for the supervising principal's personal attention. Recall W. V. Bingham's en-

FIGURE 8-2.   Record of Supervisory Follow-Up Conference

NAME _____DATE _____

SUBJECT _____DATE OF OBSERVATION _____

TIME OF CONFERENCE _____

Notes Preceding Conference: (See record of classroom visit)

_____

Topics Discussed:

_____

_____

_____

Direction and Suggestions:

_____

_____

_____

Teacher's Reactions in Conference:

_____

_____

Follow-Up:

_____

_____

during axiom, "the functions of the . . . interview are: to get information, to give information, and to make a friend."[2]

Closed, Patterned, and Open Interviews

The function of the *closed* interview is gaining or imparting information. The supervising principal may wish to make a preliminary list of questions or may formulate questions as the interview progresses, but always with the same purpose in mind.

The *patterned interview* is one wherein a series of questions is memorized or listed. The patterned interview's advantage is the certainty that desired ques-

[2] W. V. Bingham, "The Three Functions of the Interview in Employment," *The Management Review* XV (26 January 1926):36.

tions will be asked. This technique is helpful if the supervising principal has not had much skill in interviewing. As the supervisor gains skill in interviewing, the patterned interview may be utilized without its appearing formal.

The *open interview* usually is not designed to obtain answers to specific questions, but rather to permit the supervisor to set an atmosphere wherein the employee may discuss interests. This type of interview is especially helpful in permitting an employee to discuss complaints and grievances.[3]

The evolution of the open interview technique is described in *Management and the Worker*.[4] In utilizing the open interview technique:

1. Put the teacher (or other employee) at ease by careful control of the environment and of the attitude you present.
2. When conditions warrant, guarantee the teacher strict confidence with reference to anything said.
3. Encourage the teacher to talk freely. Give him/her the feeling that there is no rush; he/she has all the time needed to discuss a problem.
4. Be a good listener. Never interrupt the interviewee.
5. In the open interview, the supervising principal never disputes a point nor gives advice. Rather, he/she strives to discover how the teacher thinks, what his/her feelings are, and seeks information as to why the teacher believes as he/she does.
6. The supervising principal's attitude must be one of interest and sympathetic curiosity if this technique is to work.
7. The supervising principal must exhibit as much interest in interviewing satisfied teachers as he/she does in interviewing those who are dissatisfied.
8. The teacher takes the necessary steps to remedy a situation or solve a problem when his/her thinking has been clarified by discussing the difficulty in detail with the supervising principal. The teacher then initiates the action and assumes the responsibility.

The Control Interview

A serious offense by teacher or other staff member usually will be met by the supervising principal with dispatch. However, the control interview concerning a less serious offense—one that is not serious and barely complies with the school's policies—is the type of interview most often avoided by the supervising principal.

No matter what the nature of the topic of the control interview:

1. The interview must be planned carefully. In an emergency, it may not be possible to plan in detail, but operating on the basis of policy considerations will sustain the supervising principal and may help prevent being impetuous.
2. The nature of the control interview must be impersonal. It must arise out of

---

[3] See W. R. Spriegel, Edward Schulz, and W. B. Spriegel, *Elements of Supervision* (New York: John Wiley & Sons, Inc., 1957) especially pages 62–63.

[4] F. J. Roethlisberger, William J. Dickson, and Harold A. Wright, *Management and the Worker* (Cambridge: Harvard University Press, 1939).

the needs of the situation, with vindictiveness and personal anger being prohibited.

3. The interview must be constructive rather than punitive in nature. The purpose of the interview is to correct a situation, to help to insure that the situation will not arise again and to serve the best interests of the school, its
   students, and its classified and certificated personnel, as well as the best interests of the superintendent, the governing board, and the patrons of the school.
4. Hope must be provided for the disciplined. For as long as an employee maintains psychological integrity, self-respect, and hope for the future, there is a
   chance for improvement.
5. The employee who has been disciplined must depart with a feeling that
   he/she has paid whatever penalties required; that the supervising principal is
   not one who holds a "grudge"; and that he/she now has an opportunity to
   go ahead with a clean slate.

In evaluating the control interview, the supervisor should ask the following questions:

1. *Prior to the control review.* Did I survey the problem effectively? Did I obtain all needed data so that I would have an adequate background for the
   interview? Did I consider the background data from a viewpoint of empathy?
   Did I wait to begin the interview until tempers had been soothed and I was
   in the proper frame of mind? Was I sure that I was concentrating on the
   problem at hand rather than on the personalities (including my own) involved? Then, was I prepared to listen?
2. *During the control interview.* Did I watch the volume and intonation of my
   voice? Did I praise the employee for some recently completed task well done?
   Was I careful to protect the employee's psychological integrity, to make
   him/her feel that he/she is a person of worth to the school, and to give
   him/her an out by which to "save face"? Did I call attention to errors and
   improper approaches or attitudes, wherever possible, indirectly and with empathy? Did I show an interest in and sympathy for his/her needs and wants,
   and for his/her suggestions for solving the problem? Did I avoid arguing
   over unimportant factors? Did I build specifics into a logical construct, rather
   than challenging statements directly, so that the employee would have an opportunity to see his/her own mistakes without my having to defend and attack in a "nit-picking" fashion?
     If I was wrong, did I say so? Did I challenge the employee to demonstrate
   improvement? Did I review the interview and our plans for the future with
   the employee? Did I close the interview on a friendly note?[5]

After completing the interview, the supervisor should carefully complete
an interview memorandum for his files. He should remember to notice and praise

[5] After W. S. Ferguson, "Handling Personnel Problems (a Checklist)," *Factory Management and Maintenance,* CIX (June 1951):109; and W. R. Spriegel, Edward Schulz, and
W B. Spriegel, op. cit., pp. 292–294.

improvement and should keep the relationship with the employee on a professionally friendly basis.

The supervisor should consider the following points in evaluating the effectiveness of the interview. Was my approach during the interview one of control or correction, rather than one of punishment or revenge? Was I fair but firm; gentle but forthright in stating needs and/or requirements; kind and concerned with the employee and his/her viewpoint but clear and precise in reviewing the problem and the probable consequences of the proposed plans for solving it? Was my voice control adequate?

Remember, it is not necessary to be abusive or to shout in order to attain correction and control. Beware of overkill!

Outline for a Successful Interview

The supervising principal may wish to have the following outline duplicated for facility in planning for successful interviewing:

I. *The Problem*
   A. Purpose of the interview
   B. Positive points
   C. Weaknesses (note *facts*)

II. *Employee's Reactions Obtained*
   A. Ask, "Are these facts correct?" "Is this the way it is?" Note teacher's answer here:
   B. If the teacher presents new facts or offers a valid explanation, the supervising principal may wish to close the interview for the present and investigate the matter further.
      1. Note reasons here:
      2. Future appointment? When?
   C. If the teacher has no valid explanation, presents no new facts, and disagrees, note statement of the teacher here:
   D. If the supervising principal disagrees with the teacher, he/she should say, "Sorry, but that is not the solution"; or could say, "Even if you don't agree, I feel we should take some action."

III. *Action Consideration*
   A. Solicit the teacher's ideas concerning the problem solution. Ask, "What suggestions have you?" or "What do you think we can do?" Note suggestions here:
      1. The supervising principal should indicate that he/she sincerely wants the teacher to solve the problem and should state that he/she will help the teacher in any way possible.
      2. If suggestion requires study, or if new data are presented, close the interview, set a date for another meeting, and investigate the matter further.
   B. If the supervising principal disagrees with the suggestion, he/she

should say, "I'm sorry, but I do not believe that plan would work," or "I don't think that would do."

IV. *The Plan*

    A. It is recommended that the supervising principal have a plan worked out before the interview. If the teacher's plan does not seem feasible, or if the teacher has no plan, say, "Let us try this . . ." (Plan of action.) (It sometimes is helpful to establish a time limit for the proposal after which an evaluation interview will be held.)

    B. If the teacher objects without validity (if he/she objects to the plan but the objection is not based on valid data), the supervising principal should say, "I'm sorry, but this is a real problem and I will have to ask you to do this . . ." If the teacher has strong objections to the proposed plan, perhaps a modification of the plan made in section IV-A is called for. Note modifications here:

V. *Terminate the Interview on a Cordial Note*

    A. Insure that the teacher knows exactly what has been suggested and what is expected. The supervising principal should say, "Have I been clear?"

        1. Note date for the follow-up interview.

        2. Restate the plan. Say, "This is what we are going to do."

        3. Leave the teacher with a definite feeling that you are really interested in helping.

VI. *The Follow-Up Interview*

    A. Date of the interview

    B. Has the teacher's performance improved? Yes ( ) No ( ) Further investigation required ( ) The supervising principal should tell the teacher he/she has improved, if such is the case.[6]

    C. Interview summary:

Do

1. Remember that a follow-up conference is obligatory if visitation and observation are to improve instruction and learning; to help teachers grow in methods and techniques of instruction and in subject matter content; or for general professional development.

2. Systematically plan, appraise, and evaluate teacher growth. Have specific objectives for a follow-up conference.

3. Conduct many conferences during the year. Proper scheduling is important. Usually the follow-up conference should follow the supervisory visit within thirty-six hours. The conference should be held while the specifics of the lesson are clearly in mind.

4. Base the conference on the written analysis of the specific venture. The suc-

[6] John J. Grela, "Work Sheet Helps Supervisors Talk Constructively with Employees," *Personnel Journal* (April 1955); and W. R. Spriegel, Edward Schulz, and W. B. Spriegel, op. cit., pp. 70–71.

cessful supervising principal tries to arouse the teacher's interest and to challenge professional curiosity.

5. Include both strong points and weaknesses in the same conference. Supervisory conferences based on weak points alone are rare and should be used only as a last resort with exceptional teachers who fail to respond to any other methods and resist improvement. Human beings respond well to praise, praise that is honestly deserved and honestly given.
6. Consider conferences as essential, *cooperative* endeavors.
7. Provide a quiet, uninterrupted atmosphere.
8. Recall that if a teacher needs to discuss a problem, he/she needs to do so soon.
9. Allow approximately thirty minutes for the conference.
10. Sense how much to say, and *know when to stop*.
11. Provide for a "cooling off period" if circumstances warrant.
12. Remember that frequent visits and conferences are better than one that is drawn out.
13. Remember to be a good listener.
14. Determine a pivotal question.
15. Announce the purpose of the meeting, so as not to keep the teacher in the dark as to what to expect.
16. Strive for rapport.
17. Remember—the goal of the principal's participation in supervisory conferences is to help teachers.

Don't

1. Cover more than two or three points at one interview. When too much is planned for one interview, the entire conference suffers due to lack of time. This crowded agenda renders the conference ineffective.
2. Use the same set pattern for all conferences.
3. Use the conference to force the teacher to accept your plan.
4. Overplan for the impending conference.
5. Read directly from notes for the classroom visitation; do refer to them occasionally.
6. Schedule the conference without having a definite purpose in mind.
7. Hold the conference in a noisy place with the possibility of interruptions.
8. Keep the desk between yourself and the teacher.
9. Use formal titles; maintain   a friendly, informal air throughout the conference. Use first names.
10. Be overly verbose. Don't select vocabulary that does not communicate effectively. A beginning teacher especially may be hesitant to pry into meanings of terminology that the supervising principal may have acquired at regional, state, and national conferences, lest he/she expose either an ignorance of or reluctance to accept the practice that seems to be preferred. Do not swamp the teacher in an excess of unmeaningful verbalism. (The principal must say exactly what he/she means—effectively, succinctly, and clearly.)

TRENDS CONCERNING SUPERVISORY
VISITS AND CONFERENCES

Toward ⟶   Continued Efforts to Improve
Supervisory Visits and Conferences

Although the program of supervisory visits and conferences underwent great changes in the past, principals will continue to employ the techniques. The future will bring additional improvements. Advances in the supervising principal's skill in conducting the supervisory conference and visit as a part of the overall programs for staff and instructional development will be reflected in the general improvement of instruction.

Toward ⟶   More Group Visitations
and Conferences by the Staff Specialist

Even though the staff specialist-consultant will continue, on invitation from the principal, to visit classrooms as time permits, more of his/her work with teachers will be accomplished on a group basis. Since it allows contact with more teachers personally, this practice will have increased importance in the future.

Toward ⟶   A Greater Effort by School
Systems to Provide Needed Supervisory Assistance

Because supervising principals have felt the increased time demands and pressures of school administration, and, as a result, have had less time to devote to improving the instructional program, school systems will be forced to provide additional supervisory assistance in the form of specialist-consultants and/or assistant principals. The trend will continue to be in the direction of larger school systems that are financially capable of supporting an improved program of supervisory visits and follow-up conferences.

The mechanism of the program of supervisory visits and conferences will be improved. Data will be collected carefully for group consideration.

The objective approach, tempered with empathy and understanding—that generally has been absent from the supervisory conference and its planning—will be a vital part of the program of the future. Teachers will be helped to learn and to adapt new techniques. Individual differences in and needs of faculty members will be recognized.

| Toward | ⟶ | Greater Participation by Teachers in

Planning for Visits and Conferences

The practice of asking teachers to participate in planning will do much to improve teacher attitude toward supervisory visits and conferences.

The supervising principal will find the areas in which teachers need help. A practical, specific program will be developed that attacks underlying problems.

| Toward | ⟶ | Training Principals and

Specialist-Consultants in Classroom

Visitation and Conferences

Supervisory personnel need in-service training in supervision, just as teachers need help in teaching. Cooperative staff development programs for in-service education in supervision will be developed. Some of the larger city school systems already have taken the first steps in organizing such programs. Smaller systems will be able to take advantage of programs offered by the office of the intermediate unit superintendent of schools.

Supervisory Problem   In Basket

The problem develops in a public junior high school with an enrollment of 750 students in grades seven, eight, and nine. Mrs. Doe, who is thirty-five years old and has eight years' teaching experience, teaches girls' physical education and health. All seventh and eighth grade girls are required to take physical education. Ninth grade girls may select one class as an elective. Average enrollment in Mrs. Doe's P. E. classes is thirty-six girls. The standard uniform required is a white blouse, blue shorts, and gym shoes. These items are stocked at a local department store.

Mrs. Doe conducts an outstanding, well-rounded program for the girls that includes physical fitness and the development of poise and grace. She is well suited for this program because of her own physical appearance and abilities in dance and acrobatics.

Mrs. Doe is very severe with the girls. She tends to be sarcastic and demands immediate and unquestioning reaction to her requests. Many girls appear to be frightened of her. The supervising principal occasionally receives calls from concerned parents who question her teaching procedures. Usually an explanation is made and the parent is satisfied. Today, however, an irate parent called and announced he was coming "to have it out with Mrs. Doe." The principal determined that he must prepare her for the ordeal. He is very happy with the *results* of her program, but feels she must modify her domineering attitude. If she is offended, he may lose her.

> *How can the supervising principal approach this problem? How should he plan for the supervisory conference with Mrs. Doe?*

Questions and Suggested Activities Concerning Supervisory Follow-Up Conferences

Questions

1. How does the role of the *line* supervisor differ from that of the *staff* supervisor in conducting supervisory visits and follow-up conferences?
2. How would the personality of the teacher determine the method of suggesting means to overcome weaknesses?
3. How can differences of opinion between the teacher and supervisor concerning content and teaching techniques be resolved?

Suggested Activities

1. Suggest ways in which a supervisor could help a group of teachers who have expressed awareness of a mutual problem.
2. Prepare a debate on the topic—Resolved: group supervisory practices constitute a substitute for classroom supervisory visits and follow-up conferences.
3. Outline a plan of public relations with teachers that may assist in obtaining better communications during supervisory visits and follow-up conferences.
4. Make a list of traits that a supervisor should possess in order to work well with teachers.
5. List the points to consider in writing up the follow-up conference.
6. Note to what extent the principal and the staff specialist-consultant should interpret and/or formulate the basic goals of education to be practiced in the classroom.
7. Indicate when and under what conditions consultants from outside the local school system should be called on to conduct or participate in supervisory conferences.
8. Outline a plan for supervisory visits and follow-up conferences in a 19-teacher elementary school.
9. List the points to consider in making a record of the follow-up conference.

Selected Bibliography

Books

Bradfield, Luther E. *Supervision for Modern Elementary Schools.* Columbus, Ohio: Charles E. Merrill Books, Inc., 1964.

Brighten, Stayner F. *Increasing Your Accuracy in Teacher Evaluation.* Englewood Cliffs, New Jersey: Prentice-Hall, Inc., 1965.

Douglas, Harl R., Rudyard K. Bent, and Charles W. Boardman. *Democratic Supervision in the Secondary Schools.* Boston: Houghton Mifflin Company, 1961.

Fieldler, Fred E., and Martin M. Chemers. *Leadership and Effective Management.* Glenview, Illinois: Scott, Foresman and Co., 1974.

Gwynn, J. Minor. *Theory and Practice in Supervision.* New York: Dodd, Mead, & Company, 1961.

Kyte, George C. *The Principal at Work.* Boston: Ginn and Company, 1952.

Likert, Rensis. *New Patterns of Management.* New York: McGraw-Hill Company, 1961.

Lucio, William H., and John D. McNeil. *Supervision: A Synthesis of Thought and Action.* New York: McGraw-Hill Company, 1962.

Roethlisberger, F. J., William J. Dickson, and Harold A. Wright. *Management and the Worker.* Cambridge: Harvard University Press, 1939.

Ryan, Doris W. et al. *The Individualized System: Administration and Leadership.* (H. S. I. Studies) Toronto: The Ontario Institute for Studies in Education, 1974.

Schmuck, Richard A., and Matthew B. Miles. *Organization Development in Schools.* Palo Alto: National Book Press, 1971.

Spriegel, W. R., Edward Schulz, and W. B. Spriegel, *Elements of Supervision.* New York: John Wiley & Sons, Inc., 1957.

Stoops, Emery, and Dale Coogan. *Problems with Parents.* West Orange, New Jersey: The Economics Press, Inc., 1964.

Stoops, Emery, and James R. Marks. *Elementary School Supervision.* Boston: Allyn and Bacon, Inc., 1965.

Wiles, Kimball. *Supervision for Better Schools* 4th ed. Englewood Cliffs, New Jersey: Prentice-Hall, Inc., 1975.

Periodicals

Aubrey, Roger F. "What Is the Role of the Elementary School Teacher?" *The Elementary School Journal* LXVIII (March 1968):36.

Bingham, W. V. "The Three Functions of the Interview in Employment." *The Management Review* XV (26 January 1926):36.

Ferguson, W. S. "Handling Personnel Problems (a Checklist)." *Factory Management and Maintenance* CIX (June 1951).

Grela, John J. "Work Sheet Helps Supervisors Talk Constructively with Employees." *Personnel Journal* (April 1955).

Imin, David. "The Changing Role of the Urban Principal." *The Elementary School Journal* LXVIII (April 1968):329–333.

Nelson, W. Donald. "Supervision or Snoopervision." *The Balance Sheet* XXVII (December 1961):158–159.

Pray, Walter J. "The Climate for Supervision." *American School Board Journal* CXXIX (November 1963):12–13.

Film

Person to Person Communication. Roundtable Films, Inc., Beverly Hills, California, 1956. Demonstrates the breakdown of face-to-face communication when the participants do not consider unspoken things inferred from words: the basic assumptions, viewpoints, and feelings of each participant. Gives examples of situations in which these factors are present and absent. *Restricted to use by educational institutions only.* (14 minutes)

9

How to Provide Successful Faculty Meetings

Standard staff meetings and more specialized meetings such as workshops and institutes play a crucial role in the success of a supervisory program: they furnish the means for communicating common understanding, workable techniques, and uniform purposes. As faculty size increases, so do the number of interpersonal relationships and the problems generated by breakdowns in the communications system.

Staff meetings, workshops, and institutes should help upgrade the instructional program and solve school problems. Typically, the supervising principal serves as an interpreter, director, and coordinator for staff meetings.

Teachers and principals do not always agree on the types of activities that are the most valuable for improving instruction. Differences in points of view concerning what services are needed and how they can be provided suggest that open discussions are needed. Trends in educational thinking and practice should be discussed at faculty meetings and interpreted as they affect the school or the community. Skill must be exercised in organizing and conducting faculty meetings to enhance cooperative thinking and professional growth. Before these discussions can be fruitful, a *mutual, sincere feeling of trust* must be generated. Indeed, trust is a prerequisite to all effective communication and certainly to working with people toward instructional improvement.

This chapter includes a discussion of the following topics:

Principles and practices
How to conduct workshops and institutes
How to conduct the meeting
Do—Don't
Trends
"In-Basket" supervisory problem
Questions and suggested activities

261

Principles and Practices

If staff meetings and group conferences are to be interesting and valuable to teachers, they must be planned with teachers and concentrate on the problems of teachers. A planning committee, chosen by the staff, may help meet this goal.

The teacher is a professional worker, as is the supervising principal. With this in mind, there should be mutual respect for, and evaluation of, suggestions. Since there are many types of teachers, human relations are important in stimulating individual responses toward growth.

There are great differences in the preparation and experience of teachers. States differ as to requirements, and various colleges and universities emphasize different aspects of the teacher-education program. Nevertheless, certain basic principles concerning the improvement of faculty meetings and group conferences have been defined.

1. Groups are composed of two or more individuals who come together to solve a problem that is common to all and that cannot be solved by the individuals alone.
2. Group successes are due chiefly to individual cooperation and understanding, and to supervisory leadership.
3. The total-faculty meeting has long been used as one device for securing improvements in instruction, as contrasted to administrative purposes.
4. Groups must meet frequently to make progress. Reports, questionnaires, checklists, and bulletins cannot take the place of group interaction.
5. Cooperation with the group provides the supervisor with an opportunity for leadership.
6. The supervisor who brings about group action may be the supervising principal or another worker from within the school or may be a specialist-consultant from without.
7. The supervisor should ensure that no individual or faction dominates the meeting and speaks for the entire group.
8. Developing good leadership within the group is a function of supervision.
9. The supervisor needs to exercise patience while elevating the group to a higher level of understanding.
10. A resourceful supervisor will substitute emergent leadership from the group for his/her own directorship. This emerging leadership may revolve among various subgroups and individuals within the groups.
11. Grade level and small group meetings may have more uniformity of purpose and may be more efficient than large staff meetings.

How to Improve Staff Meetings

The following techniques may be used by the supervisor to improve the supervisory meeting:

1. The problems to be discussed should be important to the entire staff and should be chosen by the group, with leadership from the principal.

2. The meeting should contribute directly to the professional needs of teachers and administrators.
3. Throughout the meeting, teacher participation and activity should predominate.
4. The experience and knowledge of the teachers, pertinent to the discussion, should be utilized fully by a supervisory leader.
5. In very large schools, the staff should be broken into smaller groups. The large meeting should be reserved for staff decisions, personnel problems or benefits, and for all-school planning.
6. The meeting place should be as pleasant, comfortable, and informal as possible.
7. The frequency of staff meetings should be decided on by the staff itself.
8. The group should decide on the time and place of meetings, and should decide on a definite adjournment time. Meetings should be kept as brief as possible.
9. Members of the meeting should work toward a consensus.
10. Some agenda items should be merely for *information*, others should require *action*. Action should never be called for until full information has been provided.
11. A permanent record should summarize the results of each meeting. If the meeting is worth calling, something should result.
12. Each meeting should lead to improved competency and morale.

Purposes of Staff Meetings

The prime purpose of staff meetings is to improve the quality of personnel and of the school program. These meetings should provide opportunities for cooperative thinking, for staff planning, for presentation of stimulating talks by resourceful people, and for becoming acquainted with the total educational environment. In the staff meeting of today this opportunity for full teacher participation has not as yet been given.

Unfortunately, most teachers apparently feel that staff meetings deserve a low rating in providing specific help in improving the technique of instruction and in presenting new research data and subject matter findings.

Developing a staff into a working group is a long-term project. One means of achieving this goal is through effective staff meetings. It is in these meetings that the important business of the school is handled, to wit: planning for the educational experiences of students.

The old-fashioned faculty meeting at which the principal made announcements and gave directions regarding administrative routines will no longer suffice. These meetings were characterized by the issuing of orders; interpretations of orders previously given, perhaps even given in writing; or a discussion of how teachers could help lessen the noise near the principal's office. Drives and collections, and the preparation of various programs, also were discussed. The use of staff meetings for such activities is not only ineffectual but also deplorably damaging to the purposes for which they are held.

The premise that all who are involved with a policy, rule, or technique should have a part in planning it is basic to effective staff meetings. This democratic approach still reserves the right of decision making for the principal. The principal not only directs and coordinates the staff; he/she also is a member of it. It would be expected, therefore, that staff intelligence in operation, orchestrated through principal leadership, should result in a harmonious and successful working group.

A staff meeting should be concerned only with items of importance to individuals present. A cooperative solution of common problems is not only good in theory; it is the most practical and successful method known.

Meetings should inspire and stimulate a teacher's educational thinking; they should clarify or be of practical assistance in classroom, schoolwide, or school system-wide situations; and they should help the teacher to develop and maintain a consistent pattern of growth.

How to Plan Staff Meetings

The conduct and planning of staff meetings should be shifted from administrators and supervisors to teacher councils or to a planning committee chosen by the faculty. A series of meetings then are planned in accord with the supervisory plan for the school. The wishes of the staff should govern the decisions made.

During the early stages, the principal should assume considerable responsibility for the conduct of the meeting, but later these major responsibilities should be shifted to the staff. The principal's role primarily should be that of a consultant or adviser. He/she should guide without manipulating and provide leadership without dominating.

FREQUENCY AND SCHEDULING. Need determines the frequency and length of scheduled meetings. Experienced principals recognize that meetings that are held too frequently or that are too lengthy are as detrimental and ineffectual as are meetings that are held too infrequently or that do not allow sufficient time for the business to be covered.

Faculties often discover that a minimum of general meetings of the entire staff plus a few short meetings of grade levels will satisfy their needs. Staff members will be more eager to attend if they know from past experience that the meetings regularly draw to a close at the predetermined time.

It is helpful for all concerned to reserve a specific, consistent day and hour of the week for the entire school system. Such planning permits scheduling a meeting if desired. School-system policy should not require supervising principals to hold meetings at each scheduled date.

Fridays are very bad days for general meetings. Other than the usual emotional and physical condition of the staff on Fridays, it would be well to remember that the two-day weekend definitely affects desired carry-over. Tuesday is apparently a preferred day for staff meetings.

Staff members should determine whether they prefer before- or after-school meetings. Most teachers apparently prefer short before-school meetings. Generally, if teachers are required to stay one-half hour after the close of school on the day of a faculty meeting they should be permitted to leave promptly after class dismissal on the following day. *The trend is to hold faculty meetings as a part of the normal working day,* early in the day, rather than to require members of the staff to work an additional number of hours because of necessary staff meetings.

Class schedules, individual duties, and programming will affect the availability of many faculty members. Brief grade level or departmental meetings work well before school or during common conference periods. Sufficient time should be allowed for teachers to arrive and to relax, so that their powers of concentration can be more effective.

ENVIRONMENT.   The room in which the staff meeting is held should be restful in appearance and conductive to good thinking. It should be conveniently located, be permanent, and afford privacy. The faculty deserves as least one well-designed, functional, and comfortably furnished room in which to hold meetings. The room should contain a chalkboard.

FIGURE 9-1. Staff Meetings Should Be Conducted in a Restful Environment. Refreshments Should Be Served.

REFRESHMENTS.   Refreshments always are a hospitable and welcome sight to a weary, dusty traveler—especially to a teacher attending an after-school staff meeting. Refreshments not only are good morale builders but also, as the term suggests, are refreshing and physically stimulating. Usually teachers, via grade levels or other organized cooperative means, are more than happy to assist in preparation.

THE AGENDA.   Preplanned agenda are a must. Without such organization, routine matters can become lost in the last minute rush, the meeting may lapse into overtime, one may tend to digress from essential subjects, and items may be neglected or overemphasized. It is most helpful, and also a matter of courtesy, for each staff member to be given a copy of the agenda before the meeting.

How to Encourage Teacher Involvement

Teachers should be involved in planning a meeting as well as in the meeting itself. Idea memorandum sheets, distributed a week before to all teachers and returned to the meeting chairman after they have been filled in, have proven to be helpful. See Figure 9-2 for a sample of such a memorandum sheet.

In schools with large faculties, teacher planning committees, composed of grade-level representatives, may meet briefly with the principal to assist in planning the agenda.

Meetings in which teachers take an active part are more beneficial and interesting for all concerned. Demonstrations, explanations, committee reports,

FIGURE 9-2.   Memorandum Sheet

STAFF MEETING IDEA MEMORANDUM SHEET

Date _____

Topic _____

Problem _____

_____

Idea _____

_____

_____

_____

What will be accomplished _____

_____

_____

_____
Name (optional)

study-group information, and resource presentations are examples of the individual methods by which teachers might take a meaningful, stimulating, and satisfying part in staff meetings. This participation should help create staff meetings that reflect the efforts of a dynamic, harmonious working group. True discussions, in which the opinions of the staff members are as respected as are those of the principal, add a feeling of purpose, mutual respect, participation, and accomplishment for all involved.

Timing of Materials and Ideas

The timing of ideas or materials being presented can create or destroy a meeting. A highly controversial statement or question entertained at the beginning of a meeting may destroy an agenda. It could waste the time of all involved and demolish the program if much of the meeting time were devoted to arguing the point. If this same highly controversial statement had occurred near or at the end of the agenda, preferably at the end, brief discussion may have caused the participants to leave the meeting thinking and talking about the particular point. This would have enabled them to arrive at a more rational conclusion. Time and timing are basic and sensitive ingredients of decision making and require great thought and care.

How to Improve Workshops and Institutes

How to Conduct Workshops

Workshops constitute one means of stimulating professional growth. These meetings generally are called as a result of teachers' requests for assistance. T. H. Briggs and J. Justman[1] believed workshops possessed certain advantages over conventional faculty meetings.

WORKSHOP CHARACTERISTICS.   Workshops tend to have rather clearly defined and recognized purposes. These purposes usually are related directly to problems and needs emerging out of the teachers' daily work. Workshops are planned, organized, and conducted by teachers and principals.

A broadly representative membership is attracted to workshops. They are not delimited to the faculty of one school, or even of one school system. The exchange of new ideas is, therefore, facilitated.

Workshops attract people who have a special interest in the subject mat-

---

[1] Thomas H. Briggs, and Joseph Justman, *Improving Instruction through Supervision* (New York: The Macmillan Company, 1952), p. 452.

ter, a special contribution to make, or a special problem with which they need assistance. The success of the workshop depends on the quality of the collective effort of the group. Workshops usually are conducted with greater informality and with stronger emphasis on promoting good human relations than are formal faculty meetings.

Workshops tend to be fairly brief, lasting six to eight weeks in one-hour or two-hour sessions. Materials often are supplied at the workshop, although at times the teachers bring their own supplies from their individual schools. Outside preparation, which is shared with the participating members, often is required.

TYPES OF WORKSHOPS. There are many different kinds of workshops. In an art workshop, probably most of the time would be spent in actual participation, learning the skills and techniques of art activities.

In a mathematics workshop, more emphasis would be placed on analyzing and selecting appropriate learning experiences, devising instructional technology materials and methods of content presentation, and evaluating current and new programs.

The launching of the first Sputnik caused many teachers to realize that there were gaps in their knowledge of their subject areas. Workshops may supplement the backgrounds of teachers and bring the educator up-to-date with respect to advances in research in subject matter and in instructional techniques.

The needs of all teachers are not identical. Many phases of in-service education are needed in order to facilitate teacher growth. These needs are of a finite nature. Some teachers need assistance in enhancing classroom contributions in measurement and evaluation, others in content, and still others in the methods and techniques of instruction and in instructional technology.

The supervisor must make provisions for the wide variance in teachers' interests, needs, and capacities when planning the workshop. He/she should fuse personal qualities for the teacher, as a person, into the subject matter of the workshop. Even though workshops are made available through teachers' requests, it is up to the supervisor to stimulate interest in the interchange of new ideas, mutual problems, and competent solutions.

LIMITATIONS OF WORKSHOPS. Based on his investigation of workshops, J. R. Mitchell reported the following dangers and limitations to workshop procedure:

1. Too little preparation for the job at hand, little understanding of the meaning of group interaction, and inadequate skill in group techniques
2. A tendency to underestimate the potentials of the group, individually and collectively—a lack of faith in the group's ability
3. Inability to stimulate and challenge participants to critical thinking
4. Lack of personal qualities which would attract and hold the confidence of associates; lack of tact and patience in dealing with participants
5. Waste of participants' time by engaging in trivia; too much floundering
6. Promotion of social at the expense of intellectual activities; too much informality

7. Lack of flexibility; too much domination, too much lecturing . . . ; inability to get away from the classroom atmosphere
8. Insufficent sensitivity to individual needs; lack of concern for setting up and maintaining a congenial climate, emotional, physical, and intellectual for the group
9. Contempt of inadequate attempts made by members to solve problems
10. Lack of foresight, intuition, and planning
11. Fear of giving leadership and guidance (some leaders, failing to see their specific role as leaders, bend over backwards to keep from giving directions)
12. Failure to plan for getting the workshop under way expeditiously
13. Reliance on the totally indefensible notion that democratic procedure means that the leader should not lead—that situations should remain almost completely unstructured
14. Inability to control aggressive participants.[2]

How to Conduct Institutes

Institutes in various subject areas are another way in which the supervisor helps the teacher do a better job. Institutes are organized in different ways in different school systems.

Institutes differ from workshops in that less group participation and discussion occur at the former. Salary schedule credits often may be gained from workshop attendance. Workshops usually are scheduled approximately for eight to sixteen meetings. The institutes, while coordinated, generally are completed in one to three meetings.

Since teachers have a genuine interest in bettering themselves, the trend appears to be toward fewer *required* institutes. Attaching vacation pay to required institute attendance is a highly questionable practice.

PLANNING THE INSTITUTE.   Supervising principals should plan, organize, and produce institutes. However, in the planning stage, advisement and cooperation with other interested parties are essential. Early meetings are scheduled to work out a calender. Next, meetings are held with specialist-consultants in order to decide which areas will be stressed. The specialists in the fields to be covered then meet to ascertain specific needs and to discuss new techniques in their particular areas. A preview in the form of a written synopsis of each institute should be given to all concerned.

MATERIAL FOR INSTITUTES.   Institutes provide an opportunity for teachers to see the latest textbooks. New library books are exhibited for examination. Other exhibits enable teachers to become acquainted with the latest types of equipment and supplies, and with advances and current practices in such areas as audio-

2 James Russell Mitchell, "The Workshops as an In-Service Education Procedure" (Doctoral dissertation, Indiana University, 1954), pp. 67–68.

assisted learning, computer-supported instruction, computer-assisted learning, and computer-managed instruction.

Leadership opportunities should be offered by the supervising principal for teachers to work with and become a part of the institute proceedings through their participation. Teachers should be asked to bring their special skills and knowledge to the attention of others who might benefit from them. Recognition is a fine morale builder, and the realization that the contribution of work well done is appreciated generally stimulates confidence for continuing success.

How to Conduct the Meeting

Attitudes and Skills Needed in Conducting Staff Meetings

New concepts and procedures in supervision demand a variety of new skills for the principal. These skills might be grouped under five categories: (1) skills in leadership, (2) skills in human relations, (3) skills in group processes, (4) skills in personnel administration, and (5) skills in evaluation.[3]

Experience and research have provided some clues for improving group action.

1. The size of the group can be a barrier to effectiveness. As a group grows beyond thirty members, effective group action becomes increasingly difficult. A desirable size cannot be reached by arbitrarily setting up one figure, for function and make-up condition the most desirable size.
2. Physical settings must be conducive to group processes. The size and type of a room as well as physical arrangement within the room are important. For effective participation the group members must be able to hear and see each other; the seating arrangement must facilitate good human relations.
3. The plan of action that emerges should be appraised to the end that individuals in the group receive their share of work to be done. In the final analysis, a group can act efficiently only through individuals. Responsibility for action should be delegated in terms of individual interests and abilities. A division of labor is not disruptive of cooperation.
4. Sufficient time must be allowed to insure a successful attack upon a problem and the development of action suggestions.
5. Consideration of group metabolism increases effectiveness. Fatigue, tension, tempo, pace, atmosphere affect group action. Within the process, provision for brief recesses and for adjusting the length of the meetings will result in more efficiency.
6. Within the process itself the most difficult step is moving from the problem inventory and identification . . . [to *how* and *who*]. What the problem is is not usually difficult. Effective group action depends upon the how and who.[4]

[3] Kimball Wiles, *Supervision for Better Schools* (Englewood Cliffs, New Jersey: Prentice-Hall, Inc., 1955).

[4] Association for Supervision and Curriculum Development, *Group Process in Supervision* (Washington, D.C.: National Education Association, 1948), p. 49.

In order that a faculty may function successfully within the group process (thinking, discussing, planning, deciding, acting, and evaluating), the leader and the group might best be alerted to the hazards involved. The supervising principal must learn to avoid: (1) group pressures, (2) domination by a few individuals, (3) implied threats to job security, (4) the sense of extreme newness or difference, and (5) the threat of the administrative role.

Realistic leadership recognizes that all people have certain common needs. Imaginative leadership goes one step further and builds a program accordingly, with respect and appreciation toward the individuals' common needs. The principal who demonstrates a genuine respect for the professional integrity and worth of his staff will be at the helm of a dynamic and productive program designed to offer the students the best education possible.

To be an effective group leader, one must help set the emotional tone in the group. The effective leader understands and appreciates people and, what is more important, respects the unique contributions that each group member can make.

STAFF MEETING EVALUATION.   The basic concept underlying the improvement of meetings is that staff meeting evaluation must be a part of the planning. Evaluation is fundamental in achieving the purposes of a faculty and in revising purposes and procedures. The suggestion box idea has merit.

BASIC FUNCTIONS OF THE SUPERVISOR.   Cooperative action is basic to group process. The skilled supervisor can help others learn to think, discuss, plan, decide, act, and evaluate together. A leader should be skilled in the techniques of group discussion and action. His/her prime responsibility is to help the group function efficiently.

Coordinating the efforts of others is basic to effective working within the group. To be an effective coordinator, the supervising principal starts where the group is. A true leader must be accepted as a member of the group, for leader and followers are interdependent. Each needs the other for successful accomplishment of group goals.[5]

The role of the democratic supervising principal is to carry out the policies that are the result of cooperative action. The faculty must be willing to abide by the majority's decisions, although a consensus rather than a majority vote should be sought.

Basically, teacher participation is an attitude of mind more than it is the completion of a specific task.[6] It is based on the idea that collective thinking is superior to individual thought. The principal must, of course, reserve the ultimate responsibility for a major program, since he/she is the responsible supervisory leader in the school.

[5] Ibid., pp. 59–61.
[6] Willard D. Elsbree and Harold J. McNally, *Elementary School Administration and Supervision* (New York: American Book Company, 1959), p. 414.

Following the Agenda

Meetings should begin promptly, and the agenda should be followed. Emergencies and changing conditions, however, require flexibility. Attempt to hold to the schedule, but strive to reduce tension and promote informality. Insure that participants understand the reason for their attendance and attempt to obtain a commitment for positive action from them. Leaders should be very conscious of group processes and should attempt to employ proper techniques of group action.[7]

A record should be made that summarizes the discussion, conclusions, and plans for each participant. A meeting should not just end. The supervisor should attempt always to provide a plan for action that includes follow-up and evaluation.[8]

The leader should involve the entire staff and avoid domination. The leader is responsible for keeping order and should observe all members of the group.[9] Feelings that are expressed, verbally or nonverbally, are elements that the leader will have to understand and use in effective problem solving.[10]

Each participant may have a contribution to problem solving. Ideally, all should feel a responsibility for the success of the meeting and for implementing a plan for action. This will necessitate involvement, thinking, listening, and assisting the leader.

Some groups are unusually productive, whereas others consistently perform at a low level. A leader who wants to understand the individual must know the dynamics of individual roles in groups as well as the effect the groups have on the individual.

The roles typically played by participants can be classified in three categories. (1) *Roles that facilitate and coordinate group activities* include: initiator, contributor, information seeker, opinion seeker, information giver, opinion giver, elaborator, coordinator, orienter, evaluator-critic, energizer, procedural technician, and recorder. (2) *Roles that build up group attitudes and encourage group morale* include: encourager, harmonizer, compromiser, expediter, standard setter, commentator, and follower. (3) *Roles that indicate individuals are trying to satisfy their own needs* often by ill-advised methods include: aggressor, blocker, recognition seeker, self-confessor, playboy, dominator, help-seeker, special interest pleader.[11]

K. O. Benne and P. Sheats[12] delineated a three-fold classification of member roles:

---

[7] J. Minor Gwynn, *Theory and Practice of Supervision* (New York: Dodd, Mead & Company, 1961), p. 356.

[8] Harold P. Adams and Frank G. Dickey, *Basic Principles of Supervision* (New York: American Book Company, 1953), pp. 163–165.

[9] Wiles, *Supervision for Better Schools*, pp. 189–191.

[10] Daniel W. Fullmer and Harold W. Bernard, *Counseling: Content and Process* (Chicago: Science Research Associates, Inc., 1964), pp. 131, 210.

[11] Ibid, pp. 38–40.

[12] K. D. Benne and P. Sheats, "Functional Roles of Group Members," *Journal of Social Issues* XXIV (1948):41–49.

1. Roles which are focused upon the *group-task*
2. Roles which are focused upon *group maintenance*
3. Roles which are focused upon the needs of the individuals in the group.

For the discussion group, they suggested as group-task roles: (a) the initiator, (b) information seeker, (c) opinion seeker, (d) information giver, (e) opinion giver, (f) elaborator, (g) coordinator, (h) orienter, (i) evaluator-critic, (j) energizer, (k) procedural technician, and (l) the recorder.

Identifying the contributions to the group process that each role plays will enable the leader to understand more effectively what is happening. Through this understanding, the leader will be able to provide for agenda that will lead to improved problem solving and professional growth for more participants.

The Role of the Agenda

WHY HAVE AN AGENDA?   An agenda helps determine short- and long-range objectives. It assists in controlling effectively the use of time in the meeting. The agenda also helps secure the cooperative participation of the entire group by clarifying assignments and responsibilities through confining attention and time to important items.

HOW TO BUILD AN AGENDA.   The steps listed below should prove helpful in building an agenda:

1. Decide how far in advance of your meeting your agenda should be complete.
   a) Begin immediately following the close of previous meeting.
   b) Recheck several times.
   c) Change and alter if emergencies arise and as conditions are modified.
2. Provide for items of regular procedure. The use of a form helps.
   a) Welcome; rapport building.
   b) Introductions of new members or visitors.
   c) Minutes of last meeting.
   d) Unfinished business and new business.
   e) Announcement of items not otherwise covered.
   f) Announcements of appreciation and recognition.
3. List specific matters that may be considered at the meeting.
4. Rate each item on the basis of relative importance.
5. Allocate proper time to be devoted to each item.
6. Eliminate the least important items if time restrictions demand.
7. Plan for the most effective techniques and methods for presentation and participation.
   a) Make advance assignments.
   b) Employ the techniques of the symposium, panel, demonstration, and other methods.
   c) Make specific plans concerning instructional technology aids.
8. Distribute copies of the agenda in advance of the meeting to all who will or are invited to attend.

Flexibility of the Agenda

R. H. Lane[13] said that an agenda should be flexible enough to allow for change in the order in which items are to be discussed.

The planning committee, in addition to determining the agenda, may have the responsibility for the other items needed to make a faculty meeting a success, such as establishing the meeting time, selecting the meeting place, arranging the furniture, making provisions for refreshments, and securing special consultants.

The questions of how often to have faculty meetings and when they should be held present an issue that will have to be solved by the whole faculty. Ways should be devised to hold faculty meetings on regular school time, thus attempting to eliminate the feeling that faculty meetings are something beyond the regular job. If necessary, shorter meetings could be called to cover matters of an emergency nature.

Further Techniques for the Supervisor

In organizing the faculty, the supervising principal usually will act as the chairperson. The discussion leader sets the mood of the meeting, and his/her skill as an umpire determines the flow of the discussion. The leader has many responsibilities. If the staff lacks skill in leading discussions, the official leader has an obligation to help members develop the skill.

According to Wiles,[14] the principal:

1. Creates an atmosphere that is informal, yet businesslike.
2. Guides the flow of discussion by keeping in mind the main purpose of the discussion. He/she is then able to provide the transition from one question to another.
3. Clarifies questions. There are two ways in which this can be done:
   a) By asking the questioner to define certain words, or to state the question so that it will be more clearly understood by all.
   b) By restating the question in a brief, direct form. If this be done, the restatement should be accepted by the questioner.
4. Keeps the group on the subject and does not lead away from it.

The principal will have to make judgments at times concerning the degree of deviation from the issue that will be allowed. He/she must be tactful in bringing the discussion back to the subject. He/she should not offend the person who is leading the discussion in the wrong direction.

[13] Robert Hill Lane, *The Principal in the Modern Elementary School* (Boston: Houghton Mifflin Company, 1938), pp. 185–188.

[14] Wiles, *Supervision for Better Schools*, p. 214.

Wiles concluded that summarizing the discussion is one of the most valuable functions the chairperson can perform. Through this process, the chairperson gives order to the discussion.

Staff Meeting Records

P. E. Jacobson[15] pointed out vital facts concerning records of the faculty meeting. A person should be selected by the group to record, on the chalkboard, issues being discussed, the points made, and the agreements reached. In addition, there should be a permanent record kept by the faculty recorder. This record should include:

1. Date
2. Meeting place
3. Members present
4. Members absent
5. Problems discussed
6. Suggestions made
7. Problems referred
8. Decisions reached
9. Responsibilities accepted or assigned
10. Plans for next meeting

A copy of this record should be made and given to each member of the faculty. This record would keep all informed as to what has taken place and would give a sense of direction and achievement. The record would be helpful in evaluating the effectiveness of their work.

Survey of Teachers' Reactions to Meetings

In personal interviews with six teachers, opinions were obtained relating to attitudes toward meetings.

Teachers A and B were first-year teachers just out of the preparing university. Teachers C and D had taught for approximately fifteen years. Teachers E and F possessed administrative credentials. Teacher E had been teaching for five years, three in another school system. Teacher F had three years of experience. Teachers A and C were female.

SURVEY PROBLEM 1. The teachers were asked what the qualities of a good faculty meeting are. This question considered time, place, role of the principal, and material to be covered in the meeting.

[15] P. E. Jacobson, *Duties of School Principals* (Englewood Cliffs, New Jersey: Prentice-Hall, Inc., 1941), pp. 197–199.

Teacher A responded, "Faculty meetings should be held after school, once a week, and should not last more than one hour. They should cover the problems of the school and the individual problems of the teachers. They also should be used to explain district policy as well as that of the plant itself. A great deal of time should be allowed for question and answer periods, and discussion of problems which have arisen during the week. The principal should preside over the meeting and lead the discussions, but not dominate them with his opinions. This is very important, as sometimes the opinions and experiences of other teachers are far more valuable than the opinion of a man who has been out of the classroom for a period of time."

Teacher B responded, "Faculty meetings should be used to help strengthen the school curriculum. The principal should provide materials showing district policy regarding the teaching of certain subjects. What teachers learn in college and the policy of the school system are often two different things. Too much time is wasted on points that are not of interest to the entire faculty.

"The principal should not only lead the meeting but should make himself responsible for keeping it moving. His agenda should be well planned, and he should stick to it as best he can. Meetings should be held in the faculty room once a week either before or after the school day, but should not last more than one hour.

"If the principal conducts the meeting in an orderly fashion and does not allow the discussion to wander away from the main points at hand, one hour should be sufficient time. It is his responsibility to see that the meeting keeps progressing to the best interests of all attending."

Teacher C replied, "The faculty meeting should be a time of cooperation and sharing. The place is not important as long as it is one of comfort and pleasantness. Meetings should be held whenever necessary, usually once a week.

"These meetings primarily should be to help teachers who need it. Teachers should submit problems during the week so that the principal can add them to the agenda for discussion by the group. These problems should be ones of general interest and concern, and not those of individual children. Such problems as are not of general interest should be taken up with the principal privately.

"Meetings also should be a time to share good ideas and creativity. This gives the industrious teacher recognition and a better feeling of accomplishment, besides motivating the other members of the staff. This sharing of ideas should be in the form of workshops as well as informal discussions. The principal should have some control over the meeting, but should allow one of the teachers to preside and lead discussions whenever possible."

Teacher D responded, "The faculty meeting should be held one-half hour before school as this is the time of day most teachers are the most alert and will display the most willingness to cooperate. The material covered should be presented by the principal in outline form. There is a great deal of time wasted in discussions, so they should be held to a minimum by the principal. The main purpose of a faculty meeting is to inform the teachers of events, procedure, and policy. The group meeting is no place for airing individual grievances and such discussions should be avoided. Problems such as these should be discussed privately. Some faculty meetings may be skipped in preference to a printed bulletin."

Teachers E and F agreed with Teacher D. They believed teachers' meetings should be structured around general problems that concern the whole group. There should be group discussions on these problems, and provisions should be made for workshops conducted by various staff members. The meeting should be led by the principal in a businesslike manner and should include information about coming events and occasional reminders of school system policy. Any questions concerning this policy can be taken up, but opinions should be avoided since the faculty meeting is not the proper place for teachers to try changing this policy.

The meeting should not last more than an hour. Personal problems could be taken up after the meeting, either with the principal or with other teachers. Lengthy discussions that may lead to arguments and discontent should be avoided. When such a situation arises, the principal should appoint a committee consisting of interested members. This committee then can discuss the problem and submit their ideas of the next meeting. This procedure will help reduce animosities among the staff members.

SURVEY PROBLEM 2.   The teachers were asked to what degree they believed the school can and should be run democratically. Opinions on this topic ranged greatly between democracy and complete dictatorship, with the majority for democracy.

Teacher C noted, "The teachers should have total say over the way the school is run. They should elect a leader from their group and this person should preside over all meetings. The principal should have a certain period of every meeting to pass on what he has learned from the higher administration. This should be in the form of a report and be only a small part of the meeting, not the central theme of it.

"The remainder of the meeting should be devoted to discussing running the school and any problems that have arisen. In this portion, the supervising principal should have equal rights as the rest of the staff and should not be allowed to dominate the discussion."

It was interesting to note that Teachers A, B, E, and F agreed. This group included the two first-year teachers and the two holding administrative credentials. They seemed to feel that the democratic approach was far superior, but that the principal figured largely in this type of meeting. Since it is the principal's responsibility to see that the school is running smoothly and since the principal has to answer for whatever goes on, they felt he/she should have a great deal to say about how the school is run.

According to these four teachers, the principal should preside over the meetings and allow the teachers to express their opinions at all times. The principal also should allow the group to make the decisions, but always should reserve the right of veto. He/she should not lose identity or authority. If a decision of the group does not meet with his/her approval, he/she should explain why and try to work out something that would satisfy all concerned. However, as the person in charge, the principal should not be entirely bound by the teachers' decisions. By using common sense and good judgment, the principal can run the school in a democratic way without being run by the system.

Teacher D's response was slightly different. This teacher went to the opposite extreme. He felt the principal should preside as absolute ruler. Because the responsibility of efficient running of the plant rests with the principal, he/she should make all decisions as to how it should be run.

"He should be able to present his decisions as rules to be followed and not to be questioned. Any problems the teachers have should be discussed with the principal. He can help the teacher, or direct him to a teacher who can help.

"The teacher's primary function is to teach, not to run the school. Any time and energy spent on the latter can only take away from the former."

SURVEY PROBLEM 3. The teachers were asked what some common mistakes were that many principals make in running faculty meetings. The following is a collective list of the mistakes named by all six teachers interviewed. Most of the items listed were named by at least half of the group.

1. Too much time is wasted on discussing individual problems that do not interest the group as a whole.
2. The meetings sometimes run too long due to poor leadership by the principal.
3. Discussions often get sidetracked and are apt to go on for too long without reaching any conclusion about the problem at hand.
4. The principal tries to influence the thinking of the members too much instead of letting them express their own opinions.
5. Most principals do not hand out or post a copy of the agenda in advance so that the members can come to the meeting prepared for discussion.

SURVEY PROBLEM 4. The last question asked was, "If you were a principal, what one thing would you change in the way staff meetings are run?"

Teachers A and B responded, "I would set aside a definite time in each meeting for discussing school problems, instead of just using whatever time is left over."

Teacher C said, "I would select, or have the group select, a teacher to preside over the meetings."

Teacher D noted, "I would write up the meeting and run it off to be distributed to the teachers in addition to the agenda for the following week's meeting."

Teachers E and F responded (in chorus), "We would have more workshops."

Evaluation Needed

As is true with all other supervisory procedures, the staff meeting is in need of continuous, formal evaluation. One supervising principal recommended: (1) formulating a faculty study group to which would be delegated the responsibility for staff meeting evaluation; (2) developing rating instruments designed and built according to the needs and wishes of the faculty, which would be basic in evaluation; and (3) analyzing group processes with assistance from the publications and institutes of such resources as the National Training Laboratories and the National Institute of Leadership, cited in Appendix A and in chapter 5.

Do

1 Organize faculty meetings around teachers' problems in general, but not around individual difficulties. There must be a definite plan for the faculty meeting. The agenda should be developed by a planning committee selected by members of the staff. The meeting should be presided over but not dominated by the principal.
2. Set aside a definite time for the faculty meeting. Every effort should be made to stick to that time.
3. Make provisions for social activities that will provide opportunities for the staff to get to know each other better. Refreshments help set the correct social atmosphere that can improve the meeting.
4. Get the faculty organized so that the principal acts as the chairperson until other leadership is evident, then the chair should be given to another. The democratic leader will be looking to see what leadership the staff contains and to encourage the development of this leadership.
5. Give the faculty partial responsibility for determining the place, agenda, and length of a faculty meeting.
6. Hold the faculty meeting during regular school hours or as close thereto as possible, thus eliminating the feeling that faculty meetings are an added burden.
7. Set aside a definite time for discussing general teaching problems, with individual problems being solved in committees or in conferences with the supervisor.
8. Give the meeting purpose and direction and assist the staff to accomplish the desired objectives.
9. State the purpose of the meeting from the beginning.
10. Allow all staff members to state their positions briefly with regard to the topic under discussion.
11. Emphasize a variety of opinions so that the teachers may see alternate courses for action.
12. Adopt reasonable rules of order.
13. Summarize important points to show how much progress was made in that session.
14. Avoid lecturing.

FIGURE 9-3. Checklist for Group Leaders

PREPARATION

1. Were members notified about meeting time, place, and topic? . . . .
2. Were the physical arrangements right for good discussion? . . . .
3. Did I prepare an outline for the discussion? . . . .
4. Did I provide sufficient background and factual material? . . . .
5. Were the visual or other aids in place and ready for use? . . . .
6. Was a friendly, personal atmosphere developed before the discussions started? . . . .

LEADING THE DISCUSSION

7. Did my introduction state the topic? _____ Define the areas for
   discussion? _____ Relate them to the interests of the group? . . . .
8. Was it too long? . . . .
9. Did it insure that the group had enough information on which to base the discussion? . . .
10. Did the group come right into the discussion after the introduction? . . . .
11. How did I "toss the ball" to the group? . . . .
12. Did I keep the discussion moving by:
    Frequent transitional summaries? _____ Checking repetitions? _____
    Calling attention to digressions and irrelevancies? . . . .
    Pointing up differences of opinion? _____ Clarifying the discussion? . . . .
    Allowing sufficient time for each major area of the topic? . . . .
13. Were the questions and other methods I used to guide the discussion:
    Aimed at bringing out reasons, opinions, causes? . . . .
    Designed to bring out all shades of opinion? . . . .
    Presented objectively (not slanted or argumentative)? . . . .

FIGURE 9-3. (Continued)

Worded briefly and clearly? .... _____

Thought-provoking (not rhetorical or "yes—no" in form)? .... _____

Fairly and tactfully distributed among all members? .... _____

14. Did I encourage participation by:

Keeping any one member from "hogging the show"? .... _____

Drawing out the reticent members? .... _____

Expressing appreciation of individual contributions? .... _____

Re-directing questions to other members? .... _____

Maintaining good humor and fair play? .... _____

15. Did I bring the discussion to a clear and definite conclusion? .... _____

16. Did my final summary fairly review all points of view expressed? ..... _____

State the agreements reached? _____ And the points of disagreement? _____

Call attention to sources of information? .... _____

Announce the next meeting? .... _____

RESULTS

17. Were there any indications of satisfaction from members of the group? ..... _____

Any indications of dissatisfaction from members of the group? ...... _____

18. Were there any unusual problems? _____ Did I handle them properly? ..... _____

19. How many members did not participate at all? .... _____

20. Was the topic suitable for discussion? .... _____

21. Were any important aspects of the question omitted? .... _____

22. Was there a clearer understanding of the subject after the discussion? ..... _____

23. What conclusions did the group reach? _____

24. What could I have done better? _____

15. Recognize pertinent contributions of other staff members and maintain an air of impartiality.
16. Seek to obtain a consensus.
17. Help the staff to recognize that final decisions are not always possible or desirable.
18. Complete the checklist for group leaders included as Figure 9-3.
19. Use care in ascribing statements to individuals.
20. Insure that whereas some agenda items are included for informational purposes, others are calls for action.

Don't

1. Allow the group to stray from issues presented.
2. As leader, fail to give direction to the discussion.
3. Permit a statement of a derogatory nature concerning a fellow staff member to be made at a staff meeting.

Staff meetings can be interesting. By following a few proven techniques that have been used by many, they may lose their low popularity rating.

If staff meetings are to contribute to the growth of the professional staff, they require careful, cooperative planning, judicious leadership, continuous evaluation, and prompt adjournment.

TRENDS IN IMPROVING STAFF MEETINGS

Toward ⟶ Staff Meetings Planned by
Faculty Planning Committees

The staff meetings of the future will be planned by grade level or subject area representatives around staff problems. This practice is becoming increasingly prevalent today. The supervising principal will act as a director, coordinator, and resource person and will not necessarily be the discussion leader. The principal, acting as a chief of staff, will consult with the faculty planning committees in establishing the time, length, date, and agenda of the staff meetings. The meetings will be planned as an integral part of the program for staff (and instructional) development.

Toward ⟶ Staff Meetings Held on
School-System Time

There is definitely a trend toward holding staff meetings on school time whenever possible. Staff meetings are essential to the educational program. If they are justified thus, they must be sufficiently important to be conducted during school hours. A preliminary step in this direction is scheduling staff meetings before school opens in the morning.

| Toward | ⟶   Staff Meetings Devoted Mainly to
Problems Related to the Instructional Program

The staff meeting of the future will be devoted largely to problems directly concerning the curriculum and its implementation through instruction. A minimum of administrative and clerical functions will be included in the agenda of the future.

| Toward | ⟶   More Careful and Complete
Agenda Preparation for Staff Meetings

Staff meetings of the future will follow better constructed and more flexible agenda than is found in most schools today. Written agenda will be made available to the entire faculty at least two days before the meetings.

| Toward | ⟶   Improved Orientation
Programs in Elementary Education

The teacher who is new to a school system will be introduced into the system through an improved orientation program that considers the general and specific needs of beginning teachers as outlined in this chapter. The program will include an introduction to specific system policies, to the school plant, to materials of instruction, to curriculum and instructional guides, to techniques of instruction, and to an outline of subject matter content.

Supervisory Problems   In-Basket

Problem 1

Two teachers, Gary and Debbie, were standing in front of the bulletin board in the teachers' lounge when the following dialogue was spoken:

Gary: Another of Mr. B's monologue sessions.

Debbie: I'm glad the only time I could make an appointment with my doctor is for 4:30 tomorrow. These notices usually mean extra long sessions.

Gary: Then you'll have an excuse for leaving the meeting. You can feel for me. I'll be sitting at one of those terrible lunch-table benches. I really need a crane to get into one of them. You can't hear anything in the lunchroom, and Mr. B. insists on standing at the head of the table when he reads his exciting administrative announcements. Why doesn't he just put it in writing, anyway? The last meeting he called I sat at the far end of the table and couldn't hear much that he said. Mrs. P. sat across the table from me and corrected test papers.

Debbie: Did you understand what the principal meant in the last item of that handout he gave us at the last meeting?

Gary: No, and I couldn't hear what time he told us to put on the paper because of all the noise the paper made as it was passed down the line.

Debbie: What did you think of the data he gave us comparing our students' basic skills levels with those of the other schools in the school system?

Gary: He erased his figures and replaced them with another set so fast that I couldn't keep up with him. What was he driving at?

Debbie: I'm not certain. I wish he had had time to answer a few questions. By the time he had finished his lecture and reading those endless routine announcements it was too late to do anything but go home.

Gary: I wonder if he'll have time for me to report about the activities of our last association meeting?

Debbie: You'll be lucky if you get to do it, because he didn't allow me time for my science committee report at the meeting last week.

What can be done to change the environment of the staff meeting?
How can the teachers' attitudes be changed favorably toward staff meetings?

Problem 2

A teacher at the school to which you have been assigned as supervising principal has a habit of "forgetting" to attend staff meetings.

How would you proceed?

Questions and Suggested Activities Concerning How to Improve Faculty, Committee, and Grade-Level and Subject Area Meetings

Questions

1. What are the characteristics of a good faculty meeting?
2. How can faculty morale be improved or impaired through staff meetings?
3. What is meant by "restraint and acceptance" on the part of the supervisor during a staff meeting?
4. How would you solve the problem of: the talkative teacher, the poorly prepared teacher, the negative teacher?
5. As a supervisor, you are challenged by a staff member during a meeting. How would you handle the situation?
6. What influence do teachers' vested interests, that is, their special interest in their subject or in a particular grade, have on group procedures in solving a particular problem?
7. As the supervisor, you are supposed to be the leader or chairperson, of the group. How can you surrender this role to another member of the group? When, and how often, should you do this? Why?
8. Should the problem of the time for the lunch hour be settled by group discussion? The problem of the grouping of children for instruction? The problem of a new kind of report card?

Suggested Activities

1. Criticize a subject area or grade-level meeting that you have observed. Suggest how it could have been improved.
2. After observing a series of primary reading lessons, study your notes and plan for a series of meetings designed to help the teachers. Plan in detail the first of these meetings.
3. Outline the procedures to be followed in a series of six meetings planned to help the junior high school social studies teachers improve their teaching of history, or some other social study. Explain the reasons for: (a) your choice of topics for each meeting, and (b) your proposed procedure for conducting each meeting.
4. After studying new methods for teaching mathematics, plan a series of school-level meetings to be carried on throughout the year.
5. Plan a meeting with the teachers of Grade 6 to organize a program of instruction in global geography. Outline the steps to be taken.
6. Plan a social committee meeting to implement the social program for the year. Plan for such diverse functions as the orientation of new teachers and a Christmas party.
7. List as many positive and negative points as possible concerning holding staff meetings before school, at noon, after school, on Saturday mornings, and at night.

8. Present three skits. In one, a democratic leader is conducting a staff meeting, and in the other two, meetings are conducted by a *laissez faire* leader and by an authoritarian leader, respectively.

9. Prepare a sample agenda for a staff meeting. Indicate the principles of supervision that you are applying.

10. Compare and analyze the beliefs concerning staff meeting management of at least ten teachers. Indicate who should be invited to attend staff meetings and your reasons for the selections.

11. Prepare a selected bibliography of articles devoted to methods of conducting staff meetings. Delimit your selection to periodicals published during the past two years.

12. Prepare a brief article concerning the improvement of staff meetings. The article should be suitable for publication. Prepare a letter of transmittal, and forward the article and letter to a professional journal for consideration for publication. (Letters of transmittal usually contain an offer to delete, amend, and edit as the editor of the journal may suggest. A stamped, self-addressed envelope should be enclosed. The manuscript itself should be double-spaced throughout, with very wide margins to facilitate editing. If your professor assists you in securing information, writing, and/or editing the article, he probably should be named as co-author.)

Selected Bibliography

Books

Adams, Harold P., and Frank G. Dickey. *Basic Principles of Supervision*. New York: American Book Company, 1953.

Ayars, Albert L. *Administering the People's Schools*. New York: McGraw-Hill Book Company, Inc., 1957.

Barr, A. S., William H. Burton, and Leo J. Brueckner. *Supervision: Democratic Leadership in the Improvement of Learning*. New York: D. Appleton-Century Company, Inc., 1947.

Burton, William H., and Leo J. Brueckner. *Supervision: A Social Process*. New York: Appleton-Century-Crofts, 1955.

Crosby, Muriel. *Supervision as Cooperative Action*. New York: Appleton-Century-Crofts, 1957.

Culbertson, Jack A., and Curtis Henson. *Performance Objectives for School Principals*. Berkeley, California: McCutchan Publishing Corporation, 1977.

Cummings, L. L., and Donald P. Schwab, *Performance in Organizations: Determinants and Appraisal*. Glenview, Illinois: Scott, Foresman and Co., 1973.

Elsbree, Willard D., and Harold J. McNally. *Elementary School Administration and Supervision*. New York: American Book Company, 1959.

Fiedler, Fred E., and Martin M. Chemers, *Leadership and Effective Management*. Glenview, Illinois: Scott, Foresman and Co., 1974.

Fullmer, Daniel W., and Harold W. Bernard. *Counseling: Content and Process*. Chicago: Science Research Associates, Inc., 1964.

Gwynn, J. Minor. *Theory and Practice of Supervision*. New York: Dodd, Mead & Company, 1961.

Hamachek, Don E. *Human Dynamics in Psychology and Education*. Boston: Allyn and Bacon, Inc., 1968.

Jacobson, P. E. *Duties of School Principals*. Englewood Cliffs, New Jersey: Prentice-Hall, Inc., 1941.

Lane, Robert Hill. *The Principal in the Modern Elementary School*. Boston: Houghton Mifflin Company, 1948.

Lipham, James M., and James A. Hoeh Jr., *The Principalship: Foundations and Functions*. New York: Harper and Row, 1974.

Saint, Avice Marion, *Supervision of Employees—Supervision and Teaching*. Chicago: Nelson-Hall Co., 1974.

Stoops, Emery, and James R. Marks. *Elementary School Supervision—Practices and Trends*. Boston: Allyn and Bacon, Inc., 1965.

Wiles, Kimball. *Supervision for Better Schools*. Englewood Cliffs, New Jersey: Prentice-Hall, Inc., 1955.

Wiles, Kimball, and John T. Lovell, *Supervision for Better Schools*. 4th ed. Englewood Cliffs, New Jersey: Prentice-Hall, Inc., 1975.

Periodicals

Benne, K. D., and P. Sheats, "Functional Roles of Group Members." Journal of Social Issues XXIV (1948): 41–49.

Bickford, Jean F. "Weekly Team Conference." *The National Elementary Principal* XLV (January 1966): 44–45.

Foss, P. R. "Faculty Meetings and How to Make the Most of Them." *Michigan Education Journal* XLIII (Fall 1966): 31.

Hunt, Douglas. "Teacher Induction—A Key to Excellence." *The Bulletin of the National Association of Secondary School Principals* CCCXX (May 1960): 60–70.

Kline, Aubrey J., "Rhetorical Stance and the Human Element in Teaching." *Phi Kappa Phi Journal* LV (Fall 1975): 29–31.

McGrew, John F. "Improving Staff Communications." *The Clearing House* XL (April 1966): 475–477.

Ross, F. W., A. D. Erb, and F. M. Saunders. "Principals' Forum." *The Instructor* LXXV (May 1966): 25.

Winters, Kay. "Perk Up Your Faculty Meeting." *NEA Journal* LV (October 1966): 30–31.

Audio Cassettes

Conference Planning and Leadership. Development Digest, 1973. Available from Thompson-Mitchell, Atlanta, Georgia.

Films

Communication: the Nonverbal Agenda. CRM Films, 1975. Does a person really mean what he says? Discusses such topics as body language and tone. (30 minutes)

Conference Leading Skills. Thompson-Mitchell, Atlanta, Georgia: 1972. A sound filmstrip series with three color filmstrips, audio cassette tapes, and a leader's guide.

How to Conduct a Discussion. Encyclopedia Britannica Educational Corp., 1952.

Interstaff Communications. New York University, 1969. Demonstrates use of psychodrama to improve working staff communications, showing the working through of a problem between a psychiatrist in charge of a psychiatric unit and his chief resident. Introductory and closing comments by psychologist Leon J. Fine. Condensed from two-hour spontaneous workshop session. Subtitles clarify techniques and identify participants. (52 minutes)

Other Sources

Association for Supervision and Curriculum Development. *Group Process in Supervision.* Washington, D.C.: National Education Association, 1948.

10

How to Measure Teacher
Effectiveness and Improve
Methods and Techniques
of Instruction

If civilization is to advance and our nation to develop, improvements in teaching are essential. Teachers must employ the most effective instructional techniques. For this goal to be realized, those who direct the efforts of others in the field of education continuously must evaluate the effectiveness of teaching and must be aware of the results of modern research and current, up-to-date, best practice that might present implications concerning the methods and techniques of those whom they supervise.

The purpose of this chapter is to indicate several techniques and methods available for evaluating teacher effectiveness and for assisting teachers in improving instruction. The following topics are covered:

Basic principles
How to get started in measuring teacher effectiveness: organizational plans
Teacher evaluation and appraisal: How the principal should initiate the evaluation
    program
How to encourage teacher self-evaluation
How to select criteria
How to evaluate instructional efficiency
How to organize for instruction
How to help the teacher plan for instruction
Gaming
Do—Don't
Trends
"In-Basket" supervisory problems
Questions and suggested activities

Basic Principles

The several supervisory techniques are not applicable to all teachers, nor are they effective to the same degree. E. O. Melby, in 1929, made an inventory of the various supervisory techniques. He concluded:

> . . . it must be admitted that the plan of [supervision] . . . for any school system will depend upon those factors of school organization, teacher training, and educational objectives which . . . [prevail] in that system. These factors are dynamic rather than static. It is, therefore, to be expected that . . . [continuous] modification must be made in the organizations charged with the responsibility for the improvement of teaching, as well as in the [techniques].[1]

It is necessary for supervisors to be aware of all applicable techniques. The supervising principal has a responsibility to provide leadership and to apply in practice the following basic principles:

1. Teaching methods can be improved through adequate and appropriate supervision.
2. All certificated personnel have degrees of responsibility for improving classroom methods and should function as a supervisory team.
3. Supervisory personnel should practice effective democratic methods in supervision if they expect teachers to use such methods in the classroom.
4. The merit of all methods of classroom instruction should be weighed in terms of desirable student growth.
5. Good supervision promotes methods that bring about a classroom climate of satisfaction and accomplishment.
6. Supervision should provide help for individual teachers and a general methodology improvement program.
7. Supervision of methods should include preplanning, observation, and a follow-up conference.
8. Wise supervision should include freedom for teacher initiative in classroom experimentation of methods.
9. Suggestions of methods should utilize the capabilities of the entire staff.
10. All supervisors, in recommending methods, should consider the individual differences of teachers as to personal, physical, mental, and social capabilities.
11. A primary approach to methods revision is acquaintance with late research in the field.
12. Supervision should produce in teachers a genuine interest in professional improvement of teaching methods.
13. A good supervisory program of methods revision grows out of the classroom and leads to further improvement.
14. Effective supervision provides for a cooperative program of continuous evaluation and improvement of all methods used.

[1] Ernest O. Melby, *Organization and Administration of Supervision* (Chicago: Public School Publishing Company, 1929), p. 37.

How to Get Started in Measuring Teacher Effectiveness: Organizational Plans

Before a program for measuring and improving teacher effectiveness can get under way, there must be general agreement on a school system-wide basis that the chief function of modern supervision is evaluating and improving factors that affect learning. This major function clearly necessitates certain subsidiary functions.

1. We cannot evaluate except in terms of an accepted philosophy, an accepted and understood statement of aims. The cooperative formulation of this statement is a function of school supervision. Common purposes, goals, and standards are thus established.
2. A process has to be developed for carrying on an educational program aimed at achieving the objectives.
3. A staff and organization, varying in size, complexity, and relationships, must be established for implementing and improving the program. The policy, process, and organization should be of such nature as to protect and stimulate the individuality and creativity of persons included. Human relations are far more important than the mechanical efficiency of any process or organization.
4. A policy and process for community relations must be devised, stressing cooperative participation in policy making and planning.
5. A theory and practice of evaluation must be developed which is consistent with the accepted goals and philosophy.[2]

How Supervision May Differ in Definition and Practice

The historical development of school supervision explains many difficulties and strengths in modern supervision. Supervision, properly defined and understood, often differs widely from supervision as it is practiced. It is at this point that the educational worker who relies solely on experience makes the greatest blunder, both in actions and in interpretation of what is observed. What he/she, with pride, frequently calls the "practical" view as distinguished from the "theoretical" is neither practical nor theoretical, but merely the result of a lack of information.

The experience on which the naïve practical person relies usually is fragmentary and inadequate, and usually incorrectly interpreted. Experience, if it is to become a basis for conclusions, must be enlightened and illuminated by knowledge of basic principles and facts derived from philosophic reflection and from controlled research. *Critically analyzed experience* and the critical analysis of wide observation of practice are valid bases for conclusions.

The aim of supervision in the abstract has been the same throughout history—the improvement of instruction. But if one includes in this definition the connotations with respect to methods and processes that were accepted in the

[2] A. S. Barr, William H. Burton and Leo J. Brueckner, *Supervision* (New York: Appleton and Company, 1938), p. 3.

past, one will see how different the old definition really is from that of the present.[3]

The Implications of Current Knowledge for Evaluation and Improvement Programs

Avoiding errors that result from outmoded principles and practices can be insured partially by using new principles and practices.

1. Education is recognized as a basic social force affecting the development of human personality and of a stable democratic social order.
2. A consensus must be developed within the group as to the ends and values of life, hence of education, before details of education, hence of supervision, can be developed.
3. Change is recognized as a principle of the universe, affecting all phases of life and of social organization.
4. The process of social change is recognized and used.
5. Supervision is recognized as a social process; in this country it is a cooperative democratic process.
6. The chief function of supervisors is leadership and the stimulation of leadership within the group.

Teacher Evaluation and Appraisal: How the Principal Should Initiate the Evaluation Program

The principal should be able to identify good and poor teaching and be able to assist individuals in making their own evaluation of instruction. He/she should be able to make positive recommendations for improvement or to enlist the aid of those who can help. Through observation and participation, the principal should keep in close touch with classroom activities in order to be better able to help each individual.

The Principal and Teacher Appraisal

There are various types of teacher appraisal forms. Some of these forms are based on the supervising principal's expectations that list, for the most part, desirable qualities. Rating scales, observation forms, the predictive appraisal of teacher training institutions, studies of student opinion, and other diagnostic techniques are used. All of these devices provide *subject measurement of no more than a sample portion of total performance.*

[3] Edwin H. Reeder, *Supervision in the Elementary School* (Boston: Houghton Mifflin Company, 1933), p. 15.

An evaluation procedure should be used *with* teachers, rather than *on* teachers. Evaluation must be viewed as *a cooperative attempt to solve a professional problem*. Discussion of the items on evaluation forms can serve as an effective stimulus to desirable classroom results. An evaluative scale could be used well by teachers for self-evaluation and subsequent conferences with the supervising principal. Teachers must be encouraged to use whatever self-appraisal techniques are suitable.

If teachers feel that the results of evaluation will be used against them, they will be unwilling to reveal weaknesses and problems. They will be eager to participate in evaluations, however, that strengthen their own professional status.

A First Step in Teacher Appraisal

One of the first steps in teacher appraisal is to accept criteria for effective teaching. Administrators and staff members should be responsible for selecting these criteria via a cooperative process. In fact, cooperative planning and joint effort are the key to any successful evaluation program. Evaluation should be purposeful. Too often it is considered as an end in itself. True evaluation is for improvement and growth through analysis of an individual's strengths and weaknesses, and thus it should be the basis for guidance and constructive criticism.

How to Assume Supervisory Responsibility

For a successful evaluation program, the principal *must* accept the responsibility for acquainting the teachers with what is expected of them and what appraisal techniques are being used. Teachers must think in terms of the constructive concept of evaluation and must consider it a source of help. The principal must avoid giving the impression that the evaluation is the final verdict on the teacher's work and worth.

Teacher appraisal should be continuous rather than periodic. It should be accompanied by, and followed with, helpful supervision. The *purposes* of evaluation may be for retention or dismissal; for promotion, tenure, or merit pay; or for improvement of instruction. The most vitally important of these purposes is the improvement of instruction.

How to Determine the Appraisal Task
Functions of the Supervisor

A. S. Barr and others[4] have listed the appraisal and improvement task functions of the supervising principal:

[4] A. S. Barr et al., *Supervision* (New York: Appleton-Century Company, 1947).

1. Evaluating the data related to the educational products in terms of the accepted goals of education and the objectives of instruction.
   a) Determining cooperatively critical analysis of goals.
   b) Selecting the means of appraisal and applying them.
   c) Analyzing the data so as to discover strength and weakness in the product.
2. Conducting a critical analysis of the entire teaching-learning situation so as to determine the antecedents of satisfactory (anticipated) and unsatisfactory student growth as reflected in observable behavioral changes and operationally defined capabilities.
   a) Studying the course of study and the curriculum-in-operation.
   b) Studying the materials of instruction, the equipment, and the socio-physical environment of learning and development.
   c) Studying the factors related to instruction (the teacher's personality, academic and professional training, organization for instruction, use of materials, methods and techniques of instruction, and other factors).
   d) Studying the factors present in the learner which may be investigated (capacity, interest, work habits, and others).
3. Improving the entire teaching-learning situation.
   a) Improving the course of study and the curriculum-in-operation.
   b) Improving the materials of instruction, the equipment, and the socio-physical environment of learning and development.
   c) Improving those factors relating directly to instruction which may be dealt with by the supervisory team.
   d) Improving such factors as may be present in the learner which may affect his development and achievement which may be attacked in the school situation.
4. Evaluating the objectives, methods, and outcomes of supervision.
   a) Discovering and applying the techniques of evaluation.
   b) Evaluating the results of given supervisory programs, including the factors which may tend to limit the success of those programs.
   c) Evaluating and improving the performance of all who compose the supervisory team.

In performing these functions, the supervisor should call on specialists from the intermediate and state units. Local system supervisors in a given geographical area should cooperate in area meetings and in sharing materials.

Some Contrasts in Traditional and Modern Appraisal Techniques

The characteristics of modern appraisal and improvement techniques, as opposed to the more traditional programs, are summarized:

1. Modern supervision directs attention toward the fundamentals of education and orients appraisal and improvement programs within the general aim of education.

2. The aim of supervision is the appraisal (analysis) and improvement of the total teaching-learning process—the total setting for learning—rather than the narrow and limited aim of improving teachers in service.
3. The focus of appraisal is on a situation, not on a person or group of persons. All persons are coworkers aiming at the improvement of a situation. One group is not superior to another, operating to "improve" the inferior group.
4. The teacher is removed from the embarrassing position as the focus of attention and the weak link in the educational process. The teacher assumes a rightful position as a cooperative member of a total supervisory team concerned with the improvement of learning.

Traditional supervision too efficiently did well what should not have been done at all. The attention of modern appraisal and improvement program supervision focuses more on the aims, structure, and fundamental processes of education, and on how well we meet our objectives, than on the minute, specific, day-to-day devices for improving trivial aspects of classroom procedure. With improved levels of teacher and supervisor training, the invention, selection, administration, and application of devices should become more and more a question of individual initiative based on understanding basic principles. The sphere of modern supervision is the whole range of elements affecting learning.

How to Encourage Teacher Self-Evaluation

THE IMPORTANCE OF SELF-SUPERVISION.   The move away from imposed supervision, coupled with the desirable modern emphasis on cooperative group endeavor, sometimes obscures the possibilities for self-direction, self-supervision, and self-guidance. The supervising principal may wish to present the teaching analysis sheet that appears as Figure 10-1 and the checklist included as Figure 10-2 to the staff as aids in teacher self-evaluation.

The mature individual will not only serve as a leader in group enterprise and make contributions to group discussions and decisions, he/she also often will engage in individual improvement.

Specialists do this when working independently on a frontier problem. A member of the rank and file does this when engaging in an individual study or in trying new methods in the classroom, or pursuing an individual problem through the available literature. Self-initiated attention to any problem often grows out of group activities.

How to Select Criteria

Selecting the criteria for measuring teacher effectiveness probably is the most difficult and most important task in developing the appraisal program. A well-rounded program might include such items as teacher behavior and relationships

FIGURE 10-1.   Teaching Analysis Sheet

Student: Your cooperation is sincerely desired in filling out this question-naire. The following, when completed, will aid the instructor in obtaining an evaluation of the success of the methods that he has employed and the class-room environment that he has created. Because of the benefit to both instructor and future students, please be sincere in answering these questions. *Do not sign your name!* Explain items marked D and F; make any other comments on reverse side of sheet. Indicate your opinion by encircling the appropriate letter before each item.

A—Excellent   B—Good   C—Average

D—Below Average   F—Poor   O—Does not pertain to this course

INSTRUCTOR EVALUATION

A B C D F O   Knowledge of subject matter.
A B C D F O   Is willing to admit error or lack of knowledge about a certain area.
A B C D F O   Interest and enthusiasm for subject.
A B C D F O   Interest and attention of class.
A B C D F O   Ability to stimulate your interest in subject.
A B C D F O   Definite, clear-cut presentation of subject matter.
A B C D F O   Criticizes students' efforts on a constructive basis.
A B C D F O   Voice qualities (pleasant, easily heard, etc.)
A B C D F O   Awareness of students' failure to understand.
A B C D F O   Understanding attitude toward students' efforts and problems.
A B C D F O   Approachability of instructor.
A B C D F O   Freedom of student to express his own ideas.
A B C D F O   Preparation for class meetings.

COURSE EVALUATION

A B C D F O   Clarity of course objectives.
A B C D F O   Use of recent research and material in this field.
A B C D F O   Logical arrangement of topics and material.
A B C D F O   Clear examples and illustrations.
A B C D F O   Use of examples that make course interesting.
A B C D F O   Effective use of class time.
A B C D F O   Clarity and readability of text.
A B C D F O   Value of text for course.

MARKING EVALUATION

A B C D F O   Value of exams for measuring your knowledge.
A B C D F O   Clarity of assignments and exams.
A B C D F O   Fairness of grading system.
A B C D F O   Is the amount of work required appropriate for credit received?
A B C D F O   Uses tests for actual learning situations, after they have been returned.
A B C D F O   Prompt return of assignments and exams.

FIGURE 10-2.   A Checklist for Teachers

HOW DO I RATE AS A TEACHER?

KEY: Indicate A for excellent
                    B for very good
                    C for passable
                    D for poor, needs improvement

1. Do I create, a happy, relaxed, but business-like atmosphere? _____

2. Is order and control inherent in my approach to classroom management? _____

3. Am I conscious of each student's potentials and needs? _____

4. Do I avoid judging students by adult standards? _____

5. When a student does not reach my standards do I search for causes? _____

6. How do I encourage initiative and originality? _____

7. Has every student confidence that I will try to see his problem from his point of view? _____

8. Do I have conferences with each student as often as possible? _____

9. Do students come to me for advice voluntarily? _____

10. Do I recognize symptoms of withdrawal, timidity, unsociableness, and discouragement as being especially serious? _____

11. Am I impersonal in dealing with behavior problems? _____

12. Do I analyze behavior problems through a systems analysis approach? _____

13. Are specific instructional objectives, stated in terms of observable changes in behavior and performance, definitely formulated? _____

14. Do I stimulate my students by scheduling field trips, audio-video-presentations, motion pictures, special reports, open-forums, guest speakers, and other attention-getting and interest-stimulating techniques? _____

15. Do I consider both students and subject matter as I plan for instruction? _____

16. Do I use the materials of instructional technology, including the simplest audio-visual aids, regularly and with purpose? _____

17. Do I capitalize on each student's personal environment? endowments? _____

18. Am I aware of each student's interests? _____

19. Am I mindful of individual differences, abilities, and needs? _____

20. Do I give all students equal opportunities and equal attention? _____

21. Do I help students to form good work habits? _____

22. Do I teach students how to study effectively? _____

23. Are students assuming more and more responsibility for their own improvement? _____

24. Is each student's attention span increasing? _____

FIGURE 10-2.   (Continued)

25. Is there evidence that students are increasing in self-control, initiative, and originality?   _____

26. Do students attack difficult problems eagerly?   _____

27. Does a large percentage of students participate in class discussion?   _____

28. Do I summarize ideas and generalization regularly?   _____

29. Do I supply each student with knowledge of results?   _____

30. Do I make the subject so clear and vital that students are highly stimulated?   _____

31. Do I begin each class session promptly and keep things moving without appearing to hurry?   _____

32. Do I encourage students to assist each other?   _____

33. Do I expect to be more than a **good** teacher?   _____

Consider yourself as a superior teacher if you scored 25 or more items as excellent or very good. If you marked less than 15 items as excellent or very good, you may do well to enroll in a graduate course in professional education and/or psychology, to seek the aid of your colleagues in education, to consult professional texts and journals, and/or to enroll in in-service education programs.

with the staff, student growth, student-teacher relationships, student reaction, room control, participation in programs for community relations, professional growth, teaching techniques, and the like. These statements, however, are more general than they may at first appear to the reader.

R. F. Mager[5] indicated that instruction should be evaluated in terms of evidence the teacher has concerning the extent to which the objectives established by the teacher have been realized:

1. Identify the terminal behavior the educator is seeking by name; he should specify the type of behavior that will be accepted as evidence that the learner has achieved the objective.

2. Attempt to define the desired behavior more precisely by describing the important conditions under which the behavior will be expected to occur.

3. Specify the criteria of acceptable performance by describing how well the learner must perform to be considered as having mastered the task at hand and as having succeeded in reaching the desired objective. "You can test whether . . . [an] objective clearly defines a desired outcome by answering 'yes' to the following question: Can another competent person select suc-

[5] Robert F. Mager, *Preparing Instructional Objectives* (Palo Alto, California: Fearon Publishers, 1962), especially chapters III–IV.

cessful learners in terms of the objective so that you, the objective writer, agree with the selections?"[6]

Criteria for evaluation, then, must clearly communicate and be related to intended educational outcomes, and as the statements are written they must describe all intended results. Statements as to criteria are useful only to the extent that they specify what the learner must be able to *do or perform* when demonstrating mastery:

Since [no one can] see into another's mind so as to determine what he knows, [the supervisor] can . . . determine the state of the learner's development [and infer instructional effectiveness] only by observing behavior.[7]

Appraisal of instructional outcomes, then, is perhaps a more accurate description of how the supervisor should operate than is *appraisal of teacher effectiveness.* Appraisal, then, is not limited to applying a single test of value to one simple, predetermined criterion. It is a comprehensive process. Characteristics of appraisal are as follows:

1. Appraisal is an integral, complex part of education.
2. Instructional effectiveness is best determined by appraisal of growth as related to goals in the individual situations.
3. The total personality and all aspects of individual development and behavior are evaluated.
4. Many tools and procedures and many types of evidence are used in the evaluative process.
5. Evaluation means not only appraising, judging, and diagnosing, but it also means determining whether the results are adequate and desirable.
6. The evaluation process is not completed by the teacher alone; cooperative efforts by many participants are indicated.

How to Evaluate Instructional Efficiency

General questions to be answered in evaluating instructional efficiency are suggested:

1. Is there an organized instructional program?
2. Is the program known to the teachers?
3. Is the program organized to provide for continuity and completeness?
4. Is the teacher competent, well prepared, and interested in the area?
5. Is the program apparently geared to the student and his/her program of learning (e.g., stimulation, individual differences, and readiness)?

[6] Ibid., p. 12.
[7] Ibid., p. 13.

6. Are the supplies, equipment, texts, and audio-visual aids readily available for an adequate program?
7. How much time is given to the area, and how is it distributed?
8. Is the classroom environment conducive to learning?
9. Is the class size reasonable?
10. Do the students apparently enjoy and respect the program?
11. How do the teachers plan for instruction?
12. Do teachers apparently know the various approaches to learning the subject?

Questions concerning instruction in mathematics:

1. Is mathematics taught as a drill subject, is it taught incidentally, or is it taught meaningfully?
2. Is mathematics taught for generalization or as a series of individual means of working examples?
3. How is problem-solving taught?
4. What provision for teaching technical reading is there?
5. What concrete materials are used?
6. Do the students use mathematics intelligently in practical situations and when appropriate in other subjects?
7. Are there subgroups within the class? How are they formed?
8. What do objective test results show concerning learning in mathematics?
9. Are the more capable learners allowed to go beyond the customary subject matter of the grade?

Questions concerning instruction in reading:

1. How many learning groups are there within the class, and how are they determined?
2. Are there sufficient books for recreational reading?
3. What do objective test results reveal about the program?
4. Are both oral and silent reading skills developed?
5. How do upper-grade teachers adapt to the previous readiness program?
6. What provisions are there for remedial reading?
7. Does the reading program coordinate reading activities with all the other subjects depending on reading?
8. How is reading taught? Is there an emphasis on specific instruction in word-attack skills?

Questions concerning instruction in social sciences:

1. Does student behavior in the classrooms and on the school grounds offer evidence of learning citizenship and democratic behavior?
2. Are the students competent in the skills of locating data; reading charts, pictures, graphs, maps, diagrams, tables; and reading for social science understanding?

3. What objective data, other than teacher-made tests, are there to describe achievement in the social sciences?
4. What activity units have been accomplished, and how successful were they?
5. Is the emphasis on cooperative and democratic participation, as well as on learning facts in history, geography, and civics?

Questions concerning instruction in science:

1. Is the program balanced between biological and physical science?
2. Is the learning directed toward understanding scientific generalizations?
3. Is there development of scientific attitudes and the use of scientific method?
4. Is there sufficient firsthand experience to develop functional understanding of science?

Questions concerning instruction in handwriting:

1. What objective scales (Ayres, Freeman, Thorndike) are used to evaluate handwriting? Are goals and standards known to the students and the teachers?
2. What directed learning of handwriting is there after the third grade?
3. When and how is cursive writing taught? What becomes of manuscript writing?
4. What follow-up of handwriting is done throughout the day?

Questions concerning instruction in spelling:

1. How does the teacher now evaluate spelling? (Spelling lesson only? Spelling throughout the day? Or?)
2. What provisions are made to teach students to attack a previously unstudied word? Are the skills of phonetic and structural analysis taught?
3. What provisions are made for individual difficulties in spelling?

Questions concerning instruction in grammar and composition:

1. What is the range of activities and/or media utilized in teaching oral and written communication skills?
2. What do objective test results indicate as to the strengths and weaknesses of the program?
3. What follow-up is there?

Questions concerning instruction in art:

1. What are the objectives of the program (technical excellence, understanding, appreciation, production, enjoyment)?
2. What is the range of media experienced?
3. How is art used throughout the rest of the curriculum?
4. Is technical assistance in art available to the teacher who feels insecure?
5. How does the instructor evaluate art learnings?
6. Does the room environment reflect the art philosophy?

Questions concerning instruction in music:

1. What music activities are available for students?
2. What evidence of enjoyment and/or appreciation by the students is there?
3. What technical assistance is available to the teacher who feels insecure?
4. What provisions are there for musically talented children?
5. How is music correlated/integrated with other subjects?
6. How is the instrumental program coordinated with the academic time schedule?

Questions concerning instruction in physical education:

1. Is the course one of physical education and of physical exercise? How is it distinguished from recess or after-school recreation?
2. Does each teacher know the physical and health conditions of the students so that each one may have appropriate activities?
3. How are the learning outcomes evaluated by the classroom teachers?
4. Does the teacher diagnose difficulties as he/she does in academic subjects and give appropriate remedial instruction?

Figures 10-3 and 10-6 illustrate some forms that have been used in evaluating teacher effectiveness.

Evaluation and Morale

Evaluation cannot achieve its objective unless it is cooperatively approached by both teacher and principal. It seems that supervision's main tasks, therefore, are determining ways of stimulating teachers, attempting to fit methods and techniques to teacher personality, and encouraging self-evaluation with stress of strengths and weaknesses.

It must be recognized that teacher evaluation is a very potent process. If incorrectly handled, it can destroy staff morale, and high morale is an essential prerequisite to optimal teacher effectiveness. Cooperative planning of a beneficial program offers opportunities for better understanding and stronger relationships.

Factors That Influence Teacher Morale

Factors related to staff morale include:

1. Security on the job and with groups
2. Status, prestige, and recognition
3. Adequate salary, professional level, and advancement

FIGURE 10-3.   Teacher Evaluation

Circle the words or phrases which most nearly describe the classroom spirit and the influence of the teacher.

Teaching Materials and Procedures	Textbooks, dictionaries, reference material, maps, globes, wall charts
Adequate supplies	Provision for levels of abilities of students, grouping, adequate chalk-board, bulletin board space
Student-Teacher Relationships	Type of leadership, respect for students, respect for teacher, discipline-control
	Student leadership
	Stimulates students to work up to their capacity
Interest and Activity of Students	Students are nervous, fidgety, squirmy; free, relaxed; mobility about room; evidence of student activities, group activities; students courteous and mannerly
	Students appear to have a sincere desire to learn
	Students listen with interest
Classroom Management	Student responsibilities and leadership, traditional teaching, rigid control—line up and march in
	Reading center, library books, movable desks, carpet, dittoed material, student creative work, flexibility in organization
General Appearance and Poise (Teacher)	Modern, conservative, appropriate, appealing
Clothing Hair, grooming	Modern, conservative, pleasant appearance
Room Appearance and Physical Condition	Well organized, poorly organized, bulletin board materials properly displayed; adequate lighting—heating; room adjusted to curriculum or grade level taught; clean room, student work on display
Attitude toward Teaching	Professional attitude; loves to teach; enjoys class and students; encourages students to want to be teachers by actions
Command of Language	Speaks at level of students, clearly, distinctly, does not have to repeat assignments, grammatical usage correct, enunciates clearly
	Handwriting *legible and of acceptable style*

FIGURE 10-4.   Teacher Evaluation Report

_____

_____
(Teacher)   (Department)

_____
(Subjects taught)

Points of strength _____

_____

_____

_____

_____

Points where improvement might be made_____

_____

_____

_____

_____

                        _____
                                Principal's Signature

4.   Satisfying social relationships and working conditions
5.   Successful achievement of objectives
6.   A feeling that one has the support and loyalty of one's supervisor
7.   Superior leadership, with confidence in this leadership
8.   Recognition for a job well done.

Environmental factors that tend to generate a high teacher morale response include:

1.   Teamwork
2.   Positive school relationships
3.   Availability of personnel
4.   Superior performance by one's teaching colleagues.

Areas in which morale response is relatively low include:

1.   Required cocurricular activities supervision
2.   Personal security (lacking)

FIGURE 10-5.   Analysis Report

REPORT ON PRINCIPAL'S TEACHING
EFFECTIVENESS ANALYSIS VISIT
(To be retained in school files)

SCHOOL_____   Report for:

Sem. 1 _____

Sem. 2 _____

Sem. 3 _____

Sem. 4 _____

TEACHER _____ CLASS _____ HOUR _____

DATE OF VISIT _____

I. *Physical Characteristics of Classroom:*
   (Satisfactory or not satisfactory)
   1. Ventilation and lighting
      (if within control of
      teacher) _____ 3. Displays _____
   2. Seating arrangements _____ 4. Orderliness _____

II. *Teaching and Learning:*
   1. What work was actually in progress?

   _____

   _____

   2. What were the apparent student reactions to this work?

   _____

   _____

   3. Were classroom activities in line with stated objectives?

   _____

   _____

   4. General evaluation for this visit:
      Satisfactory or better _____
      Not satisfactory _____
   5. Comments: _____

   _____

   _____

(Continue on other side if necessary)

(Teacher's signature does
not necessarily mean complete
agreement on part of teacher.)
_____   _____
Teacher's Signature   Principal's Signature

_____   _____
Date   Date

FIGURE 10-6.   Teacher Evaluation Report

PROBATIONARY TEACHER EVALUATION SUMMARY REPORT
(To be filed with Personnel Division—for instructions,
refer to Principal's Circular No. _____)

Teacher's Name (Last first)   School

Subject and/or Grade

REPORT FOR: *First Year*
              1st Prob. Sem. (Internship or Regular)   _____
              2nd Prob. Sem.   _____

              Second Year
              3rd Prob. Sem. _____   4th Prob. Sem. _____

POINTS OF STRENGTH:

POINTS OF WEAKNESS:

SUMMARY:

	Is performing satisfactorily or better as a probationary teacher at this time	_____
1st, 2nd or 3rd	Should not be offered new contract	_____
Semester	Should be dismissed immediately	_____
Report	Cannot make a judgment at this time (A judgment must be made in the 4th semester)	_____

It is my carefully considered professional opinion that this teacher:

4th	Should be granted tenure	_____
Semester Report	Should not be granted tenure	_____

(Teacher's signature does not
necessarily indicate agreement)

Teacher's Signature   Date

Principal's Signature   Date

3. Recognition (lacking)
4. Negative student relationships
5. A feeling that one does not have adequate possibilities for advancement in the profession
6. Inadequate salary and/or fringe benefits
7. Too many extra-instructional duties
8. Below standard physical facilities
9. Lack of freedom from distractions
10. Poor, ineffective communications
11. Undesirable contacts with parents and/or with community pressure groups and their representatives.

Morale is contagious; in time it permeates the whole staff and is influential in determining the quality of instruction. Certainly, without high morale the teacher cannot operate with maximum effectiveness.

How to Organize for Instruction

Flexible Groupings and Individual Instruction

There seems to be a trend toward using large group, medium-sized group, small group, very small group, and individualized instruction for an identified group of students within the school. An example of one program for this technique of organization is included as Figure 10-7a, 10-7b, and 10-7c.

If such schemes for instructional organization are to be effective, the principal should insure that:

1. The teacher is given adequate time for lesson preparation and for gathering material.
2. Groupings remain flexible and the professional judgment of the teacher(s) concerned determines the placement and reassignment of students within each of the groupings.
3. Adequate time and physical facilities are made available for staff conferences.
4. Adequate physical facilities are available for teacher use with each grouping.
5. The large group is used for presentations that are not better given in medium, small, very small, or individualized sessions, such as seeing a motion picture, or listening to a guest speaker or a specialized lecture.
6. The materials of instructional technology are made available to the teachers concerned, and that these materials are strategically placed so that it is easy for the teacher to obtain them.
7. That small discussion groups are not used to go over material that has been covered in the large groupings, but rather that students bring to the dis-

INSTRUCTIONAL TEAM PROGRAM, West Community College
College Basic Skills

ACTIVITY PHASE I

Large (total) Grouping

| All Students Meeting Together |
| Total Instructional Team |
| Common Problems on Planning |
| Orientation |
| Presentations by Team Specialists and Guest Lecturers |
| Evaluation |

•••••• Student group j
oooooo Student group r
——— Student group m

ACTIVITY PHASE II

Medium Sized Groupings

| Medium Sized Group j Individual Conferences Academic Problems Seminar Group Discussion Lab. and Follow-up |
| Medium Sized Group r Individual Conferences Academic Problems Seminar Group Discussion Lab. and Follow-up |
| Medium Sized Group m Individual Conferences Academic Problems Seminar Group Discussion Lab. and Follow-up |

INSTRUCTIONAL CENTER LAB. — SMALL GROUPS

Selected Students from all 3 groups.

Instructional Team

ACTIVITY PHASE III

Small and very Small Groupings

| Very Small Group and Individual Activities related to expressive and receptive (audio-lingual and reading) communication skills Counseling Study Skills Lab.; Instructional Center Supervised Study and Reading Special Problems |
| Very Small Group and Individual Activities related to expressive (written) communication skills Counseling Study Skills Lab.; Instructional Center Supervised Study and Reading Special Problems |
| Very Small Group and Individual Activities related to computation-al and reading skills Counseling Study Skills Lab. Special Problems |

Directed by Appropriate Specialists

WEEK 1

FIGURE 10-7a.   Sample Activities Flowchart, Week 1

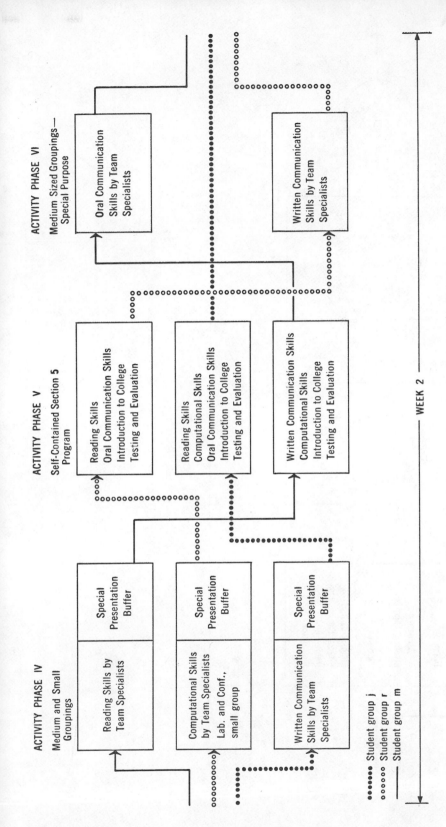

FIGURE 10-7b. Sample Activities Flow Chart, Week 2

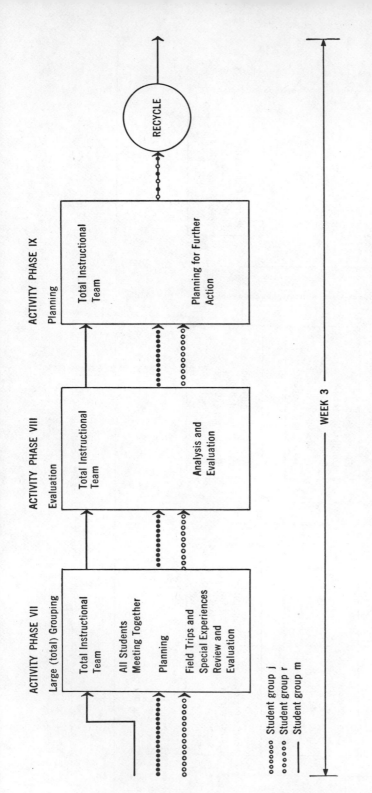

ACTIVITY PHASE VII
Large (total) Grouping

Total Instructional
Team

All Students
Meeting Together

Planning

Field Trips and
Special Experiences
Review and
Evaluation

ACTIVITY PHASE VIII
Evaluation

Total Instructional
Team

Analysis and
Evaluation

ACTIVITY PHASE IX
Planning

Total Instructional
Team

Planning for Further
Action

RECYCLE

WEEK 3

ooooooo Student group j
oooooo Student group r
——— Student group m

FIGURE 10-7c. Sample Activities Flow Chart, Week 3

cussion groups materials and notes from outside research and, in seminar session, further the points that had been developed in the large groupings.[8]

8. Individualized instruction and independent (programmed or not) work is initiated gradually, following very small group instruction.

Individualized Instruction

Individualized instruction means flexible time frames; it means allowing a student to move through an instructional program as rapidly as he/she can. It means building in exemptions and corrective subprograms. One problem is that at times faculty members do not know the entry achievement levels of their students. Some students know more than the teacher anticipates; others know less. A student who knows elements of a course should be exempt from repeating this material. A student who does not have the necessary, essential prerequisites for a specific course, should not get into the program until he/she has them.

Individualization means building in content options that relate a core of instruction to the needs or interests of the student. Students should have a choice of a learning and studying location. Everything does not have to take place in the classroom. Part of the formal program can take place in the library and in the instructional (media) center and part can be moved into the community. Individualization also means providing a choice of evaluation methods so that a student can prove that he/she has satisfied the base-line objectives for the course. At times, the objective test or an essay does not help us find out what some students know. Perhaps we should permit an oral or audio- or video-taped report.

Individualization means alternative styles of instruction. Alternative approaches should be available when they are needed: when a single method will not work in any event, students must be able to meet with the instructor directly. Research studies, such as those by Robert Diamond, Lewis Case, Travis Linn, and Bill Tucker[9] revealed that in several instances the same instructional options were at once both the most liked and the most disliked. Some students needed more structure than others. When the students who needed structure participated in an independent learning option, they had many problems.

We as supervisors cannot separate the academic program from the entire environment of the institution. We must produce more impact for the dollars available. The shotgun technique does not do the job. Supervisors must give greater support to fewer projects. In other words, the supervisor should allow projects that he/she supports to go as far as possible in the best possible way. This means putting money on the high priority projects. Furthermore, educators must design instruction with a view toward teams and groups. Often an audio-video-tutorial program dies when the teacher who put it together leaves that institution. We cannot afford such luxury. Departmental commitment and *faculty teams* are

8 See Herbert W. Wey, *Handbook for Principals* (New York: Shaum Publishing Company, 1966), p. 31.

9 See U.S. Office of Education: Implementing Instructional Development through Learning Resources Center (Dallas: The Office, 1975), vol. 1

needed so that we may have content expertise and so that we will have a program with lasting quality. Finally, the individualized program must be subjected to priorities that are derived from institutional goals. The supervisor will want to conduct a cost-effectiveness and cost-efficiency analysis. If existing resources are being used in an improved manner, then cost efficiencies are realized. If community relations are enhanced and instruction is more effective, then the program is cost effective.

How to Organize for "Nongraded" Instruction

Many faculties are experimenting with departmentalization and/or with "team teaching" techniques. The student will be with one teacher for the major portion of the day and may be with different teachers for physical education, music, art, foreign language, or other subjects. We should look for greater experimentation in this area in the future, along with further employment of the "nongraded" plans, which first were proposed shortly after the Quincy Grammar School opened its doors in 1848 with the first "graded" organization in the New World. There have been arguments, incidentally, that the first nongraded school existed in the colonies as the dame school.

The most successful type of nongraded program seems to be based on using many groupings simultaneously. Such groupings have been developed according to achievement, abilities, talents, interests, and work-study skills. In reality, it seems that many schools experimenting in this area have merely substituted twelve or more grade groupings for three, although, theoretically, at least, individuals as well as groups may move from one achievement level to the next as soon as readiness for the higher level is indicated. Students are then identified as being enrolled in the primary division rather than in grades one, two, or three.

Progress in reading comprehension seems to be the primary criterion for advancement to grade four from the primary division. In a truly nongraded situation, grade levels should not become a matter for concern until the student is about to enter grade four, and *flexible mobility* must be the keynote of the system.

There has been a lot of conflicting—but little significant—research concerning the value of the nongraded organization. Further experimentation in this area seems indicated.

Staff Utilization: Team Teaching Plans

In essence, a team is an instructional unit within a school. This unit is a combination of (1) a distinct student group, (2) a small faculty group responsible for teaching the student group, and (3) individuals who assist the teachers and students.

A *team leader* is a mature, experienced, certificated teacher of unusual talent and extensive training who has been elected or appointed to serve as the leader of a teaching team and whose major responsibilities are teaching and coordinating the team's efforts. The team leader should be paid a stipend above normal pay for this latter responsibility. Moreover, he/she receives time to plan and to coordinate team activities.

A *team teacher* is a fully certificated member of a teaching team; an *intern teacher* is a beginning teacher, not yet fully certificated. The intern teacher is given a regular teaching assignment on the team and receives supervision from both the employing school system and the sponsoring college or university.

A *student teacher* is a college student assigned to a school to observe and to teach directly under the supervision of a master teacher in that school. The *master teacher* is an experienced, regularly certificated teacher who possesses considerable advance study, unusual knowledge, and great skill in teaching.

A classified (noncertificated) individual from the community who works with the team on a paid, part-time basis is a *teacher's aide.* He/she relieves the teachers of clerical and other routine work so that they can concentrate on instructional activities.

An *auxiliary teacher* is a fully certificated teacher who is called in at the team's request. A *community resource person* is a skilled individual not ordinarily affiliated with the school. He/she can, under supervision of a teacher, assist in some specific aspect of the instructional program or can lead student study groups in his/her special area of competence.[10]

For team teaching to be successful, it must not be a thinly disguised plan for departmentalization. In team teaching, all members of the team share varying degrees of responsibility for the entire instructional program for the individuals within the class group. The supervisor must help team members increase their abilities to solve instructional problems through their individual skills, abilities, talents, and insights. The supervisor should do all in his/her power to enhance effective communication between team members and between teams. He/she must encourage the free exchange of experiences, ideas, and information.

Even though research in the area of team teaching is limited in quantity, it does indicate that members of the team must share the common abilities of being able to adapt readily to new and varied situations, of being highly efficient in self-elevation, in working well with other adults in a cooperative endeavor, and in organization, in addition to the usual attributes of the outstanding educator.

The supervisor should encourage the team to experiment with new materials, ideas, and techniques. He/she must help the team members analyze evident deficiencies in team instruction but must not discourage team members from making decisions based on sound judgment and experience. Rather, he/she must encourage the development of the strengths of the members both as individuals and as members of a functioning instructional team. Adequate facilities and time

[10] John A. Brownell and H. A. Taylor, "Theoretical Perspectives for Teaching Teams." *Phi Delta Kappan* XLIII (January 1962):150–157.

must be made available to the teaching team; adequate supervisory assistance is even more essential.

A grouping schema used in an instructional team program is illustrated in Figure 10-7b, the Sample Activities Flow Chart for week 2.

How to Help the Teacher Plan for Instruction

D. O. Weaver's[11] guidelines or "tricks of the trade" for the teacher may prove especially helpful in discussion groups studying organization and planning for effective instruction:

1. By assigning seats and keeping a copy of the plan in front of him, the teacher quickly learns the names of students. Calling a student by name makes the class a personal affair rather than a cold, formal, and impersonal experience.
2. Good questions stimulate interest and promote initiative among students. They also secure cooperation and give the teacher an idea how each student is progressing. The teacher also gets an idea as to how effective his instruction is. Make questions definite and state them clearly.
3. Remember to ask questions that will make the students think. If questions can be answered simply by a "yes" or "no," the class will not be stimulated. When a student has answered a question, ask him to explain his answer. Then request another student to comment on his explanation. In this way each student will follow every word that is being said, knowing that he may be called upon at any moment. By probing into a topic in this way, the teacher will not fall into the habit of saying, "Are there any questions?" Most students will not be willing (or able) to say whether they are in doubt or not. It is up to the teacher to find out, by proper questioning, whether the class is getting the material.
4. Take plenty of time making definite assignments. Before giving an assignment, the teacher should explain to the class what it is about and why it is being given at that time. The teacher should be specific—from page such and such to page so and so. He also should be definite about the work to be undertaken—telling the students that they are to read, memorize, outline, or whatever. The home assignment should not be put off until the end of the period when it might have to be dealt with in a hasty and inadequate manner. The competent instructor is definite about study assignments. Knowing the value of repetition and review, he gives his students frequent tasks, tests, and examinations.
5. Unless the teacher shows his students that he himself is enthusiastic about the subject matter and about teaching it, they will not attack their lessons

[11] Reprinted with permission from David O. Weaver, "The Instructor's Relationship to His Students." *Training Directors Journal* XIV (January 1960): 40–70. This Journal has much to offer the educational supervisor.

with vigor and determination. Every good instructor is, to some degree, a salesman. He is convinced he has the finest product in the world to sell. His salesmanship will largely determine the readiness with which his class accepts the product. Enthusiasm is caught, not taught.

6. Students learn by trial and error, by observation, by "transfer," and by *doing*. Trial and error is the inefficient way; doing is the most effective. The capable instructor knows that theory is good, but, as Dewey told us, theory divorced from practice is ineffectual.

7. Demonstration and illustration—appealing to the eye (or mind's eye)—are the best means of teaching as they make the most vivid impression upon the learner. Mock-ups, models, and similar teaching aids are employed by the competent instructor whenever available.

8. The good teacher shows "how" and explains "why."

9. The capable teacher does his best to arouse the students' *will to learn*. He convinces the students that the subject is worthwhile and acquirement of that particular knowledge or skill will be of immediate benefit to the students.

10. The competent teacher keeps his students informed as to their progress. He is liberal with encouraging commendation and sparing with reproof. The good teacher knows that the principle of immediate feedback of results to the student is a primary tenet of education.

11. The able teacher does his best to maintain good classroom and study periods, and keeps an eye on the physical welfare of his students.

12. The good teacher never plays Professor Know-It-All, never tries to bluff. *If he does not know the answer, he says so.* If he makes a mistake, he acknowledges that fact. He does not pose as an infallible authority.

13. At all times the competent teacher encourages student initiative and intellectual curiosity.

How to Plan for Instruction

One important factor in successful instruction is a careful, thorough preparation by the teacher. For many reasons, a written lesson plan, at least in the early part of the professional career, is a must.

The supervising principal should stress that a lesson plan first helps insure that the material is covered completely; and second, it keeps the teacher pointed in the right direction—toward a definite goal—and helps insure sequence and organization. The lesson plan acts as a guide and refreshes the memory.

There are several possible methods and combinations of methods and techniques for teaching, and there will be many differences among lesson plans.

The first problem encountered in planning a lesson is determining clearly defined objectives, for they give a purpose and direction to teaching efforts.

Next, the teacher must determine the method or combination of methods and techniques of instruction that will be used for a particular lesson. Several factors determine this choice: classroom facilities; the age level, maturity, and needs of the students; the time available for instruction; and the objectives of the lesson.

A further step is selecting and organizing supplies, equipment, and materials to be used in instruction. The teacher must study the texts, teacher supplements, and instructional guides to acquire as broad a background of information on the subject as possible. Then the information to be presented is selected. This selection will be determined by considerations similar to those governing the selection of the teaching method.

Normally, students will not be able to retain more than two or three major ideas, so the lesson material should be contained within this number of headings. The teacher should (1) determine the headings, and (2) on one-half of a folded piece of paper lay out notes under these headings so that each heading follows logically the previous one and each thought within the headings logically follows the preceding one. (The best criterion for arranging headings is what makes the most sense from the student's point of view.) The supervising principal should encourage the teacher to complete the blank side of the plan by indicating, at the appropriate points, the supplementary material to be used—references, teaching aids, or quotations.

The entire content material outline then should be incorporated into a plan, such as the one appearing as Figure 10-8. The amount of material in the plan will need to be adjusted according to the teacher's experience with the class.

In most cases, the content side of the lesson plan should have a set overall pattern. It should have three main parts:

1. The introduction
2. The body of the lesson
3. The summary

These three parts of the lesson are illustrated in Figures 10-9, 10-10, and 10-11.

FIGURE 10-8. Sample Lesson Plan Form

I. Introduction: Objectives (Specific!)	
II. Materials to Be Used	
III. Procedure:	Content Material:
A. Building readiness, including stimulation	A. Introduction
B. Body—all steps in lesson	B. Body
C. Review and evaluation (with students)	C. Summary
IV. Evaluation by Teacher of His Lesson	

INTRODUCTION

WHY

1. To establish contact; to stimulate.
2. To arouse interest.
3. To secure attention.
4. To disclose and clarify the subject.

HOW

1. Good opening statement.
2. Stories or examples.
3. Quotations
4. Questions, skits and demonstrations. Tell and show what, why and how.

FIGURE 10-9.   Introduction

Unit Plans

The unit plan is an effective way to plan a program for instruction within the classroom. A unit is planned for a period longer than a day, and it may extend for several weeks. Because the students' attention span is related to age, units in the lower grades are usually short—about one or two weeks. Attention spans become increasingly longer in the upper grades, lasting from four to eight or more weeks.

At any grade level, the learning process is implemented more efficiently when the unit is organized for more than one instruction period or one day. It is extremely difficult, if not impossible, to use teaching time efficiently when planning is on a day-to-day basis. The students cannot discover the relationship between each day's work when the teacher does not know how it fits into a larger plan.

Units may be planned on a basis of content in a single area, such as reading, mathematics, English, or science; content extending beyond a single area, such as "How Desert People Live"; a social studies unit in which history and geography are combined; and projects or problems that cross subject lines completely, as in a unit called "Understanding Our South American Neighbors," which involves reading, teaching music and art, working mathematics problems, building science concepts, and studying history and geography.

Unit teaching provides for many student activities, such as reading from several books, telling stories, listening to teacher or classmates, individualized study, group projects, group discussion, visits outside the classroom, construction

BODY

WHY	HOW
1. To present teaching points.	1. Sound organization.
2. To explain knowledge.	2. Smooth transitions.
3. To develop understanding.	3. Repetition, frequent summaries.
4. To stimulate appreciation. To change behavior. Behavioral objectives should be stated clearly.	4. Vital and interesting presentation.

FIGURE 10-10. Body

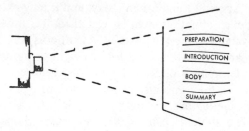

PREPARATION
INTRODUCTION
BODY
SUMMARY

SUMMARY

WHY	HOW
1. To provide an over-all view.	1. Clear up questions.
2. To emphasize.	2. Recap main points.
3. To summarize, clarify, and conclude instruction.	3. Close with a strong statement.

FIGURE 10-11. Levels of Planning for the Improvement of Instructional Materials

activities calling for creative and artistic talent, listening to records, and seeing and discussing films. For any grade, student activities and the order in which they are taken should be determined by the organization of instruction for that grade and by the successive steps required to achieve the desired outcomes.

Units are classified as resource units and as teaching units. Each has characteristics that make it adaptable to certain planning situations.

RESOURCE UNITS.   A resource unit usually is planned by a group of teachers. For example, in a seventh-grade class in which special teachers provide instruction in music, art, and physical education, the homeroom teacher and the three special teachers work out a series of resource units for that grade.

A resource unit typically has the following features:

1. A title or topic and an indication of the grade or age levels for which the unit is designed
2. An introductory statement
3. A statement of proposed objectives
4. A content guide
5. Suggested student activities
6. A list of teaching aids books for both students and teacher; pamphlets, music records, films, community resources
7. Suggested evaluation procedures.

The resource unit gives much attention to student activities and instructional materials. Organizing a resource unit helps the teacher plan activities for a given class, prepare a teaching unit, and gain a more comprehensive idea of the instructional techniques used by other teachers.

TEACHING UNITS.   A teaching unit is a unit organized by a teacher for a given class. It usually is outlined before actual instruction and has the same features as the resource unit except that the teaching unit includes only the activities, materials, and evaluation techniques that are to be used with a particular class. Thus, a resource unit might list many stories about Indian life, whereas the teaching unit, which is organized by a teacher for a given class, would list only the stories that are to be read. Materials and activities—the variety necessary to meet student needs—are listed in the teaching unit in the order in which they will be presented in the class.

Good teaching generally requires the teacher to plan in advance, especially by writing a statement of objectives, suitable learning activities, instructional materials, and evaluation techniques. After this task is completed, the teacher may ask the students to share in choosing from among the various activities. Too often, when this advance planning has not been done, a lot of class time is lost unnecessarily because the teacher does not know what can be done to good advantage and what cannot.

FRAMEWORK FOR A UNIT.   The following outline may be considered as a basic framework for a unit:

1.   Title or topic of the unit, appropriate age or grade level, and approximate time allotted
2.   Introductory statement, formulation of general purposes, and clarification of topic
3.   Objectives, including major understandings, skills, and attitudes to be acquired by the students
4.   Content guide, including the major subject matter content, problems to be solved, and suggested class activities
5.   Student activities required to achieve the objectives, including initiatory activities and developmental activities and the estimated time required for them
6.   Culminating activities, such as a summary activity or group of activities to which each student can contribute, toward which the class will direct its effort throughout the unit, which will best satisfy each student's need for approval from classmates and teacher, and which will promote favorable attitudes toward classmates, teacher, and school; and the estimated time required for these activities
7.   Materials and resources, including printed materials: the materials of instructional technology, including programmed material, single concept films and tapes, other audio-visual aids, and materials for demonstration, experimentation, or display; facilities outside the classroom that may be used; and procedures for bringing people from the community to the classroom and for taking the students on visits to the community
8.   Evaluation procedures, including ascertaining where students are when they begin work, helping students measure their own progress, and evaluating student growth in terms of demonstrated changes in behavior.

Coordinated Instructional Systems

A Coordinated Instructional System (CIS) is a collection of instructional materials and protocols that takes responsibility for achieving specified changes in behaviors and competencies for a specific population of learners. The components of such a system usually include measurable performance objectives, provision for evaluation, practice, and feedback, and a set of properly sequenced and carefully selected educational experiences. These experiences usually require the use of instructional media that are designed to achieve the performance objectives. Evaluation procedures are designed to determine the achievement of the objectives and to provide for appropriate revision of the educational experiences and materials. In *level I systems,* the teacher is involved in and available to all environments. The system extends and supports. The *level II system* is totally packaged. It does not involve any guidance by or contact with a teacher, yet it claims to provide a complete course of study. Some supervisors might argue that level II systems have no place in public education.

CIS materials should have the characteristics of reliability and validity and must be operational on an individualized or self-instructional basis, thus releasing teachers for more personalized instruction, evaluation, and counseling of students. Of course, the materials must be designed to operate using equipment and facilities available to the school.

A Coordinated Instructional System Study Unit should contain:

1. Study Unit Guidelines.
2. Lesson A.
   a. An Introduction—topics, scope, goals
   b. Descriptive Objectives—What students will learn (to do)
   c. Study Resources, Objective 1—*Specific* directions and media/modules
   d. Practice Items and Exercises, Objective 1
      (1) Relevant practice—quiz
      (2) Discussion of practice items—tell *why* an answer is correct
   e. Study Resources, Objectives 2, 3, etc.
   f. Practice Items and Exercises, Objectives 2, 3, etc.
   g. A Self-test
3. Lessons B, C, D, Etc.
4. The Study Unit Posttest

The self-test at the end of each lesson helps the student evaluate his/her own progress and identify any problem areas. It is basically the same as the practice items and their discussion. When the student is satisfied on the basis of the practice items and exercises that he/she has mastered all lessons in a study unit, he/she is ready for the study unit posttest. The posttest covers all lessons in that study unit. It helps evaluate both the student's progress and the materials' effectiveness. The posttest helps identify problems in the materials so they can be corrected.

HOW TO DEVELOP DIRECTIONS FOR COORDINATED INSTRUCTIONAL SYSTEMS. Essential to the success of the coordinated instructional unit are directions that really direct! Directions should tell the student what study resources to use, where to find them, and how to use them, and what to do with the practice items. The practice items should be built into the sequence of directions regarding the study resources. All directions are, therefore, constructed at one time.

One may deal with one objective at a time, or, in some cases, with two or even three closely related objectives at once, if all are covered by the same study resource.

Steps to follow in building directions for coordinated instructional systems include:

1. Assemble the first objective or cluster of objectives and the related study resource or resources, and the corresponding practice items.
2. Identify the objective by number.
3. Describe the study resource by type (text, tape, film) and purpose.
4. Describe the content: what is it about and why was it selected?

5. Tell what should be done with the study resource material. Be specific. If you want the student simply to read it, say so. If you want the student to prepare an outline, tell in detail how to go about it. If you want him/her to look at the practice items first, say so.
6. Tell the audience (a) where the material is located, (b) how to obtain it, (c) to do what is required, and (d) to return to the lesson.
7. Indicate (say) what tools and guides may be used and will be needed for the practice items.
8. Instruct the students to complete the practice item(s) and/or practice exercises that use the information they just obtained from the study resource. Indicate specifically whether they are to "think the answers" or write them out.
9. Repeat the above steps for any other study resources that may be relevant to the same objective and to additional practice items designed for this objective.
10. Repeat the above steps for the other objectives of the lesson.
11. Review the entire study resource and practice item portion of the lesson. Ask, "Will it be perfectly clear to the students what they are supposed to do and how they are supposed to do it?" Revise, if necessary, to make the directions as clear and unambiguous as possible.
12. Make any final revisions.
13. Test, validate, evaluate, revise.

HOW TO IDENTIFY RELEVANT RESOURCES FOR COORDINATED INSTRUCTIONAL SYSTEMS.   Since a textbook probably has been selected for the course, the developer should consider using it as a basic resource for many objectives of the lessons. Other media and resources are available. The following steps are suggested:

1. Start with one lesson. Locate the material in the textbook (if there be one) that is relevant to one or more closely related objectives. Does the material provide all of the information the student needs to complete the related practice items? Evaluate. Is there relevant material for the objectives in question? If so, identify the source by page and paragraph number on a sheet of paper.
2. Repeat the same process for each objective in the lesson.
3. Do not feel obligated to use only one text or any single source as the only source of information. Students can help conduct a search of this kind. Ask them to help find the presentations that seem clearest, easiest, and most interesting to them. An assignment of this sort can be of considerable value to the students because they have to "read for meaning," and evaluate in terms of how helpful the material is to them.
4. Identify any alternate resources that might be useful and add them to the listing. It is not necessary to make a final decision or selection just yet. At this time, we want to identify the best available set of materials, although the final selection might well have to take into account certain practical considerations and constraints. Sometimes, for practical reasons, as when the standard textbook is the most readily available source, one might have to identify the

selection as the prime source. One might also indicate that there is a clearer and easier version in another book that may be less readily available, possibly in the instructional media center, in the library, or elsewhere. Conduct this search now and list all materials that should be a part of the study resources.

5. Materials of many kinds, in a variety of media, should be identified, considered, evaluated, and selected: audio and video tapes and discs, both commercially and locally produced; slides and filmstrips, with or without some recorded audio information and/or scripts; silent and sound motion pictures; demonstration kits and materials referred to as "teaching aids"; demonstration kits, laboratory manuals, and practice exercise materials; and another old standby, the workbook, both standard and programmed, both commercially produced and in-house prepared; and presentation devices such as the Beseler See-Cue, the Bell and Howell Synchrosearch, and the Dukane techniques for individualized presentations of sound and visual materials; video cassette players; and so-called teaching machines.

6. Do not automatically reject the lecture, discussion, and conference as resources and methods for making information available and for providing instruction. Sometimes a topic can be introduced most conveniently with a lecture, and sometimes a block of information available in no other convenient format or source justifies a lecture, especially an informal lecture. For some topics, a lecture is a good method of instructing a group of students. The lecture can be put on tape. If the content is the critical element, and if the teacher does not need to be present during the particular presentation, then the tape (audio or video) could be used. The formal lecture and the tape without the teacher present, could present problems. A student who has a question must be able to ask the teacher individually and immediately!

7. Now review the list that includes the practice items. Be sure that all necessary information has been located. If there are any gaps, conduct an additional search and locate the necessary resource materials.

8. Make the final selection of the combination of materials that will be incorporated into the test version of the lesson. (The reader may wish to scan chapter 11 on instructional technology and Appendix C of this text.)

HOW TO PREPARE FEEDBACK AND EVALUATION DISCUSSIONS FOR COORDINATED INSTRUCTIONAL SYSTEMS.[12]   The program developer should have a cassette tape recorder and the list of practice items and self-test items. He/she should read the first item into the recorder and imagine that a student has asked: "Tell me what the answer is to this item, and explain *why* this is the answer." The developer should proceed through the following steps:

1. Talk to the student through the recorder. Try to be persuasive and explain clearly why the answer wanted *is* the correct answer. Avoid lecturing and do not give additional information that should have been provided before the student faced the practice item. This information should be added to the study

[12] See William A. Deterline and Peter D. Lenn, *Study Resource Materials Booklet for Coordinated Instructional Systems and the Individualization of Instruction* (Palo Alto: The Deterline Associates, 1972).

resources. At this point, we should be clarifying information already available.

2. Continue to do the same for each practice item and self-test item; do not talk about subject matter except in the sense of talking to the student about the desired response(s) to the items in question.

3. Have the first tape transcribed and typed so that it can be looked at and listened to at the same time. On the typed version, begin to make editing changes and revisions. Be careful! Do not convert it into a cold, impersonal lecture. It should be a person-to-person discussion.

4. Edit and revise. Clarify. Add any information previously omitted.

5. Record the second version. Do not use the edited version of the first discussion as a script; use it as a guide and as a reminder and simply talk through the discussion.

6. Have the second version transcribed, then edit and revise it. Consider providing the students with these discussions in taped form, so that they can examine their own answers while listening to the discussions.

7. Prepare the final version of the discussion, either in text form or on an audio or video cassette.

Instructional Methods

There is no such thing as one method of teaching or supervision that is effective for all subject matter, all teachers, and all students at all times and places. The teaching method used in any specific case must be geared to such factors as the maturity and capacity of the students, the size of the class, the length of the class period, the facilities and materials available, the teaching situation, and the lesson to be taught.

Method, considered apart from purpose, lacks both direction and meaning. Method must be conceived, applied, and judged in terms of the objective or purpose to be achieved. Although a given method may not be good for achieving a particular purpose, it may, nevertheless, be an excellent method for use at another time to reach a different goal.

The students' adjustment to teachers and to each other and the overall social climate in the classroom are more important than the method of instruction.

With these fundamental ideas in mind, let us consider the various patterns of instruction or, in other words, methods of teaching.

Teaching methods can be classified under three general headings:

1. Teacher-centered patterns
2. Student-centered patterns
3. Cooperative-group patterns

However, any such classification is somewhat artificial and another grouping may be preferred. There is so much overlapping between methods that to classify them strictly or to define them rigidly is an oversimplification. But, for the sake of a starting point, let us consider just three teaching methods that are used widely.

The basis of the *lecture method* is that the teacher relates information vocally. It is obvious that in any lesson the teacher must do some talking. The supervising principal must not withdraw in horror at the mention of the term "lecture." Rather, he/she must understand the value and strengths of this method, as well as its weaker points.

The amount of talking on the part of the teacher during a lesson varies from brief remarks interjected to guide the course of the discussion right up to the *formal lecture,* to which students merely listen.

The *informal lecture* is of greater value because:

1. Students may ask questions and participate in other ways.
2. This type of lesson presents to the class the best and most well considered thoughts of the lecturer and includes the use of instructional media.

In other words, the informal lecture should be used along with other methods in a happy combination that leads the group logically and conclusively to the goal sought—the objective of the lesson.

The *discussion method* includes the techniques of the panel, the open forum, and the symposium. It should *never* be used unless all participants have acquired a common body of knowledge pertinent to the topic to be discussed. This common body of knowledge *must* have been acquired *prior* to the discussion.

1. The *panel* type of discussion is a preset technique with panel members using prepared speeches. These speeches are followed by audience participation at the end through questions, answers, and challenges.
2. In a *symposium,* set speeches are utilized. No audience participation is permitted.
3. The (open) *forum permits audience participation and audience reaction to set speeches* during the presentation.

Discussion also utilizes the question as a technique. The directed question, with someone's name attached to the end of it, is preferred. The teacher asks the question and then states the name of the individual who is to respond.

If the teacher is asked a question he/she either responds to it, sends it back in a different form, or sends it to another student.

A sound-slide presentation showing how to use questions effectively can be borrowed for preview (and copied) from College of the Canyons, 25000 West Valencia Blvd., Valencia, California 91355.

The *role-playing method* may be used effectively in in-service education and in teaching adults. For example, one successful teacher in an adult evening school class on early American history assigned class members to play the parts of characters being studied. Whenever a quotation was to be read, the person playing the part of that particular character would read it. Whenever questions came up concerning the policies of Cortez or of Montezuma, the "player" tried to answer them as if he/she were that person.

Gaming

COMEX (the Center for Multidisciplinary Educational Exercises) is a unique learning resource center that designs, develops, applies, and disseminates, gaming-simulation exercises and other interactive communication and educational activities. COMEX is a joint undertaking of the School of Public Administration and the College of Continuing Education, University of Southern California, and is partially supported by the Fund for the Improvement of Post-Secondary Education, Health, Education, and Welfare. COMEX has been exploring the use of gaming simulation in a variety of contexts for several years. COMEX has begun to incorporate gaming simulation into some school curricula.

From preschool through graduate school and continuing education, games range from those exploring a process or concept, such as growing old or the nature of power, to those about a specific topic, such as the conditions surrounding the construction of the transcontinental railroad or the history and culture of the North American Indians.

Partly because measuring instruments have not been developed, the potency and efficiency of games in education have not been empirically established. We do know that gaming works, however, because the players tell us so.

Students on one gaming exercise really perceive the panic and frustration of progressive sensory decay, senility, and even death, through the abstract symbolism of paper clips ("money"), strings ("mobility"), and pencils ("memory"). Games can and do replicate many of the pressures, emotions, and reactions in real life.

No one has all the answers yet, but games can excite, challenge, and motivate, and therefore can be extremely effective aids to learning.

For a discussion of how to employ instructional development techniques and for a processing checksheet that might help incorporate coordinated instructional systems and individualized instruction into a staff development system, see chapters 6 and 10 and Appendix C.

Do

1. Establish a healthy working relationship with co-workers by approaching problems on a democratic and cooperative basis.
2. Strive to enhance each individual's position by delegating responsibility for instructional improvement to members of the certificated staff.

3. Evaluate continuously your own professional competencies, seeking to build on your strengths and overcome your weaknesses.
4. Work for the emerging concept of "the supervisor as a chief of staff," which will designate the principal as a staff instructional leader as opposed to a dominantly administrative figure.
5. Be aware of the staff's changing needs and be adept at devising or adapting new plans or procedures to meet those needs.
6. Use staff meetings to stimulate interest in in-service education programs.
7. Work for the cooperative study of school problems as an efficient and effective way to improve instruction.
8. Attempt to create an atmosphere in the school that will encourage experimentation.
9. Provide opportunities for teachers to share new techniques and to observe good teaching practices.
10. Rotate the personnel of subject matter and grade-level committees frequently so that each teacher has a wide familiarity with current developments.
11. Recognize and reward excellent individual teacher performance.
12. Encourage teachers to share their successes with other members of the staff.
13. Be alert to new techniques and materials, and keep teachers informed.
14. Establish a professional library and encourage teachers to use and contribute to it.

Don't

1. Rebuke any teacher in the presence of students or any other persons.[13]
2. Fail to praise teachers, and, in the fields of their special preparation, walk humbly.
3. Deal lightly with any person's problem, but treat it as if it were your own.
4. Forget the days of your youth; keep a sense of cheer and good humor.
5. Fail to honor your custodians and your teachers that your days may be long on the job that the governing board has given you.
6. Let any student be judged by his behavior alone, but seek the causes of such behavior that they may be corrected.
7. When you have a teacher who is old in the service so that he/she no longer teaches well fail to deal with him tenderly and understandingly (teachers do grow older—and they don't just fade away).
8. Fail to develop a sensitivity to the needs of your whole community, and a faith in its people, for in that faith you will find your strength to improve instruction.
9. Fail to develop vision as well as devotion, so that instruction may truly be improved and that you may use your talents for the benefit of all humanity.[14]

[13] Unfortunately, this first item frequently is broken in this list of commandments. When a teacher is rebuked or corrected by the supervising principal in the presence of students or adults, the principal is guilty of a gross breach of professional ethics.

[14] After Douglas E. Lawson, Ten Commandments for the Humane Principal in Improving Instruction," an Address at Southern Illinois University, Carbondale, Illinois, 1955.

TRENDS IN HELPING THE TEACHER
IMPROVE THE EFFECTIVENESS OF INSTRUCTION

Toward ⟶ the Evolving Role of the
Superintendent as a Coordinator and General
Director of the System-wide Program for
Improving Instruction

The superintendent of the future will operate through his/her assistant superintendent for educational services and the directors of curriculum and instruction, to provide for a general coordination of all efforts for the improvement of instruction on a system-wide basis. He/she will assure that effective communication, both horizontal and vertical, will be kept in prime working order so that efforts will not be duplicated or wasted.

Toward ⟶ the Professional Team
Approach to Educational Supervision

The alert superintendent of the future will see the trend toward team action that is beginning to develop today and will seek opportunities to develop teachers as leaders. He/she will include all of the professional staff in planning, executing, and evaluating educational experiences. Team action for better human relationships and higher morale will be a major goal.

Toward ⟶ Continuing Pressures in the
Direction of a Goals or Objectives Competency
Model Approach to Assessment

More and more we hear of *management by objectives, competency models, accountability,* and *assessment programs.* For a discussion of these schemes, refer to the research done by H. H. McAshan at the University of North Florida.[15] The supervisor must resist all attempts to impose assembly line—all-children-are-alike-and-are-capable-of-meeting-all-goals—approaches to teacher evaluation. Teaching is an art, as well as a science.

[15] See H. H. McAshan, *Goals Approach to Performance Objectives* (Philadelphia: W. B. Saunders, 1974).

Groups and children differ. This is not to say that we do not set goals and objectives for teaching and for supervision. We must! We object to the trend in some areas toward a universal, other-than-educator set, predetermined evaluation formula that ignores the individuality of children, groups, and teachers as well as denies that teaching is, indeed, an art as well as a science. Remember, *learning* is supposed to happen inside the learner. The results may or may not be demonstrated by an externally visible change in behavior or performance. *Instruction* is done to the individual with the hope that learning will occur. *Accountability* is the ASSUMPTION of responsibility for the outcomes of performance. Surely educators must have a hand in setting the goals for which they assume responsibilities. These goals vary from child to child, and from group to group. Some children and groups will be incapable of learning for some reason other than incompetency (*competency* being the potential or skill to do something). The educator, therefore, must have an escape clause, must not be reduced to "teaching the exam," must feel free to set goals and objectives for instruction.

Toward ⟶   Increased Participation of the

Professional Staff in Evaluating Instruction

An increase in the use of the professional team approach to evaluating instruction and teaching-learning effectiveness is beginning to emerge. This trend may be developing at least partially in response to the enactment of laws that require the regular, periodic evaluation of teacher performance. Principals, specialist-consultants, and master teachers will cooperate in performing the essential task of evaluating instruction.

Toward ⟶   Further Development of Level I

Coordinated Instructional Systems

The type of coordinated instructional system in which a teacher is directly involved and/or immediately available in all learning environments will become more visible. Partially self-paced modules and other individualized instructional media center and multienvironmental approaches will become more in evidence as integral components of the systems.

Toward ⟶   Some Modified Schemes of

Departmentalization and/or Team Teaching, Together

with Increased Use of Nongraded Organization for Instruction

More schools of the future will experiment with varied departmentalization and/ or with team teaching techniques. The pupil will be with one teacher for most of the day, and with different teachers for physical education, music, art, mathematics, foreign language, and other subjects. We should look for greater experimentation in this area in the future, along with further employment of the nongraded plans.

Supervisory Problems

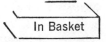

In Basket

Problem 1

Recently a rural school district in Wyoming passed a bond issue for the construction of a new school. Members of the board of education, administrators, and several teachers visited many schools in an attempt to view the most modern buildings. A building designed for flexibility to meet educational needs for future years was desired.

The staff hoped to move into a team-teaching situation and eventually a truly nongraded school. The staff at present consists of fifty classroom teachers, with approximately eight teachers in each grade division. None of the teachers has been trained in team teaching, and very few have observed team teaching in action. All of the present staff have taught in a most traditional setting.

How should the supervisor proceed in selecting personnel from the present staff for participation in the team-teaching situation?

Problem 2

The problem developed at Joseph Senior High School, which has an enrollment of nearly 2,000 in grades ten, eleven, and twelve. At Joseph, mathematics students are placed within one of three levels of ability. At each grade level there are two sections of "honors" or advanced mathematics. Mr. Tenenbaum has fifteen years of successful teaching experience and has been praised for his outstanding work with the "slow learner." He requested an assignment to the junior-level "honors" sections and taught them for two years with few, if any, complaints from parents or students.

The principal soon received complaints from students and parents relating to "boring routine" and "lack of opportunity to be creative in thought and approach to a problem," in the lower performance section. George asked to be transferred to the advanced section. This request was refused, since school policy dictates that students shall be transferred to another section only in EXTREME cases. The principal praised the teacher's past performance to parents and students and assured them that the situation would not continue. He did not confer with Mr. Tenenbaum and for a time complaints stopped. This afternoon, however, George and his mother have arrived in the principal's office, insisting that he, George, be permitted to transfer to the other section.

What do you, as supervising principal, propose to do?

Problem 3

The instructional effectiveness of the sixty-year-old teacher with tenure seems to be inadequate, boring, and causing ridicule from parents and students. His marking system apparently hinges largely on how well students get along with him.

Mr. Danks uses the formal lecture technique all period, each period, in world history. He says that after teaching thirty years, his memory is infallible, but facts, dates, names, and chronology are often wrong. Students work on mathematics, shorthand, and other subjects during his classes.

At a final year's end National Honor Society farewell banquet, which was an emotional session, a girl named Donna tearfully and emotionally gave a testimony of thanks to faculty members present. Coming to Mr. Danks, Donna thanked him for never bothering her and allowing her to practice her shorthand during his class time. Realizing what she had said, Donna was most embarrassed. The audience was amused.

On the credit side, the teacher is a fine gentleman. Generally, he is liked and respected by other faculty members.

How can the principal aproach this individual and help him become a more
*   efficient teacher, respected by his students?*
Is the problem solvable, and to what degree?

Questions and Suggested Activities Concerning How to Help Teachers Improve Methods of Classroom Instruction

Questions

1. What knowledge of instructional procedures is essential to the success of the general supervisor in improving such procedures?
2. Who is involved in the supervisory function of helping the teacher improve classroom methods?
3. How much time should the supervisor give to the "weaker-methods" teacher as compared to the resourceful teacher?
4. What techniques might be followed to convince traditional teachers to use modern methods?

5. What are some of the major obstacles to improving classroom methods of instruction?
6. Should the supervisor be responsible for preparing a formal rating of the teacher's method of instruction? Why?
7. What methods would you recommend for teaching mathematics? science? languages?

Suggested Activities

1. Develop a general instructional development supervisory program in a school that has no such program.
2. List several techniques that you would employ to aid an inexperienced teacher in the methods he/she might use to organize the class at the beginning of the school year.
3. As a principal, draw up a plan that you would follow to help a weak teacher improve methods of classroom instruction.
4. Outline a program for promoting experimentation in classroom methods by teachers.
5. Plan a staff meeting in which several teachers will discuss different methods of presenting the same lesson.
6. List several ways in which you, as a supervisor, would use superior teachers to help inexperienced and weak teachers improve their methods of classroom instruction.
7. Suggest several specific situations in which a supervisor can help teachers improve methodology without threatening teacher security.
8. Prepare a brief supporting the contention that the specialist-consultant should *not* be responsible for formal teacher performance ratings.

Selected Bibliography

Books

Anderson, R. H. *Teaching in a World of Change.* New York: Harcourt, Brace and World, 1966.

Anderson, Richard C. et al. *Current Research on Instruction.* Englewood Cliffs, New Jersey: Prentice-Hall, Inc., 1969.

Barr, A. S., W. H. Burton, and L. J. Brueckner. *Supervision.* New York: D. Appleton and Company, 1938.

Barr, A. S. et al. *Supervision.* New York: Appleton-Century-Crofts, 1947.

Bennie, William A. *Supervision of Student Teachers.* New York: Harper & Row, 1972.

Burton, William H., and Leo J. Brueckner. *Supervision: A Social Process.* New York: Appleton-Century-Crofts, 1955.

Davis, Harold S. *How to Organize an Effective Team Teaching Program.* Englewood Cliffs, New Jersey: Prentice-Hall, 1966.

Drucker, Peter. *The Practice of Management.* New York: Harper & Row, 1954.

Eye, Glen G. et al. *Supervision of Instruction.* 2nd edition. New York: Harper & Row, 1971.

Gerwin, Donald. *The Employment of Teachers.* Berkeley, California: McCutchan Publishing Corporation, 1974.

Hicks, Hanne J. *Educational Supervision in Principle and Practice.* New York: The Ronald Press Company, 1960.

Mackenzie, Gordon N., and Stephen M. Corey. *Instructional Leadership.* New York: Bureau of Publications, Teachers College, Columbia University, 1959.

Mager, Robert F. *Preparing Instructional Objectives.* Palo Alto, California: Fearon Publishers, 1962.

Marrow, Alfred J. *Management by Participation.* New York: Harper & Row, 1967.

McGregor, Douglas. *Human Side of Enterprise.* New York: McGraw-Hill Co., 1960.

Melby, Ernest O. *Organizing and Administration of Supervision.* Chicago: Public School Publishing Company, 1929.

Myers, George R., and William J. Walsh. *Student Teaching and Internship in Today's Secondary Schools.* New York: Charles E. Merrill Books, Inc., 1967.

Reeder, Edwin H. *Supervision in the Elementary School.* Boston: Houghton Mifflin Company, 1953.

Stoops, Emery, and James R. Marks. *Elementary School Supervision: Practices and Trends.* Boston: Allyn and Bacon, Inc., 1965.

Wadia, Maneck S. *Management and the Behavioral Sciences.* Boston: Allyn and Bacon, Inc., 1968.

Weber, Clarence A. *Personnel Problems of School Administrators.* New York: McGraw-Hill, 1954.

Wey, Herbert W. *Handbook for Principals.* New York: Shaum Publishing Company, 1966.

Periodicals

Adams, H., and C. R. Hollenbach. "How Can Supervisory Practices Contribute to Teacher-Pupil Growth?" *National Association of Secondary School Principals Bulletin* XXXVIII (April 1954): 151–156.

Bradfield, Luther E. "Basic Principles Underlying Techniques of Supervision." *American School Board Journal* CXXVIII (June 1954): 21–23.

Brownell, John A., and H. A. Taylor. "Theoretical Perspectives for Teaching Teams." *Phi Delta Kappan* XLIII (January 1962): 150–157.

Chalupsky, Albert B., and Jack J. Crawford. "Preparing the Educator to go Metric." *Phi Delta Kappan* LVII (December 1975): 202–265.

Coombs, Arthur W., and Harold E. Mitzel. "Can We Measure Good Teaching Objectively?" *N.E.A. Journal* LIII (January 1964): 34.

Drummond, William T. "The Meaning and Application of Performance Criteria in Staff Development." *Phi Delta Kappan* LII (September 1970): 32–35.

Ebel, Robert L., and Robert L. Green. "Opposing Views on Tests and Testing." *Phi Delta Kappan* LVII (October 1975): 83–88.

Gronamon, A. H. "Improving Classroom Instruction." *Educational Administration and Supervision Bulletin* XXXIII (May 1947): 300–309.

Kirby, David. "An Administrator Looks at the Human Side of Teaching." *Educational Forum* XIV (March 1950): 351–356.

McGregor, Douglas. "The Staff Function in Human Relations." *Journal of Social Issues* IV (Summer 1948): 6–23.

Myers, Charles A. "New Frontiers for the Personnel Executive." *Personnel* XLI (May-June, 1964): 31–38.

Myers, Charles A., and John G. Turnbull. "Line and Staff in Industrial Relations." *Harvard Business Review* XXXIV (July-August 1956): 113–124.

National Audio Visual Association. "Trends in Accountability, Competencies, and Evaluation." *Audio Visual Instruction* XX (December 1975): Special Issue.

Pearson, Evelyn. "Making Use of Teachers' Talents." *Minnesota Journal of Education* XL (September 1959): 19–20.

Stoddard, D. G. "Team Teaching for the Elementary School." *Educational Leadership* XVIII (November 1960): 89–91.

Unruh, Adolph. "Has Your School Changed?" *Educational Forum* XVIII (May 1954): 470.

Weaver, David O. "The Instructor's Relationship to His Students." *Training Directors Journal* XIV (January 1960): 40–47.

Weber, C. A. "Promising Techniques for Educating Teachers in Service." *Educational Administration and Supervision Bulletin* XXIII (December 1942): 691–695.

Films

Designing Effective Instruction. General Programmed Teaching (a division of Commerce Clearing House, San Rafael, California), 1970. A set of sound filmstrips, workbooks, and a leader's guide.

Educational Gaming. Educational Media Center, University of California, Berkeley, 1970. Concerns the production of educational and classroom games. Kinescope. (59 minutes)

Eye of the Supervisor. National Educational Media, Inc., 1975. Available from Management Development Presentations, 3460 Wilshire Blvd., Los Angeles, California 90010. Reviews the basic task of evaluating employee performance.

Performance Appraisal. Thompson-Mitchell, Atlanta, Georgia, 1973. A sound filmstrip with leader's guide. Discusses the why, what, how, and when of appraisal.

Personalized System of Instruction: An Alternative. Xerox, Inc., 1972. Introduction to the principles and techniques of Professor J. G. Sherman's personalized system of instruction. (13 minutes)

The Training Memorandum. National Educational Media, Inc., 1975. Concerns motivation and methods of changing attitudes of resistance to change and of indifference.

You Pack Your Own Chute. Ramec Productions, 1974 Concerns motivation, self-awareness, and effecting attitude changes.

Kit

Popham, W. James, and Eva L. Baker. *Teacher Competency Development System.* Englewood Cliffs, New Jersey: Prentice-Hall, Inc., 1975

Other Sources

American Association of School Administrators. *Teacher Tenure Ain't the Problem.* Arlington, Virginia: 1973.

Association for Supervision and Curriculum Development. *Creating a Good Environment for Learning.* Washington, D.C.: National Education Association, 1954.

Bennion, Adam S. *Principles of Teaching.* Salt Lake City, Utah: Deseret News Press, 1958.

Brighton, Stayner F. *Increasing Your Accuracy in Teacher Evaluation.* Successful School Management Series. Englewood Cliffs, New Jersey: Prentice-Hall, Inc., 1965.

Department of Superintendence. *Improvement of Teachers in Service.* Eighth Yearbook, Washington, D.C.: National Education Association, 1930.

Department of Supervisors and Directors of Instruction. *Newer Instructional Practices of Promise.* Twelfth Yearbook. Washington. D.C.: National Education Association, 1940.

———. *Scientific Method in Supervisory Programs.* Washington, D.C.: National Education Association, 1934.

Deseret Sunday School Board. *Teacher Training.* Salt Lake City, Utah: The Board, 1955.

Gage, N. L., ed. *Handbook of Research on Teaching.* Chicago: Rand McNally, 1963.

Hamacheck, Don E., and Joseph A. Callaman. *Evaluating Your Teachers.* New York: Croft Educational Services, 1967.

Hoover, Kenneth D. *Professional Teacher's Handbook*. Boston: Allyn and Bacon, Inc., 1975.

Lawson, Douglas E. "Ten Commandments for the Humane Principal in Improving Instruction." An Address at Southern Illinois University, Carbondale, Illinois, 1955.

Stoops, Emery, and Staff. *Report of the Study*. *Title III*. *ESEA*. Sacramento: California State Department of Education, 1970.

Torrance, Paul E., and J. Pansy Torrance. *Is Creativity Teachable?* Bloomington, Indiana: Phi Delta Kappa, Fastback Series, 1973.

Trump, J. Lloyd. *Images of the Future*. Commission on Experimental Study of the Utilization of the Staff. Urbana, Illinois: The Commission, 1959.

11

How to Select, Organize, and Facilitate the Use of Instructional Media and Library Materials

The modern educator, whatever his/her level of involvement, must meet an almost unprecedented challenge. We live in a world in which exponential expansion of knowledge and scientific breakthroughs are commonplace. Each day our professors and teachers are faced not only with the problem of transmitting the new knowledge, but also with the awesome responsibility of guaranteeing that the young people in their trust actually understand it all. The educational problems are so complex, and the needs so intense, that we no longer dare allow the teacher to work alone and unaided. Devotion to the profession is not enough.

The unique problems of individual students and of special groups (such as the socially and/or academically disadvantaged, the high-school dropout, the highly gifted, and the "average" student) are inadequately solved by the usual present-day educational facilities. A carefully formulated educational plan must provide for such heterogeneous inputs. The plan must avoid arbitrary curricular standards and decisions; it must reject the word "rejection" and substitute the concept of words such as "preliminary," "tentative," "alternate," and "auxiliary."

A systems analysis approach is implied, but whatever the approach the supervising principal must ensure that:

1. It matches the inventory and the potential of the individual to his/her present and future academic and/or career environment
2. It provides the means for transformations toward a goal with a high probability of attainment
3. It furnishes the resources to develop human talent in an optimal way
4. A program with such dimensions is self-improving, and therefore flexible.[1]

Without the application of sophisticated technology, it is difficult to see how today's teachers would be able to lead each student to explore, to learn, to

[1] The authors are grateful to Robert Gates, Dr. Philip R. Kleinberg, Shirley Marks, David A. V. Moody, and Norman Chapman for their contributions to this and other sections.

evaluate, and to master the prodigious quantities of evolving knowledge. The transforms, or paths, through which these objectives can be realized may range from using a combination of media for mass instruction (including components such as video tape) to selected media for small group and individual instruction such as the reading center, computer assisted learning and computer managed instruction, audio assisted learning, and other individual response systems. A coordinated complex including the library and the instructional technology and media center (which subsumes a programmed instruction center, a study center, and audio-visual instructional technology) is needed, so that the many facets of a subject may be explored and researched meaningfully. It may require the integration of machines and information-retrieval systems (both audio and video) with teaching teams. The reader must keep in mind, however, that the most intricate system of automated learning aids and systems of programmed instruction is irrelevant without clear, two-way channels to the instructional program(s).

Selecting and organizing materials and resources for instruction are schoolwide problems that the entire staff should consider. Teachers, principals, and specialist-consultants cooperatively should establish definite policies for selecting various instructional materials and equipment and should enumerate the steps to take in acquiring them. There are no short cuts to the wise selection of books, films, and other materials.

What procedure should be used in choosing instructional materials? Should textbooks be selected on a school system-wide basis or by individual schools? What part should the supervisor play in selecting books and other instructional materials? Who should decide what texts are to be purchased? How extensively shall community resources be utilized? These are the types of decisions that must be made in selecting materials and resources.

This chapter includes a discussion of:

Principles and practices
Curriculum improvement through the use of instructional materials and systems
How to evaluate and improve the instructional media center
How to improve the use of instructional materials
How to select and evaluate instructional materials
How to improve library services
Do—Don't
Trends
"In-Basket" supervisory problems
Questions and suggested activities

Principles and Practices

The selection of instructional materials should follow a study of the educational program and its objectives. Specialists in the various subject areas long have considered their main problem to be choosing texts and the materials of instructional technology. Selecting materials without true knowledge of their purpose is a blindfolded process. If we wish to secure the best assortment of pertinent learning materials for students we should spend considerable time in cooperative planning as a faculty, under the leadership of the supervising principal. The purposes of the instructional program, and the kinds of materials that will give the students desirable experiences and serve those purposes, must be determined.

Basic Principles

The following may be considered as a set of basic principles in this area:

1. Learning can be accelerated by the use of better instructional materials.
2. Materials promote good teaching when they fit the curriculum and are adapted to the needs, interests, and abilities of students.
3. The supervising principal should keep teachers informed about new and better materials.
4. Materials should be purchased early, be readily available for use, and be maintained in adequate supply.
5. The program for securing materials should permit representatives of all involved to participate in varying degrees in the selection.
6. Each school staff should help select its own materials, assist with storage, evaluate effectiveness, and make recommendations for improvement.
7. A Materials of Instruction Committee should make recommendations as to the appropriate grade level and subject area use of teaching aids.
8. Teachers, specialists, and supervising principals should be trained in the proper use of materials of instruction.
9. The annual appropriation per student for materials of instruction should meet some acceptable standard, such as the recommendations of experts or the findings of research.
10. There is no short cut to the wise selection of books and the materials of instructional technology.

A Source of Difficulty

One difficulty in planning for the improvement of the instructional materials in individual schools and school systems is securing the cooperation of those involved. Each teacher can and should contribute to the total school program. Materials of instruction for a particular group of learners may improve because the entire staff has cooperatively planned, studied, and experimented.

Planning Levels

Four levels of planning for the improvement of instructional materials have been identified, as shown in Figure 11-1.

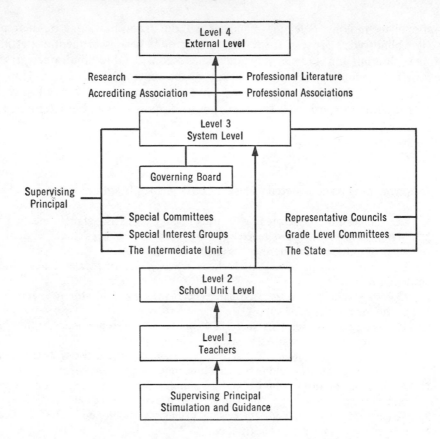

FIGURE 11-1.   Levels of Planning for the Improvement of Instructional Materials.

Of first importance is the teacher's own planning of the curriculum for his/her class. At this level, planning directly affects the students' experiences. Regardless of how sound planning at other levels may be, it serves little purpose unless it is implemented at the classroom level.

At the external level, an accrediting association may have considerable influence on local curriculum planning, although it has no legal relationship with the school. Through research studies, publications, and curriculum materials, professional associations frequently contribute directly to local planning groups.

Planning that affects local groups indirectly but sometimes forcibly is done by various organized groups who seek to influence what is taught in relation to their interests. They may work through:

1. Direct publications
2. Speakers and films for school
3. Pressure on legislatures
4. Pressure on governing boards and school curriculum planning groups
5. Pressure on publishers and/or textbook writers.

How to Determine Responsibilities for Planning

The teacher should participate in each level of planning: the teacher is the major participant at the first level; is one of the group of planners at the second level; and is represented, if not personally involved, at the third level.

The supervising principal should be involved at all levels. His/her participation at the second and third levels may be in connection with in-service education activities and cooperative experimentation and research in addition to membership in faculty planning groups.

THE SELECTION OF MATERIALS.   To the greatest extent possible, the choice of materials and resources should be the responsibility of those who use them. In school systems both large and small, the common practice has been centralization of responsibility in selecting instructional materials. In small schools, superintendents have chosen books through their contacts with book salesmen; in larger school systems, in the interest of economy, textbooks have been adopted on a system-wide basis for a period of three to five years. A number of states have some form of textbook adoption by a state agency. In Texas, Oregon, and California, textbook commissions have been established by the state legislature for statewide adoption of textbooks.

Some larger school systems, in recent years, have been moving away from the standardization and centralization of purchasing of all instructional materials. The purchase of such standard items as pencils, paper, and notebooks may be done more economically and efficiently through a central purchasing agency; but choosing textbooks and other supplementary materials is too closely related to local curriculum problems to be relegated to a central agency. Some schools have found that the individual in charge of purchasing may become involved in policy making through the selection of instructional materials.

PRINCIPLES OF PURCHASING.   The real reason for the change, however, is the desire of educators to choose materials that will be best suited to the individual school and community. In terms of adapting materials to curriculum needs, there is a real advantage in allotting each school its own budget for the purchase of instructional materials, including textbooks. Actual purchasing can still be done in the central office without increasing expenses, but the selection should be the responsibility of the individual school.

The supervising principal and the teachers can work together in choosing the types of materials that will best suit their needs and purposes. In any school system there is variation from school to school in ideas concerning the use of materials. Certainly no teacher who wants to use a variety of materials rather than a single text should be handcuffed by restrictive, outmoded regulations.

The supervising principal's job is to facilitate the choice of better, appropriate materials and to maintain lines of effective communication. Above all, his/her responsibility is to see .hat choices are made wisely in terms of the purposes for which the instructional materials will be used.

If this principle is applied seriously, the teacher, in cooperation with the students, will have an important part to play in selecting materials. One powerful incentive to experimentation is the encouragement given to the teacher through furnishing the necessary means for such experimentation in the classroom. Certainly the teacher must play a major part in selecting materials for the classroom.

Where restrictions are imposed by the state or by the board of education, some school systems have followed the practice of giving greater flexibility through adopting a list of books from which the individual school faculty may choose. This is the practice in many states that require textbook adoption at the state level.

Curriculum Improvement through the Use of Instructional Materials and Systems

As the scope of the school curriculum continually widens, the recitation method of instruction must increasingly be supplemented. In using present-day curricular vehicles to guide students to worthy goals, appropriate instructional aids must be selected out of the countless materials of instructional technology made available.

Video- and Audio-Instructional Systems, and Others

Video- and audio-instructional systems, television, video discs, and holography are coming to the front as supplementary educational aids. There are many experiments under way dealing with educational programs. Many school systems are employing television in the staff and instruction development programs.

Teachers should be alerted to the latest audio-visual and other mechanical devices that they can use to deal with the newly enriched curriculum. The principal should encourage them to keep in touch with the latest periodicals, and with books on education, including state and federal publications.

How to Evaluate and Improve the Instructional Media Center

Many large school systems and colleges have an "Instructional Technology and Media Center," "Instructional (Media) Center," "Learning Center," or "Audio-Visual Center" that provides services to students, teachers, and classrooms.[2] In

2 See Mildred L. Nickel, *Steps to Service* (Chicago: American Library Association, 1975).

FIGURE 11-2.   Two Views of the Programmed Instruction and Study Center.
Closeup of a Carrel Showing the Audio-Access Console.

some very large schools and in several colleges, an instructional media center has
been developed in the individual school unit. According to modern concepts of
instructional materials, the center should be concerned with all instructional
media (except basic course texts and most library books), including films, filmstrips, audio and video tapes and discs, exhibits, slides, specimens, objects,
pictures, maps, globes, charts, recordings, television, teaching machines and programmed materials, cross-media modules and "packages," radios, recorders, projectors, posters, information concerning field trips, and others. One programmed
study center and its control room, which is the heart of the instructional media
center, are pictured in Figures 11-2, 11-3, and 11-4.

In California, the West Los Angeles College Center for Learning and
Instructional Resources is a true instructional systems center. It combines a number of nonprint and standard traditional print media formats and includes staff
and instructional development; instructional systems development; electronic in-

FIGURE 11-3.   The Programmed Instruction and Study Center.

formation retrieval and distribution; individualized, personalized learning; and other facilities and laboratories as well as audio-visual instructional technology functions. Such centers originally were developed to support and accommodate the self-contained classroom model. Their scope and institutional patterns have evolved, resulting in a consortium of several specialties. With the emphasis on instructional systems, the evolution may well quicken in the coming years.

The premises for such a center and for its components are founded in the following principles:

1. *Media,* regardless of formats, should be viewed first for informational and stimulus possibilities and second for format and transform potentials.

2. *Schools and colleges provide an access to learning, they do not provide learning per se.* The supervisor of the instructional center activities must be a facilitator, an enabler, an engineer of learning and teaching tactics and environments, a manager of information, a teacher, a learning counselor, and an educational psychologist.

3. *Media extends a teacher* and his/her effectiveness, both supporting instruction and facilitating and improving that instruction. At times, media may provide a supplementary, peripheral, and/or reinforcing stimulus; at other times, it may provide all of the instruction. Instructional systems can give the teacher more classroom time for lecture, discussion, and individual and small group instruction.

4. *Learning and instruction are not the same.* A school or college provides for learning; group instruction is one element in the learning milieu; individualized, personalized instruction is another; and electronic support systems and instructional development are others.

5. *The wide variety in type and emphasis of stimulating media* should be developed to maximize learning potentials. The multiplicity of educational goals and goal-pathways or "transforms" must be provided for through many stimuli.

6. *An integrated and personalized approach* to learning and instruction is most economical in terms of human and nonhuman resources. Functions that can be easily integrated, such as cataloging, should be merged. Specialization, however, must continue to be recognized.

Components

The operational components of an instructional systems center include the more traditional, standard print-media services and the basic supply-support functions for such media. They also include instructional technology/media center services, which encompass supply-support, production, instructional, staff and instructional development, and coordination functions.

SUPPLY-SUPPORT FUNCTIONS. These functions encompass the activities related to providing a collection of programs, modules, materials, and equipment systems; they include basic field work, selection, evaluation, and acquisition; format transformation, and duplication; telecine[3] and electronic audio and video distribution and retrieval systems; description, storage, and inventory; and cataloging, publicity, and clerical functions.

PRODUCTION FUNCTIONS. Commercially unavailable media must be provided when needed. For example, a color television studio can provide television studio instruction and in-house production. Students can "rehearse" for oral reports and have an opportunity to evaluate and revise their presentations before going "on

---

[3] Telecine technology includes closed-circuit television and the distribution of motion pictures over video systems lines.

stage" in the classroom. Competent personnel to generate new media must be located. New media includes: holograms, computer programs, video recordings, learning modules, and program packages; posters, signs, and other printed materials; and slides and tapes.

INSTRUCTIONAL FUNCTIONS. The supervisor should help the center provide many instructional activities, such as training paraprofessionals, workshops to improve instruction, and instruction in telecine/media technology and television studio production.

How to Improve the Performance of the Media Center Coordinator

Costly and/or scarce instructional materials *must* be kept in a central pool. An adequate, efficient distribution system must be developed. In this case, the instructional media center would supplement the materials regularly kept in the classroom and would be a central coordinating agency.

Small schools need someone to perform this coordinating function. Even if a plan for distribution is established on a county-wide basis, every school should have someone who serves as a coordinator. The principal should delegate this

FIGURE 11-4. Heart of the Instructional Center: The Telecine Distribution Control Room.

responsibility to a teacher. The teacher should have some clerical assistance and also should be allocated released time.

Smaller school systems usually have a part-time audio-visual director, and larger systems and colleges generally have a full-time supervising-director. Such a person is not trained to repair equipment, but serves as a specialist-consultant who works with teachers to help them improve instruction under the direction of the local supervising principal.

A list of the duties of the instructional technology (audio-visual) consultant in one school system[4] indicates how a coordinator of the instructional media center is actually a facilitator—consultant to teachers in improving and using the materials of instructional technology, in establishing courses of study, in setting instructional objectives and long-range goals, and in developing the curriculum by:

1. Arranging sessions at which equipment can be evaluated and making recommendations to schools on the basis of these evaluations.
2. Arranging for preview of instructional materials by teachers and purchasing materials for the media center on the basis of these teacher recommendations.
3. Ordering rental and free instructional materials as requested by teachers.
4. Organizing and distributing a catalogue of owned instructional technology materials.
5. Booking materials as requested by teachers.
6. Organizing a workable system for distribution.
7. Working with the teachers who have been delegated the responsibility of serving as instructional coordinators at the local school level in planning for the future of the instructional technology/media program and in providing staff and instructional development help that can be carried back to teachers.
8. Making recommendations to teachers regarding instructional technology-instructional media that will help them reach specific goals.
9. Working with teachers to help them learn how to operate equipment, obtain materials, make materials, and use the materials effectively.
10. Working with principals and their representatives on problems specific to their schools.
11. Encouraging and working with teachers who are interested in producing materials for the instruction technology/media collection.
12. Advising community groups regarding the materials of instructional technology that will meet specific needs of these groups.
13. Interpreting the instructional media program to school personnel, the board of education, and the community.

The main function of an instructional media center director is that of instructional development facilitator or specialist-consultant. As noted above, adequate clerical service should be provided for handling details. Assistance is

[4] Ford L. Lemler, *Audio-Visual Programs in Action* (Ann Arbor: Michigan Audio-Visual Association, rev. ed., 1971), pp. 18–19.

needed in cataloging, booking and distribution, in production, and in maintenance and repair.

SOME CONTRASTS, OBLIGATIONS, AND NEEDS.   The supervisor must realize that
there are differences in the function and service philosophies of the library and
instructional media center. The difference in service philosophies exists because of
the differences in collections, functions, and roles of personnel. A print-media
specialist/librarian, for example, is not an expert in instructional media technology; a media specialist-facilitator-enabler is not a print-media specialist. A technology of instruction is becoming increasingly available and should be used as
effectively as possible. The supervisor should encourage the instructional media
center specialist to develop a viewpoint toward new dimensions in education—an
outreaching attitude.

Both the print-media librarian and the instructional media center specialist are involved actively in instruction throughout the day. Both may teach regularly scheduled courses such as "Library Science" and "Introduction to Instructional Media," as well as other subjects. In addition, they participate in the
teaching that must occur continuously in the library and instructional media
center.

Nevertheless, there are differential roles for the print-media librarian and
the instructional media center specialist. These differences result from some functional distinctions. The library is, basically, an internal operation that provides
professional services. Successful instructional media center programs demand intensive, prolonged, and close relationships between the center professionals, classified staff, other faculty, and students. Without these relationships, integrating
appropriate materials directly into instruction (into the learning environment)
would be impossible. For the instructional functions and instructional development functions to operate effectively and efficiently, the supervisor must help the
instructional media center professionals see the materials (the program packages
and electronic and other systems) in a working context.

Print-media librarians often can build collections through purchases
based on publishers' flyers, published reviews, and other sources, with very little
or no prior use/evaluation/validation/field testing of the materials required.
Offprint examination is relatively easy with books, but impossible with complex
media packages. The instructional media center specialists must buy courseware
and crossmedia packages according to how teachers will solve specific instructional problems, design and create appropriate teaching/learning modules, and
provide for continuous evaluation of materials and transforms. The instructional
media center is involved in curriculum development and in instructional design
through selecting materials aimed at solving specific instructional problems. To
attempt to do so in isolation would be foolhardy. Then, too, whereas a book may
cost twenty or thirty dollars, a simple film may cost $1,000 or more.

The supervisor must recall that instructional media center program formats are available as units and system modules that are not easily accessible,
whereas the print media librarian, especially the librarian assigned to the reference

desk, is asked to solve problems and retrieve specific data from materials that are more readily available and easily accessed. Print-media librarians, therefore, must spend more time at their desks.

The instructional media center is in the people/development/instructional programs/systems engineering/production and instruction business. The successful instructional media center coordinator *must* be outgoing. For the private institution the coordinator's success means survival of the entire institution! The instructional media center supervisor must accomplish his/her highly specialized Phase I tasks *on site* and *in the field*—with a wide array of equipment immediately at hand. He/she also needs immediate access to the engineers/staff experts and representatives of the distributors and/or professionals who already are utilizing the material.

The supervisor must not accept any excuses for lower standards for instructional media services and resources than for book services. Budget implications are enormous. The print and nonprint programs probably should be integrated for such technical services as cataloging for the patrons' convenience. The programs, however, because of their high degree of specialization, must be supervised separately. The supervisor must fight for adequate budgeting for each program.

How to Improve the Use of Instructional Materials

The following is a list of current practices that may lead to improvement in the use of instructional materials:

1. The supervising principal should work continuously with teachers in providing and improving instructional materials.
2. The teacher should continuously evaluate instructional materials in the light of student programs.
3. Consultant services should assist and instruct principals and teachers in the correct use of special materials, audio-visual equipment, and new devices.
4. The librarian should catalogue and provide care for all materials stored in the library and serve as consultant regarding their selection and use.
5. In large school systems a purchasing agent should procure materials and supervise a central warehouse where supplies are received, stored, and inventoried in readiness for distribution to schools.
6. Purchases should be made in quantity when possible, either through the system office or a central purchasing service in the intermediate unit superintendent's office.
7. Classified personnel should be given responsibility for receiving, storing, and caring for instructional materials as a means of lightening the clerical load on teachers.
8. Lay persons should be invited to help select some instructional materials, such as supplementary tapes, films, and other nontechnical aids.

9. The supervising principal should provide a workroom where teachers can construct and adapt their own instructional materials.
10. Free and inexpensive materials should be obtained from commercial, civic, and service organizations.
11. The supervising principal should help teachers instruct students in the careful use of materials as part of their education in conserving public property.

A sample checklist, developed by one supervising principal to help the teacher evaluate the effectiveness of his/her use of the materials of instructional technology, appears as Figure 11-5.

HOW'S YOUR I-T-Q?*

Score one point for each "yes."

1. Do you utilize the materials of instructional technology in regular classroom situations, avoiding auditorium showings whenever possible? _____

2. Do you utilize only those materials which are pertinent to, and serve the needs of your particular class? _____

3. Do you discuss, review, and maintain good "listening and viewing standards" as needs arise? _____

4. Do you build a readiness for viewing by establishing purposes, goals, or questions which the film will help to satisfy? _____

5. Do you, after viewing, utilize the material content for actual classroom learning by relating it to established purposes? _____

6. Do you operate all instruments of instructional technology carefully in order to avoid damage? _____

7. Do you preview the material in advance to determine content and its relationship to the specific ability of your class? _____

8. Do you check your audio-visual equipment in advance to make certain that it is in proper working condition? _____

9. Do you know where to locate your school's supply of replacement parts such as the various lamps required in your projector? _____

10. Do you return immediately all material to the proper location? _____

Total Score _____

*Instructional Technology Quotient

HOW DO YOU RATE:

10 points = Genius
9 points = Definitely gifted
8 points = Capable
7 points = Inconclusive
6 points and
below = Hide your score

---

aBased upon Los Angeles City Schools, Instructional Aids and Service Branch, "How's Your A-V-Q?" *Audio-Visual News* IX (May 2, 1960): 1.

FIGURE 11-5. Sample Checklist for Evaluating Use of the Materials of Instructional Technology.

STAFF DEVELOPMENT, INSTRUCTIONAL DEVELOPMENT, AND COORDINATION. Supervisors must work with faculty and students in selecting, obtaining, designing, developing, redesigning, and executing programs, materials, and environments. A person in authority (the facilitator) should allocate resources, tie program segments together, and stimulate evaluation. Ideally, such a person is a communicator, a specialist in educational psychology and learning theory as well as in educational technology and instruction, a public relations person, a behavioral scientist, a systems analyst, and a *change agent*.

To facilitate teaching and learning, instructional development must be based on appropriate evidence. It must both analyze the objectives and components of learning systems and engineer appropriate materials (media). The supervisor should promote innovative learning and instructional environments appropriate to Level I *Coordinated Instructional Systems,*[5] which extends the instructor's scope to meet large group, small group, individualized-personalized learning needs, and other minimally directed, packaged learning situations, and also to situations in which the learner has more control of the objective. This description fits within a general learner- and instruction-centered model (see Figures 11-6 and 11-7). To serve the learning needs of a community of students, milieus must be available for all types of learning, from corrective remediation to advanced, self-directed research activities. Remediation and tutorial activities, including the use of both media packages and human tutors, should occur within the center.

ALTERNATIVE APPROACHES TO LEARNING AND INSTRUCTION.   Alternative, nontraditional approaches to learning can be developed. They may or may not be reflected directly and physically within the center.

The supervisor must be able to plan the independent study packaging of media models for standard and minicourses, for miniunits, gaming, computer-assisted, -monitored, and -managed instruction, as well as for small and large group discussion/lecture and individualized laboratory activities. These models describe most of the formal learning activities in a school or college, but do not define the place in which the activities occur. This does not mean that department "libraries" or duplicate media "laboratories" should be developed. The individual teacher's filing cabinet is not the place to store valuable media. Duplicate "laboratories" are neither cost efficient nor cost effective. The supervisor must take a strong stand against such inefficient waste.

When a coordinated learning laboratory operation is centered in the instructional systems center, a student in a satellite location (such as a home) could dial in for audio (and video) information. In fact, the student with a touch-tone dialing pad on the telephone could remotely control "fast forward" and "rewind" functions on the school's video or audio magnetic recorder. Developing media for such activities and course application(s) and the program for con-

[5] CIS Level I involves at least partially media supported instructional modules. A teacher or professor is directly involved and/or available in all learning environments.

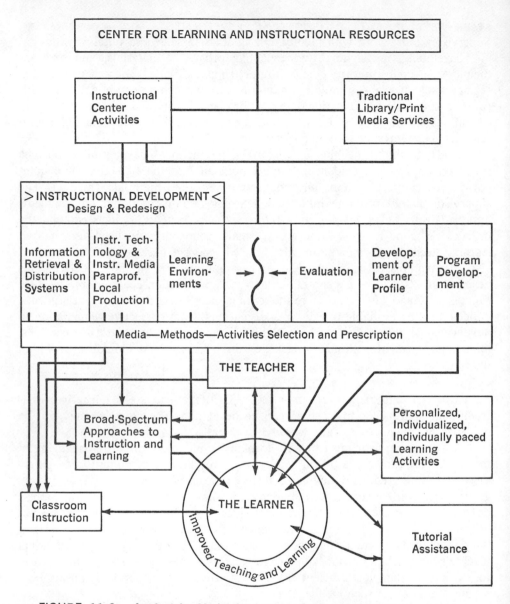

FIGURE 11-6.   An Activity Model for Learner-Centered Education.

tinuous evaluation should be centered and processed within the instructional development framework of the center.

USING AVAILABLE RESOURCES.   Central to an integrated approach to learning is the necessity of using available resources with facility. The essential related production and engineering activities must be close to (if not within) the center.

INSTRUCTIONAL PROGRAM DEVELOPMENT FLOW CHART

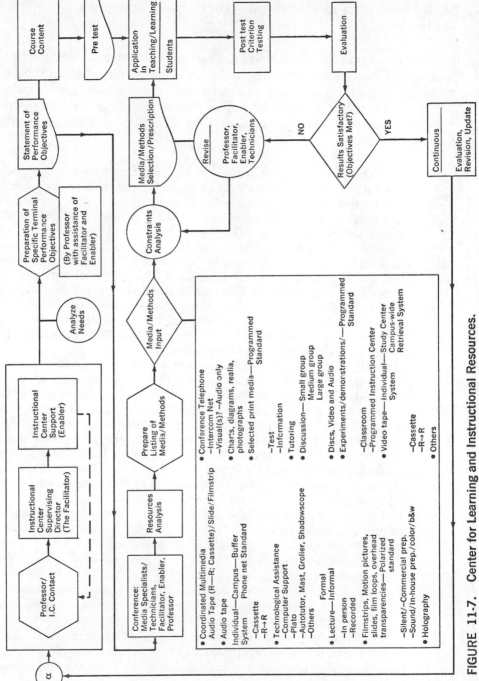

FIGURE 11-7. Center for Learning and Instructional Resources.

Many resources for such activities may be found either on campus or within the local community.

HOW TO GET STARTED.   Developing an instructional systems center is planning to introduce learning functions that initially will face some resistance.The supervisor should organize programs to involve students and faculty in the change process. These programs, while developing and implementing the general, predeveloped master plan, also will act as diffusion and adoption mechanisms within the total institution:

1. The concerned staff must be involved in all developmental activities, including initial planning. Attention should be focused on the learner and the learning process as well as on instruction and instructional strategies and design.
2. The school's concepts of individualized, personalized instruction and the individual, self-pacing learner must be extended, but not to the exclusion of successful, more traditional approaches. The self-pacing learner can *participate* in determining his/her needs, in developing a program to meet those needs, and in scheduling the rate at which he/she will proceed through the appropriate learning activities. This individualized mode is not the only way people learn. Financial constraints must be considered. Even though self-pacing is valuable under certain conditions, there is no definitive evidence that small, or intermediate sized groups are superior. For some groups the more traditional classroom approach is essential.

    Individualized, self-paced instruction provides enrichment and review and presents materials not otherwise available. There is a subsequent feedback relationship between the individualized instructional center activities and the classroom. Indeed, a special function of the facility at West Los Angeles College is distributing electronic information (both from broadcast and on-site camera and recorder sources) from Instructional Center telecine control to the classroom. This kind of multimodal instruction usually is not less expensive than traditional instruction but it may be better. The choice of personnel to handle certain developmental tasks is determined by the institution's definition of the self-pacing learner and by the resources available.
3. Existing collections must be expanded. Exploration, evaluation, and acquisition provide learning experiences. Teachers and students, as well as the center's faculty, must be involved in accomplishing these tasks.
4. Learning environments that are difficult to create must be developed. The supervisor must get educators and students to accept learning laboratories, gaming, and mass informational devices such as computers and televisions, and funds must be budgeted and allocated to support such activities. As stated in item (2) above, these activities function as an adjunct to the classroom program; they support and extend but do not replace traditional classroom instruction. Task analysis for the staff must be accomplished.
5. Plans should evolve to determine student and faculty needs and how to meet them.
6. Meetings should be held to improve learning through an objective-oriented analysis of instructional goals and strategies.

7. As the program evolves, personnel to meet needs must be selected, hired, and assigned.

Ideally, the instructional systems center can be a catalyst for significant changes in the process of education and consequently in its products. *Academic redesign is a matter of survival* for students and teachers as well as for society and its institutions.

How to Select and Evaluate Instructional Materials

The choice of materials and resources should be based on the purposes, maturity, and background of the group. Too often books and other materials for the classroom are selected on bases other than the objectives to be achieved and the students to be taught. A particular book may appear to be "teachable," it may have an attractive format, or the teacher may find that other teachers are using it. Objectives become empty statements when textbook selection is based on such criteria.

Positive Characteristics

The first characteristic for the supervising principal to consider in selecting any learning aid is its relevancy to the goal-seeking activity involved. Thus, one turns to the assignment specifications to learn about duties and responsibilities; to the dictionary to find the meaning of a word; to the microscope to examine microbes. This seemingly obvious criterion of selection is abused, however, by such practices as:

1. Using textbooks and other printed materials as sole sources of information about problems that have changed since the materials were published.
2. Using films and other visual aids as time fillers, without relation to the objectives at hand.
3. Using persons as speakers because they are entertaining, without regard to their subject matter.
4. Using the same field trips each year, without relation to particular units of work.

How to Establish Criteria for Supervising Selection of Instructional Materials

Staff members should establish criteria cooperatively for selecting materials to be purchased for the school. A committee that is responsible for choosing materials for geography should determine the criteria for selection before studying the books, maps, transparencies, or globes. Establishing criteria means that the program must be studied to see what kinds of experiences are desirable in view of the objectives. Such matters as authenticity, vocabulary, organization, consistency, teaching and study aids, style, and format should be considered.

The Criterion of Usability

The criterion of usability has at least two connotations of significance:

1. *The resources must be accessible at the time needed.* The most relevant materials can be selected from book and film catalogues but may not be usable because of lack of funds or time to secure them. The resource file may yield names of persons who can help on projects, but inquiry reveals that these persons are not available when needed. The problem of timing is a particularly complex one in relation to selecting visual aids, which frequently must be ordered (on a rental basis) weeks in advance.
2. *A learning aid must be usable in terms of its appropriateness to the particular group or individual.* Relevant materials are available on almost any topic, but they may be appropriate only to mature readers. Similarly, competent persons may have a wealth of information on students' questions but may not be able to explain this information to students. The matter of appropriateness ultimately is answered in terms of individual learners, and so far as possible supervisors and teachers must select a range of resources that provides for each individual. This criterion is violated most generally in regard to instructional materials, the selection of which may be out of the teacher's hands.

NEED FOR ACCURATE INFORMATION.   The resources for learning must give as accurate information as possible. This criterion is of special significance in relation to printed sources, particularly pamphlet materials. However, films, programmed materials, and even visiting specialists may give inaccurate information. Materials prepared with particular biases, such as those used for advertising, may be helpful resources, but the teacher is obliged to point out the biases and inaccuracies and to use any other available materials to show differing viewpoints.

THE SUPERVISOR SELECTS ECONOMICAL RESOURCES.   Other things being equal the most economical resources should be used. Often other things are not equal and teachers have difficulty in estimating the costs in time and money of different tools. However, good judgment will rule out:

1. Using expensive sound, color films, *if* more economical slides, pictures, single-concept cartridge film loops or tapes, or pamphlets are available and would be as effective.
2. Purchasing expensive motion pictures (when only one teacher wants to use the film one time per term) if rental (and even free) films are available, or renting films that are used several times each term when purchase would be more economical.

3. Taking a group of students to see a resource specialist who could come to the school and is willing to do so.
4. Sending an entire class to a set of reference books to check on the same topic if one person could present the information effectively.

The principle of economy is violated, contrary to common assumption, by using the same materials for all members of a class, when perhaps half of the group finds these materials too difficult or too boring. The same funds could be spent for materials developed at different levels of difficulty for varying interests.

In addition, the maturity and the background of the group must be considered. Students who have grown up on a farm cannot be expected to profit most from reading books based on life in the city. In recent years, more attention has been given to this problem in developing readers for the schools.

Students can participate in selecting free materials by writing for them as a committee or class project, searching for the kinds of information that will help solve their problems. The fact that material is free may make it attractive to those operating on restricted budgets.

How to Select and Evaluate Instructional Materials as Aids for Instruction

According to J. M. Gwynn,[6] instructional materials should:

1. Suit the age level and experience of the student.
2. Bring realities to the student, building upon previous experience.
3. Be introduced after careful preparation based upon thorough study and investigation.
4. Contribute to, rather than substitute for, the learning process.
5. Be of reasonable length.

Further standards concerning the use of instructional aids that the supervisor should stress are:

1. Presenting more than one image *at the same time* is of doubtful value and should occur only if there is a valid reason for such multiple imaging.
2. The effectiveness of the materials' use should be evaluated by both teacher and students.
3. The materials should be used within a well-balanced program, with one type of teaching aid being used at one time and a different teaching aid being used at another time.
4. The materials must present an air of reality, not an artificial setting that the students cannot understand.

[6] J. Minor Gwynn, *Curriculum Principles and Social Trends* (New York: The Macmillan Company, 1960), p. 561.

5. The objectives of instruction in each case must have been determined in advance before the materials will be of maximum value to the learner.
6. Materials must be used that consider the differences in students—one student sees a relationship more quickly than another, and yet all students see some relationship, for example.

The major problem the supervising principal faces in attempting to select, organize, and improve instructional materials is that varied materials are needed to provide for the individual differences of students. Most specialists tend to agree with the American Textbook Publishers Institute's definition of a modern textbook as "an assistant teacher in print."[7]

The major criticism with regard to the present manner of textbook use is that one such "assistant teacher" is not enough for the variety of needs, interests, and abilities of the typical learning group. The solution, therefore, is to increase the effectiveness of the use of this resource, and wherever possible to add other resources—not to do away with a most important resource. The methods by which these solutions are realized constitute part of the job of the supervising principal.

HOW TO HELP TEACHERS SELECT MATERIALS DEALING WITH BASIC ECONOMIC AND SOCIAL ISSUES. More books and materials should be produced that are based on the backgrounds of the students. Many kinds of free and inexpensive materials are available. The Joint Council on Economic Education in the Greater Hartford (Connecticut) area,[8] through one of its committees, developed the following criteria for selecting materials dealing with basic social and/or economic issues:

1. The source and sponsorship of literature and teaching aids should be clear, so that students may make judgments as to probable bias.
2. Resource materials should arouse interest in our economic life. They should give insight into problems inherent in our economic society, including those of human relationships.
3. In the overall selection of materials there should be a wholesome balance among the various points of view. However, the fact that an individual piece of literature has a one-sided point of view does not disqualify it as a useful aid to economic understanding.
4. Materials should be on the students' level of understanding and interest. In most classes there will be students with mature abilities and interests and others whose abilities and interests are immature. Attempts should be made to secure a variety of materials in order to meet the varied needs of a variety of students.

[7] American Textbook Publishers Institute, *Textbooks in Education* (New York: The Institute, 1949), p. 5.

[8] Greater Hartford Council on Economic Education, *Aids in the Improvement of Education for Economic Understanding,* Bulletin No. 1 (Hartford, Connecticut: The Council, 1950), p. 2.

5. The above criteria should be considered in the use of various types of resource materials including speakers, films, recordings, and field trips, as well
as pamphlets and other printed materials.

Practices in Selecting Textbooks

Practices in selecting textbooks vary widely in the United States. In general, the
supervising principal should insure that the competent, experienced teacher has
the freedom to decide whether the needs of the learning situation require the use
of a basic textbook (that is, the same book for each student) and, if so, the
additional materials that are required. If not so, the teacher should help select
cobasic textbooks (that is, multiple sets of books) and other materials. The
teacher should determine which materials to use with the class. With freedom to
make this decision, teachers may find it advantageous to select particular books
from a list already screened or adopted.

In practice, textbooks sometimes are chosen by state or local authorities
and distributed to classrooms without any consultation of teachers' preferences. In
such situations, teachers may be free to select additional materials or even to
arrange exchanges.

Authors, professional committees, and school systems have prepared extensive lists of criteria, scoring sheets, and other guides for selecting textbooks.
Although these may be valuable in making selections, the principal always must
bear in mind the unique needs, interests, and abilities of the teacher, the particular
group of learners involved, and the general goals planned for this group.

HOW TO AVOID UNDUE INFLUENCE. In selecting instructional materials, principals must guard against being influenced by outside pressures, direct or indirect,
that would limit the freedom to teach and to learn. There is no doubt that the
atmosphere of regarding new ideas with suspicion has influenced the selection of
textbooks and other instructional materials. One unfortunate result appears to
have been a tendency in some schools toward greater centralization of the selection process. Safeguards can become so formalized that it becomes difficult, or at
least discouraging, for a principal or a teacher to secure the necessary current
materials on up-to-date problems and issues.

Two steps in avoiding undue influence by such pressures to the extent that
learning is adversely affected are to: (1) work with regularly established citizen
groups in studying the kinds of materials that instruction for living in a democratic
society needs, and (2) develop written policies for selecting materials.

HOW TO IMPROVE THE SELECTION OF TEXTBOOKS. The following criteria for
evaluating books, pamphlets, and periodicals were established by one city school
system.[9]

[9] Adapted from Form 113–8, used in the evaluation of materials, in "Procedures in the
Selection and Adoption of Learning Materials in Pasadena City Schools," duplicated material
(Pasadena, California: Pasadena City Schools, 1973).

In terms of instructional merit:

1. How well does the material cover the essentials in this field?
2. How suitable is the vocabulary for the students' level of achievement?
3. How adequate is the material in scope and in interest appeal? Does it meet teacher and student needs at the grade level for which it is being considered?
4. How factually correct is the material?
5. How up-to-date is the material?
6. How well does the material suggest and discuss applications to everyday life?
7. If an anthology, how genuinely representative of the thought and the culture of the period and area to be studied are the selections?
8. How well do the problems of life presented stimulate students to meaningful consideration of right and wrong behavior?

In terms of the loyalty factor, judged on the basis of the purpose for which the particular publication is to be used:

1. How adequately presented is that aspect of American civilization with which the book deals?
2. How well does the author support generalizations with reliable information and logical deduction?
3. In the study of democracy, how well are both its accomplishments and problems considered?
4. How well does the material offer means and methods for arriving at solutions to the problems?
5. In dealing with the individual American's relationship to government, are obligations stressed as well as rights?
6. How adequately does the material help pupils develop sound methods of propaganda analysis to be applied to all situations?
7. For judging basic texts: if controversial issues are considered, how adequately are representative points of view included and treated objectively?
8. For judging supplementary materials: how well does this material contribute to an appropriate balance of all representative points of view in your school or library?
9. For judging plays, newspapers, and other periodicals: how sound is the reputation and integrity of the editorial board?

In terms of format:

1. How clear, readable, and attractive is the type?
2. How suitable is the paper for this type of textbook?
3. Is the binding attractive but still durable for extended school use?
4. Is the size of type appropriate for the students of the grade for which the material is being considered?
5. How clear, well designed, and meaningful are the illustrations?
6. How adequate for student reference work is the index?

In terms of instructional aids and authorship:

1. How well does the bibliography encourage and aid the students in carrying on research?
2. How well qualified in the field and grade level is the author?
3. How effectively are such reading aids as variations in type, center heads, side heads, and italics used?
4. How challenging and stimulating are study aids such as self-tests, summaries, reviews, and suggested activities (including instructional trips, films, tapes, and others)?
5. How adequate and practical are such instructional aids as suggested problems or projects, tests, bibliographies, appendices, glossaries, and maps?

The supervisor must ask questions such as:

1. Does the book develop the kind of ideas that are important?
2. Does it clearly distinguish between propaganda and factual information?
3. Is it suitable for use in developing the kinds of attitudes, skills, understandings, and appreciations that are important?

These kinds of questions grow out of concern for the purposes of instruction.

How to Evaluate the Use of Materials of Instruction

The need for materials and equipment to take care of a variety of individual interests, development, and abilities should be considered for every classroom. Generally, if a rich environment is provided, learning will be facilitated. Students tend to choose the more appropriate kinds of materials, if given the opportunity, through a process of self-selection. Modern classrooms should have flexible carrels equipped with audio and visual input terminals. Classrooms should serve as instructional laboratories. The classroom laboratory is essentially a *flexible* collection of the materials and equipment useful in connection with particular purposes of the learning group. Classroom laboratory materials are unique only in respect to location.

HOW TO HELP TEACHERS EVALUATE THE USE OF AVAILABLE RESOURCES. In a study of late twentieth-century schools a hundred years from now, undoubtedly the researchers will be puzzled by the great homage paid to written materials as resources for instruction. Written materials are only one kind of resource; in fact, the human elements in the learning situation are the most important kinds of resources.

Not so generally accepted or understood are the valuable resources of the teachers and students themselves. There will be students who have traveled to various parts of the country or who will have lived in other countries, and there will be students of varying backgrounds.

So many times we overlook these most valuable resources that are immediately at hand. When workshops consider resource people they ought first to look at the resources contained within the group.

In most schools are opportunities for varied experiences, such as:

1. The lunchroom or cafeteria
2. The halls
3. The school grounds
4. The books to be taken care of
5. The traffic to be regulated
6. The supplies to be inventoried and stored

There is the community, with its rich resources in:

1. Governmental institutions
2. Service organizations
3. Places of business
4. Industries
5. Homes
6. Farms
7. People who have interesting backgrounds and hobbies
8. People who have ideas that may differ from those of other people
9. People engaged in various occupations
10. Natural resources in the form of trees, soil, rock formations
11. Illustrations of erosion and conservation practices
12. Wild life
13. Tame animals

HOW TO HELP TEACHERS EVALUATE PICTURES.   The criterion of accuracy is important in selecting pictures since distorted, one-sided, or untrue concepts may result from a single picture that fails to tell the whole story or misrepresents what it does tell. This caution is applicable particularly to the attractive pictures appearing in the advertisement sections of magazines. Series of pictures, and contrasting pictures on the same topic, are most helpful. Also consider size, clarity, color, and composition.

HOW TO HELP TEACHERS EVALUATE SLIDES, FILMSTRIPS, TRANSPARENCIES, AND RELATED EQUIPMENT.   Slides, filmstrips, and transparencies may be prepared, rented, or borrowed from distribution agencies. Like pictures, they have extensive utility in learning. Filmstrips are not as flexible as slides and other transparencies, since they must be shown in a fixed series, but they are more convenient to handle. Simple concept cartridge film loops are, according to many who have used them, at least as convenient as filmstrips. In any event, the operator should be able to pause to discuss any frame as the material is projected.

Various types of projection equipment can be used for showing slides, filmstrips, transparencies, and pictures on the projection screen. The opaque projector is a particularly usable resource. It can project pictures and printed material, as well as the students' work.

Several types of equipment for projecting slides, filmstrips, "single concept" cartridge films, and transparencies are available. The overhead projector is becoming lighter and its light source more flexible; *technamation* introduces a sense of motion to the projected transparency through polarization. Slides, filmstrips, and transparencies, and equipment for their projection, offer the advantage of considerable economy over motion pictures.

The screen may be of the glass beaded lenticular type, which affords a distortion-free image to students sitting at the sides of the room. Certainly adequate room-darkening equipment should be provided, and the screen should be permanently mounted rather than portable. Two screens, one in the front of the room and one in a rear corner, angled toward the center of the room, are recommended.

HOW TO HELP TEACHERS EVALUATE SPECIMENS AND MODELS. Collections, relics, specimens, models, and other items brought from home, bought from commercial agencies, or loaned by museums, serve valuable instructional purposes. Generally, these items are used in connection with exhibits and displays that both stimulate learning and provide information. Problems of space, storage, and the preservation of these materials sometimes are acute. Unless a central school museum is practicable, it probably is best to prepare exhibits or displays when needed and then return the pieces to the original sources. Consider size and portability, as well as application.

HOW TO HELP TEACHERS EVALUATE MAPS, GLOBES, AND CHARTS. A great variety of maps, globes, and charts are available from commercial agencies. These should be selected with particular concern for their practicability in the classroom, as well as for their appropriateness for the students' achievement level and maturity. Fixed equipment has the disadvantage of taking up needed space when not in use. Central school facilities for storing maps, globes, and charts seems desirable, provided they can be readily and easily moved into classrooms when needed. Wise curriculum planning will make available a number of the most relevant, usable, and accurate maps, globes, and charts and will provide for getting adequate information about their availability and use to teachers.

HOW TO HELP TEACHERS EVALUATE THE MOTION PICTURE. Possibly the most widely used and misused instructional technology resource is the motion picture. Lack of careful planning and problems of distribution frequently result in showing films to learning groups without relation to the classroom experiences and maturity levels of the students. In fact, the criteria for selecting and using this resource are violated by practices that permit the uneconomical use of learners' time in seeing films irrelevant to their goals, inappropriate to their interests, or inaccurate in film content. It behooves supervisors to help teachers plan carefully for the wise use of a valuable resource.

Selecting films is helped by curriculum guides that suggest relevant film resources. In the absence of such guides, the teacher may find aid in annotated film guides prepared by the distribution agencies.

There is no adequate substitute for a preview of the film by the teacher concerned. In using the film, various steps should be planned for; essentially they are similar to the steps used with any other learning experience:

1. Formulating questions to be answered; that is, establishing learning goals
2. Understanding the goal-seeking activity of seeing the film
3. Answering the questions and reviewing information, evaluating the learning experience, and planning the next steps.

Properly used, the motion picture perhaps is the resource that can give to the largest number of learners the most intelligible information on the greatest variety of problems in the shortest period of time, with the possible exception of video tape and costly and complex computer-assisted learning. Hence, we may well hope to see its proper use greatly expanded.

A sample film evaluation form is included as Figure 11-8.

HOW TO HELP TEACHERS EVALUATE PHONOGRAPH TRANSCRIPTIONS AND AUDIO AND VIDEO MAGNETIC RECORDINGS. In addition to the usual phonograph records and audio tapes widely in use, several other types of recorded resources are available:

1. Transcriptions and video tapes of television and radio broadcasts make it possible to repeat the program material at more convenient times and as frequently as desired.
2. Video and audio tape and phonograph recordings of dramatizations, stories, poetry, and historical events are available commercially.
3. Various recording devices owned by schools now make possible the recording of class activities, individual student endeavors, and other events in the school and in the community.

Stereo cassette recorders offer maximum ease of use, flexibility, and the cassette cartridges have the advantage of protecting the tape within. Video and audio tape recordings of classroom sessions, speeches, assembly programs, and similar happenings can serve many purposes. These resources offer excellent help for learning experiences in most curricular areas. Community colleges, university bureaus, schools, and school systems maintain libraries of records and recordings, frequently as a part of a complete resource center. If such libraries are not available, the supervising principal should help the teacher make selections from whatever listings can be found.

If a video tape recorder is to be purchased, one that is compatible with

FIGURE 11-8.   Sample Motion Picture Evaluation Form

Film title _____ Length _____

Sound _____

Source _____ Date _____ Silent _____

Color _____

Cost _____ 1. Rent ( )   Black and White _____

2. Purchase ( )   Age Level

3. Free for   or Grade ——————
   Evaluation ( )

Subject area(s) _____

General category _____

1. Is empathy on the part of the viewer probable?

Yes _____ No _____ Don't know _____

Comments _____

2. Does the content flow and progress smoothly?

Yes _____ No _____ Don't know _____

Comments _____

3. Is the dialogue clear and well presented?

Yes _____ No _____ Don't know _____

Comments _____

4. Is the film modern in content and presentation?

Yes _____ No _____ Don't know _____

Comments _____

5. Was an adequate musical background provided?

Yes _____ No _____ Don't know _____

Comments _____

6. Was the sound track adequate as to volume, clarity, and tone?

Yes _____ No _____ Don't know _____

Comments _____

7. Would you commend the film for its photography?

Yes _____ No _____ Don't know _____

Comments _____

FIGURE 11-8.   (Continued)

8. Was this a good print?

Yes _____ No _____ Don't know _____

Comments _____

9. Were special photographic techniques used?

Yes _____ No _____ Don't know _____

Comments _____

10. Was animation used?

Yes _____ No _____ Don't know _____

Comments _____

11. Was there any attempt to indoctrinate the viewer?

Yes _____ No _____ Don't know _____

Comments _____

12. Was the content accurate?

Yes _____ No _____ Don't know _____

Comments _____

13. Was the content clearly presented?

Yes _____ No _____ Don't know _____

Comments _____

14. How would you rate this film?

Excellent_____Good _____ Average _____ Poor _____

Not suitable for school use_____

Comments _____

General comments and recommendations: _____

_____

_____

another in a neighboring school would permit sharing program materials. In spite of the comparatively moderate cost differential, a color signal video tape recorder should be considered. The supervisor should give maximum assistance in the selection and use of recordings and transcriptions, along with other learning resources.

How to Help Teachers Select and
Evaluate Blank Cassettes

The supervisor should be aware of two problems in buying blank cassettes:

1. "Bargain" tapes frequently contain faulty merchandise, which will not perform properly and usually jams, damages delicate mechanisms, and causes
   excess wear to recording heads
2. Purchasing prelabeled, standard length, commercial cassettes, especially audio
   cassettes is too expensive for most school budgets.

SELECTING AUDIO CASSETTES.   The supervisor should stress that whoever orders
such materials must specify not only the tape, but also the housing. Magnetic
media shells loaded with 3M, TDK, BASF, or AGFA are recommended. This
desirable combination meets all quality control standards (provided that loading
is totally automatic). Audio cassettes should have hard windows that are sonically
sealed; nonmagnetic shields; graphite-coated or silicone-impregnated paper or
graphite-coated polyester liners; beryllium springs with glued pressure pads; shells
with five screws; tapered and flanged rollers; steel pins and exact dimension, and
durable hubs. The use of a chromium dioxide tape is not recommended, but we do
urge the utilization of Dolby noise reduction equipped recorders/players.

The combination of exact length cassettes that satisfy all of these recommendations and that are automatically loaded with the specified tape into the
recommended shells are available from Louroe Electronics, 7908 Goodland
Avenue, North Hollywood, California 91605, and from Media Industries, Incorporated, P.O. Box 65151, Los Angeles, California 90065. A booklike binder with
intershelving capabilities and provisions for maintaining proper tape tension is
available from the same sources. These sources also provide relatively inexpensive
bulk loading, duplicating services, and labels that can be typed and pressure-
applied to the cassette.

VIDEO CASSETTES.   At the time of this writing, field experience indicates and
most experts report that 3M and Sony video cassettes are the most consistently
reliable as to tape reliability and housing performance.

HOW TO HELP TEACHERS EVALUATE RADIO AND TELEVISION RESOURCES.   Radio
and television are resources of unique significance because of their inherent values
and because of their possible uses both in and out of school. Figure 11-9 illustrates a sample brochure presented to students concerning television program
selection.

Curriculum planning for in-school use of these materials introduces the
practical problem of utilizing broadcasts at scheduled times that may or may not
coincide with convenient times in the school schedule. Taped program materials
(video and audio) help overcome this disadvantage. The primary problem in
directing the out-of-school use of educational television and radio is the difficulty

FIGURE 11-9.   Brochure Presented to Students on the Topic of Television Program Selection

---

TV!

As a study resource, your television set at home is somewhat like your school library. It can provide a great deal of helpful and stimulating material if you know how to use it to good advantage. In the library, you first study the card index to find out what's available on the subject in which you are interested. For TV, you study the program schedules.

In addition to following the daily schedules in newspapers, TV guides are available where offerings are divided under drama, music and arts, public affairs and history, and science and exploration.

Try to choose programs that:

• Are specifically related to something you'll be studying during the week.

• Will assist you in special assignments.

• Will help you have a better understanding of today's world.

• Will fit in with your own personal interests.

---

of controlling students' home schedules. Perhaps one major goal with regard to out-of-school radio and television is cooperative planning with parents as to appropriate programs for children and youth.

Selecting in-school programs involves considerable day-by-day study of program announcements. Frequently some program can be found that bears directly on current units of work and the daily program, especially in nondepartmental schools, can be adjusted accordingly. Some school systems and broadcasting stations arrange programs in series for use in schools, and plans for instructional units can be built around these series.

One effective way of using telecasts and broadcasts is through small group or individual reports. A group of students can watch a program and report to the class in the same way as with work in the instructional media center, the library, or on a field trip. This format works well for out-of-school programs. Another solution is to provide complete sets of video-taped programs in the instructional media center. Licenses must be purchased as required for some television programs.

Television sets equipped to handle *video discs* with random access capabilities should receive due consideration. The video disc system was designed for schools, industrial training programs, hospitals, and other institutions that emphasize education, training, and in-service improvement programs.

In any event, the supervising principal should remember that television, motion pictures, and the newer programmed learning devices, are teaching *aids* only. They cannot take the place of the teacher, nor should a telecast schedule be allowed to dictate the daily program for a class except at the teacher's discretion.

HOW TO HELP TEACHERS MAKE BEST USE OF AUTOMATED AND PROGRAMMED LEARNING. Automation has not taken over the classroom. The live human teacher still is required. The significant change is that the teacher has some electronic tools that make it possible to teach more effectively.

The computer can do no more than the program with which it has been provided.[10] The Beseler Cue-See, Bell and Howell Synchrosearch, Dukane sound filmstrip projectors and viewers; Bell and Howell, Caramate, Kodak, and Graflex sound-slide viewers; and other similar devices such as "spiritus" provide for programming of a sort using sound filmstrips and/or other media.

Summary of Terms Related to Instructional Technology

AUTO-INSTRUCTION. Auto-instruction is a process involving the use of carefully planned materials and machinery that are designed to produce learning, without necessarily requiring the immediate presence of a person other than the student. *Individualized* or *personalized instruction* might be the preferred terminology in most situations and learning environments.

BRANCHING. Branching is a generic term indicating a type of programming wherein students are referred to alternative items depending on their responses to a question. In intrinsic programs, the branch usually consists of a single item explaining why a particular answer is incorrect. The branch then returns the student to the original item for another attempt at the problem. A branch that would permit the student to skip over intervening material already mastered is called a *wash ahead* branch. If the student were ordered to repeat a portion of the program that had been inadequately mastered, the branch would be termed *wash back*.

PROGRAMMED TEXT. A programmed text is a program presented in book form. In the programmed text, pages may be "scrambled"; that is, successive pages need not contain successive content material. The individual who successfully masters the contents of one page is then given instructions as to the proper page to turn to. A scrambled text, then, is a special type of programmed book or text. Students are directed to pages that are not in consecutive order in terms of alternate choice or success and/or failures. A programmed book or text need not be scrambled, but all scrambled texts are programmed. In any event, a programmed book presents material in a step-by-step fashion, each step being composed of an infinitesimal body of knowledge.

---

[10] The programmed materials may be words on tape, or pictures on a screen, or images transmitted through a video tube. Many of the techniques employed are described in a book by James E. Espich and Bill Williams, *Developing Programmed Instructional Materials* (Belmont, California: Fearon, Inc., 1972).

What the Supervisor Should Know about
the Teaching Machine

Many different types of machines are designed for a wide variety of purposes. Generally, a teaching machine is used as follows:

1. The student reads assigned material.
2. He/she is asked to answer multiple choice or completion questions that follow immediately while the material is still fresh.
3. Answers may be written onto a tape, "drawn" on a cathode-ray tube with a "light pencil" (if a computer terminal is available), or recorded by selecting and pushing buttons on the machine. The materials are organized carefully in a sequence of information. Simple statements follow, idea by idea and step by step.
4. The student is led carefully by the program, much like the author of a book draws his/her reader progressively through a chain of developments. Unlike the conventional book, in programmed instruction the student is asked to respond continuously.

REMEDIAL LOOP.   A remedial loop consists solely of an explanation of an error that a student has made in selecting one of the answer choices available. The frame will refer the student to the item just left so that he/she may have another chance to answer the question inherent in the item, but the frame itself contains no question. In some textbooks the remedial loop is referred to as the *first order branch*.

SUB-SEQUENCE.   When a student has made an error on a mainstream frame, he/she may be directed to a sequence of standard intrinsic frames that contain both new material and questions on that material. New frames will provide for further remedial instruction if necessary. The subsequence returns the student to the mainstream on its completion.[11]

The teaching machine is a mechanical device that presents a program to a learner, as seen in Figure 11-10. The major features of teaching machines include:

1. They usually present a one-item frame at a time.
2. They provide some method for the student to indicate an overt response.
3. They indicate whether a response is correct or not.
4. They may or may not provide branching.
5. They maintain a record of student responses.
6. They provide for feedback.

[11] See Susan Meyer Markle, *Good Frames and Bad* (New York: John Wiley & Sons, Inc., 1964), p. 275.

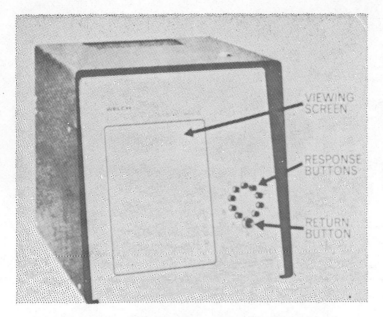

FIGURE 11-10.   The "Autotutor" Teaching Machine.
(Photo by West Los Angeles College Instructional Center)

In the homemade "machine," if one electrode is touched to the question and the other electrode to the proper response, a buzzer and a light are activated. For example, if one touches the proper city name below a map with the contact point representing the city on the map, a circuit is completed, and a buzzer sounds (or lights flash). See Figure 11-10.

Programmed learning marks a renaissance of the method of dialectic question-based teaching that was used so brilliantly by Socrates. This approach of learning is available in several formats; the teaching machine probably is the best known mechanical device that uses programmed materials.

The machines fundamentally are independent of the program material. Any type of machine that presents the program frame by frame or as distinct items and provides an opportunity for the student to respond may be adequate. Such machines can be built for less than $50, and it hardly need be said that the machines will not use all of the student's time. A child can make a simple machine using the diagram presented in Figure 11-11.

As program availability increases, more machines (the "hardware") will be needed. The cost of the program material ("software") is something else again. One recent estimate calculated that producing the manuscript for a single program would cost about $100,000.

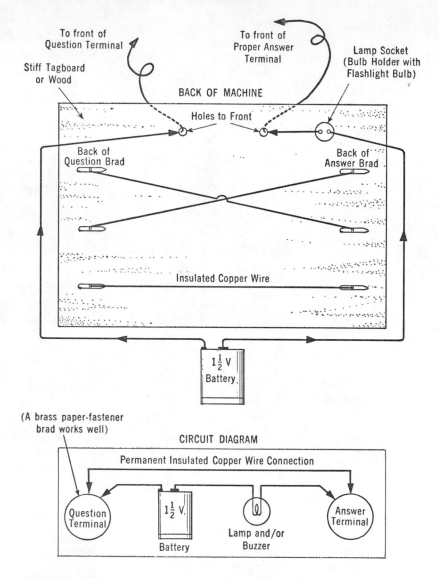

FIGURE 11-11.   Wiring Diagram of Teaching Machine.

What the Supervisor Needs to Know about "Audio- and/or Video-Tutorial," Computer-Supported Instruction, Computer-Assisted Learning, and Computer-Managed Instruction

The supervisor should be familiar with the following characteristics of "audio-and/or video-tutorial," computer-supported instruction, computer-managed instruction, and computer-assisted learning, especially with the development of minicomputers and microprocessors. The management dimension is important in *computer-managed instruction.* A student would complete one unit of work and then obtain, perhaps, the next three instructional "units" or "modules," in response to the computer's direction. The computer would have reached the "necessary" decision by analyzing the first test completed by the student. The "units" or "modules" may be programmed texts, standard textbooks, various illustrated materials or guided activities, and others.

Computer-supported instruction permits the use of the power of the computer (or minicomputer) for rapid test scoring interpretation and evaluation; keeping students continuously apprised of their progress and standing in the class; giving prompt feedback about what the teacher and perhaps fellow students consider as the weak and strong points of a presentation; for permitting rapid, complex calculations; for rapid information retrieval including multimedia programming and switching; and for meeting similar demands.

In *computer-assisted learning,* the computer is used as a compiler of educational texts and/or to control the multimedia and/or branching programs.[12] The computer permits a true interaction, and in many cases a dialogue. The student may be presented with information at the terminal, to which he responds by pushing a button, applying a light pen (a computer input device) to a cathode-ray tube (CRT) screen, by using the teletype terminal, or in some other manner. Such instruction tends to provide for:

1. Individualization of instruction, in that it provides for:
    a) Self-pacing—there is a pacing component that tells the student, in effect, words such as "You have an hour."
    b) Diagnostic preimposed testing
    c) "Modules"—unitized materials (especially in *computer-managed* learning).
2. Continuous participation through:
    a) Overt responses
    b) Varied environment
    c) Review and tutoring.
3. Evaluation and knowledge of results through:
    a) Continuous feedback
    b) Performance testing.
4. Unit revision ("module alteration") based on feedback.

Audio- and video-tutorial instruction attempts to do what has been outlined above, with audio information predominating; visual display materials are kept to a minimum. In *video-tutorial* situations the opposite is true. In *audio-video-tutorial* programs there is a balance of visual and auditory information. The medium used in the latter two situations would be a video recording. The supervising principal may wish to review the scheme developed by Norman E. Rich and Hayden R. Williams at Golden West College in California. The TRAILS project

12 Lawrence M. Stolurow, *Computer Assisted Instruction* (Detroit: American Data Processing, Inc., 1968), p. 25.

(*Total Receptive Access, Independent Learning System*) operated under the weekly format described below.

GENERAL ASSEMBLY SESSION.   All students in the course assembled at a scheduled time one hour early in each week. (Most of the traditional lecture content was incorporated into the TRAILS experience.) The general assembly session was used to heighten interest, provide historical and theoretical perspective, show longer motion pictures than was possible in the independent study session, provide guest speakers, and provide time for lectures.

INDEPENDENT STUDY SESSION.   Students had access to carrels in a center for independent study for several hours daily. This center was called the "Trails lab." In the "Trails lab" students proceeded at their own rate, worked the period of time required to master a unit, and worked at their own individual efficiency peak, independently. Each week of the semester was devoted to a major concept or principle of biology. A program on magnetic tape had been prepared for each program. This program included the materials usually found in the traditional lecture, except that the unit was programmed to include whatever combination of techniques proved most appropriate to each unit. These techniques included short tape-lectures, taped introductions to laboratory materials, study of demonstration materials, examination of specimens under taped direction, the performance of experiments, reading and study of texts and pictures, viewing brief single-concept films, studying microscope slides, and other activities of this nature. An instructor was on duty at all times to provide special assistance to those who needed it, personalizing the tutoring and maintaining the study atmosphere.

SMALL ASSEMBLY SESSIONS.   Once each week students met in groups of twenty-five or fewer in a scheduled session, always with the same instructor. During this session questions were answered; assignments were given and collected; course mechanics such as enrollments, withdrawals, absences were handled; and examinations were given. The instructor was an experienced discussion leader and functioned here as such. Students identified this instructor as their teacher in the course.

STUDENT PROJECTS.   The small assembly session instructor assigned each student two projects to be completed during the semester. A laboratory was provided for projects that required laboratory facilities. For the first project, the student was told what to do, how to do it, what data to gather, and how to use the data. For the second project, the student was counseled as to what to do and how to do it. He/she decided what data to gather and how to use the data. This practice was to give the student an appreciation of the scientific approach to problem-solving and a taste of the excitement of discovery.

HOME STUDY SESSIONS.   The students did the usual amount of outside study Assignments were made during the small assembly session.

α = Start

β = Re-enter system

* = Level of achievement on Post-Test.

FIGURE 11-12. Tutorial Decision-Making Process.

The Decision-Making Process, the Audio-Instructional System, and Teaching Machines

The tutorial decision-making process is graphically illustrated in the systems analysis chart included as Figure 11-12 on the previous page.

The audio-instructional system, which would follow the start of the tutorial program, is diagrammed in Figure 11-13.

Machines provide a *medium* for teaching, but the actual information is presented by the programmed material. Investigators are using teaching machines:

1. To test concepts that are at the heart of the educational process
2. To assist in teaching many procedures that can be broken down into some sequence
3. To train for a variety of skills in industry and in the Armed Forces.

One large factory uses a teaching machine to introduce workers to its assembly line procedures (see Figure 11-14).

How to Assess Programming and Its Advantages

The use of individualized programmed learning materials represents an important potential contribution to American education. The supervising principal must be prepared to help teachers properly use such devices.

A variety of programmed material is becoming available, but not all programs will fit all machines. Just any set of question-and-answer material does not constitute an individualized program. Individualized materials are designed to adapt to individual differences by allowing each student to proceed at his/her own rate (see Figure 11-15).

THE JOB OF THE PROGRAM.   The program's job, then, is to present to the learner an infinitesimal series of steps that lead from one behavior repertoire to the next. The program must be divided into small, equally assimilated segments. Constructing the subject matter's sequence of segments constitutes program development. Three popular programming techniques that the supervisor should bring to the attention of interested teachers are:

1. Linears with sublinears
2. Linears with criterion frames
3. Intrinsic programming.

These three paradigms are illustrated in Figure 11-16.

Programming requires the process of dividing a complex area of knowledge into a finite series of unitary facts that can be understood and mastered without error. The supervising principal must assure that there is no premature use of experimental materials that have not been tested through scientific research.

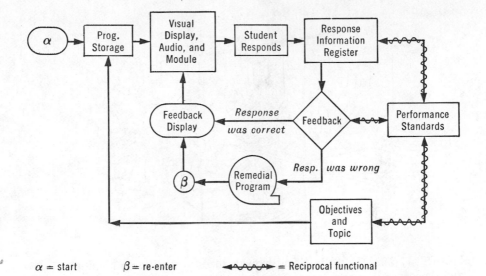

α = start β = re-enter   ◄～～～► = Reciprocal functional

FIGURE 11-13.   Audio-Tutorial Program Selection Process.
(After Lawrence M. Stolurow, *Computer Assisted Instruction*, Detroit: American Data Processing, Inc., 1968, p. 25.)

One interesting advantage of the program is that the student can arrive in the learning situation with some knowledge of the subject to be analyzed by the entire class. Bright students generally take about one-third as long to go through complex program material as do average and below average students. Even

FIGURE 11-14.   Teaching Machines and Programmed Learning: C.A.L.? C.M.I.? Holy Audio Matrix!

FIGURE 11-15.   Students Using Individualized Instructional Materials
and Devices.

though both bright and slow students can solve problems presented by the program, the more gifted students are better able to formulate concepts and generalizations than are the average and slower students. In any event, it has been said that if a teacher can be replaced by the machine, then that teacher needs replacing.

ADVANTAGES OF PROGRAMMED INSTRUCTION.   Some of the advantages of programmed instruction include:

1. Immediate knowledge of results is recorded and the effectiveness of the program can be readily assessed
2. Distraction is cut to a minimum
3. The instruction is individualized to a high degree
4. Provision can be made for students to hear a lecture missed, to receive ancillary information, or to hear an instructor describe a course in which he/she might wish to enroll.

The reader will recognize the difference between the program and a workbook. A workbook does not provide for a large number of extremely minute, carefully designed steps.

The teaching machine and programmed instruction industries are based on the work of Professor B. F. Skinner of Harvard. Skinner stressed the importance of developing *operant strength,* which was constructed through having made a successful *overt response;* but there is some question as to the value of overt response. In recent experiments conducted at a large western university, two groups of students worked with teaching machines. One group responded overtly

Technique No. 1 : Linear with Sublinears

Technique No. 2 : Linear with Criterion Frames

Technique No. 3 : Intrinsic Programming

No^A = Answer incorrect because of (or in direction of) condition A
No^B = Answer incorrect because of (or in direction of) condition B

FIGURE 11-16.   Three Program Branching Paradigms.

to questions, while the second group merely observed the program as it progressed. No significant difference in the amount of information absorbed was found.

WHAT THE SUPERVISOR SHOULD KNOW ABOUT HOW TO WRITE THE PROGRAM. The process of program writing is very expensive. It is estimated that a semester's program must consist of about 3,000 or 4,000 frames, which would cost about $50,000 to write. A sample of the charting and diagramming symbols that are used in preparing flow charts and block diagrams for program systems is presented in Figure 11-17.

One frame may take approximately three or four hours to write. The procedure followed is:

1. Try out the question with the students
2. Rewrite the question

Symbol	Translation	Symbol	Translation
→	Direction of flow	⬓	Transmittal form
	Decision function	or	Paper (punched) tape
○	On-page Connector or step identification		Magnetic tape
⬙	Off-page Connector		Punched card
□	Console operation	◇	Sort
	Terminal—halt or start sequence		Document file
	Input/output function		Verifying and other keying operations
	Program modification function		Communication Link
□	Processing function		Online storage
	Source document		Display
	Report	▽	Merge

FIGURE 11-17. Programming Flow Chart Symbols.

3. Try out again
4. Rewrite
5. Try out again
6. Rewrite
7. Try out the question once more
8. Final rewrite
9. Preliminary writing on tentative program tape
10. Try out
11. Final editing and writing
12. Reproduce on program tape

HOW TO HELP TEACHERS PREPARE TAPES FOR THE AUDIO-TUTORIAL PROGRAMS. The supervising principal should recommend the following steps to teachers who wish to use the audio-tutorial approach to instruction:

1. Define each goal in measurable terms
2. Establish a hierarchy of goals for greatest emphasis in the course
3. Determine the time to be allowed to each unit or goal
4. Arrange the units (and/or modules) in sequence—weekly wherever possible

5. Determine the best method of achieving the objective for each unit without regard to mechanics of budgeting, scheduling, or staffing
6. Assess realistically the real world constraints and proceed to achieve the objectives within the limitations that are inherent in the possible choices
7. Decide what experiences a student should have to achieve most efficiently and effectively the objectives of the unit-module
8. Assemble all equipment and materials, whether hardware or software, needed for the experiences agreed on
9. Using a cassette-type tape recorder, follow a prepared outline of the program and instruct a student lab assistant in the learning experiences. (Some reports indicated that recording the instructions in shorthand rather than recording them on tape may save time.)
10. Transcribe the tape (or shorthand notes) onto the script, which is triple spaced to permit easy editing
11. Edit the script; the instructor who produced the initial recording of the material should do the initial editing
12. Edit the script again with another instructor, reading the script as a double-check for clarity and content
13. Retype the script (at one college this was done by a student typist while another student typist was transcribing tapes for additional units)
14. Read the script onto a master tape
15. A systems analysis flow chart, which pictures graphically the general steps in program revision, is included as Figure 11-18.

FIGURE 11-18.   General Program Revision System.

The supervisor is referred to the *Program Evaluation and Review Technique* (*PERT*) for information concerning program analysis and revision.[13] In a random access system developed by Ampex Corporation, the student can select any number of programs by punching a predetermined program address number in a touch-tone remote console located in a carrel in the study center. The transistor-logic digital switching system (whose number of sources and output potential is virtually unlimited) can deliver an audio signal and any preprogrammed, recorded video signals within thirty seconds, which is almost in real time. The video portion of the program in this system is limited to still pictures that are recorded on video buffer discs. If desired, the system can permit the student to duplicate the audio portion of the signal on a special cassette duplicator. A forty-five minute program can be recorded in thirty seconds. A student could patch in his own tape recorder and take a copy of the audio information for further study.

How to Improve Library Services

The need for good library services in a modern school is recognized by effective principals and specialist-consultants. Schools that have superior library services usually seem to have a superior educational program. In a sense, the nature and scope of library service can serve as a partial index to the character and quality of curriculum and instruction.

The School Library as a Distribution Center

In a small school, just as in the larger institutions, materials accumulate, and it is impossible and not practicable for the teachers to keep all of these items in their classrooms. The central library may be the only place in the school to gather all materials required by the instructional program. The library in small schools and most elementary schools often is, therefore, the distribution center for books and for the materials of instructional technology. In the larger secondary schools and in the colleges, the instructional technology centers and libraries may be combined in a larger instructional media complex, each area being coordinated and supervised by a professional specialist.

Since small schools usually cannot employ a top-notch specialist as an instructional media coordinator, the supervising principal must make certain that the proper types of teaching aids required for proposed lessons are available. Instruction in the use of the materials also must be provided. The supervising principal also should help teachers by giving them a list of available materials.

[13] See Federal Electric Corporation, *A Programmed Introduction to PERT* (New York: John Wiley & Sons, Inc., 1967).

How to Supervise the Organization of Library Service

CENTRAL OR CLASSROOM COLLECTIONS? In some circles there still is a controversy as to whether a centralized library or separate collections in each classroom is the better plan for elementary schools. In schools without a central library, practically every teacher gradually gathers a few books that form the nucleus of a classroom collection. Some school systems make a beginning in strengthening their library resources by providing each teacher with a small annual appropriation for purchasing new books for the classroom. No doubt such a plan has merit as a way to begin; such beginnings may develop into more adequate service.

Separate permanent classroom collections have several limitations when viewed from the standpoint of library needs in a modern school program. Where teachers oppose the establishment of a central library because they are reluctant to give up their room collections, some supervising principals have used the strategy of assuring teachers that they could keep their personal collections as long as they wished. The central library merely would provide additional materials that they could borrow to augment their room collections.

The present attitude of librarians and other educational leaders is that there is no point in continuing the controversy whether a central library or classroom libraries is the better plan for schools. Both are essential parts of a comprehensive plan for library service in a school.

The temporary classroom collection should serve as a reservoir that feeds breadth of content into the instructional program in the classroom, provides recreational reading for students during spare moments, and equips the teacher with materials of different levels of difficulty to suit many and varied student interests.

The central library is the service agency that helps teachers maintain classroom collections that can be adjusted continuously to the evolving instructional program. The central library and the temporary classroom collections operate as partners that provide comprehensive library services to the school.[14] The services are diagrammed in Figure 11-19.

ESSENTIALS OF THE CENTRAL SCHOOL LIBRARY AS A TEACHING AGENCY. One's approach to the organization of library service in a school primarily hinges on whether one views the library as a direct teaching center or as a service agency.

Those who consider the library as a teaching agency will assign the librarian responsibilities for:

1. Aiding the teacher in instruction in the use of books and libraries
2. Developing in students strong motives for and permanent interests in reading
3. Guiding individual students in the selection of reading materials
4. Developing literature appreciation

[14] R. T. Calhoun, "Why Not a Central Library in Elementary Schools?" *Illustrated Elementary English* XXXVIII (January 1961): 37–40.

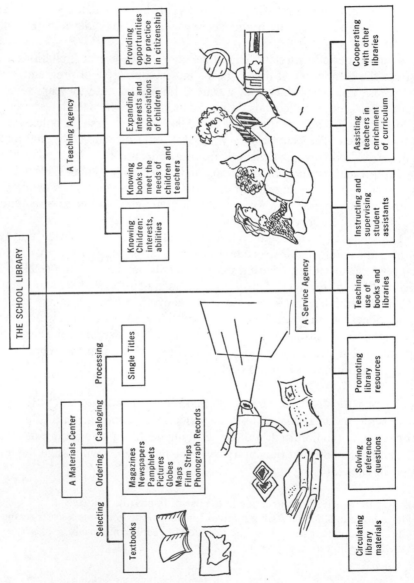

THE SCHOOL LIBRARY

A Materials Center
- Selecting
- Ordering
- Cataloging
- Processing

Textbooks

Single Titles

Magazines
Newspapers
Pamphlets
Pictures
Globes
Maps
Film Strips
Phonograph Records

A Teaching Agency
- Knowing Children: interests, abilities
- Knowing books to meet the needs of children and teachers
- Expanding interests and appreciations of children
- Providing opportunities for practice in citizenship

A Service Agency
- Circulating library materials
- Solving reference questions
- Promoting library resources
- Teaching use of books and libraries
- Instructing and supervising student assistants
- Assisting teachers in enrichment of curriculum
- Cooperating with other libraries

ᵃ From Department of Education, *Hawaii School Libraries: A Manual for Organization and Service* (Revised edition; Honolulu: The Department of Education, 1964).

FIGURE 11-19. The Function of the School Library.

5. Promoting the habit of using reading as a wholesome way of engaging one's leisure time.

It is doubtful whether a librarian should assume sole responsibility for guiding students in the selection of reading materials unless it is done under the guidance of the student's classroom teacher.[15]

Equipment in a library should be arranged to be both attractive and functional and should provide ease of supervision. It is helpful to:

1. Use all available wall space for shelving.
2. Arrange tables and chairs to allow at least five feet of aisle space for ease of movement and for the best possible light.
3. Place the charging desk near the entrance.
4. Arrange low tables and chairs near primary book shelves.
5. Place the card catalogue where it is easily accessible, but where it is away from regular traffic aisles.
6. Arrange for bulletin boards and display tables in prominent positions.

How to Supervise the Teaching of Library Use Techniques

All children should learn to appreciate the content and value of books and how to handle and care for books. They also should learn how to use the library to find most quickly the things they seek and to develop independent habits and skills of study and research and the routines essential for keeping a library in good working order. There is considerable disagreement, however, even among librarians, as to how library instruction should be organized. Some insist that there should be a graded series of lessons taught by the librarian in accordance with a predetermined schedule. This plan has the advantage of guaranteeing that the lessons will be taught.

Dynamic stimulation arises out of needs developed in classroom instructional activities. For this reason, many librarians are beginning to advocate the "integration plan," whereby classroom teachers assume responsibility for instruction in library use.

FUNDAMENTAL BOOK AND LIBRARY SKILLS.   Students at different levels need to know some fundamentals concerning the use of books and libraries. Mastery of these skills is a step toward independence.

Students need to know that:

1. Care of books is important.
2. Books are arranged in a library according to a system as an aid to the user of the library in finding the book needed.

[15] B. T. Williams, "Why an Elementary School Library?" *California Journal of Elementary Education* XXIX (August 1960): 19–23.

3. Nonfiction books are shelved alphabetically and/or numerically from left to right and section by section.
4. Fiction books are shelved alphabetically by the last name of the author from left to right and section by section.
5. Shelf labels are guides to books on those particular shelves.
6. The card catalogue is an index on cards of all books in the library. It records books according to author, title, and subject.
7. Various parts of a book have distinctive and important uses.

Students need to know how to:

1. Find books in a library by using the card catalogue.
2. Use encyclopedias and dictionaries and understand what kind of information they contain.
3. Use special reference books.
4. Take notes.
5. Make and use bibliographies.

TEACHING THE CARE OF BOOKS TO ALL GRADES. The signs of normal wear on a book over a period of time indicate that a book has been read and enjoyed. This is expected, and efforts to preserve books should never prevent students from handling them themselves. However, it is of the greatest importance that children be taught how to handle books from the first moment they are exposed to them.

The following rules help students learn how to handle books:

1. Have clean hands before handling books.
2. Put away pencils, crayons, chalk, and ink before handling books.
3. Do not eat while reading a book.
4. Keep books out of reach of very small children and pets at home.
5. Use paper book marks. Do not crease or fold pages.

The library itself should be a source of enjoyment. Students will feel secure in knowing that a corner of the library is reserved for them and their books, and that "going to the library" means a new adventure with each visit.

One supervising principal suggested activities for primary, middle, and upper grades as shown in Table 11-1.

HOW THE PRINCIPAL SUPERVISES THE LIBRARY SERVICES. The principal must take the initiative in improving library services.[16] Faculty cooperation must be encouraged so that the entire school's curricular needs will be balanced appropriately in the orders placed for books.

Another area in which leadership will be expected from the supervising principal is the actual organization and operation of the library program within the school. The organization, and the schedule under which the library operates, should be determined in the light of sound principles of library service.

[16] See A. Farelli, "Library Is a Must," *Illustrated Instruction* LXIX (November 1959): 75–76.

PRIMARY

1. Bring the kindergarten class to the library for visits. Explain the library's purpose as part of the school community.
2. Bring the class to the library for story hours. Point out the picture book section and read favorite books from the collection. Make the time spent in the library pleasurable.
3. Use library books to answer students' questions whenever possible.
4. Encourage students to look at picture books and ask them to share their favorites by showing and talking about them. The teacher may select picture books and spread them about on tables before students arrive.
5. Call their attention to displays, bulletin boards, and the like. Display work of the class in the library at least once each semester. Tie it in with books, if possible.
6. Teach students the rules for the care of books.
7. Teach students that a library is a friendly place where people are quiet and courteous so that each student may enjoy his/her own book.
8. Appoint library assistants to straighten shelves and leave the room in order for the next class.
9. Show beginning readers in the primary grades where to find their books and allow small groups to browse. Increase their desire to read independently.

MIDDLE

1. Repeat activities of the kindergarten and primary grades.
2. Show students where to find middle grade books.
3. Show them how to take a book from the shelf carefully without scraping the bottom of the book. Have them make cardboard markers with their names on them. When a book is removed from the shelf, the marker is inserted in the spot where the book was found. When the book is returned to the shelf, the book is replaced in that spot.
4. Talk about different kinds of books and stories.
5. Learn to make and use a simple bibliography.
6. Practice skills in using books. Find:
   a) The title;
   b) The author;
   c) And use the table of contents;
   d) And use an index.
7. In the fourth grade, the better readers will be using all of the library shelves and it will be necessary to teach them to locate books on these shelves. Take one section of shelves at a time and explain how the books are arranged:
   a) Explain "fiction" and "nonfiction" sections and what each means.
   b) Emphasize that each book belongs on a particular shelf and in a particular place on the shelf.
   c) All books are "named" in some way, either by a number or a letter, before they are put on the shelves. This number or letter is like a house and street number. It places the book on the shelf and makes it possible for the book to be found quickly and easily.
   d) Nonfiction is numbered according to the Dewey Decimal Classification, which divides all knowledge into ten major divisions. A book is assigned a number that stands for the subject of the book. Books with the same subject will be shelved together.
   e) Fiction is shelved alphabetically by the first letter of the author's last name. Books by the same author will be shelved together.
   f) Show how to use the card catalogue. Teach the use by actually locating a book by author, by title, and by subject. Emphasize that a catalogue is an index to the library and is used much in the same way as the students use an index to a book. Choose a title of a book and show how it can be located by noting the alphabetical arrangement of the catalogue, using the guide letter on the catalogue tray, and choosing the correct tray; finding the title card, discussing the arrangement of books on the shelf, using the labels on the shelf, finding the correct shelf, and finding the book.
8. Have students keep simple records of books they have read.
9. Discuss the Caldecott Medal books.
10. Have students give short book reviews.

UPPER

1. Review the activities of the earlier grades.
2. Supply material for practice in using the card catalogue and finding books in the library.
3. Introduce the Newberry Medal books.
4. Encourage students to give short book talks and have group book discussions.
5. Teach students to take notes on informational reading from reference materials.
6. Encourage students to make book lists on favorite subjects for others to use.
7. Promote wise book selection.
8. Promote correct use of reference materials.
9. Discuss authors and gather material on them from sources in the library.

Since the library is a service agency, its prerogative should be subordi-
nated to those of the instructional program. There should be no occasion for
teachers to say that they desire materials from the library but the library's hours
and "red tape" rules make it impossible to utilize the resources that are there.

HOW TO LOCATE RESOURCES FOR THE PROFESSIONAL LIBRARY.   Most school
systems have some kind of a school library containing professional materials. The
supervisor should evaluate the present status of the professional library. Gaps can
be filed from several sources:

1.   The public library can provide valuable assistance.
2.   Free and inexpensive pamphlets and other materials can be obtained.
3.   The school system can subscribe to various professional periodicals.
4.   Individuals in the profession may donate college texts.

It is worth the effort to develop a collection of helpful books and professional
periodicals at the school. Some publications will sell themselves to the teacher, *if*

FIGURE   11-20.   Resources for the Professional Library.

they are readily available. The supervisor may wish to promote other publications, especially in a conjunction with individual problems.

The results of recent research should be interpreted to teachers, and professional journals that emphasize such findings should be included in the library. Resources that may prove valuable in filling the gaps in the professional library are summarized in Figure 11-20.

How to Evaluate Library Services

Usually the book collection is the first item to which most supervisors turn their attention in evaluating the school library. The American Library Association has made the following recommendation regarding the book, periodical, and newspaper collection for public school libraries.[17]

Books: 6,000–10,000 titles, 10,000 volumes, or 20 volumes per pupil, whichever is greater, plus professional collection.
Magazines: Elementary—40–50 titles; jr. high—100–125 titles; high school—125–175 titles; plus 40–50 in professional collection.
Newspapers: Elementary—3–6 titles; jr. high and high school—6–10 titles.

These figures are more generous in number of titles for smaller schools than previously published minima found in bulletins of state departments of education. Table 11-2 represents an evaluation form applicable to community college libraries. For small rural schools the quotas ran as low as 250 to 500 titles for one-teacher and two-teacher schools.

Theoretically, a small school should own or have access to as wide a range of titles as a large school. The range of individual student needs and the breadth of the curriculum do not depend on school size. Some people recommend smaller book collections for small schools as a practical adjustment to the more limited financial resources of small schools. Although this is a noble recognition of reality, it is not the wisest approach to the problem.

Instead of being satisfied with the meager library resources that the local school system can afford, small schools should strive to affiliate themselves with larger library service units (such as the intermediate unit library) so that they can have access to as diversified a collection of books as the large school.

Variety of titles and total number of volumes are not the only criteria by which one judges the adequacy of library services. Recent publication often is important for books in the content fields. A book collection consisting largely of out-of-date textbooks and volumes discarded by parents has little merit.

Paper-bound bulletins and pamphlets with accurate content usually can be obtained free or at little cost from the state and federal bureaus and departments, and sometimes from commercial firms. The library should provide a verti-

[17] Mildred L. Nickel, *Steps to Service*, (Chicago: American Library Association, 1975), p. 5.

TABLE 11-2.   *Appraising Library Services in the Community College*

	RECOMMENDED	ACTUAL
A. *The Book Collection*		
Basic Collection, Volumes	20,000	
Plus 36 Volumes per Staff FTE[a]		
Plus 4 Volumes per Student FTE		
Plus 120 Volumes per Subject Field		
of Study Beyond Standard Programs		
Total Book Collection		
B. *Periodicals*		
Basic Collection, Titles	300	
Plus 1.3 Titles per		
Cert. Staff Member (FTE)		
Plus 4 Titles per Subject Field		
Plus microform		
Copying, Photocopy		
Screens, 1 per Station		
C. *Staff*		
Technical Services Staff		
Ratio: 2 clerical to 1 professional		
Audio Visual: 1 to 50–80 faculty (FTE)		
Administrative Staff: Ranges from 1 in		
college of 1,500 to 3 in college of more		
than 7,500 (FTE)		
D. *Space*		
.10 assignable square feet per		
anticipated volume		
Reading Stations for 18 per cent of full-time		
enrollment, with 25 assignable square feet		
provided for each station		
A basic complement of 400 assignable square		
feet plus 140 assignable square feet per		
FTE staff member		
Total Space		
Additional Areas	No Formula	

[a] Full-time equivalent

cal file in which such materials can be preserved for continued use. Teachers and the librarian should cooperate in a plan whereby the school can acquire a rich reservoir of pamphlets and bulletins over a few years.

Adequate records, such as a shelf list and a card catalogue, are essential if the library is to serve the school adequately. An annual inventory should be made of the materials on hand. Books that are getting out-of-date or are worn beyond repair should be eliminated. Some items should be discarded, others repaired, while still others will need replacement. Replacing worn-out titles becomes a part of the annual plan for new purchases.[18]

Most school libraries make inadequate use of the resources of other libraries. Frequently the teachers of a school never have set foot inside the door of the public library in the community, and librarians in the public library are equally unfamiliar with the activities of the school library. Often students make no contact with the public library during their entire school career.

Absence of an extensive cooperative relationship between the school library and the public library is inexcusable. A union or joint catalogue would facilitate greater use of the materials of both agencies. The time has come when those responsible for administering public services no longer can tolerate the loss of public funds such as is represented by lack of cooperative planning, financing, and utilization of a community's library resources.

HOW TO ORGANIZE THE PROFESSIONAL LIBRARY. Whether a school has a professional library for teachers and how it is used depends largely on the supervising principal. The recent interest in faculty participation in curriculum revision and other phases of school management and supervision indicates the necessity for each school system's having *an adequate professional library for teachers*. The local professional library frequently can be augmented by loan collections from the intermediate unit library, the state library, the state department of education, or the state university. Again, the principal must lead in creating the faculty organization through which these materials are utilized in study and in meeting local problems. Table 11-3 contains a summary evaluation of library services supervision.

Do

1. Accept responsibility for working with the rest of the school staff in setting up policies for selecting materials.
2. Ensure that teachers are involved in the selection of materials. Selections should not be made on the basis of friendships, of political expediency, or of unconsidered arbitrary personal opinion. Such decisions are not as efficient as are decisions that result from the combined judgment of several people who reach a decision after careful analysis.
3. Make every effort to educate the board of education as to the necessity for giving schools within the school system the opportunity to purchase materials on their own. In drawing up the budget, call on teachers for advice. Work with all of those who are concerned with using equipment.
4. Work for the allocation of a good proportion of the budget to instructional materials each year.
5. Help teachers find materials that will aid them in the classroom.

[18] M. V. Gaver, "Needed: More and Better Elementary School Libraries," *American Association of University Women* LIII (January 1960): 96–100.

TABLE 11-3. *Evaluation of Library Services: A Summary*

A. THE LIBRARY AND ITS STAFF	B. THE LIBRARY FACILITIES
1. The frequency of use of the library by students, classes, teachers, and other members of the professional staff should be determined.	1. Books should be organized according to topics or departments. They should be selected carefully in order to satisfy various interests and should be chosen according to subject and vocabulary level.[a]
2. Special subjects should be supervised by an assistant librarian who has special interest in the field.	2. It should be determined whether the card catalogue is used by the students. A chart should be present showing the Dewey Decimal System.
3. There probably should be one librarian, two or three parent volunteer helpers, a clerk, and student assistants, depending upon the size of the school population.	3. The library should have an adequate reference section.
4. Student assistants should be assigned different work from time to time so that each may gain from rich experience in the many library services. They should participate eagerly (this is a sign of a successful librarian).	4. The library should present an inviting, home-like atmosphere. Pictures and other audio-visual materials, including museum specimens, should be provided. There should be an attractive bulletin board display. The general environment should be pleasing to the eye, restful, and conducive to relaxed, quiet reading. Students should check out their own books within delimitations.
5. The librarian should have a pleasing personality and the ability to get along with others and to understand individual needs and interests. He/she should be able to deal effectively with both children and adults, and must know books, other library materials, and how to select, organize, and interpret the books and other materials present.	5. Adequate ventilation should be provided.
6. The school librarian must organize the materials for service, promote an effective and attractive reading program, serve in a teaching capacity, aid in curriculum development, and contribute to guidance services.	6. There must be adequate lighting; thirty to thirty-five candle-power is recommended.
	7. The library should be located centrally on the ground floor, accessible to both primary and intermediate classes, and away from the noise of practical arts activities in classrooms and from the playground. The reading room should have a minimum of twenty-five to thirty square feet per reader, but in no case should it be less than 1,200 square feet.
	8. Overall seating capacity should be large enough to seat the largest class expected, plus not less than ten additional students.
	9. Adequate electrical outlets should be provided on all four walls.
	10. Acoustical tile should be present on the ceiling and floors should be of a rubber tile or other noise-deadening material.
	11. The library should be painted a light, attractive color, such as light green.
	12. Adequate furniture, including tables of both twenty-five-inch and twenty-seven-inch length, with a surface area of five by three feet, should be provided. Chairs should be both sixteen and fourteen inches in height. There should be easy chairs, table lamps, and attractive reading nooks.
	13. There should be adequate working room for the library staff and for the storing of library materials, supplies, and equipment. A ten by twelve foot clear working space for the library staff should be provided.
	14. If a separate office or workroom is provided, adequate ventilation, lighting, electrical ventilation, electrical outlets, furniture, and equipment, including telephones, paper cutter, a typewriter with library keyboard, files, rack case, a bulletin board, a portable standard chair, a bulletin board, files, rack case, a sink with hot and cold water, a coat locker, adjustable shelving, and cupboards must be present.[a]

[a] See School Library Association of California, *Recommended Standards*, Bulletin of the Association (Sacramento The Association, March 1975).

6. Help establish curriculum laboratories that will serve as resource centers for teachers. One can begin with small collections secured through an exchange with other school systems, as well as through purchases.
7. Help teachers learn how to use a variety of materials. Many teachers may be afraid of taking that step since they have always depended on the security of a single textbook.
8. Give teachers an opportunity to evaluate available materials, to send for materials, and to select materials for the classroom from the central library and from the community library.
9. Work toward a coordinated complex that includes and integrates the library and the instructional center (which subsumes audio-visual instructional technology), each supervised by a professional specialist, so that the many facets of a subject may be explored and researched meaningfully.
10. Work toward an adequate staff for the library.
11. Work toward adequate clerical assistance for the professional library staff and for the instructional center coordinator.
12. Familiarize the librarian with systems such as have been developed by book processing companies such as Brodart, Incorporated, which would facilitate circulation, order, and information retrieval services.

Don't

1. Fail to study the community to determine its potential resources for learning —its institutions, people, and industries.
2. Assume the total responsibility yourself. Encourage teachers to study written materials themselves in order to find out what types will be suited for the needs and interests of different students.
3. Fail to find out all possible about the students—their abilities, skills, needs, interests, and problems—so that suitable material may be made available for each student.
4. Purchase materials too late for use in the instructional program.
5. Let material stores fall below an adequate supply level.
6. Assign responsibility for receiving, storing, and caring for instructional materials to certificated personnel. These responsibilities, along with the associated clerical work, should be assigned to classified personnel.
7. Attempt to teach *all* instructors how to use *all* of the equipment and materials available to them. Consultant services should be available to assist and instruct principals and teachers in the correct use of special materials, audio-visual equipment, and new devices developed through instructional technology.
8. Fail to encourage the developement of an instructional center and an educational materials laboratory that would facilitate teacher experimentation.
9. Be satisfied with inadequate library cataloguing systems.
10. Fail to encourage teachers to send small groups and to take entire classes to the library as well as to the instructional media center.

TRENDS IN THE PROGRAM FOR IMPROVING INSTRUCTIONAL MATERIALS

Toward ⟶   the Use of the Computer in

Improving the Use of Instructional Materials

The electronic computer will be utilized to improve the collection, organization, and utilization of instructional materials. The educational computer will be able to "talk" to any other computer through a common language, cutting from months to days the time needed to distribute statistical reports.

Toward ⟶   the Increased Use of Programmed

Instructional Modules as Integrated Parts of Level I

Coordinated Instructional Systems

The newer techniques of programmed instruction will become increasingly important teaching aids. There will not be automated teaching, nor will there be automatic learning. Rather, the teaching machine and, possibly to a greater extent, the programmed text and other packaged learning systems will assist the teacher. The supervising principal of the future will be well versed in the use and application of materials of programmed instruction, and will serve as a resource person in this area to the classroom teacher. It is expected that more information concerning the fundamentals of the art and science of teaching, as well as more data concerning the intricate processes involved in learning, will be discovered through the use of programmed instruction.

Toward ⟶   Changes in the Incidence of

Standardization and Centralization of the

Purchase of Instructional Materials

The purchase of supplies, such as paper, pencils, and notebooks will continue to be processed through a central purchasing agency. However, specific choices of textbooks and other instructional materials will be delegated more and more to the professional staff of the local school, under the direction of the supervising principal. This will make possible the purchase of appropriate materials that provide for differences among individuals and groups. Materials such as raw video tape, however, will be purchased *en banc.*

> **Toward** ⟶ Further Use of Educational Television in the Classroom and Instructional Center

School systems and television broadcasting stations will continue to cooperate in presenting educational television for classroom use. Broadcast schedules will be arranged to coincide with weekly or daily instructional program schedules of the schools. The supervising principal will assist the teacher prepare for, and follow through on, material presented in a television program. Video disc and holography, both still and motion, will be important media. Two way cable systems with three-dimensional holography and printout capabilities will combine with random access video discs to produce a new kind of publication and communication matrix system.

Supervisory Problems

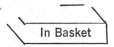

In Basket

Problem 1

A school with an enrollment of approximately 1,400 is located in a small city school system that has been quite aggressive in the areas of curriculum improvement and the purchasing of equipment and materials through its own efforts and those offered through various federal aid programs. The department with which we are concerned has obtained tape recorders, record players, audio notebooks, overhead projectors, filmstrip projectors, and motion picture projectors. Also provided have been materials such as records, transparency materials, classroom sets of various books, additional copies of resource materials, and subscriptions to various periodicals. In addition, the library staff has made an effort to provide a good supply of reference materials for this department.

   The group of teachers involved (called a department for the sake of the problem) consists of five men and one woman and is described briefly below:

1. Male, comparatively young, dynamic as a teacher, efficient, interested in improving his teaching as well as that of the whole department. In many respects acts as a department head without remuneration, authority, or released time.
2. Male, young, interested, willing to cooperate, wants to improve his teaching but still lacks some sophistication in his field.

3. Male, has been known as a good teacher, has health problems, nearing retirement age, has little interest in helping to improve the department.
4. Male, older, fairly well adjusted, in a rut so far as his teaching methods and materials are concerned.
5. Female, middle-aged, excellent background, makes students think and work, border-line in using new techniques and materials but does try to keep up-to-date in her field.
6. Male, young, member of coaching staff, possibly background in subject area somewhat weak, does not show great interest in using new materials and techniques but has shown fleeting glimpses of his ability to do so, coaching of greater interest than teaching.

Only three of the members of the department show consistent interest in improving the curriculum or their teaching. The other members seem to have no resentment toward these people, but register little interest in joining with them. Much of the teaching of the latter three is formal lecture, end of the chapter questions, notebook development, and tests. In the meantime, equipment and materials are not used as they should be, students are aware of the differences in the class structures, and those students who care openly ask for assignment to the more "progressive" teachers' rooms. The problem has been brought to the attention of the principal. The principal realizes that many similar problems exist in several departments having a number of teachers.

How can you, as a supervising principal, provide the leadership that will help improve this department and provide for the use in the proper way of the costly educational aids available? What would you do?

Problem 2

A school system-wide committee had been organized to select the basic textbook for the new required semester course in health education at the ninth-grade level. Mr. Douglas, Assistant Superintendent for Instructional Services, convened the organizational meeting and suggested that the group elect a chairman for the remainder of the work period. Following the election of one of the science teachers, the question was raised as to procedure. Mr. Douglas reported that his staff had already surveyed the available materials and had requested samples from the several book companies with textbooks in this area of the curriculum.

Mr. Lawrence, science teacher from Isadore High, asked, "Is it absolutely necessary that we adopt one book for all three high schools, or may we consider different textbooks for different schools?"

Mr. Douglas replied, "Up to now we have held to school system-wide use of textbooks for equivalent courses. However, if this committee desires to come up with any recommendations, they certainly will be considered carefully. It seems to me that this required course may call for the use of two levels of textbooks in each school. Let me suggest that perhaps the committee should establish criteria for an evaluation of the books and then should score each book in the light of these criteria."

As supervisor, you are a member of the committee.

How would you proceed to develop the criteria as suggested by Mr. Douglas? What recommendations would you make concerning:

1. Whether all schools in a single school system should be required to use single, dual, or multiple textbook adoption policies, and
2. Whether all students or classes in a single school should be required to use the same textbook or whether the policy of dual or multiple textbook adoption should extend to the individual school and/or to the individual classroom.

Problem 3

Ritter Junior High School has an enrollment of 600 students. Traditionally, English classes are scheduled by the English department head to visit the library one day per week. The school system does not have local library consultant-specialists, but the state library supervisor is available periodically.

Sources of the problem include:

1. An approach to education that provides little stimulation or time for student use of the library.
2. A study hall concept of the library that discourages the development of an affection for reading, and turns the library into a forbidding den.
3. A physical setting for the library that is not only isolated from the main stream of student traffic, but also inadequate in size and ventilation.

How will you, as supervising principal, provide leadership that will result in the teachers' wanting a flexible library in their school?
How could you, as supervising principal, improve the quality of library services in the school?
Through what steps would you proceed in accomplishing this improvement?

Questions and Suggested Activities Concerning How to Provide Improved Materials of Instructional Technology

Questions

1. How can the supervisor develop criteria and methods for procuring better materials of instruction?

2. To what extent can school and community facilities be integrated to bring about better instructional materials?
3. How can teachers be encouraged to prepare and share instructional materials?
4. How can the supervisor provide teachers with information on recent developments in instructional technology?
5. How can the supervisor insure that teachers are adequately trained in using special materials and equipment?
6. What procedures of check-out and accounting will insure the most efficient distribution of materials at the building level and from the educational materials laboratory?
7. Is the trend toward school provision of *all* materials used by students desirable?
8. What are some characteristics of good school library services?

Suggested Activities

1. Outline a plan of distribution for audio-visual materials and equipment for a twenty-teacher school.
2. Visit a nearby school district and investigate the program of procurement, storage, upkeep, distribution, use, and evaluation of instructional materials.
3. Prepare an annotated list of commercial companies that have proved to be reliable in developing instructional supplies.
4. Examine several school budgets to find the amount per student spent on materials of instruction.
5. List some techniques for evaluating teacher use of instructional materials.
6. Discuss the feasibility of trying a teaching-machine pilot program in one grade-level subject area.
7. Outline a plan for taking inventory of basic and supplementary texts, for storing them during the summer months, and for distributing them at the beginning of the school year.
8. Evaluate and compare three local school libraries. What items would you include in a list of criteria for evaluating the school library? Select any level of education you desire.
9. Prepare a series of slides or transparencies showing what you believe to be samples of outstanding organization in the school library.

Selected Bibliography

Books

Bartky, John. *Supervision and Human Relations*. Boston: D. C. Heath and Company, 1953.

Beck, Robert H., Walter W. Cook, and Nolan C. Kearney. *Curriculum in the Modern Elementary School*. Englewood Cliffs, New Jersey: Prentice-Hall, Inc., 1953.

Briggs, T. H. *Improving Instruction*. New York: The Macmillan Company, 1938.

Brown, James W., Kenneth Norberg, and Sara K. Srygley. *Administering Educational Media: Instructional Technology and Library Services*. (2nd ed.) New York: McGraw-Hill Book Company, 1972.

Brown, James W., Richard B. Lewis, and Fred F. Harcleroad. *AV Instruction, Technology, Media, and Methods*. New York: McGraw-Hill Book Co., 1977.

Dale, Edgar. *Audio-Visual Methods in Teaching*. Rev. ed. New York: Dryden Press, 1954.

DeYoung, Cris A. *Introduction to American Public Education*. New York: McGraw-Hill Book Company, 1950.

Faunce, Roland C., and Nelson L. Bossing. *Developing the Core Curriculum*. Englewood Cliffs, New Jersey: Prentice-Hall, Inc., 1951.

Federal Electric Corporation. *A Programmed Introduction to PERT*. New York: John Wiley & Sons, Inc., 1967.

Frymier, Jack Rimmel. *A School for Tomorrow*. Berkeley, California: McCutchan Publishing Corp., 1973.

Gwynn, J. Minor. *Curiculum Principles and Social Trends*. New York: The Macmillan Company, 1960.

Kinder, James S. *Audio-Visual Materials and Techniques*. New York: American Book Company, 1953.

Kinney, Lucien, and Katherine Dresden. *Better Learning through Current Materials*. 2nd ed. Palo Alto, California: Stanford University Press, 1952.

Lawson, Douglas E. *School Administration*. New York: Odessy Press, 1953.

Markle, Susan Meyer. *Good Frames and Bad*. New York: John Wiley and Sons, Inc., 1964.

Matthews, Don Q. *The Design of the Management Information System*. Philadelphia: Auerbach Publishers, 1971.

Melchior, William T. *Instructional Supervision*. Boston: D. C. Heath and Company, 1950.

Olsen, Edward G. *The Modern Community School*. New York: Appleton-Century-Crofts, 1953.

Reeder, Edwin H. *Supervision in the Elementary School*. Boston: Houghton Mifflin Company, 1953.

Saylor, J. Galen, and William M. Alexander. *Curriculum Planning for Better Teaching and Learning*. New York: Rinehart and Company, Inc., 1954.

Saylor, John Galen, and W. M. Alexander. *Planning Curiculum for Schools*. New York: Holt, Rinehart and Winston, Inc., 1974.

Stolurow, Lawrence M. *Computer Assisted Instruction*. Detroit: American Data Processing, Inc., 1968.

Stoops, Emery, Max Rafferty, and Russell E. Johnson. *Handbook of Educational Administration.* Boston: Allyn and Bacon, Inc., 1975, Ch. 13.
Wiles, Kimball, and John T. Lovell. *Supervision for Better Schools.* (4th ed.) Englewood Cliffs, New Jersey: Prentice-Hall, 1975.
Wilhelms, Fred T. *Supervision in a New Key.* Washington, D.C.: Association for Supervision and Curriculum Development, 1973.

Periodicals

Corey, Stephen M. "Imperatives in Instructional Materials." *Educational Leadership* V (January 1948): 211–214.
Eakin, Mary K. "Educational News and Editorial Comment." *The Elementary School Journal* LI (November 1950): 115–125.
Eben, Louis E. "Do-It-Yourself Slides." *Grade Teacher* LXXXVII (April 1970): 96–98.
Galanter, Eugene. "The Mechanization of Learning." *National Education Association Journal* L (November 1961): 16–19.
Garnet, Florence. "Arts and Crafts." *Instructor* LXXXV (October 1975): 115–118.
Giondomenica, William T. "What Makes a Good Media Center?" *Instructor* LXXXV (November 1975): 64–66.
Hill, Betty Jean. "Lights, Camera, Action." *Instructor* LXXXV (December 1975): 40–41.
Norberg, Kenneth D. "A New Instructional Materials Center." *The Elementary School Journal* LII (January 1952): 256–257.
Trillingham, C. C. "Selecting Books and Materials for Schools." *School Executive* LXXI (February 1952): 19–22.

Films

Designing Effective Instruction. General Programmed Teaching (a division of Commerce Clearing House, San Rafael, California), 1970. Sound filmstrips, workbooks, guide.
Educational Gaming. Educational Media Center, University of California, 1970. TV discussion with two educational gaming experts whose object has been to produce classroom games not merely educational but motivational beyond the simulated world of the game. The game discussed, played by seven 13-year-olds, is called "Manchester." It portrays a socioeconomic microcosm in the English city in which specific roles are assigned to different individuals. Also discusses ramifications such games will have in teaching, and the change this portends in teacher-student relationships. Kinescope. (59 minutes)
How to Use Classroom Films. McGraw-Hill Films, 1963. Dramatizes classroom situations in which students are seen gaining maximum educational value from films because of the teacher's thoughtful and creative approach in using them for curriculum support. (15 minutes)
Learning with Today's Media. Encyclopedia Britannica Educational Corp., 1974. Excellent introduction to the increasingly important role of media centers in the edu-

cational programs of many schools and colleges. Describes how media centers can be organized to provide resources for many instructional approaches, including individualized instruction and independent study. Focuses on four current programs: in a suburban high school in the Midwest; in a Western college; in an Eastern inner-city school; and in a modern facility that serves several schools in a small rural community in the South. (35 minutes)

Personalized System of Instruction: An Alternative. University of Nebraska, 1972. Introduction to the principles and techniques of PSI, or Personalized System of Instruction (also known as the Keller Plan). Prof. J. G. Sherman, Georgetown U., a co-orginator of PSI, discusses why he feels it is an effective educational method and answers questions from educators. Students comment on their experiences in a course in which the PSI approach was used. Statistics are presented showing that retention of material is higher than it is in traditional lecture courses. Shows a PSI classroom in basic college physics, and examines its unique relationships and climate for learning as each student works with a proctor at his/ her own rate toward clearly specified objectives. Notes that this method is also successful with other subjects and at other levels, particularly high school.

Producing Effective Audiovisual Presentations. Media Research and Development, Arizona State University, Tempe, 1975. A set of six sound filmstrips.

This is Marshall McLuhan: The Medium is the Massage. McGraw-Hill Films, 1967. Dr. McLuhan presents his thoughts, which are intercut with expertly edited filmic examples demonstrating their meaning. Employing quick-cut technique, superimposition, animation, split-screen, and collage, the film attempts to make the viewer experience the dynamic as well as didactic interpretations of McLuhan's theories of communication. In the first part, McLuhan articulates the relationship of new media to society, and other commentators present their opinions on the content and style of his writing. In the second part, the application of his ideas is presented as he explains that all media are extensions of human faculties. A film crucial to an understanding of our time; arresting, enjoyable, and easily understood. Produced by NBC. (53 minutes)

Other Sources

American Textbook Publishers Institute. *Textbooks in Education.* New York: The Institute, 1949.

Association for Supervision and Curriculum Development. *Creating a Good Environment for Learning.* 1954 Yearbook. Washington, D.C.: National Education Association, 1954.

Greater Hartford Council on Economic Education. *Aids in the Improvement of Education for Economic Understanding.* Bulletin No. 1. Hartford, Connecticut: The Council, 1950.

Lemler, Ford L., ed. *Audio-Visual Programs in Action.* Ann Arbor: Michigan Audio-Visual Association, 1951.

Los Angeles City Schools, Instructional Aids and Service Branch. "How's Your A-V-Q?" *Audio-Visual News* IX (2 May 1960): 1.

Lumsdaine, A. A., and Robert Glaser. *Teaching Machines and Programmed Learning.* Washington, D.C.: National Education Association, 1960.

Mathies, Lorraine. *Information Sources and Services in Education.* Bloomington, Indiana: Phi Delta Kappa, 1973.

Merritt, Eleanor, and Henry Harap. *Trends in the Production of Curriculum Guides.* Nashville: Division of Surveys and Field Services, George Peabody College for Teachers, 1955.

National Citizens Commission. *How Good Are Our Teaching Materials?* New York: The Commission, 1955.

National Education Association. "Selecting and Appraising Library Materials." *The National Elementary School Principal.* Thirtieth Yearbook. Washington, D.C.: The Association, 1952.

————. Department of Elementary School Principals. *Elementary School Libraries Today.* Thirtieth Yearbook. Washington, D.C.: The Department, 1951.

National Society for the Study of Education. *Audio-Visual Materials of Instruction.* Forty-Eighth Yearbook. Chicago: University of Chicago Press, 1949.

"Procedures in the Selection and Adoption of Learning Materials in Pasadena City Schools." Duplicated material. Pasadena, California: Pasadena City Schools, 1954.

Rich, Norman E., and Hayden R. Williams. "Western Trail Stories." Duplicated material. Huntington Beach, California: Golden West College, 1968.

University of California: Radio-Television Administration. "The Overrated Machine." Broadcast No. 4057—University Explorer 1771, over the Columbia Broadcasting System, Sunday, 4 June 1961. Mimeographed.

12

How to Help the Staff
Understand and Guide
Children

The teacher who does not understand the behavior of children will be in an awkward situation. The supervisor who does not effectively help the staff develop a better understanding of the nature of children will have to correct a problem that should not have raised its head—a problem that could be embarrassing for the teacher, for the supervising principal, and for the specialist-consultant. Such a problem can leave all concerned defeated and discouraged.

The supervisor who can effectively help the staff develop a better understanding of children will find that fewer problems arise, leaving the entire instructional staff freer to devote more time and energy to teaching. Helping the staff bridge the gap from the exasperated to the satisfied should be one of the supervisor's chief roles. His/her attitude is all-important since it sets the pace and can spell success or failure. A positive approach will encourage the staff, whereas a negative approach may stifle initiative and creativity.

This chapter will illustrate various methods and techniques whereby the supervisor can help the staff understand children better. A better understanding rests on general principles. Staff members, as well as children, are individuals and react as such, each with a distinct personality.

Topics covered in this chapter include:

Need for improving the staff's understanding of children
How to help the staff understand children through the in-service education
    program
Interplay of sociological factors
How to help the teacher plan for more effective parent conferences
How to help the staff understand children through health records, observation,
    anecdotal records, and related techniques
How to help the staff understand students through intervisitation
How to help the staff understand students through the interstaff conference
How to help teachers understand students through cumulative records
Case studies

How to supervise the assignment of a student to a classroom
Do—Don't
Trends
"In-Basket" supervisory problems
Questions and suggested activities

Need for Improving the Staff's Understanding of Children

The modern school is more than a place in which children are taught subjects and skills. One primary objective of education today is to help the individual live a happier, more productive, and more satisfying life. The school, therefore, must recognize and provide for the individual differences that are manifest in the school's population. All children have the right to come to school, and it is the obligation of the supervising principal to help the staff understand these children.

A Cultural Dichotomy

Certain dichotomies exist in our society and are reinforced in the schools. Aggression is a necessary ingredient in this highly competitive world, but it is viewed with much concern if employed by the developing student in the school situation. Yet the student must compete for marks and for status among peers. To reason and judge what is the right way to handle aggressive behavior in any given situation presents a confusing problem to the adult directing the student, and, indeed, to the student.

The implications are that the teacher should be many things, but this is impractical. The role of the teacher should be restricted for if the role is not clarified, frustration is inevitable.

School personnel should cultivate the habit of seeing behavior of students as the most important clue to understanding children, and also to understanding themselves. Adults often forget the many years of observation, imitation, and experience that were needed to give them their present background of behavior, and it is hard for them to go back to the world as seen by children. They need to be effective listeners and also to understand the language of children.

The social needs of children and of all human beings are deep-seated and powerful motivators to behavior. Security in social relationships is a need that influences all that people are and all that they do. Interpersonal relationships with children are a definite therapeutic tool that have a real effect on the course of total learning. Certainly there is a positive relationship between the teachers' understanding of children and the classroom environment.

Some Controversies

The most dramatic examples of the importance of understanding children are seen in situations that involve individual and group behavior and discipline. Some educators believe that teacher-training programs have not given enough attention to preparing teachers to meet these situations. Clichés that insist that the well-managed classroom does not present discipline problems have forced many a worried teacher to try to conceal problems, instead of bringing them out in the open for diagnosis and help. The teacher may feel that failure to solve discipline problems indicates professional weakness. Nor is this feeling of inadequacy restricted to the beginning teacher. The number of years a teacher has taught proves very little. In fact, a teacher may adhere to the same old ways for so long that they come to seem like the only ways. The person does not exist who is so skilled or experienced that he/she cannot increase understanding. The entire staff will benefit from a school atmosphere that fosters mutual growth and understanding. In such an environment occasional mistakes will be seen as the inevitable by-products of any genuine effort to try out new and better approaches to working with students.

Attempts to separate academic training from teaching the "whole child" are unrealistic. It cannot be done. Surely any *good* teacher must work with the entire child and understand and respect that child as an individual.

However, this is not to state that the schools should accept the total responsibility for the total child. If one considers the number of *hours* in a day and in a year, assuming six hours in class each day, the child is in the classroom, at the maximum, slightly less than one-fourth of the day and slightly less than three-sixteenths of the year. The teacher is not expected to perform as a psychiatrist, as a psychologist, or as an educational therapist; nor do the patrons of the schools expect such performance, although implications of early statements of members of the child-centered wing of the Progressive Education Association seem to point to the contrary. This does not mean, however, that the teacher is working with part of a child. Rather, it is to emphasize that the problems of the individual that adversely influence his/her ability to learn and profit from classroom instruction are legitimately a part of the teacher's professional concern. Yet the teacher must not be expected to provide psychiatric care, nor must an entire class suffer in various manners because one individual apparently has "emotional difficulties." This is correct as far as it goes, but it is incomplete.

It has been said that we teach children, not subjects. This statement is not precise. We teach children *mathematics*. We teach children *reading*. We do NOT teach children methodology; we do NOT teach children guidance and counseling. Rather, we use methodology as a vehicle for efficient and profitable instruction; and we employ the techniques of guidance and counseling to assist the individual in the task of learning and to encourage the child to learn to the best of his/her ability. To this extent the school is guidance-centered.

It is sometimes assumed that teachers are selected on the basis of (1) their interest in and love for children, and (2) their college training. Some believe it naturally follows that teachers will be able to teach and that they will have an adequate understanding of children. Unfortunately, interest in children is not necessarily synonymous with understanding. Nor is it synonymous with ability to teach. And college courses are only the starting point. Real understanding is a dynamic force that will demand unending effort on the part of the teacher as each year brings new children—each child an individual and different from all others.

General Principles

Helping teachers understand children is not a topic that can be treated in isolation. It involves all means that are at the disposal of the schools. It is hoped, but never assured, that this will produce insight, understanding, adjustment, and intellectual comprehension of the child by the teacher. It is further hoped that this comprehension will lead to more effective student learning.

The following general principles are intended to serve as guideposts to action:

1. Stimulation of student growth by the teacher depends on a better understanding of students needs, interests, and abilities.
2. Channels of communication must be established between parents, principals, teachers, and classified personnel for the better understanding of each child.
3. Supervisory help should assist teachers in providing an adequate program of testing, measurement, and evaluation for each child.
4. An effective supervisory program will provide the teacher with readily accessible records concerning each child. These records should be comprehensive and cumulative.
5. A sound program of supervision makes readily accessible to the teacher all information that has been gathered from school, home, and community sources.
6. Although general growth sequences can be roughly predicted, children have individual and unique patterns of growth and development.
7. Principals must help eliminate arbitrary and unrealistic marking standards. They must encourage teachers to work with children as individuals with varying interests, abilities, experiences, and achievements.
8. A sound supervisory program can effectively provide child study groups for teachers.
9. A supervisory program designed to help teachers understand children will establish adequate referral methods when assistance outside the province of the school is required. Adequate policies concerning follow-up for cases referred to child welfare agencies must be developed and continuously evaluated.
10. The administration can help teachers understand children by providing sufficient facilities, funds, and staff time for adequate research, study, and conferences.

How to Help the Staff Understand Children through the In-Service Education Program

The in-service education program offers an excellent opportunity for the supervisor to work with the staff in evaluating policies and practices, to discuss new methods and techniques, to review past experiences, and to coordinate future programs. Some useful approaches to understanding children through the in-service education program are discussed here briefly.

Preschool Meetings

Many school systems now utilize the week before classes commence for staff meetings and conferences. For beginning teachers it is "orientation" week. During this week, the teacher has time not only to meet with other staff members, but also to prepare his/her own room environment for the opening of school. Meeting with the supervising principal and with other faculty members, the teacher is introduced to the school plant, other teacher and classified personnel, the size and characteristics of his classes, the cumulative record system, and school policies.

During the year, follow-up conferences should be scheduled, especially with beginning teachers, to discuss the validity of assignments and policies. At the end of the year, a formal evaluation should be made in writing, indicating the successes, failures, and needs and making recommendations for the following year. If feasible, especially in the elementary school, the students' present teacher should confer with the teacher of the next grade in order to facilitate the students' transition. There is, perhaps, no better way to pass on information about children than by personal contact.

Specialists

Another aspect of the in-service education program is to bring to the school system speakers representing specialized fields. This can be done on a district level two or three times a year. Such meetings unify the staff. Specialist-consultants can be secured for a grade level or subject matter area meeting whenever a definite need arises.

System-Wide Programs

Some examples of school system-wide in-service training programs that could help the teacher understand children would be: (1) how to recognize and help the exceptional child, and (2) the selection and use of curriculum materials. Careful organization of the curriculum and selection of materials can help solve classroom problems.

Demonstration Teaching Within the School

Demonstrations within the school are helpful. A teacher could show fellow educators how a certain problem arose in the classroom, the analysis of the problem, the method of solving the problem, and the results obtained.

The use of both teachers and children as active participants in the in-service training program carries the greatest amount of learning with it, for both bring into play the people who are involved in similar situations.

Exchanging Ideas

Another valuable aspect of the in-service education program that the supervisor should not neglect is the exchange of ideas on different grade levels. This practice is especially helpful between the elementary and secondary teachers. The staff of one grade level often is ignorant of the learning that takes place at other levels. They know, of course, that reading, writing, and mathematics were taught, but they are not sure of what children really learned. Consequently, a junior high-school teacher may mutter to himself, "Jimmy didn't learn how to spell in the lower grades"; a sixth-grade teacher may wonder about how much her students learned in the fifth; and so on. If each teacher were aware of the complaints of other teachers, if effective communication were in operation, it would help each teacher evaluate his/her own program. A meeting between different grade levels enhances understanding and teaching.

Coordination and articulation between grade levels should bring about a greater understanding and unity among the staff members, a greater appreciation for the work performed by others, and a strengthening of the instructional program in general.

Collaboration between the several teachers sharing the problems of similar classes offers such obvious advantages that it may mistakenly be assumed that this will happen automatically. Every effort should be made to develop a cooperative feeling between teachers, rather than the competitive one that sometimes prevails.

Within the group setting are many ways in which the supervisor can direct the learning that occurs. Some of the most casual and informal ways are also the most effective For instance, the supervisor might relate personal impressions of appropriate articles or books that he/she is reading and stimulate staff members to read them also. The crucial factor here is that the supervisor is not telling the staff what to do; he/she is doing it and enjoying it. Having led teachers to such outstanding material, the principal will find that most of them will become so interested in the practical nature of the content that they will not require additional outside stimulation.

Another technique is giving recognition to someone taking a graduate course related to child guidance or in educational psychology. Here is a golden opportunity to draw on the opinions and experiences of specialists and experts; it is also an opportunity to give status to the teacher who is attending the class.

Teachers who are taking graduate courses should receive all possible encouragement.

Use of Instructional Technology Materials

Many fine films on child development, fear, rejection, shyness, anger, discipline, learning, and individual differences can be obtained directly from the companies producing them, from city libraries, or from the county or school district audio-visual departments. One of the best printed guides in this area is "Discipline," furnished by The Economics Press, Montclair, New Jersey. This publisher also provides "Classroom Discipline."

In the larger city school system, the supervisor logically would start with materials available within the system's audio-visual department. But these materials should not set a limit to what he/she uses, and interest and suggestions will encourage efforts by the audio-visual department to get the kind of films that the supervisor finds most useful. Some very large systems have produced their own films. "You and Your Classroom," produced by the Los Angeles City Schools, is an example. Although this film does not go into detailed student study, it does present a series of classroom incidents and asks the teacher, "What would you do?"

Such films provide a springboard for a discussion of ways of working with students. The teacher need not feel threatened, as might be the case if the discussion were on how he/she actually handled students in a given situation in their own room. The teacher could talk more objectively and freely, and also could be more open to suggestion and criticism on his/her approach to a problem.

Child-Study Groups

Child-study groups have been established in schools in cooperation with universities that offer college credit for such participation. In other schools they have been initiated by the school system or the principal. In either case, many advantages can be gained from a systematic program of child study.

The supervisor who plans to organize a child-study group within the school may wish to obtain the assistance of outside consultants. The supervisor whose district has set up such a program will want to encourage teacher participation in every way possible.

Interplay of Sociological Factors

There is one common avenue children must take in our society—they must attend school. Here all children come together and compete for status in the democratic educational system of our country. Conflicts in the total school situation can be seen between the working-class children and the middle-class criteria on which the school operates.

Techniques suitable for the middle-class student may be relatively ineffective for lower-class students. These children are likely to be found wanting in the school because of their lack of interest in intellectual achievement and the apparent lack of reinforcement in the home of the school's requirements. Indeed, some educators appear to feel that in certain cases students have been encouraged to "cause problems" through their apparent lack of effort and their disruptive behavior.

Similar conflicts exist between middle-class values of the school staff and lower-class values of many children who attend public schools. It is an important implication that commonly held values form the basis of strong group cohesion in any situation. Teachers, supervisors, and administrators must be recruited from all segments of the population to enhance effective communication and make identification more probable.

SOCIAL CLASS.   As citizens in a democracy, Americans do not like to think of their society as characterized by social class. Unfortunately, there is present in America not only social class, but also caste distinctions as well, although the latter does not have the deep connotation it has in India.

Social class has been defined in many ways; most definitions involve such variables as occupation of the head of household, source of income, housing, and education of the father. One of the most widely used definitions of social class is by A. Hollingshead and F. Redlick.[1] Their "Index of Social Position" is premised on three assumptions: (1) that social stratification exists in the community, (2) that status positions are determined mainly by a few commonly accepted cultural characteristics, and (3) that items symbolic of status may be scaled and combined by the use of statistical procedures.

The most common division of social class by sociologists, as well as by educators and psychologists, is into (1) upper class (relatively aristocratic, well-established people); (2) middle class (the great body of professional and white-collar workers); and (3) lower class, the upper-lower class being made up of skilled workers and the lower-lower class being made up of unskilled workers.

There are social class differences in tastes concerning food, clothing, social cliques, values, religion, intellectual interests, and social beliefs. Middle-class people in general espouse hard work, thrift, ambition, cleanliness, self-control, restraint of sexual and aggressive impulses, honesty and correctness in speech and action, and learning for learning's sake. The school's enrollment form may provide some clues to social class status. Such a form is included as Figure 12-1.

SUPERVISORY IMPLICATIONS OF SOCIAL CLASS STRUCTURE.   Most educators are members of the middle class, and school policy is set by middle-class people. However, their students come from a variety of homes. The gap in values between

[1] August Hollingshead and Frederick Redlick, *Social Class and Mental Illness* (New York: John Wiley & Sons, Inc., 1958), especially chapter III.

FIGURE 12-1.   Enrollment Form Completed When the Student Enters School

KENTON CITY SCHOOLS

School
ENROLLMENT FORM

Child's Name_____Male_____Female_____
        Last   First   Middle

Address_____Phone_____

Birth: Month_____Day _____Year_____City_____State_____

Father's Name_____Birthplace_____
        Last   First

Father's Occupation_____ Employer_____

Father's Business Address_____Phone_____

Mother's Name_____
             Last   First   Maiden Name

Birthplace_____

Mother's Occupation_____Employer_____

Mother's Business Address_____Phone_____

Name of Guardian or Relation_____

(If Child Is Not Living with Mother or Father)

Guardian's Occupation_____

Guardian's Business Address_____Phone_____

Person Authorized to Care for Child in Emergency if Mother and Father
Cannot Be Reached

  Name_____

  Address_____Phone_____

Family Physician_____

  Address_____Phone_____

Is Child Living with (1) Both Parents?_____

             (2) Mother Only?_____

  (3) Father Only?_____(4) Guardian?_____

  (5) Other?_____

Language Spoken in Home_____

Brothers		Sisters	
Older	Younger	Older	Younger
_____	_____	_____	_____
_____	_____	_____	_____
_____	_____	_____	_____

School last Attended: Name_____

City_____State_____Date Left_____

Kenton School Attended Previously_____

middle-class teachers and lower-lower class children is enormous. This implication is equally relevant for other groups, such as public health personnel, speech therapists, recreation specialists, probation officers, and social workers. The identification of persons with other persons who share similar cultural values, attitudes, beliefs, and customs produces group solidarity as well as group differences.

Problems in Effective Communication

Differences in social structure create barriers or tend to break down interclass communications. When there is deficiency in communication, there is little understanding, and when there is little understanding, suspicion and hostility are likely to develop. Hostility, in turn, breeds hostility.

These problems in communication and conflict of interest are particularly severe in public education. Teachers, who usually are middle-class people, must try to communicate clearly and effectively with children of all social classes. Communication problems also exist between different ethnic and national groups. The integration of minority groups into the general population is complicated by their social class position. This position is lower, on the average, than is the position of the so-called core culture. Educators, therefore, always are laboring under the heavy burden of attempting to solve the professional problem of how to balance these sociological forces so that *learning* (we would have said "optimum learning" a few years ago) may take place in the school.

Implications for the Staff

Specifically, supervisors must try to help teachers know these families better and develop a more realistic understanding of the needs of the children and their parents. The staff must examine, justify, and perhaps modify its own system of values in order to develop attitudes of objectivity and acceptance. After investigating these social and psychological problems, L. E. Harper concluded: "If the teacher makes an attempt to understand the possible cultural differences behind behavior, he may even conclude that a different way of looking at such things is as defensible as his own."[2]

How to Help the Teacher Plan for More Effective Parent Conferences

Parents come, or should come, to the teacher to learn about the child and the school. The program for community relations will falter and, perhaps, be doomed

---

[2] Louis E. Harper and Benjamin Wright, "Dealing with Emotional Problems in the Classroom," *Elementary School Journal* LXIII (March 1958): 316–325.

to fail if parent conferences are not properly handled. Only the teacher can tell the parents what his/her plans are for the student's program; only the teacher knows how he/she will attempt to help the student to learn. A child, in relating school happenings to the parents, sees such details from a child's viewpoint, and for this reason the teacher should attempt to schedule frequent interviews with parents.

It is commonly agreed that the home and the school must work closely together if a good educational program is to be developed for students. Yet establishing constructive, positive relationships between teachers and parents is often a slow business. One circumstance that can advance or hinder good parent-school collaboration is how contact between home and school is planned. The importance of satisfactory school-parent contact is directly related to teaching and to understanding children.

Purpose of Conferences

The purposes of the conference or interview with the parent are reciprocal and involve gaining information, acquiring insight, and communicating needs, status, and progress. A. Fenlason[3] noted that the interview was a purposeful conversation. The objectives of the parent-teacher interview are fourfold:

1. To help parents develop an objective concept of the student's capacities and abilities.
2. To acquaint the parents with the student's present status in the teacher's plan.
3. To establish cooperatively specific objectives for the student's growth at the present time.
4. To make plans cooperatively for achieving the objectives.

Further purposes of the parent-teacher conferences may be:

1. To interpret to the parent the student's experiences at school and how he/she is responding to them.
2. To acquaint the parent with the school, its facilities, its personnel, and its work, and thus to further the community relations program.
3. To learn about the student's home environment and relationships important to his/her development—feelings, interests, friends, health, parents' hopes and desires concerning the student.
4. To foster positive relationship between teacher and parent.
5. To discuss ways in which teacher and parent can help each other to help the student.
6. To give the student a sense of confidence and security through the friendship of parent and teacher.
7. To discuss common goals for the student appropriate to his/her stage of development.

[3] Anne Fenlason, *Essentials in Interviewing* (New York: Harper and Row, Publishers, 1952), p. 15.

8. To share observations about the student that parent and teacher interpret together.
9. To plan cooperatively with the parent so that consistent guidance can result and so that the student can meet the same kinds of demands at home and at school.

Most students welcome this planning and give valuable information and clues into their feelings and attitudes.

How to Plan for the Interview

The number of interviews or parent conferences will depend on the problem situation. For each student, if feasible, there should be several interviews. The first contact is usually the initial brief encounter, perhaps with the student present, at the beginning of the school year. Rapport should be developed in the first meeting, regardless of the brevity of the initial contact. Student and parent should feel understood and accepted.

The teacher should encourage the parent to return, but the teacher must take the initiative in planning future conferences according to his/her schedule. Students enjoy having their parents come to school, unless teacher-parent-student relationships have been strained. If negative factors are present, the teacher or staff member must rebuild rapport and understanding. This rebuilding process will be slow.

The supervising principal should stress that in planning interviews with the parent, it is advantageous first to consult the student and discuss what the parent and teacher will be covering. The following outline is a summary of steps in preparation for parent-teacher conferences. These steps should be stressed by the supervisor, and ample opportunity should be given the teacher to ask questions concerning each point.

A. *Preparation by the teacher:*
  1. Review the student's school records, such as cumulative record card, health card, anecdotal record.
  2. Confer with principal, school nurse, or other school personnel to secure most recent information.
  3. Secure samples of student's work from the folder kept throughout the term.
  4. Consider the physical factors involved when the conference is held, such as light, temperature, comfort, the privacy—free from interruptions.
  5. R. H. Hatch[4] intimated that most parents want the same type of information about their children:
     a) What are the strengths and weaknesses of the students?
     b) What special aptitudes does he/she have?

[4] Raymond H. Hatch, *Guidance Service* (Dubuque, Iowa: William C. Brown Company, 1953).

    c) What is his/her learning potential?
    d) What are his/her interests and plans?
    e) What special problems does he/she face?
    f) How does his/her achievement compare with ability?
    g) What can be done for him/her at home?
    h) How may certain home problems be *solved?*
  6. Attempt to make a positive statement concerning the student.
B. *Preparation by the parents:*
Encourage parents to:
  1. Note questions they would like to ask.
  2. Note observations about the student that they feel would help the teacher.
  3. Note unusual health factors, family situations, etc., that may have affected or do affect the student.
  4. List experiences that may explain present behavior.
  5. List special interests or abilities.

These preparatory steps serve as a base from which good parent-teacher conferences can develop. Implied is careful interpretation so that the information will be *objective* and *acceptable*. It is offered that perhaps the most important preparation that both the parent and the teacher can make is developing an attitude of accepting the other as a true partner in the joint task of helping the student enjoy school and social relationships and of creating a happy and stimulating environment in which the student will want to learn.

The Conference

ACCEPTANCE AND EMPATHY.   The first element of expertness in interpersonal relations is respect for the other person and awareness of the other person's feeling of security.[5] The teacher must be able to accept and understand individual differences in heredity, background, experience, and attitude as the basis of acceptance and understanding of both parent and student.

The teacher must be particularly aware of the parent's feelings as the parent faces the authority figure of his/her own childhood. For many parents, school has meant (and still means) a threatening place with many traumatic events and scars on the memory. There are certain limits set on the student through the behavior of parents and other people in his life, as they relive their early school experiences through their children.

Some teachers have found it wiser to play the role of naïve observer when interviewing parents. The teacher should allow the parent to be the expert regarding his child. For example, the teacher may say, "I noticed that Paul seems to be less interested in . . . and I wondered if something might have happened that

[5] See H. S. Sullivan, *The Interpersonal Theory of Psychiatry* (New York: W. W. Norton & Company, Inc., 1953).

TABLE 12-1.   Some DO's and DON'T s—Meeting with the Parent

1. Try to arrange the conference so that there will be no interruptions.
2. The teacher's greeting should be warm and friendly, with a warm-up topic to open the conversation.
3. Begin with a positive statement of the student's abilities. The parent is less defensive, and it conveys interest and liking for the student.
4. Share observations about the student, comparing responses at home and at school before making an interpretation or judgment.
5. Let any advice grow out of mutual discussion and a growing insight on the part of the parent into the reasons for the behavior.
6. Discover how the parent is thinking and feeling about the student. The teacher cannot understand the student's behavior until he/she knows the parent's attitude.
7. Listen to the parent's complaints or criticisms of the school, accepting them as evidence of interest or as suggestions to be considered.
8. If a parent gives his/her reason for the student's behavior, accept it, and, if possible, lead the discussion on to other possible causes. Behavior is a result of many causative factors.
9. Listen, and then listen some more. The teacher did not invite the parent to lecture but to obtain as well as give help. *Encourage the parent to talk, and listen to what is said.*
10. Try to close the conference with a constructive, hopeful statement.
11. It is easier to build a cooperative relationship if the teacher is not behind a desk. (Use a table if available.)
12. The educator should *not* argue with a parent. Arguing will arouse resentment.
13. The teacher should *not* try to push his/her thinking onto a parent. Conclusions and recommendations should be reached through a process of discussion and mutual thinking.
14. The teacher should *not* criticize harshly or negatively. Destructive criticism can be fatal to build a cooperative relationship in parent-teacher conferences since most parents cannot be objective about their children. The emotional involvement is too great.
15. The educator should *not* give direct advice unless it is requested, and never as the single successful solution.
16. Do *not* imply that the parent or home is to blame for the student's behavior.
17. Do *not* overlook influences other than the home on the student's life.
18. *Avoid* discussing other children in the school. Such comments direct attention from the problem at hand, encourage competitiveness, and often harm school and neighborhood relationships.
19. Do *not* use blanket words such as immaturity and insecurity.
20. Do *not* assume that the parents want help or advice. Such assumption usually brings resistance because it implies a form of criticism.
21. Do *not* criticize or blame past school experiences or teachers because such comments tend to destroy confidence in all education. Attention should be centered on present needs and on plans for the future, not on past mistakes.

you feel has caused this trouble?" For the most part, the parent will react to this invitation to be the one who knows most about the student. Parents believe they know their children better than anyone else, and perhaps they do, unless they are too emotionally involved. It is important for the teacher to remember that it is unwise to play the role of the expert with people who may feel insecure. What happens when the parents face the authority figure of their childhood?

One supervising principal listed some techniques for the conference, which appear in Table 12-1.

COMMUNICATION IN PARENT-TEACHER CONFERENCES. The supervisor may wish to encourage the teacher to have a set of carefully prepared questions that he/she introduces into the conversation tactfully at the appropriate time.

How a question is formulated has a definite bearing on responses. The teacher should realize that human beings are always protecting their egos. There is a desire to protect one's psychological integrity in all interpersonal contacts. Teachers must be sensitive to the desire of parents to impress and to repress. An attempt should be made to get the parents to say what is necessary without their feeling that their psychological integrity is in danger. The parents may have difficulty in accepting an idea they interpret as reflecting on them in a socially undesirable manner. The chief barrier to communication in such situations may be anxiety.

The supervisor should help the teacher be alert to the many factors that may detract from the interview situation. Among these are hesitancy, indecisiveness, tenseness, fatigue, apathy, sadness, overdramatics, elation, contradictory statements, mannerisms, and gestures. The teacher should attempt to establish some congruity between verbal and nonverbal behavior in the search for clues to understanding the child he/she attempts to teach.

Successful interviewing is an art and requires experience for optimum results. The relationship should permit the parents to express thoughts and feelings with the knowledge that they will be listened to and understood by a sympathetic and accepting person who, in understanding and accepting, helps the parents understand and accept both themselves and the student.

How to Help the Staff Understand Children through Health Records, Observation, Anecdotal Records, and Related Techniques

Health Records

One obvious source of information that often is overlooked is the health record. A parent often assumes that because the kindergarten teacher knew Diana had a hearing loss, this information will automatically be communicated to subsequent teachers. If the next teacher fails to talk to the nurse or to read the health card, and if this information is not in the cumulative folder, that teacher may interpret the hearing loss as dullness and inattentiveness. If success is especially important to Diana, she may learn to camouflage her handicap by copying her neighbors' work. One second-grade girl managed to conceal her deafness from the audiometrist the first time she was tested!

CUMULATIVE FOLDERS CONTAIN HEALTH INFORMATION. Cumulative folders, which can include psychological and health records, are excellent sources of information. A conscientious teacher should be encouraged to use this kind of information before the semester begins.

ADJUNCT HEALTH INFORMATION. Information concerning the health reasons for which children may be excluded from school, general information concerning communicable diseases, and other health data of concern to teachers and parents should be made available by the supervising principal.

Observation and Listening

Observation and listening are basic ingredients in all techniques that develop teacher understanding of children. Supervisors can help teachers improve their observation techniques. G. P. Driscoll suggested that teachers watch for children whose responses to situations are inappropriate, and, believing that every response must have a cause, seek out that cause. She listed four directives based on observation as the principal method in the study of children's behavior:

1. Use school situations to observe behavior.
2. Learn to describe behavior objectively.
3. Study cumulative descriptions of behavior; don't spend too much time directing behavior—study it.
4. Study the child from the standpoint of his developmental age, i.e., his physical, intellectual, and social development.[6]

   School situations provide a wide variety of opportunities for observing students. For example, the teacher can discover a lot about a student by developing an awareness of the messages conveyed through his/her creative products.
   Observing children at play can provide valuable insights into their behavior and is used widely in child guidance clinics. Much of the same insight can be derived by the teacher from studying the particular item that the student draws, writes, models, or represents dramatically.
   The teacher is not a therapist and should not try to go beyond his/her

------

[6] Reprinted with permission of the publisher from Gertrude P. Driscoll, *Child Guidance in the Classroom* (New York: Bureau of Publications, Teachers College, Columbia University, 1955), p. 27.

own role as a teacher in analyzing what he/she finds in a student's products, but the supervising principal should encourage the teacher to watch for extremes that indicate the possible need for psychological study. The teacher may be the first person to note an extreme individual difference in a student that would pass unnoticed in the student's home setting.

Take, for example, the case of twelve-year-old Joseph, who loved jigsaw puzzles but could not assemble them without extreme rigidity and tremor of the hand. His handwriting invariably was traced and retraced, until the page was smudgy and torn. In other respects he was a tidy, well-mannered youngster whose oral responses were well above average. A perceptive teacher would question the reasons for the disparity between written and oral work and look for some answers.

Learning to describe behavior objectively sharpens the teacher's awareness of how subjective we really are in our daily conversation and thinking. As he/she becomes aware of this, the teacher will discover that it is possible to accept and understand a student without judging him/her.

The importance of objective description will be most obvious in analyzing and maintaining student personnel records. Some teachers say they do not care to read cumulative records since they fear they will be prejudiced by the impressions of previous teachers. Even though the concern for impartiality is commendable, it would be more constructive if they would learn to distinguish between subjective and objective description. A discerning observer will do this and will try to base opinions on facts and on factual, objective accounts, rather than on another person's opinion.

C. E. Moustakas[7] urged teachers to listen to students as they express themselves, without trying to press their own thinking and feelings on them. The teacher who spends too much time talking will have little time to study behavior. Being a good listener is one of the best ways to maintain clear channels of communication. Teachers sometimes feel that they must have an immediate answer for everything. Teachers, and supervisors, and administrators should strive to become more skilled in the art of listening.

Anecdotal Records

Anecdotal records offer the advantage of being written. Time has a way of clouding and confusing the true picture even when seen by the most skilled listener and observer who, after all, may infect personal biases into observations and recordings.

The anecdotal record is a study device for improving professional insights that may be sparse but should eventually develop into a rather free-flowing, selective, many-sided collection of vivid and detailed information about a student. It is

[7] Clark E. Moustakas, *The Teacher and the Child: Personal Interaction in the Classroom* (New York: McGraw-Hill Book Company, Inc., 1956), p. 42.

important that the teacher feel free to give a picture of the student as he/she appears in order to facilitate recording.

It is unfortunate that some school systems are so fearful of lawsuits and/or parental criticism that incomplete, inaccurate, or even dishonest written comments by teachers are encouraged to avoid rocking the educational ship of state. These systems would do better by emphasizing objective record-keeping free from malice.

The value of anecdotal records in helping one understand the role he/she plays in the school situation becomes more apparent in their use in the study group. Here the group members can help one another with short cuts and suggestions about techniques and meanings. A kind of "co-responsibility for professional understanding of teachers' difficulties, as well as those of the child, develops."[8]

How to Help the Teacher Record and Interpret Anecdotal Records

SUGGESTIONS FOR RECORDING.   The following suggestions may be useful in helping the teacher record and interpret anecdotal records.

1. The form used for recording anecdotes should be short and informal, including the name of the student, date, situation or setting, description of behavior, and observer's name (see Figure 12-2).
2. Brief sentences are advisable, with a minimum of adverbs and adjectives.
3. Anecdotal records should contain objective statements such as, "Glenn offered to show Bruce a new game," rather than, "Glenn is a helpful student."
4. Both strengths and weaknesses should be reported.
5. Anecdotes do not suggest meaning or ideas not supported by facts. The following statement, "Bill poked Gary during reading class," is better than, "Bill poked Gary as soon as I was busy helping Esther." The latter implies deceit.

FIGURE 12-2.   Anecdotal Record Card

Name of Student _____

Date _____

Setting _____

Anecdote _____

_____

_____

Teacher _____

[8] California School Board Association of the California Teachers Association, *Sample Personnel Policies*, Third Progress Report, Joint Committee on Personnel (San Francisco: The Association, October 1954), p. 200.

6. The facts should be presented without interpretation. "Darlene is lazy" is neither objective nor descriptive of an incident.
7. Because behavior is conditioned by the situation or environment in which it occurs, it is advisable to record the setting.
8. Record the ancedote as soon as possible after the incident.

USES AND LIMITATIONS OF THE ANECDOTAL RECORD. A survey revealed the following uses:

1. Anecdotal records facilitate the understanding of personality and increase teacher ability to interpret behavior.
2. They provide a picture of the pattern of the student's behavior.
3. They help evaluate materials for sections of the cumulative record card.
4. They serve as a basis for student and parent conferences. Dated written descriptions of specific behavior are more satisfactory than vague recollections.

Teachers and supervisors have noted the following limitations with the greatest frequency:

1. Possible subjectivity of anecdotal records may lead to inaccurate or faulty interpretation.
2. The observer's personal reaction to certain types of behavior may color the description or influence the selection of incidents.
3. There may be a tendency toward regarding only negative behavior. Positive factors should be recorded in order to give a complete picture of the student's behavior.
4. Lack of setting or background can limit the interpretation of data.
5. Quiet, submissive behavior may be more significant than the aggressive, overt type, but may be more difficult to detect and record.
6. Interpretations from anecdotal records do not form conclusive evidence but are considered in the light of other findings.

Anecdotal records, then, are records of facts as objective as we can make them; they are *not* interpretations. They contain details recording specific situations. The date, the situation, a brief description of behavior, possible explanation, and the recorder's signature constitute one entry. This record often is kept for some time in order to better establish patterns of behavior.

These records may be used to gain insight into a student's development— a comparison between present behavior and that previously recorded—to determine consistent characteristics as opposed to new growth. The records may sometimes be used as a basis for a cooperative conference with parents, teacher, nurse, supervising principal, and psychologist.

The importance of anecdotal records as documentation for a principal who is considering some special action cannot be overlooked. An accurate anecdotal record often indicates the best possible solution for the student and the school.

Checklists and Rating Scales

Checklists and rating scales are used for summarizing observations of student behavior and abilities. These forms are employed widely as economical methods of categorizing information about groups as well as about individuals.

Checklists can be used to indicate teacher judgment relative to whether certain behavior traits, social attributes, abilities, interests, and personality characteristics are present. Figure 12-3 is an example of a checklist concerning student responsibility.

Rating scales may list the same type of traits and characteristics as checklists. In rating scales, however, the items are worked on gradual value scales. Rating scales also are used for evaluating students in relation to objectives of the instructional program. A rating scale in the area of work habits is shown as Figure 12-4.

USES OF CHECKLISTS AND RATING SCALES.   The following is a list of uses of checklists and rating scales that the supervisor could suggest:

1. Checklists and rating scales provide a specific situation for observation.
2. They provide an evaluation of a student's emotional and social adjustment, interests, and values.
3. They provide for observation of behavior in relation to established objectives.

LIMITATIONS OF CHECKLISTS AND RATING SCALES.   The supervisor should bring the following limitations of these instruments to the attention of the teacher:

1. Observation is limited to items on the list.
2. Data are relatively subjective in that judgments of the observer are recorded.

FIGURE 12-3.   Responsibility Checklist

Names	Usually Does His Best	Good Leader	Good Follower	Continues at Task Until Finished	Cooperates with Fellow Students	Dependable	Follows Directions

FIGURE 12-4.   Rating Scale

	Consistently	Most of the Time	Some of the Time	Seldom	Never
Follows directions					
Works independently					
Shows initiative					
Completes work					
Enjoys work					

3. Lack of common agreement concerning the meaning of behavior traits may influence the use of these data.
4. Reliability of these forms varies with the trait observed.

The Autobiography

The autobiography is a valuable technique for obtaining information about students. Teachers need supervisory help in interpretation. A student's version of his life story will give clues about his regard for self, his interests, problems, friends, and past experiences.

Autobiographies can be written either in narrative or story form, or the form may be construed to provide information in particular areas. The following outline may suggest topics for the autobiography:

1. My life before I went to school
    a) My birthplace
    b) Places I have lived
    c) My family
    d) My best friends
    e) Activities I enjoy
2. My life since I've come to school
    a) My best friends
    b) My favorite games, work, and hobbies
    c) My happiest time at school
    d) My happiest time at home
    e) My favorite subject in school
    f) My least favorite subject in school
    g) Plans for work after I complete my schooling

USES OF AUTOBIOGRAPHIES.   The uses of the autobiography include the following:

1. The autobiography is useful as a supplementary procedure for collecting information about all students and will be particularly useful in obtaining information about students new to the school.
2. It can be used to appraise changes in student adjustment.
3. Student attitudes toward school, health, teachers, parents, associates, and self are sometimes revealed through these written accounts of personal experiences.

LIMITATIONS OF AUTOBIOGRAPHIES.   The supervisor should note the following limitations:

1. Data must be interpreted in the light of their subjectivity.
2. Lapse of time between the occurrence of the event and the recording may affect recall.
3. Student may incorrectly interpret events in order to rationalize or excuse problems. This possibility presents limitations in accepting all information at face value but can be of aid in seeing the situation as the student perceives it.

Unfinished Stories and Sentences

Teachers can obtain information about students' ideas and attitudes from their written and oral compositions. Sometimes unfinished sentences and stories, designed to reveal students' attitudes about specific situations and problems, are particularly useful for this purpose. The teacher may provide pupils with a short story or a list of sentences without endings and encourage the students to complete them. The unfinished story below has been used by a supervising principal in an elementary school.

> One day Leo and Sol were walking along the street near the school. As they walked, they noticed a wallet which had evidently been dropped from a passing car. The boys hurried to pick up the wallet and examine it. They found two five dollar bills. Leo suggested that they _____
>
> _____
> _____
> _____
> _____

How to Help the Staff Understand
Students through Intervisitation

Supervisory observation takes two main forms: (1) observation by the supervising principal, specialist-consultant, or counselor for supervisory or administrative purposes; and (2) observations by the teacher of techniques used by another instructor. The latter is termed "intervisitation."

The school system should have a policy of allowing teachers to observe other teachers at least once or twice a year. These observations should be arranged beforehand, with a definite purpose in mind. For example, a teacher in the fifth grade may observe the techniques employed by another in teaching social studies as he/she presents a certain concept about the "westward movement" or initiates work on a mural about this segment of American history. While this intervisitation could quite easily be accommodated within the teacher's own school, it often is advisable to visit another school or one outside the district in order to see different viewpoints and methods in teaching the subjects, as well as for morale reasons.

The school system should provide a substitute for the teacher while he/she observes in another room. It is advisable for the principal or staff specialist-consultant to accompany the teacher. Preparation always should precede the observation. For a description of how the supervisor can prepare for and handle intervisitation, see chapter 7.

How to Help the Staff Understand
Students through the Interstaff Conference

Interstaff Conferences

Conferences with other staff members are extremely helpful in supplementing the teacher's understanding of children, and they are a good way to delve professionally into a student's problems. The most important type of conference is one with representatives from the classroom, health office, guidance, supervision, and administration. Participation in the conference would be a function of the nature of the problem. The results of the conference should be summarized and entered in the student's cumulative record.

A schedule of action for interstaff conferences in an Illinois school district follows:

Meeting 1: Describe the plan for the series of meetings. Discuss the problem areas found in the school. Each participant should keep a written record of findings. Each group or member of a group selects a student for study.

Meeting 2: Discuss the problems chosen for study. State tentative hypotheses. Agree on initial data needed for studies. Bring any sample data that may prove useful.

Meeting 3: Share initial data related to original plans, and agree on further data to be gathered.

Meeting 4: Meeting 4 is initially the same as Meeting 3, in that data are shared and an agreement is reached as to what further data are needed. Share any individual problems that have arisen. The group may try to suggest helpful answers.

Meetings
5, 6, 7:   Share further data and suggest remedies for student adjustment. Include the action in written records being kept. Agree on further data needed concerning the student.

Meetings
8, 9, 10:   Use additional data to test remedial action. Agree on further data needed. Share any progress or setbacks in individual behavior with the group.

Meetings
11, 12 13:   Report on some conclusions reached—the applications, implications, and suggestions from studies which the group has carried on.

Meeting 14:   Provide for continuous evaluation and plan for future action.

Roles in Interstaff Teamwork

By observing students at work and play, other members of the school staff may better understand them. Classified personnel also need to understand students' feelings, but they are seldom trained in this field. They must work with students in the office and on the grounds, and often they must work with a wider age span than does the teacher. Custodians, secretaries, and cafeteria workers often need help in understanding and working with students.

A friendly and interested feeling between adult and student benefits both. The supervisor may point out that the adult who is objective and sympathetic and who shows sincere interest can command a student's respect from the beginning; but preaching and moralizing will lose a student's attention almost immediately.

Tone of voice and facial expression may frighten a student before there has been any effective communication. A smile and quiet voice with secure sounding overtones help give a student a feeling of security and confidence.

Playground directors may sometimes watch student activities looking only for signs of trouble, instead of looking for positive behavior. Much real insight into the behavior of students is gained by watching them objectively at play while they are absorbed and unaware of the observation. Posture, activity, laughter, tears, and voice pitch are just a few factors that may indicate health problems or emotional strain that need further investigation. A supervisor who is aware of these factors can enlist the aid of the teacher and playground director for some really purposeful observation.

THE SUPERVISING PRINCIPAL. The principal has overall responsibility for the guidance program within the school. The program's success depends on his/her leadership in determining the needs, as well as initiating means of meeting the needs. There is no phase of the guidance program with which he/she is not directly concerned. The principal functions as leader of the guidance staff in organizing, supervising, coordinating, and administering the program. A few of the individuals whose efforts the principal coordinates are caricatured in Figure 12-5.

FIGURE 12-5.   Many Individuals May Contribute Valuable Information Based on Observation of the Student at Work and Play.

The principal provides the leadership for the teachers in increasing their understanding of, and their capacity for, molding student behavior. He/she accomplishes this by setting a good example, by coordinating in-service educational activities, by suggestion, and by furnishing or recommending materials for individual student study. The principal also arranges placement in special classes or schools, helps improve school and parent relationships, and maintains contact with all referral agencies

WHAT THE SUPERVISING PRINCIPAL CAN DO: FURTHER TECHNIQUES.   Is it true, as some believe, that the greatest weakness of supervisors, as well as administrators, is their poor relationships with teachers? The best possible place to start building an understanding of children is developing the best possible relationships between the supervisor and the rest of the instructional staff:

1.   *Teachers want supervisory leaders who create an informal atmosphere and who appreciate effective group participation.* This appreciation helps teachers place more emphasis on the cooperative clinical team approach to the diagnosis of student difficulties as a requisite for dealing with individual needs. Teachers sense the need for more assistance with problems related to diagnosis, remediation, and evaluation in working with students. The supervisor's understanding helps.
2.   *Often teachers are not sufficiently informed of effective ways and means of working with children.* Desirable supervisory assistance is democratic, provides suggestions, yet permits freedom of initiative, choice, and independence in carrying out suggestions. The supervisor who strives to understand teachers will use every contact, whether a casual comment in the hallway or a private supervisory conference, to build teacher confidence.

3. *The next step is to help the teacher understand him/herself and the roles as a teacher.* The supervisor is in a unique position to help the teacher adjust to the welter of expectations and demands that teaching roles make. No one teacher can be expert and comfortable in every role that parents, students, the community, and the administration may expect; but, with help and support to ease tensions, the teacher can discover where real strengths lie. Having learned to understand his/her own experiences, the teacher will then be better able to help students understand their reactions to the environment in which they live.

THE SUPERVISOR OF GUIDANCE.   In school systems employing a supervisor of guidance, he/she is responsible for improving the operation of the individual and group guidance programs in each school. The duties of the supervisor of guidance are as follows:

1. He/she plans and supervises programs of help for individual students by:
    a) Cooperating with the staff in gathering information about students
    b) Aiding in counseling
    c) Conferring with school personnel on strengths and weaknesses of individual students and recommending adjustment in student placement where indicated
    d) Helping with follow-up devices.
2. He/she plans and supervises the group program by:
    a) Conferring with principals on learning trends as implied from performance on standardized tests
    b) Conferring with teachers on strengths and weaknesses revealed through test results
    c) Assisting principals and teachers regarding student placement, acceleration, retardation, and changes in grouping
    d) Providing for individual needs through organization of special classes, and making recommendations for placement of students in these classes.
3. He/she assists in the construction, revision, and interpretation of:
    a) Report card forms
    b) Cumulative record cards
    c) Remedial reading record forms
    d) Welfare cards
    e) Authorization cards to administer group intelligence tests
    f) Interschool transfer data cards
4. He/she assists in research projects regarding:
    a) New tests and other techniques
    b) Articulation between schools
    c) Selection and appraisal of rapid learners
    d) Study of potential "dropouts"
    e) Reporting to parents.
5. He/she plans and conducts in-service education, which includes:
    a) Training teachers to administer and interpret group tests
    b) Orientation meetings of beginning teachers
    c) Institutes in guidance and counseling

d) Guidance workshops
e) Faculty meetings.

THE SCHOOL COUNSELOR.   The school counselor makes individual psychological studies of students who have special needs for the purpose of helping these students make a more satisfactory adjustment in school. The duties and responsibilities of the school counselor fall into two broad categories:

1. Direct service to students, teachers, principals, and parents by:
   a) Making psychological studies of students who are presenting problems of school achievement and personal adjustment
   b) Administering individual psychological examinations to these students and assembling all data necessary to understand their needs
   c) Securing the necessary assistance from other resources of the school system and community agencies in making such studies
   d) Interpreting the findings of these studies to principals, teachers, parents, and others directly concerned with the welfare of the individual student
   e) Recommending a program for the adjustment of students as determined by studies
   f) Continuing follow-up studies of students needing such help
   g) Providing consultant service to principals, teachers, and parents concerning the needs of students.
2. Staff duties and responsibilities consist of:
   a) Assisting in integrating counseling activities with the activities of other staff members within the division to promote a coordinated educational program
   b) Assisting in advancing the understanding of school personnel in the principles and recent research in the fields of mental hygiene and child growth and development
   c) Assisting with organization and leadership of teacher in-service training activities in the area of individual study of children
   d) Serving as speaker for school and community groups.

Increasingly, schools are obtaining specialists to help teachers understand and plan for students more adequately. These specialists, through diagnostic and therapeutic procedures, aid in student adjustment and educational planning. Maximum aid is given to teachers and students when efforts of the various specialists are coordinated within the school—when each special resource person is able to work as a member of a team.

FACULTY GUIDANCE COMMITTEE.   Principals may profit from the help of a guidance advisory committee. This committee serves a dual purpose. First, the committee makes recommendations about improving the guidance and counseling program. Second, questions may be referred to the guidance committee for reactions and recommendations. The chairperson of the guidance committee can do much to support the principal and improve guidance services in the school.

THE CLINICAL TEAM.   The clinical team approach is vital in obtaining adequate information about a student with special needs, in interpreting the findings, and in planning a course of action aimed at correcting deficiencies and building on strengths.

THE SCHOOL NURSE AND PHYSICIAN.   The student's health should be considered first. As guidance and counseling personnel study the student's personality development, mental growth, and attainments in basic learnings, cooperative planning with the school nurse and physician is imperative.

Through the school physician, nurse, and other related personnel, each school is given the medical service necessary to identify any defects that might impede the student's maximum development. Health personnel also are vitally interested in helping students establish proper health habits. They work in this area not only through direct contact with students but also through faculty discussions and by preparing materials for teachers to use in the health education program.

EVALUATION AND RESEARCH.   Guidance and counseling personnel work closely with those responsible for evaluation and research. In small school systems, the counselors are responsible for planning the various evaluation programs in schools and for interpreting results to the administration, the board of education, and the general public. In larger systems, a special evaluation and research section, which conducts research in various guidance areas including vocational guidance, is becoming more prevalent.

CHILD WELFARE AND ATTENDANCE PERSONNEL.   Guidance workers work closely with child welfare attendance personnel. Welfare and attendance personnel are concerned with adjustment difficulties of students as manifested by irregular school attendance. Welfare and attendance personnel usually work with problems that may be manifested in school but that are chiefly home- or community-centered, and they provide for referral to community agencies.

A WEAK LINK IN THE COUNSELING CHAIN.   Follow-up after initial study and evaluation often is the weakest link in the counseling program. Programs sometimes are planned to help a student, but due to an overloaded staff the programs are not evaluated and replanned throughout the school career of the student involved. In some instances, the student may no longer need any special guidance, but this information may not be recorded for future reference. Two forms used by one school system for referrals and reports in this area are included as Figures 12-6 and 12-7.

Since not all schools have the advantage of a full time nurse and psychologist, the principal must be able to aid the classroom teacher toward the best possible working relationships with parents and students.

The principal, as the leader in the school, can help all persons involved realize that improvement takes time and patience, as well as effort.

FIGURE 12-6.   Request for Study

(Name of School District)

Date _____

1. Identifying information:
   (to be obtained by school employee)

   Name _____

   Age _____ Birthdate _____ Grade _____

   Address _____ Phone _____
           Street   City   Zone

   School _____ Phone _____

   Father _____ Age _____
                Name

   Mother _____ Age _____
                Name

   Other Children: _____ _____

   _____ _____

2. Problem for which you wish child examined: _____

3. Description of school behavior: _____
   (Teachers, principals, counselors, etc.)

4. Record of scholastic capacity and educational achievement:
   (Copy latest test data from cumulative card)

   Date _____ Grade _____ Test_____

   Ch. Age _____ Ment. Age_____ Index_____

   XA—GP _____ Reading GP—Voc. _____

                       —Comp. _____

                       Arith. GP—Reas. _____

                       Fund._____

   Lang. GP_____ Spell. GP_____

5a. Any health data you have: _____

 b. Please list other clinics, hospitals, agencies, doctors, etc. to whom child
    and family are known: _____

6. Any social or family data you may already have: _____
   (Home calls and social history not essential.)

7 Signature of Principal_____

   Name of person who
   conferred with parent
   about referral_____

   Name of others concerned with child's problem:

   _____ _____

FIGURE 12-7.   Consent Slip

Date _____

This consent will authorize the School Guidance Center to carry out such physical, psychological, psychiatric, laboratory, and other examinations and treatments for my_____ , _____
Relation   Name of Child
as may be deemed advisable by the School Guidance Center.

_____
Parent or Legal Guardian

Success, the Teacher, and the Guidance Program

The success of the individual teacher depends largely on assistance given by others in the school, especially the technical assistance of the supervisor and the administrative assistance of the principal.

Certainly, the principal has overall responsibility for the guidance program within the school. Success of the guidance program depends on the leadership of the principal in determining needs as well as in initiating means of meeting the needs. There is no phase of the guidance program with which the principal is not directly concerned. The supervising principal functions as leader of the guidance staff in organizing, supervising, coordinating, and administering the program. It is, however, a teacher sensitive to the needs of the students who is the foundation on which any good guidance program is built. The teacher at all levels should:

1. Understand and carry out the guidance policies and procedures within the school facilities.
2. Provide classroom atmosphere that is conducive to guidance.
3. Help each student develop a sense of belonging.
4. Know each student's strengths and weaknesses and accept him/her as a person.
5. Perceive significant attitudes, abilities, behavior, and health of students; and in light of these findings provide for individual needs.
6. Provide group and individual guidance opportunities in the classroom.
7. Guide each student in developing good study habits.
8. Provide opportunities for continuous evaluation and appraisal of student growth and achievement in skills and attitudes.
9. Assist students to understand and accept attitudes and habits of good citizenship.
10. Teach basic concepts of moral and spiritual values.
11. Obtain pertinent information and records that have permanent value.
12. Select carefully, from available sources, information that can be used for effective guidance.
13 Adapt instruction to the range of individual differences.

14. Attempt to work out problems of student adjustment from the point of view that guidance is based on friendliness, mutual respect, and understanding.
15. Encourage a balance of varied experiences in curricular and extracurricular fields.
16. Make suitable referrals of individuals who need additional help or study, and contribute pertinent information.
17. Participate in case studies and conferences concerning students.
18. Follow up recommendations for improving student adjustment.
19. Participate in evaluation of school and district guidance programs.
20. Accept responsibility for professional growth.

Particularly at the *elementary school* level, the teacher should:

1. Help students cope with the transition from home to school.
2. Know the students' parents and maintain a close relationship with them.
3. Adapt instruction to the range of individual differences through grouping and adjustment of method and curriculum within the class.
4. Notify and confer periodically with parents on student achievement and social growth.
5. Prepare students for transfer to the secondary school.

Criteria for the Study of an Individual Student by the Teacher

The supervising principal should help teachers understand the characteristics of the age groups with which they are to work. Helping teachers realize the importance of listening to students and watching them purposefully is another important responsibility of the supervisor.

The supervising principal should provide data and assistance so that a teacher may study and weigh carefully the many factors involved before planning a program of adjustment for the student. The effectiveness of a teacher in classroom situations often is determined by the teacher's acquaintance with the developmental history of each student.

Perhaps the principal's most important role in this area is to insure that each staff member is familiar with the many criteria for the individual study of a student. The supervisor should stress the following:

1. *Observation.* The teacher watches for activities in which the student shows the most interest and response, has the most success, or shows the most fatigue or boredom.
2. *Health.* Cumulative health records that have been kept up-to-date are valuable. Responses to food, amount of activity shown in the classroom and on the playground, nail-biting, and frequent tardiness are other signs for the teacher to note.
3. *Social relationship.* The careful use of a sociogram may show situations in which a student lacks confidence or security.

4. *Time-sampling observation.* The teacher can observe a certain student for a week at preplanned intervals in the school day and record observations. A period of five minutes at nine o'clock, another five minutes at ten-thirty, and another five minutes after lunch can give a broad and realistic picture of a student's normal behavior.
5. *Particular situation observation.* The teacher can observe and record the different responses of several students in a special situation. This method helps the teacher plan for individual and group needs.
6. *Interests.* A questionnaire concerning daily activities, hobbies, family relationships, or any number of other things can help the teacher plan a program. In one situation, the students kept a diary, noting daily activities, books they had read, satisfactory situations and experiences, and their successes or failures. The teacher involved gained valuable information about each student's daily thinking through this method of observation.
7. *Achievement.* Test achievement does not always give a clear picture of a student's ability or daily achievement. Samples of the student's work in handwriting, arithmetic, art, and all other areas, taken at regular intervals, show any weaknesses as well as growth and improvement. The testing program per se is considered later in this chapter.

OBSERVATION BY THE PARENT.   For additional data to add to the teacher's methods of observation, the health record, the cumulative record, and an observation form for parents may be employed. Parents who are eager to help their children often welcome this personal participation. A copy of a parent observation form used in a midwest school system is included as Figure 12-8.

CLASSROOM COUNSELOR.   The teacher should know how to act in the role of classroom counselor in order to earn the student's respect and to facilitate his/her adjustment to the classroom environment. The principal should discuss this role at staff meetings. Guidance personnel and specialist-consultants from the nearby university can be called in for further assistance. The teacher should take extension or university classes to enrich his/her background.

How to Help Teachers Understand Students Through Cumulative Records

Cumulative records can be defined as permanent records of pupil progress and adjustment in school. A cumulative record may contain the following information:

1. Identification and personal data
2. School history
3. Family and home data
4. Educational and mental development
5. Emotional development and attitudes

FIGURE 12-8.   Parent Observation Form

Student's Name_____

PARENT'S OBSERVATIONS

1. Are there any health problems that may be related to the child's behavior?

2. How does he get along with his brothers and sisters? With children in the neighborhood?

3. What are the child's interests and abilities?

4 What forms of discipline have been used?
   How does he respond?

5. For what is he usually punished?
   For what is he praised?

6. What have you found to be the most satisfactory ways of helping your child with his problems?

7. How does he act when he succeeds?

8. How does he act when he fails?

9. What does he like to do in his spare time?

10. Do you approve of his friends?

11. Does he like school?

12. What jobs does the child have around the home?
    What does he do best?
    What is the most difficult for him?

13. What do you consider to be the child's chief problem, and what do you believe is the cause?

Signature _____

Date _____

---

6. Social adjustment and attitudes
7. Health and physical development
8. School experiences and plans
9. Special activities and interests
10. References to other sources of information

Cumulative records: (1) serve as a basic student guidance tool for teachers, counselors, specialist-consultants, and administrators; (2) provide assistance in planning school policy and curriculum; (3) furnish a basis for planning student programs; and (4) serve as a means for identifying student differences and group tendencies.

Suggestions for Cumulative Records

Comments should help a teacher understand the student and his/her needs. They should convey usable, accurate information. They should not be a record of the teacher's emotional reactions.

Comments should be as objective and specific as possible. Instead of using comments such as "improving" or "good worker," the subjects or character traits in which the student shows or needs improvement should be indicated.

Criteria for determining location of files that the supervising principal should consider are:

1. Safety and security of the records
2. Accessibility of records to all staff members
3. Convenience of location to those persons using them frequently
4. Available facilities.

CUMULATIVE RECORDS CAN BE TRANSFERRED AND DUPLICATED. Cumulative records generally can be transferred to another public school, public agency, private school, or private agency when a student transfers to such agency. A record of the pupil enrollment and scholarship should be retained by the school system from which the student has transferred. The following information should be kept:

1. Name of student
2. Date of birth, if student is a minor
3. Method of verification of date of birth of student being admitted to kindergarten or first grade
4. Place of birth
5. Name and address of parents or guardian, if student is a minor
6. Entering and leaving date for each school year, and for any summer or other extra session

CUMULATIVE RECORDS ARE CONFIDENTIAL DATA IN MOST STATES. Giving out any personal information concerning students in grade twelve or below, except to designated persons, is prohibited in most states, for such records constitute privileged communications. Persons to whom personal information *may be given:*

1. Parent or guardian of student, or person designated by parent or guardian in writing
2. Officer or employee of a public, private, or parochial school that student attends, has attended, or intends to enroll
3. Governmental officer or employee seeking information in the course of duties
4. Guidance or welfare agency officer or employee to whom student is going for assistance
5. Employer or potential employer of student.

CHARACTERISTICS OF AN EFFECTIVE CUMULATIVE RECORD SYSTEM.   An effective cumulative record system:

1. Reflects objectives of educational program.
2. Shows trends in student's development.
3. Contains information meaningful to teachers in understandable form.
4. Furnishes data for all students, not for problem cases only.
5. Consists of items significant in all-around development of the student.
6. Presents information from year to year in consistent and comparable form.
7. Involves simple standardized method of recording.
8. Is readily filed and used—a folder is recommended.
9. Lends itself to accurate and easy reproduction for teacher use and for other schools.

Case Studies

How to Help the Teacher Construct and Interpret the Case Study

A case study of a student is designed to give a rather complete cross-section of the student's development at a given time and should be used in conjunction with other types of information available. It might result from the coordinated needs and efforts of a number of staff members, such as the nurse, the psychologist, the teacher, and the principal.

One variation on the case study, which may be available in some situations, is the school-community conference, which involves more than school personnel. For instance, Detroit evolved a "school-community behavior project" in which a school action team consisting of a principal, one or more teachers, a visiting teacher, an attendance officer, and a nurse worked cooperatively with consultants from a wide range of community agencies, both public and private. The team attacked the problem of the early identification and treatment of delinquent or predelinquent behavior.[9]

Less ambitious approaches are available in other communities where a relatively spontaneous conference of the members of agencies working with a child can achieve greater understanding and work together to produce results more rewarding to all concerned.

[9] Detroit Commission on Children and Youth, "Handbook for Use in the Detroit School-Community Behavior Project," Prepared cooperatively by the Detroit Board of Education and the Detroit Commission on Children and Youth, revised September, 1969, p. 2. Mimeographed. R. L. Thisdell, Principal Administrative Assistant, Management Services Division, Los Angeles Police Department, stated, "It is my personal opinion that such early identification and treatment is extremely important." (Los Angeles, California, September 21, 1970.)

Types of Case Studies

There are, generally speaking, two kinds of case studies. One is the concentrated study of an individual student about whom more information is needed before a plan attempting to solve a particular problem regarding that student can be put into effect. The other is a less concentrated study of a student, usually within the so-called normal ranges, in order to learn more about children and their psychological structuring in general, so that the teacher may make practical application of the basic principles gleaned from the study.

The first study, the type most commonly encountered, begins when a teacher feels inadequate in dealing with a student. Aware that all is not well with this student, the teacher records incidents of behavior, checks the cumulative records, obtains family data, and then presents a case to the principal or counselor for guidance and opinion. Upon approval, the case is referred to the school psychologist, who should be trained to handle the more extreme cases. The school nurse is asked to conduct a health check to see if there are any outstanding physical factors involved in the case. The school psychometrist tests the student and also may interview the student's parents, teachers, and other school personnel.

It may be best to recommend halting the study at this point, with suggestions for the teacher, or to continue the study by calling for a case conference. This conference would involve the principal, the counselor, the psychologist, the student's teacher, and others as needed (i.e., the parents, assistant principal, nurse, and physician).

Upon completion of the case conference, the recommendation may be given that the need has been satisfied and the study may be terminated, or, that it is necessary to continue with further studying, testing, and conferring. The conferees will suggest actions to pursue in the classroom with this particular student. A follow-up conference always should be arranged to evaluate the results.

The case study may be brief or it may span several years, even to the extent of lasting for the student's entire school life.

Symptoms that may indicate that a case study is necessary are:

1. Marked contrasts and inconsistencies in the student's total life pattern
2. Sudden changes, shifts, and reversals in established behavior patterns
3. Evidence of undeveloped or wasted resources
4. Continued evidence of dissatisfaction with the student's adjustment in school, either on the part of the student or parents.

Types of problems calling for a referral or further testing are:

1. Group test scores and other data that indicate the possibility of mental retardation
2. Social immaturity and a lack of readiness for the academic learning in kindergarten and the primary grades
3. Referral for remedial reading

4. Evaluation as a gifted child
5. Level of achievement inconsistent with scores on mental development test
6. Factors indicating the child may benefit by retention in the same grade
7. Information needed to determine the proper grade placement of the student
8. Situations calling for a more extensive study of the student's intellectual functioning.

The second type of case study is not the study of one particular student for individual benefit as much as it is for the benefit of the class as a whole through the study of one student. This plan is best initiated with a group of teachers who will follow the study for one or two years.

By meeting as a child-study group from time to time, they can compare notes and ideas, make suggestions, and contribute to each other's work. This plan calls for selecting a student to be used as the subject of the study. Usually a student classified as being within the normal regions is selected, so that the learning gleaned from studying him/her can be applied to as many children as possible. Data regarding this student are collected and organized. Many sources of information are tapped; observations are made in the room, on the playground, and at lunch; excerpts of his/her products, such as stories and paintings, are studied; visits are made to the home; and conferences are held with former teachers and the custodians. These data are organized into behavioral patterns. The teachers base some of their actions on this information and evaluate the results.

At the end of a certain time, the study is summarized and evaluated. By conscientiously following this study plan, the teachers should become aware of the general behavioral patterns in students and be better able to understand and cope with the individual student, setting the classroom environment to meet more fully student needs. An example of a psychological referral is included as Figure 12-9. Information pertaining to specifics on how to help the teacher in testing, test interpretation, statistical concepts and assigning marks is included as Appendix D.

Information Covered by Case Studies

The case study should include the following material:[10]

I. Identifying Data
    A. Referral
       1. Source of referral _____
       2. Procedure of referral _____
       3. Date study initiated _____
       4. Date of report _____
       5. Name of person or persons to whom report is directed

---

[10] For further information that should prove helpful see Louis E. Harper and Benjamin Wright, "Dealing with Emotional Problems in the Classroom," *Elementary School Journal* LXIII (March 1958): 316–325.

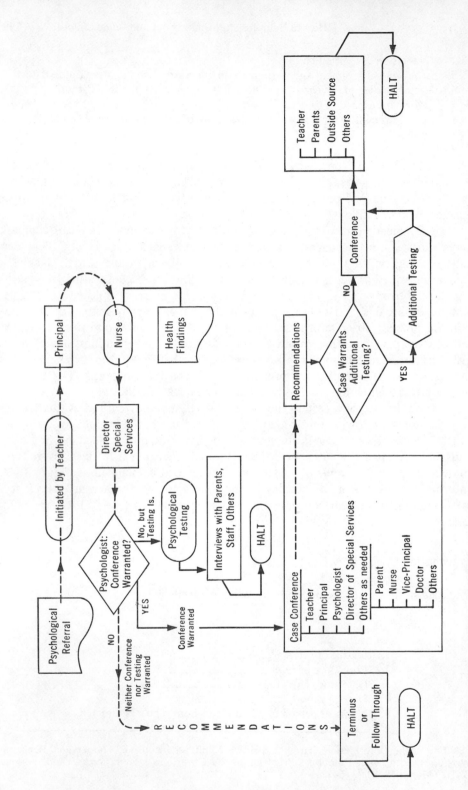

FIGURE 12-9. An Example of a Psychological Referral.

B. Subject
    1. Name _____
    2. Age _____
    3. Birthdate _____
    4. Sex _____
    5. Subject's counselor or teacher _____
    6. School _____
    7. Grade _____

II. History
    A. Developmental History
        1. Prenatal condition of mother and child _____
        2. Postnatal condition of mother and child _____
        3. Description of illnesses _____
        4. Description of infections _____
        5. Description of injuries _____
        6. History of speech and language development _____
            a) Age at which child babbled _____
            b) Age at which child used jargon _____
            c) Age at which child uttered first word _____
            d) Age at which child uttered first phrases _____
            e) Age at which child uttered first sentences _____
        7. History of development of gross motor control
            a) Age at which child held bottle _____
            b) Age at which child sat up _____
            c) Age at which child crawled _____
            d) Age at which child pulled up _____
            e) Age at which child walked _____
        8. History of social development
            a) Feeding _____
            b) Toilet control _____
            c) Dressing _____
            d) Bathing _____
    B. Family History
        1. Parents' occupation _____
        2. Parents' education _____
        3. Parents' religion _____
        4. Parents' marital status _____
        5. Socioeconomic status _____
        6. Nationality _____
        7. Racial background _____
        8. Language background of family _____
        9. Ages of siblings _____
        10. Sex of siblings _____
        11. School record of siblings _____
        12. Emotional climate of home _____
        13. Quality of parent-sibling-child relationships:
            a) Mother-infant relationship _____
            b) Disciplinary measures used _____

C. Educational History
    1. Date of entry into kindergarten or first grade _____
    2. Record of schools attended _____
    3. Summary of progress in school:
        a) Retentions _____
        b) Special learning difficulties _____
    4. Summary of social adjustment in school:
        a) With teachers _____
        b) With classmates _____

D. Results of Previous Studies
    1. Summary of results of previous
        group intelligence tests _____
    2. Summary of results of previous
        achievement tests _____
    3. Names of tests _____
    4. Grade test was administered _____
    5. Date test was administered _____
    6. Summary of previous contacts with:
        a) Special services in the school _____
        b) Community agencies _____
        c) Other professional persons _____
        Include in above:
            (1) Name of agency or person _____
            (2) Grade of study _____
            (3) Date of study _____
            (4) Findings _____
            (5) Recommendations _____

III. Test Data
  A. Intelligence
    1. Names of tests administered _____ on _____
                                           (dates)
    2. Indication of measured intelligence in terms of:
        a) I.Q. _____ on _____
                              (test)
        b) Mental age _____
        c) Grade placement norms _____
        d) Other descriptive classifications _____
    3. Analysis of student's performance on a specific type of test item
    _____
    4. Description of range of abilities _____
    5. Description of patterns of abilities _____
    6. Basic strengths included in description of range of abilities _____
    _____
    7. Basic strengths included in description of patterns of abilities __
    _____
    8. Basic weaknesses included in description of range of abilities __
    _____
    9. Basic weaknesses included in description of patterns of abilities
    _____

10. If test results are of questionable validity, evidence and supportive reasoning has been provided, such as:
    a) Variability in success _____
    b) Variability in failure _____
    c) Educational deprivation _____
    d) Social deprivation _____
    e) Sensory handicap _____
    f) Physical handicap _____
    g) Lack of rapport _____
    h) Lack of cooperation _____
11. Indication of the student's expected level of academic achievement on the basis of measured intelligence _____

B. Achievement
    1. Names of tests administered _____
    2. Skill areas tested _____
    3. Results in terms of grade placement norms _____
    4. Analysis of the types of errors committed _____
    5. Discussion of the implications for remedial classroom instructional technique _____
    6. Comparison of the student's achievement scores with actual grade placement _____
    7. Discussion of the implications for selection of the level of instructional materials _____
    8. Discussion of the achievement scores in relation to measured intelligence _____
    9. Implications concerning:
        a) Educational placement _____
        b) Classroom instruction _____
        c) Types of materials _____

C. Personality
    1. Names of tests administered _____
    2. Discussion of personality structure _____
    3. Discussion of dynamics
        a) Self concept _____
        b) Perception of others _____
        c) Interpersonal relationship _____
        d) Inner conflicts _____
        e) Defense mechanisms _____
        f) Techniques for dealing with frustration _____
    4. Discussion of the possible causes for emotional disturbances ___
    5. Discussion of the possible causes for social disturbances _____
    6. Estimation of the seriousness of the problem _____
    7. Attempt to predict future adjustment _____

IV. Test Observations
    A. Student's physical appearance _____
    B. Speech and language characteristics _____
    C. Physical activity _____
    D. Motor coordination _____

FOLLOW-UP PARENT CONFERENCE. No case study would be complete without a parent conference. This could be the parent conference that is held as a part of reporting to parents on student progress in many school systems, but it would more likely be an additional conference. It could occur at school; it would afford even greater insight if it could be held in the home. Although some people protest that teachers who visit the homes of the less economically privileged make the parents feel self-conscious and ill at ease, many parents have difficulty feeling comfortable at school.

Apart from the parents' feelings, a visit to the home deepens the teacher's understanding of a given child in many ways—some of them subliminal, some rather obvious. The teacher may find that he/she is less impatient and more sympathetic when the child forgets his lunch or misses the bus, knowing that there may not have been enough food in the house for a packed lunch or that the child had to help an ailing mother get smaller children ready for school.

The teacher may be able to see a relationship between the relative position the student holds in the family constellation and the kind of role played at school. For some childen, especially those showing signs of "educaphobia," the visit to the home may have the immediate value of bridging the gap between home and school.

If a teacher is expected to make a home visit, the time for this visit should come out of the assigned school day. Ways to permit teachers to be off campus during the school day are numerous; two of the most common and successful are asking a substitute teacher or the vice-principal to cover the teacher's classes. Such home visits must, of necessity, be few and far between, and utilized *only* in special cases in conjunction with intensive case studies. The more routine type of home visit should be handled by the counselor, nurse, or administrator.

The supervising principal should help the staff become aware of the potential of case studies—their purposes, procedures to follow in utilizing them, and what to expect in the way of results. The staff that is well acquainted with the case study program will profit accordingly.

How to Supervise the Assignment of a Student to a Classroom

The assignment of a student to a classroom can best be determined by the principal and teacher(s), working together in harmony and considering all factors involved for the benefit of the student. Correct placement can result in better adjustment.

Although the initial placement of the student is the responsibility of the principal, he/she should consult with the teacher. The specialist-consultant should help evaluate the placement from a staff standpoint *only*. Once the student has been placed, the specialist-consultant may render additional help. He/she can answer such questions as where the student should sit, and in which reading group he/she should be placed.

The students are grouped within the class at various times for instruction in reading, mathematics, singing activities, English, spelling, physical education, and committee and group work. With careful thought, the teacher places the student in order to overcome shyness, to improve study habits and skills, to develop self-confidence, to dissolve friction between classmates, to bring the isolate into the group, to remove a negative influence from a follower, to achieve maximum growth in the subject matter area. The teacher whom the supervising principal helps to see the value of correct placement will be in a more enjoyable teaching situation from a counterpart who, from apathy or lack of knowledge, does not give it much thought.

Although most placements are the result of the teacher's work, once the student has been admitted to the classroom changes in school-system policy can effect a change from without. Recently the board of education in one school system decided to accelerate the mathematics instructional program. This policy necessitated creating an accelerated group starting with the third and fourth grades. Placing the student in this group was accomplished through the coordination of the director of special services, the principal, the specialist-consultant, and the teacher.

There should be a systematic follow-up of all placement to determine:

1. If the educational program is meeting the needs of individual students
2. If the students are achieving at an optimum rate
3. If there is adequate articulation so the students are oriented for new situations and for the next grade level.

Conclusions

It might be concluded that there are implications for supervisory leadership in encouraging teachers to do their best, whether or not it is identical with approaches ordinarily used by the principal. The enlightened principal will want each teacher to use imagination and resourcefulness in working with students; the principal will not want to bind the teacher to his/her own way of thinking. If the principal is to work with a staff that continuously strives to understand students, he/she must set the example by using every opportunity to develop his/her own understandings, as well as those of the teachers.

The teacher's understanding of students will be enhanced in an atmosphere of professional democracy. It will be stifled in an empire-like situation in which administrative comfort is the fountainhead of educational dynamics.

The supervising principal can help the staff better understand students by setting the pace with his/her own attitude and activities. The studies he/she encourages, the training he/she approves, the creative ideas to which he/she is receptive, can mean the difference between personnel who merely exist and personnel who work with that extra spark because they know their work is meaningful, functional, and appreciated.

Teachers who give themselves a chance and make that extra effort to do a little better and to know a little more, and the supervisor who encourages and helps them, both by word and example, will make a teaching team that will be hard to beat.

Do

1. See that teachers are provided with accessible files of pertinent, objective information about students.
2. Encourage satisfactory home-teacher relations as a means of teachers understanding students.
3. Provide opportunities for teachers to observe students in the cafeteria, in assemblies, on the playground, and in cocurricular activities.
4. Encourage teachers to become better acquainted with parents and to take an active interest in association and community activities.
5. Encourage teachers to participate in local service organizations and community clubs in order to help teachers understand the demands being placed on students by the local community.
6. Plan meetings designed to stimulate teacher growth in developing aims, plans, methods, and procedures for learning about student needs, interests, and abilities.
7. Help teachers consider the many patterns of student growth in formulating promotional policies.
8. Discuss with teachers the common problems of group standards, conduct, and discipline as they relate to the developing nature of the student.
9. Set up panels of students for service clubs, parent associations, and others to discuss problems requiring understanding from both parents and teachers.
10. Resolve problems, needs, and frustrations by encouraging teacher-supervisor cooperation in a case study that leads to conferences with both parents and students.
11. Encourage teachers to determine personality and character traits of students by means of observation, autobiographies, diaries, and interviews with previous teachers.
12. Encourage the librarian to assemble professional reading matter on child growth and development.
13. Encourage the school nurse to report to the teacher findings from home visits and examinations and to provide the teacher with literature pertinent to developing a sound health program for students.
14. Work with the psychologist or specialist-consultant in planning meetings for teachers in order to help them observe students and write objective anecdotal records.

15. Request the instructional technology and programmed materials supervisor to obtain films on student behavior and use these services in discussions with teachers.
16. Meet with each teacher to emphasize the need for planning and organizing materials; attempt to keep a problem from developing by using a preventive method.
17. Set up a classroom observation appointment; see the problem in action.
18. Make a conference appointment with the teacher, at the teacher's convenience.
19. During the conference help the teacher to see, if there is a classroom control problem, that the problem of classroom control is not unique—that most teachers share in it in varying degrees.
20. Ask teachers how they feel about their plans and organization, whether they feel they are adequate, and what suggestions they might have for improvement.
21. Point out the need for a variety of methods (unit teaching, inquiry approach, in-depth studies).
22. Make available media materials, including records, video and audio tapes, overhead projectors, opaque projectors, models, exhibits, programmed material, picture cards, microfilm, motion pictures.
23. Recommend involvement of students in planning and evaluation.
24. Suggest books and articles that can give further guidance in planning and organizing material.
25. Suggest appropriate in-service education.

Don't

1. *Require* teachers to employ such techniques as sociograms and sociodrama.
2. Monopolize any conferences with the teacher.
3. Point out a teacher in the same building as an ideal to follow.
4 Remind the teacher that educational institutions are like industry and must be run by those in control.

TRENDS IN DEVELOPMENT OF TECHNIQUES FOR HELPING TEACHERS TO UNDERSTAND CHILDREN

Toward ⟶ Organizing More Child Study Groups by School Systems and Intermediate Units

Teachers grow professionally from participation in child study groups. When each teacher selects a child in any given grade, makes a thorough observation and study of the child's mental, physical, and social characteristics, and then shares this study with other members of the group, much greater understanding of children results.

The central offices of school systems and of intermediate (county) units have established—and will become more active in establishing—child study groups for teachers. Participation in such groups should be a part of the teacher's in-service education and should be paid for by the school system.

Toward ⟶   Greater Acquaintance with—and

Enlightened Assistance in Utilizing—Valuable Materials

for Understanding Children on the Part of the Principal

Many worthwhile materials that help teachers understand children are available. Principals will increasingly make these materials available to teachers on a regular basis. Examples of such materials for quick and easy teacher use are: *Classroom Discipline, Classroom Personalities, Discipline* (Newsletter), and *Just a Minute, Junior!,* all published by The Economics Press, West Orange, New Jersey.

Toward ⟶   the Use of Data Processing Systems

for Recording Mental, Physical, and Social Information

It is expected that the use of key punch and electronic data processing machines, along with the necessary back-up equipment, will be used to provide a file of information that would be readily available to the teacher. This system eventually may replace the cumulative record system presently used in most school systems. This is a continuing trend.

Toward ⟶   Further Use of Varied Techniques

Leading to an Understanding of Children

Sociometry and its related techniques are being utilized to an even greater extent in the schools. In this continuing trend, interest inventories, sociometric tests, and the sociogram, as well as the guess-who technique, the autobiography, the unfinished story, and anecdotal records, will be used more efficiently and to an even greater extent in the future. Principals and specialist-consultants will become more effective in helping teachers develop an appreciation for the advantages and limitations of each technique and will help them understand their use and interpretation.

| Toward |⟶   Further Use of the Interstaff

Conference as a Supervisory Aid in Helping

Teachers Understand Children

It has been noted that conferences with other staff members have proved extremely helpful to the teacher in acquiring a better understanding of the pupil. More principals of the future will plan definite programs of interstaff conferences in which further data will be furnished, suggested remedies for child adjustment will be made, difficulties will be shared, and plans for future action will be outlined.

| Toward |⟶   More Clerical Assistance for the

Teacher in Standardized Test Correction and in

Recording the Scores

It is unrealistic, and certainly not economical, to expect the teacher to correct standardized tests and to record the scores of his/her class. In one school system in the midwest, third grade teachers have been known to spend more than two and one-half hours in one week correcting standardized tests. These same teachers then had to record the scores on the cumulative record cards. In the future, we will see an intensification of the practice of providing sufficient clerical assistance, combined with the use of computers, test scoring services, and machine record systems to take this load off the teacher.

Supervisory Problems

In Basket

Problem 1

The problem develops in a public grade-school classroom. The school district is located in a rural, middle-middle class socioeconomic area. The teachers in this school are traditional in their approach to classroom control. The teacher involved in this problem, Miss Smith, is a new teacher with no teaching experience. She is burdened with an exceptionally large third-grade class of thirty-three students. Miss Smith's first month of teaching has been quite successful with the exception of one student, George, who has created continuous disturbances.

Miss Smith has tried a number of approaches in attempting to cope with George's disturbing influence on the class. She first tried to control George by verbally reprimanding him for his objectionable behavior, but this seemed to have no effect on him. Next she attempted to embarrass George by having the class stare at him whenever he said something undesirable, but still met with no success. Miss Smith asked the other teachers in the building for suggestions. They suggested that Miss Smith require George to stay in after school, and also that she could contact George's parents concerning this problem. Still no solution was achieved.

Miss Smith finally turned to her supervising principal for help. She explained the approaches that had been tried in attempting to cope with George's obnoxious behavior and requested the principal's assistance. What suggestions might the principal give Miss Smith?

Problem 2

The problem develops in a junior high-school that has an enrollment of 300; approximately 25 percent of these students are Spanish-American. Several black students also are enrolled.

Mary has had the reputation of being a "problem" since her grade-school days. When she entered junior high-school, her attitude was extremely negative and she was sent to the principal's office consistently for disciplinary reasons. Mary usually responded by saying that she was being "picked on" because she was of Spanish-American descent.

This student was below average in ability. Her parents were fairly interested in helping her become a better citizen of the school. The father was very strict and often used physical force while disciplining her. What corrective procedures might a supervisor suggest? What should he do?

Questions and Suggested Activities Concerning How to Help Teachers Understand and Guide Children

Questions

1. How can supervisors employ data processing to help teachers obtain a better understanding of children?
2. How can supervisors encourage teachers to develop democratic group situations that encourage respect for the individual?

3. How can adequate cumulative records be kept to provide a continuous longitudinal record of the child's growth and development?
4. How can teachers be stimulated to participate in faculty meetings to further their understanding of children? What topics should be covered?
5. What assistance can supervisors give to teachers for classification and promotion of students?
6. How can the information from home, school, and community sources be coordinated by the supervisor to promote teacher understanding of student needs and problems?
7. What types of problems need psychological examinations and considerations? How may the supervisor establish satisfactory methods of referral?

Suggested Activities

1. Make a student survey of your school. Put the data on data cards and run correlations on attendance and dropouts, I.Q., and physical development, or reading speed and class marks.
2. Organize a Case Conference Committee within a school to study children.
3. Evaluate various cumulative record cards and make a list of acceptable comments that can be used.
4. Make a plan for a case study listing all types of data to be included and personnel involved.
5. Keep an anecdotal record of a student over a specific period of time.
6. Outline ways of helping teachers understand and meet individual needs in a democratic manner.
7. Make and interpret a sociogram of a class.
8. Plan a simulated parent conference to discuss a student's particular problem.
9. Make and interpret a personal interest sheet to gain further information about a child.
10. What principles from child growth and development, from mental hygiene, and from the psychology of learning do you consider prime topics for discussion by the school psychologist at a series of staff meetings?
11. Which behavioral anomalies should the classroom teacher be prepared to recognize? Are there any with which he/she should be ready to cope?
12. List guidelines to which teachers may refer in employing sociometric tests and the sociogram. Note the advantages and limitations of these devices.
13. List the major causes of common behavior problems in the classroom.
14. Indicate by flow chart the establishment of system-wide planning councils, how the councils will be utilized, the membership of such councils, and the benefits that will accrue.
15. List the various referral agencies in your community and the functions of each.
16. Prepare a series of 35 mm. slides related to the problem of how the supervisor can assist teachers to understand children. Be prepared to present these to the class.
17. Indicate how teachers can participate in faculty meetings of a supervisory nature in order to further their understanding of children.

18. Show how supervisors can encourage teachers to develop democratic group situations that create respect for the worth of each individual.
19. List the types of assistance principals can give to teachers as a guide for the classification and promotion of pupils.
20. Note how the information gained from home, school, and community sources can be coordinated by the principal in promoting teacher understanding of pupils' needs and problems.
21. List the personal, health, and educational data that the teacher should have available concerning each child.
22. Indicate the advantages and limitations of the guess-who technique, the autobiography, the unfinished story, and anecdotal records.

Selected Bibliography

Books

Brim, Orville G., Jr. *Education for Child Rearing.* New York: Russell Sage Foundation, 1959.

Corcoran, Sister Mary Jerome. *The Catholic Elementary School Principal.* Milwaukee: The Bruce Publishing Company, 1961.

Cunningham, Ruth. *Understanding Group Behavior of Boys and Girls.* New York: Columbia University Press, 1951.

Cutt, N.E., and Nicholas Moseley. *Teaching the Disorderly Pupil.* New York: Longmans, Green and Company, Inc., 1957.

Driscoll, Gertrude P. *Child Guidance in the Classroom.* New York: Bureau of Publications, Teachers College, Columbia University, 1955.

Dunworth, John, Lavona Dunworth, and Emery Stoops. *Discipline.* Fairfield, New Jersey: The Economics Press, Inc., 1976.

Elkin, Frederick. *The Child and Society: The Process of Socialization.* New York: Random House, Inc., 1960.

Fenlason, Anne. *Essentials in Interviewing.* New York: Harper and Brothers, 1952.

Frank, Mary, and Lawrence K. Frank. *Your Adolescent at Home and in School.* New York: The Viking Press, Inc., 1956.

Garrett, Henry E. *Statistics in Psychology and Education.* 5th ed. London: Longmans, Green and Company, 1958.

Guilford, J. P. *Fundamental Statistics in Psychology and Education.* New York: McGraw-Hill Book Company, Inc., 1956.

———, and William B. Michael. *Intermediate Statistical Exercises.* New York: McGraw-Hill Book Company, Inc., 1957.

Hollingshead, August, and Frederick Redlick. *Social Class and Mental Illness.* New York: John Wiley & Sons, Inc.. 1958.

Madsen, Charles H., and Clifford H. Madsen. *Teaching/Discipline.* 2nd ed. Boston: Allyn and Bacon, Inc., 1974.

McCandless, Boyd R. *Children and Adolescents.* New York: Holt, Rinehart, & Winston, Publishers, 1961.

McDonald, Blanche. *Successful Classroom Control.* Boston: D. C. Heath and Company, 1963.

McKelvey, Troy V. *Metropolitan School Organization* (2 Vols.) Berkeley, California: McCutchan Publishing Corporation, 1973.

Menninger, William C. *Self-Understanding: A First Step to Understanding Children.* Chicago: Science Research Associates, Inc., 1952.

Moustakas, Clark E. *The Teacher and the Child: Personal Interaction in the Classroom.* New York: McGraw-Hill Book Company, 1956.

Neisser, Edith G., and the Staff of the Association for Family Living. *How to Live with Children.* Chicago: Science Research Associates, Inc., 1950.

Ornstein, Allan C. *Metropolitan Schools.* Metuchen, New Jersey: Scarecrow Press, Inc., 1974.

Otto, Henry J. *Elementary School Organization and Administration.* New York: Appleton-Century-Crofts, 1964.

Pearman, Jean, and Albert Burrows. *Social Services in the Schools*. Washington, D.C.: Public Affairs Press, 1965.

Phillips, C. Allee. *Educational Excellence: Key to Discipline*. Philadelphia: Dorrance & Co., 1972.

Prescott, Daniel A. *The Child in the Educative Process*. New York: McGraw-Hill Book Company, 1957.

Rasey, Marie, and J. W. Menge. *What We Learn from Children*. New York: Harper and Brothers, 1956.

Ruch, Floyd L. *Elementary Statistics in Psychology and Education*. Columbia, Missouri: Lucas Brothers, 1957.

Selye, Hans. *The Stress of Life*. New York: McGraw-Hill Book Company, 1956.

Slavson, S. R. *An Introduction to Group Therapy*. New York: International Universities Press, Inc., 1943.

Smith, Henry P., and Emerald V. Dechant. *Psychology in Teaching Reading*. Englewood Cliffs, New Jersey: Prentice-Hall, Inc., 1961.

Stoops, Emery (ed.). *Guidance Services: Organization and Administration*. New York: McGraw-Hill Book Company, 1959.

Sullivan, H. S. *The Interpersonal Theory of Psychiatry*. New York: W. W. Norton & Company, Inc., 1953.

Sylvester, Robert. *Common Sense in Classroom Relations*. West Nyack, New York: Parker Publishing Company, 1968.

White, Verna. *Studying the Individual Pupil*. New York: Harper and Brothers, 1958.

Periodicals

Adams, John C. "Teaching the Problem Child in Your Class." *Education* LXXXI (September 1961): 46–49.

Adlerblum, Evelyn D. "Social Differences among Children." *Childhood Education* XXXII (January 1956): 214–218.

Baxter, Lindley C. "What Made Johnny Run?" *The Journal of Education* CXXXIII (January 1950): 19–21.

Bradfield, Luther F. "Elementary School Teachers: Their Problems and Supervisory Assistance." *Educational Administration and Supervision* XLV (March 1959): 102–106.

Dobbs, Harrison. "Working Together for Troubled Children and Youth." *Peabody Journal of Education* (September 1958): 73–83.

Harper, Louise E., and Benjamin Wright. "Dealing with Emotional Problems in the Classroom." *Elementary School Journal* LXIII (March 1958): 316–325.

Leton, D. A. "A New Frontier in Special Education." *Education* LXXX (February 1960): 349–353.

Mathias, David. "Parent-Teacher Conferences: There *Is* a Better Way." *The Grade Teacher* LXXXV (October 1967): 55–57.

Michael-Smith, Harold. "It Takes Self-Understanding." *National Education Association Journal* XLIX (April 1960): 37–40.

Prescott, D. A. "Role of Supervisor in Reducing Tensions." *California Journal of Elementary Education* XX (November 1951): 87–97.

Smitter, Faith. "Teachers' Beliefs Regarding Control of Behavior." *California Journal of Elementary Education* XXVII (August 1958): 11–15.

Vincent, Nicholas M. P., and Helen L. Merrill. "Effective Classroom Motivation." *Peabody Journal of Education* XXXVIII (July 1960): 10–13.

West, James T. "We Found a Better Way to Have Parent-Teacher Conferences." *The Instructor* LXXVI (October 1966): 43–45.

Williams, Lois, and Sybil Richardson. "Methods of Control Teachers Find Most Effective." *California Journal of Elementary Education* XXVII (August 1958): 12–16.

Films

Each Child is Different. New York: McGraw-Hill Films, Inc., 1954. Discusses different social, emotional, and learning problems and strengths of individual children. (25 minutes)

Multimedia Package

Education Service Center. *Principals Training Program*. Austin, Texas: Region III Education Service Center, 1976. (Mailing Address 6504 Tracor Lane, Austin, Texas 78721, c/o Donroy Hafner). This extensive training package develops the rationale for returning the handicapped child to the regular classroom and alternate administrative and instructional arrangements for programming for handicapped students in the regular classroom (including filmstrip presentations of the different models of the specialist-consultant concept), as well as how to administer a building special education program. It also discusses the team assessment procedure, instructional planning, and organization for delivery of services. The package consists of two 16mm films, eight filmstrips with cassettes, seven transparencies, a book of readings, a leader's manual and participant manuals. It is well organized. Task sheets are practical. The program is flexible and can be adapted to local needs. It stresses the role of the supervising principal. Price: $350.00 (Books, parts can be purchased separately.)

Other Sources

Association for Supervision and Curriculum Development. *Growing Up in an Anxious Age*. Washington, D.C.: National Education Association, 1952.

———. *Forces Affecting American Education*. Washington, D.C.: National Education Association, 1953.

Bieker, Helen. "Using Anecdotal Records to Know the Child." *Fostering Mental Health in Our Schools*. 1950 Yearbook, Association for Supervision and Curriculum Development. Washington, D.C.: National Education Association, 1950.

California School Board Association of the California Teachers Association. *Sample Personnel Policies*. Third Progress Report, Joint Committee on Personnel. San Francisco: The Association, October 1954.

Detroit Commission on Children and Youth. "Handbook for Use in the Detroit School-Community Behavior Project." Prepared cooperatively by the Detroit Board of

Education and the Detroit Commission on Children and Youth. Revised September, 1969. Mimeographed.

Driscoll, Gertrude P. *How to Study the Behavior of Children.* ed. Hollis L. Caswell. No. 2 of "Practical Suggestions for Teaching." New York: Bureau of Publications, Teachers College, Columbia University, 1951.

Henry, William E. "The Child Tells about Himself through His Creative Products." *Fostering Mental Health in Our Schools.* 1950 Yearbook, Association for Supervision and Curriculum Development. Washington, D.C.: National Education Association, 1950.

Jennings, Helen Hall. "Sociodrama as Educative Process." *Fostering Mental Health in Our Schools.* 1950 Yearbook, Association for Supervision and Curriculum Development. Washington, D.C.: National Education Association, 1950.

————. "Sociometric Grouping in Relation to Child Development." *Fostering Mental Health in Our Schools.* 1950 Yearbook, Association for Supervision and Curriculum Development. Washington, D.C.: National Education Association, 1950.

Los Angeles City Health Department. Printed Listing of Communicable Diseases, Issued July 1956.

Stoops, Emery, and Joyce King-Stoops. *Discipline or Disaster.* Bloomington, Indiana: Phi Delta Kappa, 1972.

Stoops, Emery, and John Dunworth. *Classroom Discipline.* Fairfield, New Jersey: The Economics Press, Inc., 1958.

Willcutt, Gladys. "Informal Talks with Children and Parents." *Fostering Mental Health in Our Schools.* 1950 Yearbook, Association for Supervision and Curriculum Development. Washington, D.C.: National Education Association, 1950.

13

How to Help the Staff Study and Improve the Curriculum

"Curriculum" is the term for the sum total of the means by which a student is guided in attaining the intellectual and moral discipline requisite to the role of an intelligent citizen in a free society. The curriculum, therefore, is not merely a course of study, nor is it a listing of goals or objectives; rather, it encompasses all of the learning experiences that students have under the direction of the school.

Any school system is a part of, and consequently reflects, the unique cultural setting of its society. The school is an integral part of community life, rather than an institution set apart from that life:

> The curriculum is all that goes on in the lives of the children, their parents and their teachers. The curriculum is . . . everything that surrounds the learner in his waking hours. In fact, the curriculum has been defined as the "environment in motion." It is this concept which we try to put into practice . . . and which, of necessity, makes us a community school . . . which recognizes that everything which happens to the learner is educative either for good or for ill . . . since only in that way can the total curriculum be seen in action. Reading, writing, and arithmetic are not the curriculum, though they are part of it. Freedom, self-direction, and social growth are not the curriculum, but they are part of it. Books, tools, supplies, and material are not the curriculum, but they are used by it. School rooms, school buildings, and teachers are not the curriculum; neither are homes, churches, stores, and parents. Yet all of these are part of it.[1]

A school springs from the cultural soil of the community, and its fruits return to enrich that soil. Although the school reflects its society, it still has a responsibility to raise that society to better things. The effective curriculum capitalizes on the everyday lives of students being served by it, and the job is to move these students as far as possible up to the limit of their capabilities. The cultural

---

[1] Hollis L. Caswell et al., "Curriculum Concepts in a Community School—Glencoe, Illinois," in *Curriculum Improvement in Public School Systems* (New York: Bureau of Publications, Teachers College, Columbia University, 1950), p. 173.

values of education must be set in terms of the culture in which the student lives, rather than in terms of the culture of the past.

H. Spears[2] indicated that the conception of education that the local community has is more compelling as a curriculum determinant than is the conception of the curriculum that the superintendent brings from the graduate school. Further, the layman's complaints about the schools' accomplishments usually represent too much rather than too little faith in education.

It is entirely within reason to believe that many present-day curricula are entirely out of harmony with modern objectives of education, and hence make it relatively impossible to attain the goals assigned to the modern school.[3]

Experience has shown that failure to keep abreast of social, industrial, and scientific advancements results in a form of cultural lag that may be a factor in social unrest, and even revolution or war. But the public has always been slow to accept changes in education. Campus problems such as those at Columbia, Berkeley, and San Francisco State in the late 1960's have not made it easier for the sincere, modern educator who is in search of progress. Parents often judge schools with reference to what they recall school was like when they were students and will accept deviation from these recollections only in time of crisis.

This chapter includes a discussion of the following topics:

Basic principles and history of curriculum development
The supervising principal's role in curriculum change
How to use the systems analysis cycle in curriculum development
How to determine resources
The supervision of cocurricular activities
Do—Don't
Trends
"In-Basket" supervisory problems
Questions and suggested activities

Basic Principles and History of Curriculum Development

The following basic principles concern the role of the supervising principal in improving the school curriculum:

1. All curricula, instructional guides, and courses of study need improvement and adaptation.
2. The supervising principal should help teachers improve the techniques utilized in their attempts to improve student growth.

[2] Harold Spears, *The Teacher and Curriculum Planning* (Englewood Cliffs, New Jersey: Prentice-Hall, Inc., 1951), pp. 31–59.

[3] Henry J. Otto, *Elementary-School Organization and Administration* (New York: Appleton-Century-Crofts, 1954), p. 78.

3. The principal should help teachers understand that curriculum modification is reflected in the students' future.
4. The principal can help teachers develop fundamental skills and creative abilities in students.
5. Supervisory personnel can help teachers adapt the curriculum to the life and conditions in which the student lives and learns.
6. Adequate time, specialist-consultant help, and appropriate facilities and materials must be provided if teachers are to improve and adapt the curriculum successfully.
7. Teachers should participate in curriculum evaluation and subsequent revision.
8. Supervisors in intermediate unit offices can help school systems keep their courses of study and instructional guides up-to-date.
9. Research findings add needed knowledge to curriculum improvement.
10. Out-of-class activities concern the supervisor as well as does the regular course of study.
11. Accelerated change in the world hastens the need for curricula revision and makes revised plans and materials less permanent.
12. Teachers should participate in continuous curriculum evaluation and subsequent revision.

The Educators

A school's curriculum is part of an educational and philosophical legacy. Philosophers such as Socrates, Aristotle, Locke, and Descartes, who expounded the philosophy of Cartesian rationalism, have made contributions to education and thus to school supervision also.

Herbart, Froebel, Pestalozzi, Hand, Hutchins, Maritain, and other famous educators and sociologists have been vitally important to the development of the curriculum and its supervision.

The lives of these educators and the philosophies and sociological constructs that have most influenced supervision, and curriculum design in particular, are discussed briefly below.

THE EMPIRICISTS.   Included among the early Empiricists whose philosophies did much to implement supervision and instruction were John Locke (1632–1704) and Immanuel Kant (1724–1804). Locke believed that the mind contained no content except experience—that the mind was a passive receiver; Kant believed that although the mind contained nothing except experience, it did have forms of its own in order to classify or order what was received through experience.

Johann Friedrich Herbart (1776–1841), also an Empiricist, denied the existence of anything peculiar to the mind itself that could manufacture ideas without experience. He opposed Locke and Kant on this matter. He believed that no content, except that of experience, mediated by the senses, was present in the mind. It was false to assume that the mind had some sort of mysterious faculties.

Herbart successfully attacked faculty psychology but did not establish psychology as a true science. He believed that the power to form knowledge from experience was a function of the ideas themselves. This belief was similar to what others called "associationism." Herbart believed that the mind itself gave nothing and that contiguity was an important factor in learning. He believed that if two ideas were contiguous in time and space, that is, if they were learned together, they would stay together.

According to Herbart, the power to create knowledge was in ideas themselves, which would seek out in the mind other ideas that were related to them. These ideas, then, would enter the conscious mind and pass through it to the *subconscious mind,* where they would continue to be active rather than passive.

William James' concept that even after one ceases in his/her attempts to learn something, he/she continues learning it, goes back to the Herbartian idea of the subconscious mind. When new ideas are similar to the idea in the subconscious, the old idea can easily ascend to the conscious mind. This process was termed "apperception," which was defined as the quality of perception plus something from previous experience with which to interpret, greet, welcome, or combat the new idea or experience.

HERBARTIAN THEORY AND METHOD. Herbart was the greatest educational philosopher of his time. He was honored with a chair in philosophy at the University of Leipzig and established the experimental school. His theories had applications in the field of aims or goals of education and educational instructional methods and procedures. As a result of Herbart's influence the schools of Germany in the 1800's were the best in the world. Herbart integrated the curriculum with a central core of history—the Herbartian method. In one lesson, the famous five steps would be accomplished:

1. *Preparation* of students
2. *Presentation* of new ideas
3. *The assumption* of new ideas to old in the conscious and the subconscious
4. *Generalization,* or the extension of meanings
5. *Application* to the new situation.

ROUSSEAU. Jean Jacques Rousseau (1712–1778), a follower of Locke, believed that all learning was based on experience. He thought that direct firsthand experience without intervention of communication, coupled with removing the child from civilization and returning him to nature where he could learn from firsthand experience, would produce the optimum in education.

His famous book *Emile* attacked French aristocracy and its practice of wet-nursing and the lack of identification of child with father. Emile's tutor provided experience leading to learning without really telling Emile anything. Emile learned by himself, the hard way. Some have criticized Rousseau for his concepts as presented in *Emile,* which stated that society, not the individual, is fundamen-

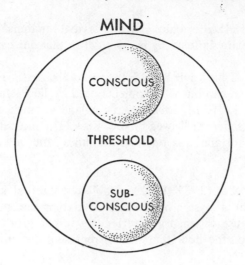

FIGURE 13-1.   The Mind: The Theater of Action for Ideas.

tally important, that education may modify the social medium, and that education really cannot occur in a social vacuum.

PESTALOZZI.   In Switzerland, the work of Johann Heinrich Pestalozzi (1746–1827) with pseudoferal orphans received much attention. He adopted Kant's philosophy, stating that the three forms that would fit into Kant's philosophy of the mind giving form to what the mind received were language, for the classifying or naming things; form, itself; and number. Pestalozzi claimed that without classification, sorting, and identification, the human intellect was of no use. He believed that the mind needed constant practice, and that experience was needed to improve its capacity and give adequate expression in language.

Pestalozzi hung tapestries on the wall and would ask the student what he saw there. He would emphasize that what the child was seeing was a representation of a line brought about through an arrangement of colors of threads that looked like a line. He believed in training students to do exercises that would improve their minds in giving forms to experience.

The purpose of education, according to Pestalozzi, was to train the mind in giving forms to broad categories of materials. Pestalozzi attempted to train the individual to observe the actual shape of things in nature by having him draw these things. He taught drawing by producing a geometric design that he claimed had all degrees and elements of drawing. His students would practice the figure over and over again. This practice was to become the basis for our own education in the twentieth century. Pestalozzi also believed that children should be prepared for vocational life as well as being prepared to better organize and interpret experience.

In summary, Pestalozzi's main concept is that firsthand experience is essential for education; reality in learning is essential so that one can give form to new experience.

Around the time of the Civil War, Edward A. Sheldon, who had gone to Canada where there was an exhibit of the objects used in the Pestalozzian school in England, brought Mrs. M. E. M. Jones from England to teach and started the first training school for teachers at Oswego, New York. The institution was called the Oswego Normal School and was open to all during the last quarter of the nineteenth centry.

FROEBEL.   Friedrich Froebel (1781–1852) established the first kindergarten in Germany in 1840. Froebel, a mystic, believed in developing the spirit. He further believed that through the use of sensory experience, spiritual growth could occur. Froebel painted a circle on the floor that was to represent the unity of mankind and God.

The students in Froebel's first kindergarten would sit around the circle holding hands. Theoretically, they were thus unified in spirit. He introduced "gifts" or playthings for the students in the kindergarten. Such gifts included the round ball (for from such contact an appreciation of the uniformity existent in universe could result), a cube (to demonstrate the strength and power of God), a pyramid, and various other solid wooden forms for a total of twelve "gifts." Froebel's curriculum consisted of playing, pleasure, learning, much sensory stimulation and contact, thinking about the forms or gifts, drawing, music, and the like.

The first German kindergarten was established on the American continent in 1855. The teacher was Mrs. Schurz. The first English kindergarten in the United States was in Boston in 1860. The teacher was Elizabeth Peabody. This institution was later to become the first teacher training school.

The great thinkers and pioneers in educational thought enunciated concepts on which modern supervision has been built. These concepts fashion the design for an evolving democratic program

The Philosophies

The philosophies that have most influenced education in general, and supervision in particular, are pragmatism, realism, and idealism. Although not new, existentialism is still in the proving laboratory.[4]

---

[4] For an interesting comparison between pragmatism and existentialism, the philosophy that teaches that philosophy is for everyone, that everyone can decide on the kind of person he wishes to be by identifying the assumptions and choosing the values by which he wishes to govern his life—that it is the individual, not external forces or environment, who is responsible for making decisions and taking action, see Nancy Gayer, "Will Existentialism Triumph Over Pragmatism?" *Phi Delta Kappan* XLIII (October 1961): 20–24.

PRAGMATISM: JAMES, PEIRCE, AND DEWEY. William James reported that the term "pragmatism" was derived from the Greek words pragmatikos and praktikos, meaning "action."[5] Our own words *practical* and *practice* are of the same origin. James noted that the term pragmatism was first introduced by Charles Peirce in 1878 in an article in *Popular Science Monthly* for January 1879, and that was translated in the *Revue Philosophique* for January 1879, Volume VII. The article was entitled "How to Make Our Ideas Clear."[6]

After noting that beliefs are really rules for action, Peirce observed that in order to develop a thought's meaning, we need only determine what conduct it is fitted to produce; "that conduct is for us its sole significance."[7]

Peirce emphasized the importance and meaning in solving problems, complaining that the absolutely unknowable was unmeaningful. To Peirce, in order to have meaning, a problem must be logical, literal, and have the quality of public understanding. He emphasized the scientific method, the standard of objective intelligibility, and stressed emphatically that meaning was equal to the sum of the verifiable consequences; that is, consequences that were verifiable through investigation. By this Peirce meant that whether a statement was true or false was irrelevant. What was important was what difference the meaning of the statement would have in the experience of the individual if it were true, as opposed to the different state of the universe that would exist if the statement were not true.

For William James,[8] statements were significant if their meaning could influence human conduct. The nature of meaning to William James could be explained on a psychological basis.[9]

John Dewey[10] thought of ideas as instruments and denied antecedent reality. Dewey noted that the kind of knowledge that was present was derived partly from the means of obtaining this knowledge. If knowledge was not from a problem, it was mere verbalism.

To both James and Peirce, an idea would produce satisfaction because the idea was true; the idea would not be true because it was satisfying. To the pragmatists, truth was scientific truth; verified experimentally for social and public value. For Peirce, two different moments, separate in time and space, were required for knowledge. The first moment was the problem, the act of looking or

5 Joe Park, ed., *Selected Readings in the Philosophy of Education* (New York: The Macmillan Company, 1958).

6 For a lucid treatment of the terms "logical positivism," "rationalism," and the application of analytical philosophy to educational supervision, see Nancy Gayer, "How to Get the Fly Out of the Bottle," *Phi Delta Kappan* XLIII (April 1962): 276–283.

7 Park, *Selected Readings*, p. 57.

8 Ibid., pp. 8, 12, 151, 163, 172, 228, 231–232, 238.

9 For a brief biological sketch of William James see Park, *Selected Readings*, pp. 55–56.

10 Ibid., pp. 73–74; John Herman Randall, Jr. and Justus Buchler, *Philosophy: An Introduction* (New York: Barnes and Noble, Inc., 1942), pp. 119, 130–132; and Merritt M. Thompson, *The History of Education* (New York: Barnes and Noble, Inc., 1951), pp. 51–52, 57. The latter reference includes an outstanding comparison between the philosophy of John Dewey and that of Giovanni Gentile and Plato.

searching for something; and the second moment was the determination of whether what was predicted was actually found. If so, there was knowledge.

To Dewey, only the second moment was required; that is, once involved with a problem did research lead to what was predicted? If so, it showed that we have knowledge. Dewey stressed that experiences must be firsthand, and that an idea worked if it would achieve goals in practical life. Therefore, students, according to Dewey, first must encounter a problem. Generalization was all right, if the generalization helped solve a specific problem. People working in school supervision have been much affected by the pragmatic approach.

EDUCATIONAL IMPLICATIONS OF PRAGMATISM.   Pragmatism has broad implications for education. Some scientists have claimed that pragmatism includes some of the best concepts of the philosophies of subjective idealism and realism. Yet pragmatism is certainly a philosophy unto itself, for it has both external and internal consistency.

If one were to follow the philosophy precisely, there would be fewer lecturers in the classroom; circumstances would be arranged to make the child see the need for learning to read and to foresee all consequences of desired actions. The teacher would change students so that they would not misbehave by helping them to see the consequences of their actions. Punishment, to pragmatists, was merely a stopgap. Effort and discipline follow interest; therefore discipline would result from cooperatively chosen goals. Since the learner's behavior changes constantly, the educator must create an optimum condition for growth and development through insight and understanding. Individual interests, value, and behavior are important. Education is to take place through experience; and through the modification of experience one would gain power, which is knowledge. If one has knowledge, one might predict the consequences of his act. Education, then, is a reconstruction process, and learning is equal to the consequences of perceiving the effects of an action.

The pragmatic supervisor operates within the scientific frame of reference. He/she stresses obtainable objectives that are of value to the individual and to society.

REALISM.   Bertrand Russell[11] was opposed to the pragmatic philosophers, including John Dewey. To Russell, when one truly *knew* everything was all right, the real state of affairs of the world was satisfactory. To the realist, reality existed before we came to know it, and our knowing it did not change the environment. This concept was in direct opposition to the ideas of the pragmatists.

According to realism, the perfect idea existed in reality. Such an abstraction as the perfect circle, or as the square root of minus one, existed in reality as the perfect idea. Moral law, to the realist, was a part of reality. The realist educator could possibly, as a first course of action in the case of disciplinary

---

[11] Park, *Selected Readings,* pp. 295, 352, 367.

action in the classroom, send the child to the principal, for the real world was independent to be learned about—the same for all people universally. The realist educator would not be worried about the individual child as such.

EDUCATIONAL IMPLICATIONS OF REALISM.   Some educational implications of realist philosophy include instruction of the great classics, in order to put the student in cultural touch with the heritage of the race. The school's task, according to the realist, is to help children understand the world in which they live, for they were born into a culture not of their own making.

To the realist, administrators and supervisors along with boards of education have the legal right to manage education but should refrain from doing so. Those who study the human mind come to know the world as it really is; therefore, specialists are better qualified than laymen concerning specialties in education. The realist educator would teach art for art's sake; the art object would possess quality all by itself. If a beautiful painting were in a dark room with no one looking at it, it would still be beautiful and have the qualities of beauty.[12]

A further purpose of the school is to help the learner identify rationally with the world in which he lives. One branch of the realist school of philosophy stresses role-playing and molding the mind and soul of the individual. These realists would control behavior in order to gain acceptance into the group. Unfortunately, the methods and objectives of this group dynamics branch of the realist school are at once both undemocratic and totalitarian. The reader should not confuse individuals who are sincerely interested in promoting better human relations through group and individual dynamics with the group dynamics branch of the realist school of philosophy.

IDEALISM: SUBJECTIVE AND OBJECTIVE.   The *subjective idealist* stressed the principle *esse est percipi*—"to be is to be perceived." According to John Locke's successor, George Berkeley (1685–1753),[13] the notion of material reality behind ideas was superfluous. Only ideas in our minds existed. Whatever exists does so only when thought of. What we can think of, we can speak of without mere verbalism. The unexperienced is the inconceivable; for everything was created within experience and could not exist without experience. Only minds or spirits were real; there was no event and an idea of an event, for they were the same thing. The danger here was solipsism, that *self* was the only existing reality.

According to Berkeley, what we get through sensations is equal to ideas in the mind. This latter thought agreed with John Locke's ideas. The only thing we know, however, according to Berkeley, is the idea of an object. In the individual mind, one is different from the world at large.

---

12 Robert L. Brackenbury, *Getting Down to Cases* (New York: G. P. Putnam's Sons, 1959), pp. 58–74.

13 Randall and Buchler, *Philosophy: An Introduction,* pp. 101, 103, 208–220.

The *objective idealist,* on the other hand, emphasized the presence of a universal mind, whereas the *absolute idealism* of Hegel (1770–1831)[14] stressed that human processes were the reflection of the universal process and absolute universal reason. The objective, real world is mental. So, to the objective or absolute idealist, each individual mind was part of the universal mind. There is just mind.

Hegel's extreme historianism—that everything eventually is a result of history—led, eventually, to the concept of the master race; such historianism had as its goal the remaking of the world. The world, according to these philosophers, had a history that went on working toward some later outcome. To evaluate experience, Hegel stressed the dialectic technique of thesis-antithesis-synthesis. The *thesis* is an established but inadequate system or idea, the *antithesis* is the clash aimed at correcting the inadequacy, and the *synthesis* is the final molding of the best elements of each viewpoint. Karl Marx was one of Hegel's disciples.

Hegel said that a kind of soul was present in humanity and it was necessary for us to promote that soul above all. This idea was somewhat similar to the ideas of objective idealists, who talked about a universal soul.

The aims and objectives of the subjective idealist were to develop the inner self in the most healthful way possible. In the Middle Ages, the philosophy of *personalism* and *humanism* was essentially subjective idealism.

If the misbehaving child were to be treated by the subjective idealist, he/she probably would be sent to the nurse. Undoubtedly he/she was not feeling well emotionally. Self-realization, then, is vital to those who believe in this mystical philosophy of subjective values.

EDUCATIONAL IMPLICATIONS OF IDEALISM. The subjective idealists placed one's personal experience in prime focus. To change one's interior self for the better and to help a person know him/herself better and achieve social approval through education would be prime goals of education for the subjective idealist. Each person in the classroom possesses traits, tenderness, talent, and desires that constantly undergo modification.

The game of life in schools should help children realize their potentials; to see themselves as others do. If a child is misbehaving in the classroom, the

TABLE 13-1. *How Subjective and Objective Idealists, Pragmatists, Realists, and Scholasticists Might Interpret the Same Sentence*

THE STATEMENT	THE PHILOSOPHIES
You	Subjective idealist stresses
should not	Scholasticists and objective idealists stress
destroy	Pragmatists stress (consequences)
school property.	Realists stress

14 Ibid., pp. 222–225.

problem exists because there is something wrong with the environment, not with the child.

The subjective idealist thinks that the children should determine what is to be taught. The school exists to help perfect the individual. As Emerson stated, what children do is foreordained; we must respect the child. Aesthetic experience was all right because such experience would lead to self-realization. The child would learn when he/she would relate the subject matter to his/her own goals. He/she must see significance to be stimulated to learn. Probably the dominant and objective idealist and scholasticist would want to emphasize one major goal for education—that one must learn to suppress urges. How the same sentence might be interpreted by subjective and objective idealists, pragmatists, and realists is presented in Table 13-1.

The following cases may help the reader further understand the major philosophies that have influenced education.

Case 1

Mary entered Mr. Books' classroom after the tardy bell rang. Mr. Books listened patiently to Mary's explanation of the reasons for her tardiness. He then decided that Mary had to learn that there were certain things that she had to do and certain things that she could not do, as was stressed in the tales of chivalry in Sir Thomas Malory's *Morte d'Arthur*. He therefore sent Mary to see the principal, Mr. Lawrence.

Mr. Lawrence, after listening to Mary's story, decided that Mary's problem was that she had not learned the consequences of arriving late at school. He therefore explained these consequences to her and helped her foresee what would happen in the future should she be tardy again, miss the beginning of the lesson, and disturb the class on her late arrival. He showed her how having missed the beginning of the lesson meant that she would miss the day's work and that she probably would not understand what had happened for the whole school year.

He convinced Mary that she should try and try again to arrive at school on time in the morning. He then asked Mary to return to class.

As he stressed the importance of the cultural heritage of the literary works of the past, as well as the existence of certain moral laws that were outside of oneself and to which one must adjust, the teacher had emphasized certain ideas with which many who followed the realist philosophy would not argue. The principal, in stressing the consequences of the act, had attempted to proceed in a more scientific and cautious manner and had been able to convince Mary of the foreseeable consequences of arriving tardy at school. He was acting as would many pragmatists. He could have determined the cause for Mary's late arrival, had he been better versed in the finer aspects of the philosophy.

Case 2

Tom got into a lot of trouble this past semester. He had been caught attempting to steal the only flute owned by the school music department, but fortunately for him he had been caught by Miss Alan.

Miss Alan had decided that Tom's real problem was that he was ill. She therefore proceeded to treat him to the best of her ability, trying to bring forth from within what was really and truly virtuous; for the individual was all-important to Miss Alan, who followed the philosophy of the subjective idealists.

Tom was lucky, however, for Miss Moffitt, the school secretary, was able to convince him that he needed to learn to suppress his urges.

In the latter case, the clerk performed as would the objective idealist, whereas Miss Alan had performed in a manner to which many who followed the subjective idealist's cause would not object.

The Sociologists

The viewpoints of leading figures in the field of sociology have had a definitive influence on the role and function of the supervising principal. John Dewey, a liberal, stressed the idea of teaching for social change. Dewey's theory was not that of life adjustment; he did not hold that we should adjust to what *is,* but rather that we should *change* what presently exists. Dewey and the famous sociological trio Smith, Stanley, and Shores[15] agreed that schools have a social function.

Harold Hand[16] stressed the need for a core program of common learnings that would include the techniques of solving problems dealing with the individual's developmental tasks. The curriculum also would include instruction in the requisites to good citizenship in a democratic society.

The developmental tasks are functions of the individual's sociological and psychological needs. Some developmental tasks, therefore, are common to children everywhere, but not all tasks are common to all children. The problems incident to this approach result from the inherent value judgments that must be exercised.

Hand disagreed violently with the theories of John MacDonald, which are explored below, and attacked a curriculum composed exclusively of traditional subjects. Hand did say, however, that value judgments enter here, and that if we are looking for traditional learnings we should employ someone who is skilled in teaching traditional subjects.

[15] John Dewey, "Education and Social Change," *The Social Frontier,* III (May 1937), 235–238; and B. Othanel Smith, William O. Stanley, and J. Harlan Shores, *Fundamentals of Curriculum Development* (New York: Harcourt, Brace & World, Inc., 1950), pp. 186–192, 726–727.

[16] Harold C. Hand, "The Case for a Common Learning's Program," *Science Education* XXXII (February 1948): 5–11.

Warner, Havighurst, and Loeb[17] stressed that education should serve as a social elevator and must exclude all implications of the caste system. They emphasized that it is democratic to have high standards and to select. They noted that value judgments must occur, but that indoctrination need not take place.

Philosophically, MacDonald[18] was a realist. He believed that the world is as it is and that there is a universal cycle of psychologically expanding worlds. He defended the traditional subjects and was opposed to the ideas espoused by Harold Hand. MacDonald stressed that no subject by itself will do the job of education; the teacher serves an equally important function. He thought that the job of education is to produce a liberally educated individual.

The intellectual virtues were emphasized by Robert Hutchins.[19] He believed that education should cultivate the mind, and that the curriculum must be organized to accomplish this task. Since the school's sole responsibility, according to Hutchins, is to develop the mind, other functions must be left to other institutions, and training must not be confused with education. There must be no "how to" in school; there should be no shop or industrial arts courses.

Hutchins believed that all men are rational to some extent. He also believed that initially we must agree on philosophy, following which we would be able to settle the problems of education. This latter belief is not concurred in entirely by the authors of this textbook, who believe that theory has a *reciprocal* relationship to practice.

As a realist, Hutchins would build the mind from a study of the great books, grammar, rhetoric, logic, and Euclidean mathematics.

The new humanism of Jacques Maritain[20] stressed the need to liberate the individual to produce the person. Leisure time education, the development of personality, and the meeting of the needs of life in community civilization were central in Maritain's system.

Smith, Stanley, and Shores were close to Dewey[21] in their beliefs about social change and education. They placed social change in primary focus as an objective of education. The sources of educational authority, according to Smith, Stanley, and Shores, are derived from the capabilities of professional experts and from the local and the national good. Professional educators, including supervising principals and teachers, determine the means, and society determines the ends.

A summary of the beliefs of these sociologists is included as Table 13-2.

[17] W. Lloyd Warner, Robert J. Havighurst, and Martin B. Loeb, *Who Shall Be Educated?* (New York: Harper & Row, 1944), see especially pp. 141–158.

[18] John MacDonald, *Mind, School, and Civilization* (Chicago: University of Chicago Press, 1952), especially pp. 85–94.

[19] Robert M. Hutchins, *The Higher Learning in America* (New Haven: Yale University Press, 1936), especially pp. 59–70.

[20] Jacques Maritain, *Education at the Crossroads* (New Haven: Yale University Press, 1943), see especially pp. 85–100.

[21] John Dewey, *Democracy and Education* (New York: The Macmillan Company, 1916).

TABLE 13-2. *Sociological Influences on the Role of the Supervisor in Curriculum Development in Terms of Goals*

THE SOCIOLOGISTS	GOALS OF THE CURRICULUM
Dewey	Social change—liberal.
Hand	Traditional subjects should be de-emphasized. Common learnings. Developmental tasks. Core program. Social and psychological needs.
Warner, Havighurst, and Loeb	Social elevators; values but not indoctrination.
MacDonald	Traditional subjects—the teacher is equally important (versus Hand).
Hutchins	Intellectual virtues. The cultivation of the mind is the only job of the school. Great books. No social amenities.
Maritain	New Humanism. Religion. The individual.
Smith, Stanley, and Shores	Social change—reconstruction for the national good, with development of the individual.

Supervisory Implications

The supervisor should seek:

1. The maximum development of individuals and groups for participation in a democratic society
2. Provision for participation of each individual in all decisions, issues, and problems
3. The development of respect for intellectual integrity and differences of opinion on educational problems
4. The cooperative participation by all staff members in the program for school supervision
5. The recognition of individual differences among staff members as well as among students
6. Initiation of the supervisory program at the attainment level of the staff
7. The utilization of scientific evidence and experimentation within a workable philosophy to secure answers to problems
8. Support for a continuous evaluation of supervisory objectives, procedures, and accomplishments.

Evolution in Curriculum Design

The last quarter of the nineteenth century began a period of expansion and reform that lasted until 1929. Some of the changes that occurred during this period were:

1. Teacher education quality was improved
2. Private schools were established
3. Individual evaluation procedures were developed
4. Modern testing practices were introduced
5. Individual differences were recognized with curricular implications
6. High schools developed rapidly.

Since 1929, there has been much progress in the basic reorganization of the school curriculum. Greater unity, reality, and democracy have been introduced into the school experiences of students.

The major types of curriculum organization that have developed include: (1) the subject-centered curriculum; (2) the broad fields curriculum, including the integrated type of organization; and (3) the core program.

The *broad fields curriculum* uses such terms as social studies, general science, and language arts, and the individual subjects tend to lose their separate identities but still maintain subject matter area boundary lines. The *core program* combines broad fields of subjects. As an example of the latter type, language arts and the social sciences could be integrated. At this point we encounter *fusion*—a process whereby broad fields or core subjects completely lose their separate identities and are no longer recognizable.

Leading educators have agreed to the need for curriculum change. The public wants the best possible program of education. This desire was reflected in the passage of the National Defense Education Act of 1958, which came about largely as an answer to the Soviet Union's orbiting Sputnik in October 1957. The Eisenhower administration answered the popular call for America to "catch up" by pushing for passage of the act, which provided for financial aid to educational institutions on a matching basis for advancement in science, mathematics, foreign languages, teacher education, and guidance.

TODAY'S INTERESTING DEVELOPMENTS. Courses that can be termed "non-academic," except for vocational or "career" education programs (especially at the community college and adult-school levels), such as supervised play and manual training, appear to be due for de-emphasis in the school curriculum. Such interesting developments as the ungraded primary system and grouping according to social maturity have implications for the school supervising principal in the area of curriculum development.

Today's state codes affecting curriculum tend generally to be permissive, with certain subjects specified as required. Prohibited is instruction that would reflect on citizens of the United States because of race, color, or creed. Generally, no sectarian, denominational, or partisan material is permitted in the public schools; and no bulletin, circular, or any other publication intended to propagandize or indoctrinate may be used in public schools.

Today, lay people, as well as educators, look at educational institutions and strongly criticize the activities they see—or think they see. They criticize courses of study, realizing that curricular inadequacy may mean the despair of the nation's future. Some criticisms are not logical; they are, however, indices of the people's interest in education and their realization of the important role of educational curricula in shaping the destiny of the nation.

Some leading educators have proposed a national curriculum. They argue that such a curriculum will provide the children and youth in schools throughout the country with the highest possible standards of education. The public is slow to accept this proposal.

DETERRENTS TO CONSTRUCTIVE CURRICULUM CHANGE.   Unfortunately, four basic deterrents to curriculum change exist:

1. Lack of adequate budgeting of time and money for curriculum change
2. Lack of a common philosophy and agreement on objectives
3. Lack of a sound program of public relations that involves the public
4. The unwillingness of teachers, supervising principals, specialist-consultants, and superintendents to discard what is familiar.

SUPERVISING CURRICULUM PLANNING.   The organization and design of the curriculum will emerge somewhat naturally when the basic goals and beliefs of the school system have been determined. A decision must be reached as to what the school system should do for students. This decision should be presented to the governing board by the superintendent and should be based on advice and counsel of administrative assistants, the teachers, and the community.

DERIVING THE CURRICULUM DESIGN.   H. J. Otto[22] stated that the design of the curriculum is derived from decisions relating to the scope and nature of the school's objectives, the psychological principles of learning to be used in teaching, the basic orientation of the curriculum, and the types of teaching-learning situations to receive major emphasis.

Supervisory functions should be planned to serve or to further the instructional program. Some implications for supervisors include:

1. Supervision should help provide a balanced program of living for students.
2. Supervision should assist in securing a curriculum that will aid students with their needs, interests, and concerns and help them relate these to broader social problems.
3. Supervision should foster a curriculum that builds competence in the basic tools and methods of work.
4. Supervision should encourage student planning and self-direction.
5. Supervision should aid in using the community as a laboratory.
6. Supervision should be adjusted to the type of curriculum planned.

These statements emphasize the importance of these basic supervisory policies: (1) supervision and administration are important means for the attainment of effective curriculum; (2) supervisory and administrative plans and pro-

[22] Otto, *op. cit.*, p. 291.

cedures should be developed cooperatively by the educational staff, the parents, and the students; and (3) the educational program should be conceived, planned, supervised, and administered as a whole.[23]

How to Focus the Forces of Supervision in Curriculum Planning

Some suggested guides for curriculum planning are:

1. Curriculum planning should focus directly on the improvement of student learning experiences.
2. Programs for curriculum improvement should be products of cooperative staff activity.
3. Programs for curriculum improvement must be flexible.
4. These programs should be included within the regular school day of the employees involved. Staff members must be freed of some regular duties if they are to participate effectively.
5. Continuous planning for curriculum improvement should be recognized as an integral part of the ideal school program.
6. The responsibilities of the administration in curriculum development should be clearly defined.

In-service education is necessary to supplement the preservice training of many teachers in order to help them in curriculum development. In a well-planned program, the administration consults the teachers about the type, variety, and quality of curriculum programs.

HOW TO USE STAFF MEETINGS AND WORKSHOPS TO IMPROVE CURRICULUM. Frequently, curriculum improvement programs are planned around a series of staff meetings and workshops. If utilized to their fullest advantage, workshops should:

1. Center about the needs and ideas of the staff
2. Enhance the social, emotional, as well as professional development of the individual
3. Provide opportunities for the faculty to contribute to the profession's body of knowledge
4. Facilitate access to assist specialist-consultants in curriculum improvement
5. Provide a stimulus to continued professional growth.

USING ALL AVAILABLE ASSISTANCE AND STIMULATING THE STAFF. The superintendent should use all local resources. Usually colleges and universities can be relied on for assistance. Other local specialists should be enlisted. Curriculum planning, experimental pilot studies, and study groups can stimulate and encourage continued professional growth in a school system.

[23] Ibid.

The Supervising Principal's Role in Curriculum Change

Even though most economic, industrial, and scientific changes are beyond the control of the supervising principal, other factors can be controlled. High morale and good human relations facilitate curriculum development at the building level.

Human Dynamics and Curriculum Improvement

The supervising principal must work to develop a creative climate within the local school. Skill in human dynamics is the essential ingredient for success in curriculum improvement.

Leadership in curriculum research and design must not be identified as a position of status; the principal must assume the role of a member of the group. He/she must be able to guide fellow staff members to gain new insight into the problem on which they are working. He/she should create an atmosphere conducive to curriculum improvement by encouraging faculty members to cooperate and use their abilities, interests, and aptitudes to solve curricular problems.

By helping the staff in this way, the principal discovers the talents and resources of each member. When these elements are put to proper uses, curriculum improvement can be achieved smoothly and successfully.

Techniques

It must be understood that in treating the problems of improving the quality of curriculum there is no one *best* way to proceed. The staff might be helped in proceeding through the steps presented by exploring a number of avenues:

1. Workshops in which the leader (a person who has done a lot of work in the area of curriculum) would draw from the group as well as have personal opinions to contribute may be employed.
2. It may be desirable to form a community-teacher-student advisory committee to make recommendations concerning what things are most important in these changing times and to agree on how best to include them in the curriculum. Due caution must be observed here, however. This statement does not indicate that input of the professional staff should be equated with community and student input.
3. Faculty committees should be organized to develop new instructional guides in a designated area or to change existing guides that seem outmoded.
4. Specialists need to be consulted. This can be done in terms of a survey, observation, and consultation, or a series of lectures in specific problem areas.
5. The department or grade-level meeting should be a source of great strength if the teachers understand that their opinions are important and will be given true and honest consideration.
6. Maintaining and improving curricular efficiency can be expedited by promot-

ing high staff morale. These two go hand-in-hand and must be maintained if an effective program is to be carried through.

THE SUPERVISOR EMPLOYS THE WORKSHOP TECHNIQUE IN CURRICULUM IMPROVEMENT. By leading the participants into various areas of possible cur- riculum change or improvement, several things may be accomplished. This does not imply that the members of the group act in a sponge-like manner. Rather, it implies that most teachers can profit from the ideas of specialists and, properly directed, these ideas can be put into operation.

In the absence of a recognized specialist, a group of teachers may con- duct their own workshop or study group under the direction of the supervising principal. This participation would be more in the nature of an exchange of ideas.

THE PROJECT METHOD APPROACH TO CURRICULUM DESIGN. In either of the foregoing situations the possibilities for change of a positive nature are unlimited. The changes evolving from the types of meetings described can be of major importance and of long-standing significance, provided the supervisor serves in the capacities of leader, specialist, and coordinator. It might be helpful to use a project-method approach. Some guidelines for the use of this technique are:

1. This procedure would be initiated by the various staff members choosing to work in an area in which change is contemplated.
2. With several groups involved, the ideas and suggestions that would be forth- coming should be helpful and meaningful. The supervisor must give the necessary direction to make the project worthwhile.
3. During the process of executing the proposed plan of action, the supervising principal must act as a counselor or adviser, insuring that the groups or com- mittees, and their discussions as a whole, do not become too labored or stray too far afield.
4. Of necessity, the principal must serve as both director and consultant. In conjunction with this role, certain areas developed by the staff may be in- corporated into particular areas of the curriculum on an experimental basis in order to see the possible reactions to the changes.
5. After a trial period, the proposals can be evaluated and reorganized to strengthen areas of weakness.
6. The revised plans, with recommendations as to their use, then can be pre- sented to the committee-of-the-whole. Even though there would be nothing binding on the committee, the possibility of new areas that have been explored in detail could have only a beneficial effect on the committee's studies.

Figure 13-2 presents a pictorial representation of the program for curricu- lum change.

In planning for curriculum improvement, the supervisor should help the faculty (1) identify school objectives, (2) decide what learning experiences will best achieve these objectives, (3) organize experiences for teaching and learning, and (4) appraise and judge. Generally, the steps involved include:

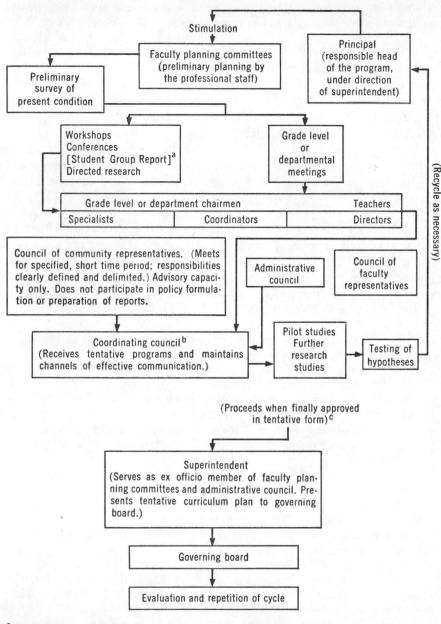

Stimulation

Faculty planning committees
(preliminary planning by
the professional staff)

Principal
(responsible head
of the program,
under direction
of superintendent)

Preliminary
survey of
present condition

Workshops
Conferences
[Student Group Report]a
Directed research

Grade level
or
departmental
meetings

Grade level or department chairmen   Teachers

Specialists   Coordinators   Directors

Council of community representatives. (Meets
for specified, short time period; responsibilities
clearly defined and delimited.) Advisory capacity only. Does not participate in policy formulation or preparation of reports.

Administrative
council

Council of
faculty
representatives

(Recycle as necessary)

Coordinating council b
(Receives tentative programs and maintains
channels of effective communication.)

Pilot studies
Further
research
studies

Testing of
hypotheses

(Proceeds when finally approved
in tentative form) c

Superintendent
(Serves as ex officio member of faculty planning committees and administrative council. Presents tentative curriculum plan to governing
board.)

Governing board

Evaluation and repetition of cycle

a If school serves pupils of grade eight or above, may include student group report

b The Coordinating Council is composed of representatives from community, administrative council, outside consultants, and faculty. It resubmits preliminary progress reports and preliminary plans to all participating above
that level in the chart for evaluation, review, and revision, in addition to function noted above.

c Reports on curriculum improvement are considered tentative rather than final, since the latter implies a closed
issue or an ultimate answer.

FIGURE 13-2.   The Program for Curriculum Change.

1. Identifying an existent curriculum program with which there is considerable dissatisfaction
2. Survey and assessment of the curriculum as it presently exists
3. Identifying a specific difficulty on which to work
4. Search for ways and means of improving the program
5. Selection and trial of promising solutions
6. Careful appraisal of consequences
7. Reconstruction of practical values
8. Suggestions put into action
9. Cycle starts again with another difficulty.

HOW TO INVOLVE THE COMMUNITY IN CURRICULUM DEVELOPMENT. The parent's association and recognized local service organizations (Kiwanis, Lions, Masonic organizations, and other fraternal, social, and service groups) should be invited to send representatives to serve as members of a lay advisory committee on curriculum design. The committee should identify an area within the curriculum as a starting point for its work. The committee then systematically attempts to discover what is being taught in the given area and what steps need to be taken in order to include those items deemed important but not yet a part of the curriculum. In this type of situation, people from the community can be of great help by letting the educators know what they feel is important.

Within any community, the people can be of assistance in the developing of any program, and of even greater value in insuring the acceptance of the program. The supervisor can be especially helpful here, serving both as the representative of the superintendent and as specialist in current practice, recent research, and legal requirements. A group of this kind should contain some lay and professional people to insure the best results in implementing the program.

COMMUNITY AND STUDENT PARTICIPATION. The discussion method must, of necessity, be a contributing part of any community-student-professional staff relationship, and is discussed in chapter 10. The method of community and student participation should be utilized with extreme caution and only when definite objectives as well as delimitations of committee functions are established. A definite date of termination should be prescribed. This is not to belittle the importance of student involvement, input, and evaluation of the curriculum in which they participate.

How to Use the Systems Analysis Cycle in Curriculum Development

The supervisor may wish to employ the systems analysis approach to curriculum design. The Task Group on the Systems Approach to Education and Training[24]

[24] The Task Group on the Systems Approach to Education and Training, Henry Lehmann, Chairman, *Eight Steps in the Design of an Education and Training System* (Washington, D.C.: The Group, 1967).

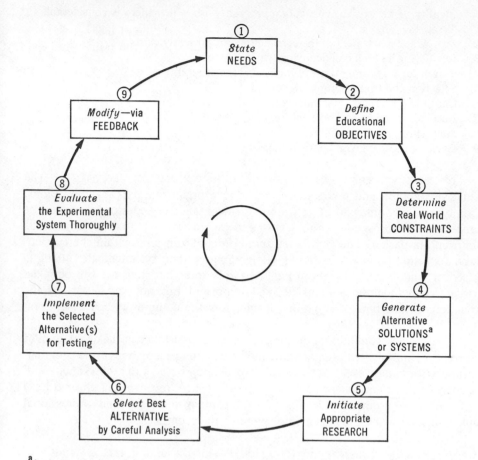

^aLook at each alternative in terms of restraints and potential for accomplishing objectives.

FIGURE 13-3.   The Systems Analysis Cycle.

has developed a simplified approach that might be employed in designing a program for curricular improvement. The systems analysis cycle is represented graphically in Figure 13-3.

Step 1: How to State the Problem

The operational statement of the real problem faced by the society under consideration is the statement that initiates consideration of an educational system as a potential solution.

1.   Start with an expression of the *generalized* need; e.g., "Our society needs better medical care."

2. Determine whether education at least partially satisfies the need.
3. Determine, in the light of present state-of-the-art, what type of man-power and what skills are needed (e.g., in a community college, the training of more knowledgeable medical technologists).
4. Define more specifically and in greater depth the group of people and skill areas required to satisfy the need.
5. Verify the need and the delineation of the group concerned through the judgment of knowledgeable people in the real world involved.

Let's evaluate and consider the following hazards:

1. Have you specified the real problem, or are you addressing a synthetic sub-problem that may presuppose a favored solution? (Have you considered the need for improved, modernized equipment, rather than adidtional personnel?)
2. Have you based the problem too heavily on assumptions and too little on verified findings?

Step 2: How to Define the Educational Objectives

Defining educational objectives involves determining and specifying the terminal capability desired of students who have successfully completed a learning experience. Figure 13-4 compares objectives stated operationally and subjectively.

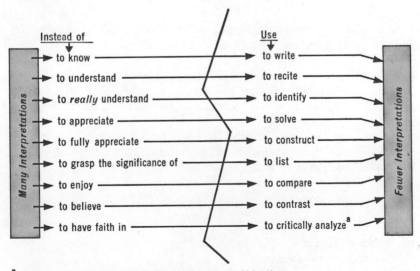

[a] After Robert F. Mager, *Preparing Instructional Objectives* (Palo Alto: Fearon Publishers, 1962), p. 11.

FIGURE 13-4.   Using More Precise Terminology in Stating Curricular Objectives.

The supervisor should:

1. Define the portion of the need that can be satisfied by the education system.
2. Describe in measurable terms the observable act(s) that will be accepted as evidence that the learner has achieved the objective.
3. Describe the environmental (stress) conditions under which the desired end behavior must be demonstrated.
4. Define the minimum acceptable criteria for demonstrating terminal behavior objectives.

Let's evaluate:

1. Are you sure that your objective contributes significantly to satisfying the real need?
2. Are your objectives stated in specific measurable terms (must be able to identify themes from Beethoven and Mozart piano concertos) as opposed to qualitative statements (must develop an understanding and appreciation of classical music)?
3. Is your definition of the test conditions realistic and valid in light of the true need?
4. Have you confined your statement of objectives to "should be able to . . .," or have you mixed in references as to how the student will in fact acquire these capabilities?

Step 3:   How to Identify Limiting Constraints

Constraints are the real-world limiting conditions that must be satisfied by any acceptable system designed to attain the educational objectives.

1. Identify the applicable constraint families (initial student behavior, facilities, financial, timing, staff limitations, administrative, political, others).
2. List specific constraints within each family and establish the source of the constraints.
3. Label the constraints by severity (physical law, short-term but inviolate, financial or political; psychological or political, subject to change).
4. Rank constraints, in order on the system design.

Let's evaluate:

1. Have you separated:
   Findings from assumptions?
   Constraints from variables?
   Intuition from bias?
   Need from unwarranted special interests and pressures?
2. Have favorite solutions introduced unwarranted constraints?

3.   Have you eliminated all but a favored answer by seeing constraints that are, in reality, nonexistent?
4.   Have the constraints been validated carefully?
5.   Has the prerequisite or presupposed student *entry behavior* been identified and defined with accuracy sufficient to permit the design of a system to bring about the required change in behavior?

Step 4: How to Generate Alternatives

Proposing alternatives involves generating candidate systems that could achieve the objectives for consideration:

1.   Gather data based on current and expected state-of-the-art with respect to potential means toward the specified ends.
2.   Solicit ideas from a wide spectrum of sources.
3.   Keep a written list of all suggested ideas. *Record all ideas,* even if they appear to be impractical or seem to violate constraints.
4.   Gather more data if the ideas are insufficient in quantity or scope.

Let's evaluate:

1.   Are ideas solicited only from a favored few?
2.   Have ideas that seem impractical or inappropriate been rejected? (If "yes," refer to item 3 above!)
3.   Are you inhibiting contributors from proposing solutions that could be termed as "radical" or unusual?

Steps 5 and 6: How to Initiate Appropriate Research and Select the Best Alternative Proposal

The systematic evaluation of all alternatives in terms of objectives and constraints in order to select the one considered the most desirable requires that supervisors:

1.   Define the criteria that will be used to select the most promising system.
2.   Establish a quantitative method for rating each alternative against the selection criteria.
3.   Evaluate the relative importance of the selection criteria.
4.   Gather data pertinent to each alternative.
5.   Relate all possible *constraints and limitations* (hazards and defects) to each alternative.
6.   Utilize analytical methods (anything from logical thinking to mathematical models) to select the best alternatives.
7.   Review the results of the analysis against mature judgment.
8.   Make final selection of alternative(s) for testing.

Let's evaluate:

1. Have you considered all pertinent selection criteria?
2. Is your evaluation system producing bias in the answer?
3. Do you balance systematic analysis and considered judgment as you proceed?
4. Are radical solutions automatically, if unintentionally, eliminated to avoid possible problems?
5. Has a predetermined conclusion been rationalized?
6. Is there objective evidence that the means selected really are effective?

Step 7: How to Implement the Selected Alternative

Implementation implies the first adoption of the selected alternative to meet the specified objective. The supervisor should:

1. Delineate the activity elements, schedule of events, and resource requirements.
2. Plan a program to evaluate the selected alternative(s) in utilizing a *pilot program* as a test phase, *if possible,* to minimize the risk factor.
3. Establish a controlled experiment and/or establish machinery to collect data (performance, financial, others) to use for evaluation.
4. Implement the program with conviction.

Let's evaluate:

1. Has the system been implemented in sufficient depth to permit success?
2. Have you planned to continue the experiment over a sufficient length of time (so that valid results can be obtained)?
3. Are you considering altering the original plan without sufficient justification?
4. *Are you ready to demonstrate active resistance to those who would have you stop after one or two early faltering steps?*
5. Are you prepared to go ahead if reasonable success is demonstrated or to repeat earlier steps if results are unsatisfactory?
6. Are you willing, and endowed with sufficient courage, to try something new?

Step 8: How to Evaluate the Results of
Your Curriculum Development Program

Evaluation implies determining the conformation or discrepancy between *all* of the objectives initially specified and the performance that was actually obtained. The supervisor should:

1. Review the original statement of operational objectives, noting particularly the statements concerning specific, measurable behavioral outcomes.

2. Review the original statement of operational objectives, noting the statements that concern the environment within which the behavior is to be demonstrated.
3. Develop as many reliable and valid procedures as may be required to determine which objectives are being met.
4. Incorporate in the procedures diagnostic features that provide definite guides for corrective action.
5. Apply the procedures to the tentative-experimental system.
6. Interpret the results of applying the procedures. Both quantitative and qualitative approaches are appropriate and are called for.
7. At regular, specific intervals, review and reevaluate the problem and *all* elements of the system.

Let's evaluate:

1. Are you evaluating with a mind to the originally specified behavior?
2. Are quantitative measures valid and reliable, and do they measure characteristics of the same parameters specified in the objectives?
3. Have you avoided subjective (it seems great!) responses?
4. Have you provided for evaluation of the *temporal stability* (lasting quality) of the behavior?
5. Have you reexamined the statement of *assumptions* to determine if they are both explicit and tenable?

Step 9: How to Use Feedback to Modify the Curricular Learning System

The final step in the systems design approach to curricular improvement involves the process of modifying the designed learning system based on deficiencies in meeting the objectives as determined through evaluation. The supervisor should:

1. Examine discrepancies between the specified system, or objectives, and the obtained system performance as determined by thorough evaluation to determine probable cause for deficiencies.
2. Analyze the entire system to ascertain where the correction can best be made.
3. Develop a specific plan for correction.
4. Make the correction during the next system cycle.
5. Conduct a new evaluation and continue this cycle until the specified performance is attained.
6. See to it that general feedback leads to continuous analysis and evaluation.

Let's evaluate:

1. Are you willing to admit that you had discrepancies that need corrective action or are you blaming them on problems "that are normal at this early phase of our operation?"

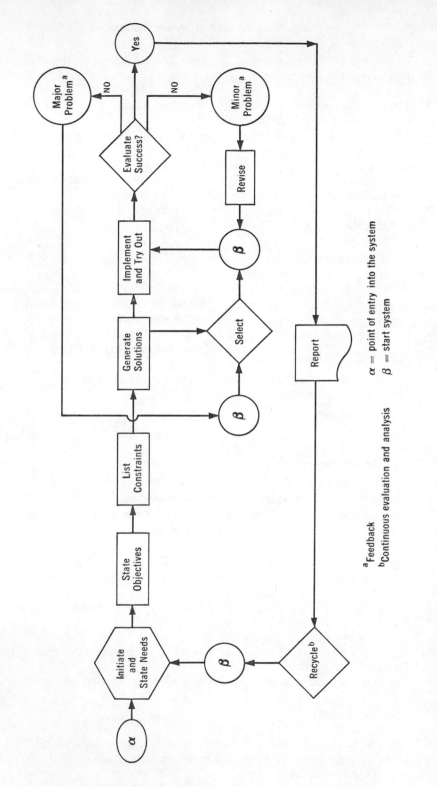

FIGURE 13-5. Diagrammatic Representation of the Systems Analysis Approach to Curriculum Development.

α = point of entry into the system
β = start system

[a]Feedback
[b]Continuous evaluation and analysis

2. Are you sure the system has actually been implemented the way you thought it would be?
3. Do not be fooled by initial success, but continue the evaluation to detect the degradation of system performance with time, and to evaluate the quality of education under real-world conditions.

Figure 13-5 depicts the process diagrammatically.

How to Determine Resources

The supervisor should seek out teachers, consultants, students, administrators, and parents in order to gather information on any phase of the curriculum.

The program of evaluation must be extended to include a wide variety of evidences of student growth. The school psychologist can be of great assistance in the evaluation of a given program or a suggested change. The opinion of the school nurse must be considered, for he/she probably has had an opportunity to view the present program and its accompanying effects on the students. In any case, the supervisor should determine if the program seems to be doing the desired job and how, if at all, a proposed change would help improve the educational program.

The Council of Faculty Representatives and the Coordinating Council

The council of faculty representatives is the advisory board selected by the teachers through which teachers are represented at scheduled meetings with the administration and community leaders via the coordinating council.

Since the trust of the rest of the faculty is placed in these agencies, the possibility of having suggestions considered with a good chance for action is greatly enhanced. No group will function with any degree of success unless there is some indication that their suggestions at least will be considered. Good staff morale is an important part of any curriculum change or improvement.

PRACTICAL ESSENTIALS.   Consideration must be given to the practical possibilities for curriculum amendments, the economy of such changes, the good that is expected from such changes, the policies that have been in practice up to this time if real progress is to be achieved.

REQUISITE ESSENTIALS: FACULTY PARTICIPATION AND SUPPORT IS ENHANCED THROUGH EFFECTIVE COMMUNICATION.   Let us consider the possibilities for success of an addition to the curriculum:

1. If this change is to be successful, it must first have the support of the faculty. This goal can be accomplished only by a full explanation of the reasons for

making the change and the additional procedures for putting this change into action. If this petition for support has been preceded by actual contributing effort on the part of the faculty, the chances for general acceptance will be greatly enhanced.

2. A second factor to be considered is the need for economy in putting the program as changed into action. The public has the right to expect efficiency, economy, and quality in curriculum development.

3. Finally, the community must be informed and must understand the need for and the procedures involved in implementing the proposed change, although the professional staff ultimately should decide what change is to be made.

How to Use Outside Specialists Effectively

Although the use of outside specialists for the *total* program of curriculum development has fallen into disuse in many situations, the need for such experts has not entirely disappeared. An expert can provide great benefits to the program in certain areas, including:

1. The specialist in a given subject area who can bring new ideas to the teachers is valuable. Also, the matter of techniques and methods can be greatly supplemented if a person from outside the school brings in suggestions.

2. The specialist also has a place in the area of advice and/or judgment concerning a particular problem area that may be causing great concern within the total structure. This person may work in various ways, such as talking to teachers, students, and administrators and making personal observations; and then bringing together all information in a report. The specialist has the advantage of not being hampered by superficial problems and can evaluate without concern for individuals.

3. The third area of expertness involves a team of specialists to evaluate the curriculum. Generally, the survey method used by this group involves the opinions of specialists in the various fields of curriculum. This can be accomplished over a period of days or weeks, but a study of this kind can help point out areas that need consideration.

Another source of valued opinion is the law enforcement and probation officers who have direct contact with students. Will this program, as proposed, help solve any problem in the area of concern?

No matter what the change, whether it be of major consequence or a change in the smallest order of business within a given subject area, the importance of making the proper choice for maximum benefit is of primary significance.

Beware the Pseudo-Experts in Curriculum Change

There have been many views concerning the best way to improve curriculum. Not long ago, the pseudo-expert emerged in the field of curriculum. Many changes occurred as a result of imitation, opportunism, and pressure from special interest groups. Although this was progress, it was of a negative quality. There is a weakness in relying on outside "experts" for the introduction of subjects into the curriculum. This phase has passed, and a more realistic approach to the problem now is pursued.

OTHER CONSIDERATIONS.   Certain subjects must be taught in the public schools, and any change must be within the limits prescribed by law.

The danger of special interest groups needs some consideration since many pressure groups seek benefits for a minority. It need only be remembered that the general interests of the public at large must, of necessity, be given first consideration.

Curriculum Improvement and Teacher Growth

During recent years, curriculum improvement has been recognized as a chief vehicle of teacher growth. Attention has been directed toward achieving change in the experiences of students with change in teachers.

Curriculum change involves what we know about students and how they learn. Public interest now is focusing on educating the talented, or gifted students. Individual needs have made the classroom a laboratory for learning.

Schools must be kept up-to-date if teachers are to accept curriculum commitments. Each teacher should have some professional help in utilizing research.

The continuing study of the curriculum in American schools is highly important. Not only is it essential that prospective teachers have a good understanding of curriculum principles and procedures, but also it is important that teachers in service continuously review and refine these curriculum essentials.

Research reveals that curriculum improvement involves many people—teachers, principals, parents, students, and others. Curriculum development is a complex social enterprise demanding the highest skills in human relationships, guidelines, respect for personalities, mutual responsibilities of individuals and groups, and good reflective thinking.

The curriculum content of the public schools constantly is being evaluated. Faculty committees, curriculum specialists, and citizens advisory committees are concerned with the courses offered and their content.

If the program for curriculum improvement has been carried on successfully, the professional staff should have:

1. Surveyed the present situation
2. Decided on school objectives
3. Decided what learning experiences would best achieve those objectives
4. Organized the experiences for teaching and learning
5. Judgd the entire program and its outcomes
6. Made a plan for further action

The Supervision of Cocurricular Activities

Basic Beliefs Regarding Student Activities

There are three basic attitudes concerning cocurricular activities operating in American schools:

1. *The strictly academic viewpoint* views the curriculum as "only those subjects for which unit credit is offered and marks are assigned," and does not recognize the activities program as a part of the curriculum.
2. *The all-inclusive viewpoint* views everything students do or accomplish while under supervision of teachers as "curricular." Nothing advocated or sponsored by the school is considered to be "extra" or outside the curriculum.
3. *The combination* views selected allied activities, such as debate and dramatics, for which credit is not assigned as considered to be part of the curriculum.

The type of program implemented depends on the school's location, background, traditions, and the attitude of the staff and the community.

THE SUPERVISING PRINCIPAL DELEGATES RESPONSIBILITY UNDER EACH TYPE OF PROGRAM. Under the academic viewpoint, there is no delegated responsibility as a rule, unless specifically assigned by the administration. Under the combination program, there are limited responsibilities to those assigned to sponsor groups. The all-inclusive program results in maximum responsibility since no real delineation is made between classroom duties and activities; both are considered vital to student learning.

CHARACTERISTICS OF THE ALL-INCLUSIVE PROGRAM. The all-inclusive program embraces the entire school community—the students, the parents, the administrators, the teachers, and the classified staff.

The program provides a natural and wholesome outlet for the energies and interests of students. With the supervision and guidance of interested teachers, students are provided with a laboratory in which to practice and test ideas taught in the classroom.

The following evaluation checklist may prove helpful in improving cocurricular activities.

1. Does the principal have control of the leadership of the activity?
2. Is a definite meeting time allotted for the activity?
3. Is the activity sponsored by a member of the faculty?
4. Are the meetings attended by a sponsor?
5. Can students elect their activities under proper supervision?
6. Is activity membership governed by approved rules of the school?

7. Is membership limited to regular students?
8. Are the meetings held on the school grounds?
9. Is the money (if any) audited by the sponsor?
10. Is there money in the school budget for defraying the expenses of the activity program?
11. Does the activity fill a social need?
12. Are students selected to office on a fair basis?
13. Is the number of organizations to which a student may belong limited?
14. Does the activity have a written constitution?
15. Is an activity record kept for each student?
16. Are the meetings and events of the activity arranged for in advance?
17. Are faculty members trained in directing student activities?
18. Does the activity fulfill definite stated objectives?
19. Does it grow out of the needs and interests of the students?
20. Are democratic group processes emphasized?
21. Is interest the primary membership requirement?
22. Does it place any other activity above it on the scale of importance, or is it equal?
23. Does the activity have educational value?
24. Is mental activity considered a form of action?
25. Is there provision for evaluation?

See Figures 13-6 and 13-7 for two devices that may prove helpful in evaluating cocurricular activities.

How to Supervise the Organization of Play Days and Sports Days in the Cocurricular Program

The California Association for Supervision and Curriculum Development[25] reported the following committees to be of assistance in carrying through the activities of cocurricular education:

1. Planning Committee
2. Reception Committee
3. Registration Committee
4. Public Relations Committee
5. Rules and Regulations Committee
6. Officials Committee
7. Communication Committee
8. Field and Equipment Committee
9. First Aid Committee
10. Refreshment Committee
11. Evaluation Committee

[25] California Association for Supervision and Curriculum Development, *Organizing and Conducting Intramural Programs, Play Days, Sports Days, and Field Days* (Sacramento: The State Professional Committee on Health, Physical Education, and Recreation, 1962), p. 7.

1. Am I interested in my activities assignment? _____
2. Do I attempt to inspire student interest in activities? _____
3. Do I believe that activities participation can be of great value? _____
4. Do I yield my "teacher" role to become a partner in the activity? _____
5. Do I provide ideas and leadership subtly? _____
6. Do I attend meetings regularly and arrive promptly? _____
7. Do I earn and keep the respect and confidence of the group? _____
8. Am I following administrative policy and decisions, and at the same time aiding students in understanding and respecting these decisions? _____
9. Do I maintain an adequate personality at neither extreme? _____
10. Do I keep a sense of humor and good nature at all times? _____
11. Do I exercise a good sense of relative values; stress only those things really important and valuable? _____
12. Do I give adequate preparation, time, and thought to my group's activities; keep aware of their progress and needs? _____
13. Do I try to expand my effectiveness in activities? _____
14. Do I try not to become discouraged easily, even if students do? _____
15. Do I ever consider when I might be wrong and admit it? _____
16. Do I have the courage to try something new? _____
17. Do I try to understand and observe regulations and procedures related to activities? _____
18. Do I evaluate activities constantly with a view toward change where the need is indicated? _____

FIGURE 13-6.   Evaluation Sheet for Activity Adviser

The following techniques should be used in a program for improving the school's curriculum:

Do

1. Determine the degree of readiness for curriculum change through opinion-aires, parents' association meetings, conferences, surveys, teacher reactions, editorials, results of standardized tests, and research.
2. Encourage laymen, administrators, teachers, and other certificated personnel to participate in curriculum development committee work.
3. Employ a curriculum specialist to facilitate the work of teacher committees.
4. Send a "kit" containing a statement of objectives and pertinent materials to teachers participating in curriculum revision.
5. Maintain a professional library containing books on curriculum, copies of

Directions:

Do not sign your name. Make your statements concise and to the point.

1. Did you attend all the meetings of this club? _____

2. Have you participated in the activities of this club as much as you would like to? _____

3. Would you like to be a member of this club next semester: _____

   Why? _____

   Why not? _____

4. Among the activities of the club, which have you enjoyed the most? _____

5. Regarding the meetings of the club, check the answers you think best apply to each of the statements below:

   a) Too long _____
   b) Too short _____
   c) The right length _____
   d) Held too often _____
   e) Not often enough _____
   f) At correct intervals _____
   g) Very interesting _____
   h) Fairly interesting _____
   i) Boring _____

6. What suggestions might the club adopt in order to be a more effective organization?

   _____
   _____
   _____

FIGURE 13-7.   Student Evaluation Sheet for School Organizations

other school systems' courses of study, and curriculum records to aid teachers in curriculum improvement.

6. Budget time for teachers to work on curriculum committees.

7. Keep a current card file on outside consultants available for help in curriculum revision.

8. See that curriculum revisions are in harmony with the education code.

9. Help teachers establish, supervise, and evaluate a tentative curriculum revision before it is adopted.

10. Encourage teachers to work jointly with other teachers of the grade behind and the grade ahead to achieve continuity in the course of study.

11. Organize staff meetings and individual teacher conferences to discuss curriculum adaptation and revision.

12. Facilitate curriculum committee work by making pertinent materials, equipment, secretarial assistance, and consultants available.

Don't

1. Lose sight of the axiom that improving the school curriculum requires the professional capabilities of the highly skilled educator.
2. Fail to allocate sufficient time, facilities, and finance so that these activities do not become a burden to the participants.

TRENDS IN THE SUPERVISION OF CURRICULUM DEVELOPMENT

Toward ——→   Including Foreign Language Instruction in the Elementary School Curriculum

To an extent, a trend to teach foreign language in elementary schools started in 1953. Usually such programs started in the third grade, but some started in kindergarten. Although research on when such instruction should begin is inconclusive, many specialists urge starting instruction in a foreign language in kindergarten, provided that the necessary teachers, materials, and funds are available.

The language department of the University of Chicago found that the achievement of younger children in many areas of foreign language competence could be compared to that of more mature groups, but that the younger children needed additional work in reading and in manipulating functional words. The method usually employed appears to be the audio-lingual approach, although the printed word, especially in a phonetic language such as Spanish, also should be utilized. Today many laboratory materials are available for teachers, and more materials will be developed and made available in the future. According to Murray and Doris Lee,[26] foreign language instruction in the lower grades should last about 15 minutes a day, and at higher levels 30 to 40 minutes should be scheduled each day.

The objectives of a foreign language program in the elementary school still are not clearly defined. Some specialists speculate that world peace is furthered by this program, but they question the translation of American patriotic songs and passages, such as "America" and the pledge of allegiance to the flag, into a foreign language. There is little evidence to indicate which pupils should study foreign languages, and it appears that this is an area where evaluation of purposes should be researched further. Probably all children who can benefit should have an opportunity to study a foreign language, at least in the elementary school grades.

[26] J. Murray Lee and Doris May Lee, *The Child and His Curriculum* (New York: Appleton-Century-Crofts, 1970), Chapter XIII.

Toward ⟶   a Compromise Curricular Organization

That Draws on the Best Factors of the "Child-centered"

and "Society-centered" Positions

Recent years have seen the emergence of what appears to be a sound and sanc midground between the so-called "child-centered" and "society-centered" positions. Some specialists have termed this organizational plan, which lacks many of the limitations inherent in the other two positions, the "interactive" position.

Toward ⟶   Achievement in Reading, Writing,

Spelling, and English Grammar and Composition as Stated

Curricular Goals with Specific Performance Objectives

There is a trend toward including statements in curriculum publications that note the three R's as definite instructional goals. Terms such as social studies, language arts, consumer effectiveness, and social living are included to a lesser extent today than in the past. It will remain for the future to demonstrate whether these changes in vocabulary and emphasis are reflected to a significant degree in classroom practice.

Toward ⟶   Less Frequent Use of Lay

Committees in Curriculum Construction

In a trend that apparently had its origin during the 1950's, the future will see a sharp decline in the use of lay committees in constructing the curriculum. Improving the elementary school curriculum requires the professional capabilities of the highly skilled educator. Although the pulse beat of the community must be taken, the professional educator must prepare policies concerning the curriculum.

Toward ⟶   Adequate Time, Facilities, and

Financial Assistance for Improving Curriculum

The supervisor should work to allocate sufficient time, facilities, and funds to guarantee that participation in curriculum construction activities does not become an undue burden on the teacher. The demands of classroom routine—marking papers, developing lesson plans, solving instructional problems, and preparing materials, among many, many other duties—are sufficient to occupy the teacher's time during the day and into "free" hours.

Supervisory Problems

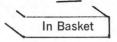
In Basket

Problem 1

Playground supervision is the responsibility of the teaching staff. The supervision of students begins when they arrive on the school grounds, includes recesses and noon hour, and does not end until the departure of the school bus at the end of the day.

A special problem involved in this area is the early arrival at school of students whose parents begin work at 8:00 A.M. Another problem is that many primary students eat hot lunches in the cafeteria. These students are on the playground before 12:00 noon, as it is necessary to stagger the lunch hour in order to accommodate the remaining students. A third problem occurs after the primary grades are dismissed at the close of school. The local students can go home, but the bus students must remain either in their respective rooms or on the playground.

How can a really effective schedule be arranged for the supervision of these students without jeopardizing the preparation time of the teacher?
How could appropriate cocurricular activities be identified and initiated?

Problem 2

Cathy R., supervising principal of the St. Anthony High School, has been under pressure by the superintendent since St. Anthony High had not been participating actively in the school system-wide curriculum study and revision committee. Although Cathy was interested in working closely with her fellow administrators and with the Citizens Advisory Committee for Curriculum Study, when she announced the existence of the curriculum study program and requested volunteer assistance on the part of the faculty, only one teacher from the staff indicated any interest.

What should Cathy do? How should she proceed?

Problem 3

A meeting of the supervising principals advisory committee (the membership of which included the two assistant principals, the coordinators of counseling and cocurricular activities, and three teachers elected by the faculty) met to discuss the school's general curricular subject pattern. Miss Rose, the principal, began the meeting by reviewing several changes made in course offerings and graduation requirements during the immediate past years. She concluded by saying, "This year's curriculum, or at least its basic pattern, can hardly be changed now. Any proposals that we make at this meeting should be for the coming school year, or perhaps even later." It was early in the fall semester.

Mr. Lewis, the science teacher, said, "I'm very concerned about the students who may complete their high school program without a course in science. Unless a student has to take science for college preparation, we have no required science course."

Miss Honey, the guidance counselor, said, "That is true, but we have encouraged all students to have at least general science or nonlaboratory biology. Also, many noncollege students elect the applied science course in their eleventh or twelfth years."

The science teacher responded, "Perhaps all of us should review the records of our last two graduating classes to determine how many enrolled in a science course."

Mr. Hart, the mathematics teacher, responded, "Regarding our requirement of one year of mathematics, noncollege students usually meet this requirement by enrolling in general math in the ninth grade. Actually, a good review course in mathematics would do them more good in their senior year. We might excuse some students from the course if they made sufficiently high scores during the junior year. If this were done, it would be easier to require a science course at the ninth- or tenth-grade level."

The counselor added, "I have often wondered why any mathematics necessary for noncollege students cannot be incorporated in the shop, homemaking, science, commercial, or other course where the mathematics is applied."

Mr. Hart responded, "Does this group have any authority to alter existing graduation requirements?"

After further discussion, it was agreed that the pattern of graduation requirements should be reviewed.

What should the supervising principal do at this point? What plans should he/she make? What should his/her answer be to Mr. Hart's question?

Questions and Suggested Activities Concerning How to Help Teachers Improve and Adapt the Curriculum

1. What advantages or disadvantages are there in assigning teacher committees to revise the course of study?
2. How often should the curriculum be adapted or revised? By whom? How?
3. How can the range of workers on curriculum development be broadened to include everyone involved and to use appropriately the contributions of each?

4. What is the process wherein persons disinterested in schools become sufficiently concerned with the schools to learn about their objectives and programs and to do something to help improve them?
5. What contributions in curriculum committees should a teacher volunteer in addition to his regular teaching load?
6. How can the school determine that it is fulfilling the needs and desires of the local community?
7. What is the supervisor's role in curriculum development?

Suggested Activities

1. Acting in the capacity of supervisor, set up criteria for determining when curriculum revisions should occur.
2. Use a fact finding survey for ascertaining whether your school or district needs a revision of its curriculum objectives, activities, and materials. Use data processing techniques where possible.
3. Make a list of desirable ways to create direct communication with all concerned in curriculum planning.
4. Tell how curriculum revision can be incorporated into in-service training.
5. Make a collection of instructional guides that improve and adapt the curriculum of your school.
6. Outline the role of the specialist-consultant in curriculum revision.
7. Draw up a budget for curriculum improvement in your district.
8. In what ways does a rapidly changing world affect the course of study?
9. Report on how participation in curriculum development can be broadened to include everyone involved and to use the contributions of each person appropriately.

Selected Bibliography

Books

Anderson, Vernon E. *Principles and Procedures of Curriculum Improvement*. New York: The Ronald Press Company, 1956.

Bailey, Larry J. *Career Education*. New York: McKnight Publishing Co., 1974.

Beck, Robert, Walter Cook, and Nolan Kearney. *Curriculum in the Modern Elementary School*. 2d ed. Englewood Cliffs, New Jersey: Prentice-Hall, Inc., 1960.

Benne, Kenneth D., and Bozidar Muntyan. *Human Relations in Curriculum Change*. New York: The Dryden Press, 1951.

Dewey, John. *Democracy and Education*. New York: The Macmillan Company, 1916.

Kelley, Janet A. *Guidance and Curriculum*. Englewood Cliffs, New Jersey: Prentice-Hall, Inc., 1955.

King-Stoops, Joyce. *The Child Wants to Learn*. Boston: Little, Brown and Co., 1977.

Krug, Edward A. *Curriculum Planning*. New York: Harper and Brothers, 1950.

————. *Curriculum for Elementary School Children*. New York: Harper and Brothers, 1950.

Lee, J. Murray, and Doris May Lee. *The Child and His Curriculum*. New York: Appleton-Century-Crofts, 1960.

Mager, Robert F. *Preparing Instructional Objectives*. Palo Alto: Fearon Publishers, 1962.

Michaelis, John U., Ruth H. Grossman, and Lloyd F. Scott. *New Designs for Elementary Curriculum and Instruction*. New York: McGraw-Hill Book Company, 1975.

Miel, Alice. *Changing the Curriculum: A Social Process*. New York: D. Appleton-Century Company, 1946.

Neagley, Ross L., and N. Dean Evans. *Handbook for Effective Curriculum Development*. Englewood Cliffs, New Jersey: Prentice-Hall, Inc., 1967.

Otto, Henry J. *Elementary-School Organization and Administration*. New York: Appleton-Century-Crofts, 1954.

Pritzkau, Philo T. *Dynamics of Curriculum Improvement*. Englewood Cliffs, New Jersey: Prentice-Hall, Inc., 1959.

Ragan, William A. *Modern Elementary Curriculum*. Rev. ed. New York: Henry Holt and Company, 1960.

Saylor, John Galen, and W. M. Alexander. *Planning Curriculum for Schools*. New York: Holt, Rinehart & Winston, Inc., 1974.

Smith, B. Othanel, William O. Stanley, and J. Harlan Shores. *Fundamentals of Curriculum Development*. New York: The World Book Company, 1950.

Smith, Vernon H. *Alternative Schools: The Development of Options in Education*. Lincoln, Nebraska: Professional Educators Publications, Inc., 1974.

Sowards, G. Wesley, and Mary Margaret Scobey. *The Changing Curriculum and the Elementary Teacher*. San Francisco: Wadsworth Publishing Company, 1961.

Spears, Harold. *The Teacher and Curriculum Planning*. Englewood Cliffs, New Jersey: Prentice-Hall, Inc., 1951.

————. *Curriculum Planning through In-Service Programs*. Englewood Cliffs, New Jersey: Prentice-Hall, Inc., 1957.

Stanchfield, Jo M. *Sex Differences in Learning to Read.* Bloomington, Indiana: Phi Delta Kappa, 1973.
Stoops, Emery, Max Rafferty, and Russell E. Johnson. *Handbook of Educational Administration.* Boston: Allyn and Bacon, Inc., 1975.
Swaab, Alexander M. *School Administrator's Guide to Flexible Modular Scheduling.* West Nyack, New York: Parker Publishing Co., 1974.

Periodicals

Albino, Joseph, and Roy Davis. "A Health Education Program that Works." *Phi Delta Kappan* LVII (December 1975): 256–259.
Beauchamp, George A. "The Elementary School Principal's Responsibility in Curriculum Improvement." *Educational Administration and Supervision* XL (February 1954): 103.
Cunningham, Ruth, and Alice Miel. "Research in Elementary School Curriculum Development." *Journal of Educational Research* LX (January 1947): 365–392.
Dewey, John. "Education and Social Change." *The Social Frontier* III (May 1937): 235–238.
Giondomenica, William T. "What Makes a Good Media Center?" *Instructor* LXXXV (November 1975): 64–66.
Lyda, Wesley J. "Suggested Conceptual System for Decision Making in Curriculum Developing." *Educational Record* XLI (January 1960): 74–83.
Olson, Arthur R. "Organizing a Faculty for Curriculum Improvement." *National Association of Secondary School Principals Journal* XII (September 1961): 178–184.

Other Sources

American Association of School Administrators. *American School Curriculum.* Departmental Thirty-First Yearbook. Washington, D.C.: The Association, 1953.
American Society for Curriculum Development. *Learning and the Teacher.* 1959 Yearbook. Washington, D.C.: The Society, 1959.
California Association for Supervision and Curriculum Development. *Organizing and Conducting Intramural Programs, Play Days, Sports Days, and Field Days.* Sacramento: The State Professional Committee on Health, Physical Education, and Recreation, 1962.
Caswell, Hollis L. et al. "Curriculum Concepts in a Community School—Glencoe, Illinois," in *Curriculum Improvement in Public School Systems.* New York: Bureau of Publications, Teachers College, Columbia University, 1950.
Ellena, William. *Curriculum Handbook for School Executives.* Washington: American Association of School Administrators, 1973.
Floyd, Earl Howard. "The Organization and Administration of Curriculum Programs in Selected City School Systems." Doctoral dissertation, University of Southern California, 1954.

Phi Delta Kappa Educational Foundation. *Three Views of Competency-Based Education*. Fastback Series, Joel Burdin, W. Robert Houston, Howard L. Jones, and Edgar Kelley, 1974.

The Task Group on the Systems Approach to Education and Training, Henry Lehmann, Chairman. *Eight Steps in the Design of an Education and Training System*. Washington, D.C.: The Group, 1967.

14

How to Improve the Work
of Classified Personnel

How often have we heard:

> "Everything seems to run smoothly when the principal is out of the office, but let his secretary be ill and utter chaos breaks loose."
> "The most important member of our whole staff is the custodian. We couldn't function without him."
> "Those bus drivers certainly can be counted on to get our children here on time each morning—and happy."
> "The staff members who contribute the most to faculty and student morale are those cafeteria workers. *Good food, served with a smile, certainly helps!*"[1]

The contributions made by these behind-the-scenes staff members are immeasurably vital to the success of each school. Consideration should be given to helping them with their respective assignments and to helping them continuously improve their job performance. Some ways in which this can be accomplished is the primary purpose of this chapter, which includes a discussion of:

Principles of classified service improvement
How to select, assign, and orient classified personnel
How to improve the quality of office management
How to improve the morale of classified personnel
How to evaluate classified personnel performance
How to do it: techniques that work
How to plan for more efficient classified personnel performance
How to get the most out of in-service education programs for classified personnel
Do—Don't
Trends
"In-Basket" supervisory problems
Questions and suggested activities.

[1] Leo B. Rotter—*connoisseur*, military tactician, and noted expert in criminal *modus operandi*.

Principles of Classified Service Improvement

A. N. Galluzo[2] suggested the following basic principles concerning the improvement of the performance of classified school personnel:

1. The most important aspect of a well-rounded personnel program is the people in it.
2. Written personnel policies should be maintained by all school systems.
3. The classification plan is the heart of the personnel program.
4. Recruitment is the responsibility of the personnel office of the school system. Selection should be a shared responsibility of the personnel office and the line supervisor.
5. Tests are valuable tools in the selection process.
6. Transfers should not be used as a means of eliminating problem employees.
7. Disciplinary action should be positive rather than destructive.
8. If an organization expects loyalty from its employee and special effort during pressure periods, the employee, in turn, is entitled to a proper claim to a similar loyalty during times in which he/she is having personal difficulties.
9. It is poor practice to demote employees for disciplinary reasons.
10. Turnover is expensive. Every effort should be made to salvage a trained employee rather than to terminate employment and hire a substitute employee.
11. The classified personnel system should be based on a principle of recognition of employee competence and performance through assignment and promotion.
12. All school systems should establish policy statements and rules governing the administration of classified personnel.
13. Each school system should have an administrative manual and a handbook for employees.
14. All school systems should establish a classification plan.
15. All school systems should establish positive recruitment programs.
16. School systems should develop, utilize, and continuously evaluate assignment specifications[3] for classified school personnel.
17. A selection of personnel should be on the basis of competitive examination. A promotional examination should be given regularly with a civil service plan developed for large school systems. In small school systems a semiformal plan is suggested. Examinations should be followed by a personal interview of the prospective employee.
18. Thorough preemployment examinations should be given all applicants concerning new developments in their specialized fields. The results of these examinations should serve as a basis for planning the in-service education

[2] See A. Neil Galluzo, "Practices in the Administration of Classified Personnel in California" (Doctoral dissertation, University of Southern California, 1955), and Emery Stoops, M. L. Rafferty, and Russell E. Johnson, *Handbook of Educational Administration* (Boston: Allyn and Bacon, Inc., 1975).

[3] James R. Marks, "An Analysis of Assignment Specifications for Certificated School Personnel in the United States" (Doctoral dissertation, University of Southern California, 1962).

program. Periodic physical examinations should be required of all employees.

19. Promotion should not be on the basis of seniority alone; however, some consideration should be given to seniority, especially if other factors are equal.

20. The orientation program should have as its main objective the establishment of a feeling of belonging on the part of the new employee.

21. The following factors should be taken into account in determining the general level of the salary schedule for classified personnel:
    a) Local-market rates
    b) Cost-of-living indices
    c) Supply and demand factors
    d) Financial condition of the school system.

22. Grievances should be settled as near to their point of origin as possible.

23. Suggestion systems should be utilized.

How to Select, Assign, and Orient Classified Personnel

Selection and Assignment

Desirable human relations begin with initial contact at the time of application or first interview. First impressions are lasting. Thus, a prime consideration must be the general atmosphere in which this meeting is held. It should be friendly but businesslike and to the point, and should invite questions. There should be a mutual exchange. Many times classified personnel are not too experienced in such situations. Every effort should be made to put them at ease immediately.

It is important that the principal, or the person doing the selecting, be thoroughly familiar with the job. He/she should be able to clarify duties, hours, and special training needed. An assignment specification (which will be discussed later) should be handy. He/she should discuss personnel policies and working conditions to the point that the applicant understands the job situation. A tour of the school grounds, including equipment and facilities, is helpful.

While discussing the assignment, the supervising principal must be able to make a valid judgment about the character and capabilities of the applicant. Both are essential for efficiency, economy, and dependability on the job. Selection, then, is finding a person to do the job, rather than attempting to fit a job to the person.

A major factor is the total plan of application and selection. If steps are defined and carried through, the job will seem important. The casual manner in which many members of the classified personnel are selected is a main reason for low morale in this group.

If selection has been made in a warm atmosphere and in a businesslike manner, if the assignment has been explained thoroughly, and if placement has been made in a position appropriate to training, the new staff member is off to a good start and looks forward to the new job with enthusiasm.

How to Prepare Assignment Specifications

Perhaps no single factor contributes more to a feeling of well being and security on the job than knowing what is expected and possessing the skills for optimum performance. Obviously, the principal cannot be an authority in all areas of operation, but he/she does carry the responsibility for supervising all personnel on the staff. Some important tools to accomplish this are concise and complete assignment specifications, well-planned orientation programs, in-service education programs, constructive supervision, and frequent evaluation. Each technique should be considered for the contribution it can make to the effectiveness of each staff member.

ASSIGNMENT SPECIFICATIONS. These documents should be available at the time of the initial interview so that each applicant can know exactly what is expected. Other purposes of assignment specifications are to make sure that necessary duties are performed, to eliminate overlapping, to upgrade efficiency, and to increase employee satisfaction. They are the basis for supervision and evaluation.

With these purposes in mind, the checklist in Figure 14-1 can be used to prepare specifications for classified personnel. Preparing assignment specifications is an excellent way to involve staff members in the recruitment-selection process.

FIGURE 14-1. Classified Personnel Specifications Checklist

1. Is it in writing?_____   Is it complete? _____

2. Is it clear?_____   Is it written in language understandable to the person applying for the position?_____

3. Are **all** major requirements for selection included?_____
4. Are staff relation responsibilities listed?_____
5. Are community relation responsibilities included?_____
6. Are hours of work and the salary schedule included?_____
7. Are line and staff relationships noted?_____
8. Are all "extra" assignments which the employee might be called upon to do from time to time included? _____
9. Are fringe benefits and tenure requirements listed?_____

No one knows the job of the maintenance man better than the head of buildings and grounds.

A complete, to-the-point assignment specification can best be used by personally reviewing it with the new staff member, by clarifying questions orally at that time, and by giving the new employee a written copy. A sample assignment specification for the school secretary includes a list of duties and minimum requisites for obtaining the position. The following qualifications were listed: neat appearance, pleasing personality, tact, ability to work well with others, skill in typing, and taking and transcribing dictation, filing, skill in written and oral English, emotional stability, poise under stress, and ability in handling general office tasks. These characteristics were spelled out specifically, as seen in Figure 14-2.

FIGURE 14-2. Qualifications for the Position of Educational Secretary

1. Either twelfth-grade education supplemented by a standard secretarial course, or an equivalent combination of education and similar experience.

2. For higher classifications the qualifications are twelfth-grade education, including or supplemented by courses in stenography and typewriting, and two years of experience in stenographic or clerical work involving contact with the public.

3. General knowledge of office methods and procedures, some knowledge of business letter-writing and business forms, knowledge of and ability to operate a mimeograph and duplicating machine, ability to perform clerical work, ability to spell correctly and use good English, ability to follow oral and written directions, aptitude and liking for office work, neatness, accuracy, pleasing personality, orderliness, good health, and mental and physical ability to do the work required.

4. Higher classifications will be required to acquire knowledge of and be able to administer first aid; and also to be able to size up situations and people accurately to adopt an effective course of action, and to get along well with students as well as with adults.

5. Ability to take dictation at a speed of not less than eighty words per minute and to transcribe it accurately at a rate of not less than twenty words per minute; ability to type at a rate of not less than forty words per minute from ordinary manuscript or printed or typewritten material.

6. For higher classifications the qualifications are the ability to take difficult dictation at a speed of 100 words per minute and to transcribe it accurately at a speed of not less than twenty-five words per minute, ability to type at a speed of not less than forty-five words per minute from ordinary manuscript or from printed or typewritten material.

How to Conduct an Orientation Program for
Classified Personnel

Orientation programs vary greatly. Ordinarily, orientation programs for classified personnel are handled poorly. The following are some items that should be on the agenda of all orientation meetings:

1. The total school program should be one of the first considerations. *All* staff members should be acquainted with *all* phases of the organization and its operation.
2. Such facts as the number of students attending, size of the staff, budget totals, and certainly the general philosophy of the school system and the school are important and should be discussed briefly. A tour of the school grounds and all facilities should be taken as soon as possible, unless this was done at the time of application.
3. The classified personnel should have the opportunity to meet as many of the certificated personnel as possible. Introductions can be made at staff meetings or by personal contact, but should be accomplished as soon as possible.
4. Personnel policies should be covered in detail during the orientation period. Salary schedules, advancement possibilities, causes for dismissal, job benefits, hours of work, provisions for health and emergency leaves, and grievance procedures should be discussed at the outset.
5. Line and staff relationships must be clarified.
6. Information should be given as to what to do in cases of accident or emergency, whom to call, and what reports to make. All bus drivers, the secretary, and at least one of the cafeteria staff should be trained in first aid. This training may be given at the school or arrangements may be made for staff members to attend courses given in the community.
7. Some suggestions should be made concerning community relations responsibilities. Although this is most important to the secretarial group, all staff members come in contact with parents and taxpayers. Because they make an important impression, it is well to discuss this at some length during orientation. It is especially important to extend information on how to handle visitors, what should be discussed with them, what questions may be answered, and what questions should be referred to the supervising principal or to other employees.
8. Information regarding use and care of equipment will vary with each group, but must not be overlooked.
9. Appearance, neatness, cleanliness, and appropriate dress should be stressed. Bus drivers and cafeteria workers usually decide on a uniform, and maintenance personnel in many schools are doing likewise.
10. Relationships with students require a fine line between being friendly and helpful or being too personal. Classified personnel should, at all times, earn the respect of pupils.
11. Staff members new to the community should learn something about it—its people, its organizations, and its services.

According to W. A Yeager,[4] a program for orientation in a school system should include the following areas:

1.   Orientation to the school, such as its philosophy, objectives, organization, program, rules and regulations, and the physical plant, together with general information such as enrollments, calendar, and the like.
2.   Orientation to the position, such as specific duties, routine, equipment, schedule, salary, and increments.
3.   Orientation to the persons with whom one will be associated, such as the superintendent or principal, both certificated and classified personnel, and the students.
4.   Orientation to the community, including its social activities.

If the orientation program has been helpful and meaningful, staff members will look forward to beginning their assignments with a feeling of confidence and security.

How to Improve the Quality of Office Management

The efficiency of a school or school system depends to a large degree on an expeditious and otherwise efficient performance of numerous office duties.[5] An introduction to the techniques of office management should be a part of the orientation program.

EQUIPMENT.   The equipment with which an employee is provided is a significant factor in determining the quality, the quantity, and the cost of the work accomplished. These materials have much to do with the mental and the physical condition of the employee, and that condition is reflected in the employee's output. In every school system, therefore, considerable attention should be given to selecting adequate equipment and comfortable, functional furniture.

MINIMUM CLERICAL SERVICES.   It is pennywise policy for boards of education to employ teachers, specialist-consultants, and principals at high salaries and then require them, or permit them, to spend their time and energy in performing tasks that clerks could perform more cheaply and, perhaps, more efficiently.

Every school needs some clerical service. A minimum standard is one full-time clerk for each 400 students. This means a half-time clerk for each 200 students.

The following is a list of some of the chief ways in which a clerk or secretary can assist the principal:

[4] William A. Yeager, *Administration of the Noninstructional Personnel and Services* (New York: Harper and Brothers, 1959), pp. 169–170.
[5] Ward G. Reeder, *Fundamentals of Public School Administration* (New York: The Macmillan Company, 1951), p. 726.

1. Taking and transcribing dictation, and copying matter on the typewriter
2. Mimeographing
3. Filing correspondence and other materials, keeping financial records, and making out payrolls, checks, and vouchers
4. Writing purchase orders and requisitions
5. Keeping inventories of equipment, books, and supplies
6. Looking after the bookkeeping for internal funds
7. Making appointments for the principal, and giving reminders to keep them
8. Meeting callers
9. Answering the telephone
10. Sending and receiving telegrams
11. Making out contracts for teachers and for other school employees
12. Selling textbooks and supplies to students
13. Issuing supplies to teachers and keeping supply records
14. Recording the minutes of school board meetings and of faculty meetings
15. Recording memoranda of conferences of the principal
16. Opening and distributing the mail
17. Typing certificates of experience for teachers
18. Posting the mail
19. Keeping the office in order
20. Receiving and sending parcel post, express, and freight
21. Receiving notes from, and making notes for, the attendance officer, the school nurse, and other employees
22. Posting school announcements
23. Completing transcripts of record of employment certificate completion.

How to Improve the Morale of Classified Personnel

The quality of service rendered by the classified personnel is directly related to their sense of belonging to a team and the awareness of their importance on this team. Each member must recognize and respect the role of the other before the degree of cooperation and teamwork necessary for the smooth running school can be attained. Each must be dedicated to the total job to be done and feel the task is a vital one.

How to Get a Positive Response

Nothing brings a positive response faster than does a friendly smile. This is particularly true of the relationship between professional and classified staff members. It is easy, in the rush of busy days, for either principal or teacher to pass by the faithful custodian in a haze of preoccupation without so much as a glimmer of recognition. And yet a warm "Hi, Rochelle! How's the new grandson?" can make a world of difference in the spirit with which the next assignment is fulfilled.

Almost as important as the greeting is knowing the name; Rochelle immediately becomes a "recognized" staff member.

Including *all* staff members, or representatives from each group, in the process of planning the school program is essential to developing team spirit. A special school function or activity might affect all staff members:

1. Responsibility for the students—the faculty
2. A special setup in the multipurpose room—the custodian
3. A change in schedule—the cafeteria staff and the bus drivers
4. Interpretation and clarification (to staff as well as to parents and community) —the secretary.

Aside from understanding the *what, when,* and *how,* each group might contribute important and helpful suggestions.

Most important is that when classified personnel are brought into planning, two things happen: (1) they will act more efficiently because of better understanding, and (2) they will develop a sense of pride and a feeling of worthwhileness.

Including the classified personnel in faculty activities whenever possible is another way of keeping them on the team. This is, at times, more difficult to schedule with the maintenance staff than it is with the office workers, but is none-the-less important. Joint coffee breaks, the Christmas breakfast, and end of the year get-togethers, can be planned to include all groups. Big dividends could accrue.

Greeting by name, inclusion in democratic planning, and inclusion in staff activities are the most obvious ways to strengthen classified personnel morale. Surveys have shown that more important than salary to these individuals is a spirit of friendliness and cooperation.

How to Measure the Nature and Effectiveness of Morale Factors

Since morale is so essential in staff personnel administration, methods must be utilized to measure its nature and effectiveness. H. H. Remmers[6] has given us five methods for determining morale:

1. The "listening in" or general impression method, in which impressions are gathered by all those in contact with personnel and cleared through the central office or individuals
2. Unguided interviews, in which persons are encouraged to talk freely to reveal the true situation about themselves or others

[6] H. H. Remmers, "The Analysis of Employee Attitudes," *Proceedings of the First Personnel Institute* (Columbus, Ohio: State University, 1938), p. 4.

3. Guided interviews, in which key individuals are interviewed through a series of carefully prepared questions designed to reveal a given situation
4. Questionnaire blanks, previously prepared and submitted to large groups requesting both information and opinion
5. Attitude scales, either specific or more general in nature.

How to Evaluate Classified Personnel Performance

Continuous Evaluation and Supervision

Orientation programs and in-service education, no matter how well planned, cannot take the place of close personal supervision. Whether this is done by the principal himself or by someone delegated by the principal, the important thing is that it be positive and creative, not negative and critical. It must be both systematic and sympathetic.

The relationship between the principal, as the supervisor, and the employee must be one of mutual respect based on sincerity of purpose. The employee should feel free to go to the supervising principal for advice and help at any time. Complete honesty is vital, for these contacts will become an important factor in evaluation and, perhaps, in settling grievances.

The supervising principal, then, must have the ability to analyze situations quickly and accurately and to help before it is "too late." He/she must be frank yet tactful, friendly but impartial. He/she must know the job he/she is supervising —its skills, materials and equipment, and methods.

Frequent Evaluation

If evaluation primarily is to be done to help the staff, then it should be done frequently. This especially is true during the probationary period of employment. It should be made on the basis of the same basic beliefs that underlie teacher evaluation. Evaluation should be:

1. Democratic
2. Fair
3. Specific
4. As objective as possible
5. Continuous

The two major considerations of evaluation should be correcting weaknesses. and improving services. Evaluation of all staff members can easily fall into three major areas:

1. The individual as a person
2. The individual as a staff member
3. The individual as a skilled worker

The evaluation itself may take one of several forms:

1. A rating scale
2. A checklist
3. An outline
4. A written essay

Ideally, the form should be planned and developed cooperatively by members of the classified personnel and their immediate supervisors. Samples of checklist and rating forms are included as Figures 14-3 and 14-4.

More important than the form, however, is the fairness of the evaluation and the use to which it is put. Opinions based on one specific instance should be avoided. Each evaluation should be discussed with the individual rated in a personal conference. The primary purpose and end result of the evaluation must be more effective service.

How to Do It: Techniques That Work

T. Jackman reported fifteen items that were rated most effective by at least 50 percent of the principals questioned:

1. Special job instruction for new employees prior to starting work, or shortly thereafter.
2. Opportunity for classified employees to work with experienced personnel during probationary period.
3. Participation of classified employees in evening or extension courses pertaining to their work.
4. Basic training course for classified employees.
5. Meetings stressing employees' part in school health and sanitation.
6. Opportunities to attend job conferences, with expenses paid.
7. Opportunities to have individual conferences with the principal.
8. Meetings devoted to job skills or problems of classified employees.
9. Planning of training programs on the basis of the results of performance evaluations of classified employees.
10. Demonstrations by commercial representatives of the use of equipment and materials.
11. In-service . . . [education] meetings for supervisors of classified employees.
12. Opportunities for classified employees to participate in salary committee meetings.
13. Opportunities for classified employees to visit other schools to observe job skills.

14. Handbook or manuals for the use of classified employees.
15. Performance ratings for classified employees.[7]

How to Evaluate Working Conditions

Each school has specific problems, but the principal always should consider: (1) physical facilities and equipment, (2) health and safety precautions, and (3) cooperation from faculty and students. Examine the checklists under each of these headings in Figure 14-5. These, then, are some techniques used to help staff members understand their jobs, learn how to do them more efficiently, and therefore help them feel more secure.

Noise is a disturbing factor. It also decreases efficiency. To minimize noise, it is helpful to:

1. Place typewriters and other machines on rubber or foam pads
2. Soften all buzzers and bells
3. Oil squeaky metal hinges or wheels
4. Use such items as staplers quietly
5. Close cabinet doors softly
6. Keep voices quiet
7. Line boxes and desk and file drawers with blotter pads
8. Cover desk surfaces
9. Play soft background music, if desired.

How to Communicate Effectively
with Classified Personnel

Without adequate communication, the best plan of classified employee supervision can be totally ineffective. One of the most important and immediate jobs of the principal is to establish lines of communication and to keep them open. If communication is to be effective, it must: (1) be well written and continuous, and (2) flow in both directions. If the purpose is to impart information, such information should be timely, pertinent, and helpful. If it is a directive, the communiqué should be clear, concise, and capable of fulfillment. It also should imply confidence.

Written Classified Personnel Policies

Every school system should have its own set of classified personnel policies that should be in writing and in the hands of every staff member. The extent to which

[7] Taylor Jackman, "The In-Service Training of Classified Employees in Elementary School Districts of Southern California" (Doctoral dissertation, University of Southern California, 1959), pp. 154–155.

FIGURE 14-3.   Classified Personnel Evaluation Checklist Form

_____   _____ Probationary Report

_____Principal_____

SERVICE REPORT

Date Due _____

(Name)_____ Classification_____

In each group place a check mark ( ) before the descriptive phrase which most nearly typifies the employee's performance.

Promptness in
Reporting for Work
( ) Nearly always late
( ) Often tardy
( ) Usually on time
( ) On time more than average
( ) Rarely if ever late

Knowledge of Work
( ) Inadequate comprehension
( ) Limited knowledge of job
( ) Adequate knowledge; knows job fairly well
( ) Well informed; has mastered most details
( ) Thoroughly familiar with all phases of his work

Work Attitude
( ) Complains or acts unconcerned
( ) Sometimes indifferent; goes about
      work half-heartedly
( ) Average interest; likes most phases of his job
( ) Definite interest in work
( ) Enthusiastic, wholehearted active interest

Initiative
( ) Needs frequent direction, or prodding
( ) A routine worker; usually waits to be told
( ) Reasonably alert to opportunities
( ) Resourceful; completes suggested
      supplementary work
( ) Seeks and sets for himself additional tasks;
      shows ingenuity

Capacity to Develop
( ) Has very little future growth; has about
      reached limit
( ) Future growth doubtful
( ) Moderate development ahead
( ) Great latent possibilities
( ) Bright future growth; shows promise

Attitude Toward
Other Employees
( ) Surly, touchy or quarrelsome; does
      not cooperate
( ) Sometimes difficult to work with
( ) Normal self-restraint
( ) Tactful and obliging; good self-control;
      cooperative
( ) An unusual and strong force for group morale

Quality of Work
( ) Poor work; frequent errors; unsatisfactory
( ) Not always satisfactory; sometimes careless
( ) Satisfactory; does fair work; few errors
( ) Work usually well done; practically no errors
( ) Work very satisfactory; quite carefully done

FIGURE 14-3. (Continued)

Quantity of Work	( ) Puts out very little work; unsatisfactory
	( ) Does not do his share of work
	( ) Average amount of work
	( ) More than average amount of work
	( ) Turns out unusually large amount of work
Ability to Under-stand Directions	( ) Carries out only the simplest directions, with help
	( ) Often misunderstands or bungles orders
	( ) Occasionally requests simple instructions to be repeated
	( ) Readily understands most orders
	( ) Requests additional information on only most complex orders
Appearance	( ) Usually unkempt, slovenly, or careless
	( ) Often neglectful of appearance
	( ) Presents a favorable appearance
	( ) Well groomed
	( ) Takes genuine pride in his appearance

Check the following only if employee has contacts with the public which are considered a necessary part of his duties:

Contacts with Public	( ) Surly, touchy or quarrelsome; antagonizes others
	( ) Lacks certain requirements of common courtesy
	( ) Complaints occasionally received; usually maintains courteous effective relations
	( ) Tactful and obliging; good self-control
	( ) Exceptionally courteous and well-mannered

Give percentage rating according to the rating guide below: _____

Rating Guide:

1. *Superior*—exceptionally qualified for the position in every way; 96 to100 percent
2. *Good*—could do the job better than most and has several positive and desirable qualities; 86 to 95 percent
3. *Average*—could do the work and has no outstanding undesirable qualities; 76 to 85 percent
4. *Passable*—probably could do the work, but some one else probably more desirable; 70 to 75 percent
5. *Failure*—either could not do the work or not desirable in the position; below 70 percent. (Not recommended for permanency.)

Signed: _____ Date _____
         Principal

Signed: _____ Date _____
         Employee

FIGURE 14-4.   Evaluation Rating Form

The following evaluation form is used for the rating of educational secretaries. It is to be made out in triplicate by the person for whom the secretary works.

NAME OF SCHOOL

Copy for:

( ) Employee
( ) Principal or
    Director
( ) Personnel Office

Name of Employee _____ Office _____

Points on Which Rated	Excel-lent	Good	Aver-age	Below Average
	Rating[a]			
1. Punctuality				
2. Accuracy				
3. Responsibility				
4. Initiative				
5. Tact				
6. Cooperation				
7. Efficient planning of work				
8. Ability in the necessary skills				
9. Completing work at the proper time; productive output				
10. Neatness of desk, files, records, reports, etc.				
General or Average Rating				

[a]Some supervisors recommend terminology such as, "Exceeds Work Standards," "Meets Work Standards," and "Below Work Standards" or "Fails to Meet Minimum Acceptable Work Standards."

---

staff members are satisfied with these policies, and the degree of their effectiveness, will be related closely to how much of a part the members had in their making. Salary schedules, fringe benefits, grievance procedures, and tenure, dismissal, and promotion policies constitute a minimum content.

FIGURE 14-5.   Working Conditions Checklist

Physical Facilities and Equipment

1. Is there adequate room for equipment, for storage, for operation?   _____

2. Are light, ventilation, and heat appropriate for the job?   _____

3. Is equipment satisfactory? If it is not new, has it been kept in good repair?   _____

4. Are supplies adequate?   _____

5. Are restrooms, lunchroom, and sanitary facilities adequate and pleasant?   _____

Health and Safety Precautions

1. Are machinery and equipment safe?   _____

2. Have potential hazards been eliminated?   _____

3. Are first-aid facilities and services available?   _____

4. Are workloads equalized? Are adjustments made under extenu- ating circumstances (peak loads and overtime)?   _____

5. Is there an adequate sick leave plan?   _____

6. Is there a health insurance program?   _____

7. Are there health advisory services?   _____

Cooperation from Faculty and Students

1. Are rooms left in good order—straightened up and picked up?   _____

2. Are lunch bags thrown on the school grounds or in the trash can?   _____

3. Is the cafeteria neat after the lunch hour?   _____

4. Is reasonable care taken of the restrooms?   _____

5. Do students evidence self-discipline and courtesy in the office, in the cafeteria, on the school grounds, and on the school bus?   _____

How to Plan for More Efficient Classified Personnel Performance

Efficiency and skill of all personnel help save money, time, and materials. Every economy that the governing board can affect leaves the way clear for providing some additional service for the students.

In developing more efficient methods, it first is necessary to determine the present state of affairs with regard to classified service in the school system. The program must be studied carefully and its strengths and weaknesses noted. Once the facts are ascertained and analyzed, it is possible to decide on a plan of action and to set it in motion. Any plan considered must be formulated after careful study and knowledge of legal requirements and governing board rules, and must be developed in the light of sound business procedures.

How to Get the Most Out of In-Service Education Programs for Classified Employees

Planned instruction and help must not stop with the orientation program. In-service education provides an opportunity for the continuous growth of the classified staff member, as well as for improved efficiency in the operation of the school. The content of the program will vary with the job category, but there are two major topics common to all:

1. *New ideas, new techniques, new equipment.* From a new directive on attendance accounting, to a new wax finish, to a new dishwasher—there constantly is something new. Staff members using new equipment first should have a part in the decision whether to purchase the item, and then should be acquainted thoroughly with both its operation and care. New ideas for method and organization of work will come constantly from the group if the mechanics for exchange of ideas are established. Videotaped presentations of a coworker using a new device or technique can be beneficial.
2. *The total school program and plans.* An advance knowledge of coming activities will help staff members anticipate peak work periods and plan ahead more efficiently.

How to Improve the Performance of Cafeteria Employees

The organization of the cafeteria staff depends on the size and type of the school. There is a definite trend toward requiring a bachelor's degree, with special training in nutrition and management, of all cafeteria supervisors. Other cafeteria employees must possess good health, regard for children, skill in cafeteria work, a pleasant personality, and neatness.

If housewives are employed part time, the cafeteria consultant or "line supervisor" must be skilled in giving both formal and informal on-the-job training. Areas requiring special attention include the ability to:

1. Read written instructions accurately
2. Prepare food in quantity
3. Learn to operate the expensive equipment with skill and safety
4. Serve the food attractively
5. Keep accurate records
6. Prepare reports.

Cafeteria workers must stress cleanliness of person and of the lunchroom.

It is important that provision be made for compensation for extra functions. Attention to the safety factors in the kitchen is vital. The supervisor should be aware of the adequacy of facilities for:

1. Food preparation
2. Food service
3. Dishwashing
4. Storage
5. Refrigeration
6. Receiving
7. Space
8. Dining area
9. Management space.

How to Improve the Work of Custodians

If a custodian works well, appreciation should be expressed and deserved praise should be rendered. A "that's fine," or "I'm glad you thought of that," is helpful. No one, including members of the classified staff, should be criticized in the presence of *anyone* else.

HOW THE CLASSIFIED EMPLOYEE ACQUIRES A BODY OF CUSTODIAL KNOWLEDGE. Custodians acquire a knowledge of the care of the school plant mostly through experience. If they are encouraged to read and study in the areas of their problems, intelligent custodians make great improvement in their services. Thus they come to know reasons for doing things in certain ways, and to learn about new materials and techniques.

One of the first problems encountered in the use of school equipment and materials is training custodians to use them properly. Most manufacturers are happy to display and discuss their products with the people who use them. The manufacturer's representative should be invited to participate in the in-service education program. Such participation must be delineated carefully, however.

Since the custodians are the ones who will be using these materials, they should have some say in their selection. This practice tends to give them a feeling of belonging to a team, rather than just having a job.

WHAT TO LOOK FOR WHEN SELECTING A CUSTODIAN. The custodian is an important representative of the school and is in close contact with students. His/her character and reputation must be above reproach. It is necessary that a custodian be physically healthy and strong, sure-footed, have good sight and hearing, and be good in housekeeping.

One of the first steps in securing, keeping, and interesting good personnel in their jobs is providing for adequate salary schedules. Higher salary schedules lead to improved custodian status and morale.

RESPONSIBILITIES OF THE CUSTODIAN.   Custodians are responsible for the health and safety of both students and teachers, and for the care of costly property. Additionally, since visitors often judge the entire school by the appearance and actions of the custodian, the custodian can do great service or harm to the school in the field of community relations. The custodian is asked questions regarding school policy and members of the staff. A careless remark can be most harmful.

The custodian is the key to making any plant functional for those who use it. The job of maintenance essentially includes four items:

1. Cleanliness and sanitation—of classrooms, drinking fountains, cafeteria, restrooms, and grounds
2. Safety—from fire hazards to loose handrails
3. Preservation of buildings—good care adding to life expectancy
4. Attractiveness—resulting in better student and teacher morale and better community impressions.

HOW TO DETERMINE CUSTODIAL LOAD.   The principal must give particular attention to the work load of the custodial or maintenance staff. To avoid disagreements and dissatisfactions and to get the job done efficiently, a detailed work schedule should be developed. Such a schedule is included as Figure 14-6.

The following factors should be taken into consideration when determining the custodial load:

1. Administration of the school and student control factors
2. Size of the school
3. Age and state of repair of the buildings
4. Attendance area location, including its general category such as residential or industrial
5. Climatic conditions
6. Type of building structure and number of windows
7. Kind of school and its age level
8. Social background of students and home cleanliness
9. Enrollment
10. Type of arrangement of rooms and desks
11. Amount and kind of floor area
12. Type and condition of heating, ventilation, and plumbing facilities
13. Amount and kind of playground and yard
14. Workshop area—location and adequacy
15. Convenience of storerooms and supply areas.

In-service education for the custodial staff must include information concerning the use of new techniques, new materials, and new equipment. "New," however, does not necessarily imply "improved." Wise planning and wise use of materials and supplies can save money for the school system.

The custodian's responsibilities for maintaining proper sanitation and for safety can be made more meaningful by providing speakers, filmstrips, transparencies, and audio materials.

FIGURE 14-6.   Sample Custodial Schedule[a]

LEVINE JUNIOR HIGH SCHOOL

Name of Custodian

School Year: 1984–85
Hours Assigned: 12:00 Noon through 8:00 P.M.

Time	Activity	Completed Check When
12:00–12:15 (15 Min.)	Prepare and check custodial equipment	_____
12:15–1:15 (1 Hour)	Sweep Kindergarten A and clean[b] and sweep Rooms 1A, 1B, and Instructional Center	_____
1:15–1:45 (45 Min.)	Cafeteria cleanup	_____
1:45–2:00 (15 Min.)	Coffee break	_____
2:00–3:30 (1½ Hours)	Clean all restrooms; clean Rooms 6, 11, 17, 18 Lower flag, secure flag; continue to clean	
3:30–4:30	rooms, clean faculty lunchroom, lock offices, deliver and set out clean trash cans	_____
4:30–5:00 (30 Min.)	Lunch	_____
5:00–7:00 (2 Hours)	Clean all ballrooms; bring in equipment left out; clean rooms 5, 8, 9, 13, 17	_____
7:00–7:30 (30 Min.)	Clean cafeteria kitchen area	_____
7:30–8:00 (30 Min.)	Clean lower and intermediate level restrooms	_____
8:00	Secure facilities and leave	

---

3. Empty waste containers and remove miscellaneous articles from floor
4. Sweep floors, return chairs to floor, where applicable
5. Dust counter tops, and all other flat surfaces including desks
6. Where applicable, clean and fill soap and towel dispensers
7. Check room again, noting general room maintenance, lights, windows
8. Lock doors (each Friday clean all erasers and spray special solution on chalkboard after dusting it.

---

[a]See Lowell G. Keith, S. Robert Infelise, and George J. Perazzo, *Guide for Elementary School Administration* (Belmont, California: Wadsworth Publishing Company, 1965), p. 122; and Emery Stoops and Russell Johnson, *Elementary School Administration* (New York: McGraw-Hill Book Co., 1967), p. 165.

[b]Includes: 1. Clean sinks, sink counters, drinking fountains, chalk trays, and chalk board
2. Clean inside of both exit doors

Safety precautions listed by J. E. Barbour[8] included:

1. Checking playgrounds for safety hazards
2. Proper storage of inflammables, acids, and combustibles.

He urged:

1. Formal training in the use of power equipment
2. Building inspection for faulty or dangerous rundown conditions
3. Practice in the use of fire extinguishers, electrical apparatus, and extension cords.

The school plant inspection report form, included as Figure 14-7, may prove useful.

HELPING THE BEGINNING CUSTODIAN.   A custodian who is new to the school will require more of the principal's time and attention. All advice to the custodian should be given tactfully.

The principal should stress every situation that may prove detrimental to human welfare. For a while the principal may find it necessary to make certain inspections that a beginning custodian might overlook, such as checking that all lights are out at the close of the school and that all windows, doors, and gates are closed and locked.

THE CUSTODIAN AND THE STUDENTS.   The students should be informed about the activities and responsibilities of the custodian and the importance of this work. The custodian's pride in this work in connection with the school buildings may become a source of inspiration.

WHAT SUBJECTS TO COVER.   Most educators and custodians alike believe that meetings devoted to the job skills or problems of classified employees are a helpful addition to formal in-service education programs. Subjects pertaining to retirement law, school rules and regulations, employment practices, and explanations of the need for additional funds are handled more easily when one instructional session for all custodial employees is held. It is possible to maintain a feeling of unity when the total school membership is kept informed regarding school issues and problems.

A well-trained custodian can affect savings by conserving water, electricity, fuel, and supplies. There should be a definite program of in-service education to help custodians in this area. Such a program should not only teach abilities and skills, but also develop desirable habits and attitudes.

---

[8] Julius Ervin Barbour, "The Selection and Instruction of Public School Custodians in Selected School Districts" (Doctoral dissertation, Michigan State College, 1954), p. 39.

FIGURE 14-7. School Plant Inspection Report

School _____ Date _____

I. *Grounds Report*

   A. Condition of surfaced area: _____

   B. Condition of nonsurfaced area: _____

   C. Please check—grounds were _____ littered

                             _____ fairly clean

                             _____ clean

   D. Condition of trees, shrubbery, flowers: _____

       _____

   E. Are there any conditions, problems, or requisitions that we should bring to the attention of the central office? _____

       _____

II. *Playground Equipment*

Please note carefully any unsafe conditions, broken equipment, or anything else which we might wish to call to the attention of the students, the teachers, and possibly the superintendent of schools: _____

_____

In your opinion, what is the most important thing we should do to have a safer playground for students? _____

_____

III. *Lavatories*

   A. Condition of urinals and commodes: _____

   B. Condition of wash basins: _____

   C. Condition of floor: _____

   D. Condition of ventilation: _____

   E. Mirrors: _____

   F. Lavatory room doors: _____

   G. Other: _____

IV. *Classrooms*[a]

Please check or answer as specifically as possible:

   A. Chalkboards: (condition?)_____

      Are chalk trays clean?_____

   B. Floors: Condition _____Clean? _____Waxed? _____

   C. Windows: When last washed?_____

      Are window blinds working?_____

   D. Desks and furniture: Clean? _____Dusted? _____Waxed? _____

   E. Locker space: Floors? _____ Shelves? _____

   F. Are teachers' closets clean?_____

   G. Condition of room lighting? _____

   H. Are thermostats working properly? _____

   I. When have seats been adjusted in this room? _____

     [a]This kind of report would have to be used for each classroom.

FIGURE 14-7. (Continued)

V. *Gymnasium and Stage*

    A. Note here any unusual or poor condition: _____

    _____

    B. Condition of gymnasium lighting: _____

    C. Condition of gymnasium floors: _____

    D. Condition of windows, shades, and screens: _____

    E. Condition of walls and ceiling: _____

    F. Are there any hazards to student's safety in the gymnasium? _____

VI. *Offices and Storage Areas*

    A. Floors: _____ Windows: _____

    B. Condition of equipment and furniture:_____

    C. Items which need repair or replacement:_____

    D. Condition of public address system: _____

VII. *Boiler Room*

Are there any conditions, safety hazards, unfilled requisitions, etc. that the central office or the superintendent of schools should know about?

_____

_____

Signed _____
                                   Head Custodian

WHAT THE SMALLER SCHOOL SYSTEM CAN DO. Smaller school systems sometimes find it difficult to provide an adequate in-service education program for their custodial staff. In order to help these school systems, as well as the larger school systems wishing to take advantage of such courses, some states offer a three- to five-day intensive training course. School systems wishing their employees to attend usually pay the expenses involved.

    These courses are of short duration because most of those attending are unaccustomed to long periods of intensive study. Smaller school systems frequently work together, cooperating with the county superintendent to provide a more adequate training program.

SPECIAL PROBLEMS FACED BY ALL CUSTODIANS. New employees must understand their duties in regard to safety emergencies, fire prevention, and civil defense drills. As mentioned earlier, a daily schedule of the custodian's work should be defined clearly. Time must be allocated in the schedule for emergency and periodic duties, and for special repairs.

    In addition, the principal should assure that:

1. Extra duties are fairly and equitably distributed among employees. All employees should be encouraged to suggest needed improvements in equipment or procedure.
2. All special or extra work desired by teachers is cleared through the principal's office. No teacher should ask a custodian to run errands. A custodian can have only *one* boss.
3. All custodial personnel are provided with a handbook. A good handbook might be *The School Custodian's Housekeeping Handbook* by H. H. Linn, or *The Custodian at Work* by N. E. Viles.

How to Improve the Work of the Educational Secretary

If you ever come into a school office and find that the secretary is home with a cold, you realize the importance of the job. The office has that empty, lost feeling.

The secretary performs services that give balance and tone to the school. Secretarial work requires skill and finesse, tact and personality. Responsibilities are detailed and routine, and these essentials contribute greatly to the smooth functioning of the school organization.

The following are identifying characteristics of a good secretary:[9]

1. A close personal contact with the immediate supervisor and a knowledge of business routines
2. A decrease in the time spent typewriting or performing stenographic duties
3. An increased reliance upon personal initiative, judgment, and knowledge of business
4. The ability to direct and supervise clerical workers
5. The ability to carry responsibility for the most important details and to assume many minor administrative duties.

HOW TO ELEVATE THE QUALITY OF THE EDUCATIONAL SECRETARY'S WORK. The techniques listed here may be employed in upgrading secretarial services:

1. Provide for guided observation tours through the office so the secretary may learn what equipment is in use and may see central storage facilities, observe the system of distribution, and examine the record-keeping system.
2. Arrange for a tour of the school to which the secretary has been assigned.
3. Require that beginning secretaries attend workshops or institutes planned for them; arrange the calendar so that experienced secretaries may attend such in-service programs if they so desire; and insist that such in-service education classes be attended by the secretary as one of the prerequisites to promotion.
4. Arrange for school system funds to pay for transportation and registration fees at the Secretarial Association's regional conferences.
5. Use available standardized and informal tests to appraise English usage,

[9] National Association and Council of Business Schools, *Secretaryship as a Career Field* (Washington, D.C.: The Council, 1959), p. 5.

office procedure knowledge, general information, and achievement in office skills including stenography and typing.

6. Schedule regular on-the-job observations of the secretary at work.
7. Schedule routine examinations of files, stockrooms, and the secretarial work area.
8. Work toward a secretarial salary schedule based on preparation, experience, and performance.
9. Arrange for demonstrations, obtain motion pictures, sound and silent film-strips, video tapes and slides, and make available publications that are pertinent.[10]

HOW TO KEEP SECRETARIAL PERSONNEL PROBLEMS TO A MINIMUM.   A good supervising principal, with a secretary, will maintain good relations between the school office and teachers, other personnel, students, and the various publics. Some problems unique to the secretary may develop because of the nature of the job. The principal must be alert to the problems and do all that is possible to prevent them from hindering the secretary's growth. Such problems include:

1. The secretary may identify with the principal, and therefore may tend to feel "superior" to the faculty. It may help to emphasize that the secretary is *ex officio* the secretary of the entire faculty, although actual secretarial duties are assigned only by the principal. The secretary must *never* even *appear* to give orders to a teacher!
2. Teachers become suspicious of an aloof secretary and lose confidence.
3. The attitudes of the students may create problems.
4. The secretary may be "in the know" concerning problems and therefore "on the spot" with the faculty.
5. Cliques may develop among the clerical personnel. Where these cliques exist, much of the spirit of cooperation is lost.

HOW TO FACILITATE THE SECRETARY'S WORK DURING TIME OF PEAK LOAD. Another task of the principal in relationship to the secretary is awareness of work load and overtime. Some hints are listed below:

1. To discover bottlenecks in job routine, a secretary may list on cards all job activities and the amount of time spent on each. In this way it is possible, over a period of time, to discover if too much, or not enough, time is spent on the various secretarial tasks.
2. A monthly or annual schedule will indicate the times of peak load and allow the secretary to plan so that nonessential duties are scheduled for times other than the peak load time. It helps to schedule ahead as new emergency work is added to the schedule.
3. In planning for peak load periods, a well-established routine, which allows for paper work to be done quickly, is necessary to ensure that time is available for the all-important job of taking care of people.

[10] National Association of Educational Secretaries, *Plan Your Work* (Washington, D.C.: The Association, 1959).

4. When load reduction can be accomplished during peak periods, accuracy and efficiency can be increased.
5. Some part-time help can be employed to handle routine tasks.
6. Where two or more secretaries work in one office, encourage them to help one another with tasks during peak loads, even though a task may be the sole responsibility of one of them.
7. Student help may be used.
8. Have all work delegated by one person.

One principal prepared the following list of suggestions for the secretary:

About yourself—

1. The educational secretary's position is a key position in the school. Since you often give the public its first impression of the school, a smile of welcome is always appreciated.
2. Poise and dignity must be maintained at all times. Cultivate a quiet, well-modulated voice. Dress carefully and in good taste.
3. You should notify the principal immediately if it is necessary for you to be absent or late.
4. Your relations with the principal, the teachers, the students, and parents should be pleasant. Learn to make adjustments with cheerful readiness. It may seem easier at times to give orders to teachers. Don't do it! It is the principal's job to supervise and administrate.
5. Accept your responsibilities willingly. Be kind and generous but do not assume more than a secretary's responsibility.
6. Loyalty is a characteristic that helps make a secretary valuable to the principal, the teachers, and the community.
7. Interruptions often are necessary and should be accepted graciously.
8. Plan your work carefully and look ahead. A last-minute rush does not enable you to perform your duties efficiently.

About the students—

1. All information concerning students in the school is confidential. Inquiries regarding them must be referred immediately to the principal.
2. Discipline and control problems are the responsibility of the principal.
3. Students may be excused to leave the school grounds only under certain conditions, as indicated by the principal.

About good office practices—

1. Your office should be neat and attractive, and all materials should be kept in the proper places.
2. All information concerning the faculty and other employees of the school is confidential, and inquiries regarding them should be referred immediately to the principal. Matters pertaining to teachers and their personal business and salary ratings should not be discussed with others.
3. Acquaint yourself with the names of members of the board of education, the

superintendent's office, and particularly the administrative and clerical employees of surrounding schools with whom you frequently communicate.

4. Telephone conversations are numerous. Remember that your telephone voice is often your first introduction to people. Learn to know whom to call for specific information. Extend a word of thanks to those who assist you.

5. Keep your calendar up-to-date! Check the "calendar of reports" that is sent to the schools each term and record the dates when reports are due. Remind the principal of appointments and meetings to be attended.

6. All bulletins and school mail should be read by you. Make arrangements with the principal to have incoming materials reach your desk as soon as they are received at school.

7. All notices and materials to be circulated within the school must have the approval of the principal.

8. School supplies and equipment are strictly for the use of the school.

9. Filing is important. Organize and mark all materials before you place them in the files. Cross index if desirable. Check out communications, reports, or other materials that are loaned to anyone. Keep your files up-to-date. Remove obsolete materials annually to make space for records of next year.

10. Your work area should be clear, with only necessities out on the desk. Other materials should be put into the desk so that you are closest to those used most often. All supplies should be kept as close as possible to the area of use, with the things used most often being the easiest to reach. Use an organizer.

THE SECRETARY'S DESK: A MOST IMPORTANT TOOL.   The desk has two work areas; i.e., the one reached by moving the forearm in an arc with the elbow close to the body, and that reached by moving the entire arm. Any space beyond this reach can be utilized only by changing the position of the body.

Instead of the conventionally styled desk, a modular type is available which increases efficiency. If both desks use the same amount of floor space, the modular design will almost double the available working area.

SHARED EQUIPMENT CAN CREATE PROBLEMS.   When other personnel or faculty members are using some of the office equipment, it helps to have certain hours reserved for this purpose so that interference is avoided. All personnel using equipment should be trained carefully in its proper use. Perhaps additional secretarial help should be provided to eliminate the necessity for the faculty's using such equipment.

A handbook for the educational secretary should be prepared by the superintendent and the professional staff, and should be presented to the governing board for official adoption. Such a handbook should provide for the necessary degree of administrative efficiency required for sound school system management and operation. The handbook for educational secretaries of one public school system includes:

1. Philosophy of the (Name) Public Schools
2. The Secretary's Position in the Educational Picture

3. National Association of Educational Secretaries
4. (State) Association of Educational Secretaries
5. (Local) Association of Educational Secretaries
6. Basic Technical Skills
7. Personal Growth and Development
8. Public Relations
9. Rating of Secretaries
10. List of Reports
11. Educational Terms
12. (Assignment Specifications)

Do

1. Be concerned about good working conditions, and make that concern known.
2. Provide for well-planned orientation and in-service education programs.
3. Provide for written personnel policies.
4. Provide for definite work schedules for all classified personnel, and involve the personnel concerned in developing the schedules.
5. Provide adequate equipment and supplies to do the job.
6. Remember to express appreciation for a job well done.
7. Introduce all classified staff members to visiting personnel when they are encountered in the course of the visit.
8. Encourage students to address all members of the classified staff as Mr., or Mrs., Miss, or Ms.
9. Work for adequate remuneration for the classified staff.
10. Provide adequate facilities (not just the boiler room!) for personal needs of the classified staff.
11. Keep lines of communication alive between the principal and members of the classified staff and remember to invite all members of the classified staff to the "staff meetings" held with the certificated staff.
12. Measure success in terms of the quality and quantity of output, the promptness with which duties are performed, individual initiative and suggestions for improvement, and cooperation with the entire staff.
13. Develop self-confidence in each classified staff member by recognizing each as an individual, encouraging creativeness, and expressing appreciation.
14. Work for the assignment of the bus driver as a full-time employee of the school system.
15. Work with other supervising principals to establish a policy wherein in-service education meetings for classified personnel will be held on school time, when the meetings are intended to improve job performance. If special meetings are held for job advancement, these may be held on the employees' time.
16. See to it that the instructional methods employed at these in-service education meetings are those preferred by the classified staff, to wit: meetings

with demonstrations, video tapes, films, and which use conference techniques.[11]

Don't

1. Assume that the new classified employee knows the job.
2. Assume that the work of the classified employee is being satisfactorily done unless you have evidence to that effect.
3. Assume that the work of the classified employee is not being satisfactorily done unless you have evidence to that effect.
4. Allow salesmen to sell a bill of goods to your secretary or custodian.
5. Disregard the problems of the custodian, the cafeteria worker, or the bus driver.
6. Permit your classified employees to attempt to repair equipment that they are not trained to repair.

TRENDS IN IMPROVING THE PERFORMANCE OF CLASSIFIED PERSONNEL

Toward ⟶ Developing Written Assignment

Specifications for Classified School Personnel

More and more school systems are developing written assignment specifications that list the major requirements, duties, and benefits of the position; compensation, fringe benefits, tenure, and promotion policies; and the qualifications requisite for obtaining the position.

The specifications will be developed cooperatively and evaluated continuously.

Toward ⟶ Establishing Written Policies

Governing Classified Personnel

School systems are developing programs for the administration of classified personnel. Such programs are formulated as written policies that are adopted by the governing board.

[11] Lowell G. Keith, S. Robert Infelise, and George J. Perazzo, *Guide for Elementary School Administration* (Belmont, California: Wadsworth Publishing Company, 1965), pp. 57–59.

Toward	→	More Realistic Salary

Schedules for Classified Personnel

If the schools are to obtain and retain the best possible classified personnel, they must maintain salary schedules that are realistic and that approximate the rate of pay in industry for the same work. Fringe benefits equivalent to those in industry must be provided.

Toward	→	Maintaining Staff Development In-service

Education Programs for all Classified Personnel

A staff development in-service education program will be established for classified personnel that will cover the major facets of the job at hand, will use many techniques, and will be practical. Such a program will include a discussion of rules and regulations, opportunities to work with more experienced personnel, individual conferences with the supervising principal and with specialist-consultants, special job instruction for beginning employees, and meetings stressing job skills and other problems of classified personnel. Instructional methods preferred are meetings featuring demonstrations, films, and conference techniques.[12]

In-service education meetings will be held on school time; the meetings are intended to improve job performance. Special meetings for individual job advancement may be held on employees' time.

Toward	→	an Increase in Benefits and Prestige

for All Classified Employees

For example, we are beginning to see an increase in the compensation and prestige of the individual who is charged with safely transporting many school children. The bus driver will be a full-time employee of the school system, rather than occupying a part-time position.

[12] Taylor Jackman, "The In-Service Training of Classified Employees in Elementary School Districts of Southern California" (unpublished Doctoral dissertation, University of Southern California, 1959), pp. 154–155.

Supervisory Problems

In Basket

Problem 1

The custodial service at Jessie Junior High was not satisfactory. The classrooms and halls were poorly swept and very little dusting was done. There was a "don't care" attitude developing among teachers and students concerning the appearance of the building. It was called to the attention of the supervising principal that the custodian was not doing a satisfactory job. Teacher morale was reflected in the appearance of the classrooms. Students were becoming careless in disposing of gum wrappers and other waste materials. There was a noticeable lack of pride in the looks of the building.

Then finally one morning, after an especially messy paper cutting art lesson the preceding day, Miss Samantha's room was untouched by the custodian. Paper scraps lay scattered about, a wastebasket remained filled to the brim, and bits of this and that were even outside the door. This scene greeted Miss Samantha when she entered her room at 8:10 A.M. Miss Samantha wrote a letter of complaint to you, the supervising principal.

What should you, as the supervising principal, do?

Problem 2

Thornwood School has been having its share of difficulties. The educational secretary, who has been employed at the school for twenty years, had as her supervisor the former principal for nineteen of those twenty years. Miss Dundy, the former principal, was of the old school; her manner was as gruff as it was insulting.

As supervising principal, you have been receiving complaints from teachers and parents alike that the educational secretary seems to think that she is *ex officio* assistant principal. Teachers complain that they are not able to obtain supplies when they needed them for instruction because "she says she's too busy!" They have further complained that the educational secretary has demanded explanations as to why certain requests have been made or certain actions taken, when the teachers believe such decisions to be in the realm of their professional domain. Yesterday a parent complained that in your absence the secretary had administered corporal punishment in the form of a "light paddling" to her child. The custodian has complained that the secretary is treating him in a manner which is unbefitting his skill and competence.

This secretary is going to retire in two years. She is a good typist and is most efficient in handling office routine.

How should you, as the supervising principal, proceed to rectify the situation?

Questions and Suggested Activities Concerning How to Assist Classified Employees

Questions

1. What are the primary and secondary duties of the clerk and the secretary?
2. How should office duties be allocated to the secretary and the clerk?
3. What are ways for making more effective use of the principal's office time?
4. What time-saving equipment would you recommend for the school offices?
5. What procedures should be adopted to handle petty cash funds for the school?
6. What office procedures should be standardized?
7. To what extent should the clerk do typing and duplicating for the teachers? Or, what clerical services provision should be made for the teachers?
8. What provision should be made when the clerk goes to lunch or is away from the office for any extended length of time?
9. What should a good office schedule include?
10. What are the ideal qualities and characteristics of the school secretary? How could you set up an in-service education procedure for your secretary?
11. What are the values and limitations of classified employee participation in supervision?
12. What should be the principal's role in providing for classified staff growth in job skills? The specialist-consultant's role? The supervisor's role?
13. What should be the principal's attitude toward employees who neglect needed growth?
14. How should a principal evaluate the effectiveness of a cafeteria worker? Of a clerk? Of a custodian? Of a bus driver?
15. What is the difference between the administration and supervision of classified employees?
16. How can the supervising principal create initiative and resourcefulness among classified employees?
17. How might the recruitment, selection, and assignment of classified employees be improved?
18. What is the difference between the authoritarian and inspirational concept of classified employee supervision?

Suggested Activities

1. Prepare an assignment specification for the secretary of a school.
2. Prepare an assignment specification for the custodian of a school.
3. Prepare a list of topics that you believe should be included in orientation meetings for classified personnel. Be sure to indicate special topics that would be included in meetings for custodians, clerks, transportation employees, and cafeteria employees.
4. Indicate what you believe to be the responsibilities of the principal and the

director of buildings and grounds in supervisir g the work of a custodian.

5. Prepare a list of in-service training activities that should be used in assisting the school secretary to improve her performance.
6. Prepare a sample table of contents for a handbook for school custodians.
7. Prepare a sample table of contents for a handbook for school bus drivers.
8. Prepare a list of equipment that you believe should be available to the school secretary and to the school custodian in order to facilitate job performance.
9. Prepare an annotated bibliography of the major works appearing in professional journals for the past year concerning the supervision of classified personnel.
10. Prepare a skit to be presented in class in which a principal introduces a new custodian to the school and its faculty.

Selected Bibliography

Books

Brainard, Alanson D. *Handbook for School Custodians*. Revised by A. E. Goedeken. Lincoln: University of Nebraska Press, 1961.

Chandler, B. J., and Paul V. Petty. *Personnel Management in School Administration*. New York: The World Book Company, 1955.

Cone, Wm. F. *Supervising Employees Effectively*. Ann Arbor, Michigan: A-W-V Co., 1974.

Grieder, Calvin, Truman M. Pierce, and William E. Rosenstengel. *Public School Administration*. New York: The Ronald Press Company, 1961.

Keith, Lowell G., S. Robert Infelise, and George J. Perazzo. *Guide for Elementary School Administration*. Belmont, California: Wadsworth Publishing Company, 1965.

Leavitt, Harold J. *Managerial Psychology*. Chicago: University of Chicago Press, 1964.

Likert, Rensis. *New Patterns of Management*. New York: McGraw-Hill Co., 1961.

———. *The Human Organization: Its Management and Value*. New York: McGraw-Hill Co., 1967.

Linn, H. H. *The School Custodian's Housekeeping Handbook*. New York: Bureau of Publications, Teachers College, Columbia University, 1958.

———. *School Business Administration*. New York: The Ronald Press Company, 1956.

Lipham, James M. *The Principalship: Foundations and Functions*. New York: Harper & Row Publishers, Inc., 1974.

McGregor, Douglas. *The Professional Manager*. New York: McGraw-Hill Co., 1967.

Mintzberg, Henry. *The Nature of Managerial Work*. New York: Harper and Row, 1973.

Morphet, Edgar L. *Educational Organization and Administration*, 3rd ed. Englewood Cliffs, New Jersey: Prentice-Hall Inc., 1974.

Mosher, William E., and J. Donald Kingsley. *Public Personnel Administration*. New York: Harper and Brothers, 1941.

National Industrial Conference Board. *Managing By and With Objectives*. Study No. 212, 1968. 834 Third Avenue, New York, N.Y. 10022.

Odiorne, George S. *Management by Objectives*. New York: Pitman Publishing Co., 1965.

Reeder, Ward G. *Fundamentals of Public School Administration*. New York: The Macmillan Company, 1951.

Saint, Avice Marion. *Supervision of Employees—Study and Teaching*. Chicago: Nelson-Hall Co., 1974.

Shane, Harold G., and Wilbur A. Yauck. *Creative School Administration*. New York: Henry Holt and Company, 1954.

Stinnett, et al. *Professional Negotiations in Public Education*. New York: The Macmillan Company, 1966.

Stoops, Emery, Max Rafferty, and Russell E. Johnson. *Handbook of Educational Administration*. Boston: Allyn and Bacon, Inc., 1975.

Strauss, George, and Leonard R. Sayles. *Personnel: The Human Problems of Management*. Englewood Cliffs, New Jersey: Prentice-Hall, Inc., 1960.

Viles, Nelson E. *The Custodian at Work*. Lincoln, Nebraska: University Publishing Company, 1941.

Walter, J. E. *Personnel Relations*. New York: The Ronald Press Company, 1945.

Weber, Clarence A. *Personnel Problems of School Administrators*. New York: McGraw-Hill Book Company, Inc., 1954.

Yeager, William A. *Administration of the Noninstructional Personnel and Services*. New York: Harper and Brothers, 1959.

Periodicals

Carlin, M. M. "The Role of the Educational Secretary." *Teachers College Journal* XXX (March 1959): 75–79.

Carson, T. E., Jr. "Is Your Janitor Work Fair?" *Nation's Schools* XXXIV (September 1944): 58.

Essex, M. W. "Practical Personnel Policies." *National Education Association Journal* XXXVII (March 1948): 159.

Handel, H. "Mr. Custodian, Partner in Education." *New York State Educator* XLV (April 1958): 492–494.

Kern, E. "On Secretaries in Particular." *National Education Association Journal* XXXVII (March 1948): 159.

McIntosh, Charles. "The ABC's of Training." *National Custodian* V (March-April 1968): 14–15, 36, 39–40, 43–44.

Melfi, Vincent A. "8 Steps to Cleaning Management Efficiency." *National Custodian* I (January-February 1968): 22–26.

National Industrial Conference Board. *The Personnel Man in Transition, Business Management Record* (December 1963): 7–10.

Ogden, L. K., and Emery Stoops. "Staff Morale: What Is It? How Do We Get It?" *Education Administration and Supervision* XLIII (December 1957): 487–491.

Saltonstall, Robert. *Who's Who in Personnel Administration, Harvard Business Review* XXXIII (July-August 1955): 75–83.

Saxe, R. W. "No Office Should Be Without One." *National Elementary Principal* XL (October 1960): 37–38.

Twenty Personnel Executives. *The Function and Scope of Personnel Administration, Personnel* XXIV (July 1947): 5–8. (Reprinted in Paul Pigors, Charles A. Myers, and F. F. Malm, *Management of Human Resources: Readings in Personnel Administration*. New York: McGraw-Hill Book Company, 1964, pp. 2–4.)

Films

Basic Job Skills: Working with Money. Coronet Films, Chicago: 1975.

Basic Job Skills: Handling Responsibilities. Coronet Films, 1975.

Basic Job Skills: Handling Criticism. Coronet Films, 1975.

Controlling Absenteeism. BNA Films (A Division of the Bureau of National Affairs, Inc., 5615 Fishers Lane, Rockville, Maryland 20852), 1975.

Managing in a Crisis. BNA Films, 1975.
Office Practice: Your Attitude. Coronet Films, 1974. (10 min.)
Office Practice: Manners and Customs. Coronet Films, 1974. (12½ min.)
Office Practice: Working with Others. Coronet Films, 1974. (13 min.)
Secretary: a Normal Day, 2nd ed. Coronet Films, 1974. (11 min.)
Working with Troubled Employees. BNA Films, 1975.

Other Sources

Barbour, Julius Ervin. "The Selection and Instruction of Public School Custodians in Selected School Districts." Doctoral dissertation, Michigan State College, 1954.

Evansville Public Schools. *Handbook for Educational Secretaries.* Evansville: Public Schools, 1955.

Galluzo, A. Neil. "Practices in the Administration of Classified Personnel in California." Doctoral dissertation, University of Southern California, 1955.

Jackman, Taylor. "The In-Service Training of Classified Employees in Elementary School Districts of Southern California." Doctoral dissertation, University of Southern California, 1959.

Marks, James R. "An Analysis of Assignment Specifications for Certificated School Personnel in the United States." Doctoral dissertation, University of Southern California, 1962.

National Association and Council of Business Schools. *Secretaryship as a Career Field.* Washington, D.C.: The Council, 1959.

National Association of Educational Secretaries. *Plan Your Work.* Washington, D.C.: The Association, 1959.

Remmers, H. H. "The Analysis of Employee Attitudes." *Proceedings of the First Personnel Institute.* Columbus, Ohio: State University, 1938.

The Association of School Business Officials of the United States and Canada. *Proceedings of the Association of School Business Officials of the United States and Canada.* Thirty-Eighth Yearbook. Washington, D.C.: The Association, 1952.

Support, Supervisory Personnel, Professional Responsibilities, and the Future of Educational Supervision

15

How to Supervise the Program for Obtaining Community Support

Our country has traveled a long way since the days when pioneer settlers built their own schoolhouses and the schoolmaster boarded with one family. Today our society is sophisticated, but there is a real need for people to renew their pioneering interest in the schools.

This country's future sits at the desks of today's classrooms. To protect America's heritage of individualism, freedom, and the right of each person to develop to the highest potential, the citizens must become working partners with school personnel in initiating supervisory programs that strengthen the schools.

The question in this area that most urgently needs an answer concerns how the supervising principal can best supervise the program for obtaining increased community support for the educational program in general, and for the program of school supervision in particular.

This chapter includes a discussion of the following topics:

Definitions and functions
Basic principles
How the staff can participate
How to build a community relations program
How to evaluate the community relations program
Do—-Don't
Trends
"In-Basket" supervisory problems
Questions and suggested activities

Definitions and Functions

Community Relations Defined

Broadly conceived, community relations refers to the harmony of understanding between any group and the publics it serves. Thus, any institution or organization affected by the will of these publics gives some consideration to public attitude and understanding, and to the influence certain of its activities have on the public viewpoint.[1]

The public relations of any institution are the sum total of all the impressions created by the institution and by the various persons connected with it. A strong supervisory program can exist only when it has faculty and community support.

Nucleus and Essence

The substance of any program for improved community relations is a continuous duologue with the several publics involved concerning the achievements, status, objec.ives, and desires of the schools.

In essence, we seek the understanding and cooperation of the entire commu.ity. The relationships of the supervising principal with the community should nᴐι be centered on *justifying* or *defending* a program—this is the task of the board ᴐі education and the administrative units within the school system. Rather, community relations should seek to *inform* and *present* to the public the "educational program," and plans concerning that program, as they exist.

Why Community Relations?

Public education, by its very nature, is an area of public concern. Since both funds and students are furnished by the several publics, the school owes those publics an accounting of its stewardship.

In a time of rapid technological change that, in turn, encourages just as rapid a change in the school's educational programs, community understanding is vital. The publics generally are suspicious of new instructional programs. Most adults view education in terms of what they experienced in their youth. An innovation may be considered a frill, and therefore unnecessary.

The main goal of supervision is improving the quality of education. Public relations can be seen as the means for obtaining community support and understanding that are essential to the success of the supervisory program.

Basic Principles

The following basic principles apply to the tasks of planning, organizing, implementing, evaluating, and improving the supervision of the program for community relations:

[1] See Jefferson N. Eastmond, *The Teacher and School Administration* (Boston: Houghton Mifflin Company, 1959), p. 250.

1.   The school is founded on the good will of people who support it. The main purpose of the community relations program must not be gaining financial support for the schools.
2.   The most important factor in gaining support for the supervisory program is developing and maintaining an instructional program that people like. Stress this factor, along with the value of facilities and improvements; not the money involved.
3.   The key to sustained community support of supervision is the instructional program that is responsive to the changing needs of the community.
4.   In planning a successful community relations program, the principal must be well acquainted with all aspects of the local community.
5.   To be effective, the principal must understand the power structure of the community and establish working relationships with individual and group opinion leaders.
6.   The principal knows that parents react to what they *think* the supervisory program is, rather than to what it *actually* is.
7.   Gaining support for the supervisory program is the responsibility of all members of the school team: board of trustees, administration, faculty, classified employees, students, and parents. The school principal should provide leadership.
8.   In developing support for the supervisory program, the teacher-supervisor relationship is the focal point.
9.   The basis of effective community support from parents, taxpayers, and businessmen is participation through shared responsibilities in the plans, goals, and activities of the school.
10. The principal should establish two-way communications concerning the plans, purposes, and results of the supervisory program with the school and community.
11. The student is the key to effective communications because he/she is the vital link between the home and the school.
12. The projection of a positive attitude by the school team is an indispensable factor in gaining support for the supervisory program.
13. Besides assuring that all employees know their community relations duties, responsibilities, opportunities, and limitations, it is well to appraise their effectiveness at regular intervals.

Through adequate planning, one can use all available avenues leading to the goal of enhanced public relations in the most efficient, effective, and economical manner.

Information must be geared to the several publics that are the intended receivers. This means that both the wording and the instruments used must be aimed at reaching these publics. Good publicity will not substitute for poor public relations. Good public relations involves the ability to take criticism, admit faults, and rectify shortcomings. The best road to travel in community relations is one paved by the achievement of excellence in the instructional program.

The necessity for keeping the publics well informed is recognized by all well-run organizations. School officials should help the people become intelligently and completely informed and thereby guided into sympathy and under-standing toward school problems. The responsibility of the school supervisor is: (1) to gather, (2) to organize, and (3) to present information.

Honesty is the best and only policy in supervision, as well as in all other areas of the educational enterprise. We must be prepared to present all pertinent facts in a truthful and sincere manner. No effective school-community relationship can exist without this prerequisite. Education is big business, but it must be differentiated from commercial big business. The goals of the school are not reached by the "hard-sell" of its commercial brothers.

An essential fact in public relations is that once the community supports school employees, support for the supervisory program will follow. This is a necessary outgrowth if we wish to advance the general educational program in general, and the supervisory program in particular.

WHAT THE PRINCIPAL CAN DO WITHIN THE SCHOOL ATTENDANCE AREA.   The principal in each school is the catalyst that makes the supervisory program sparkle with action and use. If the principal is aware of the personality of the school's neighborhood and understands its many facets, then the supervisory program can be geared to meet these needs:

1. Each school-community has needs to be met as each has its own pattern of social, religious, commercial-industrial, and recreational life.
2. Each community, though individual, has an obligation to relate itself to the local school system, to the state, and to the nation.

The supervising principal has a unique position in today's society. He/she can become a modern-day town crier and reawaken the people to the needs of educating their children.

THE SCHOOL AS A REFLECTION OF THE COMMUNITY.   Each school is a mirror of the community. The school's curriculum reflects what the citizens desire for their children. If the citizens do not participate in the school's life, then the activities within its walls are static and unchallenging.

Community relations seek harmony between any groups and the publics served. The supervising principal enhances this harmony by (1) informing, (2) rallying support, (3) developing an awareness of the importance of education in a democracy, (4) developing the partnership between parents and the school, (5) integrating the program for community relations, (6) evaluating the status of the program, and (7) correcting existing misunderstandings.

If well planned, such a program will be truthful, unselfish, intrinsic in the instructional program, positive, continuous, comprehensive, interesting, and sensi-tive to the needs and desires of the school patrons. It will be expressed clearly so that it is understood easily.

THE GOVERNING BOARD AND COMMUNITY RELATIONS. The governing board should develop an adequate statement concerning public relations. This statement should appear in the official handbook. Suggestions for implementing the provisions should be listed.

Definite board policies should be developed that will (1) facilitate cooperation with other community agencies, and (2) insure working conditions that will attract and hold competent employees.

The governing board can further public relations by:

1. Planning community programs
2. Erecting schools that have areas for meetings
3. Maintaining open channels of effective communication between industry and the school
4. Providing adequate financial support for the program for school supervision.

THE SUPERINTENDENT AND PUBLIC RELATIONS. The person responsible for planning and coordinating public relations for supervisory programs must be the superintendent. Under the superintendent's leadership, the supervising principal performs to the best of his/her ability. The superintendent must encourage the supervising principal to adapt activities to suit his/her own personality, the personalities of the teachers and students of the school, and the personality of the community. In-service education courses for the superintendent and for the supervising principal are recommended. Technical assistance is essential.

In many school systems, one person is assigned the task of coordinating news releases. The superintendent, as well as the supervising principal, should stress the importance of every member of the staff participating in the program for community relations. The educators should maintain broad, professional contacts outside of the school system. All must work to eliminate the teacher stereotype, and to hold to high professional standards in the selection of school employees.

HOW SCHOOL MANAGEMENT INFLUENCES COMMUNITY RELATIONS. Generally speaking, planning and managing school business should be done at such a high level that public confidence will be created and maintained. Up-to-date instructional materials must be provided. Organizing and preplanning help to avoid confusion. The amount of direct lay participation in educational planning, even in an advisory capacity, should be delimited sharply in amount and kind. The community is represented through its elected representatives on the governing board.

WHAT THE PRINCIPAL CAN DO IN THE AREA OF SCHOOL FINANCE AND COMMUNITY RELATIONS. The supervising principal has definite responsibilities in maintaining the community's confidence in the fiscal management of its educational enterprise. Several suggestions are:

1. The supervising principal should have national, state, and local school finance data available at all times.

2. He/she should be ready to interpret the relationship of financial support to the quality of education.
3. Generally speaking, the principal should insure that no fees are charged to parents or to students, nor should teachers be encouraged to purchase materials from their own funds.
4. If a piece of equipment or material has a place in the instructional program, the school system should purchase the item.

HOW TO ORGANIZE AND ASSIGN PRIORITIES FOR PUBLICITY.   A list of criteria for organizing a publicity program follows:

1. Unfounded attacks by "taxpayers" organizations should be met with a counterattack of facts.
2. Reports should be issued to the public concerning what is happening with bond funds that have been voted.
3. Easy to read, interesting financial reports should be published regularly.
4. All publicity should be accomplished through selected media.
5. As many types of media should be utilized as possible.
6. Selected material should be distributed throughout the year, with a few good stories released each week.
7. One individual should be in charge of school publicity.
8. The material produced should be checked by a second staff member.
9. All material should be simple, honest, direct, and up to date.

Some priorities for publicity, listed in descending order, follow:

1. Student programs and welfare
2. The instructional program
3. Guidance and health services
4. Attendance, discipline, and control
5. Enrollment trends
6. School staff members and the administration
7. The building program
8. School management and finance
9. Parents' association
10. General student activities.

How the Staff Can Participate

The Supervising Principal Obtains
Participation of the Staff Members

In developing support for the supervisory program, the principal must work not only with the community, but also very closely with the professional staff. He/she must insure that each person on the staff understands and sees the need for improvement through supervision and discerns its relationship to the total school program. The school program should be planned cooperatively with the total staff. Specialists[2] know that sharing in formulating decisions concerning one's working world contributes to realizing the profession's goals.

How to Educate the Members of the Staff

The supervising principal should develop, in cooperation with staff members, a program for keeping parents and citizens informed. He/she also must acquaint the staff with the techniques of good public relations. Certainly it is beneficial for the students to arrive at home happy and excited about their class, but all this can come to a halt if the parents have unsatisfactory experiences with the school. Many unpleasant situations and misunderstandings can be avoided if the professional staff of the school is well versed in basic public relations methods.

The principal, in planning the in-service program, should devote much time to making the staff aware of the need for successful relations with the public.

FIGURE 15-1.   Home Assignment Data Form

Name of School

Date _____

To the Parents of _____

Homework which was due today was not turned in by _____.
_____ . As it is the policy of the Board of Education that homework be assigned according to individual and class *needs*, his/her achievement in the subject area within which the homework was assigned may suffer considerably.

_____   This is the first time he/she has failed to complete a home assignment in this class.

_____   This problem has occurred in the past.

_____   He/she has failed repeatedly to turn in home assignments.

_____   An appointment has been made for a conference at school on

_____ , at _____ . Please notify me if this time is not convenient.

Thank you for your kind attention to the above matter.

Sincerely,

(Principal)

---

[2] Robert E. Wilson, *The Modern School Superintendent—His Principles and Practices* (New York: Harper and Brothers, 1960), p. 422.

FIGURE 15-2.   Exceptional Progress or Improvement Form

Name of School

Date _____

Dear _____ ,

   I am pleased to inform you that _____ 's progress has been most satisfactory this past week.

Sincerely,

_____
(Principal)

The use of forms, such as those in Figures 15-1 and 15-2, should be discussed with the teaching staff. No school employee, nor any correspondence emanating from such employee, can be disregarded. "Every employed member of the school system must know every aspect of the program well enough to believe in it and to interpret it in its proper perspective to the public."[3] All have a very important part to play in obtaining the community's respect and support.

How the Custodian and the Secretary Can Help

Many times the first person whom a visitor to the school sees or talks with is the custodian or the school secretary. Their appearance, tone of voice, and knowledge of the school's program frequently will determine the visitor's opinion of the school. If a visitor is met at the school by a person of careless grooming and uninteresting personality who does not know the school plant and its personnel, the visitor constructs a negative mental picture of the school.

   Many times lasting impressions are made by the telephone voice of the school secretary. Is it sharp, listless, annoyed in tone, or is it warm, pleasing, and helpful? These qualities do much to create displeasure or good will toward the school. If a visitor is met at the school by a person of careless grooming and "for a system is constantly judged by the way its telephones are answered and visitors are received, and by the quality of its correspondence."[4]

   The supervising principal should offer reminders such as the following to school secretaries in connection with the community relations program:

1.   Remember that the child comes first.
2.   Avoid generalizing, whether at school or away from it. Weed out of your

[3] Howard Stephenson, _Handbook of Public Relations_ (New York: McGraw-Hill Book Company, Inc., 1960), p. 739.
[4] Ibid., p. 740.

conversations such phrases as "trouble with parents is . . ." or "kids now-adays . . ."

3. Be loyal to coworkers. A negative comment about one reflects on all. Positive comments foster higher public respect for the secretary as well as for all the teachers and administrators in the school.
4. Do not breach a confidence whether it is about a student, parent, teacher, or other coworker.
5. Again, avoid, however, giving the impression that the school has any "secrets" to be kept from the public. Even though there may be confidential information about an individual, it should be made clear that the overall public information policy is frank, honest, and forthright.
6. Remember that a telephone voice must be friendly, cheerful, interested, and helpful. Avoid sounding busy. Be a good listener.
7. Be cordial to visitors. Show that you are concerned with whatever the visitor is inquiring about. Make the visitor feel that the school welcomes the call and appreciates the visit.
8. Do not procrastinate or stall. Handle complaints and requests promptly.
9. Do not presume to answer for the principal or for the governing board.
10. Remember that there is no individual who is a true *enemy* of the school. There are critics and there are cranks; the well-informed, uninformed, and misinformed; the biased and the prejudiced. You must operate on the premise that everyone's views, no matter how haywire they may sometimes sound, are aimed toward improving education.
11. Treat every school patron alike, no matter how troublesome some of them seem to be. Be willing to listen. Be patient and friendly.

How Cafeteria Workers Can Help

In addition to the custodian and the school secretary, the cafeteria workers can help in the public relations program. These staff members are instrumental in creating positive or negative feelings toward the school and its supervisory program. They can help by being (1) courteous to all, (2) scrupulously neat and clean in appearance, (3) skilled in their craft, (4) the recipients of the benefit of continuous supervision, (5) made to feel that they are an important, integral part of the total school family, and (6) made aware of the vital part they play in community relations.

The School Nurse and the Community

The duties of the school nurse take him/her into the homes of many of the students. He/she can be a positive force for the good of the school. By knowing the supervisory program and understanding public relations techniques, he/she can create positive reactions to the school. The principal must arrange time for this staff member to be present at many in-service meetings.

How Teachers Can Provide Fuel
for the Program's Progress

The principal must be alert to the latest knowledge and information in education. The public relations program for teachers must be complete and must cover various techniques for communicating with parents; it should be interlaced with thoughtful, professional guidance, for teachers provide a window through which the public can view the supervisory program. Teachers must be made to realize that the school is evaluated in the minds of the parents by their response to the teachers' relationships with the home. Corrected papers, homework assignments, notes reporting on how well a student is doing in school, and person-to-person contacts have impact on the parents. Chapter 12 contains specific suggestions on how the supervising principal can help the teacher plan for more effective conferences with parents.

From the Principal's Desk

The principal can do much to gain parental support through bulletins and notices. Many parents are unable to attend the parent's association meetings. Printed information from the principal's desk is of great importance.

A monthly newsletter, dealing with some area of the curriculum or with some unmet need, is a valuable device. The letter should be well written, readable, informative, and brief. This friendly information missive may stimulate parents to participate.

By having a perforated tear-off section on the lower part of the news-letter, a principal can ask for questions and suggestions. These topics can be discussed in the following month's letter. This contact can benefit both home and school.

Every Day Is Visiting Day

Each classroom should have a planned program for inviting parents to visit the school. Parents share their children with teachers for a school year. They should feel comfortable in visiting their children's classrooms.

In the past, a teacher and the curriculum were classified information as far as parents were concerned. In many cases, parents were never given such basic information as their children's reading levels. Fortunately, due to the impact of Sputnik I on the American parent, more parents became interested in what was happening in the schools. The challenge of the future demands that educators establish and maintain a close understanding and working arrangement with the parents. Without it, the program for supervision will be ineffective.

The supervisor should remember the difference both in philosophy and implementation between parent-teacher conferences and parent-teacher-child conferences. Improving the skills of all school personnel who handle these different conferences is important to the community relations program.

Parents should be encouraged to participate actively in the several instructional and corollary programs of the school. A *Volunteer Parents Program* should be established, with goals, delimitations, selection procedures, and in-service development programs worked out cooperatively by the faculty and the parents' association.

The parents may profit from and enjoy planning for and participating in group conferences, parents' choice days, and early morning conferences, which often are better attended and more productive than conferences and programs held later in the day. Parents and teachers are less fatigued early in the day, and some baby sitting problems are solved by scheduling morning programs and conferences.

How to Build a Community Relations Program

Major steps in building a community relations program follow:

1. A competent person should be employed to organize and direct the public relations work.
2. The public relations director should be used in a counseling capacity.
3. The publics involved should be located and defined.
4. The reactions of the various publics to the objectives, services, policies, and ideals of the program involved should be analyzed.
5. The needs of the schools should be examined.
6. All public relations activities should be coordinated.
7. The efforts of the schools and the institutions of higher education should be coordinated.
8. Every policy proposal should be considered carefully in order to decrease the possibility of hasty or unwise action.
9. All possible procedures for improving relations between the schools and each of the various publics should be analyzed.
10. All possible sources of adequate funds and personnel should be examined.

To create an interest that eventually will lead to community participation in educational activities, a supervising principal should proceed through four basic steps:

1. The supervising principal should publicize and support the local parents' association.
2. The supervising principal should know the desires of the school and community. He/she should form a joint parents-community information committee. This joint group would represent better home-school coordination. It would involve both professional people and civic leaders contributing.
3. The supervising principal should utilize student help. Students provide the

community with living proof of the merits of the educational program. Teachers should be encouraged to conduct a ten-minute review of "what we learned today" just prior to dismissal each day.

4. The supervising principal should encourage attendance at board meetings. By introducing lay citizens to the benefits gained from attending school board meetings, the supervising principal will have a group with greater understanding of the many problems confronting the schools.

Once these four areas are explored, they should provide a breeding ground for many new approaches aimed at inducing a high level of positive citizen participation.

One sees in this analysis that good public relations are the result of a well-planned and well-defined program. Emphasis is placed on the need for an awareness of the various publics and their characteristics, desires, and beliefs.

How to Use the Instruments of Communication

Those in charge of the program for bettering public relations should know that several vehicles can and should be used. These media should be used when and where they will be most effective. They should be used as informative or preventive media, not as crisis media.

W. G. Reeder[5] divided public relations activities into four major categories: (1) written, (2) visual, (3) oral, and (4) social. One can readily see in the following list of communications media that many activities overlap, and thus may fall into more than one category.

1. The press
2. Radio and television
3. Exhibits
4. Commencement exercises
5. Report cards
6. Alumni gatherings
7. Debates, panels, and open forums
8. Excursions
9. Personnel
10. Bulletins
11. School newspapers
12. The local parents' association

In dealing with the vast number of media, the supervising principal must realize that in order to reach the general public, he/she must not rely on any one method of presentation. He/she must decide which medium will transmit the message to the greatest number of people in the most satisfactory manner. To rely on one medium could prove disastrous, not only because of the limited publics that may be reached but also because of certain limiting characteristics inherent within the medium.

E. Stoops and M. L. Rafferty[6] cited just such an example in the relation-

[5] Ward G. Reeder, *An Introduction to Public-School Relations* (New York: The Macmillan Company, 1937), p. 13.

[6] Emery Stoops, M. L. Rafferty, and Russell E. Johnson, *Handbook of Educational Administration* (Boston: Allyn and Bacon, Inc., 1975), p. 524.

ship between a local newspaper editor and a superintendent. The study cited below, although limited in the number of respondents is, nevertheless, of interest. It illustrates how the two disagreed on the relative importance of items included in a list of thirteen topics, in rank order:

The Editor: Rank No.		The Superintendent: Rank No.
1	Cocurricular activities	12
2	Parents' Association	11
3	Board of education and administration	8
4	Student progress and achievement	2
5	Teachers and school officers	9
6	School buildings and building program	4
7	Courses of study	5
8	Business management and finance	7
9	Discipline and behavior of students	13
10	Health of students	3
11	Value of education	1
12	Methods of instruction	6
13	Attendance	10

How to Work with the Press

The press usually publishes releases issued by the local governing board and also observes and interprets. For the most part, educators are aware of the need for a good working relationship with the press. The question is how to set about establishing and maintaining good press relations. L. W. Kindred[7] offered the following points as suggestions for improving newspaper publicity:

1. In planning the publicity program, discuss with the newspaper editor the types of stories in which he is interested and the style in which news should be presented.
2. One person should coordinate the news service. He should be available to the newspaper as needed.
3. Daily contact with the press should be established. Report possible news stories and supply requested copy.
4. Reporters should be treated with professional courtesy.
5. Honesty and frankness are essentials of news releases.
6. Confidence in the reporter is essential and advisable. Background information should be provided.
7. All copy should have news value.
8. A directory of the names, addresses, office hours, and telephone numbers

[7] Leslie W. Kindred, *School Public Relations*, © 1957, p. 336. Reprinted by permission of Prentice-Hall, Inc., Englewood Cliffs, New Jersey.

of city editors, department editors, reporters, and photographers should be kept up-to-date.

9. A weekly calendar and future events ("suspense") book should be maintained. These may be shared with reporters and photographers.

10. Reporters should be permitted a reasonable amount of freedom to interview the professional staff.

11. Reporters should be briefed in advance of governing board meetings. They should know what problems and issues will be brought up for discussion.

12. A press conference should be held when something significant and newsworthy occurs.

13. All newspapers must be treated alike, even though one may feel a dislike for the personnel and editorial policies of a particular paper.

14. Editors and reporters should receive deserved praise for the way they have written and presented a story, but *not* for having published the story.

15. The *community press* also should be employed as a means of gaining support for the supervisory program. This vehicle provides an excellent source for focusing community attention on the school.

The educator should be aware of the press's impact on the community. It long has been known that the press is one of the boldest molders of public opinion. The press reaches almost all segments of the population and can serve education well.

How to Make Use of Radio and Television

In recent years, radio and television have served as vocal arms of community-school relations. Radio and television broadcasts reach segments of the population that normally might be missed by other media. Federal law requires that the commercial stations devote a certain portion of their broadcast time to public service programs. A recent trend has been to have numerous "specials" that deal with education—in both local and national surroundings. Some educational television stations have been approved by the Federal Communications Commission.

A combination of public interest and school effort has brought these programs to the waves. A point worth considering is that much of the public will listen to or view these broadcasts although they would not take the time to read articles conveying the same information.

Television has a unique quality that the educator would be foolish to overlook. Through television, several devices may be incorporated into one. Thus, many current programs may have speakers, slides or filmstrips, live performances, charts and graphs, and a host of other techniques, all in one program.

Some Inherent Limitations of Broadcast Media

Although radio and television can serve the educator, certain difficulties are inherent in the uses of these media. For one, the problem of time is of major importance. Since radio and television are highly commercial, the desirable hours usually are devoted to commercial programs. Additionally, television time is sold in increments of fifteen, thirty, sixty, or ninety minutes. The script may be either padded or overedited, thus becoming distorted or losing its force.

Television offers an additional drawback in terms of production. It is a highly technical medium. Producing a television script may require the use of technically trained personnel whose sympathies lie in producing an "entertaining" product.

How to Evaluate the Community Relations Program

Public education, by its very nature, is an area of extreme public concern. Since funds for its maintenance are taken from the public pocket according to set formulas, the various publics must feel that their monies are being spent in an appropriate and wise manner.

A publication of the American Association of School Administrators[8] suggested the following set of criteria that may be employed to evaluate factors influencing the community relations program:

1. The governing board should develop and constantly improve the educational program, provide adequate personnel for staffing the school program, provide and maintain an educationally efficient physical plant, secure adequate financial resources, maintain a two-way contact with the adult community and the schools, and choose the chief executive and work harmoniously with him.
2. The superintendent should serve as a partner and executive officer of the board as well as a member and leader of the professional staff, and should keep open the lines of communication between the board, the coworkers, and the community.
3. The superintendent's dual role as champion of the teachers' needs and representative of the governing board provides a challenge to administration which must be faced explicitly and honestly.
4. Due deliberation should precede any policy decision.
5. Ignorance of school problems on the part of the press frequently is the cause for poor public relations. An explanation should be provided for the press in order to avoid unjustified criticism.
6. Schools should have an open board press policy.
7. Board members cannot escape being identified with schools twenty-four hours per day, and people expect them to give answers to questions. These questions can be answered only on the basis of stated board policy.
8. Supervising principals must be wise listeners also, and confine answers to questions to stated board policy and professional levels.

[8] American Association of School Administrators, *School Board-Superintendent Relationships,* Thirty-Fourth Department Yearbook (Washington, D.C.: National Education Association, 1956).

FIGURE 15-3.   Sample Service Award Form

```
┌─────────────────────────────────────────────────────────────┐
│                    (Name of School System)                   │
│                       SERVICE  AWARD                          │
│  This is to certify that _____    │
│  is presented this                                            │
│                                                               │
│                    AWARD  CERTIFICATE                         │
│                                                               │
│  in recognition of outstanding service.                       │
│                                                               │
│  _____                             │
│       Date                                                    │
│                              _____ │
│                                          Teacher              │
└─────────────────────────────────────────────────────────────┘
```

9. Board members, superintendents, and supervising principals must be able to "take the community pulse" and evaluate pressures.
10. Potential value of all local professional associations should be tapped.
11. Economical use of funds and assurance of value received are major responsibilities.
12. Awards earned by students of the school system, such as appear in Figures 15-3 and 15-4, should be publicized.
13. A booklet indicating when and where governing board meetings are held, the usual pattern of board procedure, and how one may have a subject included on the agenda should be readily available to all patrons of the school and should be presented to all who visit board meetings. Excerpts from such a booklet are included as Figure 15-5. Such a booklet should contain:

FIGURE 15-4.   Sample Attendance Record Certificate

```
┌─────────────────────────────────────────────────────────────┐
│                        CERTIFICATE                            │
│                This certificate is hereby awarded to          │
│                                                               │
│              _____                │
│              who has an outstanding record of attend-         │
│              ance and promptness, and whose citizenship       │
│              has been commendable at all times                │
│              during the term.                                 │
│                                                               │
│  _____                             │
│       Date                                                    │
│                              _____ │
│                                          Teacher              │
└─────────────────────────────────────────────────────────────┘
```

a) A message of welcome
b) A card which may be utilized to ask questions from the floor and/or to request that an item be put on the agenda
c) Instructions for utilizing the card noted in "b" above
d) A list of school system facilities
e) A summary of usual board procedure
f) A summary of the duties and sources of authority of the governing board
g) A list of board meeting dates.

What the Supervising Principal Should Consider

Every supervising principal and community relations committee should consider:

1. Specific yearly *goals.*
2. Some sort of *publication,* annual report, etc.
3. *Good relations* with the local press.
4. *Contact with local service clubs* and other community organizations.
5. A *plan* for a continuous community relations project at each of the pre-Area Council meetings.
6. A *"leadership membership"* in the National School Public Relations Association.
7. *Representation* at the Public Relations Conferences.
8. During the fall season, representation at the public relations session of the nearest state professional association field conference.
9. Purchasing subscriptions to *Report Card,* published by the California Teachers Association, Southern Section, Los Angeles, California, for members of the local board of education, parents' association presidents, presidents and/or education committee chairmen of chambers of commerce and service clubs, and other lay leaders.
    a) Subscription prices are more advantageous when one purchases in packets and personally handles mailings (committee members can help here).
    b) Many local associations precede the first issue with a letter explaining the complimentary subscription and indicating the hope that the publication will be helpful.
    c) At the end of the term, some groups follow up with a questionnaire.
    d) Some member of the public relations committee might be designated to submit news or feature stories of broad interest for inclusion in *Report Card.*
10. *Assuming leadership* in United Way, Community Chest, Salvation Army, Blood Bank, and other such drives; and arranging to have publicity in local newspapers when large association checks are presented to such agencies.
11. *Cooperation* with other supervisors and the administrators of the local school system in setting up regular channels for collection of articles, or ideas for articles, in school system or association "house organs" and community newspapers.

FIGURE 15-5.   Sample Booklet of Information for Board Meetings

---

WHAT TO DO IF YOU WISH TO ADDRESS
THE BOARD OF EDUCATION

If the Item is on the Agenda—

If you wish to speak on an item which is on the agenda, fill out the attached card, indicate the item number, and hand the card to the secretary prior to the start of the meeting. You will be called upon by the chairman at the time this subject is under consideration. He will grant you a maximum of ten minutes in which to make your comments.

If the Item is not on the Agenda—

It is impossible for the Board to make intelligent decisions on important questions without complete information. It will not act on an item which is not on the agenda.

If there is a subject which you wish the Board to consider, you may fill out and submit the attached card stating your desires. When the chairman reaches the topic, "Questions from the Floor," he will call upon you. You may have the floor for a maximum of five minutes to make your presentation and to request that your problem be placed on the agenda for a subsequent meeting. The Board will act on this request following your comments.

Board Procedure:

Adoption of the agenda for the meeting is the first item of business acted upon by the Board. The agenda then becomes the scheduled order of business.

The agenda, with its extensive background material, has been studied by each member of the Board for at least three days preceding the meeting. Board members have had an opportunity to call the district offices for clarification of items on the agenda. This procedure enables the Board members to handle more efficiently the many, many items which come before them.

[Sample Card]

Agenda Item ———————————————— Date ——————

Subject, if not on the agenda: ————————————————

————————————————————————

————————————————————————

Name ————————————————————

Address ————————————————————

Telephone ————————————————————

(If additional space is necessary, use reverse side)

a) Each teacher should be alerted to the need for a continuous flow of such ideas in order to give complete coverage and proper balance to news about school activities.

b) One person in each school might be delegated to contact others, on regular deadlines, for such contributions.

c) Emphasis might be on future events and human interest stories, rather than past events. Care should be exercised in selecting human interest materials.

d) A specialist familiar with journalistic writing may be appointed to edit copy in conformity with the style sheet of publications to which stories are submitted.

12. *Four elements that contribute to good community relations are:*
a) A fundamental belief in public education
b) A questioning attitude of "Why is this so?"
c) Belief in the democratic process
d) *A sense of humor!*

13. *Cooperation in publicizing* and promoting school system participation in American Education Week and Public Schools Week observances.

14. *Purchasing* leaflets produced by state associations, such as the California Teachers Association, for mass distribution during Public Schools Week (sold at or below cost—from one to two cents per copy).

15. *Cooperation with parents' association leaders* and unit organizations as fully as possible.

16. *Strong and continuing emphasis* on the fact that every teacher, in and out of the classroom, is contributing (consciously or otherwise) to public attitudes toward schools.
a) Reporting (regardless of the type used in the district) presents a problem and a challenge. Insofar as possible, some good words should be a part of every report about student progress.
b) A recent NSPRA publication on this subject is "Person to Person." Its contents would be helpful to many teachers.
c) There is a high rate of turnover in the "publics" in many school systems. Teachers should be genuinely hospitable to newcomers.

17. *Cooperation with the National Professional Associations,* the state associations, and the state legislature, in initiative and other campaigns.

18. *Urging educators (and others) to register and vote* at all elections.

19. *Purchasing,* for members of the committee, copies of "Freeways to Friendship" (a handbook for local associations public relations committees). Order from Field Service, CTA, 1125 West 6th Street, Los Angeles, California 90017.

Some Further School-Community Relations Aids

Some sources of materials and services are:

1. *Trends*—a monthly digest of important developments in school public relations in all parts of the country.

2. *It Starts in the Classroom Newsletter*—a monthly roundup of classroom-inspired, classroom-tested public relations ideas developed by teachers.
3. *Public Relations Leads for the Elementary School Principal*—a quarterly report on outstanding public relations case studies and how-to-do-it techniques written expressly for the elementary school principal.
4. *Public Relations Leads for the Secondary School Principal*—a quarterly review of successful public relations projects designed to help the secondary school principal plan an overall public relations program.
5. *Public Relations Leads for the Local Association Leader*—includes case studies, techniques, and publicity tips especially planned for use by local association leaders.
6. "Public Relations Research Memo"—a quarterly service of the National School Public Relations Association and the National Education Association Research Division designed to channel to subscribers new findings and background data on significant public relations topics and trends.
7. "Public Relations Guide"—a quarterly listing of new public relations books, pamphlets, films, and television and radio programs designed to spark the school public relations program.
8. "Exchange File"—a monthly mailing of outstanding printed materials produced by school and nonschool sources.
9. NSPRA handbooks:
   Let's Go to Press—a guide to better school news reporting
   Contacts Plus—a handbook of ideas for improving school-community relations
   Janie Learns to Read—a handbook to help parents understand the school's reading program, and how they can help.

The aforementioned listings may be obtained through the National School Public Relations Association (a department of the National Education Association), 1201 Sixteenth Street, N.W., Washington, D.C. 20006.

The California Teachers Association, Burlingame, California, and 1125 West Sixth Street, Los Angeles, can provide, in quantity and at minimum cost, many helpful pamphlets for distribution to the public. Among these publications are:

1. *There's a Flag Flying at Your Public School*—tells how schools are teaching American history, government, and citizenship.
2. *Assignment for Today: The 7 R's*—shows how schools are teaching the "3 R's" plus reasoning, responsibility, resourcefulness, and respect for law.
3. "The Truth About Our Public Schools"—a reprint of an article in *Changing Times,* the Kiplinger magazine, showing factually that modern children are getting a better education today than they ever could have received in the public school before. (This is one of the most effective articles written for showing the strong points of public education in the United States.)[9]

[9] See also C. W. Scott and C. M. Hill, *Public Education Under Criticism* (Englewood Cliffs, New Jersey: Prentice-Hall, Inc., 1954). This is a comprehensive anthology of three parts: major criticisms of public education, analyses of such criticisms, and suggested procedures used in meeting the criticisms. Contains more than 100 pertinent excerpts from a wide range of authors.

4. *Freeways to Friendships*—an entertaining and informative guide to beginning a public relations program.

Other sources:[10]

1. National Association of Manufacturers, 532 Emerson Street, Palo Alto, California. *This We Believe About Education*—a booklet published in the interest of greater education-industry cooperation. *National Association of Manufacturers News,* August, 1954, "Our Public Schools and Their Financial Support"—a statement of the problem, and how businessmen may help.
2. United States Chamber of Commerce, 1615 H Street, N.W., Washington, D.C. 20006. "Education—An Investment in People"—a research brochure which documents the interdependence of business and education; probably the finest and most complete publication in its field. (Due to its cost this publication is not for quantity distribution, but is invaluable when strategically placed.)

Do

1. Distribute periodically prepared materials, brochures, newsletters, and special notices concerning the school to the several "publics."
2. Arrange for speeches before the community organizations by qualified school personnel to help gain support for the supervisory program.
3. Encourage the use of research programs, studies, tests, and surveys to build an understanding of the school program and how supervision has helped.
4. Encourage citizens' advisory committees to participate actively in support of the instructional program.
5. Arrange for demonstrations and exhibits by teachers and students that can present the school program in a positive light.
6. Make information available to the local press regarding all school functions, including supervisory activities and educational accomplishments.
7. Plan for a program of teacher and supervisory conferences with the parents to share student progress and educational accomplishments. This is an excellent medium of public relations.
8. Invite the parents' association and other organized groups to participate in the responsibilities of the school program as an effective technique in gaining community support for supervision.
9. Use Open House activities to present the school program to the community.
10. Have supervisors present radio and television programs (and encourage teachers to do the same) to publicize outstanding features of the educational program.
11. Encourage school forums on important issues as a service to promote the community-school concept and draw attention to its program.

[10] See also R. F. Campbell and Elaine A. Ramseyer, *The Dynamics of School-Community Relationships* (Boston: Allyn and Bacon, Inc., 1959). This is an excellent approach to working with citizens' committees.

12. Use governing board (trustees) meetings to create understanding of the role of supervision in the educational program.
13. Encourage special curriculum area gatherings, such as Business Education days, which reach an important public.
14. Stress the importance of making sure that each student leaves school with a clear idea of what he has learned that day.
15. Take steps to strengthen staff relations. Money and time spent in this manner are investments, not an expense. They could pay enormous dividends in improved community relations.

Don't

1. Threaten, denounce, or bring pressure on an editor to print or to withhold a story.
2. Employ *destructive* criticism or become emotional when the facts of a story are reported incorrectly, when headlines give the wrong impression, when individuals are misquoted, when unfavorable news stories are published, or when a story is not published.
3. Refuse to release timely information to the press and broadcast media or pretend to be unacquainted with the details of a story.
4. Send out many news releases that really do not have news value.
5. Be drawn into controversies on a personal basis when the school is criticized or attacked in a news story.
6. Play favorites with television and radio stations or with the morning or evening (or daily or community) newspapers.
7. Create the impression that you know more about listener, viewer, or reader interests than does the commentator, reporter, producer, director, or editor.
8. Fail to invite representatives of all communication media (press and broadcast) to special school affairs that should be reported or, having invited them, fail to show them the courtesy and hospitality that is expected.
9. Cause the commentators and reporters to wait for a long time for an interview with a school official.
10. Always be on the "asking end" in your relations with the press.
11. Fail to obtain support for the community relations program through a functional in-service education plan, strengthened by a professional staff that practices good public relations every day.
12. Neglect pushing for an adequate budgetary provision for the program for community relations.
13. Neglect the professional associations, which can be of great help in planning your program for improved community relations.
14. Plan for improved community relations on the basis of a particular past experience in a stable present, for the materials, content, and procedures of the requirements of education are changing so rapidly that these changes must be taken into account if the program for school-community relations is to have validity.

TRENDS IN OBTAINING COMMUNITY SUPPORT

Toward ⟶   the Assigning of an Individual to
Serve as Community Relations Coordinator

Medium- and large-size school systems of the future will assign an individual who is trained, perhaps at the doctoral level, in community relations. This individual will be the chairperson of a committee composed of certificated and classified personnel and will devote much time to publicizing the supervisory program. He/she will have on the staff an experienced communications officer. Broadcast facilities will be utilized extensively. Through such a program, sufficient support for the educational complex will be obtained. Planning for community relations will be done on the basis of past experience and present conditions. Planning for improved community relations cannot be made on the basis of a particular past experience and a stable present, for the materials, content, and procedures of the requirements of education are changing rapidly, and these changes must be taken into account if the program for school-community relations is to be a valid one.

Toward ⟶   a Community More Fully Educated
Concerning Both the Educational Program of the
School and the Supervision of Instruction

The program of community relations of the future will lay the foundations for introducing new policies and practices and will invite community cooperation in connection with school improvement. It will educate the pupil more fully with regard to the work of the school through courses of study devoted to examining the school system. It will awaken community concern for public education, will develop a more friendly feeling toward the school system, and will point out the contributions of the school to children and to society. The manifest need for more adequate financial support will be emphasized.

Research in attaining, maintaining, and enhancing community support for education as a whole, and for educational supervision in particular, will be conducted at the university level and by the supervisors in the field. Professional associations will continue to participate in this research.

Supervisory Problems

Problem 1

Candy machines have been placed in five of six secondary school buildings. Carbonated soft drink vending machines are available to students in the senior high schools. In one junior high school there is a milk and orange drink dispenser. Students have access to the machines throughout the school day.

This practice is in violation of district policy. The policy, written and in effect before candy machines were installed, stated:

> During regular school hours candy and soda pop shall be sold only in the school cafeterias and only during regular lunch hours. This policy does not prohibit the sale of milk in vending machines.

Teachers have complained that accessibility of vending machines during the school day increases *a permissive attitude* and affects adversely the discipline in the school. It has been charged that educational objectives are being ignored by "not practicing what we preach about dental and personal health practices." The state administrator of federal hot lunch programs has registered a complaint that the sale of candy is contrary to regulations of federal hot lunch programs. Five principals have stated that revenue from the machines is essential to help pay for increased costs of student activities. The revenue from the candy machines is significant.

The local distributor who supplies the machines and keeps them stocked has an investment in the machines. He has said that he would resist removal of his machines and the ensuing loss of business.

As supervising principal, would you decide that the existing policy be enforced and the vending machines removed? If so, how should this be done? What would you do?

Problem 2

At a recent meeting of the administrative council, the superintendent presented her views concerning community relations. She indicated that she felt that good community relations should be within the skill and scope of the school community; that is, that it should be attainable. She stressed that community relations should be a continuous effort, based on truth and honesty, which would unfold and develop naturally. She emphasized the importance of interest and the stimulation of enthusiasm and good will, and of the importance of good two-way, open channels of communication. She said that she felt all available avenues should be used so that the program could be comprehensive, and concluded by saying that the community relations program should be balanced in time and emphasis as well as planned, guided, and flexible. At the following meeting of the administrative council, the superintendent reported that she believed that the success of a community relations program depends, to a large extent, on the school personnel and the students. She assigned various tasks to the individuals attending the meeting.

Your task, as supervising principal, is to prepare a checklist to be used in evaluating the community relations program with respect to the local school, the classroom, and the teacher association group.

How would you proceed?
Whom would you involve in solving your problem?
What would you do?
What checklist would you come up with?

Problem 3

The superintendent of schools, once again, has become concerned about the adequacy of the community relations program. He indicated that he felt that time and/or money spent in fact-finding research could well prove to be good insurance in a community relations program. He indicated that he felt that the power structure and decision-making machinery in the community was difficult to discern; that some facts were deeply imbedded and required especially careful study.

Although you know that you will not have to go to the public in the near future to ask for a tax rate increase or for a bond issue to be passed, nevertheless the superintendent has indicated that he feels it is necessary to know more about how the public feels about its schools. Your assignment is to gather that information.

How would you proceed?
What would you do?

Problem 4

As supervising principal of an elementary school with 800 pupils, you have noticed a steadily declining attendance at the functions that currently are planned for parents.

How can you increase parent attendance and participation and involvement?
How would you proceed?

Questions and Suggested Activities Concerning
How to Obtain Support for the Supervisory Program

Questions

1. What are the most important areas in your curriculum that are causing friction in the community? What, if anything, should be done about them?
2. What are the key activities in your school that have positive public relations value? How much time is being spent by personnel in your school on these functions?
3. What in-service functions have been planned in your school to acquaint school personnel with modern public relations techniques?
4. What are the most important attitudes, values, traditions, and customs in your school community? How do they manifest themselves?
5. Who are the official and unofficial opinion leaders in your community? In what ways do they exert their influence?
6. What is the attitude of your school personnel toward the school system? How are these attitudes projected to the community?
7. What are some of the common misunderstandings about supervisory programs? On the part of the teacher? Parents? Students?
8. Are public relations as important in education as they are in business or industrial enterprises, labor organizations, professional associations, and governmental agencies?

Suggested Activities

1. Prepare summaries of daily class activities that the child can take home to parents.
2. Prepare a school letter, meaningful to parents, on an interesting new unit of study, materials, or techniques being developed in your school.
3. Write a newpaper release covering an unusual feature of your school program, such as dropout level, programmed learning, computer supported instruction, team teaching, or flexible scheduling.
4. Prepare a program to initiate or improve open house activities in your school system.
5. Review the report card system in your school from a public relations point of view and recommend ways this device may be used more effectively to communicate with parents.
6. Study the methods by which the telephone is answered in your school and recommend ways to improve telephone techniques.
7. Review the parents' association program for the year and recommend ways by which activities can be improved to gain maximum public relations value.
8. Study the extra class activities of your school and recommend ways to involve parents in problem-solving activities that will have optimum community relations value.

Selected Bibliography

Books

Adler, Irving. *What We Want of Our Schools—Plain Talk on Education, from Theory to Budgets.* New York: The John Day Company, 1957.

Arnold, William E. et al. *The Administration of Public Education.* New York: The Ronald Press Company, 1952.

Bennett, Margaret E. *Guidance in Groups: A Resource Book for Teachers, Counselors, and Administrators.* New York: McGraw-Hill Book Company, Inc., 1955.

Bernays, Edward L. *Public Relations.* Norman: University of Oklahoma Press, 1957.

Brown, Rex V. *Research and the Credibility of Estimates.* Homewood, Illinois: Richard D. Irwin, Inc., 1971.

Campbell, R. F., and Elaine A. Ramseyer. *The Dynamics of School-Community Relationships.* Boston: Allyn and Bacon, Inc., 1959.

Cook, Lloyd. *School Problems in Human Relations.* New York: McGraw-Hill Book Company, Inc., 1957.

Davies, Daniel R., and Kenneth F. Heller. *Citizens Committees.* New London, Connecticut: Arthur C. Croft Publications, 1954.

Eastmond, Jefferson N. *The Teacher and School Administration.* Boston: Houghton Mifflin Company, 1959.

Frey, Sherman H., and Keith R. Getschman. *School Administration: Selected Readings.* New York: Thomas Y. Crowell Company, 1969.

Gray, John Wylie. *Communication and Leadership.* Reston, Virginia: National Association of Secondary School Principals, 1973.

Jones, James J. *School Public Relations: Issues and Cases.* New York: G. P. Putnam's Sons, 1960.

Kindred, L. W. *School Public Relations.* Englewood Cliffs, New Jersey: Prentice-Hall, Inc., 1957.

McCloskey, Gordon. *Education and Public Understanding.* New York: Harper and Brothers, 1959.

Nance, Everette. *Community Council: Its Organization and Function.* Midland, Michigan: Pendell Publishing Co., 1975.

Reeder, Ward G. *An Introduction to Public-School Relations.* New York: The Macmillan Company, 1937.

Scott, C. W., and C. M. Hill. *Public Education Under Criticism.* Englewood Cliffs, New Jersey: Prentice-Hall, Inc., 1954.

Stearns, Harry L. *Community Relations and the Public Schools.* Englewood Cliffs, New Jersey: Prentice-Hall, Inc., 1955.

Stephenson, Howard. *Handbook of Public Relations.* New York: McGraw-Hill Book Company, Inc., 1960.

Stoops, Emery, and Max Rafferty, Jr. *Practices and Trends in School Administration.* Boston: Ginn and Company, 1961.

Stoops, Emery, Max Rafferty, and Russell E. Johnson. *Handbook of Educational Supervision.* Boston: Allyn and Bacon, Inc., 1975.

Whitt, Robert, and Larry Burdan. *The Community School Principal: New Horizons.* Midland, Michigan: Pendell Publishing Co., 1973.

Wilson, Robert E. *The Modern School Superintendent—His Principles and Practices.* New York: Harper and Brothers, 1960.

Zirbes, Laura. *Spurs to Creative Teaching.* New York: G. P. Putnam's Sons, 1959.

Periodicals

American School Board Journal. "Try This Common Sense Little Way to Win Community Support for Your Schools." *American School Board Journal* CLXII (January 1975): 50.

Independent School Bulletin. "Public Relations and the Press." *Independent School Bulletin* XXXIV (December 1974): 55–56.

Soverly, Ron et al. "The Newspaper as a Tool for Teaching Kids to Read." *Phi Delta Kappan* LVII (December 1975): 260–261.

Mauro, Carl. "Partners in Education." *Educational Leadership* XV (April 1958): 401–406.

Nations Schools and Colleges. "Public Relations: Community Involvement, Cost Control." *Nations Schools and Colleges* I (September 1974): 56.

Ressing, Clinton. "Education's Bad Press." *Phi Delta Kappan* LVII (December 1975): 272–273.

Audio Cassettes

Crisis in the Schools. Rochester, New York: Xerox, Inc., 1971. (58 min.) Community involvement and changes in curricula and voting procedures.

Public Opinion in a Democracy. Rochester, New York: Xerox, Inc., 1969. (26 min.) Professor Peter Odegard points out the differences between opinion, attitude and culture, and analyzes mass media's considerable role in molding public opinion.

Other Sources

American Association of School Administrators. *Public Relations for America's Schools.* Twenty-Eighth Department Yearbook. Washington, D.C.: National Education Association, 1950.

———. *School Board-Superintendent Relationships.* Thirty-Fourth Department Yearbook. Washington, D.C.: National Education Association, 1956.

Educational Policies Commission. *Strengthening Community Life: Schools Can Help.* Washington, D.C.: National Education Association, 1954.

Mass Media in Education. Fifty-Third Yearbook of the National Society for the Study of Education. Chicago: University of Chicago Press, 1954.

National Citizens Commission for the Public Schools. *How Can Citizens Help Their Schools?* New York: The Commission, 1954.

National School Public Relations Association. *Public Relations Gold Mine.* Volume II. Washington, D.C.: National Education Association, 1959.

———. *Public Relations Gold Mine, Brightest Ideas of 1957.* Washington, D.C.: National Education Association, 1957.

————. *No News Is Bad News Where Schools Are Concerned.* Washington, D.C.: National Education Association, 1955.

————. *Person to Person—The Classroom Teacher's Public Relations.* Washington, D.C.: National Education Association, 1956.

————. *Contact Plus—A Handbook of Ideas for Improving School-Community Relations.* Washington, D.C.: National Education Association, 1954.

————. *Action and Reaction—Public Relations for Educational Secretaries.* Washington, D.C.: National Education Association, 1957.

Williams, Catharine. *Community as Textbook.* (Fastback Series #64.) Bloomington, Indiana: Phi Delta Kappa, 1975.

16

How to Select Personnel
for Supervisory Positions

School systems have two types of supervisors. The first type is the *line* supervisor, such as the building principal. The building principal is responsible to the central office for the supervision of both personnel and programs within his unit. The second type of supervisor holds a *staff* position and is responsible as a specialist for one segment of the program. Staff supervisors hold titles such as coordinator, reading specialist, psychologist, or health supervisor. Staff supervisors participate mostly in building-level programs, usually at the call of the principal. Staff supervisors must work for and with the principal since he is held responsible for what goes on at the building level.

Selecting supervisors is complex since there are many kinds of positions, particularly among the varied specialists among the staff support group. The school system, therefore, must set up varied criteria for the selection of line and staff supervisors, including the several kinds of specialists.

This chapter includes a discussion of the following points:

Selection and recruitment
How to appraise candidates for supervisory positions
How to set priorities for candidate qualities
How to match candidate with position
How to decide whether to reject or accept a candidate
How to make probationary assignments
How to evaluate the selection process
Do—Don't
Trends
"In-Basket" supervisory problems

Selection and Recruitment

Any selection process must be preceded by a strong recruitment program. The recruitment program must attract as many qualified candidates as possible before the techniques of careful selection can take place. An effective recruitment process usually will produce a large group of applicants, many of whom obviously are underqualified. The underqualified candidates should be rejected and courteously informed. This early weeding out is best for both the candidate and the school system.

Selection Policies and Procedures

Before vacancies arise, the board of education should adopt specific policies and procedures. These policies should be adhered to strictly in all cases for selecting any type of supervisor. For example, the policies should state that no position at the supervisory level should be filled unless the candidate completes every step of the stipulated process. The policies should state that all positions *will be filled strictly on the basis of merit,* and that no discrimination will be permitted concerning such conditions as marital status, sex, race, age, or ethnic background. These policies should be based on the fact that the schools belong to the people and that the people who pay for the operation of schools deserve the most qualified and capable supervisor for each available position.

After the selection committee has agreed on a candidate for the supervisory position, there should be well-established procedures for completing the contractual relationship and beginning an orientation process. The superintendent should see that the whole selection process is reviewed, evaluated, and revised as changing conditions point to the need for improvement.

Importance of Selection

Mediocre supervisors run mediocre educational programs. Educational programs in a school rarely rise above the competency of the principal. A strong line supervising principal, backed up with highly capable staff supervisors, can establish and maintain "lighthouse" programs. W. Castetter has stressed careful selection as leading to the assurance that merit will be the key factor.[1]

Business and industry have led the way in recognizing the importance of careful selection with respect to supervisory and executive positions. One engineering firm in Dallas, Texas, with highly technical government contracts, budgets as much as $20,000 for recruitment and selection of each key line and staff officer. Through experience this company has learned that the most meritorious candidates must be secured if the company is to compete with others who are seeking the same government grants. Likely candidates, therefore, are flown into Dallas from any part of the world and kept for the required number of days at company expense as a means of determining the candidate's capabilities, attitudes,

[1] William B. Castetter, *The Personnel Function in Educational Administration,* 2nd ed. (New York: Macmillan Publishing Co., Inc., 1976), p. 168.

family status, eagerness, health, and overall likelihood of advancing the company's welfare. This same care and expense should be provided for selecting line and staff supervisors for our schools. Better selection will insure better educational programs.

Careful selection serves the best interests of both the school system and the candidate. It is obvious that when strong supervisory candidates are selected, and they build strong programs, the school system will benefit. It is less obvious but equally true that when unqualified candidates are selected for supervisory positions, and suddenly find themselves treading water over their professional heads, they have been harmed. Placing an unqualified teacher in the principalship is a disservice to that teacher. A good teacher is lost and a poor principal is a continuing problem. Due to social and political pressures, poorly prepared candidates have been professionally boosted into supervisory positions. Then when they have failed to render satisfactory performance, they have lost the esteem of their colleagues, the students, and the community. We cannot over stress the importance of improved selection.

The case of John Flagel (name changed) is a perfect example of poor selection. John had taught for two years in a small district in Iowa. His father was the superintendent of schools in an adjoining district and his mother was socially prominent in the community where John taught. John's superintendent, a close friend of John's father, wished to "make points," and instead of recruiting outside the district and going through good selection procedures, he just announced that John Flagel would be principal.

Young principal John went through a very brief "honeymoon" with his more mature faculty, and then laughter turned to derision among the primary teachers. John had taught only two years at the sixth-grade level. Even the upper grade teachers with 10 to 15 years experience took his suggestions lightly or rejected them altogether. Discipline deteriorated and faculty morale plummeted. This school discontent seeped into the community, so that in the middle of the second year, John resigned under pressure and enrolled in an eastern university. Both the school and John Flagel suffered needlessly due to poor selection policies and procedures. Stoops, Rafferty, and Johnson say that "The success of the educational program is dependent upon the selection of qualified [candidates] . . ."[2]

Criteria for the Selection of Supervisory Personnel

The superintendent has the responsibility for developing criteria for the selection of supervisory personnel. These criteria should be reported to, and approved by, the board of education. The criteria should specify that written policies and procedures be prepared and made available to all candidates. Selection must be an open process. When policies and procedures are clear and understood, selection

[2] Emery Stoops, Max Rafferty, Russell E. Johnson, *Handbook of Educational Administration: A Guide for the Practitioner.* (Boston: Allyn and Bacon, Inc., 1975), p. 623.

proceeds orderly and effectively. The practice of selecting cronies over a glass at the bar or in a smoke-filled room is *passé*. The wife's cousin or a good friend of the board's chairman should go through the selection process with all other applicants and be judged on the basis of merit only.

Again, let us state that policies for selection should clearly state that there will be no rejection due to sex, race, age, nationality, or religion. The reverse is equally important. The policies should state that there will be no affirmative selection just because of sex, race, etc. This places selection back where it belongs: *on the basis of merit only*. As far as the school system can discern, using the most refined techniques in existence, the candidate that ranks highest in training, experience, and personal qualifications should be given the contract.

Position Specifications

During the recruitment process, detailed position specifications should be given to all applicants. These specifications must identify the candidate qualities most desired. The selection committee then must choose the candidate who best fulfills the position specifications regardless of social, racial, or political thrusts.

Figure 16-1, courtesy of Dr. Paul E. Dundon, superintendent, Garden Grove (California) Unified School District, illustrates good practice in setting forth position specifications in employing a music supervisor.

FIGURE 16-1.   Garden Grove Unified School District.

Office of Personnel Services

Announcement of Application and Screening for the Position of:

MUSIC SUPERVISOR (K–12)

Basic Responsibilities:
   Under the Supervision of the Director of Instruction, the Supervisor of Music (K–12) is responsible for the planning, coordinating of the vocal and instrumental music curriculum for grades K–12.

Typical Duties:
   1. Initiates and coordinates the vocal and instrumental music program and curriculum in grades K–12.
   2. Assists in planning and implementing an articulated music program.
   3. Assists teachers who have special problems in techniques and methods of teaching music.
   4. Consults with principals on the implementation of the music curriculum.
   5. Organizes and presents pertinent workshops.
   6. Consults with Office of Personnel Services and principals on the employment and evaluation of music personnel.
   7. Makes recommendations for the purchase and distribution of materials.

8. Visits the music teachers and consults with principals on such visitations.
9. Coordinates music festivals and special music programs.
10. Cooperates in the supervision and evaluation of special teachers of
    music.
11. Develops schedules for special teachers of music.
12. Serves as district representative on all music committees.
13. Accepts reasonable share of the responsibility for the operation of the
    general school program.

Requirements:
   General Administration Credential
   Standard Administration or appropriate K–12 Supervision Credential
   Presently employed in the GGUSD

Salary and Length of Assignment:
1. Range 10, Administrator's Salary Schedule
2. Twelve contract months, 216 contract days

Application Procedure:
   Applicants are requested to submit a letter of interest and a resume to
   the Office of Personnel Services.

Who Should Select?

Who should administer the selection process? In very small schools, the superintendent must perform and direct many of the steps in recruitment and selection.
He/she should utilize as much as possible the help of other supervisors and
teachers. A middle-sized school system usually has a Director of Personnel or a
Director of Instruction who handles personnel procedures. This office organizes
and develops all necessary selection processes. The personnel office chooses a
selection committee whose members will be responsible for the new supervisor,
along with people who will be supervised. Whenever feasible, school systems
should employ the services of university professors, county offices (intermediate
unit), or supervisors with similar duties in nearby school districts.

It is easy to prescribe policies and procedures that state *what* to do in
selection, but much harder to follow the *how* in securing the best possible candidates.

How to Appraise Candidates for Supervisory Positions

The appraisal of candidates for supervisory positions is one of the most important
functions of school administration. Teachers, too, should be of highest caliber, but
a teacher affects the educational program for a classroom of about 30. If a
supervisor works with 30 teachers, then that supervisor is affecting the educa-

tional program for 30 times 30, or about 900 students. Once employed, a good supervisor can raise the level of instruction. The proper appraisal of candidates should lead to rejection of the unfit and selection of the outstanding. The questions that arise in any good selection are: *Who* does *what? How* is it done and *when?* Figure 16-2 suggests answers. It must be understood that procedures outlined in Figure 16-2 should be changed to fit different size school systems, and that the items might be shifted on occasion from one administrative officer to another. Adapting the suggested activities can help in the selection process.

The techniques involved in selecting candidates often determine the degree of success that a school district has in selecting the best candidate. Many selection

FIGURE 16-2.   Illustration of Selection Responsibilities and Functions.

Board of Education
1. Approves good employee benefits
2. Adopts selection policies and procedures
3. Approves candidate recommendations by superintendent

Superintendent
1. Recommends good employee benefits and working conditions
2. Organizes the selection process
3. Recommends candidate(s) to board
4. Evaluates the selection process
5. Appoints selection committee

1. Designs selection policies and procedures
2. Formulates selection criteria
3. Plans improvements in the selection process

Asst. Supt.— Personnel
1. Administers the selection process
   a. Recruits and sends position specifications
   b. Gathers data on candidates
   c. Rejects unqualified applications
   d. Sets schedules
   e. Keeps records
   f. Supervises selection committee
   g. Reports ratings to superintendent
2. Issues eligibility lists (in large districts)
3. Initiates improvements in selection process

Selection Committee
1. Examines and rates candidate papers
2. Gives oral interviews and rates candidates
3. Makes suggestions for better data, interviews, and process

procedures are available. The list of procedures can be changed to meet varying conditions.

Whatever techniques or procedures are used, the purpose of the school district should be to identify the best possible training, experience, and personal qualifications of candidates. These qualifications should best match the position requirements as set forth in the position specifications.

A standard list of selection techniques includes such procedures as:

1. Getting as complete information as possible on the application blank.
2. Calling for references from those who know the candidate best.
3. Administering physical, mental, psychological, and emotional tests.
4. Investigating academic transcripts and all other information related to training.
5. Visiting and telephoning the candidate's previous place of employment.
6. Making preliminary and final interviews.
7. Setting priorities with respect to the value of candidate qualities.
8. Matching candidate qualities with requirements of the supervisory position.
9. Deciding to reject or accept the candidate.
10. Assigning the candidate on a probationary basis as a means of on-the-job performance testing.

This standard list of selection techniques should be revised and varied to meet the differing needs brought about by diverse supervisory positions and by changing conditions within the school system.

The Application Blank

Application blanks now in use range from shallow and irrelevant to exhaustive and ponderous. Some where between is the most usable application blank. The form should comply with all legal requirements with respect to nondiscrimination and should contain blank spaces with proper instructions to secure valuable and complete information. If the information is relevant, it is difficult to get too much, but very easy to get too little. It also is easier to get inconsequential information than to get highly significant information.

The best thing for a school system to do with its application form is to *revise it*. Too many school systems make the mistake of depending on one standard form to be used for all positions. This scatter gun approach usually gets a conglomeration of inappropriate information and misses key facts vital to a specialized position. The application blank should be designed to zero in on the vital information needed.

The Los Angeles City Unified School District has designed an application form for supervisory positions that covers seven legal-size pages. In all instances, the candidate has plenty of space to give complete information and to add significant supplementary data. The Los Angeles application form calls for the regular personal data, certificates and credentials, complete records of education and training, verified experience, written references, space for biographical data and philosophical statements, and human relations questions that reflect on the supervisor's cooperativeness, regard for colleagues and subordinates, interest in program advancement, and outside obligations. Nearly a page is devoted to community participation. The time and energy required to prepare such a blank automatically screens out half-hearted candidates. The accuracy and thoroughness with which a candidate prepares such a blank gives good between-the-lines evidence to the selection committee.

Written References

Written references from people who know the candidate best may be open or structured. Generally, the referent is free to write anything that he/she wishes about the candidate. This kind of writing often omits vital points, and only occasionally or accidentally hits on the qualities most needed in the specific supervisory position.

The school system can improve its information by providing structured reference forms that call for judgments concerning vital competencies. The structured forms that the candidate hands to the referent may be in the form of a rating scale with respect to training, experience, and personal qualifications, or it may call for written statements in answer to specific questions. The best written reference forms include both rating scales and space for written comments.

In several states, court decisions have all but destroyed the confidentiality of written references. When this is true, referents tend to omit all negative statements and sing the praises of the candidate. These references are about as meaningless as the traditional "to whom it may concern" letters. Written references always should be substantiated with personal visits or telephone calls to the person who wrote the reference.

Testing as a Technique for Supervisory Selection

No test has ever defined the supervisor's perfect profile. On the other hand, various tests do contribute data that offer evidence of possible success on the job. Tests are more effective in determining who cannot succeed as a supervisor than who *will* succeed. Test results do offer predictive value, but as King-Stoops[3] points out, the predictive value of tests is open to question. Because of low validity and reliability of tests, the changing conditions in the school system, the community, the candidate and family, tests can offer only evidence as to who *may be able* to succeed, rather than giving a numerical assurance of success.

The director of personnel (or the equivalent) may compile the results of

[3] Joyce King-Stoops, *The Child Wants to Learn*. (Boston: Little, Brown and Company, Inc., 1977), chapter 16.

intelligence, achievement, personality, aptitude, interest, performance, physique, and present health testing. Results may be used, misused, abused, or unused. The real value of testing lies in the proper use of the results. Castetter[4] indicates that the information derived from tests alone should not be used in making hiring decisions. The test results should be but one source of total data necessary for decision making.

Most school systems require regular and arduous duties of their supervisors. It therefore seems reasonable that school systems should require candidates to have a physical examination. Supervisors must have the vitality and the good health necessary to fill the rigorous requirements of the position. It also is reasonable to believe that supervisors cannot be successful if they are less intelligent than those whom they supervise. Good supervisory service does not necessarily correlate with increasing steps on the I.Q. scale, but there is a lower cut off point at which supervisors could face little but disaster if assigned to a supervisory position. Certainly the supervisor must be interested in the challenges of the position and must be able to work harmoniously and effectively with colleagues. Unfortunately, the interest and personality inventories in these areas have low predictive value. Yet with proper interpretation, they are better than no evidence at all.

The results of tests should be interpreted and used as one segment of the total required data for selecting the supervisor.

Transcripts and Other Information Related to Training

Transcripts and all other information that substantiates adequate and appropriate training for the candidate are essential. Candidates may hold valid supervisory credentials but be poorly trained in a specialized area. For example, the supervisor of music, K–12, must have more specialized training than would be expected of the general subject supervisor. The principal as a line supervisor should be expected to have more training in organization and administration than would the coordinator of federal projects.

The selection committee should have access to the candidate's total training record. This record should be examined to determine whether the candidate would have acquired the competencies necessary to succeed in the specified position.

Visitation to Determine Candidate's Successful Experience

Experience claimed on the application blank or referred to in written references may not always have been completely adequate or appropriate. Since the super-

---

[4] William B. Castetter, *The Personnel Function in Educational Administration.* 2nd ed. (New York: Macmillan Publishing Company, Inc., 1976), p. 191.

visor in education is so important, the school system seeking a candidate should not hesitate to send emissaries to the candidate's last place of employment. Personal conferences and telephone calls should be used to verify and supplement the experience as reflected from other sources. School systems that fail to follow this necessary technique may be taken in by a good first appearance but may wind up with mediocre service in the position. Personal investigation is one technique that adds to the total precedure of knowing the candidate's total capability.

Interviews in the Selection Process

If possible, the director of personnel should meet each candidate in order to acquaint the candidate with all conditions in the school system and to determine whether the candidate is qualified to proceed through the several techniques of the selection process. Obviously if the candidate does not have the required certificates or credentials there should be early rejection. This rejection due to lack of qualification, for whatsoever reason, is best for both the candidate and the school district.

A final interview by the selection committee is a must. It is true that interviewers differ greatly in their reaction to candidates. It also is true that the interview process is subjective. But in spite of the shortcomings, certain bits of evidence may be picked up that would not be revealed in any other way.

Interview sessions can be good or poor, depending on the planning and abilities of the interviewing committee. Interviews without planning or organization can be hit-or-miss affairs with little accomplished. Proper planning and training of the interview committee can overcome many of the weaknesses inherent in the interview technique.

Interviews should be carefully planned. Specific questions should be written out. The whole process should be designed to fit the candidate and the position requirements. For example, a candidate for the vice-principalship should be asked questions that reveal attitudes toward student discipline, toward supporting the teaching staff, and toward cooperating with the principal. If the candidate were applying for art supervisor, another set of questions would be equally important. In all cases, the candidate should be allowed to do most of the talking during the brief session.

Since the interview process is subjective, the interview committee should not waste time by asking for information already available on the application, in written references, or on transcripts. Occasionally, it may be appropriate to ask for a supplement to or an extension of a fact already known. It is more worthwhile to ask questions that will reveal the candidate's interests, attitudes, biases, enthusiasms, dedications, conflicts, and determinations. This technique allows the committee to receive invaluable impressions about the candidate's ability to control composure, respond harmoniously to colleagues, to maintain a different opinion without being obnoxious or bigoted, to show interest in the school system's goals and objectives rather than just the dollar amount of the salary, and to give evidence that he/she and the family will be adjusted in the community, and to show promise of both accomplishment and continuing development after assignment to the position. The interview technique, then, will be as valuable as the committee's planning and its ability to ask the right questions and properly judge the candidate's responses. Impressions derived from the interview give clues that would never surface from the candidate's stack of papers. Despite interview weaknesses, it remains an essential technique for selecting supervisory personnel.

How to Set Priorities for Candidate Qualities

Establishing priorities among the candidate's qualities should begin when the vacancy is announced and not end until final selection. The selection committee, during and after the interview, should determine and redetermine what qualities are of most worth. Some positions require a high degree of factual information. Others require in an equally high degree the ability to work successfully with those being supervised. Some candidates may be strong in qualities of average priorities, but weak in those that are indispensable. Others may be strong in the qualities that really count and weak in areas that can be strengthened later. The committee must make these priority judgments.

Too often, priorities are not discussed or placed in proper order. When this happens, the selection committee judges the candidate according to each member's own bias rather than on uniform priority standards developed by the total group. The setting and resetting of priorities is necessary before the candidate can be matched with the requirements of the position.

How to Match Candidate with Position

The selection committee has at hand all possible information along with its own priority scale. The selection committee also has the specified requirements of the position to be filled. The committee's function then must match the qualities of the candidate with position requirements.

A committee usually does not have sufficient time to make the best possible match. For best results, deliberation time should be extended just as it is for juries in the judicial system. Both the fate of the candidate and the success of the school program hang on the committee's ability to best match candidate qualities with position requirements. Supervisors should be hired to fit positions; job specifications should not be changed to match the given qualities of a candidate.

How to Decide whether to Reject or Accept the Candidate

Following the matching process, the interview committee should use a form similar to that outlined in Figure 16-3. Composite scores should be totaled, and the candidate receiving the highest score should be recommended for employment. The runner-up candidates can be listed in score order and their tests filed in the personnel office. Unless some disqualifying evidence surfaces following the decision of the selection committee, the superintendent should recommend the committee's chosen candidate to the governing board.

FIGURE 16-3. Selection Committee Rating of Supervisory Candidates.

Interview Date: _____ Position: _____

Applicant Number	Interviewer							Composite Score
	1	2	3	4	5	6	7	
1								
2								
3								
4								
5								
6								
7								
8								
9								
10								
11								
12								

Choice #1 _____ Score _____

Choice #2 _____ Score _____

Choice #3 _____ Score _____

Choice #4 _____ Score _____

How to Make Probationary Assignments

There are good arguments for and against making probationary assignments. A probationary trial period is the best means of on-the-job testing. Paper and pencil tests cannot compare with the experience of actually doing the job. Even though a probationary assignment gives a supervisory candidate a chance to prove his/her abilities, the uncertainty surrounding the trial period tends to weaken the status of the position and makes the new employee more vulnerable to criticism. Offering a probationary contract may not attract the most capable candidates.

Actually, few supervisors have tenure. Most school systems, by state code, offer tenure for teachers, but not for supervisors and administrators. In that respect, the supervisor's assignment has to be made on the basis of future success and satisfaction in the position. Even though school systems may have the right to terminate the supervisor's assignment, every effort should be made to give the position the earmarks of permanency.

Even the strongest candidate has no guarantee of infallibility. Castetter points out that the position and the person occupying the position make frequent changes of such severity that decisions made by the selection committee have limited relevance.[5] A divorce or death in the employee's family or a change in employee benefits or working conditions can quickly turn successful performance into satisfactory production. Both the employee and the school system must be flexible enough to change with unavoidable changing conditions.

When Should Supervisors Be Selected?

Supervisors should be selected when the school system has the best possible chance of securing top-notch candidates. Announcing supervisory openings during the Christmas season is not ordinarily a good time for selection. Candidates still have contracts to fulfill. The announcement of openings will receive more attention when possible candidates are about to complete their academic year assignments. The spring of the year usually is the best time.

Some school districts procrastinate in announcing supervisory openings. Then, when applications have been made, they also procrastinate in going through the necessary techniques for selection. This continued procrastination allows most of the best candidates to be sorted out and selected by rival school districts. In general, the school system should make its announcement of intention to employ as early as possible and then move progressively through the necessary selection steps, allowing sufficient time for thoroughness, but moving toward final selection at the earliest possible time.

[5] William B. Castetter, *The Personnel Function in Educational Administration*. (New York: Macmillan Publishing Company, Inc., 1976), p. 17.

Official Selection and Assignment

Final selection assignment, and orientation should quickly follow the selection committee's recommendation. Few things can be more exasperating to an eager candidate than to have reason to believe that the position will be offered and then to have to wait until the superintendent can return from summer vacation or until the board of education finally decides to handle personnel matters. Under such circumstances, the best qualified candidates can and should accept offers from other systems.

As soon as the candidate is officially selected for supervisory service, *assignment should be made in writing.* This is one of the first and most important steps in the orientation and induction process. An assignment in writing leaves less doubt in the minds of the newly selected supervisor and the responsible administrative officer. The written assignment should conform to the previously announced position specifications. An oral conference should clear any doubt concerning the meaning of the written assignment.

After Selection

The administrative officer responsible for the newly employed supervisor should consider official selection not the end of the selection process, but the beginning of the supervisor's continuing contribution to the school system. A scheduled program of orientation, induction, in-service help, and career development should be the goal of the responsible administrative officer. The stimulation of growth and improvement following the selection committee's decision makes possible supervisory success and enriches instructional programs.

How to Evaluate the Selection Process

No selection process is perfect. All components of the process, from formulating selection policies to the in-service improvements of supervisors, should be studied, revised, and improved.

Revising and Improving Selection

Since one of the most important functions of the superintendent and the staff is selecting the best supervisors, the process of selection should be continuously evaluated and changed to meet varying needs. State codes and court decisions render yesterday's forms and procedures ineffective or illegal. Supervisor supply-and-demand calls for changes in selection techniques. Changes in the school system or community may necessitate a revision in position requirements.

The superintendent, director of personnel, some members of the selection committee, and supervisees should form a group to review all aspects of the selection process and determine needed change. When school systems are concerned enough to study the strengths and weaknesses of how they select supervisors, then that concern will lead to improvements not only in the selection process but also in the total instruction of children. The evaluation of supervisory selection is as important as the application blank.

School systems can improve their selection of supervisors by following a few specific Do's and Don't's. The following list may be helpful.

Do

1. Write out supervisory selection policies and procedures. If you already have policies and procedures, add needed new ones and revise the ones that are outdated.
2. Design more effective ways for recruiting supervisory candidates.
3. List as many reasons as you can why supervisory selection is vitally important. Discuss the list with your superintendent or personnel director.
4. Prepare a list of criteria for selecting supervisory personnel.
5. Write out position specifications for the position, elementary school principal, K–6.
6. Revise your school system's application forms.
7. Write the best possible reference that you can for a super/isory candidate.
8. Volunteer to serve on the selection committee. In preparation for this service, read periodical articles, chapters in personnel books, and disc ss the duties and responsibilities of a committee member with your director of personnel.
9. Outline the planning and training that a selection committee should be involved in before meeting a candidate.
10. Write a few simple questions to ask a candidate applying for the position, supervisor of science, K–12.
11. Consider the position, general elementary supervisor, K–6. List candidate qualities in priority order.
12. Study all aspects of the selection of supervisors. Volunteer to help your school evaluate its own selection process.

Don't

1 Interpret paper and pencil tests as if factual numbers were valid predictors of success. Be assured that tests have value when properly interpreted, but be wary of drawing false conclusions from tests that may have low validity and reliability.
2. Conclude that successful experience in another district guarantees successful

experience in your district. Conditions may be different in the other district; or conditions may change in your district after employment of the supervisor.

3. Fail to be cautious about relying on certain factual information for selection as much as you rely on that information for rejection. For example, a candidate with an actual I.Q. of 70 would surely fail as a supervisor, but a candidate with an I.Q. of 130, or even 150, would not necessarily succeed. Tests and other factual data can predict the negative better than they can predict the positive.

4. Rush through the selection process and select supervisors on inadequate evidence. On the other hand, when the best possible techniques have been used and a judgment has been made, don't let the prospect dangle and cool off in the limbo of indecision.

5. Throw a new supervisor into the arena of confused assignments and let the lions of neglect tear him/her into professional shreds.

TRENDS IN SELECTING SUPERVISORY PERSONNEL

Some clearly defined trends in selecting supervisors are visible in well-administered school systems These trends are leading to better selection and, therefore, to better educational programs for children and adults.

Toward ⟶ Improving General Working Conditions and Benefits for Supervisors

As general working conditions and employee benefits improve in school systems, supervisors will be easier to recruit and select. With the increase of federal funding, supervisory positions not only have increased in number but also have received greater recognition. The salaries of both line and staff supervisors have improved.

Toward ⟶ Formulating and Adopting Policies and Procedures that Affect Supervisory Selection

More school systems throughout the United States have designed and written policies and procedures for supervisory selection. These policies define the process and make possible the elimination of hit-and-miss techniques and the utilization of professional devices in supervisory selection. Sound policies and procedures can eliminate discrimination and place selection where it belongs, on the basis of merit.

Toward ⟶   the Use of Refined Techniques that
More Nearly Objectify the Selection Process

Selection is subjective enough at best. Using proven selection techniques places the process on a more impartial and objective basis. This use of proven selection techniques better matches the candidate's qualities with position requirements.

Toward ⟶   Evaluation and Improvement of the
Selection Process

As long as individuals, the school system, and the world around change, just so long will a continuing evaluation of the selection process be essential. Evaluation is the prelude to improvement, and improvement in the selection process is the way to secure candidates who can improve the educational program.

Toward ⟶   Greater Administrative Help for
Beginning Supervisors

Newly selected supervisors need adequate administrative help during their orientation, induction, and in-service growth. The supervisor who enters a new position and stands still professionally is a discredit to him/herself and to the school system. School systems must make sure that their supervisors continue to grow professionally and productively on the job.

Supervisory Problems

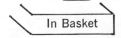

Problem 1

You are on the selection committee and have reviewed the papers of many candidates. The committee has rejected all but five, who have just been called in for interview. Following the final interview, the composite scores of all committee members ranked Abel Armstrong as number one. But last evening your best friend called to tell you that his reputedly reliable friend had reported that Abel Armstrong was guilty of a highly immoral and illegal act in his previous place of employment. Your friend's friend believed that this was the real reason for his application in your school district. Your selection committee is ready to recommend Abel Armstrong as number one candidate for the position.

> *What should you do? Keep still? Report this hearsay evidence to the selection committee? Talk over the report with your director of personnel? Risk the chance of damaging a capable candidate in case the information were false? Risk a libel suit in case you repeated false and damaging evidence?*
>
> *What would you do?*

Problem 2

Your school system is promoting several teachers to the rank of line or staff supervisor. You have been selected to serve on the selection committee for health coordinator. Rumors are that you, yourself, would be the strongest contender for an upcoming elementary principalship. Jane Willoughs, daughter of Thomas F. Willoughs, III, superintendent, is one of the candidates for health coordinator. In your honest opinion, she should rank number 3. The other committee members are placing her number 1.

> *Would you go along with other members of the committee and rate Jane Willoughs number 1, when you actually feel she should be ranked number 3?*
>
> *If you vote your conscience and place her number 3, will this spoil your chance of becoming the next elementary school principal?*
>
> *If you vote Jane Willoughs number 1, and she causes the health program for children to deteriorate, will you be able to live with your professional conscience?*
>
> *How will you vote?*

Problem 3

You have been employed as the new director of personnel in a small- to medium-size school district. Selection of supervisors has previously been done on the whim of the superintendent or by pressure from certain members of the board of education. Little or almost nothing exists in the way of selection machinery for supervisors. In a reasonably short time, a principal and a supervisor of reading must be selected.

> *How will you proceed?*
>
> *Will you follow a less than adequate system?*
>
> *Will you ask the superintendent to delay until you have time to organize a respectable selection process?*
>
> *What recommendations for change will you make and to whom?*

Selected Bibliography

Books

Beach, Dale S. *Personnel: The Management of People at Work.* 3rd ed. New York. Macmillan Publishing Co., Inc., 1975.

Bolton, Dale L. *Selection and Evaluation of Teachers.* Berkeley, California: McCutchan Publishing Corporation, 1973.

Carroll, Stephen J., Jr., and Henry L. Tosi, Jr. *Management by Objectives.* New York: Macmillan Publishing Co., Inc., 1973.

Castetter, William B. *The Personnel Function in Educational Administration.* 2nd ed. New York: Macmillan Publishing Co., Inc., 1976.

Chruden, Herbert J., and Arthur W. Sherman, Jr. *Readings in Personnel Management.* Cincinnati, Ohio: South-Western Publishing Co., 1972.

Culbertson, Jack A., Curtis Henson, and Ruel Morrison, eds. *Performance Objectives for School Principals.* Berkeley, California: McCutchan Publishing Corporation, 1974.

Dunnette, Marvin D. *Personnel Selection and Placement.* Belmont, California: Wadsworth Publishing Co., 1966.

Fear, Richard A. *The Evaluation Interview.* 2nd ed. New York: McGraw-Hill Book Co., 1973.

Gellerman, Saul W. *Management by Motivation.* New York: American Management Association, 1968.

Gerwin, Donald, ed. *The Employment of Teachers.* Berkeley, California: McCutchan Publishing Corporation, 1974.

King-Stoops, Joyce. *The Child Wants to Learn.* Boston: Little, Brown and Co., 1977.

Lopez, Felix M. *Personnel Interviewing,* rev. ed. New York: McGraw-Hill Book Co., 1975.

Preskin, Dean B. *Human Behavior and Employment Interviewing.* New York: American Management Association, 1971.

Stoops, Emery, Max Rafferty, and Russell E. Johnson. *Handbook of Educational Administration.* Boston: Allyn and Bacon, Inc., 1975.

Tagliere, Daniel A. *People, Power, and Organization.* New York: American Management Association, 1973.

Yancy, Joseph P. *Reaching Organizational and Human Goals.* Columbus, Ohio: Charles E. Merrill Publishers, 1975.

Periodicals

Wanous, John P. "Tell it like it is at Realistic Job Previews." *Personnel* LII (July 1975): 50–60.

Sharf, James C. "How Validated Testing Eases the Pressure of Minority Recruitment." *Personnel* LII (May–June 1975): 53–59.

17

How to Make Effective Decisions and Evaluate a Supervisory Program

S. H. Moorer[1] reported that an effective supervisor continuously seeks to narrow the gap between what *is* and what *might be* in the supervisory program.

This chapter includes a discussion of the following topics:

Principles for the evaluation of supervision
Psychological aspects of decision making for the supervisor
Stages in decision making
How to develop and appraise written evaluations of performance
How to describe and appraise the status of the supervisory program
Teachers and principals view supervision in action
Evidence of an effective supervisory program
Some questions the supervising principal can ask
Do—Don't
Trends
"In-Basket" supervisory problems
Questions and suggested activities

Principles for the Evaluation of Supervision

Supervising principals have suggested the following criteria for evaluating a supervisory program:

1. Supervisors must accept the principle that supervision is a cooperative service activity (specific, cooperative planning being at its heart), and that its goal is to help teachers perform more efficiently and more effectively.
2. Supervision must release the energies of the professional staff in creative ways to solve both individual and common problems.[2]

[1] Sam H. Moorer, *How Good Is Your Supervisory Program?* (St. Augustine: Florida State Department of Education, 1950).

[2] See Jane Franseth, *Learning to Supervise Schools*, Circular No. 289 (Washington, D.C.: Office of Education, n.d.), p. 3.

3. The evaluation of a supervisory program should be a fundamental part of the program itself.
4. Evaluation is continuous—and occurs at regular, frequent intervals.
5. The aim of evaluation is to improve supervision and, ultimately, instruction for students.
6. A supervisory program should be evaluated in terms of its own objectives and the instructional improvement that it achieves.
7. Evaluation should encourage improvement of the school's organization for supervision.
8. The evaluation of a supervisory program helps form harmonious relationships between school staff members.
9. Statistical data-gathering and interpretation form the basis of supervisory evaluation.
10. Evaluation considers the total teaching-learning situation.
11. Outside consultants occasionally are needed to make more objective evaluations and to bring new points of view.

The Department of Elementary School Principals of the National Education Association[3] has defined four minimum essentials for the program of supervision that may be considered as evaluation points. To what extent does the supervisory program provide for:

1. The appraisal of specific learning situations to ascertain the needs of students and the efficiency of instruction?
2. Technical service to teachers in the form of instructional aids, specific suggestions for improving instruction, and assistance in diagnosis and measurement?
3. Research for the purpose of curriculum construction and revision, and for improving materials, techniques, and methods of instruction?
4. Professional leadership of and cooperation with teachers through individual and group conferences, through stimulation to further professional study, and through cooperative development of a program of in-service education?

In the search for ways to evaluate the supervisory program, emphasis is placed on an effective, cooperative approach to a professional problem. School supervision, however, usually does not begin with cooperation and democratic action, but that is where it may arrive under proper guidance. In the end, "supervision" will constitute something slightly different for each one who supervises and for each one who is supervised.

Good supervision is based on a belief in democracy and uses the scientific method, continuously improving and evaluating its products and processes. It proceeds by means of an orderly, cooperatively planned and executed series of activities and is judged by its results. Effective supervision requires, then, a sound knowledge of decision making and problem solving techniques, since it seeks to evaluate (1) personnel, (2) procedures, and (3) outcomes.

---

[3] Department of Elementary School Principals, *The Elementary School Principalship—Today and Tomorrow,* Twenty-Seventh Yearbook (Washington, D.C.: National Education Association, 1948), p. 104.

Psychological Aspects of Decision Making for the Supervisor

Before we can proceed further, we must discuss decision-making and problem-solving techniques that we will need as the evaluation program progresses. B. M. Bass[4] presented a valuable analysis of the psychological aspects of decision making in industry. He reported that according to classical principles of organization, conflict can be eliminated or resolved by programs of rules that can be applied to each problem as it arises to provide appropriate answers. Conflicts over returned goods can be resolved, for instance, if the firm has a routine, standard operating procedure for handling customer complaints. An applicable rule might be that refunds are automatic for all merchandise returned within a year costing less than $100. Other refunding is on a pro-rata basis reflecting cost and use. All problems about refunds can be categorized and decisions made according to rules for each category.

Even though it often is possible to apply such programming, particularly for the simpler problems, a variety of human judgments and discriminations are involved when the problem becomes more complex and cannot be solved routinely. For example, before appropriate rules can be applied to the problem of whether to discontinue or redesign a particular instructional procedure, it is necessary to classify the problem or to see if the problem can be classified according to acceptable categories for which rules are available. Even before this, someone may have to decide whether there is a problem—whether there is dissatisfaction with the current situation or procedure.

Decision making proceeds in at least five stages: (1) perceiving the problem, (2) searching for and/or inventing solutions, (3) evaluating the solutions, (4) making the decision, and (5) providing for prototype or "pilot" field testing, reporting, and continuous appraisal. Various characteristics of the problem and the decision maker affect outcomes at each of the five stages. At each stage it is seen that despite an intention to be rational, various attitudinal and motivational factors limit the decision maker. Much can be done at each stage to reduce these restrictions on creativity, inventiveness, and accuracy of decision.

Decisions on how to handle problems may be reached through discussion, persuasion, delegation, or by accident. Supervisors from two different divisions of an organization may happen to meet in a hallway and decide, as a consequence, on a subsequent curriculum development plan. If they had not been in the same hallway at the same time, they might never have decided on such a plan.

Decisions may be *random*. Administration might be indifferent as to which of two departments will switch to a new plan first, so a coin might be tossed to decide the matter. Sometimes random decisions are a rational or best possible solution to a problem. But organizations are unlikely to survive if all their decisions are made accidentally, randomly, or as a consequence of power. Of course,

---

[4] Bernard M. Bass, *Organizational Psychology* (Boston: Allyn and Bacon, Inc., 1965), p. 75.

the old adage "Wisdom is knowing what not to do next" sometimes holds true, and the best decision can be to make no decision—at least for the present.

Stages in Decision Making

Three broad stages complete the decision process. (1) First, the problem must be sensed and analyzed. Applicable elements must be discerned. (2) Then, solutions must be discovered, invented, or identified. To do this, known information is appraised and corrected for bias. Unknown factors are isolated. (3) Third, the solutions must be evaluated to identify the one or more that best copes with the problem. For this to be done, we need to (a) establish criteria for evaluation, (b) weigh the pertinent alternatives and unknowns, (c) project expectations of the impact on objectives (real-world constraints must be identified), and (d) synthesize our findings with a course of action.

Figure 17-1 displays a flow chart of logical steps that might be involved in a complete or ideal decision-making process.

The process usually begins with a sense of dissatisfaction with the current state of affairs. A memorandum may be written to the safety chairperson viewing with alarm the increasing number of minor accidents to custodians. If the safety chairperson can assure the dissatisfied memo writer that the rise in accidents is only a random departure from expectations and that the alarm is not warranted, the process may stop. If, however, he/she agrees that the situation is unsatisfactory, he/she may call an *ad hoc* committee to define the problem. They may raise numerous questions. Is the unsatisfactory situation due to a change in reporting methods? Is it due to the moving of the health center nearer to the workplace? Are only major accidents increasing? Are the definitions of minor and major accidents in terms of days work lost meaningful and do they help clarify the nature of the current problem? Are minor accidents on the increase in all or only selected departments and shifts? Has there been any recent change in worker morale? Has there been a slackening in the safety program? Are new employees more prone to accidents, or is the introduction of new, faster equipment with more risks for operators confusing the issue?

Following this examination, are we in a position to classify the problem? For example, can we say that the increase in minor accidents is due specifically to faster equipment? If it is, then we have a routine solution for the problem. We have available a special staff development program to be used when new equipment causes difficulties for employees. Therefore we can follow standard operating procedure and end the decision process at this time by contacting the staff development facilitator about the matter.

But suppose our analysis suggests that rather than being routine, the problem is due to several causes, and remains outside the bounds of routine classification and treatment. We then must search for alternatives until all options have been identified or continued exploration for solutions is deemed not worth-

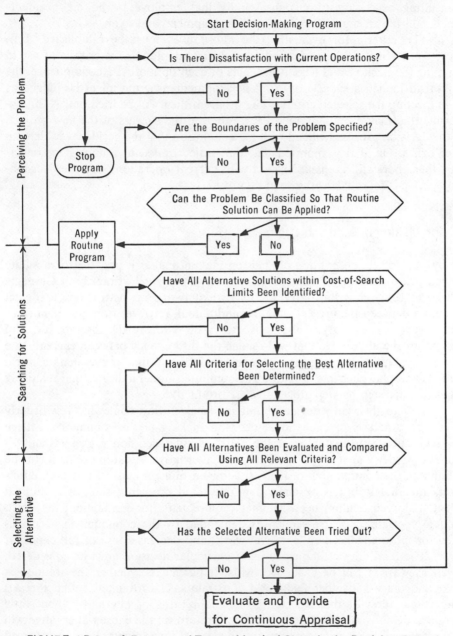

FIGURE 17-1. A Program of Tests of Logical Steps in the Decision Process.

while. We may generate such alternatives as starting a special safety campaign, providing special programs for supervisors on attitudes toward supervisors, hiring a consulting psychologist to counsel individual employees who are accident-repeaters, hiring an engineer to redesign the equipment, and so on.

The criteria for evaluating the alternatives must be established. Efficiency, constraints, cost, and feasibility might be adopted as the criteria to use in evaluating the positive and negative aspects of each option. As a consequence, the proposal to launch a supervisory staff development program might be judged as best in meeting the selected criteria. The program then will be tried out. A follow-up evaluation may eventually report favorably on the success of the new project, and the decision process will end with the conclusion that the accident problem no longer exists. Or, if it is reported that the project failed to reduce minor accidents, then there still is dissatisfaction with current operations and the decision-making cycle is repeated, as shown in Figure 17-1.

Decision Making by Man and Computer

Step-by-step logical description of decision making makes it possible to stimulate this heuristic process by computer programs. A program written by a Carnegie Tech-Rand research group develops its own network of instructions to detect differences between the present situation and a goal, retrieves from its memory or through search and analysis alternative ways of reducing the discrepancy, and then applies the alternative that will reduce the discrepancy between current state and objective. Similar programs have been designed that prove mathematical theorems and play checkers or chess. The computer model indicates that relatively straightforward step-by-step procedures are productive.

Left to their own devices, humans usually follow somewhat less orderly procedures. Analysis of educational decision making at the community college level suggests, unfortunately, that the actual human decision process is not as rational or orderly as it might be. Thus, one alternative to cutting costs might be to eliminate the continuation of high-cost-low-enrollment classes. But such elimination immediately brings on many new unwanted problems, such as unfulfilled student major curriculum needs; unmet requirements for graduation; failure to complete specialized course sequences demanded by the community and/or required for more advanced college-level work; and decreased use of full capacity.

The feasibility of implementing a particular decision must be considered, as well as ways it can be evaluated. Most important is whether the solution is within budgetary and other real-world constraints. Unfortunately, often there is some examination of the expected costs and returns of alternatives, but little attempt to demonstrate that the expected net return on the chosen alternative will equal or exceed the expected return on alternative investments. But when forced into more orderliness, human beings become more successful decision makers.

Whereas computers *must* adopt such orderly processes, humans may find it advantageous to do so, for there is some evidence that a step-by-step orderly attack on problems increases the effectiveness of human problem solvers. Orderly decision making proceeds in three stages: (1) delineating the problem, (2) creating and/or searching for alternative solutions, and (3) evaluating prospective solutions. Decision makers are most effective when they thoroughly consider one stage before moving to the next.

A Systems Approach to Decision Making Is More Likely Among More Effective Supervisors

Further evidence on the profitability of outlining the problem and screening alternatives before taking action is seen in the results of "in-basket" tests given to 232 supervisors. These tests were a collection of facsimiles of letters, memoranda, and other contents likely to be found in a typical supervisor's in-basket. The supervisor responded to the 32 problems posed by the contents of his in-basket by placing in his out-basket instructions for his secretary, memos, letters, reminders, and appointment calendars. Analyses disclosed that the supervisors with more ability (as measured by aptitude tests) and supervisory knowledge (as measured by a special achievement examination) were most likely to concentrate on preparing for a decision rather than on taking immediate action.

Searching for Solutions

EFFECTIVE VERSUS INEFFECTIVE APPROACHES TO PERCEIVING THE PROBLEM. More and less effective ways of viewing a problem can be suggested from studies of successful and unsuccessful decision makers. Those likely to succeed almost immediately perceive through some familiar stimulus, word, or phrase a point at which they begin their attack. They break the problem into smaller parts, parts with which they are likely to have had some past experience. They eliminate redundancies while retaining the important points and tend to sharpen and bring the major elements of the problem into focus. They systematically reorganize the problem into a series of subproblems, extracting key terms and ideas and simplifying their perceptions without losing the essentials. They handle each part of the problem methodically.

Unsuccessful problem solvers fail to understand the problem. They become confused. Worse still, unsuccessful problem solvers are more likely to distort the problem and attack a newly perceived problem—one that is so dissimilar from the original that the solution has no relation to it. Unlike the potentially successful decision makers, those likely to fail refuse to break up a problem into its parts.

In generating solutions, those who ultimately fail to solve a problem satisfactorily have no logical plan of attack. They jump from one part of a problem to another and from one stage to another, neglecting the important details; they become sidetracked by external considerations; they wander off on tangents when some word suggests an irrelevant idea or an interesting incident. Before they have sufficiently considered alternatives, the failing decision makers select one solution on the basis of feeling that it "seems right." Often some trivial or irrelevant point is used to justify such a selection.

For ultimate success in solving a problem, alternatives need to be identified, classified, discovered, and invented. Many of the perceptual tendencies that describe how problems are recognized also describe what happens in the search for solutions. Particularly important is the *set* one adopts.

Increasing Search for Alternatives by Using a Set

THE BRAINSTORMING SET.   Fundamental to improving the search process is promoting a set to increase the number of alternatives to be considered.

Brainstorming has been offered as a generally useful method for improving the quality of decisions by forcibly increasing the quantity of alternatives generated by the problem solvers. Four rules are prescribed to create a brainstorming set. (1) Evaluation and criticism of any presented idea is withheld during brainstorming. (2) Idea generation as such is unrestricted in this search phase. (3) "Wild" ideas are as acceptable as pedestrian solutions more easily seen as relevant to the problem. (4) Quantity of output is stressed. Inhibitors to creative output such as: "it's not part of our job, we've never done it that way, we haven't the time, we tried that before, our situation is different, it's too hard to administer, or somebody would have used it before if it were any good" must be avoided.

Some research points to the possibility that real groups become more effective than isolated individuals as members become more familiar with each other. Presumably members learn to build on each other's ideas.

A QUESTIONING SET FACILITATES SEARCH.   The search process is facilitated if the decision maker adopts a *questioning set*. To help generate alternatives, he/she may ask in a systematic sequence: Why? Where? When? Who? What? How? What current resource could be adapted? Modified? Substituted? Transformed? Combined? Omitted? Reversed? Along the same lines, merely adopting *a set to be original* increases the originality of ideas generated. That is, if we are given instructions to try to discover or invent unique solutions rather than just any solutions, we increase our production of such out-of-the-ordinary alternatives. Adopting a *constructive set* rather than a negative or critical set towards ideas helps to promote greater and more successful search for creative solutions.

In the search for alternatives a number of criteria or tests can be made on how well the search has proceeded. Is the search broad enough and clear in its directions? Have some alternatives been ignored because they customarily are solutions to different problems? Has there been a failure to consider alternatives that are considerably different from the initially proposed solution? Have some alternatives been rejected without full consideration or because they are misunderstood? Are we holding onto one alternative because it has worked successfully before on a different problem or in a different situation?

Venturesomeness and wide-ranging search for new and better ways of doing things are likely to be inhibited if the payoff is to those who maintain stability and order rather than to those who innovate. On the other hand, creativity will be enhanced when the school administration approves attempts to experiment, to innovate, and to challenge old ways of operating.

Divergent Versus Convergent Search

So far we have concentrated primarily on the *divergent* search for alternatives. That is, we have been concerned with producing as many diverse solutions to a problem as possible. In many situations the search becomes *convergent,* starting with many possibilities available and continually narrowing the range of alternatives or creating the best alternative out of some or all of the available possibilities.

Convergent search usually is involved when one seeks to discover the proof of a mathematical theorem, what move to make next in a game, or at what point there has been a communication breakdown:

> In . . . convergent thinking there almost always is one conclusion or answer that is regarded as unique, and thinking is to be channeled or controlled in the direction of that answer. . . . In divergent thinking, on the other hand, there is much searching about or going off in various directions. This is most easily seen when there is no unique solution . . .[5]

Convergent thinking occurs when one tries to find the answers to multiple-choice questions. All alternatives are provided, but only one answer is correct or best. Divergent thinking occurs on any completion test requiring the generation of as many correct answers as possible.

Evaluating and Choosing

Following the search process, particularly the divergent kind that has generated many solutions to the problem at hand, how does supervision evaluate the alternatives it has assembled? How does it decide on which alternative or alternatives to select to apply in solving the problem?

Evaluation is affected by how orderly and systematically it proceeds. Evaluation is affected by the error of the estimates of the cost of each alternative

---

[5] J. P. Guilford, *A Revised Structure of Intellect,* Reports from the Psychological Laboratory, No. 19 (Los Angeles: University of Southern California, 1957), pp. 6–7.

as well as the potential utility of each alternative. Evaluation depends on the *risk* and *uncertainty* of each prospective outcome. (We are involved in a 50 percent risk if we bet that a coin will land as a head instead of a tail; we are involved in 50 percent uncertainty when we have only half the information about what is affecting a particular outcome.)

An Orderly Approach to Evaluation

It appears profitable to adopt a systematic screening procedure. First, the *criteria* on which evaluation will be based should be examined. Weights may be attached to each of these criteria. A series of questions about risk preferences may guide our choices: Do we seek the anticipated outcome yielding the greatest probability of gain? Are we interested in the least risk of loss? Do we prefer the greatest gain regardless of risk or the least loss regardless of probabilities? What material, monetary, and human constraints limit what we may do? What are the real-world *consequences* of implementing each alternative? What new problems will be generated by each particular solution?

WEIGHING ALTERNATIVES.   After screening out obviously unfeasible or irrelevant alternatives, an orderly evaluator proceeds to examine and weigh the advantages and disadvantages of each alternative, using the selected criteria. A checklist of pros and cons often is advisable. Each criterion in the checklist need not be given the same weight, but the checklist forces the decision maker to be systematic in evaluating every alternative by means of each criterion. No one alternative is treated with favoritism. Wherever possible, supporting evidence and the confidence in evaluations is examined. A choice matrix may be worked out and gaming techniques applied in a search for an optimum choice.

INTEGRATING SOLUTIONS.   Such systematic exploration often makes it possible to see ways of combining and integrating solutions, particularly if one makes an effort to do so. To promote such integration, it appears more profitable to look at each alternative solution with a positive constructive attitude than with a negative set. When a college staff, for instance, reviewed ideas by asking, "What's good about these proposals?" they were more likely to incorporate the suggestions in the final solution. When they focused on what was wrong with the proposals, the ideas were likely to be rejected completely.

QUALITY OF FINAL DECISION BY SUPERVISOR OR SUPERVISOR AND STAFF.   One supervisor may believe that he/she should obtain the advice and consent of subordinates about a problem and possible solutions to it. Yet the supervisor still feels that he/she alone must make the decision about which alternative to adopt. Another executive collaborates with the group in making the final decision. Is one approach better than another?

If the supervisor is trying to capitalize on the values of group consensus, but reserves the last step, the final decision for him/herself, he/she risks selecting an unfavored one through misunderstanding how the problem and the solutions to it were seen by the group. On the other hand, if the supervisor maintains the group approach to the end of the process, hammering out a jointly constructed agreement, does he/she risk reaching a decision that is personally regarded as less than the best?

Actually, if the supervisor and staff are pursuing similar goals with similar knowledge of constraints, have achieved agreement on the problem, and have searched and evaluated the various alternative solutions to the problem, the final choice is likely to be similar whether the supervisor makes it alone or it is made by the supervisor and the group. The *quality* of the decision usually is superior when the supervisor has the benefit of staff consultation.

Factors Affecting the Final Choice

Classical economics assumed that a decision maker was completely informed about the available choices as well as about their consequences. He/she was infinitely sensitive to this information and was completely rational. As such, he/she chose the alternative whose consequences would give the greatest value or utility with the least cost. If utilities for different alternatives were the same, the decision maker became indifferent about the choice. If these assumptions were correct, then there would be no need to study the behavior of the decision maker, for we would only need to understand the decision maker's environment and the available choices. Then we could determine mathematically what the choice would be.

Unfortunately most organizational decision makers are not completely informed, are not infinitely sensitive, and exhibit only limited rationality. Although the decision maker sees him/herself as orderly, systematic, and rational, he/she must estimate the likely consequences of each prospective choice, how much it will cost, whether it will work, and how much utility lies in making the given choice. In making these estimates, the decision maker displays certain cognitive tendencies and judgmental errors.

Although the quality of the decision may not differ after the group has deliberated, the group's decision is likely to involve taking more risks than would the decision made by a lone individual. Discussion, consensus, and the diffusion of responsibility leads to increased tolerance for risk. We may infer that bank committees are likely to approve more risky loans than are individual loan officers.

AN IRRATIONAL GROUP DECISION MAY EMERGE FROM RATIONAL CHOICES OF ITS MEMBERSHIP.   A purely rational person is transitive in his choices. If Mr. Black prefers apples to bananas, and bananas to cherries, then he will also choose apples over cherries. (If $a > b$ and $> c$, then $a > c$.) Consider that Mr. Black, Mr. Brown, and Mr. Green prefer the fruits in the following order:

	MEMBERS		
	BLACK	BROWN	GREEN
First Choice	Apples	Bananas	Cherries
Second Choice	Bananas	Cherries	Apples
Third Choice	Cherries	Apples	Bananas

For Mr. Black, $a > b > c$; for Mr. Brown, $b > c > a$, and for Mr. Green, $c > a > b$. Suppose the trio votes on which fruit to choose. In each case a majority of two of three voters can decide the outcome. Apples are favored over bananas by Mr. Black and Mr. Green; so for the trio, if a vote is taken, $a > b$. Bananas are favored over cherries by Mr. Black and Mr. Brown; so for the trio, $b > c$. If the trio vote is completely rational it should be transitive. Since $a > b$ and $b > c$, then $a > c$; apples should be voted for over cherries. Yet in such a vote both Mr. Brown and Mr. Green favor cherries over apples $(c > a)$ and so the trio majority would be irrational or intransitive despite the fact that each of its members, Black, Brown, and Green, are completely rational.

SYSTEMATIC DISTORTION OF OBJECTIVE PROBABILITIES. Understanding of choice is made more difficult by the increasing distortions that occur in an individual's subjective estimates as the objective odds rise. Slot machine players in particular are usually playing against impossibly unfavorable odds. Classical economics would suggest that no one would play a slot machine after observing the pattern of payoff, for the player should act completely rationally. The player would maximize holdings by not playing at all and keeping what money was on hand. But the 24-hour-a-day casinos in Nevada prove otherwise.

Confidence in the Decision

Our willingness to risk obviously is directly related to our confidence that we know what outcomes are likely as a consequence of our choice. Studies of confidence provide clues as to how we move to reduce the uncertainty in situations before making a final decision.

As might be expected, we tend to be more confident that an alternative will work as a direct consequence of our previous experience of success or failure with that alternative. Certainty and speed of decision also depend on the intensity with which one emotionally favors one alternative over another. One is less likely to deliberate over choices about which one already has strong attitudes, regardless of the reason for the development of those attitudes.

We tend to be more confident when we receive more information about an alternative and when the information is more constant. We attempt to increase our confidence before making a decision that could prove expensive by reviewing the probable costs and projected gains.

Judgment is fraught with other errors. We have mentioned the general tendency to accept or agree rather than to object or disagree. This tendency becomes more pronounced if we are confronted with more uncertainty and ambiguity. We also become more acquiescent if we are bored or indifferent.

Our judgment of one alternative will be affected by its contrast to other alternatives. It may look good simply because other solutions look bad. In the same way we may accept an alternative because it is embedded in a context of optimistic and hopeful statements, or because it is connected to other actually more promising solutions that are to be tried.

Following Up a Final Decision

The decision process is not complete even after we have made our final decision. We must follow up the decision to see whether the consequences were as expected. If the outcomes have occurred as predicted, then the problem is solved. Otherwise a reexamination of the problem may be needed, initiating again the cycle of steps in the decision process.

In the follow-up phase, a particular judgmental phenomenon that is likely to affect accuracy adversely is the tendency to seek justification and validation of one's decisions rather than an objective appraisal of the decision.

THE TENDENCY TO CONFIRM RATHER THAN REJECT DECISIONS.   Francis Bacon noted 350 years ago:

> The human understanding when it has once adopted an opinion . . . draws all things else to support and agree with it. And though there be a greater number and weight of instances to be found on the other side, yet these it either neglects or despises, or else by some distinction sets aside and rejects; in order that by this great and pernicious predetermination the authority of its former conclusions may remain inviolate.

Once we have made a decision, we tend to concentrate on corroborating its correctness rather than taking equal note of subsequent contradictory evidence. We become blind to contrary evidence, particularly if the after-effects of decisions are ambiguous or difficult to evaluate. Since cognitive balance is favored over cognitive dissonance, if the evaluation of the wisdom or efficacy of a decision that has been made depends on subjective judgment, it is likely that we will perceive the decision to have been beneficial rather than detrimental when actually if may have had no utility for us. Errors of judgment in reaching the final decision are thus reinforced, and our subsequent evaluations biased accordingly. For instance, most supervisors, when queried about the effects of some special training they have received, will respond favorably about the effects on them. And if they must decide on whether the program should be continued, they are more likely to vote to continue than to suspend it regardless of its actual worth or lack of value.

Confucius said, "The superior man understands what is right; the inferior man understands what will sell."

How to Develop and Appraise Written Evaluations of Performance

The written characterization of performance must be a true record of evaluation based on measurement that is as objective as possible. Evaluation must be a positive critique; it should not be laudatory anymore than it should be defamatory. Deserved praise should be included. In the case of a beginning teacher, the individual must be evaluated in terms pertinent to the experience of the individual, but the issues should not be evaded.

If the written characterization is to serve its purpose, an account of performance should be provided that includes the whole truth uninfluenced by personal motives, fear, or pity. A frank appraisal of the strengths and weaknesses of the individual should be included so that a program of professional growth may be planned.

If a check sheet is used, the principal should be sure that any written comments apply to professional competencies, and that they are not duplications of phrases included in the checklist. Written comments may explain, but they also should amplify the check sheet section of the evaluation so that a clearer picture of the individual and his/her needs will be provided.

Specific information that should be found in the evaluation form includes:

1. Personal characteristics
2. Professional competence and knowledge of subject matter
3. Ability to work with and control students
4. Classroom management and instructional efficiency
5. Interpersonal relationships
6. Needs (specific)
7. Recommendations
8. Prognosis

The important consideration is that written records, and supervisory conferences as well, will be helpful to teachers. If they are not, recommendations should be made to alter the written record form (and/or the conference procedure).

How to Describe and Appraise the Status of the Supervisory Program

The supervising principal will not be satisfied to know merely the adequacy of the product; rather, he/she will want feedback concerning the status of the many conditions that limit or facilitate educational outcomes.

Knowledge of status is important. Also important is feedback on the supervisory program's present conditions and effectiveness in terms of goals met.

The feedback can help interpret the many kinds of data that the principal might receive about the program for supervision and its objectives. Furthermore, such knowledge can lead to revision, innovation, and subsequent improvement, continuous evaluation, and further feedback, which is so vitally important to educational supervision.

Normative Survey of the Effectiveness of Supervision

Generally speaking, the supervising principal should proceed through the following ten steps in conducting a normative survey of the supervisory program in order to determine present status.

1. Prepare statements of the objectives of the normative survey
2. Define the population to be sampled
3. Decide the nature of the data to be collected
4. Delineate techniques for collecting the data
5. Delimit the study and the sampling unit
6. Select a method for determining the sample
7. Decide on methods for treating nonrespondents
8. Conduct exploratory of pilot surveys, follow with the final study
9. Prepare a summary and analysis of data received
10. Prepare the survey report.

When the supervising principal asks questions of opinion concerning the supervisory program, every effort should be made to formulate wording that will not invoke bias in the respondent. Some opportunity should be given in the survey to permit respondents to record general remarks on special points. These remarks should direct attention to facts that are relevant to the problem at hand, but that were not included in the list of questions.

In reporting the results of the sampling survey, the supervising principal should consider the following list of suggested material:

1. A general description of the survey should be included. Purposes of the survey, descriptions of the material covered, methods used in collecting the data, nature of the information collected, sampling method, accuracy, repetition, period of time, responsibility, and basic references should be indicated.
2. The design of the normative survey should be presented carefully, with limitations and delimitations of design reported.
3. The method of selecting sample units should be noted.
4. All materials and personnel utilized in conducting the supervisory survey should be included in the report.
5. The cost of conducting the evaluative survey should be noted.
6. Precision and the efficiency of the survey, as indicated by the degree of agreement observed between independent investigators and from a comparison with other sources of information, should be reported.

FIGURE 17-2.   Which Is Worse? No Suggestion Plan at all, or the Wastebasket
Approach?

7. A summary of the findings, conclusions, and recommendations for further
   study should be included.

Remember that the ultimate purpose in studying causes is to be able to
predict the effects of certain causes with a view to controlling the cause-effect
continuum. Collecting enumerative data may provide important source data for
analytical investigation of the effectiveness of the program for school supervision.

The purpose of the normative survey in an analytical problem situation is
to inquire into the underlying factors or causes that may have given rise to an
observed condition or situation. In the enumerative problem situation, however,
the objective of the normative survey is to determine certain characteristics of the
population without inquiring into the reason that these characters appear as they
do. The latter situation does not appear to have as much value as does the former
in evaluating the program for supervision.

Teachers and Principals View Supervision in Action

D. Benjamin[6] reported teachers' and principals' reactions to supervisory techniques, listed in rank order and based on frequency of occurrence. Teachers and
principals differed widely concerning their concepts of helpful supervision. A
combination, however, is possible.

[6] Dayton Benjamin, "How Principals Can Improve Instruction," *American School Board
Journal* CXXXII (May 1956): 37–39.

Teachers' Views

Teachers viewed the following as effective supervisory behavior:

1. Occasionally relieving the teacher of classroom duties so the teacher may attend to pressing professional commitments; respecting plans made by the teacher.
2. Building the teacher's confidence by demonstrating knowledge of teaching procedures.
3. Observing the class and conducting follow-up with a clear, direct evaluation of the teacher's work.
4. Using the formal evaluation conference as an objective agreement concerning strengths and weaknesses previously discussed.
5. Supporting the teacher in relations with children and parents.
6. Relieving the teacher of clerical details to allow more time for preparation and actual teaching.
7. Granting teachers' requests for help from outside specialist-consultants.

Principals' Views

Principals viewed the following as effective supervisory behavior:

1. Becoming thoroughly acquainted with the teacher's capabilities before suggesting a new procedure; observing for a length of time to assess the teacher's capabilities.
2. Waiting until the beginning teacher becomes acquainted with the students, the philosophy of the school system, and its routines before suggesting major changes in routine.
3. Waiting until the teacher is emotionally ready to accept suggestions for change.
4. Listening sympathetically to the teacher's personal problems and offering assistance when asked for it.
5. Arranging visits to other classrooms, making certain that no stigma is attached to a visitation, and discussing the visitation thoroughly.

Teachers and Principals Combine Their Views

A combination of views of both teachers and principals is possible.

1. Continuing to work with the teacher in developing new techniques and procedures; continuing to bring new ideas to the teacher.
2. Helping the teacher improve classroom control by giving suggestions that apply directly to the problem area.
3. Providing direct assistance in the utilization of instructional materials.
4. Considering the teacher's preferences and ideas when making suggestions.

5. Demonstrating teaching procedures in such a way that the students' respect for the teacher is preserved.
6. Giving direct praise for specific accomplishment.
7. Giving reassurance when possible that the teacher is doing a good job.
8. Giving the teacher an assignment in which the teacher feels important before other school and community adults.
9. Complying with the teacher's request for expediting additional plant facilities and instructional supplies.

Evidence of an Effective Supervisory Program

The symptoms below may be indicative of a supervisory program that works. There is evidence of:

1. Increased understanding of the nature of the student.
2. Increased knowledge of skills and techniques of directing, improving, measuring, and recording the intellectual and social growth of the student.
3. Increased knowledge and skill in planning and adapting learning materials and activities to individual (and group) abilities and interests.
4. Increased knowledge in the subject matter fields.
5. Understanding and skill in the use of "newer" classroom procedures and devices of worth.
6. Knowledge of modern concepts dealing with the problems of discipline and control.
7. Increased understanding and skill in counseling young people.
8. Constructing a curriculum related to local, state, and national needs, pertaining to present and future needs of the student.
9. Establishing better relationships with students, professional colleagues, and members of the community.
10. Developing greater interest in reading, in research, and in professional writing.

Evidence of the supervisory program's effectiveness may be gathered through the review of tests and inventory results as well as through the survey technique. The following should be investigated:

1. Results of achievement tests
2. Results of intelligence and aptitude tests
3. Results of adjustment inventories
4. Anecdotal records of student behavior
5. Records of teacher's estimate of student achievement
6. Records of the reactions of students, parents, and the community to the school program
7. Classroom visits and supervisory conferences.

A general survey of supervisory organization and administration by outside consultants should be completed occasionally. A committee composed of local staff members should be appointed and asked to evaluate the supervision program. The evaluation committee should compare the budget expenditures for supervision with those of other school systems.

Some faculty meetings should be devoted to evaluating supervisory services. An unsigned opinionnaire, answered by teaching personnel, is a technique for uncovering attitudes toward supervisors and supervision.

The supervising principal should determine if goals have been met and whether or not the goals were desirable in the first place. He/she should examine the validity of the instruments or records used to conduct the evaluation. All results must be recorded and, if the evaluation is to be worthwhile, it should result in some sort of action. Evaluation per se is worthless!

Some Questions the Supervising Principal Can Ask

The following list of questions to be answered by the supervising principal may help evaluate the supervisory program:

1. Do I maintain cordial relationships with teachers?
2. Is communication with the staff on a personal basis?
3. Do I seek out the strong points in teachers and build on these?
4. Do I seek and accept the contributions of all members of the staff, no matter how inconsequential the contribution may seem at the time?
5. Do I provide opportunities wherein teachers can make decisions in matters in which they are vitally concerned?
6. Do I seek to uncover and encourage the development of leadership on the part of staff members? (It is the supervisor who knows that the more people who feel a personal responsibility for the supervisory program, the more successful it probably will be.) [7]
7. Do I pretend to be expert in all subjects and grade levels, or am I a specialist in working with teachers on the requirements of successful instruction?
8. Do I provide an ample supply of textbooks and supplementary materials and equipment, and then make sure that it is easy for teachers to obtain these materials?
9. Do I keep teachers informed about free and inexpensive materials that are available?
10. Do I facilitate the participation by teachers and students in educational field trips?
11. Are my plans for supervision concrete and specific?
12. Are my plans for supervision consistent with the aspirations, goals, and

[7] Moorer, *op. cit.*

level of development of the teaching personnel and the citizens of the community?

13. Do I base planning, so far as possible, on the realities of the situation that are discovered through the use of the techniques of research and careful experimentation?

14. Do I consult parents to find out what they think the school should be doing?

15. Do I contribute to and help coordinate and integrate the efforts of all agencies and institutions in the community that are interested in improving education?

16. Do I actively cooperate with, and draw on, the available local, state, national, and international departments that are interested in improving education?

17. Do I establish a schedule for my supervisory activities on a yearly, monthly, weekly, and daily basis?

18. Do I judge my success by the progress of the school program toward goals accepted by the group?

19. Do I encourage teachers to assume more responsibility for self-supervision?

20. Have I been successful in elevating the quality and quantity of cooperative planning among staff members?

21. Have I been successful in stimulating more teachers to experiment and do research related to the instructional program and the curriculum?

22. Am I flexible, making changes easily when pertinent and qualified data indicate changes are in order?[8]

23. Do I realize that self-evaluation is the key to the effective analysis of my contribution to the improving instruction?

Do

1. Recommend a general survey of supervisory organization and administration by outside consultants periodically.

2. Seek the appointment of a staff committee from the local school system and give it the task of evaluating the supervision program.

3. Make certain the supervisor and all personnel engaged in the process of supervision are encouraged to make observations concerning the effectiveness of the supervisory program.

4. Conduct interviews with the teachers, students, parents, and others to determine the effectiveness of the program.

5. Evaluate the supervisory range, scope, and function in light of research findings.

6. Use an unsigned opinionnaire filled in by teaching personnel to discern attitudes toward supervisors and supervision.

7. Institute a suggestion box. (Such a device, utilized by teachers and supervisors, may aid constructive evaluation.)
   Employ preschool workshops to evaluate aims, objectives, plans, purposes, and goals with respect to the supervisory process.

[8] Harvey L. Roach, Lieutenant, Los Angeles Police Department, in the Leadership Training Conference Series, Los Angeles, September, 1970.

9. Remember that evaluation should accompany and follow each supervisory activity.
10. Invite intermediate unit (county) or state consultants to help evaluate the school's supervisory program.
11. Examine records and note what changes have occurred in the curriculum.

Don't Forget

Let us state again what Confucius said; it's worth repeating—and remembering. "The superior man understands what is right; the inferior man understands what will sell."

TRENDS IN EVALUATING THE SUPERVISORY PROGRAM

Toward ⟶ Continuous Evaluation of the Program of Educational Supervision

Although supervising principals have been willing to evaluate the work of their professional colleagues, they have been unwilling to evaluate adequately their own supervisory programs. In the future, more evaluation of supervisory services will be conducted on a continuous basis.

Toward ⟶ Faculty Planning for the Evaluation of Supervisory Services

Evaluation of the program for educational supervision will be planned by the professional staff under the leadership of the supervising principal.

Toward ⟶ The Use of the Techniques of Scientific Research in Evaluating Supervisory Services

The normative survey, as well as experimental methods and techniques, will be utilized in evaluating the program for supervision. Specific performance objectives will be set carefully, terms used in a unique or arbitrary manner will be defined, procedures will be selected, hypotheses will be set, and research will be conducted in a scientific manner. Attempts to whitewash the program will be rare; supervising principals will realize that a continuously improving instructional program can be realized through an improving program of supervision.

Toward ⟶ Greater Emphasis
on Criterion-Referenced Evaluation

Testing and evaluation traditionally have been norm-referenced. Comparisons are made to the performance of other subjects or to standardized averages. There is a definite trend toward criterion-referenced testing and evaluation that uses individualized tests and objectives for evaluation. This procedure will be applied to administrators, teachers, and other personnel, as well as to students, in spite of the hazards and limitations of applying the techniques universally, as noted in the trends section of chapter 10.

Supervisory Problems

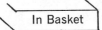

In Basket

Problem 1

The existing policy for supervision has been enforced in School District No. 35 for the past eight years. A university evaluation study of the total district organization and program resulted in a series of faculty and administrative council meetings.

All concerned seemed to agree that there is a need for some revision in the policy for supervision for the district.

How would you, as supervising principal, determine what additions, changes, or deletions you might suggest?

Problem 2

The evaluation program in the Coldwood Unified School District requires the principal to evaluate probationary teachers twice a year and permanent teachers once a year. The evaluation form is a checklist covering such items as: teaching ability, classroom control, personal characteristics, and professional growth. Under each topic are several subitems and a small space for comments. Principals are required to fill out the checklist and schedule a teacher conference. At the end of the conference, the teacher is asked to sign the checklist, indicating that it has been discussed with him. One copy of the evaluation is given to the teacher and one is sent to the personnel office. A record of classroom visitations is also required.

The teachers have raised many objections to the evaluation system. They say that some principals do not visit their classes and others stay only a few minutes. (Secondary principals retort that with over 80 teachers, it is impossible to visit all of them.) Teachers feel that the checklist is an outdated evaluation procedure; that evaluations by a single person—the principal—are not satisfactory and often show personal bias; that evaluation conferences are not always a two-way exchange of ideas and more often are dominated by the principal.

Permanent teachers feel that they should be exempted from yearly evaluation.

The teacher's association, as a result of the compaints, has asked the superintendent to appoint a committee to revise the evaluation procedure. The superintendent has delegated this responsibility to the personnel director.

Whom should the personnel director select for the committee?
What schedule should be established for committee meetings?
What procedure should the committee follow as it works at developing a new evaluation policy?
If you were a member of the committee and were asked for your ideas about an evaluation policy, what would you recommend?

Questions and Suggested Activities Concerning How to Evaluate the Supervisory Program

Questions

1. How can the principal get group participation in evaluating supervision?
2. What statement of facts could be given to the governing board to get the board's support in a proposed evaluation program?
3. What outside evaluation help do you feel the school board should be willing to consider?
4. How much of a supervisor's annual allotment of time should be used in evaluating the supervisory program?
5. What steps would you take to assure the superintendent that you, as principal of the school, had given the board "the most supervision for its money?"
6. What are late trends in instruction and how would you evaluate their worth?

Suggested Activities

1. Interview a principal of a school to discuss the methods used in evaluating the supervisory program.

2. You are the assistant superintendent of instruction of a large school system. Prepare a list of criteria you would use in evaluating the work of specialist-consultants.
3. Prepare a plan for evaluating supervision in a school or school system of your choice.
4. The board asks for a specific evaluation of mathematics supervision. Prepare a report for the superintendent showing how you would go about evaluating mathematics supervision in your school that has an enrollment of 900.
5. Devise a check sheet that you could use to evaluate supervisory services in a junior high school.
6. Write an article suitable for publication in a professional periodical concerning the importance, purposes, and techniques of evaluation for supervisory programs at the junior high school level.
7. Evaluate your supervisory organization for the handling of innovations in curriculum, buildings, in-service education, and public relations.

Selected Bibliography

Books

Barr, A. S., William H. Burton, and Leo J. Brueckner. *Supervision: Democratic Leadership in the Improvement of Learning.* New York: D. Appleton-Century Company, 1947.

Barr, Arvil S., Robert A. Davis, and Palmer O. Johnson. *Educational Research and Appraisal.* Chicago: J. B. Lippincott Company, 1953.

Bass, Bernard M. *Organizational Psychology.* Boston: Allyn and Bacon, Inc., 1965.

Bradford, Eugene et al. *Elementary School Evaluation.* Los Angeles: Parker & Son Publications, Inc., 1972.

Browder, Lesley H. *Developing an Educationally Accountable Program.* Berkeley, California: McCutchan Publishing Corporation, 1972.

Collings, Ellsworth. *School Supervision in Theory and Practice.* New York: Thomas Y. Crowell Company, 1927.

Conant, Eaton H. *Teacher and Paraprofessional Work Productivity.* Lexington, Massachusetts: Lexington Books (Div. of D. C. Heath), 1973.

Crosby, Muriel. *Supervision as Co-operative Action.* New York: Appleton-Century-Crofts, 1957.

Etzioni, Amitai. *A Comparative Analysis of Complex Organizations.* New York: The Free Press, 1961.

Fiorino, John A. *Differentiated Staffing.* New York: Harper & Row Pubs., Inc., 1972.

Granger, Robert L. *Educational Leadership: An Interdisciplinary Perspective.* Scranton, Pennsylvania: Intext Educational Publishers, 1971.

Hummel, Raymond C., and John M. Nagle. *Urban Education in America: Problems and Prospects.* New York: Oxford University Press, 1973.

Lewis, Arthur, and Alice Miel. *Supervision for Better Instruction: New Challenges, New Responses.* Belmont, California: Wadsworth Publishing Co., Inc., 1972.

Lipham, James M., and James A. Hoeh, Jr. *The Principalship: Foundations and Functions.* New York: Harper and Row, 1974.

Lucio, William H., and John D. McNeil. *Supervision—A Synthesis of Thought and Action.* New York: McGraw-Hill Book Company, Inc., 1962.

Meranto, Phillip. *School Politics in the Metropolis.* Columbus, Ohio: Charles E. Merrill Publishing Co., 1970.

Nunnery, Michael Y., and Ralph B. Kimbrough. *Politics, Power, Polls, and School Elections.* Berkeley, California: McCutchan Publishing Co., 1971.

Spears, Harold. *Improving the Supervision of Instruction.* Englewood Cliffs, New Jersey: Prentice-Hall, Inc., 1953.

Thurley, Keith, and Hans Wirdenius. *Supervision: a Reappraisal.* New York: Russak and Co., Inc., 1973.

Wiles, Kimball. *Supervision for Better Schools.* Englewood Cliffs, New Jersey: Prentice-Hall, Inc., 1955.

Wiles, Kimball, and John T. Lovell. *Supervision for Better Schools.* 4th ed. Englewood Cliffs, New Jersey: Prentice-Hall, Inc., 1975.

Periodicals

Benjamin, Dayton. "How Principals Can Improve Instruction." *American School Board Journal* CXXXII (May 1956): 37–39.

Ebel, Robert L. "Educational Tests: Valid? Biased? Useful?" *Phi Delta Kappan* LVII (October 1975): 83–88.

The Editors. "Trends: Accountability, Competencies, and Evaluation." *Audio Visual Instruction* XX (December 1975): special ed.

Green, Robert L. "Tips on Educational Testing: What Teachers and Parents Should Know." *Phi Delta Kappan* LVII (October 1975): 89–93.

Kyte, George C. "This Is the Kind of Supervision That Teachers Welcome and Appreciate." *Nation's Schools* XLVIII (July 1951): 33–34.

Maier, Norman R. F. "Leadership Principles for Problem-Solving Conferences." *Michigan Business Review* XIV (May 1962): 8–15.

Stodolsky, Susan Silverman. "Identifying and Evaluating Open Education." *Phi Delta Kappan* LVII (October 1975): 113–117.

Audio Cassette

Evaluation of Training. Development Digest, 1970. Available from Thompson-Mitchell, Atlanta, Georgia.

Films

ABC'S of Decision Making. Washington, D.C.: Creative Media, Inc., 1974. Management consultant Joe Batten outlines a practical approach to making decisions, stressing the need to identify problems and to use a logical process that analyzes alternatives in terms of people, money, materials, time, and space. Also considers why decisions go wrong, the ways decisions should not be made, the two basic types of decision, and when decisions should be made. (29 minutes)

Decision Making Skills. Thompson-Mitchell, Atlanta, Georgia, 1973. Shows the steps in decision making and how to implement and validate decisions. Filmstrip.

Effective Decisions. Washington, D.C.: BNA Films, 1968. Peter Drucker investigates the process of managerial decision making. Noting that executive decision is at best a choice between two alternatives, neither of which can be proved right, Drucker points out that the effective executive's job is to discover the reasons behind alternative opinions. In this way all pertinent facts can be uncovered and brought to bear. (25 minutes)

Other Sources

Arkansas State Department of Education, Division of Instruction. *Guide to Effective Elementary School Supervision.* Little Rock: The Department, n.d.

Clark, C. H. *Brainstorming.* New York: Doubleday, 1958.

Department of Elementary School Principals. *The Elementary School Principalship—Today and Tomorrow*. Twenty-Seventh Yearbook. Washington, D.C.: National Education Association, 1948.

DeNovellis, R. L., and Arthur J. Lewis. *Schools Become Accountable*. Washington, D.C.: Association for Supervision and Curriculum Development, 1974.

Editorial Staff, U.S. Supreme Court Reports. *Decisions of the U.S. Supreme Court*. Rochester: The Lawyers Co-operative Publishing Co., 1973.

Franseth, Jane. *Learning to Supervise Schools*. Circular No. 289. Washington, D.C.: Office of Education, n.d.

Guilford, J. P. *A Revised Structure of Intellect*. Reports, Psychological Laboratory, No. 19. Los Angeles: University of Southern California, 1957, 6–7.

Harris, Lewis E., and Clyde B. Moore. *Keys to Quality—Quest for Quality*. Washington, D.C.: National School Boards Association, American Association of School Administrators, 1960.

Moorer, Sam H. *Supervision: The Keystone to Educational Progress*. Tallahassee: Florida State Department of Education, 1952.

———. *How Good Is Your Supervisory Program*. St. Augustine: Florida State Department of Education, 1950.

Reavis, William C. "Evaluating the Work of the School." *Proceedings of the Ninth Annual Conference for Administrative Officers of Public and Private Schools*. Volume III. Chicago: University of Chicago Press, 1940.

Texas Education Agency. *Work-Conference on Educational Leadership and Supervision*. Austin: The Agency, 1949.

———. Curriculum Division. *Supervisor's Exchange*. Austin: The Agency, 1951.

18

Professional Responsibilities
of the Supervisor

An educator needs to develop technical skills, but his/her concern must go beyond the scope of those skills. A good educator cannot delimit activities and perform only as a technician.

The motivations that are basic to education do not operate on an eight-hour day—they are a constant part of daily life. In a sense, the educator has no choice of being in a profession or a trade. The vital function of education in all areas of national concern has established the status of education.

The discussion of professional responsibilities calls attention to the need for identifying current practices and for defining the term "professional." Theology, law, and medicine long have been considered the learned professions, and in themselves involve many educational activities. During the Renaissance, doctoral degrees were earned in these three areas. To these areas have been added professional degrees in engineering, the sciences, pharmacy, and education.

A true profession involves a desire to serve mankind through its accumulated skills and knowledge. A profession has a well-defined body of established factual material that can be verified by research. A scholarly concern for truth and continual dedicated search for new material and applications are in evidence. A profession involves both the present and the future—the long-range goals and hopes as well as daily practice.

The points discussed in this chapter include:

Requirements for professional status
Qualities of a profession
The educator's responsibilities
Ethics for the supervisor in handling personnel matters
Professional organizations
Moving toward professional status
Do—Don't
Trends
"In-Basket" supervisory problems
Questions and suggested activities

614

Requirements for Professional Status

Each profession undergoes misuse of position, forays into the mystical, and unfounded and untrue claims and practices. However, a true profession can meet the tests of truth: serious research and scholarly study.

Education is approaching the definitive criteria of a profession. During the last century, the world saw the rise of active study and research in education and the establishment of the sociological, psychological, and philosophical foundations of education. Knowledge of the field of educational statistics is growing. Educators have become increasingly articulate in writing for publication.

Many universities have established professional schools of education devoted to training educators and furthering the profession. Professional degree programs established at the Master's and Doctor's levels train highly qualified individuals for work in professional education.

A professional worker originally professed or was committed to a recognized system of values and standards. This original meaning is still implicit in the broader use in which the term ordinarily is employed.

A physician professes—i.e., publicly commits him/herself—to the codes and standards of that group. So do the lawyer and the clergyman. Each of these individuals *follows a calling* rather than holds a job.

The professional worker who follows a calling has engaged in a rigorous program of preparation. Presently, this means preparation well beyond the requirement of the first academic degree. After meeting the minimum standards for admission to practice of the profession, one continues to study. By engaging in research, attending meetings and conventions where colleagues present their research findings, and by other means, one increases a grasp of the subject matter and enhances the quality of practice.

The professional keeps abreast of developments in the field. The physician, the attorney, or the engineer who does not read professional journals or study important new books written by colleagues, soon falls so far behind and loses effectiveness, as well as patients or clients.

Because the professional person can exercise independent judgment, he/she decides what procedures and materials are called for.

Of course he/she confers and seeks advice, but the action adopted—the medication prescribed, the dimensions of the structural beams in the building, the precedent cited when in court—are the individual, informed, and responsible decisions of the professional.

The professional person must accept responsibility for his/her decisions, even wrong ones. The professional person who violates the ethical code is subject to disciplinary action or even expulsion by the action of peers in the profession.

Education must be judged by these criteria. The professional educator should be prepared to work independently and should be able to decide, *on the basis of sound knowledge and informed judgment,* how best to proceed in the always complex and constantly changing situations in the classroom.

Education will not be recognized as a *mature* profession as long as many educators hold jobs rather than follow a calling, or as long as many educators fail to keep abreast of developments in their field. When educators themselves set the standards for admission to their ranks, and when they make the decision about who may be retained and who is to be expelled, then the profession will have come of age.

In the light of what has been said, we can see that any *ethical* means by which the educator can better perform the work to which she is dedicated are by definition appropriate for a person who operates on a professional level.

Qualities of a Profession

The following may be considered as a set of criteria for determining whether professional status has been earned, based on present-day qualities of professionals. A profession possesses:

1. A craft that is comparatively conservative in practice
2. Requirements for extensive and intensive training
3. The maintenance of high standards for admission to the craft—an exclusiveness in selection
4. A strict code of ethics
5. A high level of social status accompanied by a high rate of remuneration
6. An intellectual aura
7. A program of research on both an organized and an individual level
8. The practical application of research within the craft
9. Techniques that can be taught, but only with difficulty
10. A brotherhood—almost a caste
11. Responsiveness and service to the public
12. Foresight about the nature of elements relevant to the profession
13. Advanced training and certification.

Generally, people in a profession cannot agree as to what constitutes a profession, but everyone stresses service to the public. When young people choose service as a way of life, they may be ready to become professional educators.

Professional Activities for the Supervisor

Supervisory personnel should exhibit:

1. An active interest and noticeable pride in being a member of the profession.
2. A positive approach toward the status of the profession and the gains made toward professional status.
3. A willingness to do the "extra" expected of the strongly motivated individual.

4. Interest in working with fellow educators and citizens to solve educational problems and to plan for improvement and evaluation.
5. Academic advancement in general degree work and also within the particular field, or fields, of the educator's responsibilities.
6. Willingness to endure temporary setbacks while working toward long-range improvements.
7. An insistence (when deserved) on recognition as a professional in matters of student-teacher, supervisor-teacher, citizen-educator, and other personal relationships.
8. Courage to speak out when a situation demands attention.
9. A dissatisfaction with the unprofessional and unethical activities and conduct of other educators, such as a manifest lack of interest in in-service education, pettiness in attempting to gain favor by reporting trivial mistakes of a fellow educator to the administrator, attempting to obtain a position already held by a professional educator, or undermining efforts of groups endeavoring to advance the effectiveness of education.
10. An awareness of the deep responsibility those in education bear to the nation's needs as well as to the needs of each student.
11. An image of the profession to the lay public as well as to other professions as one of purpose, quality, and high standards.
12. An insistence on progress toward financial support for educators that will permit their elevation from mere subsistence levels of living.
13. A development of mutual respect for other professional members in education, going beyond employee-employer relationships found in other vocations.
14. A desire to correct a situation when necessary. The creation of a labor versus management situation, which may tend to degrade one segment of the educational team, should be avoided.
15. A realization that moderation in most instances is a virtue, and that patience must be a constant companion in progress toward professional goals. Students have been taught, and will continue to be taught, under the direction of many who never have attained professional status, just as some persons have been helped by other than fully licensed practitioners for hundreds of years.

The Educator's Responsibilities

Responsibility 1—To Self

Only when one has learned self-respect can one gain the respect of others. Certain attitudes of the educator toward self and work have considerable bearing on total professional efficiency. The educator must respect him/herself and his/her own ideas without becoming dogmatic or intolerant of the ideas of others. The educator also should be able to view matters according to their relative importance because otherwise there might be danger of devoting all of the time and energy to trivial or routine items.

The personal life of the educator also needs to be considered. He/she should attempt to lead a life as normal and as rich as possible. A well-rounded personal life will make a person a more effective leader.

Responsibility 2—To Students

Students constitute an educator's most important professional responsibilities, taking up a good share of the thinking and effort throughout tenure. An educator must know the entire program of public education, not merely at his/her own level—elementary, secondary, or higher—but at all levels.

The educator should employ all available resources to provide leadership in developing the instructional program. Merely having a dedicated attitude toward children is insufficient. This attitude must be reflected by actual practice, and frequently this is not an easy task.

To provide the most profitable experiences to students, the educator must set up machinery to study their needs. The present *and future* needs of the students always should be in the foreground, and the educator should use these needs as the bases for all educational planning.

Responsibility 3—To the Patrons of the School

The effective educator recognizes a responsibility to the community. If he/she is seen as a competent individual in whom the citizenry can trust, then success and the smooth operation of the school will be enhanced. The educator's relationship with the public, with the students, and with the parents must be characterized by honesty, sincerity, and integrity.

Responsibility 4—To the Members of the Staff

The supervising principal who believes and practices the basic democratic tenets in relations with teachers in the school finds it easier to stimulate similar practices and attitudes in classroom teachers.

Supervisory leaders occasionally find it necessary, in order to protect the rights of individuals or groups, to uphold principles that may be unpopular in the community. Although he/she will exercise the greatest tact in such situations, the leader of stature will not shrink from the role of advocate of a just cause.

Responsibility 5—To the Superintendent
and the Governing Board

The principal has certain responsibilities to those who appoint him/her. These responsibilities encompass loyalty to the general purposes and welfare of the school system as a whole:

[Problems should be] dealt with impersonally, in a friendly but forthright manner, and through the proper channels. The effective principal is both honest and co-operative in his relations with those who select him.[1]

Any person who assumes the great responsibility of becoming a supervisor should be acutely aware of professional responsibilities to the superintendent. He/she can be outstanding in all other areas, but faltering in this association means failure.

Ethics for the Supervisor in Handling Personnel Matters[2]

To fulfill special responsibilities to students, parents, the community, and the profession as an executor of board policies, as adviser to the board on policies and procedures, and as a professional leader in the school district, the educator employed in a supervisory position recognizes and adheres to these standards of personnel administration:

In selecting and employing new personnel, he:

1. Spares no effort to maintain and increase professional standards, utilizing professional placement agencies to obtain properly qualified, full-time teachers and administrators before employing provisionally credentialed or part-time personnel.
2. Provides opportunities to employees to make known their desires for transfer or advancement and gives consideration to their wishes.
3. Considers no position vacant and seeks no applicants for it before the present employee has resigned or has been notified that he will not be re-employed.

[1] Henry J. Otto, *Elementary School Organization and Administration* (New York: Appleton-Century-Crofts, Inc., 1954), p. 20.

[2] The statement on ethics in personnel matters was developed by a special committee composed of representatives of the California Association of School Administrators, California Association of Secondary School Administrators, California Elementary School Administrators Association, and the California Teachers Association Personnel Standards Commission. This definition is aimed primarily to serve as a guide to supervisors to aid them in avoiding unethical personnel practices. It also may serve as a basis for interpreting specific acts when malpractice is charged.

4. Adheres strictly to adopted salary schedules in employing new personnel.
5. Describes as accurately as possible the employment policies and educational philosophy of the district, the salary schedule and the grade level, subject areas, or other assignment for which the candidate is being considered.
6. Makes no offer of employment for a period of time concurrent to that covered by a contract to another district unless that district has first sent notice of its willingness to release the employee.

In the supervision and leadership of the staff, he:

1. Assumes responsibility for promoting the success of all employees, realizing that the difference between the success and failure of an employee may depend on efforts in selection, in supervision, and in assignment.
2. Makes sure that as soon as significant weaknesses are observed they are called to the attention of the employee and that assistance toward their correction is extended.
3. Makes no formal criticism of any employee to superiors or the board without having first discussed this criticism with the employee involved.
4. Informs superiors and the board about the good performance and contributions of employees.
5. Values the professional suggestions and criticisms of staff members, according to each the recognition to which he/she is entitled as a fellow professional in the field of education.
6. Provides opportunity for employees to discuss their problems or complaints freely and assists in the cooperative development of systematic channels for reporting and discussing employee problems and suggestions.

In recommending re-employment or dismissal of employees, he:

1. Establishes a systematic procedure for periodic written evaluation of probationary teachers. Teachers are kept informed of their employment status as it will effect re-employment, tenure, or dismissal.
2. Recommends that an employee be rehired unless the employee has been notified regarding weaknesses and has been given time for and assistance toward their correction.
3. Does not jeopardize the educational welfare of students in order to avoid an unpleasant dismissal relationship.

In respect to recommendations for former employees, he:

1. Realizes that an honest appraisal is necessary to do justice to the teacher, the profession, and to the students in any district contemplating employing this teacher.
   fied regarding weaknesses and has been given time for and assistance to-
   sonable time.
3. Keeps confidential the content of confidential professional papers.

To meet responsibility to the profession, he:

1. Endorses the principle that the profession must accept responsibility for the conduct of its members and understands that his/her own conduct will be regarded as a sample of the quality of the profession.
2. Makes professional life one of continuous growth.
3. Maintains an attitude that strengthens public respect for the teaching profession and for the school system of which he/she is a part.
4. Maintains active membership in professional organizations and works through them to attain objectives that will advance the status of the profession.
5. Exercises the right to participate in the democratic processes that determine school policy.
6. Follows ethical business procedures. He/she:
   a) Does not underbid for a position or apply for a specific position until it is vacant.
   b) Works for the appointment and advancement of those who are best qualified by ability and experience.
   c) Conducts school affairs through the established channels of the school system.
7. Acts with consideration in contacts with fellow teachers. He/she:
   a) Is kind, tolerant, and loyal, and avoids pettiness, jealousy, and rancor.
   b) Takes pride in their achievements, is grateful for their assistance.
   c) Respects their confidence.
   d) Criticizes with discretion, knowing only that valid criticism stems from a desire to improve the educational process and is directed at issues rather than personalities.

Professional Organizations

The principal of a school is an important member of a great profession. This membership carries with it the obligation to carry out responsibilities in a manner that will reflect credit on the entire profession.[3]

Membership in Professional Organizations

One basis of in-service growth that the educator can promote is membership in professional organizations. These professional organizations and their publications have proven to be a major source of growth and intellectual stimulation during the preparatory years and throughout the professional career of the supervisor. Virtually every facet of education has a professional organization and a periodical through which the educator can keep abreast of current developments in the field and publish contributions and critical reactions.

[3] Otto, *op. cit.*, p. 24.

The educator of today usually belongs to more than one association because each organization serves a particular need. Research and creative writings in education are emphasized in organizations such as Phi Delta Kappa. However, the supervisor cannot effectively be active in more than a few organizations even if one of the organizations, in reality, is a local edition of a second organization.

Some representative organizations for education and educational supervision are:

Various state elementary, secondary, and community college school administrator's associations
The National Education Association
American Association of School Administrators
National Association of Elementary School Principals
National Association of Secondary School Principals
Association for Supervision and Curriculum Development
Various state teachers' associations
National Audio Visual Association
National Society for the Study of Education
Phi Delta Kappa
Pi Lambda Theta
Association for Childhood Education International
Many content and special interest associations

The supervising principal who never attends the local, regional, state, or national meetings of professional organizations will suffer from the lack of opportunity to mingle and to exchange ideas with others. There are many branches of the national association in which an educator may enroll, according to personal interests.

Membership in the Most Powerful Associations

All supervisors should be members of the strongest professional organizations available. Supervisors should realize that education association or teacher-union membership per se is neither professional nor unprofessional. It is possible for any local organization to come under the domination of malcontents who become obsessed with shortsighted goals and who conceive their ends selfishly and apart from the ultimate considerations of the educational welfare of students.

A number of arguments, pro and con, concerning teacher unions are listed for the edification of the supervising principal:

Pro—people say:

1. Academic freedom is stressed.
2. Tenure provisions are strengthened.

3. Pay increases, as do fringe benefits.
4. Administrators and teachers should not be in the same organization under present conditions. Administrators and quasi-administrators are responsible to the governing board as employees and will take over the organization. (This often does happen, and is natural, for administrators usually are known to more people.)
5. Prestige increases for large organizations.
6. Other professional organizations are encouraged to take stronger stands. For example, the teachers of one midwestern state now take a stronger stand concerning academic freedom than they did in the past.

Con—people say:

1. Teachers teach children from homes of *both* labor and management.
2. Unions lower prestige and status, and are unprofessional.
3. The teacher becomes a civil servant.
4. Fringe benefits are degrading.
5. The tone of union arguments often is abusive.
6. Union methods are overly aggressive and are degrading.
7. The union implies that teachers and administrators are *not* all educators working on a professional level.
8. Associations are as militant as are unions, and therefore the more vigorous posture is already assumed by the association, rendering the union unneeded.

Questionable arguments include number (4) in the "pro" grouping and numbers (2), (4), and (6) in the "con" section. The merger of the local association and union in Los Angeles in 1970 was a most interesting development. If education is to be considered as a true profession, then the supervising principal and the teacher must think of themselves as fellow *educators,* rather than as manager and employee.

Broad Interests

A profession, we have seen, requires a high regard for the codes of professional conduct. This regard should be demonstrated by the supervising principal's relationship with fellow principals and in the performance of duties. The supervising principal can contribute to the profession by *actively supporting* professional organizations.

Moving Toward Professional Status

The demands of supervision are so varied that versatility is one basic requisite for proficiency on the part of the principal.

Roles in a Profession

The job of a supervisor is such that he/she must be able to assume many roles with ease. The supervisor must be:

1. An executive officer
2. A stimulator
3. An expert
4. An adviser
5. A coordinator
6. A mediator
7. An interpreter
8. An evaluator
9. An educational prophet

An ever-growing group of educators have reached professional levels. As the ranks swell, the acceptance and desire for professional status grow also. Those professional educators sincerely working toward improving their profession, and thus the effectiveness of their efforts to educate, have definite responsibilities for leadership and for encouraging others within the vocation.

The listings included in the Do—Don't sections below may be considered as sets of criteria that, when met, may help gain recognition for the educational endeavor as a true profession.

Do

1. Everything possible to combat anti-intellectualism.
2. Everything possible in the area of basic research.
3. Remember that there is nothing wrong with being concerned with remuneration. The way the concern is carried into action is important. Students are entitled to be taught by the most capable teachers possible. If they are to be taught by these capable individuals, there must be concern with pay and fringe benefits.
4. Everything in your power to increase standards of professional training.
5. Be active in a few professional organizations, but strongly resist efforts to require membership in many professional organizations.
6. Participate actively in the internship program. Encourage professional training in conjunction with practice teaching and internship.
7. Work to produce and elevate a professional code of ethics.
8. Use your best judgment in making recommendations.

Don't

1. Apologize for the profession.
2. Run down theory unless it is completely cut off from practice and is proven inaccurate. (Remember: teaching is an art with a scientific basis.)

3. Be tempted into the sin of pettiness; it can be stifling. (Show that you respect your colleagues!)
4. Gossip; it endangers privileged communication.
5. Make remarks concerning students in public.

When thinking of a medical doctor or of a lawyer, the lay person assumes a rigorous professional preparation and also a dedication of purpose beyond mere earnings. This type of thinking can and needs to be encouraged in the field of education.

A Final Don't

DON'T OVERDO IT.

TRENDS: EMERGING PROFESSIONAL RESPONSIBILITIES

Toward ⟶ the Creation of One Strong
Professional Association for the Educator

The educator of tomorrow will, it is hoped, belong to a professional association that will be unique in the field. It will have all of the power and prestige now possessed by the National Bar Association and the American Medical Association. The organization will be on a national level and will be subdivided into state and intermediate unit professional associations. Membership in one area of the association will automatically include membership in other areas. The national association will have various departments, but one will not gain membership to a department directly. The educator will join the national association and, for various purposes, will be assigned to one of the several departments.

Toward ⟶ True Professional Standing
for the Educator

Not only the supervising principal but all other educators will be considered true professionals in the eyes of the public. The requisites for professional standing, outlined in this chapter, will be met as the indispensable quality of education is recognized more and more.

Toward ⟶ Professional Remuneration
for the Educator

All educators will receive remuneration equivalent to that now received by the members of other professions. As the required training, internship, and certification for membership in the profession increases, the realization that the members of the profession deserve professional remuneration in the form of salary and fringe benefits will be put into action. As school systems obtain sufficient funds through state-wide tax programs operating on an equalization basis and through federal participation in educational finance, funds will become available for increasing the remuneration of the educator.

Toward ⟶ the Development of and Strict
Adherence to a Code of Ethics for the Professional Educator

The professional educator of the future will be bound by an oath similar to that of Hippocrates. The pettiness that, at times, has been observed in the field of education, will be a thing of the past.

Supervisory Problems

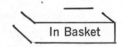

In Basket

Problem 1

A teacher in the school to which you are assigned reports to you that a coworker has made an error in judgment.

How would you handle the situation?

Problem 2

You have been asked by the superintendent to indicate how policies could be developed and submitted to the governing board, which would indicate to the professional staff and to the lay public that the superintendent and the governing board consider the professional staff to be true professionals.

How would you proceed?
What policies would you recommend?

Problem 3

You have been asked by the state professional association to prepare a suggested bill for submission to the legislature that would establish procedures under which professional educators would select those to be admitted to the profession, and by which the professional educators would pass judgment on those who may have to be asked to retire from the profession.

How would you proceed?
What policies would you recommend?

Problem 4

You find a memorandum in your in-basket. In the memorandum a member of your staff indicates that he is applying for a position that is already held by a co-worker.

How would you handle the matter?

Questions and Suggested Activities Concerning the Supervisor and Professional Responsibilities

Questions

1. What do you consider the main reason for education's not being considered as the leading profession in our country? Why is it so considered in some other nations?
2. How can a professional approach by supervisors and teachers develop morale?
3. Why should all educators be interested in a code of professional conduct and ethics?
4. What can teachers and supervisors do about colleagues whom they believe are engaging in unethical or unprofessional conduct? (Recall the term *unprofessional* has certain legal implications in some states; i.e., it may be a cause for dismissal and/or credential revocation.)

Suggested Activities

1. Report on the effect professional organizations have had on professional status and morale.
2. Determine what influence the medical and legal professions have had on

standards that determine who shall practice in those professions and indicate to what extent educators should follow their examples.

3. Investigate what has been done by the leading national organizations in education concerning professional standards and evaluate the influence of the organizations in upgrading professional relationships among educators.

4. Prepare an article suitable for publication concerning steps that should be followed by the supervising principal who hopes to make education a profession.

5. Prepare an oath for the supervising principal and for the teacher embodying ideas similar to those in the Hippocratic oath.

6. Prepare a bibliography of articles appearing in professional journals applicable to the subject of professional responsibilities. Delimit your study to articles published during the past twelve months.

7. Indicate reasons for exhibiting (or not exhibiting) the educator's framed credentials on the wall of the room within which he/she works.

8. List what you consider to be the ten most vital professional responsibilities of the educator. Indicate how managing physical facilities could be related to the professional responsibilities of the educator.

9. Prepare a debate in which you and other members of the class argue whether increased membership in a teacher's union could enhance education's status as a profession.

10. List the fringe benefits that you believe the educator should receive. Support your presentation with reference to practices and trends in industry, public administration, and education.

11. Prepare a skit in which you as the supervising principal speak out concerning procedure or policy that you believe requires immediate remediation. This policy, in the past, has had the wholehearted support of the superintendent and of the governing board.

Selected Bibliography

Books

Bennis, Warren G. *Changing Organizations.* New York: McGraw-Hill Book Co., 1966.

Drucker, Peter F. *The Effective Executive.* New York: Harper & Row Co., 1967.

Frazen, C. G. *Foundations of Secondary Education.* New York: Harper and Brothers, 1955.

Frey, Sherman H., and Keith R. Getschman. *School Administration: Selected Readings.* New York: Thomas Y. Crowell Company, 1969.

Grinnell, J. E., and R. J. Young. *The School and the Community.* New York: The Ronald Press Company, 1955.

Hicks, Hanne J. *Administrative Leadership in the Elementary School.* New York: The Ronald Press Company, 1956.

Jacobson, Paul B., and William C. Reavis. *Duties of School Principals.* Englewood Cliffs, New Jersey: Prentice-Hall, Inc., 1941.

Jordan, William C. *Elementary School Leadership.* New York: McGraw-Hill Book Company, Inc., 1959.

Kyte, George C. *The Principal at Work.* Boston: Ginn and Company, 1952.

Marchus, Sando. *Mr. Principal, How Do You Do?* Martinez, California: Sandemark Enterprises, 1956.

McDill, Edward L., and Leo C. Rigsby. *Structure and Process in Secondary Schools.* Baltimore: Johns Hopkins Press, 1973.

Miller, V., and W. B. Spaulding. *The Public Administration of American Schools.* Yonkers, New York: World Book Company, 1952.

Mort, Paul R. *Principles of School Administration.* New York: McGraw-Hill Book Co., 1946.

Myers, M. Scott. *Every Employee a Manager.* New York: McGraw-Hill Book Co., 1970.

Otto, Henry J. *Elementary School Organization and Administration.* New York: Appleton-Century-Crofts, Inc., 1954.

Perry, Charles R., and Wesley A. Wildman. *The Impact of Negotiations in Public Education.* Worthington, Ohio: Jones Publishing Company, 1970.

Pierce, T. M. et al. *Community Leadership for Public Education.* Englewood Cliffs, New Jersey: Prentice-Hall, Inc., 1955.

Reavis, W. C. et al. *Administering the Elementary School.* Englewood Cliffs, New Jersey: Prentice-Hall, Inc., 1953.

Reeder, Ward G. *Public School Administration.* New York: The Macmillan Company, Inc., 1949.

Roe, William Henry, and T. L. Drake. *The Principalship.* New York: Macmillan Publishing Co., Inc., 1974.

Sears, Jesse B. *Public School Administration.* New York: The Ronald Press Company, 1947.

Stoops, Emery, and Russell E. Johnson. *Elementary School Administration.* New York: McGraw-Hill Book Co., 1967.

Wiles, Kimball, and John T. Lovell. *Supervision for Better Schools.* 4th ed. Englewood Cliffs, New Jersey: Prentice-Hall, Inc., 1975.

Periodicals

Armstrong, G. O. "His Teacher Must Advance His Profession." *Minnesota Journal of Education* XLI (April 1961): 15–17.

Goodland, John I. "A Perspective on Accountability." *Phi Delta Kappan* LVII (October 1975): 108–112.

Kinnaird, Virginia. "Privileges Entail Obligations." *National Education Association Journal* XLIII (April 1954): 245.

Robinson, T. E. "The Ten Best Public Relation Devices." *The School Executive* LXVIII (August 1949): 36–38.

Sobel, Harold W. "Is Open Education a Fad?" *Phi Delta Kappan* LVI (April 1975): 551–553.

Stoops, Emery. "The Principal as Personnel Coordinator." *The Overseas Principal* I (Autumn 1963): 1–3.

The Editor. "News and Trends." *National Education Association Journal* LI (January 1962): 4.

Wardner, Philip. "They Teach Themselves." *National Education Association Journal* XXXIX (December 1950): 675–676.

Yeager, H. V. "Profession Anyone?" *Journal of Teacher Education* XI (December 1960): 460–463.

Audio Cassette

Goal Setting for Professionals. Thompson-Mitchell, Atlanta: 1975. Interview with Lee Danielson.

Film

What's the Matter with Alice? Newsfilm, USA, 1972. Designed to stimulate thinking about career advancement, upward mobility, and equal opportunity for minorities and women. First part consists of series of short interviews with members of a hospital staff as well as shipyard and factory workers who have had experience with job retraining, affirmative action, and other career advancement programs. Second part enacts an office situation in which a bright young black woman who is an excellent worker decides to quit, and shows how her supervisor, when he tries to find out why, learns that his own unconscious refusal to advance her to a more challenging and rewarding position has caused her to seek work elsewhere. Demonstrates that the consequences of not carrying out a career advancement program may often be human waste, inefficiency, and loss of profit. (25 minutes)

Other Sources

American Association of School Administrators. *Staff Relations in School Administration.* Washington, D.C.: National Education Association, 1955.

Hall, Roy M. *Achievements and Changes in Educational Administration.* Austin: The Southwest School Administration Center, University of Texas, 1956.

Haring, Roy J. *The Role of the Superintendent in the Interrelationship of School and Community.* New York: Columbia University, published for the Pennsylvania Association of District Superintendents, 1953.

Midcentury White House Conference on Children and Youth. *Platform Recommendations, and Pledge to Children.* Washington, D.C.: Government Printing Office, 1950.

National School Public Relations Association. *Eighty-Eight Techniques in School Public Relations for Teachers and Administrators.* Washington, D.C.: National Education Association, 1951.

The Conference. *Education for Professional Responsibility. A Report of the Proceedings of the Inter-Professions Conference on Education for Professional Responsibility.* Pittsburgh: Carnegie Press, 1948.

19

Further Trends and Issues·
The Supervisor Looks
to the Future

What does the supervisor of today need to know about supervisory practices of the future? How will the supervisor's role change? What issues will he/she confront? What emerging trends will he/she encounter?

This chapter includes a discussion of the following topics:

Factors producing changes
New directions in educational supervision
The supervisor faces the issues of today and tomorrow
Trends
"In-Basket" supervisory problems
Questions and suggested activities

Factors Producing Changes

It is impossible to enumerate all factors that will affect supervision in the future. Some are so subtle in their influence that relationships are difficult to establish. Others have not yet appeared. The following list, though far from complete, will be discussed: population factors and urban renewal, automation, scientific discovery and invention, rediscovery of liberal education, increased leisure time, the cold war, earlier maturity of children, and child development and learning.

Population Factors and Urban Renewal

Our population is leveling off. Soon we will become a nation of older people. Providing for this changing population has become a major challenge in this country.

As our population expanded, people who could afford to leave the city moved into the suburbs. Overproduction on the farm resulting from the use of machinery and improved agricultural procedures made it necessary for the younger generation to leave the farm and move to the city and suburbs to seek other employment. In many areas, the suburbs of one city have reached those of another to form one gigantic sprawling metropolitan area.

When the economically more fortunate families moved out of the cities, slums developed. Although these slums have been tolerated for many years, our great cities are at last awakening, and real urban renewal is on the way.

These population changes and their consequences will continue to create problems in the areas of personnel staffing, physical facilities, and class size. Population mobility usually means a high rate of teacher and pupil turnover.

Good urban renewal means more than providing decent new housing. Adults must be re-educated to a new way of life, and their children must receive a kind of education different from that given to students who have been raised in more favorable home environments.

Supervisory programs must be geared to help teachers acquire know-how in helping children to become independent learners.

Space for teaching and learning will continue to be at a premium. The school of the future will have to become a learning center for six days a week and twelve months a year. More and more schools are being used during the evening hours. The twelve-hours-a-day, six-days-a-week, twelve-months-a-year schedule will create numerous supervisory problems. Supervisory personnel may find themselves working in shifts or even in an "on call" status. Supervisors may be working with more individuals. The use of the same physical facilities and instructional materials by several different groups of teachers also may present some morale problems for the supervisor.

Supervisors must become even more creative and imaginative in developing instructional materials and procedures for the many city youngsters who now receive a substandard education. It is unrealistic to expect to meet their needs by subjecting them to the same educational fare served in most of today's classrooms. Certainly new types of relationships must be formed with colleges that have teacher-education programs.

Technology

Research in automation and electronics is progressing so rapidly that a machine can scarcely be built and put into use before it is obsolete. In every line of work we find machines taking over some tasks formerly done by human beings. If schools will accept the challenge, the machine can be made to serve people.

It is safe to predict that advancing technology will affect supervision in a number of ways. Not only will the content of the curriculum be changed, but the purposes, program, techniques, procedures, and the entire scope of education also will be affected. Data-processing equipment already is a valuable aid in curriculum revision and in the learning process itself. In addition, the entire process of educational research can be speeded up by using such tools as minicomputers.

Will it be necessary to alter the basic theory of curriculum? How can children who experience repeated success through programmed instruction be encouraged to face possible failure in group competition? Answers to these and other questions must be sought.

Rediscovery of Liberal Education

Voices that clamor for more book learning have always been present. Here in the United States we have always admired the well-read, scholarly individual. In recent years, frequent comparisons have been made between the difficult educational fare of Chinese, Japanese, and European children and the less exacting menu of American children. This concern is affecting education from kindergarten to the university. Is a more rigorous education the way to meet the industrial might of other nations?

It is safe to predict that there will be a rebirth of the humanities. A liberally educated individual must be a patron of the arts. Movements throughout the world for cultural exchange programs will supply needed stimulation.

Increased Leisure Time

Unions are predicting a five-hour work day and a twenty-hour week. As people have more free time, they must be equipped to engage in a wide variety of worthwhile leisure time activities. The supervisor must start planning now to fill this real void in the curricula.

Scientific Discovery and Invention

Many of nature's secrets have been discovered. New foodstuffs are being created daily, as are new household appliances and products, building materials, fuels, wearing apparel, and medicines. Devices and machines have been invented to amuse people and to perform many unpleasant and/or difficult tasks. The atom has been harnessed and the mysteries of the universe are now being fathomed. Just as the discoveries of science are revolutionizing other areas of living, they will continue to affect supervision. Through the use of new building materials, improved lighting, air-conditioning, and acoustical treatment, the learning environment of students will be greatly improved.

Developments in the field of instructional technology will greatly increase the repertoire of teaching and learning aids. Communication satellites will bring history to the classroom as it is being made any place on the earth, and from outer space as well.

New chemical compounds will be discovered that will assist the learning process. Auto-conditioning and hypnosis some day may be used as aids to learning.

As transportation becomes swifter and cheaper, field trips to any point in our nation and to other continents will become common.

More science will be taught. Current events will play an increasingly more important role in the curriculum. The language arts (and foreign languages) may be in for some surprises because of inventions now being perfected. The English language may become completely phonetic in structure. Electric typewriters that automatically type dictated material will place greater emphasis on learning correct spoken English. Other devices, as yet unnamed, armed with minicomputer components, will translate any spoken language into any other language by the flick of a switch. Visual literacy as well as audio (listening) literacy will be demanded.

New Directions in Educational Supervision

New Knowledge and Disciplines

As knowledge accelerates, new disciplines are developed and new roles and responsibilities emerge for the school and the teacher. An example is the emergence of educational psychology as a field of study. The impact of educational psychology on the schools has resulted in a wider variety of roles being required of school personnel.

Sociology and its related disciplines can be seen to have increasing impact on the education process.[1] Supervisory practices will reflect this development. Teachers will need new insights and skills in processes if they are to be effective in moving children from school into a complex, dynamic society. Educational supervision will address issues such as inner city power structures and economic blight. Social awareness training programs will be developed in order to effect more dynamic and effective working relationships in the classroom and community.

Because of the many social forces impinging on the classroom, dynamic in-service education experiences will relate to increasingly diverse topics, including areas such as housing, zoning employment, leisure-time activities, health, stress, innovation, and economic planning.

Changing Structure of the School

As the school continues to be pushed into cooperation and collaboration with increasingly powerful governmental agencies, influential business forces, and a

[1] Jack Culbertson et al., *Social Science Content for Preparing Educational Leaders.* (Columbus, Ohio: Charles E. Merrill Publishing Co., 1973).

multifaceted society going in many directions at once, the structure of the school will adjust, adapt, and ultimately change. The school is being forced to innovate, evaluate, and innovate again. These processes will tend to have increasingly greater impact on all aspects of supervision.

With innovation and extended roles, new specialists will be needed. Teachers will continue to be re-educated for positions in areas such as instructional technology, reading instruction, systems development, and drug education. A proliferation of roles and tasks will result in increased development of the school hierarchy. More supervisory specialists will be needed to manage and supervise departments and to coordinate, evaluate, and direct programs for change and changing programs. A more complex school organization will cause supervision to become more specialized and specific, and, perhaps, more polarized as departments compete for status and funding.

Role Clarification

With increasing size and complexity of supervisory positions, difficulties of role clarification will demand greater formalization of structure. Communication channels will need to be developed in order to apprise everyone in the supervisory hierarchy of the positions and responsibilities outlined in the organization charts. If supervision is to be effective as roles become more diverse, both duplications and omissions of efforts must be avoided. Functions of line and staff will require continual coordination. All personnel, from the superintendent to the classroom aides, will be involved in the process of defining their roles preliminary to successful evaluation.

The Supervisor Faces the Issues of Today and Tomorrow

Wasting Human Resources

In the 1970's, we continued to waste human resources. This extravagant use of our most highly trained professionals, coupled with an increasing unwillingness of our most capable scholars to emerge from the pack cannot be tolerated in the supervisory world of the future.

RETIREMENT—MANDATORY OR NOT?   Should we continue the practice of forcing some of our most competent educators to retire at some set age? Surely the schools of the future cannot afford to continue such outmoded, inefficient, discriminatory, and costly practices.

OBSOLESCENCE.   The supervisory staff must address itself to the problem of how to maintain technical vitality. Table 19-1 lists some newer problems and the competencies needed by the supervisor in order to meet them.

TABLE 19-1.   Meeting Challenges to Supervision.

AS A RESULT OF:	THE SUPERVISOR NEEDS:
1. Mass media communications: radio, TV, newsstand publications, video disc publication, holography	1. To know how to use these media and knowledge of policies and practices in other schools
2. Intergroup, intercultural, religious, and racial problems	2. To gather information on experiments, materials, and practices, and develop an ability to help develop impartial approach
3. Overcrowded facilities	3. Information on multishift and other organizational programs and utilization schemes, and knowledge re. how to organize to solve this problem
4. Cooperative reports re: pupil progress. Teachers, students, and parents cooperatively will assess pupil progress	4. Knowledge of successful practices in student progress
5. Teaching controversial issues	5. Ability to identify propaganda, to secure source and factual materials on each side, and to identify the issues
6. Helping parents understand what the school is trying to do	6. To know when, how, and where, and what to communicate with, and to meet the several publics
7. The expanding role of the supervisor in planning school buildings	7. Familiarity with blueprint reading and specifications
8. Expanding work experience programs	8. Information about types of programs and how they operate
9. Attacks on public education in general and supervision in particular	9. Familiarity with and analysis of types and sources, and how other communities have met such attacks
10. Lack of trained, competent leaders in education	10. To know how to develop leadership qualities in existing staff
11. Action research and other types of experimentation	11. Skills in search techniques
12. Providing more adequately for the talented pupil	12. Information on current practices, grouping, types of programs, and ability to organize to meet this challenge
13. Increased participation of faculty in supervisory processes	13. Strategies for cooperative development of goals, policies, techniques

Human Research

Invasion of privacy has become standard practice in too many environments. With ever-increasing technological advances, the supervisory team will have to be alert to the hazards inherent in such practices.

In the past, the students and teaching assistants have been used to spy on teachers and supervisory personnel alike. Data processing devices also have been used. In fact, one report in the California Courts noted that the computer has been used to keep track of the number of times employees use the rest room. The supervising principal must be alert to such challenges to liberty and freedom.

The Supervisor and Collective Bargaining

Are staff and instructional development negotiable? That is not *the* question, but it is one question always asked when the words "negotiation" and "staff development" appear together. Luke reported:

> Setting aside precise legal distinctions, two functional generalizations can be made. One is that in-service education programs can quite legitimately be designed to meet the institutional needs of the school system. The other is that the program—with equal legitimacy—should be designed to meet the in-service needs of teachers.[2]

But even though this distinction may clarify, it does not simplify. Dillion, writing in *Educational Leadership,* supported the point that some in-service education is overly pragmatic. She observed,

> Show teachers in an in-service activity how to make something for use in the classroom out of four pipe cleaners and they will go home satisfied, but try to give them anything related to learning theory and it's instant turn-off.[3]

Although this illustration may be a bit extreme, we have no quarrel with the general accuracy of the observation. Teacher involvement in decision making as it affects in-service education has implications for the financing of the in-service education program. Often, both administrators and teachers think that any talk about in-service education over the negotiating table is automatically equated with an increased expenditure. This is not necessarily so. Most school budgets build in a sum for in-service education. Frequently, it is not labeled as such; it often is scattered through various administrative units of the school system. One useful outcome of professional negotiations is the incentive to analyze supervision expenditures.

[2] Robert A. Luke, "Collective Bargaining and In-Service Education," *Phi Delta Kappan* (March 1976), pp. 468–469.

[3] Elizabeth A. Dillion, "Staff Development: Whose Job Is It?" *Educational Leadership* (November 1974), pp. 137–140.

Perhaps the needs teachers express for more "relevant" supervision can be met by reallocating existing funds. Some items in which teachers seek a meaningful voice are not budget items, such as being represented in developing and analyzing a continuing needs assessment process.

Even though concern is expressed for in-service education as a negotiable item, it does not follow that this concern automatically will find its way to (or through) the bargaining table.

Two broad alternatives for action exist:

1. Provisions designed to preserve an existing in-service education program. *Caution: a program that is incorporated into the collective agreement cannot easily be abandoned.*
2. Provisions designed to bring about changes in the existing programs. The school district must make available expert technical and professional supervisory assistance.

How do adults learn? How do they acquire new skills? How can teachers be motivated to try new teaching techniques and to develop delivery systems? What reports of research and best practice point to new goals? What new course content is needed?

Whether to use existing professional development staff, hire additional personnel, or employ specialist-consultants may be items for negotiation. The manner of securing accountability of the supervisory program itself is negotiable.

Cooperative appraisal of programs as well as of personnel performance is here. Tomorrow it will be even more widespread and institutionalized. Teachers are becoming less content to permit others to make needs assessments and to determine teaching methods and appraisal techniques. They demand a voice in determining needs and in designing delivery systems. These issues demand the attention of today's supervisors.

Education and Management

Who will run the schools? Will a business manager make all decisions? Shall the supervisor of the future face a situation in which the school is a battlefield, with teacher against administrator, and both fighting the board of education?

What's Next?

Humanity does not leap into the future. A Chinese proverb states: "a journey of a thousand miles begins with a single step." People have learned to creep, to crawl, to walk, to run, and now to move forward with giant steps. They have produced machines to help conquer the physical environment. But there are physical and psychological dangers in this relationship. People must not let themselves be controlled by machines or outstripped by technology.

The supervising principal must help teachers and parents define what they want to teach youngsters and then use modern technology to achieve those ends. We must be aware of the psychological impact of the newer media on the teacher who is concerned primarily with interpersonal relationships. More research is needed in the area of instructional technology.

New techniques and methods of teaching mean that teachers and supervisors must change their ways of thinking. New teachers must be trained differently by the colleges and universities. If the schools adopt the new ideas presented in this book, they must change their methods and patterns of organizing and thinking. Articulation of the elementary school with the secondary school and college is important if the advantages of new techniques of teaching are to be successful. Subject-matter time allotments and the length of the school day may need to be changed. New material or subjects cannot be added to the educational program forever. The school day is not long enough. Something must be eliminated. A lot of research, thinking, and planning are needed to determine what is best. This is a challenge to the supervising principals as they face the new frontier—*the cutting edge of education.*

As education changes, supervision also will change. Individuals serving in supervisory roles in the schools of the future will have at their command many new instructional techniques and procedures. Continuous curriculum development will be one of the most important supervisory tasks, as patterns of cultural change evolve in the world community. The wonderful world of the future is with us, and we live in a tomorrow of promise. Can we be equal to the challenge and, as educational leaders, guide teachers and pupils to that brighter tomorrow?

TRENDS

> Toward ⟶   Increased Involvement of Government
> and Other Agencies in Supervision

In addition to the many bulletins, circulars, and pamphlets that are issued, the *Biennial Survey of Education,* including statistical and textual résumés of educational conditions in the United States, the *Education Directory,* the *Vocational Division Bulletins, Higher Education,* and *School Life* are published.

Many biographies have been issued that apply to the field of supervision, as have Guidance Leaflets, Higher Education Circulars, Home Economics Circulars, Industrial Circulars, International Education, Kindergarten Circulars, and posters, charts, and similar materials.

The supervising principal should write to the Librarian, U.S. Office of Education, Department of Health, Education, and Welfare, Washington, D.C.

20025, as well as to the Superintendent of Documents, Government Printing Office, Washington, D.C. 20025, for lists of publications referring to particular topics. Complete information, specifically delimiting the data needed, should be included in the request.

Some educators have suggested that the Commissioner of Education become in effect a national superintendent of schools. The U.S. Office of Education would be established as a nonpartisan, independent agency, governed by a national board of education. This board would be composed of individuals assigned for overlapping terms by the president, with the consent of the Senate. The commissioner would serve as the executive officer and the secretary of the board.

The office would be responsible for coordinating educational functions for the Federal Government, but with all federal participation and publications in education being transmitted through the departments of education of the several states.

Surprisingly, an overwhelming percentage of federal monies is expended for education through agencies other than the Department of Health, Education, and Welfare. Such agencies govern the military academies and the Department of Defense; the Department of Justice and prison education; the school for postal inspectors in the Post Office Department; the Library of Congress; the Copyright Office; the Government Printing Office; the Pan-American Union; the Office of Indian Affairs; the Smithsonian Institute; the National Academy of Sciences; the Commission of Fine Arts; the American Printing House for the Blind in Louisville, Kentucky; and the Columbia Institute for the Deaf in Washington, D.C.

The Tennessee Valley Authority maintains public schools and educational facilities for children as well as for adults, and special schools have been established where there exists a large concentration of federal employees overseas.

The present system of American public education, decentralized as it is, does not and will not preclude an improved federal program of cooperation, leadership, and support.

We may look to a Committee report of the past for a glimpse of the future. The Advisory Committee on Education stated:

> Education is, in a large sense, an individual matter, but individuals compose neighborhoods and communities, communities compose states, and in the United States the states compose the nation. As are the neighborhoods so will be the states and nation.
>
> Since the formation of the Union, Americans have been citizens both of the state and of the nation. Most Americans now feel that the federal government is their agent as much as is their state government.[4]

In light of today's needs, it is safe to predict increased research activities by the federal office in instructional techniques and instructional technology. A

[4] Advisory Committee on Education, *Report of the Committee* (Washington, D.C.: Superintendent of Documents, Government Printing Office, 1938), p. 35.

system of education that can do the job required for modern institutions requires national coordination. This does not necessitate a system managed from Washington, however.

Toward ⟶   Expanding Influence of Other Outside

Agencies on School Supervision

Funding agencies and foundations have and will continue to have a profound influence on supervisory practices and procedures. A good example of this is the National Science Foundation's commitment to financial aid for teachers in selected training areas, to supplemental training of teachers of science and math, and to improving curriculum studies by financial support for approved programs.

The National Science Foundation recently has broadened its influence to include funding programs in the social sciences. Twenty-three percent of the N.S.F.'s 1972 budget was allocated to social science projects.[5]

A funded project in the school tends to develop its own hierarchy. Certain pledges must be kept, conditions maintained, and results proven. Schools engaging in funded project activities will have unique methods and modes of supervision, and usually their teachers will experience more supervision.

Toward ⟶   Further Changes in Evaluation and

Decision-Making Process

Evaluation promises to become more specific and technical. Decision-making processes will continue to shift from the local school district to state and national levels, and personnel will need increasing sophistication in setting goals and objectives and in making assessments and evaluations.[6] More specialists and consultants will be employed to work with faculties in an effort to upgrade instructional outcomes. New organizational patterns, innovative methods, and experimental materials require that outcomes be recorded, evaluated, and communicated. In today's world of grantsmanship, supervisory skills frequently will make the difference between funds being granted or denied. It is apparent that many supervisory efforts have undergone a change in emphasis. This trend will continue.

[5] National Science Foundation, *Twenty-Second Annual Report for Fiscal Year 1972* (Washington, D.C.: U.S. Government Printing Office, 1972), p. 68.

[6] Roald F. Campbell, Luvern L. Cunningham, Raphael O. Nystrand, and Michael D. Usdan, *The Organization and Control of American Schools* (Columbus, Ohio: Charles E. Merrill, 1975), pp. 406–407.

| Toward | ⟶ | Changing Roles and Personnel

Relationships in Supervision and Evaluation

Teachers have become better trained, better organized, and increasingly militant in their demands. Teachers' organizations have and will continue to have an impact on the process of supervision. No longer will in-service programs be conducted on the teacher's own time or at the teacher's expense. Released time for teachers' institutes and workshops will be increased. The teacher and teacher organizations will have increasingly important input as to conditions of selection, assignment, supervision, evaluation, and rating.

The supervising principal is emerging as the expediter or organizer of supervisory programs and as a change agent. The supervisor will not be the originator or director to the extent he/she is today. The principal will encourage, motivate, and stimulate the flow of ideas, and will bring in consultants rather than act as the training or resource person. Teachers will look more frequently to grade chairpersons or department heads for instructional leadership. The teacher's role increasingly will include planning and development of in-service education experience for peers and self, in concert with other teachers pressed with similar problems. The supervision will be "on call."

As teachers have more voice in program development and improvement, they also will have a greater voice in disseminating information about the programs.

| Toward | ⟶ | Increased Teacher Involvement in the

Total Process of Supervision

Without question, the teacher will be more involved in the total process and program of supervision. Teachers and supervisors cooperatively will set goals, establish priorities, and design programs. Appraisal will be a cooperative task of supervisors, administrators, and teachers.

| Toward | ⟶ | Increased Involvement of the Supervisor

in the Physical Facilities' Improvement Program

The supervisor of the future will be more directly involved in designing new educational facilities and in planning for the improvement of existing physical plants. A facilities team or task force cooperatively will develop goals, plans, do necessary field work, meet with outside experts, and visit schools that recently solved similar problems. The input from teachers and from supervisory personnel will have a greater impact on the finished facility than presently is the case.

Toward ⟶   an Improved Physical Environment

through the Use of Modern Techniques and Materials

Classrooms of the future will be designed, operated, and maintained so that they will contribute to the education, health, safety, happiness, and development of the pupils and of the community. Temporary citizens' committees will participate, in an ad hoc advisory capacity only, in improving the physical environment.

Flexibility will be the watchword for the functional surroundings. Forced-air heating and air conditioning, possibly of the heat-pump variety, will be commonplace. The plastic illuminated ceiling will improve visibility and performance and will reduce fatigue.

Each classroom will be equipped with room darkening equipment, record and video disc players, audio and video recorders, an adequate supply of earphones and connectors, provisions for both front and rear projection, loudspeakers with wall-input receptacles, and a radio. Giant screen television monitors, capable of receiving color (and three dimensional holographic) broadcasts, will be built-in, as will wall receptacles for closed-circuit television reception.

Toward ⟶   Increased Use of the School Plant

as a Community Center

The modern school, with its electronic aids to speech and hearing, its athletic facilities, and its recreational equipment, is the natural choice for a community social and civic center. The decline of the church's and the home's roles in social and recreational life presages the increase of the school's role in community living.

Toward ⟶   Regional Educational Centers

Regional educational centers will provide space and specialized personnel for some educational programs. School buildings constructed to serve wide areas will be paid for from state monies rather than from local bond levies. Satellite centers or sharing of extraordinarily expensive instructional technology will be established on the school campus on a regional basis.

Toward ⟶ Clusters and "Open-Space"

Environments

There is a somewhat tentative trend toward a less formal and more unstructured internal space arrangement in the schools. Since architectural innovations freeze into steel and concrete what may prove to be transient educational theories, they always should be analyzed in the planning stage with an eye toward long-range goals, as well as economy of construction and operation.

Toward ⟶ Accepting the Supervisor as an Aid,

Consultant, and Professional Advisor

As noted earlier, the supervising principal of the past was considered to be a super-inspector. It is hoped that in the future the supervisor will be accepted as an aid, consultant, and professional advisor to the classroom teacher and to classified personnel. Signs are already appearing to indicate that this change has begun. The road is uncertain and rocky, however, and is a slow one to travel. Perhaps with the cooperative development of assignment specifications in this area, and the granting of tenure to supervisors, this journey will be smoothed and speeded.

Supervisory Problem

 In Basket

You are the Instructional Development Coordinator in a large city school system. You found a memorandum in your in-basket this morning from Superintendent Moriarity. She asked that you organize a "District Commission for New Dimensions in Education." The Commission would be given the task of devising new instructional delivery systems for the school system's adult education program.

How will you proceed? What do you need in order to get started?
What problems will you note? What goals will you set?
Whom will you involve? Why? How? When?
What plans for action do you predict will come out of the Commission's activities?
What provisions for appraisal might be established?
What problems in communications do you foresee as a result of establishing such a Commission? As a result of its probable report to the superintendent? What about communications with the Board of Education?

As before, you may assume any facts not given in the statement of the in-basket problem. Good luck!

Questions and Suggested Activities

Questions

1. A school district has experienced a sudden population shift. What supervisory problems might the district face as a result of the rapid change in population? (Assume any change you wish.)
2. What instructional problems are faced by an elementary school staff in a culturally deprived area? If you were serving in a supervisory position in this school, how would you proceed in solving these problems?
3. What implications for the instructional program are there in recent research on creativity?

Suggested Activities

1. Describe a school in the year 2085 that has an instructional program and curriculum based on several predictions made in this chapter. Depict what you believe the job of the supervisor would be like in this school.
2. Make a list of recent articles on supervision. Write a short critique of each.
3. List some important guides to action for the beginning supervisor of the future. Include things not to do, as well as things to do.
4. List the qualifications of the ideal supervisor as to training, experience, and personal qualities. What principles are involved?
5. Write a short article suitable for publication in a professional journal. It should be related to one of the topics covered in this chapter.
6. Prepare two skits to be presented in class. In one skit, show the traditional supervisor in action; in the other, show how the supervisor of tomorrow will perform.
7. Indicate the major organizations concerned primarily with school supervision; trace the development of these organizations; and predict how their role might change in the future. (Or, will the roles remain static?)
8. Indicate briefly how developing social movements have influenced supervision. Prepare charts, graphs, and/or diagrams that will assist in interpretation. Be sure to include demography, sociology, and theories of educational sociology, government, communication, transportation, and agrarian movement.

Selected Bibliography

Books

Campbell, Roald F., Luvern L. Cunningham, Raphael O. Nystrand, and Michael D. Usdan. *The Organization and Control of American Schools.* Columbus, Ohio: Charles E. Merrill Publishing Co., 1975.

Culbertson, Jack et al. *Social Science Content for Preparing Educational Leaders.* Columbus, Ohio: Charles E. Merrill Publishing Co., 1973.

Smith, Louis M., and Pat M. Keith. *Anatomy of Educational Innovation: An Organizational Analysis of an Elementary School.* New York: John Wiley and Sons, 1971.

Stoops, Emery, Max Rafferty, and Russell E. Johnson. *Handbook of Educational Administration.* Boston: Allyn and Bacon, Inc., 1975.

Periodicals

Dillion, Elizabeth A. "Staff Development: Whose Job Is It?" *Educational Leadership* XXII (November 1974): 137–140.

Luke, Robert A. "Collective Bargaining and In-Service Education." *Phi Delta Kappan* LVIII (March 1976): 468–469.

Other Sources

Advisory Committee on Education. *Report to the Committee.* Washington, D.C.: Superintendent of Documents, Government Printing Office, 1938.

National Science Foundation. *Twenty-Second Annual Report for Fiscal Year 1972.* Washington, D.C.: U. S. Government Printing Office, 1972.

Appendix A

Useful Sources for the Supervisor

Publications and Films Related to Human Relations for the Supervisor

1. Publications of the National Institute of Leadership[1]

   a) *The Identification, Education, and Evaluation of Leaders*—a 100-item checklist for determining the training needs and evaluating the executive's, manager's, or supervisor's performance of leadership functions, by Russell H. Ewing and Nadine R. Ewing. Price $2.00.

   b) *The Leadership Functions of Executives and Managers*—an evaluation of current leadership theory and practice, by Russell H. Ewing and Nadine R. Ewing. Price $2.00.

   c) *Leadership, Principles, and Practices Chart*—a series of charts that contain more than 500 items of information about leaders and leadership training, by Russell H. Ewing and Nadine R. Ewing. Price $1.00.

   d) *Sensitivity Training for Permissive Leadership—A Critical Analysis and Evaluation,* by Russell H. Ewing and Nadine R. Ewing. Price $2.00.

   e) *Train Future Leaders Today—Tomorow May Be Too Late,* by Russell H. Ewing and Nadine R. Ewing. Price $2.00.

   f) *Management by Motivation—Checklists, Questionnaires, and Bibliography,* by Russell H. Ewing and Nadine R. Ewing. Price $2.00.

   g) *Training by Motivation—Checklists, Questionnaires, and Bibliography,* by Russell H. Ewing and Nadine R. Ewing, Price $2.00.

   h) *The Motivation of a Nation—Production, Distribution, and Consumption,* by Russell H. Ewing and Nadine R. Ewing. Price $2.00.

   i) *The Crisis in the Colleges and Universities—Causes, Consequences, Cost, and Cures of Student Riots,* by Russell H. Ewing and Nadine R. Ewing. Price $2.00.

[1] National Institute of Leadership, 9015 Wilshire Boulevard, Beverly Hills, California 90210.

j) *Checklist for Evaluating Fraternity Leadership Training Programs,* by Russell H. Ewing and Nadine R. Ewing. Price $2.00.

k) *The Education, Training, and Evaluation of Fraternity Leaders—A Fraternity Personnel Performance Checklist,* by Russell H. Ewing and Nadine R. Ewing, Price $2.00.

l) *How to Conduct Successful Seminars,* by Russell H. Ewing. Price $3.00.

2. *Explorations in Human Relations Training: An Assessment of Experience, 1947–1977.*

3. Selected readings series—approximately 100 pages each:

a) *Group Development,* edited by Leland P. Bradford, 1971.

b) *Leadership in Action,* edited by Gordon L. Lippitt, 1971.

c) *Human Forces in Teaching and Learning,* edited by Leland P. Bradford, 1961.

d) *Issues in Human Relations Training,* edited by Edgar Schein and Irving Weschler, 1962.

e) *Conferences for Learning, Planning, and Action,* edited by Richard Beckhard, 1962.

4. Research-training series:

a) *Interpersonal Perceptions of Teachers, Students, and Parents,* by David H. Jenkins and Ronald Lippitt. 119 pp. An action-research project for teacher in-service education.

b) *Emotional Dynamics and Group Culture,* by Dorothy Stock and Herbert A. Thelen. 314 pp. An interpretation of research concerned with factors of group productivity and with personality changes occurring in groups, which was conducted over a five-year period at the Human Dynamics Laboratory of The University of Chicago and NTL sessions in Bethel, Maine.

c) *Interdisciplinary Team Research: Methods and Problems,* by Margaret Barron Luszki. 384 pp. A study of problems arising when researchers from various disciplines attempt to work together—made possible by a grant from the National Institute of Mental Health. (Books 2 and 3 in this series were published for NTL by the New York University Press, Washington Square, New York, New York 10003.)

5. Research reprint series:

a) *Bibliography of Research—NTL—1947–1977.* Compiled by Lewis E. Durham and Jack R. Gibb. 10 pp. Free.

b) *An Annotated Bibliography of Research—NTL—1947–1977.* Compiled by Lewis E. Durham and Jack R. Gibb. 22 pp. An annotated listing of forty-nine publications resulting from research performed entirely or in part at the National Training Laboratories.

c) *Defense Level and Influence Potential in Small Groups,* by Jack R. Gibb. 25 pp. (This, and the following four items, result from Office of Naval Research sponsorship.)

    d) *Some Effects on Group Problem Solving of an Enforced Separation of Problem-Solving Stages,* by Jacqueline Goodchilds, Jacob Schonfield, and Jack R. Gibb. 17 pp.
    e) *Group Effects on Perceptual Behavior,* by Dorothy Stock. 23 pp.
    f) *Effects of Group Activities upon Member-Performance,* by Jack R. Gibb. 24 pp.
    g) *Effects of Group Goals upon Personal Goals,* by Alvin F. Zander. 20 pp.

6. NTL *Trainers Workbooks,* each approximately 100 pages:

    a) *Group Observation and Recording.*
    b) *Sample Group Evaluation* (Post-Meeting Reaction) *Forms.*
    c) *Large Group Meetings, Conferences, and Institutes.*

7. Free Materials

NTL distributes without charge such items as the following:

    a) "Brand-New Breakthrough in Management Development" by George A. Hoy, reprinted from *Factory* magazine. 8 pp.
    b) "New Thrust for Community Leadership Training" by Edward E. Moe and H. Curtis Mial, reprinted from *Adult Leadership.* 5 pp.
    c) "Partial List of Resources in the Field of Human Relations Training," 2 pp.
    d) "What Makes a Small Group Tick?" reprinted from *Business Week.* 4 pp.

8. *Supervisor's Survival Kit.* (By Elwood N. Chapman, published by Science Research Associates, 259 East Erie Street, Chicago, Illinois 60611.)

9. *Supervisor's Development Program.* An excellent program for the supervisor from National Foreman's Institute, Waterford, Connecticut 06386. Their "Standard Manual for Supervisors" is most helpful

Films

1. "Laboratory Training for College Student Leaders and Faculty." 12 minutes.
2. "Our Invisible Committees." A 25-minute training film.
3. "Role Playing in Human Relations Training." A 25-minute training film.

For additional films, see individual chapter bibliographies. See also the excellent Thompson-Mitchell & Associates newsletter (Thompson-Mitchell & Associates, 2996 Grandview Avenue, Atlanta, Georgia 30305). This newsletter contains annotated entries for filmstrips, audio cassettes, multimedia programs, and other materials, as well as for 16mm motion pictures related to supervision.

Major Published Sources for Educational Research

1. *The Encyclopedia of Educational Research*—published in 10-year cycles by the American Educational Research Association.
2. *The Education Index.*
3. *The Review of Educational Research.*
4. Professional journals.
5. *The Journal of Educational Research.*
6. Professional books.
7. *Theses and Dissertations Accepted by the United States Office of Education* —published biennially.
8. Dissertations.
9. *Monograph Series*—Teachers College, Columbia University; University of Chicago; University of Southern California; and others.
10. Publications of organizations—such as the American Association of School Administrators, The National Society for the Study of Education, The Department of Elementary School Principals, The National Association of Secondary School Administrators, The Association for Childhood Education International.
11. *The Vertical File Index*—a bibliography of pamphlet materials.
12. *Books in Print*—published annually.

Educational Bibliographies

W. S. Monroe and L. Shores[2] compiled a summary of more than 4,000 published bibliographies and summaries in education. Annotations indicate the number and character of references, degree of completeness, format, kind of annotations, and further material.

Educational Dictionaries

The Dictionary of Education[3] is a scholarly and accurate work of more than 16,000 technical and professional terms covering the entire area of education. Foreign educational terms most frequently employed in a discussion of education, and significant in educational psychology, philosophy, and sociology, are included. The work is an indispensable part of the library of a professional school supervisor.

[2] Walter S. Monroe and Louis Shores, *Bibliographies and Summaries in Education to July 1, 1935* (New York: H. W. Wilson Company, 1936).

[3] Carter V. Good, ed., *The Dictionary of Education* (New York: McGraw-Hill Book Company, Inc., 1945).

Educational Encyclopedias

The Encyclopedia of Modern Education[4] presents a concise treatment of basic items as well as some biographies. *The Cyclopedia of Education*[5] presents excellent bibliographies and is extremely useful for bibliographical and historical research purposes. The *Encyclopedia of Educational Research*[6] is indispensable in its field; it presents a critical and evaluative synthesis of the literature of educational research arranged alphabetically by subjects. Each topic is presented with a critical summary and evaluation of research, as well as a list of needed research in the area.

Educational Yearbooks and Government Publications

The yearbooks of the National Society for the Study of Education[7] and The Year Book of Education[8] are valuable; the latter contains annual surveys of educational developments in most European countries. Major educational problems throughout the world and attempts at their solutions are indicated.

All educators should be familiar with the publications of the United States Government.[9] Access to most special documents is available through the Government Printing Office.

Alexander and Burke[10] presented an outstanding listing of government publications and documents in the field of education. They recommended bringing a government list up-to-date by listing important publications only, and through exhaustive searching.

Periodical Sources

The following is a list of major professional journals. These sources should be helpful in determining present status as well as recent developments and practices in the field:

[4] Harry N. Rivlin and Herbert Scheuler, eds., *The Encyclopedia of Modern Education* (New York: Philosophical Library, 1943).

[5] Paul Monroe, ed., *The Cyclopedia of Education* (New York: The Macmillan Company, 1911–1913).

[6] Walter S. Monroe, *Encyclopedia of Educational Research*, rev. ed. (New York: The Macmillan Company, 1950).

[7] National Society for the Study of Education, *Yearbook* (Chicago: University of Chicago Press, 1902 ff.).

[8] *The Year Book of Education* (Yonkers-on-Hudson, New York: World Book Company, 1932–1940 and 1948 ff.).

[9] United States Government Publications, Superintendent of Documents, *Decennial Cumulative Index*, 1941–1950 (Washington, D.C.: Government Printing Office, 1953).

[10] Carter Alexander and Arvid J. Burke, *How to Locate Education Information and Data* (New York: Bureau of Publications, Teachers College, Columbia University, 1958). Access to federal documents, as well as to the documents of state and local governments, is treated on pp. 272–283.

1. *American School Board Journal*—presents problems of public school administration, and attempts to promote better administration and supervision.
2. *Art Education Bulletin*—designed for teachers; presents new developments.
3. *Audio Visual Instruction*—published by the Association for Educational Communications and Technology.
4. *Curriculum Bulletin*—reports current, timely curriculum materials; each issue is complete in itself.
5. *Educational Outlook*—presents trends as well as a discussion of broad issues and problems.
6. *Educational Research Bulletin*—presents summaries of research in education.
7. *Elementary English Review*—reports modern methods.
8. *English Journal*—presents teaching techniques and content material.
9. *Health, Physical Education, and Recreation*—an outstanding summary of news, especially in the area of health education. Administrative problems also are treated.
10. *Hygiene*—developments in medicine are treated.
11. *Journal of Education*—presents problems of elementary and high schools.
12. *Journal of Educational Research*—a scientific study of education.
13. *Journal of Experimental Education*—reports statistics and scientific investigations concerning curriculum and methods.
14. *Journal of Girls' Physical Education*—especially helpful to those teaching physical education to girls or to coeducational classes.
15. *Journal of School Health*—emphasizes coordinated activities of the school nurse, the principal, and the teacher.
16. *National Education Association Journal*—presents suggested solutions to classroom problems.
17. *National Elementary Principal*—attempts to keep members informed.
18. *Nation's Schools*—attempts to improve school administration and public education by presenting research, current practice, and theory.
19. *School and University* (formerly *Overview* and *School Executive*)—presents school news, practices, and advanced thinking in connection with educational problems.
20. *Research Quarterly*—presents abstracts of research in health, physical education, and recreation.
21. *Review of Educational Research*—includes an excellent bibliography and summaries of research in education under fifteen topics in a three-year cycle. Published five times per year.[11]
22. *School Administrator*—a news bulletin.
23. *School Business Management*—promotes efficient business procedures within school systems.
24. *School Management*—keeps school administrators abreast of new developments in school administration, maintenance, equipment, supply, and building construction.
25. *Phi Delta Kappan*—an invaluable resource in educational research, supervision, administration, curriculum, and instruction.

[11] For an outstanding review of recent research concerning instruction, see Richard C. Anderson et al., *Current Research on Instruction* (Englewood Cliffs, New Jersey: Prentice-Hall, Inc., 1969).

Other valuable periodicals include:

1. *Audio-Visual Instruction*
2. *Audubon Book*
3. *Bulletin of the National Association of Secondary School Principals*
4. *Current History*
5. *Education Digest*
6. *Educational Leadership*
7. *Grade Teacher*
8. *Journal of Health, Physical Education*
9. *Journal of Higher Education*
10. *Journal of Home Economics*
11. *Journal of Research in Music Education*
12. *Journal of the National Society for Programmed Instruction*
13. *Life* (past issues)
14. *National Geographic*
15. *Personnel and Guidance Journal*
16. *Quarterly Journal of Speech*
17. *Scholastic Coach*
18. *School Activities*
19. *School Arts*
20. *School Life*
21. *School Shop*
22. *Speech Teacher*

Other Sources

1. David W. Zuckerman and Robert Horn. *Guide to Simulations and Games.* (Hicksville, New York: Research Media, 1975.) An indispensable guide to finding the right game. A comprehensive directory!
2. Ronald G. Havlock, *The Change Agent's Guide to Innovation in Education.* (Englewood Cliffs, New Jersey: Educational Technology Publications, 1974.) Shows the supervisor how to be an effective catalyst or change advocate.
3. *Designing Effective Instruction,* a program developed by General Programmed Teaching, Quail Hill, California 94903, is good for developing instructional objectives and criterion test items within coordinated instructional systems or within any instructional system.
4. *Coordinated Instructional Systems,* Palo Alto, California: Sound Education, Inc. This program is a "self-study course for teachers," and it also can be used profitably by supervisors. Order the audio cassettes as well as the "Lesson Book" and the "Study Resource Materials Book."

Appendix B

Flanders[a] System of Interaction Analysis and Accompanying Forms for Recording and Charting Results

TABLE B–1. *Categories for Interaction Analysis*

TEACHER TALK	**INDIRECT INFLUENCE**	1.* *ACCEPTS FEELING:* accepts and clarifies the feeling tone of the students in a nonthreatening manner. Feelings may be positive or negative. Predicting or recalling feelings are included.
		2.* *PRAISES OR ENCOURAGES:* praises or encourages student action or behavior. Jokes that release tension, but not at the expense of another individual: nodding head, or saying "go on" are included.
		3.* *ACCEPTS OR USES IDEAS OF STUDENTS:* clarifying, building, or developing ideas suggested by a student. As teacher brings more of his own ideas into play, shift to category five.
		4.* *ASKS QUESTIONS:* asking a question about content or procedure with the intent that a student answer.
	DIRECT INFLUENCE	5.* *LECTURING:* giving facts or opinions about content or procedures; expressing his own ideas; asking rhetorical questions.
		6.* *GIVING DIRECTIONS:* directions, commands, or orders to which a student is expected to comply.
		7.* *CRITICIZING OR JUSTIFYING AUTHORITY:* statements intended to change student behavior from nonacceptable to acceptable pattern; bawling someone out; stating why the teacher is doing what he is doing; extreme self-reference.
STUDENT TALK		8.* *STUDENT TALK—RESPONSE:* talk by students in response to teacher. Teacher initiates the contact or solicits student statement.
		9.* *STUDENT TALK—INITIATION:* talk by students which they initiate. If "calling on" student is only to indicate who may talk next, observer must decide whether student wanted to talk. If he did, use this category.
		10.* *SILENCE—CONFUSION:* pauses, short periods of silence and periods of confusion in which communication cannot be understood by the observer.[a]

[a] Ned Flanders, "Intent, Action, Feedback: A Preparation for Teaching," *Journal of Teacher Education* XIV (September 1963), no. 3. Reprinted by permission.

* There is NO scale implied by these numbers. Each number is classificatory; it designates a particular kind of communication event. To write these numbers down during observation is to enumerate, not to judge a position on a scale.

CLASS CODE NO. _____ OBSERVER _____ DATE _____

		Teacher Talk							Student Talk		Silence Confusion	
CATEGORY	1	2	3	4	5	6	7	8	9	10	TOTAL TALLIES
Teacher Talk — 1											
2											
3											
4											
5											
6											
7											
Student Talk — 8											
9											
Silence or Confusion — 10											
TOTAL TALLIES											
Percent of Total											
	Teacher Total: _____							Student Total: __		Silence: _____	

FIGURE B-1.   Observation Matrix Tally Sheet.
Explanation: The tally mark in the box at the intersection of column 6 and row 10 indicates, by reference to the preceding page, that the teacher was giving directions and the response was silence and/or confusion.

FIGURE B-2.   Scatter Sheet—Working Matrix.

Appendix C

Program Evaluation Checklist for Staff and Instructional Development Programs

Introduction

The purpose of this checklist is to help the reader evaluate the developmental procedures that are considered necessary to systematic staff and instructional development programs. Use the checklist guidelines as you assess your own programs prior to and following tryout.

Remember, do not just identify the *presence* of a program development component. Make a qualitative assessment of the degree to which the program element meets the stated standards or criteria for judging the adequacy of the element's application in a program.

In the columns labeled "Yes," "No" or "Unsure," indicate that a criterion has or has not been met by placing a check ($\sqrt{}$) in the appropriate column. If you think the element is at a high qualitative level, place a plus ($+$) sign in the "Yes" column.

FIGURE C-1.   Checklist.

I.   *Needs Assessment:* Does the program element meet the stated principle?

Yes	No	Unsure		
			A.	Have we identified specific staff and learner needs and problem elements clearly and concisely (*i.e.,* gap between current and desired knowledge, skills, and attitudes, etc.)?
			B.	Has the audience (target population) been identified carefully (*e.g.,* age, sex, expectations, abilities, current knowledge, skills, and attitudes, etc.)?
			C.	Have we stated broad program *goals* derived from 1 and 2 above (*i.e.,* changing environment, increasing motivation, instruction, etc.)?
			D.	Have management organizational tasks, responsibilities, time schedules, etc., been specified clearly?

II. *Strategy Development* (techniques, media, etc.): Does the program element meet the stated principle?

Yes	No	Unsure	
			A. Have *instructional objectives* that are observable, measurable, and specific expected behavior standards (quality or quantity) been derived from the goal statements? Are the objectives stated in correct format, with base-line qualitative and quantitative standards for expected behavior or performance noted?
			B. Have we designed criterion tests or measures *prior* to program development?
			C. Have we stated entry or prerequisite behaviors for learners (*e.g.*, experience, performance level, skills, etc.)?
			D. Has the best alternative for meeting each identified need been identified as (1) environmental change, (2) motivational incentive, or (3) instructional or educational process?
			E. If instruction is called for, have we identified and developed possible strategies to accomplish instructional objectives as (1) partially self-directed study, (2) interactive strategies (*e.g.*, seminars), (3) problem solving, simulation and games, or (4) other strategy types? (List them here:)
			_____
			F. When appropriate, has provision been made for the use of media in instruction?
			G. Have we specified:
			1. Resources now available?
			2. Resources to be developed, including finance, personnel, equipment, supplies, facilities, and others.
			H. Where appropriate, has a prototype of the proposed program been constructed that includes:
			1. Appropriate practice (experience)?
			2. Opportunities for feedback to learner so he/she can have rapid, true knowledge of results?
			3. Provisions for maintaining interest, motivation?
			4. Flexible strategies in activities and media to provide for differentiation?
			5. Other characteristics? (List them here:)
			_____
			6. Is a complete package ready for tryout with a sample of the target population?

III. *Evaluation of Program:* Does the program element meet the stated principle?

Yes | *No* | *Unsure*

A. Have provisions been made for assessing the accomplishment of each stated objective in the program so that we will know whether or not the performance is met to the base-line mastery level specified?

B. Have evaluation techniques (both objective and subjective) been clearly specified well in advance of prototype development (tests, self-report, and observational techniques)?

C. Is the evaluation *technique* matched properly to the base-line *criterion* of success stated in the instructional objective?

D. In planning for testing the prototype:
  1. Has a small sample of target population been identified?
  2. Are evaluation standards and criteria well stated for an external observer?

E. Have provisions been made to utilize such devices as tests and/or questionnaires for analyzing evaluation results in relation to:
  1. Program objectives?
  2. Strategies employed?
  3. Evaluation methods and results?

F. Is data from tryouts efficiently summarized for use by the program initiators or evaluators to use in making revisions? (Please note that this item applies *only* after tryout.)

IV. *Redesign:* Does the program element meet the stated principles?

A. Has provision been made for program revision based on changes suggested from the program tryout? Have personnel been appointed, forms developed, procedures for tryout developed, and schedules published?

B. Are basic suggestions regarding program revision based primarily on criterion data from objectives?

C. Have learner/user responses during or immediately following the program been considered as sources for program improvement? (Caution: such responses generally are quite subjective.)

D. Have provisions been made for an operations analysis, in which we appraise and record the strengths and weaknesses of the procedures that were employed in designing the total program?

E. Is the revised program now ready to be implemented with the intended audience or target population?

Appendix D

Applied Educational Psychology for the Supervisor: Growing, Learning, and Testing

Society in America is particularly conscious of children, and children differ from each other in a variety of ways. This appendix presents an outline of applied educational psychology for the supervisor, with special attention to the principles of growth and development and the psychology of the learning process for supervisors; how to help the teacher in testing; assigning marks; and understanding statistical measures; and a look at the future.

Principles of Growth and Development for the Supervisor

Studying Individual Development

THE INTUITIVE UNDERSTANDING OF CHILDREN.   Any firsthand dealings with children have a concrete quality. It therefore is vital that those who have dealings with them understand children as children. The study of how children behave and how this behavior differs from that of adults might well be called the psychology of childhood, as opposed to psychology of adulthood. There is additionally the psychology of development, which examines the process of becoming mature, the influences of the child's environment, personality, and potentials.

INTUITIVE UNDERSTANDING AS OPPOSED TO SCIENCE.   The reason that children seem so inconsistent to the adult observer is that the adult is likely to interpret their behavior from an adult point of view. The child's behavior may therefore, at times, make no sense at all. To understand children, there is no substitute for direct experience. We must develop some explanation of child behavior that goes beyond intuitive understanding if we are to effectively communicate our understanding and account for the aspects of behavior that are beyond the present understanding of our wisest parents and teachers.

If our understanding of behavior is completely intuitive, we shall have difficulties in communicating this understanding. Our explanations may tend to be in the form of analogies and metaphors. If we speak of behavior in terms of objective detachment instead of in analogies and metaphors, the concepts derived will be useful in explaining a variety of child behavior. These concepts may be testable.

The difference between intuitive understanding and a scientific explanation is, therefore, that a scientific explanation permits behavior to be observed or deduced logically. The explanation applies to a wide range of child behavior. Superficially, the range does not resemble the original incident, whereas an intuitive understanding is more limited to actual incidents, although intuition is also somewhat generalizable to some new situations. The most important difference between an intuitive understanding and a scientific explanation of child behavior is that the latter may be tested and may be applied to further hypotheses, suggesting further areas of research.

Major Concepts of Growth and Development

All members of the professional staff should know and understand certain basic factors about human growth and development. In human development, four areas always should be considered in understanding the growth and development of the child: physical, intellectual, emotional, and social. Each area of development in the child follows a schedule from birth until death.

On the biological or physical level, this cycle is easily seen when the child first sits up, then crawls before walking, and so on. There are certain tasks at each level that must be mastered, so that the tasks at the next level can be mastered. Where development is too deviant or uneven, certain problems arise. Every developmental task may pose a problem for some children. Some children spend more time on one phase of development than do others. For example, in developing motor skills, research has shown that some children never crawl; they progress immediately from the standing stage to the walking stage. Others will spend a long time in the crawling stage, and some will crawl for only a short period of time. Provision for, and recognition of, these differences by line, staff, and instructional personnel is imperative.

An example of misunderstanding in this area is the practice of some educators that was based on the finding that "large" muscles develop and are usually controlled before "smaller" muscles. These well-meaning individuals gave children extremely thick pencils and crayons, in the belief that the muscles of the hand and fingers were "small" muscles and were not sufficiently developed to control smaller objects. Actually, these finger and hand muscles, both extensors and flexors, are relatively large muscles and are sufficiently well coordinated to permit the efficient use of normal-sized crayons and pencils in even the lowest grades.

Such research findings and their educational implications, should be evaluated continuously by supervisory personnel. Channels for communications concerning this topic must be kept open and active.

Major concepts relating to growth and development, which can help teachers in working with individuals and groups, are:

1. Growth is determined by capacity and experience.
2. There is a continuous, predictable pattern of growth even though any student may be accelerated or retarded within this pattern.
3. Growth or development follows a sequential order, and students are not likely to skip a stage of growth.
4. All aspects of growth are interrelated.
5. Growth creates needs. All students have certain basic needs even though the intensity of the needs will vary.
6. Growth proceeds at different rates.

Table D-1 contains an outline of the stages in the growth and development of a child and what the supervisor can suggest to the teacher concerning each stage.

EMOTIONAL DEVELOPMENT AND IN-SERVICE EDUCATION.   A child first learns to listen by imitating others. He/she watches adults, and if they listen to one another with interest and respect he/she comes to sense the rightness of having a give-and-take relationship with people. Even more important to the person he/she will become is how parents and teachers listen. If at home are talkers but no listeners, he/she may take problems elsewhere, or worse, seal them inside. The supervisor should help the teacher to realize that the little child who is talking so big, and with so much bravado, may well be seeking security and attention.

An example of two areas that were discussed by the school psychologist in an in-service education program planned by the supervisor in one school system in the midwest follows:

1. Recent developments in research related to three causes of reading retardation, including sensory immaturity, in which the perception areas of the brain have not yet reached maturation; emotional difficulties; and brain damage.
2. Recognition of the overaccepted (overprotected), rejected, and dominated child; the brain-damaged child, who exhibits the action-for-action's sake pattern; and the behavioral-epileptic child, who may respond with aggressive movements that are intense and that the child does not remember after the occurrence.

IMPLICATIONS FOR THE SCHOOL.   Since all students approach the task of maturing in a unique fashion, all students will not master specific learnings at the

TABLE D-1. *Supervisor's Outline of Growth and Development Stages*

	PHYSICAL FACTORS	REACTION PATTERNS	SUPERVISORS STRESS HOW TEACHERS CAN HELP
EARLY CHILDHOOD Ages 5, 6, and 7	1. Growth is slower, more stable than during infancy and preschool years.	1. These children are active, vigorous, and noisy. They tire easily.	1. Ample provision should be made for active, vigorous games as well as simple group work and play. Rhythmic and dramatic activities are important. Because of short attention span, work periods must be short and frequent change of pace is important. Teachers should be aware and help parents to become aware that academic progress, particularly in reading and writing, can be affected by perceptual immaturity, by immaturity in eye muscles, and by poor eye-hand coordination.
	2. By age six, girls are likely to be a year or more ahead of boys in physical maturation.	2. They have short interest span and will become restless and fidgety if activities require concentration over long periods.	
	3. Motor skills will continue to develop during this period, although large muscles of the arms and legs are more developed than the small muscles of the hands and fingers.	3. There is great interest in activity. Increasing motor control gives them increased ability in skipping, hopping, keeping time to music, catching and throwing balls.	2. Adequate rest is vital. Provision should be made for quiet, relaxing activities and rest periods at school as well as co-operative planning with parents. Children need from eleven to twelve hours of sleep.
	4. Eye-hand coordination is improving but may still be incompletely developed throughout this period. Children are likely to be far-sighted as they enter school; eyes still are not ready for much close work at age seven.	4. They will be interested in other children as they enter school but will also be highly individualistic. Many will play "along side of", not *with* another child at first, then with one or two children before developing skill in team and group activities. Usually they are sensitive to the opinions of both adults and classmates by age seven.	3. Encourage independence at home and school while permitting the child to fluctuate between self-sufficiency and extreme dependence on adults. At home the child can brush teeth, dress him/herself, and help with household chores. But the child will need some help. At school, with the teacher's help, the child can assume monitor duties, learn to observe safety precautions, and help to plan and evaluate individual work.
	5. There is great susceptibility to childhood diseases. There is particular need to guard against strain during convalescence.	5. There is gradual growth toward greater independence although they will fluctuate between apparent self-sufficiency and extreme dependence on adults. They may seem more cooperative at age five because of greater dependence on adults. At ages six and seven they are likely to be more interested in being first, more self-assertive, more competitive. Growing ability in self-evaluation is apparent. By age seven the child is likely to be quite self-critical.	4. The teacher can help by planning a daily program in accord with children's need for routine and by giving children opportunity to help with the planning and setting up their own standards.
		6. There is beginning awareness of fairness and justice.	

TABLE D-1. *(Continued)*

	PHYSICAL FACTORS	REACTION PATTERNS	SUPERVISORS STRESS HOW TEACHERS CAN HELP
EARLY CHILDHOOD Ages 5, 6, and 7 (continued)		7. Concrete, first-hand experiences and active participation promote effective learning at this time.	
		8. They like the familiar, the routine. They like a great deal of repetition and will play the same game, tell the same joke, or listen to the same story over and over.	
		9. Their sense of humor may seem silly and "slapstick" to adults.	
		10. Boys' and girls' interests usually are beginning to differ by ages six or seven.	
MIDDLE CHILDHOOD Ages 8, 9, and 10	1. There is slow, steady physical growth with a growth lag occurring just before adolescence.	1. They usually have boundless energy. They are eager and enthusiastic and may seem careless and hurried.	1. There should be ample provisions for active team games. Competition is likely to be strong and teams should be evenly matched. The need for group approval creates increasing need for a child to "hold one's own" with the group. The teacher can help and can encourage parents to help them develop skills that will enhance their prestige with the group.
	2. Some girls, because of more rapid physical development, may reach a period of rapid (preadolescent) growth by the age of ten.	2. There is a longer interest span and ability to work for longer periods, independently. Wider interests are developing.	
	3. Large muscle control and coordination improve rapidly and are excellent during the latter part of this period. The control of very small muscles as well as eye-hand coordination	3. There is great interest in organized team games and at this age they will work hard to develop specific skills.	2. Adequate rest is very important. During this period, children often are fatigued if special provision is not made for rest periods. They need ten to eleven hours of sleep.
		4. There is greater sensitivity to the opinion of peers and increasing participation in peer society. During this period, approval of age-mates begins to be more important than approval of adults. Peer loyalty results in extreme interest in "gangs" and clubs in most nine and ten year olds. Best friends are of the same sex; "gang" loyalty is likely to be stronger in boys.	3. Encourage growth in independence. Ample provision should be made for many group activities. Clubs, committees, and special group projects are valuable and all require different skills and

TABLE D-1. (Continued)

	PHYSICAL FACTORS		REACTION PATTERNS		SUPERVISORS STRESS HOW TEACHERS CAN HELP
MIDDLE CHILDHOOD Ages 8, 9, and 10 (continued)			5.	There is increased ability in self-evaluation. They not only are critical of themselves but are developing a critical attitude toward adults.	abilities and serve to meet differing interests. At these ages, they are capable of effective committee work and need practice in being a good leader and a good follower.
		4.	By eight years of age the eyes of most children accommodate both near and far vision; by age ten the eyes usually function as well as at the adult level.	6.	A strong sense of justice and fairness is developing.	4. Increased provision should be made for them to set up their own standards and help plan their activities. Reasonable explanations to their questions from teachers and parents are particularly important at this period in keeping with their sense of justice and fairness. They need, at school and home, to feel that they are in on the plans.
		5.	They normally will be energetic and in good health; toward the end of this period they will have had most contagious diseases.	7.	There is a growing ability to learn through vicarious experience, though concrete, first-hand experiences are still necessary for all children.	
				8.	Interest in routine develops into conscious appreciation of a well-organized program that they can help plan.	
				9.	A definite sense of humor may manifest itself in rough-house activities, much poise, and giggling. This is particularly apparent at the beginning of this period.	
				10.	Close friends and "gangs" are of the same sex. Differences in interests are widening. They are learning to assume their masculine and feminine roles.	
LATER CHILDHOOD (PREADOLESCENCE) Ages 11, 12, 13	1.	There is a growth lag prior to a very rapid growth spurt. Growth at this stage is uneven.	1.	Rapid and uneven growth is likely to result in awkwardness and restlessness. Poor posture may develop during this period. There is a wide range in both physical and emotional maturity among children of this age.	1. There should be provision for more highly organized games like handball and softball, although competition is keen and they will be self-conscious about trying any activity in which they lack skill.
	2.	Girls mature, physically, as much as two years ahead of boys.	2.	Interests are more mature and increasingly more diversified.	2. Adequate rest is important. From nine to ten hours of sleep are needed.

TABLE D-1. (*Continued*)

	PHYSICAL FACTORS	REACTION PATTERNS	SUPERVISORS STRESS HOW TEACHERS CAN HELP
LATER CHILDHOOD (PREADOLESCENCE) Ages 11, 12, 13 (continued)	3. Muscular growth is very rapid. Rapid, uneven growth may result in poor muscular control.	3. There is increased interest in highly organized games, particularly among boys.	3. Encourage and provide opportunity for many self-directed activities both on an individual and a group basis. They are ready now, if they have had practice, to assume real leadership roles. They can engage in effective committee work and learn to become good group members. They want to and are able to assume real responsibility. Membership in student councils or other self-governing groups at school is helpful as is membership in a "family council."
	4. Eye function is usually well established.	4. Peer codes are extremely important although there tends to be a shift from "gang" interest to interest in one or two close friends. There is increasing ability to sacrifice personal desires and self-interest for the good of the group.	4. Teachers can help greatly by providing opportunity for them at this age to discuss problems either in a teacher-student conversation or with their group. They can and want to evaluate their plans and decisions but resent being told what to do or "talked down to." Above all, teachers realize that they, at this age, are growing away from dependence on adults. Their efforts to establish independence will be clumsy, at first and they will seem antagonistic and uncooperative.
	5. During the transitional period there may be more minor illnesses. There is susceptibility to fatigue.	5. There is increased ability in self-evaluation and much interest in self-improvement, which includes improving personal appearances. The "rift" between children and adults is widening so that children nearing adolescence are likely to seem highly critical and uncooperative toward adults.	
	6. Secondary sex characteristics are developing.	6. There is increased need to feel that adults are just and fair but a tendency to feel that they are not. They want to feel that they are in on planning that involves them, that they are sharing in the decision making.	
		7. There is rapid growth in ability to see relationships between ideas; to generalize.	
		8. Their growing independence increases their need to help plan and evaluate their activities. At these ages they are able to effectively analyze situations and problems.	
		9. Sense of humor is becoming more "adult" and will likely manifest itself in verbal cleverness. There is much giggling, however, when boys and girls are together.	
		10. Closer identification with masculine and feminine role is developing. While interests are different, at the same time their interest in each other may lead to a "scornful," antagonistic attitude	

same chronological age. The interrelatedness of all phases of growth makes it possible to help students progress in one phase of development and reinforces growth in other areas.

Even though teachers are aware of the tremendous variation among the students they teach, they also observe that no student differs completely from all other students. No student, however puzzling, is entirely baffling to a teacher because of what the teacher knows and understands about *all* students.

SIMILAR PATTERNS. Noting specific capacities, interests, experiences, and needs of children emphasizes the differences between them. However, as the *total* child is viewed in light *of basic needs and stages of growth, similarities among children are apparent.* An understanding of normal growth and development, along with an awareness of the total sweep of the developmental processes, provides the framework or context within which teachers interpret the behavior of individuals and lends perspective and direction to educational planning.

Psychology of the Learning Process for Supervisors

Learning for the sake of learning is not a child's attribute, for learning is work. To learn, the child must subordinate the pleasure principle, play, to the reality principle, work. An immature child needs understanding and time to move in the direction of learning. Since children identify with their families and carry this relationship into the classroom, the teacher must know what feelings the child has brought. If the child feels disliked at home or dislikes the teacher, who may be a parent-surrogate, he/she does not have the motive to learn. Positive feelings stemming from home influence and develop the child's attitude toward learning.

The understanding educator is aware of the child's wish to please parents and teacher, and depends on this motivation. The educator attempts to direct, stimulate, and gratify the student's curiosity and wish to learn and know. Before a supervisor can attempt to help teachers improve instruction, the supervisor must be aware of the basic principles concerning the learning process.

Theories of Learning

William James, eminent anatomy teacher, turned to philosophy, becoming the first exponent of the pragmatic philosophy that later influenced John Dewey. William James conducted research work in memory training. To James, learning was a matter of forming connections within the nervous system. Then connections resulted in the formation of habit.

Wilhelm Max Wundt, whose initial psychological laboratory in Leipzig in 1879 has become famous as the first laboratory in the field of psychology, saw cortical action as the basis for the mental act. David Hume (1711–1776) previously had developed a theory that there was a principle of connection between various thoughts and ideas; David Hartley, at about the same time, perceived a factor of association in learning. Alexander Bane, an evolutionist, probably was of great influence in the development of the theories of trial and error learning as set forth by the great psychologist Thorndike.

EDWARD LEE THORNDIKE.   Edward L. Thorndike, undoubtedly a genius, originally worked with William James at Harvard and then moved to Columbia University, where he worked with J. McKeen Cattell, a student of Wundt. Thorndike's initial work was in the field of animal intelligence, which was the topic of his doctoral dissertation. Thorndike was the first teacher of statistics in the United States. After turning from the study of animals to the study of children, he wrote a three-volume set in psychology. This work was followed by the famous *Briefer Course*.

From 1913 to 1930, Thorndike's stimulus-response connectionism was omnipotent in the field of educational psychology. Some outstanding points of view of Thorndike that have implications for the supervisor are those concerning stimulus-response bonds that are fixed and made permanent by success or pleasure.

Thorndike's three laws of learning were readiness, effect, and use. The law of *readiness* stated that if the organism was ready to act, being permitted to act would be satisfying, whereas not being permitted to act would be quite dissatisfying. The law of *effect* stated that the success of trial and error learning depends on the effective and satisfying result of the successful movements. The law of *exercise* or *use* brought forth the idea that—other items being equal—learning is a factor of repeating a response over and over again.

The supervisor should be acquainted with the supplemental principles of Thorndike, such as the laws of multiple response, set, partial activity, analogy, and associated shifting, and should realize that Thorndike has shown that we must teach for transfer, making our materials more lifelike. This transfer theory has proven a most valuable lesson to educators.

Thorndike helped us in the field of discipline. He showed us that if we must punish, the undesirable character of behavior must be eclipsed with a new positive, acceptable behavior response that is made available to the child. It is easier to obtain a more desirable outcome with a positive response in the form of acknowledgment from the teacher in the first place, with undesirable reactions not being rewarded.

He has shown us that with no knowedge of results, there is no motivation. Thorndike considered motivation as essential to the learning situation. Thorndike also stressed that there is to be drill, but only in the form of meaningful practice, with materials proceeding from the simple to the more complex, and from the specific to the general.

On the negative side, one must admit that this system is atomistic, with the whole being developed by a synthesis of the parts—a view not held today by many educational psychologists. In spite of this limitation, one inevitably must return to the completeness of the system and to the logic with which it has been developed.

OTHER THEORIES.   The supervising principal also must be familiar with the theories of psychologists who developed the theory of contiguous conditioning. This theory was propounded by Edwin R. Guthrie in 1935. If one applies the teaching of this school to the classroom, he/she will find it is unnecessary to apply reward for correct behavior responses. *We learn what we do,* and in the situation in which we have a series of movements we learn the last thing we do. Therefore the child must be informed that he/she is through with a particular impinging stimulus he/she has been working on, and that he/she has learned the particular item.

Material must be presented in a variety of ways in a variety of situations, such as on the blackboard, on paper, vocally, kinesthetically, and through various audio-visual media. The teacher must give clues that help the child discover the correct answer, provided the child is sufficiently mature to make the desired reactions.

The supervisor should be familiar, also, with the works of Clark L. Hull and E. R. Hilgard, who developed a behavioral system that stressed that the child must be taught how to live in this social world, for inadequate learning would result in maladjustment. Since *learning occurs by doing,* there must be an emphasis on the activities of the student. Problems must be presented so as to insure reinforcement of the habit hierarchy needed for adequate response.

DESCRIPTIVE BEHAVIORISM AND THE SUPERVISOR.   Of special interest to the student of programmed learning are the implications for education of B. F. Skinner's system termed "descriptive behaviorism." An educator who utilizes Skinner's system of education will wait until the child does the correct thing in the classroom and then will reinforce the response. A positive reaction always will be reinforced. Skinner said that punishment will not reinforce a reaction that is desired.

One must build up another response with reinforcement, thereby building up *operant strength* in desired directions. In the classroom, one must reinforce the appropriate moves, building operant strength, and must show the correct moves in the case of adverse response. The appropriate move must be reinforced when it is made.

According to Skinner, the selection of stimuli is of optimum importance. The individual's growth and development should be taken into account. Skinner's theories and findings are valuable when applied to the area of programmed learning, which is treated in chapter 11.

GESTALT PSYCHOLOGY.   The supervisor should be familiar with the works of Kurt Koffka, Wolfgang Koehler, Max Wertheimer, and Kurt Lewin. These scientists treated learning as a problem in figure and ground, as traces on the cerebral cortex, as sudden flashes of insight, and as field forces with valance and vector potentials, respectively. They did not view learning as atomistic nor as a trial and error behavior. Insight was stressed.

When one learned something new, one modified the whole trace system; one did not add a new part. When two or three learnings came at the same time, there would be a more complex change in the trace system than if they came at one time. Instruction must be geared to the maturity of the learner, with individual differences being taken into account.

The instructor must take into account the learner's intellectual level, provide for motivation, and present the curricular materials in a pattern rather than an atomistic form. Periodic checks of each child's growth and development must be accomplished. The gradual development of discernment as the organism matures is considered as the prime measure of the learning that has taken place.

It would seem that some background of material or experience of a trial and error nature would be needed in at least some of the learnings that occur, but this has been negated by Koehler. Lewin, the field psychologist who emphasized the importance of the student's level of aspiration, stated that the individual must become ego involved with the task presented. The instructional materials, therefore, must be neither too difficult, nor too simple.

FUNCTIONALISM. The psychologists James R. Angell, John Dewey, Harvey Carr, Charles H. Judd, Edward F. Robinson, and Robert S. Woodworth were the leaders in the school of functionalism. Robinson's experiments seem to indicate that the teacher must present the learner with a series of tasks that are evenly spaced and that will not result in interference with prior learning. The materials selected must not be so similar as to result in retroactive inhibition. The teacher must watch for trophism and be very aware of the four basic laws of *contiguity, frequency, assimilation,* and *intensity* in presenting material; the teacher must be certain that the correct associations are emphasized.

One must, according to the functionalists, teach the *whole child*. Schools must assure that habits that have gone through a previous stamping-in process are retained. Continuous supervision by a teacher who assumes an active role in a learning environment is essential.

John Dewey, who has been identified with the functionalists of the University of Chicago, was a pragmatic philosopher as well as a functionalist with a touch of Gestalt in him; he did not care for the functionalist idea of Stimulus-Organism-Response (S-O-R). He stated that the organism *learns by doing* and was convinced that there is not the slightest worth in Herbartian pouring in of subject matter. Dewey felt that many isolated facts and figures are of little value in our social world. Education must be the child's becoming aware in his/her own right, thereby acquiring the ability to solve individual problems in the society that is his/her environment. The child must have the freedom needed to be peripatetic and to solve problems collectively, thereby gaining a sense of self-reliance and adequacy.

Dewey stated in 1938, in *Experience and Education,* that there must be a curriculum with objectives, law, and order, but without the ancient pouring in. To him, the only truisms were the facts that would accrue from experimental work, with the eternal verities thus being cast in disrepute except as they have been verified in the laboratory.

Guthrie had stated that we learn what we do; Dewey said that we learn by doing. Dewey's project method, which took into account the basic needs of the learner, included the five steps of learning, which he identified as follows:

1. Realization of the problem—locate the problem
2. Search for clarity—specifications and size
3. Statement of the proposal or hypothesis—for solving the problem
4. Rational application—an attempt to solve the problem
5. Experimental verification—ascertain what has happened in the attempted solution of the problem.

If there were no solution, one would start again with number (3), pragmatically trying hypotheses after hypotheses until the desired results were obtained, or another alternative was accepted as a solution.

Dewey saw learning as an item that must be founded on the everyday problems of social democracy, and as a procedure by which the organism was to be guided in life by ascertaining the solutions to problems that inhibit personal and social growth.

IMPLICATIONS FOR THE SUPERVISING PRINCIPAL.   Dewey's five steps in learning, and the project technique, can be used by the classroom teacher in the education of the "whole child." Teachers should utilize the method that works, no matter what it is, with no pet beliefs or detriments to location of new knowledge.

The teacher must act as a guide and counselor in the learning environment. Individual differences must be taken into account, for the individual is all-important in the learning situation. Dewey said that stimulation and motivation, especially of the intrinsic variety, are essential, for children learn best from activities and materials in which they are actively interested.

Dewey's critics may have overlooked the statements regarding the curriculum and other related matters in 1932, although one must admit that the system apparently falls short in the area of the formation of habits in the child. One may criticize the concept of discarding all of the so-called eternal verities, except those that can be experimentally proved in a laboratory.

One should, therefore, take this concept of truth along with Dewey's pragmatically extreme views in a buffered fashion for optimum classroom results. Again, one must remember that Dewey was angered by the manner in which many of his ideas were being stretched and compressed, especially by the followers of the child-centered wing of the Progressive Education Association. He was most emphatic in stating that he considered reading, studying, experimenting, and purposeful practice as activities that constituted "doing," just as surely as did such enterprises as dramatic representations and construction. Surely, such activities as dramatic play, construction, and playing and working with blocks may have certain social values in the primary grades. Their extensive use in the middle and upper grades is to be questioned seriously. If it is true, as we have seen, that play *is* a natural expression of childhood, should the student spend extensive time receiving instruction on how to play when this time could have been spent in studying mathematics, oral and written language, health, science, spelling, reading, and even foreign languages?

A positive answer to the question would seem both to be inaccurate and illogical, and the supervisor of tomorrow is cautioned lest the temptation to have the classroom turned into a showcase rather than a learning laboratory be too much to withstand. It may be more entertaining for classroom visitors to see children engaged in dramatic activity than in learning certain processes in mathematics. The temptation on the part of the supervisor to force the teacher to utilize such techniques as dramatic representation, block play, and construction is to be avoided when there is no real need for their utilization, or when the class or the teacher does not work best with these techniques.

The parents of the school at the lower grade levels, for instance, have the right to expect that the students are being taught reading, mathematics, spelling, grammar, science, geography, history, and, in some instances, a foreign language. Instruction in other areas certainly has a place, but there is no justification for spending several hours per week from the regular instructional program preparing for a "culmination" show for parental consumption in the name of public relations, as has been the practice in certain elementary schools of this country, any more than there is for spending hours in dramatic play or "free rhythmic representation" activities with children who probably would benefit more from direct instruction in the so-called eternal verities.

Summary of Learning Principles for the Supervisor

When one studies the theories of the psychology of learning as espoused by Skinner, Thorndike, the Gestaltists, and the functionalists, it becomes evident that there is a need for an eclectic point of reference for the supervisor. The following summary is an attempt to provide a brief outline:

1. Learning has been defined as the modification and development of tendencies that govern the psychological function.
2. Learning takes place when there is a felt need on the part of the individual. Reinforcement apparently is important.
3. Learning is greatly influenced by frequency and distribution of practice, generalization, opportunity to transfer, and sensory modality (the use of various colors, sounds, odors, and tactile stimulations).
4. Learning must be stimulated. It should be noted that stimulation may be accomplished by the teacher, but motivation is from within. We should therefore, refer to what we do to influence the learner as *stimulation,* which is done with the hope that the learner will be *motivated* to respond.

5. Many theories have been advocated to explain learning phenomena, but no one theory accounts for all phenomena and research findings. Among the theories most widely discussed are those of Koffka, Koehler, Lewin, Wheeler, Robinson, Dewey, Thorndike, Guthrie, Hull, Skinner, and Tolman.

We must stimulate, but we must keep the stimulating material at the proper maturity level, and the material must be patterned. The material that we are stimulating the individual to learn must be adjusted to the level of maturation.

We must evaluate progress that is being made by the individual, otherwise motivation will lag. Knowledge of results, then, is essential to learning. Finally, we must work toward a broad integrated development for basic skills, mental health, physical health, understandings, appreciations, hobbies and interests, and social development, including the essential social skills and the amenities. It is the job of the supervisor to help the teacher become increasingly familiar with the more basic teachings of the psychologists in the field of learning.

Evaluation of Learning

The findings of educational psychology in the area of tests, measurements, and evaluation should be brought to the attention of the certificated staff. These findings and developments should be interpreted to the staff. Recommendations for the utilization of selected methods and techniques of measurement and evaluation should be made on an individual basis. Clearly, techniques applicable to Grade 6 or Grade 9 may not be applicable to Grade 1.

The supervisor must use due caution when working with teachers in the area of measurement and evaluation. The difference between measurement and evaluation should be understood clearly by both teacher and supervisor.

As used in this text, measurement refers to a mathematical determination. This determination may be either exact, as in the case of three correct answers, or approximate, as in the case of a line three inches long. In the former, it should be noted that one may count accurately how many answers are correct according to an answer key. However, even with the highly advanced electronic measuring devices of the space age, one may never be absolutely certain that a line is EXACTLY three inches long. There will be an error, even though this error may be only in the millionths of an inch.

The second area is evaluation. Unlike measurement, evaluation implies a comparison or subjective judgment of worth. It usually includes measurement as a preceding step, but measurement does not necessarily include evaluation.

Teaching through understanding is the heart of the learning process. It is a skill developed only through discipline and constant practice. The supervisor must help the staff develop this skill. Regardless of the individual behavioral manifestations, there are certain general principles that apply to the understanding of all children. Everyone has certain basic needs that must be met, no matter how different the surface behavior may be. All need a fairly comfortable opinion of the self with which to live. This may be achieved in a variety of ways.

Regardless of the behavior differences, all children need a good opinion of themselves. The psychological integrity of the individual must be preserved. The following seven items are guides to the preservation of individual integrity:

1. *Acceptance.* Students need to be accepted as they are.
2. *Consistency.* Consistency can be used effectively to contribute to a student's security.
3. *Negative emotions.* Students need to be allowed to express negative emotions. This expression, however, should be routed into positive channels.
4. *Reassurance.* Reassurance must be given by interest in the student as a person.
5. *Routine.* An explanation of routine assignments and plans should be given on the student's level of understanding.
6. *Force.* Verbal and physical coercion should be avoided as much as possible.
7. *Objectivity.* Objectivity should be a goal in understanding the student and should contribute to the effective employment of the principles of interpersonal relationships.

A basic tenet is that no two students are exactly alike. Supervising principals are reminded constantly, as they observe students, of the countless ways in which they differ. In any class, students vary in height and weight and amount of energy output. They differ in capacities, interests, and background of experiences. They differ in how they feel about themselves, how they feel about others, and in what they think is important. These latter are subtle forces not readily observable perhaps, but powerfully influencing how a student acts and learns, thereby affecting the rate and manner in which she masters the task of "growing up."

How to Help the Teacher Test, Assign Marks, and Understand Statistical Measures

Testing provides basic information regarding the student's ability to learn and his/her educational achievement, personality, needs, and interests. This information should be considered in relation to information about health and physical development, reactions to daily learning activities, social relations, and attitudes. As no one test successfully defines the student, the teacher should be encouraged to compare the results from many tests in order to secure a more valid profile.

Test results help the teacher better understand and plan for the class as a whole and to spotlight the student who may merit special attention. Groups of teachers representing one grade level or subject matter area can meet to study certain tests, evaluating their ideas and impressions with each other. The school psychologist can help teachers analyze the significance of the intelligence or achievement test scores, the aptitudes, and the relations between tests. The principal, assistant principal, director of curriculum, counselor, specialist-consultant, and other specialists should help evaluate test results.

The Use of Tests

The teacher who knows how to administer, use, and interpret tests will have a better understanding of the students in the classroom and will be able to give them better counsel. Principals should help teachers better understand tests and measurements. Standardized tests, including the following, should be made available to the staff by the principal. Recommended—(1) intelligence tests, group and individual; (2) achievement tests; (3) aptitude tests. Optional—(4) interest inventories; and (5) personality tests.

The following is a listing of just a few of these tests:

1. Intelligence tests—group
   a) Kuhlman-Anderson Intelligence Test (Grades 1–9)
   b) Otis Classification Test
   c) Otis Group Intelligence Scale
   d) Otis Quick-Scoring Mental Ability Tests
   e) California Tests of Mental Maturity (all levels)
   f) Terman-McNemar Test of Mental Ability
   g) Thurstone SRA Primary Mental Abilities (ages five through seven, seven through eleven, eleven through seventeen)
   h) Progressive Matrices (Lewis and Company, London)
2. Intelligence tests—individual
   a) Latest Stanford Revision of the Binet-Simon Intelligence Scale
   b) Wechsler Intelligence Scale for Children (WISC) and the WAIS (Wechsler Adult Intelligence Scale)
   c) Gesell Development Schedules
   d) Arthur Point Scale of Performance (cubes, form board, maze)
3. Interest inventories
   a) Kuder Preference Record (occupational interests)
   b) Pressey Interest-Attitude Test
   c) Guilford Interest Survey
4. Achievement tests
   a) Metropolitan Achievement Test
   b) Gates Modern Scholastic Achievement Tests
   c) SRA Iowa Tests of Educational Development
   d) Stanford Achievement Test
   e) SRA Achievement Series by Thorpe, Lefever, and Naslund
   f) American School Achievement Tests (reading, arithmetic, language)
   g) Diagnostic Reading Test
   h) California Achievement Tests (reading, arithmetic, language)
   i) Monroe Reading Aptitude Tests
   j) Iowa Silent Reading Tests
   k) Iowa Every-Pupil Tests of Basic Skills (silent reading, study skills, arithmetic, language)
   l) SR/SE Survey of Reading and Study Skills (SRA)

m) Sequential Tests of Education Progress (STEP)
n) California Phonics Survey
o) Lee-Clark Arithmetic Fundamentals Test

5. Aptitude tests
   a) Differential Aptitude Tests (verbal reasoning, numerical ability, abstract reasoning, space relations, mechanical reasoning, clerical speed and accuracy, language usage)
   b) Lee-Thorpe Occupational Interest Inventory
   c) Detroit Mechanical Aptitudes Examination
   d) Clerical Aptitude Test
   e) Seashore Tests of Musical Aptitudes
   f) Employment Survey Tests
   g) SCAT and SAT

6. Personality tests
   a) Ohio Guidance Tests for Elementary Grades
   b) California Test of Personality
   c) Allport A-S Reaction Study
   d) Vineland Social Maturity Scale
   e) Kuder Preference Record—Personal
   f) Mooney Problems Test Sheet

Test Functions and Factors

Reading readiness tests assist teachers and principals in ability grouping for reading instruction and in preparing individuals for reading programs (kindergarten and first grade). Achievement tests assist teachers in diagnosing individuals' and classes' strengths and weaknesses for planning instruction, assessing progress (student and class), and reporting to parents.

Teachers and principals also should consider achievement test results in class placements. These tests provide measures (in grade-placement or percentiles) of reading vocabulary, reading comprehension, total reading, arithmetic fundamentals, arithmetic reasoning, total arithmetic, spelling, and English (punctuation, grammar, and usage).

Tests of mental maturity, or "intelligence tests," normally provide a "verbal," a "performance" or "nonverbal," and a "total" I.Q. The major purpose is estimating intellectual or scholastic capacity and expected achievement. These tests help indicate "overachievement" (a misnomer, at best), "underachievement," and potential superior intelligence, which should be tested individually.

The *Iowa Tests* have been given the second semester of the eighth grade to assist students, staff, and parents in planning a program for high-school years. Evaluating overall academic knowledge, they compare the student with local class average and with national average.

A good test is readily and easily scored; is objective, valid, reliable, easily administered; and is as free from contaminating factors as possible.

Assigning Marks, Statistical Concepts, and Interpreting Statistical Measures

The supervising principal should help the teacher become familiar with such basic statistical tools for test interpretation as the *median, mode, mean, average deviation, standard deviation, correlation, chi square,* and with the basic methods of assigning marks.

The supervising principal may wish to recommend the following technique utilizing the average deviation from the median (middle) score of the distribution for use in assigning marks.

Assuming five raw scores for illustrative purposes:

Raw Scores	Deviation from Median (*Midscore*)
30	12
20	2
Median or Midscore 18	0
17	1
10	8

N = 5   Σ (sum) of deviation = 23 all deviations are treated as positive

1. Arrange the test scores in sequence, with the highest score first.
2. Calculate the median or midscore. If there is an even number of cases (N) go up and down the distribution of $\left(\frac{N}{2}\right)$ scores, and find the average of the two middle scores. If there is an odd number of cases (N) go up or down the distribution $\left[\left(\frac{N-1}{2}\right)+1\right]$ scores, where N = the number of cases (the number of scores in the distribution). In the event that N is even, it is possible to round off the median to the nearest whole number as follows:
   a) If the fraction is less than 0.5, delete it;
   b) If the fraction is more than 0.5, round up;
   c) If the fraction is exactly equal to 0.5, round up if one would obtain an *even* number in so doing. If one would have obtained an *odd* number in rounding up, delete the fraction and *do not* round up. In this manner the calculations that result in fractions exactly equal to one-half are rounded up and down approximately the same number of times, and should, by chance, result in no significant differences in the quantities obtained. *Example:* 3.4 would be rounded to 3; 3.5 would be rounded to 4, since 4 is an even number; 3.7 would be rounded to 4; 2.5, however, would be rounded down to 2, since rounding up would have resulted in an odd number. Note that one need not be concerned whether the resulting rounded number would be even or odd *except* where the fraction is exactly equal to one-half.

3. Calculate the deviation of each score from the median. All deviations are treated as positive. A raw score minus the median equals the deviation.
4. Obtain the sum of the deviations.
5. Obtain the average deviation (AD): the sum of the deviations divided by the number of scores, or $\left(\dfrac{\Sigma d}{N}\right)$ where Σ = sum, d = deviations, and N is as above. In our example AD $=\left(\dfrac{\Sigma d}{N}\right)=\left(\dfrac{23}{5}\right)=4.6$. To facilitate computations, one should always round off the AD to the nearest tenth.
6. Obtain the *scale unit* or range of each letter mark. Assuming a letter-grade assignment of five letters, as A, B, C, D, F, the scale unit is equal to the average deviation multiplied by the constant figure 1.5. In our example SU $=(4.6)\times(1.5)=6.9$, rounded to the nearest tenth. It should be noted that 1.5 is a constant, and is always used as a multiplier when five letter marks are to be assigned.
7. Find the range of the C marks: one-half of a scale unit above and one-half below the median.

   a) $\dfrac{SU}{2}=\dfrac{6.9}{2}=3.45=$ on-half of a scale unit in our example.

   b) The median plus and minus one-half the scale unit equals the lower and upper limits of the mark C:

   $18+3.45=21.45=$ upper limit of C.
   $18-3.45=14.55=$ lower limit of C.

8. Find the upper limit of B by adding one scale unit to the upper limit of the mark C:

$$21.45+6.90=28.35$$

9. Find the lower limit of D by subtracting one scale unit from the lower limit of C:

$$14.55-6.90=7.65$$

10. What is left equals the marks A and F:

   A = 28.36 and up
   B = 21.46 to 28.35
   C = 14.55 to 21.45
   D = 7.65 to 14.54
   F = Lower than 7.65

   The extremes of each letter mark may be indicated by plus and minus marks. The score 21.45 would be a C+, and 14.55 a C−.

Since it is assumed that there will be approximately six standard deviations (σ) under the curve of the normal or standard distribution, if there are five letter marks to assign, each will occupy 1.2 (6 divided by 5) standard deviations along the baseline of the curve. About 3.9 percent of the population would receive a mark of A, and the same percent would receive F's; 23.84 percent would receive a mark of B, and the same percent would receive D's; 45.14 percent would receive a mark of C. It should be noted that these percents change from class to class; often there will be no F's or no B's, and so forth.

Since 1.2σ is approximately equal to 1.5 average deviations, a constant of 1.5 was used as a multiplier in the example given in the text. In the event that

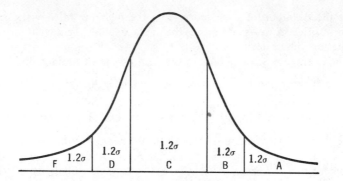

FIGURE D-1.   Sample Curve Showing Five Letter Marks Assigned Within the Normal or Standard Distribution.

TABLE D–2.   *Table of Areas Under the Normal Distribution Curve*

$\frac{x}{\sigma}$	0.00	0.01	0.02	0.03	0.04	0.05	0.06	0.07	0.08	0.09
0.0	0000	0040	0080	0120	0160	0199	0239	0279	0319	0359
0.1	0398	0438	0478	0517	0557	0596	0636	0675	0714	0753
0.2	0793	0832	0871	0910	0948	0987	1026	1064	1103	1141
0.3	1179	1217	1255	1293	1331	1368	1406	1443	1480	1517
0.4	1554	1591	1628	1664	1700	1736	1772	1808	1844	1879
0.5	1915	1950	1985	2019	2054	2088	2123	2157	2190	2224
0.6	2257	2291	2324	2357	2389	2422	2454	2486	2517	2549
0.7	2580	2611	2642	2673	2704	2734	2764	2794	2823	2852
0.8	2881	2910	2939	2967	2995	3023	3051	3078	3106	3133
0.9	3159	3186	3212	3238	3264	3290	3315	3340	3365	3389
1.0	3413	3438	3461	3485	3508	3531	3554	3577	3599	3621
1.1	3643	3665	3686	3708	3729	3749	3770	3790	3810	3830
1.2	3849	3869	3888	3907	3925	3944	3962	3980	3997	4015
1.3	4032	4049	4066	4082	4099	4115	4131	4147	4162	4177
1.4	4192	4207	4222	4236	4251	4265	4279	4292	4306	4319
1.5	4332	4345	4357	4370	4383	4394	4406	4418	4429	4441
1.6	4452	4463	4474	4484	4495	4505	4515	4525	4535	4545
1.7	4554	4564	4573	4582	4591	4599	4608	4616	4625	4633
1.8	4641	4649	4656	4664	4671	4678	4686	4693	4699	4706
1.9	4713	4719	4726	4732	4738	4744	4750	4756	4761	4767

EXAMPLE: between the mean and a point 1.96 σ ($\frac{x}{\sigma} = 1.96$) are found 47.50 percent of the entire area under the curve.

NOTE: $x = X - M$, where X = a score and M = the mean of the distribution. σ = a standard deviation. Therefore, $\frac{x}{\sigma}$ = the distance from the mean in terms of σ; the number of σ's.

TABLE D–2.   (*Continued*)

2.0	4772	4778	4783	4788	4793	4798	4803	4808	4812	4817
2.1	4821	4826	4830	4834	4838	4842	4846	4850	4854	4857
2.2	4861	4864	4868	4871	4875	4878	4881	4884	4887	4890
2.3	4893	4896	4898	4901	4904	4906	4909	4911	4913	4916
2.4	4918	4920	4922	4925	4927	4929	4931	4932	4934	4936
2.5	4938	4940	4941	4943	4945	4946	4948	4949	4951	4952
2.6	4953	4955	4956	4957	4959	4960	4961	4962	4963	4964
2.7	4965	4966	4967	4968	4969	4970	4971	4972	4973	4974
2.8	4974	4975	4976	4977	4977	4978	4979	4979	4980	4981
2.9	4981	4982	4982	4983	4984	4984	4985	4985	4986	4986
3.0	4986.5	4986.9	4987.4	4987.8	4988.2	4988.6	4988.9	4989.3	4989.7	4990.0
3.1	4990.3	4990.6	4991.0	4991.3	4991.6	4991.8	4992.1	4992.4	4992.6	4992.9
3.2	4993.129									
3.3	4995.166									
3.4	4996.631									
3.5	4997.674									
3.6	4998.409									
3.7	4998.922									
3.8	4999.277									
3.9	4999.519									
4.0	4999.683									
4.5	4999.966									
5.0	4999.997133									

This table gives the percent of the area under the distribution curve between this $\frac{x}{\sigma}$ point and the mean. Fractional parts (10,000ths) of the total area under the curve are shown. It should be recalled that $\frac{x}{\sigma} =$ how many standard deviations you want from one side of the mean. To obtain both sides, multiply by two.

there are more than five letter marks to assign, the amount of σ to assign to each letter mark is determined by dividing six σ (constant) by the number of marks to assign. One then determines the percent to be assigned to each letter mark by referring to Table D-2, which gives the percent of the distribution under the normal curve in terms of standard deviations from the mean of the distribution.

The material that follows demonstrates a few of the methods commonly used to calculate standard statistical measures.

Three Measures of Central Tendency

1. THE ARITHMETIC MEAN.   The total of all measurements or scores divided by the number of such measurements. For grouped data, see the example included below:

ci	MP	Tally	f	d	fd	x(x = MP − True Mean)	fx
90–94	92	1	1	4	4	25	25
85–89	87	11	2	3	6	21	42
80–84	82	111	3	2	6	16	48
75–79	77	111111111	9	1	9	11	99
70–74	72(am)	–5–5–1–1	12	0	0	6	72
65–69	67	5–5	10	–1	–10	16	10
60–64	62	5–1111	9	–2	–18	4	36
55–59	57	1111111	7	–3	–21	9	63
50–54	52	1111	4	–4	–16	14	56
45–49	47	111	3	–5	–15	19	57
40–44	42	11	2	–6	–12	24	48
35–39	37	1	1	–7	–7	29	29

$$N = 63 \quad \Sigma fd = -74 \qquad\qquad \Sigma fx = 584$$

ARITHMETIC MEAN for grouped data = AM =

$$am \pm \left[\frac{\Sigma fd}{N} \cdot ci \right] = 72 - \left[\frac{(74)}{(63)} \cdot (5) \right] = 66.15$$

ci—class interval. (Originally determined as follows):

$$\frac{\text{Highest Score} - \text{Lowest Score.}}{\text{Number of Intervals Wanted}}$$

am—assumed mean (mispoint of ci with most tally marks)
d—number of intervals away from the interval containing the assumed mean.

Note that in reality we compute the *algebraic sum* of the assumed mean and the correction factor (which is derived from the formula) in order to obtain the true mean. In the example, we subtract because Σ fd is negative.

2. THE MEDIAN. The frequency above or below which is found 50% of the total frequency; the score above and below which 50% of the scores fall. Determined by counting up the distribution to find $\frac{N}{2}$ (use $\frac{N+1}{2}$ if there is an odd number of scores). $\frac{N}{2}$ = one-half of the total number of scores. For grouped data, use the formula $L + \left[\dfrac{\frac{N}{2} - F}{fm} \right] \cdot$ (i or ci)

where F = the sum of scores for all intervals *below* the interval upon which the median falls
     fm = frequency (number of scores) *within* the interval upon which the median falls
       i = the length of the class interval

3. THE MODE. The score that occurs most often in a distribution of scores; the "fashion."

Two Measures of Deviation from the Arithmetic
Mean (AM) (All Deviations Treated as Positive)

1. AVERAGE DEVIATION (AD).   The sum of the deviation of each score from the
arithmetic mean, ignoring positive and negative signs, divided by the number
of such scores:

$$AD = \frac{\text{Sum of fx}}{N}, \text{where } f = \text{the frequency (number}$$
$$\text{of scores), and}$$
$$x = \text{the difference of the}$$
$$\text{midpoint of a class}$$
$$\text{interval minus the mean}$$
$$\text{(AM) of the distribution}$$

Referring to the example given under Arithmetic Mean, above, especially to
the two right hand columns,

$$AD = \Sigma \frac{fx}{N} = \frac{584}{63} = 9\frac{17}{63}$$

2. STANDARD DEVIATION (σ).   The square root of the sum of the squared deviations of each score from the mean divided by the number of scores. A
more powerful measure of deviation than the average deviation, but somewhat
more difficult to calculate.

$$\sigma = \sqrt{\frac{\Sigma d^2}{N}}$$

Correlation Analysis

Correlation analysis focuses on determining whether two variables are related to
one another in ordering individual differences between people. The maximum
correlation index is $= 1.00$, with both variables ordering people in the same way.
An index of -1.00 indicates an ordering in reverse directions. An index of 0.00
indicates no relationship between the variables. In no instance can we draw a
conclusion concerning cause-effect relationship based on correlation analysis and
none is implied.

SPEARMAN RHO CORRELATION.   Rank the scores of individuals within the two sets
of data—1, 2, 3, 4, 5. Then apply the formula RHO $\rho = 1 - \frac{6 \Sigma d^2}{N(N^2 - 1)}$ where
$d^2 = $ the difference between the individual's rank on one test and his/her rank on
another test ($r_1 - r_2$).

The advantage of the average-deviation method, as well as that of the chi
square method, described below, over the correlation and the more complicated
(but increasingly popular) analysis of variance methods, is the ease with which
the calculations can be performed. The teacher may, of course, use the above

system in combination with others, such as finding the so-called natural breaks in a distribution. It should be noted that the latter, when used in isolation, gives data, generally, that are not treatable statistically.

Chi Square

The supervising principal may wish to recommend the use of the chi square statistic to the teacher who wishes to research some problem within the classroom where chi square may prove a helpful tool. J. P. Guilford[1] noted that chi square is a general purpose statistic with many diverse applications. It is intended to test the hypothesis of no relationship between two variables.

H. E. Garrett noted that the chi square test represents a useful method of comparing experimentally obtained results with those to be expected theoretically on some hypothesis:

> The differences between observed and expected frequencies are squared and divided by the expected number in each case, and the sum of these quotients is x^2. The more closely the observed results approximate to the expected, the smaller the chi square and the closer the agreement between the observed data and the hypothesis being tested. Contrariwise, the larger the chi square the greater the probability of a real divergence of experimentally observed [results] from expected results.[2]

Further discussion of the properties of this statistic may be found in Ruch.[3]

Interpreting Statistical Measures

Certainly honesty is essential in dealing with statistical data. One overzealous school system in the midwest, in the struggle for enhanced public confidence in the educational program, printed inaccurate norms to the achievement test used locally. The students obtained scores which indicated that they were ahead approximately one to two years of where they really were in educational achievement. What was forgotten in this little bit of educational dishonesty was that such procedures definitely do delimit the scope, or universe of application, of the examination results.

One must bear in mind, also, when interpreting examination results, that

---

[1] J. P. Guilford, *Fundamental Statistics in Psychology and Education* (New York: McGraw-Hill Book Company, Inc., 1956), pp. 229–239.

[2] Henry E. Garrett, *Statistics in Psychology and Education*, 5th ed. (New York: Longmans, Green and Company, 1958), pp. 253–254.

[3] Floyd L. Ruch, *Elementary Statistics in Psychology and Education* (Columbia, Missouri: Lucas Brothers, 1957), pp. 1–14.

FIGURE D-2.   Normal Distribution Curve.

those scoring in the so-called average range would have scored there only two-thirds of the time, whereas those in the far extremes would have scored these extreme scores approximately but one-sixth of the time. This is illustrated in the normal distribution curve (Figure D-2.)

Again, it is the supervisor's rightful role to aid the teacher and administrator in interpreting examination results, and to assist in the maintenance of honesty in this interpretation.

A Look at the Future

As supervisors help teachers plan educational experiences for students, continuous attention to the ways in which students differ and are alike is vital. Thus teachers, through observation, conferences, and the various other techniques described in this text, will do a better job on the instructional firing line. In the future, teacher training institutions will stress not the *fundamentals* of educational philosophy, psychology, and sociology, but rather the *application* of these principles.

As the various states increase the requirements for the license or certificate authorizing service in school supervision, the preparing institutions will require the completion of additional professional course work in scientific research methods. Such courses will help prepare the supervisor for advanced research that, it is hoped, will help solve many professional problems. Advanced work in research design for the school supervisor who elects to obtain training beyond that required for the basic license or certificate in school supervision will become the rule rather than the exception, with such a program being required of all who enter the doctoral program in educational administration and supervision.

Author Index

Adams, Harold, P., 272
Alexander, Carter, 48
Alexander, Marvin, 67
Alport, Gordon W., 4

Baldwin, R., 122, 123
Barbour, Julius Ervin, 520
Barr, A. S., 89, 172, 173, 175, 291
Bartky, John A., 185
Bass, Bernard M., 103, 146, 147, 148, 190, 589
Beckley, J., 122, 123
Beneditti, Eugene, 43, 45
Benjamin, Dayton, 602
Benne, K. D., 272
Bent, Rudyard K., 12
Bernard, Harold W., 272
Bingham, W. V., 250
Boardman, Charles W., 12
Borden, Richard C., 134
Brackenbury, Robert L., 465
Bradford, L. P., 144
Briggs, T. H., 96, 267
Brownell, John A., 313
Browning, Bruce D., 97
Brueckner, Leo J., 12, 89, 172, 173, 291
Buchler, Justus, 463, 465
Burke, Arvid J., 48
Burton, William H., 12, 89, 172, 173, 175, 291
Butts, Freeman R., 8, 9, 11, 45, 51

Calhoun, R. T., 383
Campbell, Clifford W., 139
Campbell, Roald F., 559, 642
Cartwright, Dorwin, 199
Castetter, William B., 569, 576, 580
Caswell, Hollis, L., 457
Cleland, David I., 110
Cooper, Shirley, 27, 33
Cremin, Lawrence A., 8, 9, 11, 45, 51
Culbertson, Jack, 635
Cummings, H. H., 44
Cunningham, Luvern C., 642

Deighton, Lee C., 62
Deterline, William A., 323
Dewey, John, 468
DeYoung, Chris A., 46, 47
Dickey, Frank G., 272
Dillion, Elizabeth A., 638
Dimock, Gladys Ogden, 14
Dimock, Marshall Edward, 14
Douglass, Harl R., 12
Driscoll, Gertrude P., 418

Eastmond, Jefferson N., 540
Elsbree, Willard S., 94, 271
Engelhardt, Fred, 30, 31
Evans, Albert R., 176
Evans, N. Dean, 189
Ewing, Russell H., 137, 138

Farelli, A., 386
Fayol, Henri, 94
Fenlason, Anne, 413
Ferguson, W. S., 252
Fielstra, Clarence, 92
Fitzwater, Charles O., 27, 33
Flanders, Ned, 220, 655
Franseth, Jane, 587
Freese, Theron, 90
Frost, S. E., 6
Fullmer, Daniel W., 272

Galluzo, A. Neil, 501
Garrett, Henry E., 684
Gaver, M. V., 391
Gayer, Nancy, 462, 463
Glasser, William, 209
Good, Carter V., 651
Goodwin, Jack C., 11
Grela, John J., 254
Gronlund, Norman E., 167
Guilford, J. P., 595, 684
Gwynn, J. Minor, 50, 130, 204, 272, 357

Halpin, Andrew W., 98
Hand, Harold C., 468
Harper, Louis E., 412, 439
Hatch, Raymond H., 414
Havighurst, Robert J., 469
Havlock, Ronald G., 654
Hill, C. M., 558
Horn, Robert, 654
Hutchins, Robert M., 469

Infelise, S. Robert, 529

Jackman, Taylor, 511, 528
Jacobson, P. E., 275
Johnson, Russell E., 26, 27, 30, 140, 501, 550, 570
Justman, J., 96, 267

Keith, Lowell G., 529
Kindred, Leslie W., 551
King-Stoops, Joyce, 575
King, William R., 110
Kyte, George C., 100, 244

Lane, Robert Hill, 274
Lawson, Douglas E., 99

Lee, Doris May, 492
Lee, J. Murray, 492
Lemler, Ford L., 347
Lenn, Peter D., 323
Lippitt, R., 144
Loeb, Martin B., 469
Lucio, William H., 221
Luke, Robert A., 638

McClure, W. P., 27
MacDonald, John, 469
McGovern, E., 35
MacKintosh, H. K., 55
McNally, Harold, J., 94, 271
McNeil, John D., 221
McNerney, Chester T., 173
Mager, Robert F., 298, 299
Maritain, Jacques, 469
Markle, Susan Meyer, 370
Marks, James R., 92, 501
Marks, Shirley, 444
Medley, Donald M., 220
Melbo, Irving R., 79
Mitchell, James Russell, 269
Moehlman, Arthur B., 27, 28
Monroe, Walter S., 651
Moorer, Sam H., 587, 605
Morphet, Edgar L., 67
Moustakas, Clark E., 419

Neagley, Ross L., 189
Nickel, Mildred L., 342, 389
Norton, Monte S., 213, 216
Nutt, Hubert Wilbur, 89
Nystrand, Raphael O., 642

Otto, Henry J., 13, 97, 458, 472, 473, 619

Park, Joe, 463, 464
Perazzo, George J., 529
Perkins, Hugh, 220
Pfiffner, John M., 14
Piety, Donald, 88

Rafferty, M. L., 26, 27, 30, 44, 47, 140, 501, 550, 570
Ramseyer, Elaine A., 559
Randall, Herman John, Jr., 463, 465

Reeder, Edwin H., 175, 213, 216, 217, 292
Reeder, Ward G., 506, 550
Reisner, Edward H., 15
Remmers, H. H., 508
Rich, W. B., 55
Roethlesberger, F. J., 103, 251
Ruch, Floyd L., 684
Ryan, Charles O., 67

Schulz, Edward, 119, 121, 251, 252
Scott, C. W., 558
Sheats, P., 272
Shores, J. Harlan, 468
Shores, Louis, 651
Simons, A. H., 14
Smith, B. Othanel, 468
Spears, Harold, 11, 34, 169, 188, 215, 458
Spriegel, William B., 119, 121, 251, 252
Spriegel, William R., 119, 121, 251, 252
Stanley, William O., 468
Stephenson, Howard, 546
Stolurow, Lawrence M., 373
Stone, Charles A., 200

Stoops, Emery, 26, 27, 30, 44, 47, 92, 140, 176, 501, 550, 570
Sullivan, H. S., 415

Tannenbaum, A. S., 145
Taylor, H. A., 313
Tead, Ordway, 79, 115, 126, 127
Trillingham, C. C., 35

Usdan, Michael D., 642

Warner, W. Lloyd, 469
Weaver, David O., 314
Weller, Gerald M., 91
Wey, Herbert W., 311
Wiles, Kimball, 184, 185, 189, 270, 272, 274
Williams, B. T., 385
Wilson, Robert E., 545
Withall, John, 220
Wright, Benjamin, 412, 439

Yeager, William A., 14, 15, 506

Zander, Alvin, 199
Zuckerman, David W., 654

Subject Index

Accreditation and approval:
  as function of state, 53–58
  visitation and inspection, 60–61
Administration. *See also* Superintendent;
    Principal.
  ten commandments for, 99
Advisory Committee on Education, 50
Agenda:
  flexibility of, 274
  for faculty meetings, 272
  purposes of, 273
American Association of School Admin-
    istrators, 90, 184, 553, 622
American education:
  as big business, 43
  history of, 43, 45
  local-state-federal relationships, 44
Art, evaluation of instruction in, 301
Assistant principal, duties of, 91
Assistant superintendent, instruction,
    duties and functions of, 89–90
Association for Supervision and Curricu-
    lum Development, 18, 118, 270–71,
    288, 622
Attendance laws, compulsory, 54
Audiovisual media, 337–95
Authority, lines of, 147–49

Beginning teachers:
  and disturbed child, 183
  helps for, 175, 181
  opening of school, 183–84
  orientation meetings, 184–87
  self-evaluation, 182

California Teachers Association, 558
Case studies:
  information covered, 439–43
  preparation and interpretation, 437–39
Change in education:
  agent of, 123–25
  as slow process, 99–100
Chief state school officer, 50–53
  historical development, 51
  position today, 51–53
Child, children:
  growth and development, 661–67
  guidance of, 403–52
Child welfare and guidance, 430
Classified personnel, 500–532
  activities, 531–32
  assignment specifications, 503–504
  cafeteria, 516–17
  communication with, 511
  do's and don'ts, 528–29
  evaluation checklist, 512–14
  in-basket problems, 530
  in-service for, 516–20
  morale of, 507–508
  orientation of, 505–506
  performance evaluation, 509–11
  policies for, 511

Classified personnel (*continued*)
  questions, 531
  secretarial, 523–27
  selection and assignment of, 502–503
  trends in improving performance, 527–28
Classified personnel services, 500–532
  checklist for, 515
  improvement of office management, 506–508
  planning for, 515–16
  principles for improvement of, 500–502
Communication:
  and personnel policies, 135–36
  channels of, 104
  in state departments, 69
  in understanding children, 412
  listening skills, 134
  principles of, 134–35
  skills in, 131–33
Community relations, 477–564
  activities, 564
  administrative roles in, 542–45, 555–57
  basic principles of, 540–42
  classified staff and, 546–48
  communication in, 550–51
  curriculum and, 477
  definition of, 539–40
  do's and don'ts, 559–60
  evaluation of program, 553–54
  governing board and, 543
  in-basket problems, 562–63
  program development, 549–50
  publicity for, 554
  questions, 564
  radio and television, 552–53
  resources, other, 557–59
  school's place in, 542
  staff participation in, 544–46, 548
  trends, 561
  working with press, 551–52
Community support, 539–65
Competency, 163
Computers:
  for decision making, 592–93

instruction by, 373
Conferences:
  inservice growth, 174
  post-visitation, 237
  state departments of education, 59, 64–65
Counselor, counseling:
  in the classroom, 434
  problems of, 430
  role in guidance, 429
Cumulative records:
  case studies, 437–43
  characteristics, 437
  confidentiality, 436
  transfer and duplication of, 436
Curricular activities:
  characteristics of, 488–89
  evaluation of, 490–91
  play and sports days, 489
  role of principal in, 488
  supervision of, 488
Curriculum:
  activities, 496
  co-curricular activities and, 488–92
  community and, 477
  definition of, 471–72
  deterrents to change, 472
  do's and don'ts, 490–91
  history and philosophy of, 459–72
  improvement of, 458–96, 474–75
  in-basket problems, 494–95
  project method, 475
  questions, 496
  research in, 481–82
  role of principal, 474
  staff meetings and workshops, 473
  state development of, 61, 62
  students and, 477
  supervision of, 473–74
  trends, 492–94

Decision making:
  evaluation of, 596–97
  process of, 375–76
Democratic leadership:
  applications of, 141, 143
  classroom observation and, 212–13
  for quality education, 144, 145

Democratic leadership (*continued*)
  undemocratic staff member and, 189
  vs. authoritarian, 141
Department of supervisors and directors
  of instruction, 170
Discipline and classroom control:
  beginning teachers and, 178
  building room standards, 180
  student perceptions of, 176

Educational improvement:
  decision making for, 375–76
  democratic leadership in, 141–45
  supervision for, 78–79
Educational personnel
  administration of, 14
  developmental trends, 15
  evaluation of:
    classified personnel, 509–514
    teachers, 91, 289–328
Evaluation:
  by state departments of education, 59,
    69
  curriculum development and, 483–85
  instructional media checklist, 350
  of classified personnel, 509–514
  of community relations program, 553–
    54
  of decision making, 596–97
  of group action, 200–201
  of instructional outcomes, 299
  of instructional systems, 323–24
  of interview, 252
  of media center, 342–45, 389–91
  of personnel selection process, 581–82
  of staff meeting, 271, 279
  of subject areas:
    art instruction, 301
    handwriting instruction, 301
    mathematics instruction, 300
    music instruction, 302
    physical education instruction, 302
    science instruction, 301
    social science instruction, 301
  of supervising program, 587–610
  of teachers, 91, 289–328
  rating instruments, 228–32

Faculty:
  activities, 285
  conferences, 250–52
  professional development of, 4
  reactions to faculty meetings, 277
Faculty meetings, 260–86
  activities, 285
  agenda for, 272
  do's and don'ts, 279–82
  evaluation of, 271
  improvement of, 262–63
  planning for, 264–65
  principal's role, 274
  principles and practices, 262
  purposes of, 263–64
  questions regarding, 285
  records of, 275
  teacher involvement in, 266
  teachers' reactions to, 277
  techniques for, 171, 270–71
  trends, 282–83
Federal role in education
  constitutional provision for, 43, 45
  governmental agencies, 49
  supervision, 43–50
Financial support, state department, 54
Flanders System, 220
  interaction analysis, 655–58
Follow-up conferences, 243–60
  activities, 258
  do's and don'ts, 254–55
  evaluation, 252
  in-basket problems, 257
  outline for interview, 253
  preparing for, 244
  principal's, 246–47
  principles and purposes of, 243
  questions regarding, 258
  recording results, 248
  report of, 249
  time and place for, 245–46
  trends, 256–57
  types of interviews, 250–52

Games and simulations, 166–67
Grades, grading, 678–84
Group action, 126–27

Group dynamics. *See also* Human dynamics.
   effectiveness, 193
   group techniques, 172–73
   stages of development, 192
Groups, working with:
   achieving consensus, 194–95
   activities, 206
   character and performance, 191
   checklist for leaders, 198
   clear and unclear expectations, 195
   competitiveness, 195
   conference for classroom control, 181
   do's and don'ts, 202–203
   evaluation, 201
   growth and development of, 191–93
   guidelines for work with, 190–91
   in-basket problems, 205
   need for feedback in, 196
   problem-solving in, 196–97
   questions regarding, 206
   techniques of, 172–73
   trends, 204
Guidance, understanding of children, 403–452
   activities, 451–52
   anecdotal records, 419–22
   autobiography, 423–24
   case study, 437–43
   checklist and rating scales, 422–23
   child growth and development, 661–67
   child welfare and, 430
   cumulative records, 434–37
   do's and don'ts, 446–47
   in-basket problems, 449–50
   inservice program, 407–412
   instructional technology for, 409
   inter-staff teamwork, 425–27
   observation and listening, 418–19
   parent observation, 434–35
   principles of, 406
   questions, 450–51
   role of teacher, 432
   study by teacher, 433–34
   study groups, 409–412
   trends, 447–49
   use of health records, 417–18

Handwriting, evaluation of instruction, 301
Health records, 417–18
History of supervision, 6–9, 12–13, 46
   constitutional provision, 43, 45, 51
   in Colonial period, 45
   in dame schools, 43
Human dynamics, 116–54
   and criticism, 121–23
   and supervision, 121
   group techniques, 172–73, 191–203
   interaction in, 146, 193
   social product, 127–28
Human relations. *See also* Human dynamics.
   communication in, 131–35
   films and publications, 648–54
   staff relations, 103

Individual differences, 126–28
Individualizing instruction:
   flexible grouping for, 307
   student materials for, 378
Inservice education, 163
   child guidance and, 407–412
   classified personnel, 516–23
   principles of, 169–70
   self-directed, 173
Institutes, 172
   how to conduct, 269–70
   improvement of, 267
   planning of, 269
Instruction:
   development of, 4
   improvement of, 3
   individualization of, 307–312
   nongraded, 312
   organizing for, 307–320
   principles of, 4
   state role in, 50–71
   systems of, 320–24
   team teaching, 312–14
Instruction, methods of, 324–26
   discussion, 325
   gaming, 326
   lecture, 325
   media, 337–95
   role-playing, 325
   sessions of, 374

Instructional development, 164
  programmed learning and, 379–80
  purposes of evaluation in, 167–68
  stimulating faculty in, 164
Instructional materials. *See also* Instructional media.
  audio system, 375
  care of books, 386
  evaluation of, 350, 361–69
  for curriculum improvement, 342
  for instructional systems, 322–23
  for social sciences, 358
  media and library, 337–95
  planning and selection, 355–58
  standards for, 59
  use of, 349–355
Instructional media, 337–95
  activities, 398
  checklist for evaluation of, 350
  criteria for usability, 356–58
  development of center, 354–55
  do's and don'ts, 391–93
  evaluation of, 350, 361–69
  evaluation of media center, 342–45
  improving performance of coordinator, 346–47
  in-basket problems, 395–97
  planning and selection, 341, 355–56
  principles of, 338–39
  programmed instruction, 343–45
  questions, 397–98
  staff development for, 351
  systems of, 342
  teaching machines, 375
  trends, 394–95
  use of, 349–55
Instructional systems, 320–24
Intermediate unit:
  activities, 39
  county unit, 27–28
  do's and don'ts, 36
  functions of, 30
  in-basket problems, 38
  organizational status, 31
  questions regarding, 39
  role of, 26
  services of, 31–36
  specialist consultant, 33–35
  supervisory functions, 32–33

  supervisory union or township, 28
  trends, 37
Interviews:
  evaluation of, 252
  outline for, 253
  types of, 250–252

Leadership, 116–54
  activities, 154–55
  authority and subordinates, 147–48
  by principal, 97
  change agent, 122–25
  communication in, 131–35
  delegation of, 120
  democratic vs. authoritarian, 141–46, 173
  do's and don'ts, 150–51
  human dynamics in, 123
  in-basket problems, 153–54
  individual and group action, 126, 127
  keys to, 149–50
  problems in, 17
  purposes of, 116
  questions regarding, 154
  self criticism, 123
  self image related to, 128–29
  trends, 151–52
  types of, 137–40
Learning theories, 668–72
  summary of, 673–74
Lesson plan, 316–17
Library:
  as distribution center, 382
  as teaching agency, 383–84
  care of books, 386
  evaluation of, 389–91
  for teachers, 161
  improvement of, 382
  principles of, 338–39
  professional, 391
  supervision of usage, 385–88
Library materials, 337–95
  activities, 398
  do's and don'ts, 391–93
  in-basket problems, 395–97
  planning for, 341
  principles of, 338–39
  questions, 397–98
  selection of, 341

Library materials (*continued*)
  selection of textbooks, 359–61
  trends, 394–95
  use of, 349–55

Master teacher consultant, role of, 93
Mathematics, evaluation of instruction, 300
Media coordinator, 346–47
Media development, 165, 348–49
Micro-Teaching, 221
Music, evaluation of instruction, 302

National Association of Manufacturers, 559
National Defense Education Act, 46
National Education Association, 18, 27, 33, 97, 558, 622
  Department of Elementary School Principals, 588
National Society for the Study of Education, 622
Needs assessment, 165

Objectives:
  curriculum development, 479–80
  follow-up conference, 243–44
Organization:
  activities, 110
  as shared responsibility, 82
  communication, 104
  conflicting demands of, 103–105
  county unit, 27
  do's and don'ts, 106
  evaluation of, 105
  for curriculum development, 63
  in-basket problems, 108–109
    internal and external, 80–82
  legal bases for, 83–84
  of library service, 383
  principles of, 76, 80
  questions regarding, 110
  state central system, 27
  superintendent roll, 102
  supervisory, 87–89
  supervisory union or township, 28
  trends, 107
  vertical and horizontal, 82

Parent observation, 434–35
Parent-teacher conferences:
  acceptance and empathy, 415
  communication, 417
  follow-up, 444
  planning for, 412–15
Parent-teacher-school relations, 175–76
  visiting day, 548
Permissiveness:
  consequences of, 145–46
  expectations and, 148
Personnel policies, and communication, 135–36
Personnel, supervisory, 568–85
  appraisal of candidates, 572–74
  assignment, permanent, 581
  candidate qualifications, 578
  do's and don'ts, 582–83
  in-basket problems, 585
  position specifications, 571–72
  probationary assignments, 580
  selection and recruitment, 567–78
  trends, 583–84
Phi Delta Kappa, 622
Phi Lambda Theta, 622
Philosophy of education:
  empiricists, 459–60
  Froebel, 462
  Herbartian theory, 460
  idealism, 465–67
  Pestalozzi, 461–62
  pragmatism, 463–64
  realism, 464–65
  Rousseau, 460
Physical Education, evaluation of instruction, 302
Placement of teachers, 32
Planning, 77
  for faculty meetings, 264–65
  for instruction, 314–20
  for instructional materials, 340
  for parent conferences, 412–15
  for responsibilities, media, 341
  format for plan, 181
  supervisory, 94, 96, 170, 213–14
  techniques for, 170–73
Policies:
  handbook of, 77
  systems approach to, 77

Principal:
  and classroom control, 179
  and classroom visitation, 235
  and community relations, 543–45, 555–57
  and curriculum, 474
  and faculty meeting, 274
  and follow-up conference, 247–48
  and teachers evaluation, 292–93
  as chief supervisor, 18
  as instructional leader, 97, 100–101
  as library supervisor, 386
  coordination with others, 100
  definition of, 5
  delegation of duties, 101–102
  organizing supervisory program, 96
  perceptions of supervision, 602–604
  positive climate by, 98
  preparation of, 101
  role in guidance, 426–28
  supervisory responsibility of, 16, 98
Program revision, 168
Programmed instruction, 343–45
  advantages of, 378–79
  and teaching machines, 377
  text of, 369–70
Publicity:
  press relationships, 551–52
  radio and television, 552–53

Rating. *See also* Evaluation.
  instruments for, 228–32
Reading, evaluation of instruction, 300
Reinforcement, 143
Research:
  by state department, 67–69
  by U.S. Office of Education, 48
  director of, 91
  publications, references, 651–52

Science, evaluation of instruction, 301
Secretary, 523–27
  community relations for, 546–47
Selection and recruitment. *See* Personnel.
Social studies:
  evaluation of instruction, 301
  material selection, 358
Sociology of education:
  humanism, 470

liberalism, 468
rationalism, 469
traditionalism, 468–69
Specialist consultant, 5, 18
  at state level, 66
  role of, 92–93
Staff development, 163–200
  for media usage, 351
Staff relations, 103
State department of education, 50–70
  accreditation and approval, 53–58, 60–61
  activities, 72
  chief state school officer, 50
  curriculum materials, 66
  do's and don'ts, 69–70
  evaluation, 59
  functions of, 53, 58
  growth of departments of education, 50
  improvement of programs, 54
  in-basket problems, 71
  questions regarding, 72
  special committees in, 63–64
  specialist consultants, 66
  supervisor, 66, 67
  trends, 70–71
Statistical measures, 678–84
Students:
  assignment of, 444–45
  and curriculum, 477
  disturbed child, 183
  homework assignments, 179
  and library skills, 385–88
  perceptions of classroom control, 176
  unsatisfactory work, 178
Superintendent:
  as instructional leader, 102
  community relations, 543
  supervisory responsibility, 16
Supervision
  activities, 22–23
  as educational leadership, 10
  as inspection, 10
  by intermediate unit, 26–36
  curricular services, 32
  definition of, 291
  democratic, 6, 10
  do's and don'ts, 19

Supervision (*continued*)
 evaluation and changes in, 8–9, 13, 16, 17
 federal role in, 43–50
 history of, 6–8, 46
 in-basket problems, 21
 methods of, 171–72
 of library, 385
 of cafeteria personnel, 516–17
 principles of, 5
 problems in, 17
 productivity and, 143
 questions regarding, 22
 role today, 15
 self-supervision, 18
 traditional vs. modern, 12
 trends, 19–20
Supervision, evaluation of, 587–610
 activities, 609–610
 computer use in, 592–93
 decision making, 589–99
 do's and don'ts, 606–607
 effective programs for, 604–605
 in-basket problems, 608–609
 performance appraisal, 600–601
 principal's perceptions, 602–604
 principles of, 587–88
 questions, 609
 teachers' perceptions, 602–606
 trends, 607–608
Supervisor
 activities of, 617
 and evaluation, 294
 decision making, 589–99
 from state department of education, 66–67
 new type of, 94
 planning by, 96
 power of, 140
 principal, 16
 professional characteristics, 616–17
 professional organizations, 621–23
 professional status, 615–16
 role in guidance, 428
 self-control, 131
 specialist, 16
 superintendent, 16
Supervisory program:
 evaluation of, 587–610

 of intermediate unit, 26–35
 planning for, 4, 6
Supervisory responsibilities, 614–28
 activities, 627–28
 do's and don'ts, 624–25
 in-basket problems, 626–27
 professional status and, 623–24
 questions, 627
 to students, patrons, and administration, 617–19
 trends, 625–26
Supervisory visits, 210–40
 activities, 240
 and democratic leadership, 212–13
 do's and don'ts, 238
 Flanders System, 220
 in-basket problems, 239
 interschool, 234
 micro-teaching, 221
 planning for, 213–14, 235
 post-visit conference, 237
 principles and purposes of, 211–12
 questions regarding, 240
 record keeping for, 221–28
 scheduled and unscheduled, 95, 217–18
 techniques of, 171, 214, 218–21, 234–35
 to experienced teachers, 216–17
 types of, 216
 videotape recordings of, 221
Systems analysis, for curriculum development, 477–80

Teacher evaluation:
 activities, 332
 and morale, 302
 by principal, 292–93
 by supervisor, 294
 checklist, 297
 criteria, for, 295
 do's and don'ts, 326–27
 in-basket problems, 330–31
 organizing for, 291
 principles of, 289–90
 questions related to, 331–32
 report of, 304–306
 self-evaluation, 295
 traditional vs. modern, 294–95

Teachers:
  collective bargaining, 638–39
  emotional health, 130
  guidance role of, 432–33
  helps for:
    beginning teachers, 175, 181–87
    dissenting teachers, 188–89
    senior teacher, 188
    superior teacher, 187–88
  individuality of, 100
  perceptions of supervision, 602–604
  preparation standards, 58, 59
  professional growth of:
    helps for beginning teachers, 175, 181–87
    preparation standards, 58–59
    self-supervision, 18
    supervision of, 187–89
  reactions to faculty meetings, 275–77
  restrictions in early days, 142
  self-evaluation, 295
  self-supervision, 18
  study of student, 433–34
  supervisors and, 3
  work with principal, 98
Teaching, criteria for, 293
Teaching machines, 375
  and programmed learning, 377
Teaching unit, 317–20
  framework for, 320
Team teaching, 312–14
Technology:
  instructional materials, 361–69
  uses in guidance, 409
Television, evaluation of materials for, 361–69
Tests and measurements:
  assigning marks, 678–84
  helping teachers with, 675–78
  statistical measures, 678–84
Texas Education Agency, 60, 61

Textbooks, selection of, 63, 359
Trends and issues in supervision, 632–46
  activities, 646
  changing structures of school, 635–36
  collective bargaining, 638–39
  discovery and invention, 634–35
  future of supervision, 639–40, 685
  in-basket problems, 645–46
  liberal education, 634
  new knowledge and discipline, 635
  obsolescence, 637
  population factors, 632–33
  questions, 646
  retirement, 637
  summary, 640–45
  technology, 633–34
  use of human resources, 636–37
  use of leisure time, 634

Understanding children. *See* Guidance.
U.S. Chamber of Commerce, 559
U.S. Commissioner of Education, 48
U.S. Department of Health, Education, and Welfare, 43
U.S. Office of Education, 46–48
  history of, 46–47
  research activities, 48
  supervision activities, 47–48
U.S. Supreme Court, 44–45

Video- and audio-tutorial systems:
  audio and video instruction, 373
  auto-instruction, 369
  making audio-tutorial tapes, 380–81

Workshops, 172
  for curriculum development, 473, 475 76
  improvement of, 267
  limitations of, 268–69
  types of, 268